THE SELECTED CORRESPONDENCE OF MICHAEL FARADAY

VOLUME 1 1812-1848

*Edited on behalf of the Royal Institution
of Great Britain by*

L. PEARCE WILLIAMS

with the assistance of
Rosemary FitzGerald & Oliver Stallybrass

CAMBRIDGE

AT THE UNIVERSITY PRESS

1971

Published by the Syndics of the Cambridge University Press
Bentley House, 200 Euston Road, London N.W.1
American Branch: 32 East 57th Street, New York, N.Y.10022

Library of Congress Catalogue Card Number: 77–138377

ISBN: 0 521 07908 X

Printed in Great Britain
at the University Printing House, Cambridge
(Brooke Crutchley, University Printer)

Portrait of Michael Faraday

Frontispiece

CONTENTS

EDITOR'S PREFACE

Michael Faraday was born on 22 September 1791; he died on 25 August 1867. During his lifetime, science and its function in society underwent a profound transformation. When he was born, physical reality was to be sought in the interactions of corpuscles moving in empty space. The generation that followed him was to find the causes of physical phenomena in the stresses and strains of the (hypothetical) luminiferous ether, with no place for particles. The pursuit of science, at his birth, at least in England, tended to be firmly in the hands of the amateur. When he died, science was a profession in which force of intellect, rather than modest talents supported by material advantages, determined a man's place in the scientific community. In 1791, the idea of science as an important, nay fundamental, instrument for the betterment of man's earthly condition was just that – an idea. In 1836, when pressed during a debate on education in the French Chamber of Deputies to give an example of the utility of science, a member could only cite the lightning rod. By 1867, only those who would not see could fail to recognize that the application of science to the problems of agriculture and industry held out the promise of unimagined material wealth.

Faraday contributed to all three of these transformations. His *Experimental Researches in Electricity* subtly undermined the prevalent orthodoxy until, in the hands of James Clerk Maxwell, his ideas became the new orthodoxy of the second half of the nineteenth century. Faraday was firmly committed to the idea of the professionalization of science. Under the tutelage of Sir Humphry Davy, he had received a rigorous scientific education and he was one of the ardent advocates of the introduction of science into general education. He also early entered the lists against the application of the standards of the dilettante to the determination of scientific merit. This struggle took place in the Royal Society and Faraday, although not a leader, was a faithful adherent of the group which desired reform. Although he himself did not develop the technological applications of his own inventions, he was keenly aware of them and encouraged others to put his ideas to work. While he followed up the theoretical implications of his revolutionary discoveries in electricity and magnetism, others attempted to make his invention of the dynamo and the electric motor bear fruit in industrial applications.

All this and more is reflected in Faraday's correspondence. My principle of selection has been determined by my desire to illustrate all the facets of Faraday's life. Most of the letters by Faraday in this collection are previously unpublished but I have not hesitated to reprint those which contribute to an understanding of the hitherto unpublished letters and to crucial events in

Faraday's life. This part of these volumes, I would hope, should serve as the foundations for any future biography of Michael Faraday.*

Faraday corresponded with a relatively large number of fellow scientists. Their letters to him provide some extraordinary glimpses into *their* scientific ideas and *their* problems. My selection from these letters has been guided by my desire to present historians of nineteenth-century science with sources of interest to them. In general, I have not included simple gossipy letters, although I am aware of the fact that one man's gossip is another's *pièce justificative*. Sometimes, for the sake of the completeness of an exchange of letters, I have violated this rule but this is an infrequent occurrence.

Every effort has been made to transcribe the letters to and from Faraday exactly as they were written, with one exception. I have omitted reproducing the name and titles of the person to whom the letter was addressed which usually (but not always) appeared to the left and below the signature of the sender. Idiosyncrasies of spelling or usage have been retained; only where there is the possibility of confusion have notes been added or editorial emendations made. These latter are included within square brackets. The one insoluble problem was Faraday's punctuation. Faraday followed no system whatsoever. In many letters, he omits all use of a final period in all sentences; in others, he mingles periods with dashes; in others, periods appear in the most unlikely places. The confusion is compounded by the fact that Faraday does not always begin new sentences with a capital letter. I have tried to apply common sense here; where the absence of punctuation merely causes temporary inconvenience, I have left the letters as Faraday wrote them. If what seemed to me to be the sense of a passage was rendered obscure, I have provided the minimum of punctuation. But periods are not all. There are many cases where it is impossible to tell if a mark is a comma, or just some spray from Faraday's pen; or whether a mark is a semi-colon or a colon or a double splash. Reason is no guide, so, once again, I have tried to follow Faraday until the result was obscure. Then, I have come down on the side of clarity and eliminated what may, or may not, have been punctuation marks.

I have adhered to a Spartan standard of simplicity in my annotations. This has been dictated by two considerations: (1) I have not wished to take up precious space with lengthy footnotes which every scholar could reproduce with a minimum of effort; (2) the nineteenth century is very well provided with scholarly aids for the history of science. With few exceptions, a scientific publication can be easily located in the Royal Society's Catalogue of Scientific Papers or in Poggendorff and the repetition of these citations did not seem

* The ready availability of the letters which passed between Faraday and C. F. Schoenbein has led me to exclude them from this selection. The reader is referred to Georg W. A. Kahlbaum and Francis V. Darbishire, editors, *The Letters of Faraday and Schoenbein, 1836–1862*, Bâle and London, 1899.

worthwhile. What I have done is to give specific references when this seemed appropriate; when a large number of papers was involved, I have referred the reader to one or the other of the above-named sources. I have, similarly, kept identifications of individuals to the bare minimum. Most are easily found in obvious places such as Poggendorff or the numerous national dictionaries of biography. Where no identification is offered in a footnote, I have been unable to find anything on the individual involved.

No project of this size can be completed without the help of a number of people. I should like to take this opportunity to thank them.

Kenneth D. C. Vernon, formerly Librarian of the Royal Institution, gave me invaluable help before he departed for the London Graduate School of Business where he is now the Librarian.

The Reference Librarians of the Cornell University Library have been unfailingly kind and helpful to me. Each, at one time or another, has patiently searched out some essential piece of information for me. It is a pleasure to thank Barbara Brown, Mary Burlitch, Evelyn Greenberg, Pamela Gunnell, Martha Landis, L. Frederick Pohl, Virginia Reid, and Caroline T. Spicer.

Mrs Roberta Ludgate transcribed the letters and I thank her for the care and intelligence with which she performed her task.

Lady Rosemary FitzGerald carefully checked the typescripts against the manuscripts and discovered many errors of transcription which had escaped me. What errors remain are solely my fault; they are far fewer than would have been the case without Lady Rosemary's care for which I here thank her.

My deepest gratitude and sympathy are due Mr Oliver G. W. Stallybrass who entered upon his duties as Librarian of the Royal Institution only to face a growing stack of transcripts in which no principle of order could be discerned since none was present. It was he who patiently sorted things out, prepared innumerable indices, and constantly spurred me on when the pressure of other business seemed to require the temporary abandonment of this project.

Finally, I can only wonder at the patience of my wife who watched silently while first one room of our house, then another, was gradually filled with photostats, reference works and various copies and transcripts of the letters. For the care with which she trained my children not to touch a single paper, and for their obedience, my feeble thanks is small repayment.

L. PEARCE WILLIAMS

Ithaca, N.Y.
May, 1971

LIST OF ABBREVIATIONS FOR JOURNALS, PUBLISHED WORKS AND MANUSCRIPTS

ABLP	*Annuaire* du Bureau des Longitudes, Paris
AC	*Annales de Chimie et de Physique*
AE	*Archives d'Electricité*
AJS	*American Journal of Science*
AKAWB	*Abhandlungen* der Königlichen Akademie der Wissenschaften zu Berlin
AOP	*Annals of Philosophy*
AP	*Annalen der Physik*
ASPN	*Archives des Sciences Physiques et Naturelles*; Supplément à la *Bibliothèque Universelle et Revue Suisse*
BAAS	British Association for the Advancement of Science
BAASR	British Association for the Advancement of Science; *Reports*
BASB	*Bulletin* de l'Académie Royale des Sciences, des Lettres, et Belles-Lettres de Bruxelles
BF	*Biblioteca Fisica*
B.J.	Henry Bence Jones, *The Life and Letters of Faraday*, 2 vols., London, 1870
BSd'E	*Bulletin* de la Société d'Encouragement pour l'Industrie Nationale
BU	Bibliothèque Universelle des Sciences, Belles-Lettres et Arts, faisant suite à la Bibliothèque Britannique rédigée à Genève
CDMJ	*The Cambridge and Dublin Mathematical Journal*
CGA	L. de Launay, editor, *Correspondance du Grand Ampère*, 3 vols., Paris, 1936–43
CR	*Comptes Rendus Hebdomadaires des Séances* de l'Académie des Sciences, Paris
DJMCS	*Dublin Journal of Medical and Chemical Science*
EJS	*The Edinburgh Journal of Science*
ENPJ	*The Edinburgh New Philosophical Journal*
EPJ	*The Edinburgh Philosophical Journal*
ERCP	M. Faraday, *Experimental Researches in Chemistry and Physics*, London, 1859
ERE	M. Faraday, *Experimental Researches in Electricity*, 3 vols., London, 1839–55
IEE	Institution of Electrical Engineers
JGC	*Journal de Génie Civil*
JP	*Journal de Physique, de Chimie, et d'Histoire Naturelle*

JRAS	*Journal* of the Royal Agricultural Society of England
JRI	*Journal* of the Royal Institution of Great Britain
LG	*The Literary Gazette*
LPW	L. Pearce Williams, *Michael Faraday, A Biography*, London and New York, 1965
MAS	*Mémoires* de l'Académie des Sciences, Paris
MASB	*Mémoires* de l'Académie Royale des Sciences, des Lettres et Belles-Lettres de Bruxelles
MASN	*Memorie* della Reale Accademia delle Scienze, Napoli
MAWB	*Mémoires*; Akademie der Wissenschaften, Berlin
MCASB	*Mémoires Couronnés* publiés par l'Académie Royale des Sciences, des Lettres et Belles-Lettres de Bruxelles
MNASL	*Monthly Notices* of the Astronomical Society of London
MNGB	Mittheilungen der Naturforschenden Gesellschaft in Bern
MSA	*Mémoires de Physique et de Chimie* de la Société d'Arcueil
MSIM	*Memorie di Matematica e di Fisica* della Società Italiana delle Scienze residente in Modena
MSSN	*Mémoires* de la Société Royale des Sciences, Lettres et Arts de Nancy
NASN	*Nuovi Annali delle Scienze Naturali*
NBSP	*Nouveau Bulletin des Sciences* de la Société Philomatique de Paris
NJ	*Nicholson's Journal of Natural Philosophy, Chemistry and the Arts*
NM	*Nautical Magazine*
NRRS	*Notes and Records* of the Royal Society of London
PM	*The Philosophical Magazine*. After 1832, *The London and Edinburgh Philosophical Magazine and Journal of Science*. After 1840, *The London, Edinburgh and Dublin Philosophical Magazine and Journal of Science*
PRI	*Proceedings* of the Royal Institution of Great Britain
PRS	*Proceedings* of the Royal Society of London
PT	*Philosophical Transactions* of the Royal Society of London
PVSP	*Extraits des Procès-verbaux* de la Société Philomatique de Paris
QCM	Quételet, *Correspondance Mathématique et Physique*
QJS	*The Journal of Science and the Arts* edited at the Royal Institution of Great Britain (known as the *Quarterly Journal of Science*)
QR	*The Quarterly Review*
RI	The Royal Institution of Great Britain
RS	The Royal Society of London
RSAE	*Recueil des Travaux* de la Société Libre d'Agriculture, des Sciences des Arts et des Belles-Lettres du Département de l'Eure

RSCSP	*Catalogue of Scientific Papers* compiled and published by the Royal Society of London, 19 vols., London, 1867–1925
TCPS	*Transactions* of the Cambridge Philosophical Society
TLCS	*Transactions* of the London Chemical Society
TLES	*Transactions* of the London Electrical Society
TRSE	*Transactions* of the Royal Society of Edinburgh
TSM	Richard Taylor, *Scientific Memoirs*, selected from the Transactions of Foreign Academies of Science and Learned Societies and from Foreign Journals, 5 vols., London, 1837–52
VEKNIW	Verhandelingen der Eerste Klasse van het Koninklijk Nederlandsche Instituut van Wetenschappen, Letterkunde, en Schoone Kunsten te Amsterdam

THE
CORRESPONDENCE

———

I

1 M. FARADAY to B. ABBOTT,[1] 12 July 1812

[*R.I., Warner mss., B.J. 1, 16ff*]

Sunday Afternoon
July 12th 1812

DEAR A.

Ceremony is useless in many cases, and sometimes impertinent; now tho'
between you and me it may not be the last; yet, I conceive it is the first, therefore I have banished it at this time. But first let me wish you well, and then I will
proceed on to the subject of this letter: Make my respects too if you please to
Mr. & Mrs. Abbott, and also your brother & sister.

I was lately engaged in conversation with a gentleman, who appeared to have
a very extensive correspondence: for within the space of half an hour, he drew
observations from two letters that he had received not a fortnight before; one
was from Sicily; and the other from France. After a while, I adverted to his
correspondence; & observed that it must be very interesting, and a source of
great pleasure to himself: He immediately affirmed with great enthusiasm that
it was one of the purest enjoyments of his life: (observe he like you and your
humble servant is a Bachelor.) – much more passed on the subject, but I will
not waste your time in recapitulating it; however let me notice, before I cease
from praising and recommending epistolary correspondence, that the great
Dr. Isaac Watts,[2] (great in all the methods respecting the attainment of Learning;) recommends it, as a very effectual method of improving the mind of the
person who writes, & the person who receives; Not to forget too another
strong instance in favour of the practice, I will merely call to your mind the
correspondence that passed between Lord Chesterfield & his Son: In general,
I do not approve of the usual tendency of Lord Chesterfields Letters, but I
heartily agree with him respecting the utility of a written correspondence. It,
like many other good things can be made to suffer an abuse, but that is no
effectual argument against its good effects.

I dear A——, naturally love a letter, and take as much pleasure in reading
one, (when addressed to myself:) and in answering one as in almost any thing
else; & this good opinion which I entertain, has not suffered any injury from
the circumstances I have noticed above: I also like it for what I fancy to be good
reasons, drawn up in my own mind upon the subject; and from those reasons,
I have concluded, that letter writing improves; first, the hand writing secondly,
the ——. . . At this moment occurs an instance of my great deficiency in letter
writing: I have the Idea I wish to express full in my mind, but have forgot the
word that expresses it; a word common enough too: I mean the expression, the
delivery, the composition a manner of connecting words. thirdly, it improves
the mind, by the reciprocal exchange of knowledge. fourthly, the ideas; it tends
I conceive to make the ideas clear and distinct, (Ideas are generated or formed

1-2

in the head, and I will give you an odd instance as proof. fifthly, it improves the morals: I speak not of the abuse, but the use of Epistolations, (if you will allow me to coin a new word to express myself) and that use I have no doubt, produces other good effects. Now, I do not profess myself perfect in those points, and my deficiency in others connected with the subject you well know; as Grammar &c therefore it follows that I want improving on these points, and what so natural in a disease, as to revert to the remedy that will perform a cure; and more so when the Physic is so pleasant: or to express it in a more logical manner, and consequently more philosophically, MF is deficient in certain points, that he wants to make up. Epistolary writing is one cure for these deficiencies. therefore, MF should practice Epistolary writing.

Seeing that I have thus proved, from both Reason and Logic, and the last is almost equal to Mathematics in certainty; that I should Write Letters; it merely remained to obtain correspondents: Now do not be affronted Mr. Abbott at my looking towards you before you have heard my reasons; I am happy to say that my disposition is somewhat like your own, Philosophically inclined; and of course I wish to improve in that part more than in others: you too have I presume time to spare now & then for half an hour or so: your Ideas too I have ascertained whilst conversing with you, are plentifull, & pretty perfect; I will not say quite, for I have never yet met with a person who had arrived at perfection so great as to conceive new ideas with exactness & clearness. & your – vide above, where I failed; your composition, or expression, pleases me highly. for these reasons I have presumed to conceive, that the interchange of ideas & Information would not be unpleasant to you, & would be highly gratifying to me. You may if you choose take this   (insert some word here) as a specimen of what mine would be, & return me an answer similar to what you promised me, before *Yes* or *No*.

On looking back I find dear A——, that I have filled two pages with very uninteresting matter; and was intending to go on with more, had I not suddenly been stopped by the lower edge of the paper. this circumstance, (happily for you, for I should have put you to sleep else,) has "called back my wand'ring thoughts," & I will now give you what I at first intended this letter should be wholly composed of, Philosophical Information & Ideas.

I have lately made a few simple galvanic experiments merely to illustrate to my self the first principles of the science. I was going to Knights, to obtain some Nickle, & bethought me, that they had Malleable Zinc: I enquired & boght [*sic*] some. – have you seen any yet? The first portion I obtained was in the thinnest pieces possible; observe in a flattened state. It was as they informed me, thin enough for the Electric Snake,[3] or as I before called it, de Luc's Electric column. I obtained it for the purpose of forming discs, with which & copper to make a little battery. the first I completed contained the immense number of seven pair of Plates!!! and of the immense size of half-pence each!!!!

I, Sir, I my own self, cut out seven discs of the size of half-pennies each! I, Sir, covered them with seven half-pence and I interposed between seven or rather six pieces of paper, soaked in a solution of muriate of Soda!!! – but laugh no longer Dear A—— rather wonder at the effects this trivial power produced, it was sufficient to produce the decomposition of the Sulphate of Magnesia; an effect which extremely surprised me, for I did not – could not have any Idea, that the agent was competent to the purpose.––––––––– a thought has struck me – I will tell you, I made the communication between the top & bottom of the pile & the solution with copper wire: do you conceive that it was the copper that decompose [sic] the [earthy] sulphat? [sic]. that part I mean immersed in the solution;——that a galvanic effect took place I am sure, for both wires became covered in a short time with bubbles of some gas, & a continued stream of very minute bubbles, apping [appearing] like small particles, rose through the solution from the negative wire. My proof that the Sulphate was decomposed, was, that in about 2 hours the clear solution became turbid, Magnesia was suspended in it.

Seeing the great effect of this small power, I pr[ocured] from Knights some plate Zinc, or Sheet Zinc; I think they call it; about the thickness of pastboard. from this I cut out discs; & also obtd [sic] some sheet copper, & procured discs of that Metal; the discs abt [sic] $1\frac{3}{4}$ inch in diameter: these I piled up as a battery, interposing a solution of the Muriate of Soda by means of Flannel discs of the same size; as yet, I have only made one trial, and at that time had I believe about 18 or 20 Pair of Plates. With this power I have decomposed the Sulphate of Magnesia, the Sulphat of copper, the Acetate of Lead, & I at first thght [sic] also Water. but my conclusions in that [respect] were perhaps too hastily made.

I inserted the wires [into a por]tion of water that I took out of the cistern, and of course [in a short time] strong action commenced: a dense, I may really say dense w[hite cloud] of matter descended from the Positive wire; & bubbles rose rap[idly and] [ms. missing] in quick succession from the Negative wire. On perceiving this effect take place, I concluded I had decomposed the water; but after a time, I perceived that the action slackened, the white cloud was scarcely perceptible at the wire, tho' by the former action the lower part of the solution was perfectly opaque: & the bubbles nearly ceased. I thought that the action of the battery was exhausted, but in philosophy we do not admit sup-position, & therefore to prove whether the battery was inert, or whether any principle in the water was exhausted, I substituted a fresh portion of water for that which had been galvanized. Then the action commenced again, & went on as at first; the white precipitate again appeared, & bubbles rose as before, but after a while it ceased as in the first instance

I make no affirmative conclusion from these phenomena, but this I presume that the water was not decomposed; our water comes through Iron pipes, & is

5

retained in a leaden cistern: I have also ascertained that it holds a small portion of Muriatic Acid, & have no doubt but that it contains Carbonic Acid. Now do you think that any part of the lead, or Iron, the lead I should rather fancy, is held in solution by the Muriatic or Carbonic Acid? and that the bubbles are formed by the precipitation of the metal, whilst the Acid – what a blunder I mean that the bubbles are formed by the escape of the Acid, & the precipitate is the Metallic oxide? – explain this circumstance to me, will you; either by your pen, or your tongue.

Another Phenomena [*sic*] I observed was this, on seperating [*sic*] the discs from each other, I found that some of the zinc discs had got a coating, a very superficial one; in some parts, of Metallic copper, & that some of the copper discs had a covring [*sic*] of the Oxide of Zinc; in this case the Metals must both have passed through the flannel disc, holding in the solution of Muriate of Soda: & they must have passed by each other. I think this circumstance well worth notice, for remember no effect takes place without a cause. the disposition too of the oxide of Zinc in the flannel was curious, & will tend to illustrate the passage of the metals from one side to the other. I cannot describe it with any effect, you must see it. – but think of these things, & let me – if you please Sir, if you please let me know your opinion.

Thus far have I scribbled & have still got to apologise; but Philosophy must bear sway a little longer. I had a contest with some Gents, respecting a perpetual motion, which induced me to go & see what they affirmed to be one. it was an application of the ball pendulum to a time piece, a very neat piece of workmanship; you may likely have seen it: but if not it is in the window of a Watchmakers situated in a passage at the East side of the Royal exchge [*sic*]. by inquiring I ascertained that – it was called the inclined plane clock, – was not invented by a watchmaker, (negative). – required winding up once in fourteen days —— & was estimated at the value of fifty Guineas or more definitely at 52 10 0. – Guineas change in value so much now a days.

And now dear Sir; to conclude in a manner requisite for this occasion, I humbly beg pardon for thus intruding on your time, your patience, & your good sense. I beseech you if you will condesend [*sic*] so far, to return me an answer on this occasion: & pray let the refusal of your correspondence be as gentle as possible————hoping dear A—— that the liberty I have taken will not injure me in your good opinion, I cannot conclude better than by wishing you all the happiness you can enjoy: the completion of all your good & honest wishes; & full health [illeg.] until I communicate with you again; & for ever after.

I am dear A——

Yours Sincerely

M. FARADAY

Monday Morning

DEAR A——

I am just now involved in a fit of vexation. I have an excellent prospect before me and cannot take it up for want of ability had I perhaps known as much of Mechanics, Mathematics Mensuration & Drawing as I do perhaps of some other sciences that is to say had I happened to employ my mind there instead of other sciences I could have obtd [*sic*] a place an easy place too and that in London at 5.6.7. £800 per Annum. Alas Alas Inability————I must ask your advice on the subject and intend if I can to see you next Sunday.

I understand from my brother that you was [*sic*] in good health & spirits yesterdays [*sic*] you will be sure I was happy to hear it – I heartily hope too that your brothers health improves make if you please my best wishes to him Fail not to give my respects to your Father & Mother & also your Sister.

I am Dear A——
Yours Sincerely
M. FARADAY

One necessary branch of Knowledge would be that of Steam engine and Indeed any thing where Iron is concerned. – Paper out. Pen worn down so

Good day to you   MF

1 Benjamin Abbott was Faraday's best friend in the period of his early manhood. He was a cut above Faraday, socially, earning his living during this period as a clerk in a counting house. He also had received a better education than Faraday, and Faraday turned to him naturally when he needed help with a subject.
2 Dr Isaac Watts (1674–1748) was a clergyman who wrote a number of popular philosophical works for students who did not have the opportunity for a formal education. For his influence upon Faraday, see *LPW* 12 ff.
3 Bence Jones here reads 'stick' but this is not correct. 'Snake' is a somewhat doubtful reading; I have never run across the word in this context.

2   M. FARADAY to B. ABBOTT, 20 July 1812
[*R.I., Warner mss., B.J. 1, 23ff*]

July 20, 1812
Monday Evg. 10 o'clock

DEAR ABBOTT,

Were you to see me instead of hearing from me I conceive that one question would be how did you get home on Sunday evening I suppose this question because I wish to let you know how much I congratulate myself upon the very pleasant walk or rather succession of walks runs and hops I had home that evening and the truly Philosophical reflections they gave rise to.

I set off from you at a run and did not stop untill I found myself in the midst of a puddle and quandary of thoughts respecting the heat generated in animal bodies by exercise. The puddle however gave a turn to the affair and I proceeded from thence deeply immersed in thoughts respecting the resistance of fluids to bodies precipitated into them I did not at that time forget the instances you and your Brother had noticed in the afternoon to that purpose

My mind was deeply engaged on this subject and was proceeding to place itself as fast as possible in the midst of confusion when it was suddenly called to take care of the body by a very cordial affectionate & also effectual salute from a spout. this of course gave a new turn to my ideas and from thence to Black-Friars Bridge it was busily bothered amongst Projectiles and Parabolas At the Bridge the wind came in my face and directed my attention as well and as earnestly as it could to the inclination of the Pavement Inclined Planes were then all the go and a further illustration of this point took place on the other side of the Bridge where I happened to proceed in a very smooth soft and equable manner for the space of three or four feet. This movement which is vulgarly called slipping introduced the subject of friction and the best method of lessening it and in this frame of mind I went on with little or no interruption for some time except occasional and actual experiments connected with the subject in hand or rather in head.

The Velocity and Momentum of falling bodies next struck not only my mind but my head my ears my hands my back and various other parts of my body and tho I had at hand no apparatus by which I could ascertain those points exactly I knew it must be considerable by the quickness with which it penetrated my coat and other parts of my dress This happened in Holborn and from thence I went home Sky-gazing and earnestly looking out for every Cirrus, Cumulus, Stratus, Cirro-Cumuli, Cirro-Strata and Nimbus that came above the Horizon[1]

I almost fear dear Abbott that you will envy me my walk and for that I should be sorry I do not wish to give rise by any means to so bad so disagreeable a passion in the breast of any person. I myself was well pleased with it (the walk) and had it not been that through it I was deprived of the pleasure of your company I should have blessed my stars for such amusing weather.

> To an honest man, close buttoned to the chin
> Broad cloth without, and a warm heart within.[2]

Hear [*sic*] am I dear Sir on the third page of my paper and have not yet began [*sic*] to answer your very kind free friendly instructive amusing and very wellcome letter but now I will turn to it and "say my say."

For the first part I thank you and here note that I shall keep you to the following words "But will not fail to give them a thorough investigation.' I like your Logic well. – Philosophical Accounts, Scientific inquiries Humble

8

trials, ha, ha, ha, hah! – Don't *you* charge me with Ceremony yet, or whilst your style runs thus "but this I overlook &c. &c. &c." – you know the rest – apply it.

I am exceedingly obliged to you for the observation & quotation you have given me respecting Cupid & Galvanism and return my most gratefull thanks [to] you for the remedy you have pointed out to m[e] against the attacks of the little God-Demon, [ms. missing] by Le Sage's pardon. You no doubt are aware that this is not the first time that he has been conquered by Philosophy and Science The last named person informs us very minutely in what manner he was shut up in a glass bottle and rendered incapable of doing mischief – oh that I were as wise as that Sage – that I could shut little Cupids in glass bottles what exquisite presents they would be to the Ladies and how irresistible would the fair sex be to all who knew not how to oppose them thus armed tho' I must confess they are not quite so absolute since the discovery of this anti-amorous remedy Galvanism. You will not have forgot too when we set the Nitrous Oxide in opposition to him and since Galvanism now aids the Gas it is not possible for the little Urchin to keep his ground. Farewell to him

I am now going to set my piles in action in which state I shall leave them all night and in the morning I will note down what Phenomena I shall perceive. –––Alas. alas. the salt-box is empty and as it is now too late to procure a fresh quantity I shall wish you all Health and Happiness, and wish you a Good-Night –

Tuesday Morning, half-past 6
o'Clock and a fine Morning

Goodday to you Sir I now intend to proceed on with my letter from the point where I left off – not exactly tho' for as yet I have no salt and I do not like to substitute any other solution or any Acid because I suspect both the Acid and the Alkali bear a part in the transmission of the Metals. I am exceedingly obliged to you for your Ideas on this subject, and I think I need not say I received it with good-will I never yet dear Abbott received any thing from you but what I met with that feeling and for the rest of the sentence had I thought that your mind was so narrow as to be chagrin'd at seeing a better solution of this Phenomena from another person I certainly should never have commenced a correspondence with You.

I beg your pardon for an error I committed on Sunday Afternoon. Malleable Zinc is 2/6 per lb. as for the Copper I am not exactly aware of its value I have calculated as correctly as I could that 1 lb. of Sheet Zinc contains 130 Square inches superficial measure on each side.

I was this Morning called by a trifling circumstance to notice the peculiar motions of Camphor on water You no doubt know that when a very small piece of Camphor is placed on the surface of some clean water it commences mostly a rotatory motion I have both heard and read of it before but I was

9

greatly impressed when I beheld it The piece of Camphor was cracked and when on the surface of the water it immediately split and a sharp rapid motion commenced between the two halves the end(s) were alternately attracted and repelled in a very curious manner. I should not have mentioned this simple circumstance but that I thought the effect was owing to Electricity and I supposed that if you were acquainted with the phenomena you would notice it. I conceive too, that a Science may be illustrated by those minute actions and effects almost as much as by more evident and obvious phenomena Facts are plentifull enough but we know not how to class them many are overlooked because they seem uninteresting but remember that what led Newton to pursue and discover the Law of Gravity and ultimately the laws by which Worlds revolve was – the fall of an apple. –

Whilst conversing some time since with a young Lady I learned that there was a kind of glass of such a nature or so prepared as to have a singular effect when employed to glaze windows and placed in them with one particular side outwards Any person in the room could observe another on the outside who could not in return look into the room he could not see what was passing tho' done before the windows It struck me a few days since whilst passing by a fine house that appeared to have in the Window frames very bad glass that this peculiar glass was of the kind called plate and ground smooth only on one side the rough side being outwards perhaps the diversity of reflection would hinder a person from seeing what passed in the interior – If you are acquainted with this circumstance explain it to me. –

(My knife is so bad that I cannot mend my pen with it – it is now covered with Copper having been employed to precipitate that Metal from the Muriatic Acid – this is an excuse – accept it).

Tuesday Evening, 11 o'Clock

Thus far had I got kind A——, when I received your very friendly Epistle and inclosure. I heartily thank you for both but more particularly the first tho' I cannot refrain from being discontented at your hunger as it shortened your communication and with it my pleasure I would complain much more but that I cannot spare paper at present.

I have just finished putting the battery, as you term it, in action and shall now let it remain for the night acting upon a solution of the Muriate of Ammonia thus is the disposition made Fifteen plates of Zinc and as many of Copper are piled up with discs of Flannel interposed, Fifteen other plates of each Metal are formed into a pile with pasteboard, both it and the Flannel being soaked in a solution of Common Salt. These two piles are connected together and their combined action employed as I before stated. The flash from it when applied to the Gums or Eyes is very vivid and the action on the tongue when in contact with the edges will not allow it to remain there.

With respect to your second solution of the Passage of the Metals, I have not time at present to think of it nor have I room to say more than that I thank you for [a]ll on that subject, wait till I have heard of your experiments. [ms. missing] Good-night.

Wednesday Morning 6 o'Clock –

I have doubled in as much paper as I could in order to gain room never mind the shape –

I can now only state facts Opinions you shall have next time On looking at the pile this morning I found that the M[uriate] of A[mmonia]. had been decomposed the Alkali separated at the negative wire and escaped this was evident last night by the cloud it formed with M[uriatic] A[cid]. – The Acid acted on the Copper wire and a M of C was formed this was again decomposed and now I find the negative wire covered with a vegetation of Copper and the P wire eaten away very considerably the solution is of a fine blue colour owing to the Ammoniate of Copper – On turning to the piles I found the action of one considerable the other was exhausted the first contained the flannel discs and they were yet very moist the other had the paper discs and they were quite dry of course you know why the action ceased On looking to the states of the plates particularly I found but one in the pile containing flannel that was in the state I before noticed that is it being Zinc and possessing a coat of Copper, in the paper pile not a single Zinc plate was affected that way the Copper plates in both piles was [sic] covered very considerably with the Oxide of Zinc

I am aware with you that Zinc precipitates Copper and that the Metals are oxided before solution in Acids but how does that effect their motion from one disc to another in contrary directions – I must trust to your experiments mor[e] than my own – I have no time and the subject requires several.

Remember me to all Friends Yours Unceremoniously,   M. FARADAY

[1] This terminology had only recently been introduced into meteorology. See Luke Howard, 'On the modifications of clouds, and on the principles of their production, suspension and destruction,' *PM*, 16 (1803), 97–107, 344–57.
   'The natural history of clouds,' *NJ*, 30 (1812), 35–62.
[2] The couplet appears in *B.J.* but not in the manuscript.

3   M. FARADAY to B. ABBOTT, 2 August 1812

[*R.I.*, *Warner mss., previously unpublished*]

August 2, 1812.

DEAR ABBOTT,

What is the longest, and the shortest thing in the world: the swiftest, and the most slow: the most divisible and the most extended: the least valued and the most regretted: without which nothing can be done: which devours all that is small: and gives life and spirits to every thing that is great?

It is that, Good Sir, the want of which has till now delayed my answer to your wellcome letter. It is that which the Creator has thought of such value as never to bestow on us mortals two of the minutest portions of it at once. It is that which with me is at the instant very pleasingly employed. It is Time.

To be brief dear A—— amidst this circumlocution it is solely to the want of the above valuable article that you are at this time to attribute the apparent mark of Carelessness that so delayed an answer would induce you to suppose I had evinced. At the moment I read your letter my ideas marshalled themselves into the form of an answer and were extremely willing to issue out to paper immediately but that could not be and I will now call them up by a re-perusal in the best manner I can.

In compliance with your request I return you with thanks my first – (not Scrawl (for that is a very un-philosophical word and fit only to be used by feminine males, man-miliners [sic] – ladies footmen &c. and sounds or rather reads very badly I will assure you amongst Voltaic Experiments) but first introduction to your correspondence, and in that view (and that alone) I respect it – It is not "inclosed in a long account of curious usefull and entertaining experiments" but want of time and ability will – must, excuse me.

When I first took in hand the pen I was not aware that I could any way manufacture a decent letter for really I have nothing to say but somehow I suspect I shall as usual fill the paper & I wish you were inclined to copy my example somewhat more than you do I mean in length not in quality I am obliged to you for the philosophical experiment you have described to me so clearly; yet, as you know that the eyes are by far more clear and minute in the information they convey to the sensorium than the tongue or rather Ears you must allow me to defer any observations untill I have repeated and varied it myself It was my intention to do so on the same day that I received your letter and for that purpose arranged the pile and connected it by Copper wires to a solution of the Muriate of Soda my real intentions were to connect it by a copper & Zinc wire to the solution and then consider it as a circular or endless battery but by an oversight both connecting wires were Copper I will not describe to you the Voltaic effects for I did not pay to it sufficient attention, but I will inform you that from it I obtained a result not at all connected with my intentions but to me gratifying you well know there is two oxides of Copper the Black & the Orange the Protoxide and the Peroxide. The Black or Per-oxide is obtd by heating Copper for a few minutes in a bright fire and then plunging it into water that I could do but I could not easily indeed not at all obtain the Orange oxide untill on looking in the Morning to my battery I found a considerable deposit of it at the bottom of the solution the Salt was first decomposed & the Acid had acted on the Copper & then again the M of Copper in time gave way to the Voltaic influence at least I suppose that was the process.

With respect to the Camphor and Glass I will tell you my reason for noticing them. I wish to make our Correspondence a deposit of Philosophical facts & circumstances that will perhaps tend to elucidate to us some of the laws of nature for this reason I shall insert in the form of Queries or otherwise all the facts I can meet with that I think are as yet unexplained they will be as subjects for investigation and if you think fit to chime in with my fancy and will propose such things as you are acquainted with that are yet unresolved or any thing else that your better judgment may choose it will give a peculiar feature to our communications and cannot fail of laying under obligations your most Obedient.

I was in hopes dear Sir that I should before now have received the promised long epistle containing your Electrical Experiments since I have been aware that you intended making some I have felt much interested in the result do not delay to inform me at all times as early as convenient and let me caution you not to wait for my answers consider the disparity between your time and mine and then if you do feel inclined to communicate alternately I hope you will give tha[t] notion up

I am not sure that I acted properly when I addresse[d my] [ms. missing] correspondence to you alone and not jointly to you and your Brother. My reason for entertaining this doubt is the oneness of spirit that appears to actuate you both and the truly Brotherly parts you support – I do not know exactly whether your Brother has that enthusiasm for writing that I have but as at one time he proposed to translate a French Book on Philosophy into English I fancy he is not quite averse to it

Once and once only I had the *pleasure* of being ingaged [*sic*] in a friendly controversy with your Brother respecting the Universality of the Deluge He opposed it I cannot say I maintained it but I thought it was so If your Brother has no objection to lay down his arguments on paper and will transmit them to me by Post I shall not forget the obliging condescension on his side and the gratifying honor on my own but observe I do not so ask to infringe on convenience inclination or other employment Remember me Sincerely to him and wish him good health. HEALTH[1]

In the Epistle I return you of mine I find I promised you an instance as proof that ideas were formed in the head It is scarcely worth having but as it costs nothing take it Six or seven years ago whilst standing at the door of a gentlemans house and waiting untill my knock should be answered I thrust my head through some iron railing that separated the door way from another and then I began to consider on which side of the rails I was. In my mind I affirmed that the side possessing my head was my station for there was my perception my senses I had just sufficient time to ascertain this when the door opened and my nose began bleeding by the contact of the rails and such matter as that quickly put flight to my rude metaphysics. Simple as is this instance it did more in illustrating this case to me than all the arguments I have heard since on the subject or all the affirmations that have been made.

I wish to add something more if I can and therefore will not at present conclude Mr. Huxtable[2] left town I believe on last Monday On the Saturday before we made two of a party that went down the river to the Botanical Gardens at Chelsea belonging to the Company of Apothecaries I was very well pleased with the excursion and wished for you two or three times

I have at this time a small Galvanic trough in my hands it is on the construction of Cruickshanks[3] that is it has glass partitions The plates of metal are about $2\frac{1}{2}$ inchs [*sic*] long & 2 wide the trough contains 36 cells but I have in my hands only 18 pair of plates The owner is a young man who has attended several of Tatum's[4] Lectures I know him slightly before he has his trough again I shall make free to use it and see whether I cannot decompose water the M of Ammonia &c. and I will try at animal & vegetable matter.

Pyrotechny will be exhibited in considerable perfection on Tuesday evening at Ranalagh Gardens alias Manor Vauxhall alias Kings Arms &c. Will you go to see it If I receive no denial from you I shall transmit under cover a couple of double tickets Your Brother of course will come & if your Sister conceives the place will afford an hours amusement to her I hope she will make one of your Party. I am not quite certain I can be there myself but if convenient I will make my appearance about 9 or 10 say $\frac{1}{2}$ past 9 o'clock The pleasure I expect will be the walk & your company. ' Till then, I

> Remain, Dear Abbott
> Yours Sincerely
> M. FARADAY

I have left the enclosure at Weymouth St[5] & I am now here you shall have it next time.

> Blandford St[6] Mondy Morn.

[1] The word 'health' was written in large script, not capitals, in the manuscript.
[2] T. Huxtable was one of Faraday's early friends. See *B.J.* 1, 13.
[3] See William Cruickshank, 'Account of some important experiments in Galvanic Electricity,' *PM*, 7 (1800), 337–47.
[4] John Tatum was the moving force behind the City Philosophical Society to which Faraday belonged. See *LPW*, 15 ff.
[5] During the last years of his apprenticeship, Faraday lived in Weymouth Street.
[6] 2 Blandford Street was the address of Mr Riebau's bookbindery where Faraday was just completing his apprenticeship. See *LPW*, 10 ff.

Aug. 11, 1812.

DEAR A——.

I make all imaginable haste to assure you that Idleness is a fault which never in my mind was associated with any ideas respecting you nay so opposite to that is my opinion that I conceive were it not for your good sense you would sooner be doing mischief than doing nothing but understand here dear Sir once for all, that I never wish to invade your conveniency in any manner on the contrary I would rather add to it by any means in my power.

"Pyrotechny is a beautifull art" but I never made any practical progress in it except in the forming a few bad squibs so that you will gain little from me on that point I have a book at home which amongst other things contains a considerable number of Receipts in the Art and several illustrative plates It if you choose is at your service and I have no doubt would be of considerable use.

I thank you for your electrical experiment but conceive the subject requires a very numberous series and of very various kinds I intend to repeat it for I am not exactly satisfyed of the division of the charge so as to produce more than one perforation I should be glad if you would add to your descriptions any conclusions which you by them are induced to make They would tend to give me a fairer idea of the circumstances

I have to notice here a very singular circumstance namely a slight dissent in my ideas from you it is this You propose not to start one Query untill the other is resolved or at least "discussed and experimented upon" but this I shall hardly allow for the following reasons – Ideas and thoughts often spring up in my mind and are again irrevocably lost for want of noting at the time I fancy it is the same with you and would therefore wish to have any such objections or unresolved points exactly as they appear to you in their full force that is immediately after you have first thought of them for to delay untill the subject in hand is exhausted would be to lose all the intervening ideas Understand too that I preserve your communications as a repository into which I can dip for a subject requiring explanation and therefore the more you insert the more will it deserve that name nevertheless I do not mean to desert one subject for another directly it is started but reserve them for after subjects of consideration

Thank your Brother for me if you please for his assent to my desire I am exceedingly sorry you should have to urge ill health and need not tell you that I wish it were otherwise most heartily.

I will attend to your advice respecting the Aether and shall carefully catch and preserve as much of it as extends thus far I have no doubt but that you diffuse a very fragrant atmosphere about Bermandsy.[1] [*sic*]

Sr H. Davys book is I understand already published but I have not yet seen it nor do I know the price or size it is entitled "Elements of Chemical Philosophy."

That Oxy-Muriatic Acid gas is obtained by heating a mixture of the Peroxide of Manganese Muriate of Soda and Sulphuric Acid is I conceive no objection to S^r H D. theory I have not heard the particular fact explained but conceive it to be thus. Sulphuric Acid we will consider as a simple substance The Per-oxide of Manganese as a lesser oxide and Oxygen and the Muriate of Soda is a compound of Chlorine and the metal Sodium This perhaps you are not fully convinced of but the experiments of Davy prove it In the process of disengaging Chlorine the Sulphuric Acid decomposes both the oxide and the Muriate it combines with the Manganese when united to a lesser portion of Oxygen and of course Oxygen is liberated The Muriate being composed of but two parts Chlorine and Sodium can only be resolved into those principles The Chlorine is given out as a gas and is received in jars The Sodium combines with the Oxygen liberated from the Oxide and Soda is formed which is dissolved by the Sulphuric Acid.

This I conceive to be the theory of the process [ms. missing] and if you refer to the discoverers Scheele's Theory[2] [ms. missing] you will find it is exactly the same indeed I would wish you not to be surprised if the old theory of Phlogiston should be again adopted as the true one tho I do not think it will entirely set aside Lavoisiers but the "Elements" will inform you – If you find in your mind the least objection to the above explanation let me know it as I do not wish to adopt an error.

I beg your pardon for puzzling you without cause with respect to the galvanic experiment in which the Muriate of Soda was decomposed you enquire "where is the Acid" I did not pretend to give a minute description of the experiment or otherwise I should have noticed an apparently continued corrosion of the Copper at the Positive wire and a continual deposit of the oxide at the negative wire so that as the Salt was decomposed at one pole the Acid was employed in forming a fresh portion at the other so that when the action of the battery was exhausted still a portion of the Muriate of Copper remained in solution tho' perhaps three or four times as much had been decomposed Its presence was evident by the blue colour of what remained.

Having thus dear A———. noticed all the topics of your letter I will add a little matter of my own and first a few queries for future discussion.

You must know well the appearance of a window when covered with the frost as it is termed the figures often possess very great regularity what is the cause of it? I am aware that the crystallization of the water or rather ice is one *affecting* circumstance but I suspect from some appearances I have noticed that the Electric state of the glass has also its influence.

In the northern parts of Europe and America a very singular Phenomena is noticed in Metals – Iron I believe The Laplanders will offer a stranger a piece of Iron that has been in the air and obtained the common temperature and it will on touching the flesh bring away the skin somewhat like a burn The same Phenomena is evident or rather takes place in the Northern parts of Russia Siberia &c. and at Hudsons Bay in America how is this effect to be accounted for. The *Gents. Mag.* contains some very foolish explanations of it[3]

Definitions dear A – are valuable things I like them very much and will be glad when you meet with clever ones if you will transcribe them I am exceedingly well pleased with Dr. Thomsons definition of Chemistry he calls it the Science of insensible motions "Chemistry is that Science which treats of those events or changes in natural bodies which consist of insensible motions"[4] in contradistinction to Mechanics which treats of sensible motions

How do you define Idleness?

I forgot to insert a Query when at the proper place tho I think an investigation of it would be of importance to the Science of Chemistry and perhaps Electricity Several of the Metals when rubbed emit a peculiar smell and more particularly Tin Now smells are generally supposed to be caused by particles of the body that are given off if so then it introduces to our notice a very volatile property of those metals But I suspect their Electric states are concerned and then we have an operation of that fluid that has seldom been noticed and yet requires accounting for before the Science can be completed.

Thus dear Abbott I have given you all the Philosophy I can spare at present and now I will ask you how your time is engaged for next Sunday afternoon My Brother as well as myself wishes much to see where the Surrey canal passes by locks over the hill and as you proposed it to me the last time I saw you I considered it as not unallowable If you feel inclined to a like treat [on say next Sunday and will] [reading doubtful][5] accept the company of your humble Servants it would be I hope gratifying to all We would be with you at whatever time you should be ready to start and will appoint after 1 o'clock but observe this is if perfectly convenient and agreeable Let me know if you please your pleasure on the subject.

I will see you before the 20th at all events.

Let me hear from you shortly. Remember me to all Friends. Health Happiness and Prosperity be with you and believe me continually

Yours Very Sincerely,

M. FARADAY

[1] Benjamin Abbott lived in Long Lane in Bermondsey.
[2] See Mary Elvira Weeks, *The Discovery of the Elements*, 6th ed., Easton, Pa., 1956, 729ff. for Scheele's work on chlorine.
[3] *GM*, 81 (1811), 124, 234, 412.
[4] Thomas Thomson, *A System of Chemistry*, 2nd ed., 4 vols., Edinburgh, 1804, Vol. 1, p. 3.
[5] Omitted from *B.J.*

August 19th, 1812.

DEAR ABBOTT,

Never do I feel so well able and so well inclined to answer a letter as at the time of receiving it or rather at the first reading I have just reperused yours but having seen you since I received it I find that by far the greater part of it is answered It is probable therefore that this letter will be a dull one for I have but few subjects and the heat of the weather has so enervated me that I am not able to treat those I have in a proper manner – But rouse up Michael and do not disgrace thyself in the opinion of thy Friend –

I have again gone over your letter but am so blinded that I cannot see any subject except Chlorine to write on but before entering upon what I intend shall fill up the letter I will ask your pardon for having maintained an opinion against one who was so ready to give his own up – I suspect from that circumstance I am wrong – I am happy to find from the conclusion of your Epistle that your views are so comprehensive and indulge largely the pleasures of anticipation in expectation of a rich harvest (in the winter) of new and important information

With respect to Chlorine if we intend to debate the question of its simple or compound nature we have begun at a wrong point or rather at no point at all Conscious of this I will at this time answer your present objections but briefly & then give the best statement I can of the subject – The Muriate of Soda is a compound of Chlorine and Sodium and as Chlorine in this theory is esteemed a simple substance I conceive that the name of Chlorate of Sodium is improper *ate* and *ite* are the terminations of the generic names of Salts, and convey to our minds an idea of the Acid that the base is combined with but Chlorine is not an acid it is a simple substance belonging to the same class as oxygen and therefore its binary compounds should I conceive be termed in imitation of Oxydes, Chlorides. The Muriate of Soda is therefore a Chloride of Sodium and the Oxymuriate of Soda is a compound of that Chloride with Oxygen

I will not say more at present on your objections since you will now be able to answer them yourself in the same way that I should do but I will proceed to the more simple and elementary parts of the subject – In the present case I conceive that Experiments may be divided into three classes 1st Those which are for the old theory of Oxy-muriatic Acid and consequently oppose the new one 2ndly Those which are for the new one and oppose the old Theory and 3rdly Those which can be explained by both theories – apparently so only for in reality a false theory can never explain a fact – I am not aware of any belonging to the first class what appeared to be such at first have on consideration resolved themselves into the third class Of the second class I will propose a few to you and of the third class is that we have already been engaged upon

Be not surprised my dear Abbott at the ardour with which I have embraced this new theory – I have seen Davy himself support it I have seen him exhibit experiments conclusive experiments explanatory of it and I have heard him apply those experiments to the theory & explain and enforce them in (to me) an irresistible manner Conviction Sir struck me and I was forced to believe him and with that belief came admiration[1]

As you are already acquainted with the properties of Chlorine it will be improper to say anything about its particular characters. I shall therefore enter immediately upon such experiments as I am acquainted with that tend to prove it a simple body that is an undecomposed one – You well know that when a taper is immersed burning in Chlorine gas the combustion becomes very dim the flame appears of a dull red & a great quantity of smoke is emitted This smoke is the carbonaceous part of the taper Now on the supposition that Chlorine or Oxy-muriatic Acid is a compound of the Muriatic Acid and Oxygen how happens it that [the] Hydrogen of the combustible burns and not the Ca[rbon]. Carbon is considered as having the strongest affinity [for] [ms. missing] Oxygen of any combustible yet here Hydrogen will burn and Carbon will not Carbon which has the strongest affinity cannot do what Hydrogen does Several of the Metals will burn spontaneously in this gas a proof that the supporter of combustion is not held by so strong an affinity from them and tho the Carbon will decompose the Oxides of those Metals it cannot combine with the Oxygen of the gas The fact is no oxygen is present nothing but Chlorine a simple substance and with Chlorine Charcoal has no apparent affinity[2] Hydrogen possesses a strong attraction for it and therefore we see why that part of the combustible burns & not the Carbon. As a still more simple and decisive experiment I will relate the following of Davys He had a glass globe filled with dry Chlorine gas and by means of a Voltaic Battery he ignited in this gas two points of charcoal but no change took place both the combustible and the gas remained unaltered Carbon at a white heat could abstract no oxygen from Chlorine gas whereas at the same time he made Gold a metal which has the least affinity for Oxygen burn in the same portion of gas & by the same power It combined with the Chlorine.

When Chlorine gas is mixed with Hydrogen gas equal parts of each being put together and are submitted to the action of the Sun's rays or electric sparks are passed through them it is affirmed that the Hydrogen combines with the Oxygen and both Muriatic Acid gas & Water are formed but this affirmation is false it is not so if the gasses are both perfectly dry no condensation takes place no water is formed nothing but Muriatic Acid remains – This is a very decisive experiment and therefore particular attention has been paid to it it has been performed with every possible care both by the French Chemists and by Davy and the result has been as I have stated it no water was obtained nothing but pure Muriatic Acid gas and as Chlorine & Hydrogen were present it follows that Muriatic Acid is composed of these two bodies.

The experiment I last stated is a synthetical proof of the compound nature of Muriatic Acid I shall now in order to complete the circumstances relate an analytical one – If a piece of Potassium is enclosed in a portion of dry Muriatic Acid gas and its temperature is somewhat raised it will inflame the Acid gas will disappear and Hydrogen will be found remaining The Metal has united to the Chlorine forming a Muriate of Potash & the Hydrogen remains behind The same effect may be produced by other metals but more slowly Tin Antimony Arsenic Copper &c. all are capable of decomposing the Muriatic Acid gas

By Lavoisier's Theory you would explain it thus The metal say you decomposes a portion of water combines with the oxygen and the Hydrogen remains – But no water is present – it is impossible that water sufficient to supply so much Hydrogen can be present & escape detection it cannot be the Hydrogen proceeds solely from the decomposition of the Muriatic Acid gas.

I will before I conclude this long letter just notice another synthetical experiment respecting Muriatic Acid – When steam & Chlorine gas in proper proportions are passed through a red hot porcelain tube a decomposition of the water takes place. Its Hydrogen combines with the Chlorine and forms Muriatic Acid and its oxygen comes over accordingly Muriatic Acid Gas & Oxygen gas comes over and nothing else By Lavoisier's Theory the fact would be explained thus The steam caused a decomposition of the Oxy-Muriatic Acid and Muriatic Ad & Oxygen came over – but what becomes of the steam? no water in Davy's experiment came over – none at all – but by Lavoisier's theory the disappearance of that is unaccounted for – and the decomposition of the Oxy-Muriatic Ad & it is very unaccountable when it does not combine with either of its parts – in fact it is not so the water is decomposed and thus it disappears and thus is the Muriatic Acid composed –

Thus far dear Friend for the present in my next I will continue the subject and in the mean time transmit to me any objections you have to what I have already drawn

I have not time, dear Ben at present to close my letter in a proper manner I shall be at Ranelagh tomorrow evening (if fate permits) & if we do not meet before will take my station exactly at nine under the orchestra

Yours Truly

M. Faraday

[1] For an account of Faraday's attendance at Davy's lectures, see *LPW*, 25ff.

[2] This was a point which bothered Faraday a good deal. Surely if chlorine were a supporter of combustion it *must* combine with carbon. It was this conviction which led Faraday to the discovery of compounds of chlorine and carbon in the 1820s. See his papers, 'On two new Compounds of Chlorine and Carbon, and on a new Compound of Iodine, Carbon, and Hydrogen,' *ERCP*, 33ff. 'On a new Compound of Chlorine and Carbon' (with R. Phillips), *ibid.*, 53ff.

[*R.I., Warner mss., previously unpublished*]

Sept. 1st, 1812.

DEAR OBLIGING ABBOTT,

I acknowledge the receipt of your last letter dated Aug 28ᵗʰ and intend to preserve it sacredly not only as a part of our correspondence but as a proof of your kindness & industry. I am sorry & beg pardon of you for reproaching you not knowing your situation and promise not to offend so again – I condole with you most sincerely on account of your indisposition – I am surprised and that not agreeably at its remaining on you so long – Your situation (for the view of which I thank you) is certainly not the most agreeable it is almost pitiable but I conceive it will not last long and then all will be right again nevertheless in order to support you by giving you a little relaxation and bringing to your mind other objects I will again take up the subject of Chlorine & back the opinion I conceive to be correct and have affirmed by experiments & reasonings in the best manner I can.

In my last if I remember rightly I gave as proofs that Chlorine gas contained no Oxygen experiments in the following import – That the Carbonaceous part of a taper would not burn in it – That ignited Carbon or Charcoal would not burn in it – That when Chlorine and Hydrogen were united no results containing Oxygen appeared – That when Steam & Chlorine were made to act on each other all the Oxygen obtained came from the water and as a proof that Muriatic Acid is a compound I noticed an experiment in which it is decomposed by Potassium the chlorine being taken from it by the metal & I slightly adverted to the peculiar combinations of other metals & Chlorine.

It was necessary dear Abbott that I should thus recapitulate what I had before said on this subject for so many things have since engaged my attention and draw it off from that point that it was essential to re-collect my thoughts again to avoid saying largely now what I had said before. Sept. 2. – (Last night dear A——— I saw you and heard some of your objections but shall not answer them untill I have them in writing thus then I proceed).

At this time my arguments in favour of the simplicity of Chlorine will be drawn from the nature of the results when it pure is made the supporter of combustion and when it is combined with other bodies – I have already observed one of these combinations i.e. when Hydrogen was united to it – Hydrogen when united to Chlorine forms a pure unmixed uniform binary compound Muriatic Acid and no water is produced in weight too the weight of the Acid is exactly equal to the weight of its ingredients or rather components used With Oxygen the other supporter of combustion it forms water a body very different to Muriatic Acid and different also are the combinations of the other inflammables with the two supporters.

Look into your Lavoisier[1] into your Nicholson[2] into your Fourcroy[3] and what other Chemical books you have at the article Oxy-Muriatic Acid they will tell you that its Oxygen is held by an affinity so weak that the combustibles burn in it very easily and compounds of the Oxygen and inflamables are obtained as well as Muriatic Acid – You will think me bold dear A if I deny all these authorities but Davy[4] has done so & I will do it too on the strength of his experiments One has copied the errors of another & all are wrong.

As a proof of their want of experiments on this point and their abundance of assertions I will again tell you that Carbon has not yet been made to combine with Chlorine or if you please the Oxygen of Oxy-Muriatic Acid it has not even apparently been made to do so that I know of and yet they affirm that all the combustibles burn in it and produce the same results as in oxygen gas They were not acquainted with the peculiar fact of its non-combination but took it for granted that as it combined with Oxygen it would also burn in Chlorine – but these are a kind of negative facts tho very very importan[t ones.] [ms. obscured] let us now turn to the other combustibles

Phosphorus I believe generally burns spontaneously in this gas with a pale flame and a solid compound is formed but not Phosphoric Acid tho that is solid too but a body very different from it One essential character of PA is its great degree of fixedness it will not sublime or rise in vapour at an heat less than white ignition but this compound my good Sir is volatazable at an heat below $212°$ (I myself saw it rapidly rise from the heat of a small spirit lamp) and this is a very distinguishing difference let me tell you

This substance the Chloride of Phosphorus as we will call it combines with Ammonia – here I fancy I hear you crying out "an Acid an Acid it combines with an Alkali"!!! but softly my good Sir we have no Acid as yet – tho it does combine with Ammonia no Phosphat is formed but a dry powder This powder is very different to the combination of PA & Ammonia and possesses different properties & characters It is exceedingly fixed in the fire it will not rise at a white heat whereas the Phosphat of Ammonia is decomposed at an heat far below that point consequently it must be a different substance & Chlorine must be a simple body

There is another compound of Phosphorus and Chlorine besides the foregoing which will afford some very strong proofs that Chlorine is a simple substance or rather that it is not & does not contain Oxygen This compound is not in a solid form like the former but is a dense liquid it is obtained by distilling the Corrosive Sublimates of Mercury & Phosphorus together now what according to Lavoisier's Theory would you suppose this liquid to be? Phosphoric Acid? or perhaps a mixture of Phosphoric & Muriatic Acids but no my good Sir either supposition would be wrong or any other that supposes an acid or Oxygen present The liquid is no acid but a compound of Phosphorus & Chlorine it does not possess Acid properties If a portion of it is dropped on to

22

litmus paper or any other test paper for Acids it will cause no changes of colour except round the edges of the drops and that circumstance I will otherwise explain

Another proof that the Phosphorus exists in this compound uncombined with Oxygen is the following pour some of it on a surface as paper a film of Phosphorus will quickly form and if it is brought towards the fire it will inflame and burn it then combining with Oxygen a sufficient proof that it was not combined with it before What then was it combined with? Chlorine a substance containing no Oxygen but a simple supporter of Combustion.

This liquid compound is decomposed by & decomposes water & then Sir Abbott we have Acids in plenty If a portion of it is poured into a small quantity of water de- and re-combinations take place and a mixture of Phosphoric and Muriatic Acids are formed During this or those actions no gas is evolved except it may be Muriatic Acid gas but no Oxygen or Hydrogen from the water is given out They are both taken up in the re-compositions They are both necessary to form the Acids The Oxygen of the Water unites to the Phosphorus and produces Phosphoric Acid The Hydrogen unites to the Chlorine & forms Muriatic Acid and thus all the constituent parts are employed The Hydrogen & Oxygen evolved from a certain portion of water is exactly sufficient to saturate both parts of a proper quantity of the compound of Phosphorus & Chlorine.

If now you apply it to Litmus paper the effect of an acid immediately takes place because acids are present and yet it is diluted with thrice its quantity of water before when strong and concentrated it produced no effect on the test now by the addition of water it does a proof that there was no acid in it in the first case tho there was in the latter and a proof also that it was by the decomposition of the water the Acids were formed

I will now explain the reason of the change of colour observed when the compound was dropped on to Litmus paper it took place round the edges The compound having so strong an affinity for water attracts it in a very effectual manner from the Atmosphere and forming such strong acids by its decomposition it immediately decomposed it and then the results acted on the paper now it is evident that this action of the compound would take place at the surface of the drop and as the only part where the surface touched the paper was round the edges it was there only that a change of colour could take place

If you (as I suppose you do still oppose this theory of Davy's consider this experiment with care and account for it otherwise if you can Remember that this compound of Chlorine & Phosphorus possesses not Acid properties That the phosphorus in it will unite to Oxygen and therefore is not previously so that when poured into water it is not a dilution but an action a strong action that takes place and great heat is evolved That both the Oxygen & the Hydrogen of the water is employed and – That then Acids are present The Phosphoric Acid is readily accounted for it is produced by the union of the Phosphorus & the Oxygen but the Muriatic Acid how is that produced nothing but Chlorine

23

& Hydrogen at present remaining nothing but these form that Acid, and nothing else is necessary.

There is a compound of Sulphur & Chlorine similar to the above described one of Phosphorus & Chlorine it is a red liquid & is obtained by heating sublimed Sulphur in Chlorine gas This liquid like the former possesses no Acid properties tho with water it forms two strong Acids Sulphuric & Muriatic This decomposition of water by the compound is exactly similar in its action with the before mentioned one tho not in all its circumstances The Hydrogen liberated unites to the Chlorine & the result is muriatic Acid The Oxygen unites to the Sulphur & forms sulphuric Acid but it so happens that the quantity of Sulphur in the compound is greater than can be saturated by the liberated Oxygen If we conceive a certain portion of the compound to be decomposed and also as much water as will afford Hydrogen sufficient to combine with all the Chlorine of the compound then the Sulphur separated from that quantity is far too much for the Oxygen liberated from the decomposed water consequently Sulphur is separated & remains pure

I have thus dear Abbott detailed the principle facts that I am acquainted with respecting the reciprocal action of the inflamables and Chlorine They all of them afford convincing proof that Chlorine is as yet an undecomposed body & Sulphur & Phosphorus combine with it the first in one proportion & the second in two These three compounds are new & singular ones and exhibit very curious Phenomena They are not neither do they contain any acid – Carbon will not or at least has not yet been made to combine with Chlorine a striking proof that it contains no oxygen – Hydrogen unites to it and is the only one of the combustibles that forms with it an Acid namely the Muriatic Acid – In my next I will continue the subject but positively will first hear from you so that I may know my opponent & his objections.

Adieu, dear Ab[bott. I am] [ms. obscured]

M. F A R A D A Y

Sept 4. [Friday Evening.

Received] [ms. illegible] of Mr. B. Abbott the sum of 24 lines contained in a letter dated Sept. 3, 1812 [illeg.] by me MF. MF congratulates Mr. A on his acquisition of Accum[5] and thinks he has made a good bargain he will enquire about the Phosphorus shortly & thanks Mr. A.—— for his promise of a letter & experiments and expects them impatiently and to conclude he will be exceedingly obliged to him for Admission to Mr. J. Tatum's lectures on the Alkalies he of course even hopes of seeing Mr. Abbott that evening and till then remains Mr. A

Obedient Humble Servant

M. F A R A D A Y

Ha. Ha. Ha. Hah!!!

[Written in pale red ink – Cannot bring initials out.]

[1] Antoine Laurent Lavoisier, *Elements of Chemistry*, translated by Robert Kerr, Edinburgh, 1790; Faraday had not learned French in 1812, hence he probably refers to this English translation.
[2] William Nicholson, *A Dictionary of Practical and Theoretical Chemistry*, London, 1808. See under article, Acid (Muriatic, Hyperoxigenised).
[3] Probably the reference here is to Antoine François Fourcroy, *Elements of Chemistry and Natural History*, Translated by R. Heron, 4 vols., Edinburgh, 1796, Vol. 1, 361ff.
[4] The reference here is to Davy's lectures at the Royal Institution but see also H. Davy, 'Researches on the Oxymuriatic Acid, its nature and combinations, and on the elements of the Muriatic Acid, with some experiments on Sulphur and Phosphorus,' *PT* (1810), 231ff.
[5] See Friedrich Christian Accum, *System of Theoretical and Practical Chemistry*, probably the 2nd ed., 2 vols., London, 1807.

7 M. FARADAY to B. ABBOTT, 9 September 1812

[*R.I., Warner mss., B.J. 1, 31ff*]

September 9th 1812.

"Read it through."

You wrong me, dear Abbott if you suppose I think you obstinate for not coinciding in my opinion immediately. On the contrary I conceive it to be but proper retention I should be sorry indeed were you to give up your opinion without being convinced of error in it and should consider it as a mark of fickleness in you that I did not expect – It is not for me to affirm that I am right & you wrong – speaking impartially I can as well say that I am wrong and you right or that we both are wrong and a third right I am not so self opinionated as to suppose that my judgment & perception in this or other matters is better or clearer than that of other persons nor do I mean to affirm that this is the true theory in reality but only – that my judgment conceives it to be so Judgments sometimes oppose each other as in this case and as there cannot be two opposing facts in nature so there cannot be two opposing truths in the intellectual world consequently when judgments oppose one must be wrong – one must be false – and mine may be so for aught I can tell – I am not of a superior nature to estimate exactly the strength & correctness of my own and other mens understanding and will assure you dear A – that I am far from being convinced that my own is always right

I have given you this theory not as the true one but as the one which appears true to me and when I perceive errors in it I will immediately renounce it in part or wholly as my judgment may direct – From this dear Friend you will see that I am very open to conviction but from the manner in which I shall answer your Letter you will also perceive that I must be convinced before I renounce

You have made a blunder in your letter Abbott. You say that you will first answer my experiments and then relate others but you have only noticed one of mine and therefore I suppose the answers to the others are to come – " With

25

respect to the taper" do you mean to say that none of its Carbon is burnt in Atmospheric air or Oxygen gas I understood Davy that none of it was burned in Chlorine gas and as for your Query of water being formed I do not believe there was any not the slightest condensation took place – I did not insist much on this experiment by itself but had connected it to another where charcoal would not burn you should have answered them both together.

p m
Wednesday Night, 10.30.

I thank you dear A – most heartily for the amusement and pleasure I have just experienced I was instructed at the Lecture[1] but expected to see (hear) more of the particular nature of the Alkalies the subject was copious enough Order was not sufficiently attended to yours I have no doubt will abound in that respect.

You wish to alter the tenor of our arguments you conceive that if you prove oxygen to exist in Muriatic Acid you have done enough – not so – if you do that you will do wonders and I shall certainly pay that respect to it it deserves but the experiments I have related must also be answered before I change opinions I understand it is possible to support a new theory of Chlorine namely that it is a compound of an unknown base and Oxygen but which have never yet been detected separate – but this will not alter our arguments since still MA is considered as the Chlorine and Hydrogen united and whilst this Chlorine is undecomposed we must consider it as simple –

I was considerably surprised to hear you charge me last night with having denied facts I am not aware that I have denied any nor do I wish to do so – I have denied some which have been accounted facts but those cannot be what you alluded to – pray point them out to me

I shall now answer all your conclusive experiments and must confess I do not see that difficulty I expected – Do you remember the first experiment you quoted the solution of a metal in Muriatic Acid in which experiment you consider the Metal as being oxidised at the expence of the Acid – By this means you have arrived at a discovery which has drawn the attention of all great chemists the decomposition of the Muriatic Acid – for by informing us what remains by the de-oxidation of the Acid by the Metal we shall have its other constituent part and thus our dispute – no not dispute – friendly controversy will end – I fear dear A – you will find it hard to decompose M A by the solution of a metal in it It has never knowingly been done by any of Lavoisier's disciples yet or at least they have never allowed it It has been done and I have before related the experiment to you – but to return to your experiment. When a metal is dissolved in M A; I believe it is generally the case that Hydrogen is evolved – from whence is this Hydrogen but from decomposed water and in what manner is the Oxygen employed but by combining with the metal – the oxide is then dissolved – as very prominent instances of this kind I will notice the action of M A on Iron & Zinc – other metals are dissolved by this Acid

26

but I have never noticed the phenomena attendant – If you say the metal obtains Oxygen from the Acid inform me what part of the Acid is left and in what state.

2nd, Oxygen I know may be obtained from the Oxy-muriates because they contain it they are formed by double combination first a Muriate is formed being a compound of Chlorine, & the metallic base of the Alkalies and with this compound Oxygen combines – by applying heat the only operation that takes place is the driving off of Oxygen – but more of this when I have detailed further to you Davy's theory tho' you must perceive the experiments are as easily explained thus as by Lavoisier's opinion

3rd, You can refer I presume to J Davy's experiment[2] and therefore I shall give here only my opinion on it whether mechanical or chemical if the oxide is held mechanically in the ferrane as he supposed it makes no part of the compound of Chlorine & Iron and of course does not affect the subject at all in my idea and if chemically which is not at all probable it does not make its appearance until water is added and then it is easily accounted for but in order to estimate the experiments exactly it would be necessary to consider the manner in which the Ferrane is formed.

I come next to your remarks of which I own the propriety and tho I do not suppose that at any time I can make experiments with more exactness & precision than those I have quoted yet certainly the performance would give us a clearer idea I accept of your offer to fight it out with joy and shall in the battle experience & cause not pain but I hope pleasure nevertheless I will if you will allow me give whilst I have time & opportunity & whilst my ideas are fresh & collected what little more I know of this theory not requiring your immediate answer to it but leaving it to your leisure consideration.

One circumstance amongst many others which makes the difference between Chlorine & the Acids is the change it causes in vegetable colours it does not turn them red as the Acids do but it destroys them entirely and makes the body white and the colour can be restored by neither Acids or Alkalies Pure Chlorine has no effect on vegetable colours at all as has been proved but when water is present it decomposes it and the oxygen causes the change of colour Acids act by combining with the colour without decomposition but Chlorine by presenting oxygen to them having first liberated it from water by taking to itself the Hydrogen – Muriatic Acd is formed

Sr H. Davy I believe was first induced to make an experimental inquiry into the nature of M A by observing that it could never be obtained from Oxy-muriatic acid or the dry Muriates unless water or its constituent parts were present – Having noticed that this phenomena never took place in his general experiments he made some directly to ascertain the point and found that he was incapable of obtaining that Acd from the dry Muriates or from what has been considered as a combination of it with oxygen. Neither Oxygen or M A can be obtained or at least has been obtained from the Oxy-muriatic Acid – This circumstance it was that first induced Davy to prosecute the inquiry and is a high stumbling block to the Lavoisierian theory of this Acid.

There is an experiment of the reciprocal decomposition of Ammonia & the Oxy-muriatic gas that appears directly opposite to this theory of Chlorine So it appeared to Davy and of course he examined it in order to see what conclusions it would lead to He found that it had generally been too loosely made and the opinion that water is formed too hastily adopted he found that when those gases pure & dry were mixed in the proportions of one of Chlorine to 3 of Alkali no water was formed but the product was dry & solid M of Ammonia with about $\frac{1}{10}$ of nitrogen gas The Chlorine had decomposed a part of the Ammonia the nitrogen of which was liberated The Hydrogen it united to forming M A & then a M of Ammonia was formed.

Chlorine forms binary compounds not only with Hydrogen Phosphorus & Sulphur but also with several of the metals amongst which are the bases of the Alkalies and Alkaline earths – When Tin is heated in Chlorine gas both the metal & gas disappear and a liquid being the liquor of Libavius or a Muriate of Tin is obtained This substance is a binary compound only – if ammoniacal gas is added to it no decomposition takes place but the gas & the Stannane (as Davy terms it) combine & a solid volatile body is obtained – What is this Volatile body by the Lavoisierian theory?

Some of the combustibles (including metals) have a stronger affinity for Chlorine than for Oxygen Others have a stronger affinity for Oxygen than for Chlorine – When the affinity of the Chlorine exceeds that of the Oxygen it can be employed to decompose the Oxides in which case it separates the Oxygen – When a piece of Potassium is inflamed in Chlorine gas it unites to the Chlorine and a dry M of P[otass] is formed If an oxide of Potassium (not Potash that is an Hydrat) is used the Chlorine combines with the metal and the oxygen is liberated a Muriate is formed – If the Red Oxide of Mercury is heated in Chlorine gas the Metal & gas unite and the Oxygen is given out Corrosive Sublimate is formed If lime is heated in Chlorine gas the base or Metal Calcium unites to the Chlorine, & the Oxygen is given out & in this way can the Alkalies & Alkaline earths be decomposed I know well your answer to this, "O the Acid parts with Oxygen & then the simple M A & the base combine" but not too fast if so then the same quantity of Oxygen should always be liberated from the same quantity of O M A gas but that is Not the case The quantity of oxygen varies with an equal portion of Chlorine gas but is always in exact proportion to the quantity contained in the oxides a clear proof that it is given out by them and not by the Chlorine Indeed it appears singular to say that the Oxygen is given out by a body (Chlorine) from which it has never yet been directly (or any other way) obtained when other bodies are present containing it in exactly similar proportions.

Amongst other experiments S H. Davy heated some dry Muriatic Acid gas in contact with the per-oxide of Manganese also very dry – water was rapidly formed & Chlorine gas was liberated – how do you explain this – I know well your theory but you cannot account for the production of the water – in reality the M A was decomposed its Hydrogen united to the Oxygen of the Oxide & formed water & the Chlorine remained free – I should have observed that the black oxide was reduced to the brown oxide of Manganese.

I have before adverted to the peculiar action of Chlorine on vegetable colours but I shall now intimate that in reality it does not act on them at all S H. Davy made some experiments where the dry & pure gas produced no effect on Litmus paper tho the contact was continued some time His gas was freed from water by the Muriate of Lime and then it did not at all affect dry Litmus paper or other vegetable colours at the same time Litmus paper that had been dried & heated when exposed to gas not standing over the M of Lime was instantly rendered white & also paper not previously dried when immersed in the dry gas slowly underwent the change but when no water was present no bleaching powers were exhibited This certainly proves Chlorine to be of a very different nature to the Acids since it in reality has no action on vegetable colours It only destroys them by decomposing water & by liberating & giving to them Oxygen.

Davy in his Bakerian Lecture[3] says that "most of the salts which have been called Muriates are not known to contain M A or any Oxygen. Thus Libavius Liquor tho' converted "into a Muriate by water contains only Tin & Oxy-muriatic gas and horn silver seems incapable of being converted into a true muriate."

With respect to the affinity of the Metals & Inflammable bodies with Chlorine and Oxygen he says that Potassium Sodium, Calcium, Strontium, Barium, Zinc, Mercury Tin Lead and probably Silver Antimony & Gold seem to have a stronger affinity for Oxy-muriatic Gas than for Oxygen but Boron, Phosphorus Iron & Arsenic have apparently a stronger affinity for Oxygen than Chlorine.

It is now time to conclude dear A – which I do with best wishes to yourself & friends In my next I will conclude the subject with Euchlorine when I will again subscribe myself,

Your Sincere Friend,
M. FARADAY

Friday Evg. 7 o'clock
(Postscript)

Dear Abbott I have received yours of today the perusal of which has raised in my mind a tumult of petty passions amongst which are predominant vexation Sorrow, & regret I write under the influence of them and shall inform you candidly of my feelings at this moment You will see by the foregoing part of this letter that I have not acted in unison with your request by dropping the subject of chlorine and for not having done so I feel very considerable sorrow I had at various short intervals as time would permit drawn it up & felt, I will own gratified on reading it over but the reception of yours has made me most heartily regret it Pity me Dear Abbott in that I have not sufficiently the mastery of my feelings & passions – In the first part of this long Epistle you will see reasons I have given for continuing the subject – but I fancy that I can now see the pride & self complacency that led me on & I am fearful that I was influenced by thinking that I had a superior knowledge in this particular subject – being now aware of this passion I have made a candid confession of it to you in hopes to lessen it by mortifying it & humiliating it – You will of course understand that I shall not now enter on Euchlorine untill it is convenient for both of us when I hope to take up the subject uninfluenced by any of those humiliating & to a Philosopher disgraceful feelings.

I am heartily obliged to you for your Queries but have not time to consider them at present – the Philosophical adventures of your Friend were laughable & I hope the sentiment you express namely caution will also strike him least he should err in more important cases – I am glad you are pleased with Accum you must at some opportunity let me look into it I wish to see you shortly (perhaps tomorrow at noon) when I will bring the MS Lecture & the P. M. – and thus having made my confession I subscribe myself with humility

Yours Sincerely,
M. FARADAY

¹ The reference here is to a lecture at the City Philosophical Society which met on Wednesday nights. See Letter 3, fn. 4 for references.
² For John Davy's work on 'Oxymuriatic acid' (chlorine) see: 'Some remarks on the observations and experiments of Mr. Murray on the nature of Oxymuriatic Acid, and its relations to Muriatic Acid,' *NJ*, 28 (1811), 193ff. 'On the nature of Oxymuriatic Gas, in reply to Mr. Murray,' *ibid.*, 29 (1811), 44ff. 'An account of a new Gas, with a reply to Mr. Murray's last observations on Oxymuriatic Gas,' *ibid.*, 30 (1812), 28ff. 'On the nature of Oxymuriatic and Muriatic Acid Gas, in reply to Mr. Murray,' *ibid.*, 31 (1812), 310ff.
³ Humphry Davy, 'The Bakerian Lecture. On Some of the Combinations of Oxymuriatic Gas and Oxygene, and on the chemical Relations of these Principles, to inflammable Bodies,' *PT*, 1811, Pt. 2, 32.

8 M. FARADAY to B. ABBOTT, 20 September 1812

[*R.I., Warner mss., B.J. 1, 41ff*]

Sept. 20ᵗʰ 1812.

What? affirm you have little to say and yet a philosopher! – what a contradiction! – what a paradox! – 'tis a circumstance I till now had no idea of nor shall I at any time time [*sic*] allow you to advance it as a plea for not writing – A Philosopher cannot fail to abound in subjects and a Philosopher can scarcely fail to have a plentifull flow of words ideas opinions &c. &c. &c. when engaged on them – at least I never had reason to suppose you deficient there – Query by Abbott – "Then pray Mike why have you not answered my last before now since subjects are so plentifull" Tis neither more nor less Dear A—— than a want of time Time Sir is all. I require and for time will I cry out most heartily – O that I could purchase at a cheap rate some of our Modern Gents spare hours nay days I think it would be a good bargain both for them & me – As for subjects there is no want of them I could converse with you I will not say for ever but for any finite length of time Philosophy would furnish us with matter & even now 'tho I have said *nothing* yet the best part of a page is covered.

How prone is man to evil and how strong a proof have I of that propensity when even the liberal breast of my friend Abbott could harbour the vice of covetousness nevertheless on a due consideration of the cause and a slight glance at my own feelings on the same subject (they will not bear a strict scrutiny) I pass it over thus.–––––––––––

I fear that by this time you are partly disappointed in the effect you expected to gain from your water-coated battery When I first made my machine I adopted the same plan tho in a minor degree but the effect was in proportion to that of a properly coated apparatus but little this I attributed at the time to the lesser conducting power of water it being much below the metals in that quality – Inform me in your next if you please how it answered

Your commendations of the M.S. Lectures[1] compell me to apologise most humbly for the numerous – very – very numerous errors they contain If I take you right the negative words "no flattery" may be substituted by the affirmative "Irony" be it so I bow to the superior scholastic erudition of S[r] Ben. There is in them errors that will not bear to be jested with since they concern not my own performance so much as the performance of S[r] H. – and those are errors in theory There are I am conscious errors in theory and those errors I would wish you to point out to me before you attribute them to Davy.

With respect to Nicholson I like him exceedingly and more particularly his method of explaining the nature of a lever I have read the 1st. Vol through and am now going to study those parts I more particularly wish to be acquainted with[2]

I thank you for the observations you make on the smell of Brass I attribute it more to the Copper than the Zinc Hydrogen will dissolve several of the Metals – Hydrogen gas I should suppose was formed by the action of the M A on the Zinc and by dissolving the Copper conveyed it with such effect to your olfactory nerves – want of time deters me from prosecuting the subjects at present.

Thus have I answered your last letter and now I will take in hand the one previous to it tho this retrograde mode of proceeding does not confer on me the character of an orderly being but it suited me best at this time and – so it is.

Cracked & smoked-plastered-ceilings – (what a jaw spoiling word) is the first subject requiring attention at present – Presuming that the smoke ascends in nearly a perpendicular direction upwards it will then take an horizontal path beneath and close to the ceiling according as it is influenced by those currents that enter into & pass out of the room If as I suspect to be the case tho I have never ascertained it the clear side of the crack is on the side farthest from the approaching current then I should from theory account for it thus – Each crack or rather the edges project in some degree – consequently that side which is nearest to and is first reached by the dingy stream will present a surface more directly opposed to it than what the other side does it will be more opposed to it than even the ceiling itself and the farthest side will be less opposed to it than the ceiling – from this it follows that the particles of smoke must strike with a force much greater perh[aps] by five or six times on the near side than on the far [ms. missing] one & consequently the momentum being greater they will [ms. missing] there attach themselves – I could enlarge on this point and notice other circumstances accordant with this solution but there is no need to be explicit to one of thy quick discernment "A word to &c"

Your query respecting the variety of colour in paper or rather the difference of shade I am not prepared to answer – very possibly it is produced in the press of the paper-maker.

I shall now draw off & resign the occupation (not the task) of writing untill I have again heard from you Make my respects to all Friends at Long Lane & accept for yourself Dear A. the warmest wishes of

Yours Sincerely
M. FARADAY

Is Mr. Bowyer happily admitted to the dignity of M.C.P.S.

1 Faraday took careful notes of the lectures he heard Davy deliver at the Royal Institution. He then wrote them up and bound them together in a volume now in the possession of the R.I.
2 William Nicholson, 'An Introduction to Natural Philosophy, 1st ed., 2 vols., London, 1782. Other editions, 1787, 1790 and 1796.

9 M. FARADAY to B. ABBOTT, 28 September 1812

[R.I., Warner mss., B.J. 1, 42ff]

Sept.ʳ 28.ᵗʰ 1812.

DEAR ABBOTT,

I plead guilty to your criticism on the word task and earnestly beg pardon for any offence my expression may have been calculated to give I trust so much in your goodness I have no doubt you will grant it and set at ease and liberty your Humble Servant – least I should err again I will hurry on to Philosophy where I am a little more sure of my ground – Your card was to me a very

32

interesting and pleasing object I was highly gratifyed in observing so plainly delineated the course of the Electric fluid or fluids (I do not know which)[1] It appears to me that by making use of a card thus prepared you have hit upon a happy illustrating medium between a conductor and a non-conductor had the interposed medium been a conductor the Electricity would have passed in connection through it it would not have been divided – had the medium been a non-conductor it would have passed in connection and undivided as a spark over it but by this varying and disjoined conductor it has been divided most effectually Should you pursue this point at any time still farther it will be necessary to ascertain by what particular power or effort the spark is divided whether by its affinity to the conductor or by its own repulsion or if as I have no doubt is the case by the joint action of these two forces it would be well to observe and ascertain the proportion of each in the effect These are problems the solution of which will be difficult to obtain but the Science of Electricity will not be complete without them and a Philosopher will aim at perfection 'tho he may not hit it difficulties will not retard him but only cause a proportionate exertion of his mental faculties.

I did not before know the date of your Lecture 'tis a long time I hope to hear you before then – It is somewhat singular that your volunteers are so forward it will make up for the deficiency of your regulars Had they come after yours it would have been better I thank you for a view of the outline of Electrical Lectures when do they commence – As they will last so long I hope to hear the greater number of them as an M.C.P.S. – Mr. Shepherd[2] is apparently a very frequent Lecturer I hope he satisfies *you*

I had a very pleasing view of the Planet Saturn last week through a refractor with a power of ninety I saw his ring very distinctly 'tis a singular appendage to a planet to a revolving globe and I should think caused some peculiar phenomena to the planet within it I allude to their mutual action with respect to Meteorology and perhaps Electricity.

Some time since I had soaked some flannel discs in a strong solution of the Muriate of Soda but not having immediate use for them I threw them wet into a cupping glass there they have till now remained and on looking at them lately I was highly pleased to see the effect that had taken place by the evaporation The salt did not crystallize in the flannel or at least not all of it but had issued out as it were from the edges of the discs up the sides of the glass in irregular but concentric lines forming shapes very similar to currant leaves these crystallizations increase in size even now and at present one part of them has turned over the top of the cupping glass and descended above half an inch on the outside – does the increase of size in these crystallizations take place at the edges of the flannel discs which is a kind of center to the crystals or at their circumference?

Tatum in his last Lecture on the Alkalies[3] observed that Litharge may be employed to decompose the Muriats [*sic*] soap Ley – I thought of this whilst looking at the above mentioned discs of flannel a pen had fell into the glass and where the head and point rested on the flannels an oxidation of the Metals had taken place it was apparent by the stain of the copper I have little doubt that some portion of the Muriate of Soda was decomposed as it appeared not to be the oxide but the M of C that coloured the disc

Whilst on this subject I will notice the state of a small galvanic battery that was piled up six weeks or two [months] ago Tho its apparent galvanic action has ceased [ms. missing] action is not dead in it an oxidation of the Zinc [ms. missing] even now [*sic*] the oxide as it is formed exudes (if I may so say) from the edges of the discs and falls down so as to cover all round the base of the battery with a white coat or carpet – This formation of the oxide takes place more rapidly at the bottom of the pile than at the top.

I cannot spare more time at present than to desire my respects to all friends and to ask where & how is your brother You know well that to yourself belongs the earnest & hearty wishes of

Your Friend
M. FARADAY

I humbly apologise to you Dear A——— for the careless manner in which I have noted down the phenomena of the *stale* battery I just wrote down what appeared to be the fact and then proceeded to prove it thus doing last what required the first attention On separating two of the discs & applying my tongue to the powder between them I found a strong alkaline taste On collecting some of the powder and pouring on to it a little hot water I obtained an Alkaline solution of considerable strength as proved by its effects on test paper On adding an Acid Carbonic acid gas was liberated which of course was before combined with the Alkali. From these circumstances I draw the following conclusions During the galvanic action the Muriate had been decomposed the Alkali for the most part proceeding towards the copper discs a Muriate of Zinc would then be formed On the cessation of the Galvanic action the Alkali began a decomposition of the Metallic Muriate by its own superior affinity for the Acid and it is by its thus regaining its former station that the oxide of zinc is set free. The slowness of action is to be attributed to the want of moisture

I am ashamed to dwell so long on so trivial a subject but the former error made a clear explanation necessary as such I have given the above and shall now cease – waiting with impatience for a letter to

M. FARADAY

[1] It is interesting to notice Faraday's change here from adherence to a two-fluid theory in 1810. See *LPW*, 17ff.
[2] Mr Shepherd was a member of the City Philosophical Society.
[3] See Letter 7, fn. 1.

[*R.I.*, *Warner mss.*, *B.J. 1*, *43ff*]

Octr 1, 1812

– no – no – no – no – none – right – no Philosophy is not dead yet – no –
O no – he knows it – thank you – 'tis impossible – Bravo.

In the above lines dear Abbott you have full and explicit answers to the first
page of yours dated Septr 28. I was paper hanging at the time I received it but
what a change of thoughts it occasioned what a concussion confusion con-
glomeration what a revolution of ideas it produced – Oh 'twas too much –
away went cloths shears paper paste and brush all – all was too little all was too
light to keep my thoughts from roaring high connected close with thine

With what rapture would a votary of the muses grasp that inimitable page
how would he dwell on every line and pore on every letter and with what
horror dread disgust and every repulsive passion would he start back from the
world BARILLA to which I now come I cannot here refrain from regretting my
inability (principally for want of time) to perform the experiment you relate to
me I mean not to reflect on any want of clearness in your details on the contrary
I congratulate you on the quickness with which you note and observe any new
appearances but the sight possesses such a superiority over the other senses in its
power of conveying to the mind fair ideas that I wish in every case to use it –
I am much gratified with your account of the Barilla but do I read right that
part of your letter which says that the salt you obtained from the first treatment
of it was *efflorescent* As I went on to that passage I did not expect that you
would obtain any crystals at all but only an uniform mass but that crystals
containing so great a quantity of Alkali in I suppose nearly a free state should
give out water to the Atmosphere surprised me exceedingly – explain if you
please.

With respect to the combination of Carbon with the fixed Alkalies I can say
nothing to the point – With the volatile Alkali Ammonia you well know that
it forms Prussic Acid – But Ammonia differs from Potash & Soda – true the
two last are Oxides or rather Hydrats of Potassium and Sodium[1] & Ammonia
is a compound of Nitrogen Hydrogen and Oxygen[2] now if as we have some
reason to suppose is the case Nitrogen & Hydrogen are volatile Metals the
difference between Ammonia & the fixed alkalies will be perhaps none and then
the plea of similarity will induce us to suppose that Carbon is capable of
uniting to all the Alkalies With respect to the last observation you make on
the subject – when Potash is ignited on charcoal it undergoes I believe no
other change than when ignited by itself in both cases it assumes a greenish
colour.

"Ether." – How are the fragrant atmospheres of Bermondsy situated at
present – do they kindly accomodate themselves to each other or are they at

perpetual variance neither is the case one is completely dissipated "lost lost for ever lost" whilst the other remains and will remain to clear the fatigued spirits of all who like M. F. will gladly go miles to see B. A. – Thus ends the response to Abbotts Letter dated as above. Hear [*sic*] beginneth an answer to Benjamins last letter.

Dear Ben.

I rejoice in your determination to pursue the subject of Electricity & have no doubt but that I shall have some very interesting letters on the subject I shall certainly wish to (and will if possible) be present at the performance of the experiments but you know I shortly enter on the life of a Journey-man and then I suppose time will be more scarce than it is even now

I partly repine at learning that I cannot be admitted before Christmas I understood from the old laws that it could take place any private night nevertheless to make a virtue of necessity I will persuade myself that second thoughts are best and therefore employ the time in considering it over again I am greatly obliged to you for your offer of admissions an[d ms. missing] afraid I am so covetous as often to acept them.

I am obliged to you for your information respecting ['respecting' re-written in margin as part of word cut out] that species of crystallization which may be called vegetative I have very seldom observed particularly any instance of it 'till the one I last described came under notice A series of confused thoughts came across my mind at that instant which induced me to describe it so minutely – I supposed that it might be only certain salts as the Alkaline ones that would thus crystallize or perhaps thought I those whose crystals are primary or plates then again I conceived that their [*sic*] might be a difference in the appearance of the vegetation peculiar to each salt & lastly I fancied that a knowledge of these things would add to the science of crystallography – These are ideas of the moment and are therefore loose & erroneous of course but an investigation of the subject might lead to other things of importance

Venus I find is amongst your visible planets – tis – a – beautifull – object – certainly.

I am suddenly stopped

yours Hastily
M. FARADAY

[1] This was the opinion entertained on the Continent, particularly by Gay-Lussac and Thenard.

[2] Faraday would appear to be referring here to the aqueous solution of ammonia.

[*R.I., Warner mss., B.J. 1, 47ff*]

Sunday afternoon,
Octr 11, 1812.

DEAR ABBOTT,

I thank you heartily for your letter of yesterday the which gave me greater pleasure than any one I had before received from you – I know not whether you will be pleased by such commendation or not it is the best I can bestow – I intend at this time to answer it but would wish you before you read the ensuing matter to banish from your mind all frivolous passions It is possible that what I may say would only tend to give rise (under their influence) to disdain contempt &c. for at present I am in as serious a mood as you can be and would not scruple to speak a truth to any human being, whatever repugnance it might give rise to Being in this state of mind I should have refrained from writing to you did I not conceive from the general tenor of your letter that your mind is at proper times occupied on serious subjects to the exclusion of those which comparatively are frivolous

I cannot fail to feel gratified, my dear Friend at the post I appear to occupy in your mind and I will very openly affirm that I attach much greater importance to that interest since the perusal of your last I would much rather engage the good opinion of one moral philosopher who acts up to his precepts than the attentions and common place friendship of fifty natural philosophers This being my mind I cannot fail to think more honorably of my Friend since the confirmation of my good opinion & I now feel somewhat satisfied that they are correct.

As for the change you suppose to have taken place with respect to my situation and affairs I have to thank my late master that it is but little Of Liberty & time I have if possible less than before tho I hope my circumspection has not at the same time decreased I am well aware of the irreparable evils that an abuse of those blessings will give rise to These were pointed out to me by common sense nor do I see how any one who considers his own station and his own free occupations pleasures actions &c. can unwittingly engage himself in them I thank that cause to whom thanks is due that I am not in general a profuse waster of those blessings which are bestowed on me as a human being I mean health sensation time & temporal resources – Understand me clearly here for I wish much not to be mis-taken I am well aware of my own nature it is evil and I feel its influence strongly – I know too that – but I find that I am passing insensibly to a point of divinity and as those matters are not to be treated lightly I will refrain from pursuing it – all I meant to say on that point was that I keep regular hours enter not intentionally into pleasures productive of evil reverence those who require reverence from me and act up to what the world calls good I appear moral and hope that I am so tho' at the same time I consider morality only as a lamentably deficient state

I know not whether you are aware of it by any means but my mind delights to occupy itself on serious subjects and am never better pleased than when I am in conversation with a companion of my own turn of mind I have to regret that the expiration of my apprenticeship hath deprived me of the frequent company and conversation of a very serious and improving young companion[1] but I am now in hopes of a compensation by the acquisition of at times a letter from you – I am very considerably indebted to him for the sober turn or bent of my reason and heartily thank him for it In our various conversations we have frequently touched on the different parts of your letter and I have every reason to suppose that by so doing we have been reciprocally benefitted

I cannot help but be pleased with the earnest manner in which you enforce the necessity of precaution in respect of new acquaintances I have long been conscious of it and it is that consciousness which limits my friends to the very small number that comprises them I feel no hesitation in saying that I scrutinized you long and closely before I satisfyed the doubts in my breast but I now trust they are all allayed

It appears that in the article of experience you are my superior You have been tried If the result of the trial satisfies your own good sense and inward admonitions I rest satisfied that you acted rightly I am well aware that to act rightly is at times difficult Our judgment & good sense is oftentimes opposed and that strongly too by our passions and wishes That we may never give up the first for the sake of the last is the earnest wish of your Friend

I have made use of the term friend several times and in one place I find the expression of common place friendship It will perhaps not be improper at this time to give you my ideas on true friendship and eligible companions – In every action of our lives I conceive that reference ought to be had to a superior being and in nothing ought we to oppose or act contrary to his precepts These ideas make me extremely displeased with the general and also the ancient idea of Friendship A few lines strike upon my mind at this moment they begin thus

> ("A generous Friendship no cold medium knows
> But with one love with one resentment glows &c.)

and convey sentiments that in my mind give rise to extreme disgust According to what I have said a few lines above I would define a friend a true friend to be "One who will serve his companion next to his God" nor will I admit that an immoral person can fill completely the character of a true friend – Having this idea of Friendship it was natural for me to make a self inquiry whether I could fill the character but I am not satisfyed with my own conclusions on that point I fear I cannot True friendship I consider as one of the sublimest feelings that the human mind is capable of and requires a mind of almost infinite strength and at the same time of complete self-knowledge such being the case and knowing my own deficiency in those points I must admire it but fear I cannot attain it

The above is my opinion of true friendship a passion or feeling I have never personally met with and a subject that has been understood by very few that I have discussed it with Amongst my companions I am conscious of only one who thinks the same of it that I do but who confesses his inability to fill the character

When meditating and examining the character of a person with respect to his fitness for a companion I go much farther than is generally the case A good companion in the common acceptation of the word is one who is respectable both in connection & manners is not in a lower rank of life than oneself and does not openly or in general act improperly This I say is the common meaning of the word but I am by no means satisfied with it I have met a good companion in the lowest paths of life and I have found such as I despised in a rank far superior to mine A companion cannot be a good one unless he is morally so and however engaging may be his general habits and whatever peculiar circumstances may be connected with him so as to make him desirable Reason & Common Sense point him out as an improper companion or acquaintance unless his nobler faculties his intellectual powers are in proportion as correct as his outward behaviour What am I to think of that person who despising the improvement & rectitude of his mind spends all his efforts in arranging into a nice form his body speach habits &c is he an estimable character is he a commendable companion no surely not nor will such ever gain my commendation

On recollecting myself I fancy I have said enough on this subject I will therefore draw towards a conclusion your wellcome letter arrived in Weymouth Street precisely at my dinner hour consequently I got it immediately If at any time you wish to communicate in haste and will so express it on the exterior of the letter it will be brought to me immediately. I am in hopes of again hearing from you at some of your serious moments at which time you of course will express yourself as I have done without ceremony but I must conclude in confidence that you are an eligible companion and wishing that you may attain even to the character of a true friend I remain

Yours dear Abbot Very Sincerely,
M. FARADAY

I will give you my opinion of the Lecture in my next.

---

[1] The only source for Faraday's life as an apprentice, other than his own later, and very meagrely reported, recollections is Benjamin Abbott. There is, in the Warner mss. at the Royal Institution a document written by Abbott after Faraday's death, entitled, 'Jottings from Memory in reference to my dear and deceased Friend M. Faraday.' There mention is made of Faraday's two fellow-apprentices (neither identified by name) one of whom, Abbott states, later became a comedian and the other a professional singer. Which of these two is the one Faraday here mentions is impossible to tell.

London,
October 18, 1812.

DEAR HUXTABLE,

You will be at a loss to know what to think of me, inasmuch as near two months have expired, and you have not, in that time, received any answer to your agreeable communication. I have to beg your pardon for such delay, and scarce know how satisfactorily to account for it. I have indeed acted unadvisedly on that point, for, conceiving that it would be better to delay my answer until my time was expired, I did so. That took place on October 7, and since then I have had by far less time and liberty than before. With respect to a certain place I was disappointed, and am now working at my old trade, the which I wish to leave at the first convenient opportunity. I hope (though fear not) that you will be satisfied with this cause of my silence; and if it appears insufficient to you, I must trust to your goodness. With respect to the progress of the sciences I know but little, and am now likely to know still less; indeed, as long as I stop in my present situation (and I see no chance of getting out of it just yet), I must resign philosophy entirely to those who are more fortunate in the possession of time and means.

Sir H. Davy is at present, I believe, in Scotland. I do not know that he has made any further advances in Chemical science. He is engaged in publishing a new work, called "The Elements of Chemical Philosophy"[1] which will contain, I believe, all his discoveries, and will likewise be a detail of his philosophical opinions. One part of the first volume is published. It is in price 11s. or 12s. 6d. I have not yet seen it. Abbott, whom you know some little about, has become a member of the City Philosophical Society, which is held at Tatum's house every Wednesday evening. He has sent me a ticket for admission next Wednesday to a lecture; but as you know their rules, I have no need to enter further into them.

With Abbott I continue a very intimate and pleasing acquaintance. I find him to be a very well-informed young man. His ideas are correct, and his knowledge, general as well as philosophical, is extensive. He acts too with a propriety of behaviour equal to your own, and I congratulate myself much on the acquisition of two such friends as yourself and him.

How are you situated now? Do you intend to stop in the country, or are you again coming up to London? I was in hopes that I should see you shortly again. Not that I wish to interfere in your arrangements, but for the pleasure it would give me. But I must not be selfish. It is possible that you may be settled where you are at present, or other strong and urgent reasons may exist that will keep you there. If it is so, I wish they may be such as will afford you pleasure, and tend to increase the happiness and comfort of your life.

I am at present in very low spirits, and scarce know how to continue on in a strain that will be anyway agreeable to you; I will therefore draw to a close this dull epistle, and conclude with wishing you all health and happiness, assuring you that I am sincerely yours,

M. FARADAY

[1] H. Davy, *Elements of Chemical Philosophy*, Pt. 1, Vol. 1 (all published), London, 1812.

13 M. FARADAY to B. ABBOTT, 7 December 1812

[*R.I., Warner mss., previously unpublished*]

Decr 7th 1812.

DEAR ABBOTT,

I thank you most heartily and sincerely for the pleasure I received on hearing your Lecture[1] of last Wednesday and I have to transmit to you also the acknowledgements of both my Friends for the high gratification it afforded them Of the Lecture, its Character, and Delivery, to you I shall say nothing but that all was excellent, you are so far able to judge as to be well satisfied in your own mind with your own efforts.

I expect that by this time you are considerably advanced in the arrangement of a second Lecture for I presume that you will not delay longer than is convenient and necessary the continuation of your subject The Society too will expect it and look forward to it with pleasure as you made a partial promise to them to continue it It will I conceive shew your whole course to more advantage as the more connected a subject is the better it appears By the by I was highly gratified with the order observed throughout the last Lecture when I perused it it was not so evident but it appeared in an eminent degree in the delivery and conferred on it a degree of clearness & simplicity even beyond what I expected

My Port-folio in which is contained our correspondence makes a singular appearance the last six letters in it are from you not one of them having drawn back an answer You know me well enough to be satisfied that it is not owing to want of inclination or even intention but solely to inability & the same cause even extends to this Letter and obliges me to shorten it long before I should wish it nevertheless you I hope will not relax or shorten your correspondence making my slackness a plea but will continue to gratify your friend by an epistle whenever agreeable to yourself or whenever subjects *which are always plentiful* occur

I must now resign my occupation 'till a future time but would first desire my respects to Mr. & Mrs. Abbott & your Sister I have no doubt but that your Father & Sister were gratified on Wednesday evening at least as *much* as at any of Tatum's Lectures but adieu dear A—— for the present & believe me ever yours.

M. FARADAY

[1] See Letter 3, fn. 4 for references.

[*R.I., Warner mss., previously unpublished*]

Monday night
April 5 1813

Thanks to my dear Ben for his letter 'twas so long since I had before obtained one from him that my pleasure was if possible heightened at the reception of it perhaps as much by the long and silent interval preceeding it as by the letter itself. There is no occasion for me to inform you that I feel influenced by the same hopes and fears as yourself 'tho they are considerably abated by knowing that you will and that I intend if I can to support each our part. But before I proceed farther let me congratulate you on the safe and happy return of a beloved brother from a long and dangerous voyage after a tedious & extended absence and I feel much pleasure mental pleasure in knowing the increase of happiness that it will occasion in the breasts of his relatives. I cannot refrain from again desiring of you to remind him that there is such an one as myself who feels the most earnest interest in his welfare – just jog his memory so that he may not entirely forget me

You desire me to inform you at times of any thing new in philosophy that may fall in my way and I shall accordingly obey your desires by detailing to you at present some circumstances relating to the newly discovered detonating compound[1] This I do with more eagerness as I have been engaged this afternoon in assisting Sr H. in his experiments on it during which we had two or three unexpected explosions

This compound is formed by inverting over a solution of the Nitrat or Muriate of Ammonia an air jar full of fresh made pure clean chlorine gas all contact of oil grease or inflammable matter being carefully guarded against it was at first supposed necessary to surround the solution with ice but it is of no importance to do so it in fact forms better without it.

Immediately that the jar is inverted over the solution an action commences This is evident by the gradual the slow rise of the solution in the jar as the absorption of the gas takes place quickly spots are evident on the surface of the solution in the jar which increase in size and appear as drops of an high colored oil As the action goes on these drops become so large as at last to fall from the surface and sink to the bottom of the solution.

I am not exactly aware what change it is that takes place in the solutions In that of the Nitrate of Ammonia the action is not apparently so strong as in the other. The solution of the Muriate becomes as it absorbs the gas of a fine amber colour and a continual ascending shower of bubbles pass through its whole length. In the Nitrate of Ammonia the colour is scarcely at all affected and the action is not so energetic

The substance in question possesses very many singular properties amongst which its immediate decomposition is not the least remarkable as soon as a globule is formed & has fallen to the bottom of the solution it begins to decompose this it does by giving off azote a minute bubble of gas appears at the top of the globule which when it has attained to some size separates & rises to the surface another is immediately formed which rises in turn & thus the whole may be decomposed This gas is ascertained to be azote.

The Specific gravity of this body appears to be very considerable that is to say three or four times as heavy as water during its spontaneous decomposition the bubble of gas will sometimes carry up with it to the surface the globule of the compound but becoming separated at the surface the globule falls with considerable rapidity through a strong solution of the Muriate of Ammonia a salt not deficient in solubility & of course the solution is somewhat dense

At the bottom of the solution or of water the globules appear to exert a considerable power in the attraction of aggregation and they there appear compact close & dense but if a small portion happens to rise by the gas attached to it and gains the surface and contact of the atmosphere it immediately expands as would oil and quickly evaporates and is lost in this state that is whilst evaporating it affects the eyes in a very disagreeable manner bringing forth tears in abundance it excites also a very disagreeable sensation in the nostrils and lungs.

It appears therefore that this body quickly assumes an elastic form and this afternoon I witnessed its solidification a portion of it in the solution was placed in a freezing mixture of ice and the Muriate of Lime The compound quickly became solid and appeared like butter in cold weather and the solution itself appeared to freeze sooner in consequence of its having dissolved a small portion of it. Alcohol or spirits of wine dissolve this compound very readily but I have not seen the solution.

With respect to its detonating power it exhibits them with many bodies when a small portion of it is placed in a bason [*sic*] and covered with water and oil or Phosphorus is then brought in contact with it it explodes violently The bason is shattered to pieces and the water is thrown in all directions but I can inform you of a very easy and safe method of inflaming it by oil which is thus drop a small portion of it on an oily surface and an instantaneous inflamation will ensue but without noise Heat also explodes this body and was by this means that Sr H. met with his very unpleasant accident

Another mode of exploding it was discovered this afternoon in the Laboratory here but I must first inform you of the other experiments Having made a considerable quantity of the compound and gathered it together (that being my business) Sr H. proceeded to make his experiments on it and first with the acids A small glass was filled with Muriatic Acid and a tube closed at one end and answering the purpose of a receiver was filled and inverted in the same a globule of the compound was then introduced into the glass and the end of the tube placed over it the rapidity with which the globule was decomposed increased very much bubbles of gas rose in quick succession which expanded as they ascended in a beautifull manner to fourteen or fifteen times their original bulk and the tube quickly became full of gas this gas was transferred to a water trough examined and found to be pure chlorine excepting about one fortieth part of pure oxygen gas. on examining the Muriatic Acid in which the decomposition had taken place Muriate of Ammonia was found to have been formed

When the compound was tried in the same way in Nitric Acid Azote gas only was formed

The same gas was given out when it underwent spontaneous decomposition in a solution of pure potash but when decomposed in Ammonia it was decomposed indeed S^r H bade me repeat the experiment with Ammonia as I had done with the Acids accordingly a glass was filled & a tube inverted and then a portion of the compound was introduced but lo! instead of sinking to the bottom it rose to the top a strong action took place and a considerable quantity of smoke was produced As it was evident the body was decomposed it shewed that something could be done in this way and therefore we modified the arrangement of circumstances a little glass was filled with water & a tube full of liquid ammonia inverted in it a globule was then put in the glass which sank to the bottom and the tube was placed over it a bubble of gas formed which ascended in the tube and at the top appeared like smoke a second rose and inflamed in the middle of the tube the compound being all decomposed I put in a much larger portion a bubble formed in it which in rising took up the globule of the compound with it it ascended till within about one third from the top when an explosion took place and the vessel was shattered to pieces

So far has S^r H proceeded with his experiments on this body and so far have I got on in my letter he has ceased his experiments untill tomorrow and I must cease scribbling until another time This letter I know is too long but I will not increase its length by apologising. I am dear Abbott

Yours truly
M. F A R A D A Y

I had almost forgot an important part of my letter. Robert[2] wishes to know how you are engaged for next friday week but it is scarcely possible to arrange anything without verbal communication if you will give me leave I will call on you some evening this week I would ask you here but that Sr H. goes out of town next monday which renders his presence here more continual at this time besides I hope to see both you & your Brother here in his absence when I shall be more at liberty I wait your answer. Farewell.

[1] This is chloride of nitrogen which is very unstable. The scientific journals of the day carried a number of accounts of accidents involving those working with it. See H. Davy, 'On a new detonating Compound', *PT* (1813), 1, and 'Some further observations on a new detonating substance', *ibid.*, 242.

[2] Faraday's elder brother.

[R.I., *Warner mss.*, B.J. 1, 60ff]

Thursday Evng
April 9th, 1813

DEAR ABBOTT

A stranger would certainly think you and I were a couple of very simple beings since we find it necessary to write to each other tho we so often personally meet but the stranger would in so judging only fall into that error which envelopes all those who decide from the outward appearances of things he would perceive that we meet and that we write and he would perceive no more unless he possessed more than common sagacity – but I trust that not only mine but your intentions also in writing are for the improvement if not of yourself yet of me & as I know or at least believe that you are very willing I should burnish myself up a bit you must suffer me to write you another (perhaps) long letter – When writing to you I seize that opportunity of striving to describe a circumstance or an experiment clearly so that you will see I am urged on by selfish motives partly to our mutual correspondence – but tho selfish yet not censurable.

Agreeable to what I have said above I shall at this time proceed to acquaint you with the results of some more experiments on the detonating compound of Chlorine and Azote and I am happy to say I do it at my ease for I have escaped (not quite unhurt) from four different and strong explosions of the substance of these the most terrible was when I was holding between my thumb and finger a small tube containing about 7 1/2 grains of it my face was within twelve inches of the tube but I fortunately had on a glass mask. It exploded by the slight heat of a small piece of cement that touched the glass above half an inch from the substance and on the outside – The expansion was so rapid as to blow my hand open, tear off a part of one nail and has made my fingers so sore that I cannot yet use them easily – The pieces of tube were projected with such force as to cut the glass face of the mask I had on – but to proceed with an account of the experiments

A tube was filled with dry boiled mercury and inverted in a glass containing also mercury a portion of the compound was thrown up into it & it was then left to act all last night on examining it this morning the compound was gone a substance was formed in the tube and a gas obtained This gas was azote the substance Corrosive [reading doubtful] Mercury evidently proving it to be a compound of Chlorine or O[xy] M[uriatic] A[cid] G[as] and azote – On repeating the experiment this morning as soon as it was thrown up it exploded and the tube and a receiver were blown to pieces. I got a cut on my eyelid and Sr H. bruised his hand

A portion of it was then introduced into a tube of this form and a stop cock connected to it it was then taken to the air-pump and exhausted until we

45

supposed the substance to have rose and filled the tube with vapour. it was then heated by a spirit lamp and in a few moments an inflammation took place in the tube but all stood firm on taking it off from the pump in order to ascertain the products it was found that so much [com]mon air had passed in from the barrels of the [pump] [ms. missing] as to render the experiment indecisive and therefore it was repeated this morning with a larger portion of the substance – when put in the pump it was exhausted and there stood for a moment or two and then exploded with a fearfull noise both Sr H. & me had masks on but I escaped this time the best Sr H. had his face cut in two places about the chin and a violent blow on the forehead struck through a considerable thickness of silk & leather & with this experiment he has for the present concluded.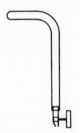

The specific gravity of this substance as ascertained yesterday by comparing its weight with the weight of an equal bulk of water is 1.95. so that my former estimate is incorrect but you will excuse it as being the estimate of a tyro in chemical science

Such are some few of the properties of this terrible compound and such are the experiments in which those properties are evinced from these it appears to be a compound of Chlorine and Azote for the presence of any other body has not been satisfactorily proved It is a body which confers considerable importance on azote which has till now been celebrated chiefly for negative properties it shews its energy when united in this combination and in this compound too azote is rendered capable of decomposing the Muriatic Acid as shewn by the experiment related in my last it combines with the Hydrogen to form Ammonia and the Chlorine of the compound & of the Acid are liberated

This compound is of such explosive power as to render it imprudent to consider it at any time and in any state as secure often times it will explode in an experiment that has been before made five or six times with perfect safety and in which you have been lulled into a dangerous security. I was yesterday putting some into a clean dry tube when it exploded on touching the glass & rushed in my face so that it is as I before said improper to consider it at any time as secure

I shall now leave this subject for the present and look forward to the end of this letter as well as to the beginning of one from you but before concluding I shall make a few remarks which yet I do not deem necessary. – I have dear Ben in all of my letters where Chemical Philosophy has been touched upon accounted for things by that theory which appeared to me most correct. This I do without any apology or hesitation as knowing you to possess a mind too enlarged to be offended at it On the contrary I conceive you will be pleased with it as you will more readily perceive where I err and can more properly seize the fit opportunity to set me right In the experiments themselves you can very easily subtract theory from fact and may account for them as is most agreeable to yourself Thus we shall each be a check on the other which will be equivalent to each one of us seeing the same object on different sides – but away with Philosophy for the present – remember me to all friends within the æthereal atmosphere of Bermondsey and believe me to be what I hope shortly to assure you personally I am

Yours Truly
M. F A R A D A Y

16   M. F A R A D A Y to B. A B B O T T, 12 May 1813
[*R.I., Warner mss., B.J. 1, 63ff*]

May 12, 1813.

The monk for the chastisement of his body and mortification of sensual lusts and worldly appetites abstains from pleasures and even the simple supplies that nature calls for. – The miser for reasons as strong tho' diametrically opposite the gratification of a darling passion does exactly the same and leaves unenjoyed every comfort of life – but I for no reason at all have neglected that which constitutes one of my greatest pleasures and one that may be enjoyed with the greatest propriety – 'till on a sudden as the dense *light* of the electric flash pervades t'horizon so struck the thought of Abbott through my soul.

And yet Ben tho I mean to write to you at this time I have no subject in particular out which I can cut a letter I shall therefore (if you will allow me a second simile) follow the pattern of the expert sempstress who when she has cut out all her large and important [works] collects and combines as fancy may direct pieces of all sorts sizes shapes and colours and calls it patch work such a thing will this epistle most probably turn out begun one day yet most likely finished on another formed of things no otherwise connected than as they stand upon the paper things to [*sic*] of different kinds it may well be called patch work or work which pleases none more than the maker

What is the matter with the thumb and fore-finger of your right hand and yet tho' they be ever so much out of order it can scarcely excuse your long silence I have expected something from you before now even tho' it might be wrote thus[1]

"He that hath not music in his heart etc." confound the music say I. – It turns my thoughts quite round or rather half way round from the letter You must know Sir that there is a grand party at dinner at Jacques Hotel which immediately faces the back of the institution and the music is so excellent that I cannot for the life of me help running at every new piece they play to the window to hear them[2] – I shall do no good at this letter tonight and so will get to bed and "listen listen to the voice of" bassoons violins clarinets trumpets serpents and all the other accessories to good music – I cant stop Good-night

May 14th. What a singular compound is man – what strange contradictory ingredients enter into his composition – and how completely each one predominates for a time according as it is favoured by the tone of the mind and senses and other existing circumstances – at one time grave circumspect & cautious – at another silly headstrong and careless – now conscious of his dignity he considers himself as Lord of the creation – yet in a few hours will conduct himself in a way that places him beneath the level of beasts – at times free frivolous and open his tongue is an unobstructed conveyor of his thoughts – thoughts which on after consideration makes [*sic*] him ashamed of his former behaviour – indeed the numerous paradoxes anomalies and contradictions in man exceed in number all that can be found in nature elsewhere and separate and distinguish him if nothing else did from every other created object organised or not – The study of these circumstances is not uninteresting in as much as knowledge of them enable [*sic*] us to conduct ourselves with much more propriety in every situation in life Without knowing how far we ourselves are affected by them we should be unable to trust to our discretion amongst other persons and [without] some knowledge of the part they bear or make in the[ir own] [ms. missing] position we should be unable to behave to him unreserved & with freedom.

It was my intention when I again sat down to this letter to obliterate all the former part of it but the thoughts I have just set down were sufficient to alter my determination I have left them as being the free utterance of an unemployed mind and delineating a true part of my constitution I believe too that I know sufficiently of the component parts of my friend as to justify my confidence in letting them remain unaltered

For much more I have neither room nor time to spare nor had I – would I lengthen what is already too long yet as a clock after giving warning passes on for a few moments before it strikes so do I linger on the paper. It is my intention to accept of your kind invitation for sunday *morning* (further your deponent knoweth not) and I shall therefore take the liberty of seeing you after breakfast at about 9h. 45m, till when I remain with respects to all friends

Yours Truly,
M. FARADAY

1 'thus' was written in mock shaky handwriting in the manuscript.
2 Faraday was given rooms at the Royal Institution when he was hired there on 1 March 1813. See *LPW*, 29.

[R.I., Warner mss., B.J. 1, 65ff]

June 1st 1813

DEAR ABBOTT

Again I resort, for pleasure and to dispel the dullness of a violent head-ach to my correspondence with you tho perfectly unfit for it except as it may answer the purpose of amusing myself The subject upon which I shall dwell more particularly at present has been in my head for some considerable time and it now bursts forth in all its confusion

The opportunities that I have latterly had of attending and obtaining instruction from various Lecturers in their performance of the duty attached to that office has enabled me to observe the various habits peculiarities excellences and defects of each of them as far as they were evident to me during the delivery I did not wholly let this part of the things occurrant escape my notice but when I found myself pleased endeavoured to ascertain the particular circumstance that had affected me: also whilst attending Mr. Brande[1] and Mr. Powell[2] in their lectures I observed how the audience were affected and by what their pleasure & their censure was drawn forth.

It may perhaps appear singular and improper that one who is entirely unfit for such an office himself & who does not even pretend to any of the requisites for it should take upon him to censure and to commend others to express satisfaction at this, to be displeased with that according as he is lead by his judgement when he allows that his judgement is unfit for it but I do not see on consideration that the impropriety is so great If I am unfit for it 'tis evident that I have yet to learn and how learn better than by the observation of others If we never judge at all we shall never judge right and it is far better to learn to use our mental powers ('tho it may take a whole life for the purpose) than to leave them buried in idleness a meer [sic] void[3]

I too have inducements in the C. P. S. to draw me forward in the acquisition of a small portion of knowledge on this point and these alone would be sufficient to urge me forward in my judgment of

$$\left\{ \begin{array}{l} /\text{men} \\ /\text{lectures} \end{array} \right. \text{ and } \left\{ \begin{array}{l} /\text{things} \\ /\text{apparatus} \end{array} \right.$$

In a word Ben I intend to give you my ideas on the subject of lectures and lecturers in general. The observations and ideas I shall set down are such as entered my mind at the moment the circumstances that gave rise to them took place. I shall point out but few beauties or few falts [sic] that I have not witnessed in the presence of a numerous assembly and it is exceedingly probable or rather certain that I should have noticed more of these particulars if I had seen more lecturers or in other words I do not pretend to give you an account of all the falts possible in a lecture or directions for the composing & delivering of a perfect one

On going to a lecture I generally get there before it begins indeed I consider it as an impropriety of no small magnitude to disturb the attention of an audience by entering amongst them in the midst of a lecture and indeed bordering upon an insult to the lecturer by arriving there before the commencement I have avoided this error and have had time to observe the lecture room.

The best form for a lecture room in general is without dispute a circular one tho in particular circumstances deviations may with propriety be adopted The seats should be so arranged that no obstruction intervene between the spectator & the lecture table if there is a gallery each person in it should be situated in a manner the most convenient for observation and hearing Those in which I have seen company and which please me most are the Theatre Royal, Haymarket, the Automatical Theatre and the Lecture room here for the last of which I must give the preference In a lecture room I would have the lecturer on a levell with the lowest person in it consequently the pit should ascend very considerably an object which cannot be attained in a theatre also in the two I have mentioned the lecturer is too far backward and a part of his audience is placed in a direction by far too oblique with respect to him – I allude to the side seats of this theatre

In considering the form of a lecture room we should take into account the time at which it is intended to be occupied inasmuch as the modes of lighting by means natural and artificial are very different In this particular the theatres in a large way have one advantage i.e. in the site of their stage lamps which illuminate in a grand manner all before them tho at the same time they fatigue the eyes of those who are situated low in the house but tho Walker[4] has shewn in the most splendid and sublime manner that Astronomy may be illustrated in a way the most striking by artificial light yet from what little I know of these things I conceive that for by far the greater part of Philosophy day light is the most eligible and convenient

When a Lecture room is illuminated by the light of the Sun it should constantly be admitted if convenient at the top not only as rendering the whole of the interior more uniform and distinct but also for the convenience of darkening the room in the instance of the Lecture room here you will readily recognize the mode of attaining that end to which I allude.

There is another circumstance to be considered with respect to a Lecture room of as much importance almost as light itself and that is ventilation how often have I felt oppression in the highest degree when surrounded by a number of other persons and confined in one portion of air how have I wished the Lecture finished the lights extinguished and myself away merely to obtain a fresh supply of that element The want of it caused the want of attention of pleasure and even of comfort and not to be regained without its previous admission Attention to this is more particularly necessary in a lecture room intended for night delivery as the lights burning add considerably to the oppression produced on the body.

Entrance and Exit are things too, worthy of consideration amongst the particulars of a Lecture room but I shall say no more on them than to refer you to the mode in which this is arranged here – a mode excellently well adapted for the convenience of a great number of persons.

Having thus thrown off in a cursory manner such thoughts as spontaneously entered my mind on this part of the subject it appears proper next to consider the subject fit for the purposes of a Lecture Science is undeniably the most eminent in its fitness for this purpose There is no part of it that may not be treated of illustrated and explained with profit and pleasure to the hearers in this manner The facility too with which it allows of manual and experimental illustrations place it foremost in this class of subjects after it comes (as I conceive) Arts and Manufactures, the Polite Arts, Belles Lettres etc. a list which may be extended untill it includes almost every thought and idea in the mind of man Politics excepted – I was going to add religion to the exception but remembered that it is explained and laid forth in the most popular and eminent manner in this way

The fitness of subjects – however is connected in an inseparable manner with the kind of audience that is to be present since excellent Lectures in themselves would appear absurd if delivered before an audience that did not understand them Anatomy would not do for the generality of audiences at the R. I. neither would Metaphysics engage the attention of a company of school boys. Let the subject fit the audience or otherwise success may be despaired of.

A Lecturer may consider his audience as being Polite or Vulgar (terms I wish you to understand according to Shuffletons new Dictionary)[5] Learned or unlearned (with respect to the subject) Listeners or Gazers – Polite Company expect to be entertained not only by the subject of the Lecture but by the manner of the Lecturer; they look for respect, for language consonant to their dignity and ideas on a levell with their own The vulgar that is to say in general those who will take the trouble of thinking and the bees of business wish for something that they can comprehend. This may be deep and elaborate for the Learned but for those who are as yet Tyros and unacquainted with the subject must be simple and plain Lastly Listeners expect reason and sense whilst Gazers only require a succession of words

These considerations should all of them engage the attention of the Lecturer whilst preparing for his occupation each particular having an influence on his arrangements proportionate to the nature of the company he expects he should consider them connectedly so as to keep engaged completely during the whole of the Lecture the attention of his audience

If agreeable this subject shall be resumed at a future time till when I am as always

Yours sincerely
M. FARADAY

[1] William Thomas Brande (1788–1866) was a chemist who succeeded Davy as Professor of Chemistry at the Royal Institution. For many years he offered lectures on chemistry to medical students in London and it is of these that Faraday here speaks. Brande was also the editor of the *Quarterly Journal of Science* which, though officially not connected with the Royal Institution, often served to present views held by people connected with it.
[2] There is no record of a course given at the Royal Institution by Mr Powell. The reference may be to a course of lectures at the City Philosophical Society.
[3] For Faraday on the art of lecturing, see *LPW*, 323ff.
[4] William Walker (1766–1816) was a very popular lecturer on astronomy in London in the late eighteenth and early nineteenth centuries.
[5] Not listed in the *British Museum General Catalogue of Printed Books*, London, 1964.

18   M. FARADAY to B. ABBOTT, 4 June 1813

[*R.I., Warner mss., B.J. 1, 7off*]

June 4, 1813

DEAR ABBOTT,

Not having room in my last letter I must apologise in this for the extraordinary length to which it was spun out – a length which would have made it unpardonable to any one but yourself. However I am so confident that I can judge aright of you at least that I take it for granted you will allow me the liberty of resuming the subject dwelt upon before and so without further ceremony I shall proceed

The hour at which a Lecture should be delivered should be considered at the same time with the nature of the audience we expect or wish for. If we would suit a particular class of persons we must fix it at the hour most convenient for them If we would wish to exclude any let the time be such that they cannot attend at it In general we may distinguish them according to their times into morning and evening Lectures each being adapted for different classes of persons

I need not point out to the active mind of my friend the astonishing disproportion or rather difference in the perceptive powers of the eye and the ear and the facility and clearness with which the first of these organs conveys ideas to the mind – ideas which being thus gained are held far more retentively and firmly in the memory than when introduced by the ear 'tis true the ear here labours under a disadvantage which is that the Lecturer may not always be qualified to state a fact with the utmost precision and clearness that language allows him and that the ear can understand and thus the complete action of the organ or rather of its assigned portion of the sensorium is not called forth. But this evidently points out to us the necessity of aiding it by using the eye also as a medium for the attainment of knowledge and strikingly shews the necessity of apparatus.

Apparatus therefore is an essential part of every lecture in which it can be introduced but to apparatus should be added at every convenient opportunity illustrations that may not perhaps deserve the name of apparatus and of experiments and yet may be introduced with considerable force and effect in proper places. Diagrams & Tables too are necessary or at least add in an eminent degree to the illustration and perfection of a Lecture.

When an experimental Lecture is to be delivered and apparatus is to be exhibited some kind of order should be observed in the arrangement of them on the Lecture table Every particular part illustrative of the Lecture should be in view no one thing should hide another from the audience nor should anything stand in the way of or obstruct the Lecturer. They should be so placed too as to produce a kind of uniformity in appearance no one part should appear naked and another crowded unless some particular reason exists and makes it necessary to be so at the same time the whole should be so arranged as to keep one operation from interfering with another If the Lecture table appears crowded – if the Lecturer (hid by the apparatus) is invisible if things appear crooked or aside or unequal or if some are out of sight and this without any particular reason the Lecturer is considered (and with reason too) as an awkward contriver and a bungler.

Diagrams tho ever so rough are often times of important use in a Lecture The facility with which they illustrate ideas and the diversity they produce in circumstances occurrant render them highly agreeable to an audience By diagrams I do not mean drawings (nor do I exclude drawings) but a plain and simple statement in a few lines of what requires many words a sheet of cartridge paper and a pen or a black board and chalk are often times of great importance I in general allude to temporary diagrams and would resort to temporary means to obtain them

A diagram or a table (by which I mean constituent parts or proportions wrote out in a rough enlarged way) should be left in the view of the audience for a short time after the lecturer himself has explained them that they may arrange the ideas contained in them in their minds and also refer to them in any other parts of the theory connected with the same subject and (if they choose as is often the case) also to copy them

With respect to illustrations simply so called no regular rules can be given on them They must be in part extempore and suggested to the mind of the Lecturer by particular circumstances They may be at one time proper at another improper but they should always be striking & to the point

53

June 5th 6 o'clock, P.M.

I have but just got your letter or should have answered it before For your request – it is fulfilled – For your invitation – I thank you but cannot accept it – For your orders – they shall be attended to – For to see you – I will come on Tuesday evening and – For want of time – I must conclude with respects to all friends,

Yours Sincerely
M. F ARADAY

19   M. F ARADAY to B. A BBOTT, 11 June 1813
[*R.I., Warner mss., B.J. 1, 72ff*]

June 11th 1813.

D EAR A BBOTT,

Having fulfilled your part so well and so completely with respect to a Lecture it is now my turn to begin At this time I shall speak of the qualifications requisite to form a Lecturer and do it with the less hesitation because having so lately a display of many of them they are impressed on my mind with the more force and clearness.

The most prominent requisite to a Lecturer 'tho perhaps not really the most important is a good delivery for tho to all true Philosophers Science and Nature will have charms innumerable in every dress yet I am sorry to say that the generality of mankind cannot accompany us one short hour unless the path is strewed with flowers In order therefore to gain the attention of an audience (and what can be more disagreeable to a Lecturer than the want of it) it is necessary to pay some attention to the manner of expression The utterance should not be rapid and hurried and consequently unintelligible but slow and deliberate conveying ideas with ease from the Lecturer and infusing them with clearness and readiness into the minds of the audience A Lecturer should endeavour by all means to obtain a facility of utterance and the power of cloathing [*sic*] his thoughts and ideas in language smooth and harmonious and at the same time simple and easy his periods should be round not too long or unequal they should be complete & expressive conveying clearly the whole of the ideas intended to be conveyed if they are long or obscure or incomplete they give rise to a degree of labour in the minds of the hearers which quickly causes lassitude indifference and even disgust

With respect to the action of a Lecturer it is requisite that he should have some tho it does not here bear the importance that it does in other branches of Oratory For 'tho I know of no species of delivery (divinity excepted) that requires less motion yet I would by no means have a Lecturer glued to the table or screwed on the floor he must by all means appear as a body distinct and separate from the things around him and must have some motion apart from that which they possess

A Lecturer should appear easy & collected undaunted & unconcerned his thoughts about him and his mind clear and free for the contemplation and description of his subject His action should not be hasty and violent but slow easy and natural consisting principally in changes of the posture of the body in order to avoid the air of stiffness or sameness that would otherwise be unavoidable His whole behaviour should evince respect for his audience and he should in no case forget that he is in their presence no accident that does not interfere with their convenience should disturb his serenity or cause variation in his behaviour he should never if possible turn his back on them but should give them full reason to believe that all his powers have been exerted for their pleasure and instruction

Some Lecturers choose to express their thoughts extemporaneously immediately as they occur to the mind whilst others previously arrange them and draw them forth on paper Those who are of the first description are certainly more unengaged and more at liberty to attend to other points of delivery than their pages but as every person on whom the duty falls is not equally competent for the prompt cloathing and utterance of his matter it becomes necessary that the second method should be resorted to This mode too has its advantages inasmuch as more time is allowed for the arrangement of the subject and more attention can be paid to the neatness of expression.

But 'tho I allow a Lecturer to write out his matter I do not approve of his reading it at least not as he would a quotation or extract he should deliver it in a ready and free manner referring to his book merely as he would to copious notes and not confining his tongue to the exact path there delineated but digress as circumstances may demand or localities allow.

A Lecturer should exert his utmost efforts to gain completely the mind and attention of his audience and irresistably to make them join in his ideas to the end of the subject he should endeavour to raise their interest at the commencement of the Lecture and by a series of imperceptible gradations unnoticed by the company keep it alive as long as the subject demands it – No breaks or digressions foreign to the purpose should have a place in the circumstances of the evening no opportunity should be allowed to the audience in which their minds could wander from the subject or return to inattention and carelessness a flame should be lighted at the commencement and kept alive with unremitting splendour to the end For this reason I very much disapprove of breaks in a Lecture and where they can by any means be avoid[ed] they should on no account find place If it is unavoidably necessary to complete the arrangement of some experiment or for other reasons leave some experiments in a state of progression or state some peculiar circumstance to employ as much as possible the minds of the audience during the unoccupied space – but if possible avoid it.

Digressions and wanderings produce more or less the bad effects of a complete break or delay in a Lecture and should therefore never be allowed except in very peculiar circumstances – They take the audience from the main subject & you then have the labour of bringing them back again (if possible)

For the same reason (namely that the audience should not grow tired) I disapprove of long Lectures one hour is long enough for any one nor should they be allowed far to exceed that time The only instance in which I have seen a Lecturer succeed in occupying the attention of his audience for a time eminently [reading doubtful] longer than an hour was at Walkers orrery[1] in which the subject has occupied time to the amount of two or three hours But here we have peculiar attendant circumstances from the nature of the place itself (a theatre) we expect to remain there a considerable time & tho the subject differs from such as usually draw us there yet we in part associate the ideas together – Again Mr. Walker very judiciously leaves the audience at intervals to themselves during which time they are entertained by harmony well suited to accompany such a subject by these interruptions he allows the minds of his company to return to their wonted level and they are in a short time again ready to accompany him into the celestial regions

Nor fancy dear Abbott that I here utter sentiments contrary to those I have just expressed and that I now approve of what I so strongly condemned I have not spoken without thought nor uttered undigested opinions 'Tis true I may be wrong I am but an inexperienced and unfit director but still those ideas I have expressed still appear to me correct

The science which Mr. Walker undertakes to explain and describe has for its object the most stupendous and magnificent work of the great the universal creator The subject is so immense that the mind is lost in the contemplation of it and the mode in which it is illustrated in the case in question is not at all deficient in grandeur and beauty but is well calculated to explain such a subject A mind engaged for too great a length of time amongst such illustrations and on such matter would become lost & confused and unable to follow rightly the path of reasoning that the subject requires Mr. Walker does well therefore to allow opportunities for the re-arrangement of our thoughts and we become by the vacation instead of less, more capable of again following the subject

These interruptions too are made at those parts of the subject where the science naturally separates into divisions so that our thoughts are not drawn *from* & then *to* one point but are merely taken from one when finished to be placed renovated on another we may indeed consider Mr. Walkers Lecture as a continual series of three or four distinct ones on the same subject & thus we easily become reconciled to the interruptions and admit their utility and good effects

But I have said enough for once on this subject and must leave it in order to have room for other things I had arranged matters so as to accept your kind invitation for Sunday and anticipated much pleasure from the meeting but am disagreeably disappointed circumstances being such as to hinder my seeing you at that time this I much regret but hope however to enjoy the full measure of pleasures expected at some not far distant time

I had a conversation with Mr. Hume[2] of Long acre this afternoon at which time he partially stated to me his opinion of Silex being the base of oxygen gas he promised me some papers on the subject and if I obtain them you shall of course see the foundation of so singular an opinion but farewell dear Abbott for a few days when you shall again hear from yours, most Sincerely

M. FARADAY

[1] See Letter 17, fn. 4.
[2] Joseph Hume (1756–1846) was a chemist in London. See his 'On the identity of Silex and Oxygen,' PM, 30 (1808), 165, 274, 356; 31 (1808), 161.

20 M. FARADAY to B. ABBOTT, 18 June 1813
[R.I., Warner mss., B.J. 1, 76ff]

June 18th 1813

Dear Abbott As when on some secluded branch in forest far and wide sits perched an owl who full of self conceit and self created wisdom, explains, comments condemns ordains and orders things not understood: yet, full of his importance still holds forth to stocks and stones around – so sits, and scribbles Mike; so he declaims, to walls, stones, tables chairs, hats, books pens, shoes, and all the things inert, that be around him – and so he will to the end of the chapter.

In compliance with that precept which desires us to finish one thing before we begin another I shall at once fall to work on the Lecturer & continue those observations which I have from time to time both made & gained about him Happy am I to say that the fault I shall now notice has seldom met my observation yet as I have witnessed it & as it does exist it is necessary to notice it

A Lecturer falls deeply beneath the dignity of his character when he descends so low as to angle for claps & asks for commendation yet have I seen a lecturer even at this point I have heard him causelessly condemn his own powers I have heard him dwell for a length of time on the extreme care and niceness that the experiment he will make requires. I have heard him hope for indulgence when no indulgence was wanted & I have even heard him declare that the experiment now made cannot fail from its beauty its correctness & its application to gain the approbation of all – yet surely such an error in the character of a Lecturer cannot require pointing out even to those who resort to it its impropriety must be evident & I should perhaps have done well to pass it

Before however I quite leave this part of my subject I would wish to notice a point in some manner connected with it In Lectures & more particularly experimental ones it will at times happen that accidents or other incommoding circumstances take place on these occasions an apology is sometimes necessary but not always I would wish apologies to be made as seldom as possible and generally only when the inconvenience extends to the company I have several times seen the attention of by far the greater part of the audience called to an error by the apology that followed it

An experimental Lecturer should attend very carefully to the choice he may make of experiments for the illustration of his subject they should be important as they respect the science they are applied to yet clear & such as may easily & generally be understood They should rather approach to simplicity & explain the established principles of the subject than be elaborate & apply to minute Phenomena only I speak here (be it understood) of those lectures which are delivered before a mixed audience and the nature of which will not admit of their being applied to the explanation of any but the principal parts of a science If to a particular audience you dwell on a particular subject still adhere to the same precept tho perhaps not exactly to the same rule let your experiments apply to the subject you elucidate [ms. missing] do not introduce those that are not to the point

'Tho this last part of my letter may appear superfluous seeing that the principle is so evident to every capacity yet I assure you dear Abbott I have seen it broken through in the most violent manner A meer [*sic*] ale-house trick has more than once been introduced in a Lecture delivered not far from Pall-Mall as an elucidation of the laws of motion.

Neither should too much stress be laid upon what I would call small experiments or rather illustrations It pleases me well to observe a neat idea enter the head of a Lecturer the which he will immediately & aptly illustrate or explain by a few motions of his hand a card a lamp a glass of water or any other thing that may be by him but when he calls your attention in a particular way to a decisive experiment that has enterd his mind clear and important in its application to the subject and then – lets fall a card I turn with disgust from the Lecturer and his experiments

'Tis well too when a Lecturer has the ready wit and the presence of mind to turn any casual circumstance to an illustration of his subject Any particular circumstance that has become table talk for the town any local advantages or disadvantages any trivial circumstance that may arise in company give great force to illustrations aptly drawn from them and please the audience highly as they conceive they perfectly understand them

Apt experiments (to which I have before referred) ought to be explained by satisfactory theory or otherwise we merely patch an old coat with new cloth and the whole (hole) becomes worse If a satisfactory theory can be given it ought to be given If we doubt a received opinion let us not leave it unnoticed & affirm our own ideas but state it clearly & lay down also our objections If the scientific world is divided in opinion state both sides of the question – & Let each one judge for himself assisting him by noticing the most striking and forcible circumstances on each side Then & then only shall we do justice to the subject please the audience & satisfy our honour the honour of a philosopher.

I shall here cause a slight separation in the subject by closing this epistle as it is now getting late so I shake hands 'till tomorrow at which time I hope to find all as well as is at present

Yours Sincerely
M. FARADAY

21 M. FARADAY to B. ABBOTT, 1 May 1814
[*R.I., Warner mss., B.J. 1, 128ff*]

Rome,[1]
May 1, 1814

DEAR BEN,

It was with much pleasure that I began a correspondence with you nor was the feeling diminished at any time during its continuance and though at present the interval between us is much greater than it was before which necessarily will render the progress of our epistolary communication much slower yet it is not at all my intention to drop it & I am in hopes that as it becomes more tardy in its advancement it will also become more important more instructive & more interesting Certainly I cannot now advance an excuse for the uninteresting strain of my letters a want of matter for every day presents sufficient to fill a book As I hope and expect that the good understanding still continues between our family & yours I expect that when they get a letter in Weymouth Street you will hear that I have thought of you I shall therefore fill this paper princi-pally with philosophical matter & as far as my feeble powers will permit me will endeavour to make it interesting I have commenced at this 1 day of May 1814 in the ancient city of Rome & hope to send it off on Wednesday by favour to England but if it cannot go then I shall keep it by me & add to it as to a journal and send it when an opportunity arises and opportunities I hope will soon be frequent

Here the thing which is uppermost in the mind of every person is the strange chain of events which have brought about the downfall of Napoleon the Great (the title he had taken) & of the system of government that he had established These events are so singular & have occurred with such rapidity that it appears as a waking dream passing rapidly over the mind & of which it is difficult to form an idea of reality To see the Bourbons on the throne of France was never expected & though a universal European peace was earnestly desired no hopes of it were entertained at present those events appear close at hand God grant they may come to pass Amongst these occurrences England has shone out most conspicuously & her firm & steady virtue & constancy are held up to the whole world as a model of imitation & England meets with her due in the praises of every one In France I found every one laud the English at Paris they all praised the English & since we have left the French dominions we have been received with testimonies of pleasure & gratitude as strong as it was possible for the tongue to express At Lucca we found the whole population without the gates waiting for the English It was said that the Army which had debarked at Leghorn would enter Lucca that day & the inhabitants had come out to receive them as brothers The town was decorated in the most brilliant manner by colours drapery and embroidery flying from every window & in the evening general illuminations took place done as expressive of their joy at the deliverance from the French government & the English were hailed every where as their Saviours

24 July, Geneva.

This morsel of paper dear Ben has made a longer voyage than that I intended for it and instead of being in London it is now at Geneva but I hope that it will not be long before it is at its original destination and procuring me the pleasure of a letter from you On perusing the last (and the first) page I found the matter so different from that at present in my head that I was suddenly urged to destroy it but second thoughts induced me to leave it unaltered since it conveyed the ideas of that moment which to you will not be more uninteresting than those of the present As it is my intention to well fill this paper I shall write it as much in the style of description as in that of a letter or rather I shall write it as my thoughts run – too much indeed out of order. You will find in this letter not a regular description of my journey but a few observations on those things which I have found most remarkable and which have been most under my notice for as all parts of my travels have pleased me it will be useless to say I liked Aix or I liked Nice, etc. It is now 9 months ago since I left London but I have not forgot and never shall forget the ideas that were forced on my mind in the first days. To me who had lived all my days of remembrance in London in a city surrounded by a flat green country a hill was a mountain and a stone a rock for though I had abstract ideas of the things and could say rock & mountain and would talk of them yet I had no perfect ideas conceive then the astonishment the pleasure and the information that entered my mind in the varied county of Devonshire where the foundations of the earth were first exposed to my view and where I first saw granite limestone etc in those places and in those forms where the ever working and all wonderful hand of nature had placed them No Ben it is impossible you can conceive my feelings and it is as impossible for me to describe them The sea then presented a new scene of information and interest and on approaching the shore of France with what eagerness and how often were my eyes directed to the south When arrived

60

there I thought myself in an uncivilized country for never before or since have I seen such wretched beings as at Morlaix. But I must break this train of thoughts Dear Ben and carry you in haste to Paris where art exerts her power to inform and astonish man There are many things at Paris calculated in an eminent degree to arrest the progress of the traveller but these things consist in the works of men & I would rather talk to you of the works of nature however I must not forget to tell you of what I suppose you have heard at least I earnestly hope so namely *Iodine* on which Sir H. Davy has made many experiments and he has written to the Royal Society papers on the subject[2] This substance adds a fourth body to the class of supporters of combustion or to the class of undecomposed bodies attracted by the positive pole of the Voltaic apparatus and which by their strong and opposed attraction to other bodies produce light & heat and it is the only one of them which has been obtained in a *separate piece & solid* form It is very heavy of a dark colour similar to plumbago and has much the appearance of that body when heated it melts and gives off or rises in the form of a beautifully coloured violet gas of great intensity and when cooled it appears in minute crystals but otherwise unchanged It combines readily with many other bodies with all the metals except two that I have seen it tried on – the two are Platinum & Gold and I have seen the compounds it forms with Iron Tin Lead Silver Copper Mercury etc. It forms acids by combining with very different bodies thus Chlorine Hydrogen Phosphorus & Tin all form acids with it & possessing new and singular properties. It unites to Azote & like chlorine forms a detonating compound with it and with potassium sodium Baryum etc it forms substances very similar to the compounds of these bodies with Chlorine indeed it resembles this body more than any other in its combinations. When added to Potash in solution two new compounds are formed one being a binary compound of iodine & potassium similar to muriate of potash as it [is] [ms. missing] called and the other parallels with oxymuriate of potash for it contains all the oxygen of the alkali and detonates very readily with nitre I am however but wasting time in writing that of which you have a complete account as far as it goes in England and shortly I suppose that Sʳ H——will send you further accounts for he works upon it every day Before I leave iodine however I must ask you & also desire you to inform me of the state of your sentiments respecting chlorine whether you class that substance & fluorine with oxygene or whether you insulate the last body as in former times On leaving Paris we visited Lyons rested at Montpellier for a few weeks and afterwards saw Aix, Nice etc. between Nice and Turin we crossed the Maritime alps by the Col de Tende in the Month of Feby. not the most favourable season in the year for crossing these many mountains The col de tende cost a day to cross it and at the summit we were elevated above 6000 [feet] higher than the level of the sea. From Turin we went to Genoa where I first saw a torpedo[3] and a water spout The torpedos here were small too small for the experiments which Sr H.——— wished to make with them These experiments were to ascertain whether the electric power of the torpedo could be made to decompose water The apparatus used was that of Wollaston and the fluid solution of potassa it being a very good conductor but though the animal gave several shocks which there is reason to suppose passed through the water yet no satisfactory result was obtained & no effect appeared to be produced Sr H.——— has repeated these experiments since at Rimini with the torpedo of the adriatic Sea but they were also too small to give certain results – Leaving Genoa we proceeded by water to Lereche [*sic*] [Lerici] and from thence to Florence a beautiful city where we remained some days here is a fine Museum of Natural History containing an immense quantity of things curious & instructive and some wax works in anatomy & botany of the most delicate kind The collection of apparatus is numerous and rendered invaluable by the instruments of Galileo & the Duke of Tuscany. The first telescope of Galileo & that with which he discovered the satellites of Jupiter is carefully preserved as an invaluable philosophical relic and also the first lens which he made which is set in a fine worked [reading doubtful] frame with an inscription It is cracked in two. There is also a vast quantity of electrical machines and apparatus there is a machine of Red Velvet passing under a rubber of black silk & there is a collection of jars broken singularly by extraordinary explosions Magnets here are numerous and very strong & there is a compound one which supports some Cwt. S^r H took the opportunity whilst here of making many experiments on the diamond with the great lens of the Grand Duke[4] a noble instrument belonging to the academy and in these pursuits as in every other his attentive mind observed & demonstrated new facts In the first experiment on the combustion of the diamond it was placed in the middle of a glass globe of 18 or 20 cubical inches capacity supported in a cradle of platinum fixed on a prop of the same metal The cradle was pierced full of holes to admit a free circulation of air i.e. oxygen for the globe was filled with the gas procured from hyperoxymuriate of potassa On placing the apparatus thus arranged in the focus of the lens it (the diamond) shortly entered into combustion & on removing it from the instrument the combustion was observed to continue for above 4 minutes during this time the diamond gave off intense heat & a beautifull vivid scarlet light it diminished rapidly in size and became at last a mere atom when it ceased to burn but on placing it again in the focus the whole rapidly disappeared The globe was found to contain nothing but a mixture of Carbonic and Oxygene gases. This experiment was repeated several times and in all the cases the same striking phenomenon was observed a phenomenon which lessens considerably the difference existing between diamond and charcoal Sir H burned also by the same instrument a piece of plumbago in oxygen and he heated also diamonds in Chlorine & Carbonic acid gases but no change was produced no compound no muriatic acid was formed in the first place and no carbonic oxide in the second These experiments on carbonaceous substances were continued at Rome at which time charcoal obtained from Alcohol from Turpentine & from wood were weighed & burned and from all these experiments it appeared that the diamond was pure crystallised carbon and that the black compounds of carbon contained hydrogen though none of them in great quantities plumbago also contained hydrogen and when heated in chlorine the hydrogen was separated and fumes of muriatic acid clouded the globe of the charcoals that obtained from turpentine by sulphuric acid appeared the purest then that from alcohol and lastly the charcoal of wood by purity I mean a want of hydrogen and the purest contained the least hydrogen the charcoal of wood the most S^r H—— wrote an account of these experiments which has been sent to the Royal Society & I hope received – From Florence we went to Rome that City of Wonders but they are wonders created by a former nation & in a former age You know Ben my turn is not architectural nor though I can admire a beautiful picture do I pretend to judge of it but certainly the things here would affect any one and that mind must be dull indeed that is not urged to think & think again on these astonishing remains of the Romans when they appear in sight at every corner I shall not pretend to describe them dear Ben since descriptions far more perfect than those I can give you are in England The two things here most striking are the Coliseum & St. Peters and one is not more worthy of the ancients than the other is of the moderns The Coliseum is a mighty ruin & indeed so is Rome & so are the Romans & it is almost impossible to conceive how the hardy warlike race which conquered the globe has degenerated into modern effeminate idle italians St. Peters appears to have been erected on the plan of some fairy tale for every luxury every ornament & every embellishment & species of embel-lishment have been employed in its erection Its size is mighty – it is moun-tainous its architecture elegant its materials costly They consist of Marbles of every hue & every kind mosaics statues casts bronzes Jewels Gold & silver not spread sparingly but shining & glittering in every part The mosaics are numerous and large and amongst the many designs that ornament this edifice there is but one painted picture – But I must for the present leave description and employ the rest of my paper on other matter matter which I have deferred to the last – because I wish it to remain clearest & strongest in your mind And in another letter I will give you such accounts of Naples Vesuvius etc. as I am able to do. (The burning mountain I have been up twice once in the day time and once at night) As communications are so free between this place and England you will I hope not delay many days in answering this letter The time of communication is I believe only 7 days and the letters must be franked reciprocally out of each country. You will be so good as to let my Mother & friends know this and I hope I shall hear from more than one person and by more than one letter There are two persons nearly strangers to my mother to which if you would go I should be much obliged Mrs. Greenwell[5] of the R. Institution to whom give my warmest thanks and remembrances for her kind treatment of me when there and my warmest wishes for here [*sic*] prosperity & happiness & Mr. Newman[6] of Lisle St. to whom I feel grateful for his readiness in communicating to me such things as were useful and instructive and whose success in life is I hope proportioned to his merits To my Mother & My brother you will of course go and you will say all you can to them without any fear of outrunning the warmth of my wishes. I have wrote many times to them & by such hands as I suppose could not fail & I hope to hear now how they do & how affairs move Give them all for me every warm feeling that can flow round the heart To Mr. & Mrs. Abbott & to your Brother & Sister I present my respects & would if I durst my affections & to you Dear Ben I give the dearest feeling that can enliven the days of man friendship May you ever be happy & honorably so and may you never have cause to censure the feelings of

Your Friend, M. FARADAY

Direct to Me at Geneva Post restant

[1] On 13 October 1813, Sir Humphry and Lady Davy began a continental tour. Faraday was included in the company as a 'temporary' valet to Sir Humphry. For an account of this trip drawn from the journal which Faraday kept, as well as from the letters that follow, see *LPW*, 31ff.

[2] H. Davy, 'Some experiments and observations on a new substance which becomes a violet-coloured Gas by Heat,' *PT* (1814), 74, and 'Further experiments and observations on Iodine,' *ibid.*, 487.

[3] Davy, like Faraday later in his life, was fascinated by electric fish.

[4] See H. Davy, 'Some experiments on the combustion of the Diamond and other carbonaceous substances,' *PT* (1814), 557.

[5] Mrs Greenwell was the housekeeper of the Royal Institution.

[6] John Newman was a scientific instrument maker who later was to make the instruments which Faraday used in his experimental researches in electricity.

22 M. FARADAY to B. ABBOTT, 6 September 1814
[*R.I., Warner mss., B.J. 1, 152ff*]

Geneve,
Sept 6th 1814

DEAR BEN

It is with extreme pleasure that I pursue a correspondence which I find is not to be impaired either by time absence or distance a correspondence which has been dear to me from the first moment of its existence which I have found full of pleasure and which I have never regretted and its continuance continually gives me fresh proofs that it will ever remain as it has been a strong & irreproachable source of instruction and amusement. I thank you Dear Ben as earnestly as I can do for your long and kind letter which I shall endeavour to answer as well as I can though not in such a manner as it ought to be I have not I can truly assure you enough time to write you a letter as long as your own I have a great deal of occupation which leaves me but little time to myself and my Journal is much behindhand and as we leave this place in eight or nine days I shall have difficulty in arranging my things and clearing up my papers My head at this moment is full of thoughts respecting you and me respecting your uneasy situation and mine which is not at all times pleasant and what I expected your last letter has partly collected those thoughts, and I shall probably state some of them on this sheet of paper – I must beg of you to acknowledge on my part the receipt of your brother's second letter and the receipt of a second one from my brother. I had them both on Augt. 31. eight days after the post date they gave me great pleasure and I shall not delay longer than is convenient thanks under my own hand but I will here desire of you Dear Ben to inform my friends that I wish whatever letters they will send me may be directed to me alone or to me at Sir Humphry Davy or chez Monsieur le Chevalier Davy I have already given this notice in a letter to my brother but for security (for I should wish it to be attended to) I give it again to you well knowing that you will do every thing I can wish – I feel a pleasure which I cannot describe on perceiving the interest you take in my i.e. our friends in Weymouth Street and I hope to return and be grateful for your attentions they are such as I expected from a friend and they deserve better acknowledgments than I can give but I trust words are as little wanting from me to Ben as from Ben to me In my last letter to my brother I wrote a few lines to Peggy[1] but I unaccountably forgot to thank her for her present which I received with yours and I know of no way of compensating for my slip than by engaging you to thank her for me I feel great very great interest in Peggy she has talents in a high degree accompanied by a strong and rapid memory and a willing mind and were knowledge to be communicated to her by those who know how to lead a child by attention to its numerous and simple questions and a soft and pleasing demeanour I should hope to see her at some time what I should like to be myself With the thanks you will give my love and answer fully if you please any questions she may put to you respecting me or the country where I am or may be I was very happy to hear of Mrs. Greenwells[2] health and hope you will repeat your commission and my remembrances Sir Humphry was glad to hear that she was well. I hope you will see Mr. Newman[3] again and name me to him and if he would remember me to Mr. Fincher [4] I should feel much obliged I remember Mr. Fincher on more account than one and he will understand me if Mr. Newman tells him that I often think on our conversations together and wish I were at home. Some doubts have been expressed to me lately with respect to the continuance of the Royal Institution[5] Mr. Newman can probably give a guess at the issue of it. I have three boxes of books etc. there and I should be sorry if they were lost by the turning up of unforeseen circumstances but I hope all will end well (you will not read this out loud) – Remember me to all there if you please – and "now for you and I to ourselves."

I was much hurt in mind to hear of your ill health and still more so to understand your uncomfortable situation for from what I have felt at times I can judge of your feelings under such a painful bondage I am as yet but young Ben very unacquainted with the world with men and manners and too conscious of my ignorance to set up for a moralizer but yet dear friend I have not passed on to this day without a little experience and though not endued with the acutest powers of mind I have been forced to notice many things which are of service to me and may be useful to you if they are I shall not repent the trouble I give you; and if they are not, you must attribute them to the warmth of my feelings for you – You are you inform me in a situation where gain only is the object where every sentiment is opposed to yours where avarice has shut out every manly feelings [*sic*]; where liberal thoughts and opinions are unknown where knowledge except as it is subservient to the basest and lowest of feelings is shut out and where your thoughts if not looking to the acquisition of money are censured and where liberality and generosity never enter These are things which I know to be so opposite to your mind and inclinations that I can well conceive your feelings and, as if it were to increase those feelings, this disagreeable situation follows one that was perfectly pleasant and aggreeable In passing through life my Dear Friend everyone must expect to receive lessons both in the School of Prosperity and in that of adversity and taken in a general sense those schools do not only include riches & poverty but every thing that may cause the happiness and pleasure of man and every feeling that may give him pain I have been in at the door of both those schools nor am I so far on the right hand at present that I do not get hurt by the thorns on my left. With respect to myself I have always perceived (when after a time I saw things more clearly) that those things which at first appeared as misfortunes or evils ultimately were actually benefits and productive of much good in the future progress of things sometimes I compared them to storms and tempests, which cause a temporary dyrangement [*sic*] to produce a permanent good sometimes they appeared to me like roads stony, uneven hilly and uncomfortable it is true but the only roads to a good beyond them and sometimes I said they were clouds which intervened between me and the sun of prosperity but which I found were refreshing reserving to me that tone and vigour of mind which prosperity alone would enervate & ultimately destroy I have observed that in the progress of things circumstances have so worked together without my knowing how or in what way that an end has appeared which I could never have fancied and which circumstances ultimately show could never have been obtained by any plans of mine I have found also that those circumstances which I have earnestly wished for and which ultimately I have obtained were productive of effects very different to those I had assigned to them and were oftentimes more unsatisfactory than even a disappointment would have been I have experienced too that pleasures are not the same when attained as when sought after and from these things I have concluded that we generally err in our opinions of happiness and misery.

I condole with you Dear Ben most sincerely on the uneasiness of your situation but at the same time I advise you to remember that is an opportunity of improvement that must not be lost in regret & repining It is necessary for man to learn how to conduct himself properly in every situation for the more knowledge he has of this kind the more able is he to cope with those he is at times sure to meet with You have under your eye a copy of thousands and you have the best opportunities of studying him in noticing his errors you will learn to avoid them what he has good will by contrast appear more strongly you will see the influence of the passions one on another and may observe how a good feeling may be utterly destroyed by the predominance of an opposite one you will perceive the gradual increase of the predominant sentiment and the mode in which it surrounds the heart, utterly debarring the access of opposite feelings – At the same time, dear friend you will learn to bear uneasy situations with more patience you will look to the end which may reward you for your patience and you will naturally gain a tone of mind which will enable you to meet with more propriety both the prosperity & adversity of your future fortune Remember that, in leaving your present situation you may find a worse one and that though a prospect is fair you know not what it may produce

You talk of travelling and I own the word is seducing but travelling does not secure you from uneasy circumstances I by no means intend to deter you from it for though I should like to find you at home when I come home and though I know how much the loss would be felt by our friends yet I am aware that the fund of knowledge and of entertainment opened would be almost infinite but I shall set down a few of my own thoughts & feelings etc. in the same circumstances In the first place then my dear Ben I fancy that when I set my foot in England I shall never take it out again for I find the prospect so different from what it at first appeared to be that I am certain if I could have foreseen the things that have passed I should never have left London In the second place enticing as travelling is and I appreciate fully its advantages and pleasures I have several times been more than half decided to return hastily home but second thoughts have still induced me to try what the future may produce and now I am only retained by the wish of improvement I have learned just enough to perceive my ignorance and ashamed of my defects in every thing I wish to seize the opportunity of remedying them. The little knowledge I have gained in languages makes me wish to know more of them and the little I have seen of men & manners is just enough to make me desirous of seeing more added to which the glorious opportunity I enjoy of improving in the knowledge of

5-2

Chemistry and the Sciences continually determines me to finish this voyage with Sir Humphry Davy. but if I wish to enjoy those advantages, I have to sacrifice much; and though those sacrifices are such as an humble man would not feel yet I cannot quietly make them Travelling too I find is almost inconsistent with religion (I mean modern travelling) and I am yet so old-fashioned as to remember strongly (I hope perfectly) my youthful education and upon the whole malgré the advantages of travelling, it is not impossible but that you may see me at your door when you expect a letter

You will perceive Dear Ben that I do not wish you hastily to leave your present situation because I think that a hasty change will only make things worse you will naturally compare your situation with others you see around you, and by this comparison your own will appear more sad whilst the others seem brighter than in truth they are for like the two poles of a battery the ideas of each will become exalted by approaching them – But I leave you dear friend to act in this case as your judgment may direct hoping always for the best I fear that my train of thoughts have been too dull in this letter; but I have not yet attained to the power of equalizing them and making them flow in a regular stream If you find them sad remember that it was in thinking on you they fell and then excuse them.

I felt much interested in reading the philosophical part of your letter and congratulate you upon the advances which you must now make and it was doubly pleasing to me as it showed me that no circumstances could overpower the industry of your active and vigilant mind I felt highly flattered in understanding the good opinion that was entertained of my friend at the Surrey Institution but I was still more pleased at learning his determination since it shews me that he can so easily and successfully combat & overcome pride by humility

With respect to Boyle's Statical Baroscope I am not sure that I know the instrument I suppose it is an exhausted flask that is balanced The experiments are I supposed made with several at a time of different sizes and of different glasses for as glasses vary in their particular ratio of expansion by heat it will cause variations in the results but I can give no opinion on it – Sir Humphry works often on iodine and has lately been making experiments on the prismatic spectrum at M. Pictet's[6] these are not yet perfected but from the use of very delicate air thermometers it appears that the rays producing most heat are certainly out of the spectrum and beyond the red rays Our time has been employed lately in fishing and shooting and many a Quail has been killed in the plains of Geneve and many a trout and grayling have been pulled out of the Rhone[7] – Go as usual to Weymouth Street and give my kindest love to them all and if you have not time ask them to do so in the City remember me to Boyer Magrath Castle[8] etc and kindly to Mr. & Mrs. Abbott & Your Brother and Sister I need not say dear Ben how perfectly I am yours,

Adieu

M. FARADAY

1 Faraday's younger sister, Margaret.
2 See Letter 21, fn. 5.
3 See Letter 21, fn. 6.
4 Joseph Fincher was Assistant Secretary of the Royal Institution.
5 For the difficulties which the Royal Institution faced in these years see Henry Bence Jones, *The Royal Institution: Its Founder and Its First Professors*, London, 1871.
6 Marc Auguste Pictet (1752–1825) was a resident of Geneva who did his most important scientific work in meteorology.
7 Davy was an avid hunter and fisherman.
8 All friends of Faraday's from the City Philosophical Society. The only one I can identify is Edward Magrath. Magrath tutored Faraday in English writing style during these years of his scientific apprenticeship. He later became Secretary of the Athenaeum Club to which Faraday belonged from its inception.

23   B. ABBOTT to M. FARADAY, 20 November 1814[1]

[*R.I., Warner mss., previously unpublished*]

London,
Sunday 20th Nov.ʳ 1814.

MY DEAR MICHAEL!

The knowledge that the receipt of my letters affords you any pleasure would I can assure you be sufficient to induce me to write them even was the doing it a task instead of what it is – a pleasure – Impressed with this Sentiment it is with a great degree of readiness & alacrity that I seize the present Opportunity of continuing a correspondence which affords us mutually so much Entertainment & which [illeg.] distance will have no effect in impairing however much it may in impeding.

I have some fear at this time that the present text will find you already at Rome, which it was not my intention it should do but so many circumstances have lately intervened to prevent my [persuing it more that I found it impossible & can therefore only say] [passage doubtful] that should it arrive later than you have expected, its length must compensate for its delay. I say its length for I intend to fill this Sheet at all costs & with the utterance of this intention I shall without further preamble proceed.

First then I must acknowledge the receipt of yours of the 6th Sept. from Geneva which reached me the 17th same & afforded me new proof, if such had been wanted, of your friendship for me, [the interest you feel in my welfare] [reading doubtful]...I thank you My Dear Michael...[whole passage of 10 lines illeg.]. Besides the inhabitants of this house & those of Weymouth Street...[illeg.]...Your Mother Brother & Sister I believe are well; they were so a fortnight since. When I was there, Peggy, you will be interested to hear has with the assistance of my beloved Sister succeeded in prevailing on her mother to permit her to spend the day with us & if I can judge by her talk she would have no objection to repeat the visit. When this will be allowed I know not. – I particularly notice what you say respecting her & can assure you I conceive her worthy of all the affection you can feel for her, that she feels the same for you I doubt not. She talks of you incessantly, you are her perpetual theme of admiration. "Michael" she says, "taught me to read & to write, he encouraged me to learn, & yet I was afraid of him, but nobody takes any pains with me now, I wish Michl [*sic*] was home again." – This is her constant idea. I much wish I could take upon myself the occupation you have left & could attend to her improvement, so far as I am able but circumstances forbid it, do you therefore accept the will for the deed & do me the justice to believe that was it in my power I should not fail to [*sic*] all I could towards it. – Robert does not often visit us for which I can assign no reason except so far as report goes – Peggy tells me he is seldom at home; that when he comes in he cleans himself & goes out again immediately. The report is that he is over head & ears in love! I say the report for he has not told me so; I heard it from Mrs Gray & Betsey,[2] therefore when you write to him do not mention it lest he feel vexed with me (you know his temper) for saying any such thing to you. – Mrs. G. & your Sister I have also called on as desired & I am truly happy to say found both well & their family the same. They desired that when I wrote to you I would say for them all that they could say if you were present or that I could say were I in their situation. More than either of these I need not say. I called on Mr Newman 2 Sundays ago (I had no opportunity before) but unfortunately was unable to see him. I however saw Mrs. N. who having seen me before politely asked me in & gave me all the information in her power, promising to desire Mr N. to tell Mr Fincher what you wished. Respecting the R. I. you need be under *no* apprehension. The members have this Summer submitted to a great sacrifice & all the debts are paid off so that altho' eventually the Expences will eat up the Principal of their Funds yet a dissolution in consequence cannot take place within a period of time much larger than it is even probable you will be absent. You may therefore be at ease on this Head – but should any thing *par possibilité* occur, Ben will not lose sight of any thing that concerns his Friend Michael. Mrs Greenwell

Nov. 22, 1814.

Unfortunately this Sheet was last night left in the City by mistake where I had taken it for the purpose of submitting the part already written to the pressure of the Copying Machine, & I therefore fear instead of its being forwarded to day as I intended I shall be forced to postpone it till tomorrow. I shall now proceed somewhat more philosophically than in the foregoing part. – In your last you congratulate me on the Progress I must have made & term my mind active & vigilant – now I do not think I am *lazy* but yet I am afraid my Dear Michl you are a flatterer & you well know that is not a character I am fond of & I should be particularly sorry to find your travels had caused any tendency in you towards it – with respect to my progress in Science I am sorry to say it has been much less than I could have wished since your departure, for though I have in the Institution an excellent Library & still more a decent Laboratory yet I have no scientific companion – it is true some indeed most of my acquaintances are philosophically inclined – that is – they like to hear a Lecture & to see a few dashing Experiments – but they are not so fond of Science as to stand at a furnace till their Eyes are scorched or risk a convulsion of their Muscles from the unexpected touch of a Voltaic Battery – such a one as this would be a treasure to me such a one as could catch my ideas & pursue them in conjunction with me & to whom half a word might suffice to convey more than a whole lecture does to some – but for such a one as this I must wait till *you* return & then I shall have all I wish in this way till that time I must content myself with what progress I can *alone*, & look forward to the time when you, with all the knowledge you will have gained shall once more be my companion my Friend I believe you still are & I trust will still continue however inferior I may be in attainments to you when you will have completed your Tour – Notwithstanding the drawback on the rapidity of my progress (to which I may also add another – viz. – Expence, I would not have you suppose I am idle – by no means, such opportunities as I have I endeavour to profit by as much as I can & the Laboratory in the Institution is principally valuable you know on account of the Furnaces for which the Institution supply [*sic*] fuel & as I am the only one who uses them I have no fear of interruption. They are certainly very good ones – a short time since I procured a specimen of Silver Ore from Potosi in So. America 100 grains of which I [illeg.] etc. & submitting it to cupellation obtained 2 buttons weighing together 62 grains besides a small portion (about 3 grains) which were lost in consequence of the (vat?) cracking when one changed with lead – the hour being late I am inclined to believe I did not push the firing so far as I ought to have done & I therefore suspect it is still somewhat impure tho' in a very small degree – a second cupellation will put it beyond doubt – The richness of the ore arises I should inform you from it being part of a specimen sent over as a rarity – some of their mines are far from cont[ainin]g such a proportion of the precious Metal. – I sometime since saw a specimen from Peru (I believe) of white Marble spangled with grains of Gold nearly pure. – It was really beautiful. –

The Lectures at the Surrey Institution have commenced. There are 4 courses 1st on Chemistry by Mr Wheeler, 2nd on Extemporary Eloquence by Mr Rippingham 3d On the Passions & affections of the Mind & their Influence on Language & the Polite Arts by I M Good – 4th On Music by Dr Crotch – the two first are commenced but I have not yet heard Mr Rippingham he has delivered only one & from that I was unluckily detained by Business – my Sister however (who subscribes also) was there & she says he is an Orator I therefore expect some pleasure from hearing him. – Mr Wheeler has delivered 2 Lectures – he is a young man who has never before appeared in Public & therefore labours under a great disadvantage from diffidence This however will be soon overcome & I think he then bids fair to be a decent Lecturer a first-rate one he cannot be from a slight defect in utterance – from Mr Goode I anticipate a course deeply fraught with Enquiry & delivered in a very excellent Stile [*sic*] – When I have heard them I shall send you my ideas on them Dr Crotch will as usual please the Ladies – Mr Spencer still notices me & constantly stiles me – "my Scientific Friend –"3 The Librarian calls me "a Philosophical Gossip. – I here commence a new Sheet for from the appearance I fear the 2 last pages will be scarcely legible on this thin paper & I am unwilling to give you more trouble in deciphering them than is necessary. –

In a former Letter you promised me a full Sheet with a little of Vesuvius in it but I have not received it my last Epistle I suppose chased the Volcano out of your head. I hope by your next it will have returned – I have an extraordinary wish my Dear Mike to see one of these flaming Furnaces & I think tho' you know I am not famous for Courage that my nerves would allow me to take a tolerable quiet look at it. – Pray have you seen many Cataracts? Mr K. my Companion in the County Ho has travelled in America & has seen the Falls of Niagara – he lent me his Manuscript Account & also gave me some verbal particulars – from his relation it appears to me the Scene can scarcely be less awful than a Volcano tho' of course differing much in its nature. The noise he compared to all the Cannon in the World keeping up an incessant roar all around you: as to what some persons have said of its being possible to go between the stream & the rock over which it falls he denies it altogether & says the place looks more like the Mouth of the Infernal Regions than any thing else, & that any person attempting to go there would meet instant suffocation from the Spray & from the violent agitation of the air which he describes as so great 30 feet from the Stream as to oblige you every moment to turn round to recover the use of the Lungs. –

A native of the Country you are now in lately opened a Shop here for the Sale of Fulminating Objects particularly small Balls as large as large Peas – These being crushed under the Foot or thrown with violence against any Substance exploded with a very considerable Report. – The Streets, Theatres, & even Chapels were annoyed by them & many persons were taken into Custody & fined in the mean time others made them & they were sold at almost every Chemists Shop at last the Magistrates found out they were Fireworks & Fined many for selling them among others a young man who brought forward our Friend *Banks*4 – & tried to prove they were not Fireworks to do which he was about to explode one in a [bbl.] [reading doubtful] of Gunpowder. This was not permitted but he stated Sir H. had performed the Expt & the Gunpr *never* was nor could be inflamed & insisted on trying with a smaller portion – he did so, tho' the Gunpowder blew up but he even then declared he would have fixed one in a barrel of powder without fear – had he not become then convinced – his Friend was fined £5 – it is almost needless to say – they were fulminating Silver in a Glass Bubble. –

When you write next to me indeed whenever you do I shall feel a particular pleasure if you will give me all the intelligence you can concerning your Route & the probable time of your Return – agreable to what I told you before your departure you will bear in mind that your Letters are shewn to no one if they contain any thing private – if they do not your Mother & Brother have the perusal of them. – I merely [mention] this now to freshen your memory & to let you know *if you are ignorant of it* that you may place confidence in me & my promises. –

I must here my Dear Michael think of drawing towards a conclusion of this tolerable long Letter – remember I shall be glad to see your writing if only three Lines – Therefore do not delay to answer it in any way as [reading doubtful] most convenient – should I not previously hear from you I intend to write again in about 3 or 4 Weeks – Boyer Castle Magrath &c desire their kind remembrances – my brother requests you will bear in mind his Commission[5] & unites with my Father, Mother & Sister in every heartfelt wish for your Welfare it is almost needless for me to add how cordially I do the same. That you my Dear Michael may be ever Happy as you deserve & that our Friendship may only gain strength from its age is the constant Prayer of

Yours most truly & sincerely
BENJ. ABBOTT.

Que croyez vous des Femmes Italiennes? sont-ils aussi belles que les Anglaises

Orig¹ sent via Paris 24th Novʳ 1814 Recd by MF at Rome

1 None of Abbott's original letters to Faraday have survived. What is printed here is a copy made by Abbott with a letter press. Over the course of years, this copy has faded so that it can now be read only under an ultra-violet lamp. Even with this help, however, much of it is illegible. Nevertheless, as one of two surviving specimens of Abbott's end of the Faraday–Abbott correspondence, it deserves publication.
2 Mrs Gray was probably a neighbour. Faraday's elder sister was Elizabeth.
3 The Surrey Institution was one of many similar establishments in early nineteenth-century London, providing both education and recreation for its members. It sponsored lectures, paid for by members' subscriptions, offered the use of a library and, as Abbott hints, provided laboratory facilities. There is a real need for a scholarly and thorough investigation of the role such institutions played in the scientific sphere in these years when science was being transformed from the pastime of amateurs to the full business of professionals.
4 Sir Joseph Banks (1743–1820), then President of the Royal Society.
5 Abbott's brother had asked Faraday to buy him a snuff box on the Continent. See Letter 26.

[*R.I.*, *Warner mss.*, *B.J. 1*, *169 ff*]

Rome,
Saturday. Nov.ʳ 26ᵗʰ, 1814

What have I done or what have I said that I am to hear no more from England day passes after day week after week but passes without bringing me the long-wished for letters. Did you but know the pleasure they give me did you but know the importance they are of to me certain I am that compassion would induce you to write Alone in a foreign country amongst strangers without friends without acquaintances surrounded by those who have no congenial feelings with me whose dispositions are opposite to mine & whose employ-ments offend me where can I look for pleasure but to the remembrances of my friends? At home I have left those who are dear to me from a long acquaintance a congeniality of mind a reciprocal feeling of friendship affection & respect as well for their honor & their virtues here I find myself in the midst of a crowd of people who delight in deceiving are ignorant faithless frivolous and at second sight would be my friends their want of honor irritates me their servility disgusts me & their impertinence offends me and it is with a painful sensation I think of my friends when I remember I cannot do more Why then do you delay so long that which is the greatest service you can do me and since I have lost your company let me at least have your thoughts since I can not see you let me see the work of your hand Through my own imprudence I have lost for a time that source I did possess for I have left at Geneva with books – those letters I have received from you my brother & yours and which I ought never to have separated so far from me It is possible I may never see them again and my fears tell me I may never receive any more and even that the possibility exists of my being for ever separated from England Alas! How foolish perhaps was I to leave home to leave those whom I loved & who loved me for a time uncertain in its length but certainly long and which perhaps may stretch out into eternity and what are the boasted advantages to be gained knowledge yes knowledge but what knowledge knowledge of the world of men of manners of books & of languages things in themselves valuable above all praise but which every day shews me prostituted to the basest purposes alas how degrading it is to be learned when it places us on a level with rogues and scoundrels how disgusting when it serves but to shew us the artifices & deceit of all around How can it be compared with the virtue and integrity of those who taught by nature alone pass through life contented happy their honour unsullied their minds uncontaminated their thoughts virtuous ever striving to do good shunning evil and doing to others as they would be done by Where [*sic*] I by this long probation to acquire some of this vaunted knowledge In what should I be wiser Knowledge of the world opens the eyes to the deceit & corruption of mankind of men serves but to shew the human mind debased by the vilest passions of manners points out the exterior corruptions which naturally result from the interior of books the most innocent occasions disgust when it is considered that even that has been debased by the corruptions of many & of languages serves but to shew in a still wider view what the knowledge of men & of manners teaches us. What a result is obtained from knowledge and how much must the virtuous human mind be humiliated in considering its own powers when at the same time they give him such a despicable view of his fellow creatures Ah Ben I am not sure that I have acted wisely in leaving a pure and certain enjoyment for such a pursuit but enough of it I will turn to more pleasant recollections I am so confident in you and the few friends I have in England that I am quite sure it is not from any change of feeling but from unfavourable circumstances that I have not yet received any letters from you at Rome The Post is from here to England much more difficult & uncertain than at Geneva and is at least 40 days in going & returning One may frank from here to Calais or to Florence only and I am advised to do the last because if the Postage is paid before hand the letters seldom go I am sorry for this expence which will thus fall upon you but I am willing to believe that you do not repine at the postage of a chance letter from me and I hope for an opportunity when the debt may be cleared I would not do it but that if they are paid the chance of their going is reckoned as 4 to 1. Your health dear Ben is I hope fixed in a state of vigour but I feel some doubts least the season which is now winter with you may not incommode you Mr. & Mrs. Abbott are I hope well & Miss Abbott & my friend Robert and all in the enjoyment of health my *love* to all and if you would be so good as to give the same to my mother brother sister &c. you would add still more to the obligations I owe you I wrote to my mother by favour a few (about 10) days ago and hope the letter will reach home I shall write immediately to the two B's[1] but I hope also I shall soon read as well as write I am in excellent health & have been continually We have passed over much ground since we left Geneva & have seen many things & many places very curious & interesting in themselves and in the information they afforded On leaving Geneva we immediately entered Switzerland a country very interesting not only from its history its boasted freedom & its situation but also from the peculiarity of its customs manners dresses & the character of the people and all these things we had many opportunities of observing in the towns of Lausanne Vevay Berne Zurich Schaffhause Uberlangen & many smaller ones as well as on the roads Switzerland claims and with a good deal of justice the preeminence in beauty of country consisting of mountains it abounds in all those forms of grandeur & majesty which strike the mind with awe and even fear and is washed by many torrents which rushing from the mountains change for a while their azure blue into the whitest foam The dress of the various Cantons were very interesting & amusing

They differed from each other considerably and form an excellent object for the designer series of costumes which included from thirty to forty varieties each peculiar to its town or canton & very well executed are sold in the Print shops of Berne Zurich &c. The observation of the dress of various countries shews in a very perfect manner the variety & invention of the female mind The dress of the men differ also in different countries but when compared with the changes in the habilement [of] [ms. torn] women it appears stationary The general form is the same in England France Italy & Germany changed slightly by lesser alterations but the women appear in every form that one can conceive sometimes the head undergoes a thousand changes & sometimes the body and to the passing traveller the change of place is shewn first by the change of the womens dress. The people are generally free goodnatured & somewhat more hospitable than the French or Italians but they are great cheats and experience lessened extremely the opinion I had formed of them They speak German generally but it is not the pure language but a corrupted Patois We saw in Switzerland amongst other things the famous fall of the Rhin [sic] at Schaffhause it is the largest waterfall in Europe but it is not very high nevertheless the immense body of water which falls over makes it tremendous & magnificent On leaving Switzerland we entered Germany by the dominions of Wurtemburg but remained in them only two days What we saw of the country was flat & monotonous The weather was here very cold & on the 2nd of Oct. we had a sharp frost On leaving Wurtemburg we entered Bavaria and stopped for 3 days at Munich a very pretty busy looking place with streets well formed & well peopled But intending to make no stay untill we got to Rome we soon left it and found ourselves amongst the mountains of the Tyrol This beautiful country which rivals & perhaps even surpasses in many parts Switzerland furnished us with the sublimest scenery for many days we found the weather here much more moderate than at Munich At an elevation of above 6000 feet I found wild strawberries growing We were at Trente on the 10th of Oct the day on which the Vintage commences a long walk gave me all the pleasures of this jovial day & I found the vineyards full of the happy labourers The year was not considered as abundant but to me the quantities of fruit appeared enormous The roads were soon filled with men & women laden with grapes who carried them to the wine press The first process (which was going on every [where]) was to tread the fruit a vat raised upon a waggon served for this purpose the fruit was thrown in & two or three men trod it down the juice ran out by a small hole into vessels placed to receive it & was then taken away to be fermented We passed from Trente by Bassano Vicenza &c. to Padua & then turned off to the left hand to Venice a place I had long wished to see My curiosity was perfectly satisfyed we stayed there but 2 days but that was sufficient to see the place in a general manner You will know the peculiarities of Venice & its situation too well to render it necessary that I should endeavour to describe it

From Venice we proceeded by Ferrara Bologna Florence Levano Arizzo [*sic*] Foligno Narni &c. to Rome & arrived here on 2nd of November & intend to stop here some time Between Bologna & Florence at a little distance from the last city we stopped at Pietro Malo to see a phenomenon in natural history called *il fuoco di Pietro Malo* At a little distance from the small village of the same name there is a place in the side of a mountain where much gas continually issues out of the earth from between some loose stones and in another place in an opposite direction where a small puddle exists the same phenomena [*sic*] appears when a light is applied to this gas it inflames At the first place a large flame of 4 or 5 feet high & 3 or 4 in diameter arises & in the second it spurts to a little distance over the water The carriage was stopped at Pietro Malo in the midst of a heavy shower Sir Humphry went to the first place & I went to the second accompanied by a peasant carrying some straw & fire on arriving at the spot I found the above-mentioned puddle apparently formed by the present rains and the gas bubbling up in considerable quantities through it I could find but a very slight smell somewhat resembling spirits of wine the peasant applied fire to the ground & disturbed the earth a flame immediately spread over the surface to the distance of 4 or 5 inches & burnt for several minutes untill the wind extinguished it on apply[ing] a light to the surface of the water the gas arising also inflamed & burnt some moments The flame was very pale & in the day time scarcely perceptible but readily set fire to paper matches &c. it was like the flame of spirits of wine I filled a bottle with the gas it had a very faint smell & on pouring water into a bottle full of it & holding a light at the mouth a jet of flame was obtained It did not explode with its volume of atmospheric air I brought a bottle full of the gas away & some of the water & at Florence Sir Humphry made experiments on it. (The ground was perfectly cold & also the water) Thursday 27 Oct[r] was occupied at the Academy at Florence with the above gas $2\frac{3}{4}$ of the gas were detonated with $5\frac{1}{4}$ of oxygen and the remainder equaled 3. but on agitating it with a solution of pure potassa it diminished to $\frac{1}{2}$ a volume From this experiment considered the gas as being light hydro carburet pure When detonated with $2\frac{1}{2}$ times its volume of chlorine which was done to separate & demonstrate the presence of the charcoal it diminished to 1 & charcoal lined the tube The water was nothing more than rain water The phenomena is extremely singular & I believe unique in its nature The quantity of gas that issues out from the principal place is enormous and there is no proof that fire has anything to do with the formation of it The country is not at all volcanic & it is doubtfull whether the source of the gas is near at hand or at a great distance Sir Humphry Davy observes that it may originate from a mine of fossil charcoal but every thing is conjecture & it still remains a source of investigation.

In my last letters I gave you a rough account of various things that had occurred up to Rome & meant to continue it on but as we are now on the same ground & shall go over the same roads again I shall continue the subject on from this letter My time is extremely occupied so that I can scarcely look in my Italian books & I have been three days in manufacturing this letter I beg pardon for the inattention you will find in it & hope that you will not be guided by it in writing to me but will give me some of your usual interesting letters I hope that long before you receive this I shall hear from you I again desire you as a favour & a service to see my friends for me Tell me in your answer how Margaret goes on in her learning I feel much interested in the Institution & should much like to know its probable issue Remember me to Mr. Newman and Mrs. Greenwell

I hope that if any change should occur in Albemarle Street Mr. Newman would not forget my books I prize them now more than ever. Give my Love again to your family & mine Adieu dear Friend

M. Faraday

Wednesday, 30 Nov. 1814.

P.S. Thermometer 60° Fahrenheit!!! not much above the ordinary temperature – Barometer 29.7.

[1] His brother Robert (Bob) and Abbott's brother, Robert.

25 B. Abbott to M. Faraday, 25 December 1814[1]
[R.I., *Warner mss., previously unpublished*]

London,
Sunday 25th Decr 1814

My Dear Michael,

Last evening between 5 & 6 O'clock I was while at dinner most [agreeably] [reading doubtful] interrupted by the Postman's Rap announcing the arrival of your still [reading doubtful] friendly letter dated Rome, 26th & 30th ult. [reading doubtful] you may judge it was not long unopened nor long unread, nor shall it remain long unanswered. The first page aroused in my mind feelings of every kind but pleasant, ideas of every species but brilliant, and those ideas & feelings would have increased in [illeg.] had not the second informed me you still felt confident in my friendship may you ever feel so [illeg.] as I feel so in yours; that I may never give cause for you to do otherwise shall be my constant endeavour.

I wrote you on the 20th ult. & forwarded the L^r etc on 24th via France. I confidently hope that long ere this it will have reached you & have calmed in some degree the tumult which it grieves me to see my neglect should have tended to raise in your Heart – a tumult which I cannot condemn tho' I am very sincerely sorry to witness it & feelings which endear you to me though I regret sincerely having so painfully aroused them if by so doing I have occasioned you any uneasiness (which I well know I have) I can only say in extenuation it was unintentionally – This & our friendship are my only pleas – tho' the latter ought rather to appear against me than in my favor – You will have perceived by my last (if it has arrived) that I refrained from saying much or indeed any thing on your uneasiness as expressed in your [last] of 6th Septr because I was fearful lest it might fall into hands where its operation might only tend to increase that uneasiness . . . but at this time I shall not suffer that fear to operate & I trust if such a circumstance should occur, you will acquit me of blame & lay the cause where it is truly to be laid; to the warmth of my feeling for your Happiness, a warmth which will not suffer me to be silent on such an occasion.

To say that I know by your letter you are not as you could wish & to say that I am sorry for it, would be alike futile & a waste of words, since the first is a sure action of commonsense, & of the latter I trust you are long ago convinced so fully as to need no arguments to establish your belief. But altho' I know you are uncomfortable I know not the *precise* cause of your being so & it [will seem] I reperuse your sentences & form conjectures almost innumerable as to what it may be. Excuse me my friend, on asking information on this subject. I know my power in moralizing & speaking comfort to affliction is very small yet would I fain have ample scope for its action in such case as may come in my way. I therefore must request you to inform me the whole & to open your mind to me to confide to my Bosom the causes of those agitations so much disquiet yours & I need not say your confidence will not be abused. I need not say that I ask not for the purpose of idle curiosity but believe me I ask it only that I may participate in the burthen & bear my share of the galling oppressive weight. & I trust you will not deny my request. If any part of it has for its cause me or any word or action of mine let me know it & if written & I hope at a future day expressed concessions can atone I will acquit myself & fully. I am well aware my dear Michael of your strength of mind & of your fortitude but I can still perceive the truth of your observation that you have not yet attained to the power of equalizing your feelings – your letter now before me affords me proof of this where you give way to your thoughts concerning your return, & begin to reflect on the past with such painful sensations. I am as I said before very inadequate to say much that will afford you any solace but I may venture to suggest that all things are for the best, & the blows you are now receiving tho' painful *may* & I doubt not *will* ultimately turn to your great advantage. Remember [reading doubtful] [passage illeg.] & disappointment are every one's portion & you & I must not forget that we are not exempt from the common lot of mankind. Your ideas of knowledge as expressed in your letter are in my view *true* but I would ask you, are they your constant ideas or only dictated by the feelings of the moment? Whatever they may be the view you have taken of the subject is partial & consequently one from which no just conclusion can be drawn. You say "how degrading it is to be learned when it places us on a level with rogues & scoundrels, how disgusting when it serves but to shew us the artifices & deceit of all around." I need not copy more as you doubtless have a transcript; – what? then does learning do this? it does in some degree you will say – but does it *nothing more* – does it shew you *nothing* but the degradation of the human mind & further, in what respect does it place you on a level with rogues? because perhaps you have some brilliant talents prostituted to infamous purposes are you hence to judge that all learning has such an effect? & because you have seen a self-taught or rather nature-taught person glide so happily along like a rill among the gnats are you to suppose that ignorance is synonymous with happiness & comfort? If you say yes, then I must say I think your views are altered since I saw you & not only altered but *reversed*. Am I to refuse to ascend a lofty eminence in order to enjoy the glorious sight of the rising sun   "Ocean & Heaven rejoicing in his Beams"

merely because near its base some offensive manufactory cants its stinking vapors which annoy me in my ascent & at the summit or because some town involved in smoke deprives me of a part of the prospect? You will doubtless despise in such cases the petty inconveniences & will be content to overlook them & what other imperfections may appear so that you can obtain the object of your toils & in like manner my dear friend would I have you regard the vice & deception which knowledge leads you to see in the world not as the effect of learning but as spots & imperfections which only obscure & sully a part of the glorious Horizon which you must be content to [illeg.] if you would wish to embrace all things in your view. I may be wrong but as yet I am not inclined to believe that knowledge ends *only* in disgust vexation & disappointment, & I am much mistaken if *you* will not one day think with me. I am certainly at this time inferior to you in acquirements but yet suppose you & I chatting together & then introduce a person ignorant & untaught. I am not learned nor perhaps are you so much so as one day may see us both, and yet what a figure would such a one cut! What a triumvirate! we should converse, if he has any sense he would listen but could not afford an argument by taking part. If he had none, he would talk, but what would he excite but contempt, or at best Pity! – I have done – I will not say more on this subject. You have my view; let me have yours *when you are calm.* –

   Robert called on us on Wednesday Evening last & informed us that all Friends in Weym.² Sᵗ are well; you will be surprised to hear I have not been there since my Lʳ of 20th Novʳ but I can assure you it has only arisen from Occupation & the very wet weather we have lately had. I called a short time since (about 3 Weeks) on Mr. Gray who with his wife & family is in full health & desires their kindest affection may be expressed to you. – I have been placed rather in a dilemma lately, out of which I have been scarcely able to extricate myself *fully*. You must know that all your L^rs to Weym. St have been shewn to me by your Mother & she has accordingly wished & *expected* to see mine. The first I shewed her, but the second I *did not* well knowing it w^d only render her uneasy & uncomfortable, I called however immediately on receiving it & acquainted her with it stating you were well & also what you said respecting them. Now it has since appeared she has supposed because I did not shew the Letter that there were some *secrets* in it. "& what could they be which concerned A & not me." nothing replied her Fears but that Mich. is not quite comfortable. – When I found this was the case you may judge my Dear Mich. my feelings – what could I do – to shew the Letter would make it worse – I therefore read to your Brother the greater part of it particularly what related to *my* situation & he engaged to satisfy his Mother that I only kept it to myself because it contained affairs of MINE improper to be divulged – & to tell her *he* had seen & read the *whole*. – I therefore hope this incident will not lessen me in her esteem but I thought it proper you should know of it as I wish all my actions towards *our* Friends should be *fully* open to you at all times. I trust you will approve of the [wd. illeg.] I have still been unable to see my [illeg.]

[whole page illegible]

ends, "Since the date of that letter I have become a good deal less uncomfortable than before from more than one Circumstance. firstly I have learned to look with contempt on all the pure proud Speeches & behaviour which were at first so much annoyance to me & 2ndly he has taken into the Counting House a Gent who knew him Years ago & who is not only an intelligent Companion but also by his Presence prevents some of the hauteur so oppressive to me when alone – add to this [illeg.] that an undeserved sharp Speech to me always produces a twinging Reply whose justice sometimes (I believe) bites at the moment – all these things added to there being not quite such close work as formerly has rendered me much more at ease in the City – & I am happy to say others have done the same here at home (for which you know there was room). –

Notwithstanding all this I am still resolved to keep a watchful Eye to any thing likely to prove more advantageous to me & with this View I have all along made constant Enquiries among my Friends after any thing that might suit me but hitherto without Success. I mentioned in my last it was possible I might visit the Continent the fact was, I was in treaty with a Merchant here to go & reside at Bordeaux to take [the] place of Chief Clerk in a House he was endeavouring to establish there & I should have gone had the Posture of affairs there rendered the design practicable – my father thought it would be of essential Service to me both for Health and information – this not succeeding the same person who I believe has taken a fancy to me – offered me a Situation on the River Plate in So. America of 1000 Dollars a Year & Board & Lodging but I declined it on account of the immense distance & the unwillingness of Father & Mother I should go *so far* – I am still in Hopes he will serve me if in his power. –

With respect to what you say concerning your own Situation I could say as much or more than I have said of my own were we confabulating together, but I do not think it prudent for obvious reasons (which you will well comprehend) to commit to Paper what I think on the Subject you must therefore my Dear Friend consider that I think of you as you think of me, with a warm Heart – & that I feel from your descriptions as much as you feel from mine – when we meet (which I trust we may do happily) we shall no doubt have many mutual communications to make not to be made now

26 Decr.

As to your present communication I shall transcribe such part as relates to your Route etc. etc. & send to Weym. St so abridged as to seem the entire contents & this plan if it meets with your approbation I shall pursue in future, but if you can point out one more reliable I will immediately accede to it with pleasure My only wish is to merit & obtain the Esteem & Friendship of both them & you & to that effect to act with perfect propriety to both with which view I have thus fully stated to you the occurrence & my conduct in it which as I before said and I trust will meet your approbation should it not, I hope you will not hesitate to say so that I may act otherwise in future. – Concerning Margaret I can only say what I said in my last – I will take the first opportunity of seeing her and informing you of her progress in learning – *since* the rept. [abbreviation doubtful] of yours you are of course aware it has not been possible & I am unwilling to miss the opportunity of Tuesdays mail (tomorrow) by which I shall forward this Sheet for all imperfections in which I ask excuse on the ground of being very busy in the City & somewhat agitated in my feelings on your account. –

I am sorry you should have made the Postage of your letters an object of consideration for a moment. Send them only the surest way. Trust me I shall not grumble at an extra shilling. You perhaps are not aware that it is merely charged here by Countries, thus a French letter is [3/4] [reading doubtful] an Italian [7]/11 etc. – I paid no more for those of yours from Rome than for your last from Geneva – therefore you see it is of little importance the difference is so trifling & so pray never think of this matter more – I expect shortly to have a little bit of News to tell you but it is not yet ripe & I dare not forestall the market it is something which I expect you will be glad to hear. –

Concerning the Royal Institution I wrote you fully in my last to which I have nothing to add but confirmation & an assurance that you may depend on my care. – I shall endeavour ere long to call on Mrs Greenwell & Mr Newman.

I was highly gratified at your account of your Route & still more at the promise of its being continued – & I must tender you my sincere thanks for sacrificing your time for my amusement & can only say in return I will do my Endeavours to return the Obligation by rendering my correspondence as interesting as my circumscribed Horizon will allow – a propos – the word Obligation brings to my recollection the way in which you use it – a way in which I hope I shall not see it again employed in your letters Pray – what obligations are you under to me I am your friend – & the execution of your friendly commissions are only so many pleasures to me. – I thank you for your kind wishes for my Health which is tolerable at present the Winter set in yesterday with a fall of Snow but I have as yet felt no ill effects from it My Father, Mother Brother & Sister are also well & desire their love – Robert I expect will write you shortly. –

I have little Philosophical News to send you – the Lectures at the Surrey Inst: – are suspended this Week but resume on 5th Jany. when they are finished I intend giving you my Ideas soi-disant Criticisms on them – You doubtless have heard of the Earthquakes at Lyons & at Palermo – but perhaps not of one which has taken place in Luzon the largest of the Phillipine Islands in the East Indies it was accompanied by an explosion from a Volcano long since apparently extinct so violent as to render it nearly dark for two days! which together with the Earthquake destroyed Five Towns!! Such Scenes as these may you & I never witness! much as I wish to see a Volcano I have no desire to see a town buried in Ashes and Lava!

It seems as if your letter & my last were written by Sympathy. I ask you for your Route you have given it me. I enquire concerning cataracts you mention the best in Europe pray are you a Conjurer! I however did not ask because I had never heard of the Fuoco de Pietro Malo which is certainly a singular Phenomenon & I am entirely at a loss how to account for it tho I should suppose it may originate from decomposing vegetable matter. – I imagine I see you in the rain with a bottle under each arm & the peasant with a bundle of lighted straw – (of course wet straw) catching Gas & stirring up the muck with a stick I think what with Gas – Rain & Smoke those must have been a laughable combination – Were I a caricaturist you should have an elegant design of my ideas at this moment. – talking of Gas – the Gas lights get on here like a house on fire[3] – Westminster Hall & all the streets thereabouts are lighted – Westminster Bridge is contracted for – Bishopsgate Street is also lighted i.e. the Shops – & a new company has built an apparatus at the bottom of Dorset Street & is about to light that Street & the Strand Tatum's Room is to be splendidly illuminated Tatum by the by has had a serious Accident about 10 days ago when preparing some Fulminating Silver for a Society's Lecture – it by some accident exploded & shattered the containing bottle to pieces which with some pulverised Marble entered his Eye & nearly blinded him he was incapable of lecturing but is now recovering by degrees. – The Society there goes on as usual the London Society has been patronised by a Royal Duke & is like I hear to become permanently established.

I have not opportunity at this time to write much more you must therefore excuse the briefness of this letter & attribute it to my wish not to delay forwarding it – ere long I shall write again (if I be alive & well) & I also expect shortly to hear from you as I suppose my last would reach you about the 14th inst. – I shall go as usual to Weym[outh] St. The Inst. Mr Gray, Mr Newman etc. & endeavour to fulfil your wishes to the utmost of my power. May every blessing attend you & may you always have cause to feel pleasure in the Friendship of him who subscribes himself

Yours most truly & sincerely
BENJ. ABBOTT.

Fire Side – 9th M.

¹ See Letter 23, fn. 1.
² Abbott's abbreviation for 'Weymouth' looks like 'Weym' followed by a small 'o' on the top of the line.
3. London was beginning to light its streets with gas lights. The gas works were to play an important role in Faraday's scientific life. His analysis of a strange "oil" that accumulated at the bottom of the pressure cylinders led him, in 1825, to the discovery of benzene. See *LPW*, 107ff.

26   M. FARADAY to B. ABBOTT, 25 January 1815
[*R.I., Warner mss., B.J. 1, 18 off*]

Rome,
Jany 25th, 1815

DEAR BENJAMIN

I begin this letter in a very cheerful state of mind which enables me to see things with as correct an eye as it is possible for my weak judgement to do unless indeed I see them too favourably but at all events I hope that you will not have occasion in your answer to this letter to repeat what you have said in your last. I have received both the letters you have directed to me at Rome. I have too much to say at present to waste words in thanking you for them you know how great their value is to me and the return I can give that will be most wellcome [*sic*] to you is to answer them It happens fortunately indeed that the first is in part answered and I am not sure I can say much more in return for it on this sheet of paper or even on another if I happen to extend my blotting It was my intention when I read it to give you some account of the various waterfalls I had seen but now I have more important & fresher subjects to treat of & shall reserve them for another time by important I do not mean important in itself but only with respect to the waterfalls and you must understand the word in that sense I cannot however refrain from saying how much I feel obliged to you for your information respecting the health &c. of my mother & our family and hope that you will always have the charity to continue such information as far as lies in your power.

Though it may appear somewhat consequential that I begin the letter with my own affairs yet such is my intention at present You found me in the last squabbling almost with all the world and crying out against things which truly in themselves are excellent and which indeed form the only distinction between men and beasts I scarce know now what I said in that letter (for I have not time to take copies of them as you supposed) but I know I wrote it in a ruffled state of mind which bye the bye resulted from a mere trifle Your thoughts on knowledge which you gave me in return are certainly much more correct than mine that is to say more correct than those I sent you which indeed are not such as I before and since have adopted but I did not mean to give them to you as any settled opinion They ran from my pen as they were formed at that moment when the little passions of anger and resentment had hooded my eyes.

You tell me I am not happy and you wish to share in my difficulties – I have nothing important to tell you or you should have known it long ago but since your friendship make you feel for me I will trouble you with my trifling affairs. – The various passions and prejudices of mankind influence in a greater or less degree every judgement that men make and cause them to swerve more or less from the fine love of rectitude and truth into the wide plains of error Errors thus generated exert their influence in producing still greater deviations untill at last in many points truth is overthrown by falsehood and delusive opinions hold the places of just maxims and the dictates of nature Nothing shews this truth more plainly than the erroneous estimation men make of the things the circumstances and the situations of this world Happiness is supposed to exist in that which cannot possibly give it Pleasures are sought for where they are not to be found Perfection is looked for in the place from which it is most distant and things truly valuable are thrown aside because their owner cannot estimate them Many repine at a situation others at a name and a vast multitude because they have neither the one nor the other

I fancy I have cause to grumble and yet I can scarcely tell why If I approve of the system of etiquette and valuation formed by the world I can make a thousand complaints but perhaps if I acted influenced by the pure & unsullied dictates of common sense I should have nothing to complain of and therefore all I can do is to give you the circumstances

When Sir Humphry Davy first made proposals to me to accompany him in this voyage he told me that I should be occupied in assisting him in his experiments in taking care of the apparatus and of his papers & books and in writing and other things of this kind and I conceiving that such employment with the opportunities that traveling would present would tend greatly to instruct me in what I desired to know & in things useful in life consented to go. Had this arrangement held our party would have consisted of Sir Humphry & Lady Davy the Lady's maid la Fontain Sir H.'s valet & myself – but a few days before we came off la Fontaine diverted from his intention by the tears of his wife refused to go & thus a new arrangement was necessary When Sir H——— informed me of this circumstance he expressed his sorrow at it and said he had not time to find another to suit him (for la Fontaine was from Flanders and spoke a little Italian as well as French) but that if I would put up with a few things on the road untill he got to Paris doing those things which could not be trusted to strangers or waiters and which la Fontaine would have done he would there get a servant which should leave me at liberty to fill my proper station & that alone I felt unwilling to proceed on this plan but considering the advantages I should lose & the short time I should be thus embarrassed I agreed At Paris he could find no servant to suit him for he wished for one that spoke English French & a little German (I speaking no French at that time) and as all the English there (ourselves excepted) were prisoners and none of the French servants talked English our want remained unsupplied but to ease me he took a Lacquis [*sic*] de Place and living in a Hotel I had few things to do out of my agreement It will be useless to relate our progress in the Voyage as it relates to this affair more particularly a thousand reasons which I have now forgot caused the permanent addition of a servant to our family to be deferred from time to time and we are at present the same number as at first Sir Humphry has at all times endeavoured to keep me from the performance of those things which did not form a part of my duty and which might be disagreeable and whenever we have been fixed I have had one or more servants placed under me we have at present although in an hotel two menservants but as it is always necessary to hold a degree of subordination in a house or family and as a confidential servant is also necessary to the master and again as I am the person in whom Sir Humphry trusts it obliges me to take a more active share in this part of my present occupation than I wish to do & in having to see after the expenses of the family I have to see also after the servants the table and the accomodations [*sic*].

I should have but little to complain of were I travelling with Sir Humphry alone or were Lady Davy like him but her temper makes it often times go wrong with me with herself & with Sir H. She is haughty & proud to an excessive degree and delights in making her inferiors feel her power she wishes to roll in the full tide of pleasures such as she is capable of enjoying but when she can with impunity that is when her equals do not notice it & Sir H. is ignorant of it she will exert herself very considerably to deprive her family of enjoyments – When I first left England unused as I was to high life & to politeness unversed as I was in the art of expressing sentiments I did not feel I was little suited to come within the observation and under the power in some degree of one whose whole life consists of forms etiquette & manners I believed at that time that she hated me and her evil disposition made her endeavour to thwart me in all my views & to debase me in my occupations This at first was a source of great uneasiness to me and often times made me very dull & discontented and if I could have come home again at that time you should have seen me before I had left England six months as I became more acquainted with the manners of the world and those things necessary in my station and understood better her true character I learned to despise her taunts & resist her power and this kind of determined conduct added to a little polishing which the friction of the world had naturally produced in your friend made her restrain her spleen from its full course to a more moderate degree At present I laugh at her whims which now seldom extend to me but at times a greater degree of ill humour than ordinary involves me in a fray which on occasions creates a coolness between us all for two or three days for on these occasions Sir H—— can scarcely keep neuter and from different reasons he can scarcely choose his side

Finally Sir H—— has no valet except myself but having been in an humbler station and not being corrupted by high life he has very little occasion for a servant of that kind & tis the name more than the thing which hurts – I enjoy my original employment in its full extent and find few pleasures greater than doing so. – Thus Dear Ben I have answered your kind enquiries by a relation of my circumstances things which were not of consequence enough to put in a letter before you asked for them – As things stand now I may perhaps finish the voyage in my present company though with my present information I should not hesitate to leave them in any part of the world for I now know I could get home as well without them as with them At all event [sic] when I return home I fancy I shall return to my old profession of Bookseller for Books still continue to please me more than any thing else

I shall now my dear friend turn the subject or rather change it for Philosophy and hope in so doing to give you pleasure in this letter I say this more confidently because I intend to give you an account of a paper just finished by Sir Humphry, of which one copy has already been sent by Post as a letter to the Royal Society and all the experiments & demonstrations of which I have witnessed.[1]

When we were at Naples the Queen gave Sir H—— a pot of colour which was dug up in their presence it contained a blue paint in powder. At Milan a gentleman had some conversation with Sir H—— & gave him some pieces of blue glass from Adrian's Villa at Rome and since we have been here this time the opportunity afforded & the former hints have induced Sir H.—— to undertake an examination of the ancient Grecian & Roman colours with an intent to identify them & to imitate such as were known I shall give you a very brief account of this paper putting down results discoveries & such parts as I think will be most interesting to you

The introduction speaks of the art of painting as it existed in Greece and as it flourished truly greek in the midst of Rome. many arguments and authorities are brought forward to shew that even in Italy during the (early part at least of the) Roman ages the art was grecian and was cultivated by & flourished under the care of natives of its own country he concludes the introduction by announcing his chemical labours on this subject.

The second part speaks of the red colours of the Ancients these and indeed almost all the colours came from the ruins of the Baths & Palace of Titus which stand at a little distance from the Coliseum and are wonderfully interesting from their extent their perfection and their richness of three reds found in a pot in these baths two were ochres and the third proved to be red lead these colours Sir H—— recognized again on the walls in various parts of the ornaments – In the chamber & the niche where the Laocoon is said to have been found another red prevails which proved to be Vermilion – A *classical* account is then given of those colours but the history of Vermilion is the most interesting anent [reading doubtful] the reds It was prepared by roasting the ores of quicksilver & from its beauty and scarcity held a very high price It used to be placed amongst the precious ointments at feasts & the body of the victor at the Olympic games was coloured with it

The third part treats of yellows a large pot in the ruins of the baths of Titus contained a yellow colour which was an ochre The author notices two other yellows which were spoken of by Vitruvius & Pliny auri pigmentum & Sandarach The first he considers as massicot or the yellow oxide of lead and the second as an oxide of lead obtained by a different degree of heat or calcination Orpiment has not been found amongst the ancient colours

Fourthly blue colours Sir H.—— found several shades of blue in the baths of Titus on the walls and on pieces of stucco but he found them to be the same colour mixed with different quantities of chalk or whiting when separated from the carbonate of lime a fine blue powder rough to the touch unalterable in its colour by heat but when urged agglutinating together By analysis it gave Silica Alumina lime potash and oxide of copper and some pieces of blue frit found in the chambers gave the same colour when powdered & the same products by analysis It appears therefore that this colour is a deeply tinged frit powdered & is probably the same as that the ancients called cerulium

Some blues mentioned by Pliny appear to be preparations of lapis lazuli & of the arseniates & carbonates of copper.

The Greeks appeared to be acquainted with a species of indigo

Blues on some fragments of fresco from ruins near the monument of Caius Castius others in a celebrated antique picture now at Rome and that alluded to as found at Pompeia appear all to be produced from this blue frit.

Pieces of blue transparent glass which have apparently been used for mosaic work and which are very frequent in the ruins are coloured with cobalt & it appears that all the transparent blue glasses are tinged with the same metal and it must be supposed that the knowledge of this metal or at least of its ores has been unjustly denied them by the moderns

The greens come next in order and these appear to be produced principally by copper & to be the carbonates of that metal. In the vase however a portion of the green earth of Verona was found – Sir H—— considers the substance called chrysocolla as a green color a combination of copper He points out the error of those who suppose borax to be chrysocolla and shews that there is no reason for supposing that the Borate of Soda was known to the ancients

The ancients had beautiful green glasses which were tinged with copper but they did not use them in the state of powder as colours.

The fine Tyrian purple of the ancients comes next under consideration but here more of uncertainty prevails The circumstances of its being prepared from animal matter prohibits any hope to find it in its original state after a period of 1700 years but not discouraged by the difficulties the author has given some very interesting observations & conjectures on this point From the description given of this colour by the ancient authors Sir H—— was induced to try many experiments on a pale rose coloured powder found in a vase at the baths of Titus This colour was destroyed by heat by acids & alkalies It appeared to be composed of siliceous aluminous & calcareous earth with a little oxide of iron When mixed with the hyper oxymuriate of potassa & heated a slight scintillation was perceptible and the gas given of [*sic*] precipitated lime water & from these & various other experiments it was evident that the colouring matter was of animal or vegetable origin but which Sir H—— was not able to determine though the probability is in favour of the first and of its being the Tyrian purple of the ancients

Other purples were mixtures of red ochre & the blues of copper.

The blacks & browns of the ancients were easily made out such specimens of black as were found in the baths on pieces of stucco were carbonaceous matter Pliny speaks of the ink of the cuttle fish of ivory black & of some fossil blacks The first Sir H—— observed is a compound or rather mixture of carbonaceous matter with gelatine – the second was discovered by Apelles – the third were probably ores of iron & manganese – and the author considers the ancients as being acquainted with the ores of this last metal

The browns are all mixtures of red & yellow ochres with black.

The whites which have been found in the ruins at Rome are all either carbonate of lime (chalk) or of fine aluminous clay – The ancients were acquainted with ceruse but Sir H—— has not met with it

The paper then gives some observations on the mode in which the ancients applied these colours Their stucco is described which was formed of powdered marble cemented by lime Three coats of the stucco were laid on & the powder of each diminished in size from the first to the third when dry & polished it was ready to receive the colours.

The encaustic process is referred to and Sir H. endeavoured to discover if any such a process had been performed upon the walls of the chambers in the baths or on the Aldobrandine picture but could gain no evidences in the affirmative

In some general observations with which Sir H——— concludes the paper he gives a process for making the Azure or Alexandrian frit 15 parts of carbonate of soda 20 parts of powdered flints & 3 parts of copper filings strongly heated for 2 hours will produce the frit which when powdered gives the same fine deep sky blue

Those colours which are the most permanent are pointed out Frits are placed first and after frits saturated combinations of metals Animal and vegetable colours are the least permanent

The colours which the refinements in Chemistry have given to modern artists & which excell the ancients colour in tint & durability are noticed and the cause of their superiority is pointed out & in the last lines some ideas are given on the materials which are best calculated to receive the picture and on the modes of pressing Canvas impregnated with Asphaltum or bitumen is considered as being superior to wood copper or any other substance that is used for this purpose.

I am ashamed Dear Ben to send you this imperfect account of so valuable a paper but I trust that my willingness to give you news will plead my excuse I hope you will soon read a copy of the paper at large and have no doubt you will perceive in every page the enquiring spirit of the author. – I have long inquired after a sure opportunity of sending a little parcel home and if it were in my power I should pack up a few of these colours for you with your brothers snuff box[2] some books of mine & other little things but as yet my search has been useless however at Naples I may meet with better luck.

I have within the last few weeks altered the plan of my journal and for that purpose have made free with your name but I hope you will allow me to continue the liberty I have already taken I found myself so much more at ease in writing to you than in writing in my book that latterly I have written in it as if I were talking to you and from this it arises that your name now & then occurs and though not in bad yet perhaps in foolish company and for this I attend your pardon.

I have heard nothing at all of the earthquakes and eruptions you spoke of but expect to be more in the country of them soon – and then for a little of Vesuvius if I have time

I must not forget the proof you have given me of your feelings truly of friendship in the dilemma and I am extremely sorry that I should in any way have occasioned you embarrassment I am indebted much to you for your care in concealing such things as you supposed I intended for you alone They were written for you alone but at the same time I did not wish that my mother should remain ignorant of them I have no secrets from her and it was the insignificance alone that made me quiet on the subject I would rather my mother should see or hear the first sheet of this paper [than] [ms. torn] otherwise for where the causes are open the conduct can be better judged of with this part you may do as you please but there is as yet little in it can interest her and I do not know that I shall add much more

I must however tell you that we are in the midst of the Carnival a scene of great mirth & jollity amongst the Romans last Tuesday 24*th* it began by the horse race which takes place in the Corso in the middle of the city Having in London heard of these races I felt much inclined to see them and paid my five baiocci (3d.) for a seat Before the race commences the people that fill the corso open to the right & left & leave an open space about 18 feet wide The horses were brought out and placed before a rope at the top of the Corso & on sounding a trumpet the roap [*sic*] falls & the animals start They go without riders They have a slight harness on just sufficiently strong to hold some leaden balls at the end of a chain These balls are set with short sharp spikes one is hung on each shoulder & one on each flank and as they run the play of the balls pricks them on to their utmost speed. On Thursday & Saturday these races were repeated & today also and on Thursday the masquerade began this takes place also in the Corso & continues from about 3 till 6 o'clk. Today it was very good & all Rome glittered with Princes Princesses Dukes Lords Spaniards Italians Turks Fads [?] &c. all of which were in procession I went this morning to a masquerade ball between 2 & 5 o'clk and found it excellent.

Now for news!!! We shall part in a few weeks (pray write quickly) for Naples and from thence proceed immediately to Sicily Afterwards our road is doubtful but this much I know that application is made for passports to travel in the Turkish Empire & to reside in Constantinople that it is Sir H——— intention to be amongst the Greek Islands in March and at Athens early in the spring[3] – Thus you see Ben a great extension is made to our voyage an extension which though it promises much novelty & pleasure yet I fear will sadly interrupt our correspondence – Have the goodness therefore to write quickly & tell all my friends that you can to do the same or I shall not get the letters – I shall make a point of writing to you as long & as late as I can.

I will not pretend to know whether it is time to leave off or not but I think it is impossible for you to get through this letter of 12 pages in less than three or four readings how it has got to such a length I know not for I have as yet read no part of it over and even now I find I could write you a long letter were this and the subjects of it anihilated [*sic*] but I must cut it short Pray remember me with strongest affection to my mother & friends & to your family (excuse the repetition) and at your opportunity repeat your commission of remembrance to Mrs. Greenwell Mr. Newman and others – Castle Rupert McGrath &c. I am in a great passion with your brother for not writing to me and must beg of Miss Abbott to scold him well having more time than you

Adieu dear Friend with you I have no ceremony the warmest wishes that friendship can dictate are formed for you by

M. FARADAY

P.S. Do you know any thing of a young lad of the name of George Bramwell Mrs. Meek my Companion has a cousin in London of that name who is in a counting house on the river side with a Mr. Abbott. She heard me mention the name & supposed that her cousin might be with your Father. Should that be the case she wishes to be remembered to him and to know how he is in a letter from himself if convenient.

Le Donne [reading doubtful] Italiani sono sfacciato pigrichissimo e sporchessimo come dunque valete fare una comparazione fra loro e l'Inglese.

Adio Caro Amico

[1] H. Davy, 'Some experiments and observations on the Colours used by the Ancients,' *PT* (1815), 97.
[2] See Letter 23, last paragraph.
[3] These plans were abandoned when Davy discovered that he would have to go through quarantine in Constantinople.

27 M. FARADAY to B. ABBOTT, [27?] June 1815
[*R.I., Warner mss., B.J. 1, 225ff*]

June [27?], 1815

DEAR BEN,

I shall now endeavour to recommence on my side our two-penny post correspondence, though without much hopes of success for I have nothing to write about and that being the case it is evident that no end can be obtained though a form of something may be visible however as most important things commence by an exhibition of mere forms and as it is only between you and me and still more as I shall get out of debt I am not deterred from proceeding

It strikes me Ben that I have made a bold affirmation in saying that I shall get out of debt i.e. that my letter containing nothing and of course worth nothing is still equivalent to and a sufficient counterpoise for your *six* but you know we wind up our accounts in a manner somewhat out of the common mode and therefore without any disparagement to your *epistles* I shall still hold to my words

The Enemy having been completely beaten in the contests that took place notwithstanding the reinforcements which he endeavoured to bring into action his party was obliged to quit the spot contested for *and* retire and I last night found all hindrances removed and the place as ready for my reception as the short time would allow of[1] Since then I have been arranging my affairs & forming a plan of occupation suited to the best of my powers for the employment of the advantages now presented to me These advantages are as you well know many and not the least of them is that I shall have frequent opportunities of seeing you here and if you would allow me to employ that advantage tomorrow evening I shall be very glad – Tomorrow bye the bye is Lecture night in the city if it is a good lecture, come and take me there – I should like to know more exactly how that Society stands at present & I intend to join it as soon as can be

You perceive Ben that I have held to my words & that my letter is worth nothing nor are my thoughts at present & it is not worth the trouble of putting in more of them Remember me to all at home & believe etc. etc. etc. etc.

M. FARADAY

[1] Faraday experienced some difficulty in getting back his room at the Royal Institution after his return from the Continent.

28 M. FARADAY to B. ABBOTT, ca. July 1815 [1]
[R.I., *Warner mss., previously unpublished*]

DEAR BEN

Within these last few days I have been hammering my brains to remember whether 'twas me or you who wrote last but I dare not as yet affirm it of either one or the other 'till lately I entertained no doubts but considered myself as out of debt – your long silence has however made me put the query, & lest it should be me that is deficient I have ventured to scratch a line or two. I want to see you I want to talk to you I want to hear from you indeed I want to know whether you are among *sub-lunary* things or whether you have gone to the moon in search of wits – I have been looking over our lanterns several times but I want you to look at them too, but I dont know when you will – indeed I dont know when to ask you Friday is my only spare evening this week but it may not be so with you if it is not suppose you come down on Monday but at all events drop me a line soon – When you come I promise to chatter so much as to make up the deficiencies of this letter

Adio Caro Mio
Vostro Amico
M. FARADAY

[1] On the back of a note dated 4 March 1816.

29   M. FARADAY to B. ABBOTT, 1 August 1815[1]

[*R.I., Warner mss., previously unpublished*]

"L'I.R.,
Aout 1er, 1815"

CHER AMI

Je serai a la porte a l'heure que vous avez fixée et Je ne doubt pas que nous ferons un jour bien interessant pour tous Cependant Je serai faché si on ne peut pas faire un moyen d'eviter l'engagement avec le Duc, parceque l'esprit prend souvent tous les foiblesses et la debilité du corps mais comme il est possible que nous serons obligés de diner a la Humphrie Je prendrai guarde d'avoir assez du pain extraordinaire chez moi de rapasser nos appetits terrestre

Adio Caro Amico
M. FARADAY

Où est votre Francais?

[1] This is Faraday's first and, so far as I have been able to determine, only letter written in French.

30   M. FARADAY to B. ABBOTT, 13 September 1815

[*R.I., Warner mss., B.J. 1, 228*]

R.I.,
Wednesday, 13th Sept., 1815

DEAR ABBOTT

French with me is out of the question at present so you must be content for a while to double your own portion I can hardly find time to write english Had you come last night you must have been content with the laboratory for I did not leave it (& could not) 'till $9^h.30^m$. I fancy therefore you were better where you were and what with the "jeune Demoiselle" & the music must have been better pleased there than you could be with me However tomorrow evening if you have nothing else to do & will condescend to visit Albemarle St (which by the bye you have not done lately) no one will be more glad to see you (excepting your sweetheart) than

Your Friend
M. FARADAY

"Jeune" I am half afraid of the word for if you like it it is possible the essay may never advance any farther.

31 M. FARADAY to B. ABBOTT, 10 January 1816

[*R.I., Warner mss., B.J. 1, 228*]

R.I.,
Jany 10th, 1816

DEAR ABBOTT,

Many persons spend years in seeking honor but still being unsuccessful call themselves miserable and unfortunate but what are their cases to mine who when honor waits for admission am obliged to refuse her entertainment. But so the fates or the unlucky stars or the gods or something else have decreed and I am obliged to dissent from your arrangements for Thursday. – It happens that my time for this week is completely cut up and so that I cannot cut it over again On Thursday evening I expect my old Master Mr. Riebau at the Institution and I shall be out both Friday and Saturday Evenings

It is impossible to look forward so clearly into the next week as to fix a day at present[1] I mean, to mention one. I can scarcely see any thing in it but Wednesday. But I will write you again at the end of the week in answer to your first and hope I shall not write in vain. Accept my Sorrow & excuses on this occasion and believe me as ever

Yours Sincerely
M. FARADAY

---

[1] The words 'to fix a day at present' were crossed out in the manuscript.

32 M. FARADAY to B. ABBOTT, 9 February 1816

[*R.I., Warner mss., B.J. 1, 229ff*]

R.I.,
Friday Evg. (Feb. 9) 1816

DEAR ABBOTT,

Be not offended that I turn to write you a letter because I feel a disinclination to do anything else, but rather accept it as a proof that conversation with you has more power with me than any other relaxation from business, – business I say, and I believe it is the first time for many years that I have applied it to my own occupations, but at present they actually deserve the name; and you must not think me in laughing mood, but in earnest. It is now 9 o'clk P.M., and I have just left the Laboratory and the preparations for tomorrow's two Lectures. Our double course makes me work enough, and to them add the attendance required by Sir H.—— in his researches, and then if you compare my time with what is to be done in it you will excuse the slow progress of our correspondence on my side – Understand me I am not complaining the more I have to do the more I learn but I wish to avoid all suspicion on your side that I am lazy, – Suspicions by the bye which a moments reflection convinces me can never exist

95

Mr. Wheeler[1] attends both our courses of chemical lectures very closely and I perceive with surprise that that singularly acetous physiognomy which I first saw at the Surrey Institution belongs to him naturally and that instead of being caused by the dread of an attending company he wears it at all times – But it is time I should reperuse your letter & answer it by something more allied to it than this unconnected irregular coarse material

I thank you for the promise you give me of taking up the subject I proposed and expect much information on it. If with your original observations you sometimes give me the ideas of others as concuring with or opposing your own and if you can point out to me such a course of reading or study as might bring me a little acquainted with the subject and can direct me to such books as you know to be good it will enhance the value of your communications

Having thus noticed what comes before your "First" then I will answer to that and say that I have seen the combustion of the taper in the flame of Alcohol, – but before I go further I will enter a little more minutely into the subject which I fear I badly explained to you.[2] Newton, I believe, defines flame to be red hot vapours but perhaps ignited vapours would have been better because all flame is not red – This definition is I think a good one and by flame I understand nothing more than what is expressed in it and of course I do not consider vapour not ignited or not emitting light as flame It must however be evident to you that in every case of combustion where flame is produced from a pure combustible, vapour in both those states is present, i.e. ignited vapour & vapour not ignited In the flame of a candle for instance there is a small dull halo round the wick within the flame & this I do not consider as a part of the flame but merely the vaporized tallow which not being luminous must of course diminish the effect of that part of the whole flame and make it appear inferior in power to the superior parts where the whole body is luminous Now in this central and nonignited space I do not think any thing will burn because no oxygene is there present for if it were the vapour would burn & be luminous but above this part and where the flame appears uniform and luminous throughout, there I say that oxygene exists even in the centre of the flame and if any body is intruded into that part having a stronger affinity for oxygene than the hydrogen & charcoal of the tallow it will burn and its flame will be seen within the flame of the candle. – It is the same with Alcohol but in the large flames we can make with it the circumstances are more distinct I made a little experiment this evg. [= evening. Abbreviation doubtful] thus: Into a small wedgewoods basin (diameter 2 inches) I poured Alcohol having previously fixed a taper of an inch in height in the middle of it the alcohol was level with the edges & the bottom of the flame of the taper when it was lighted was about 1/2 inch above the alcohol. I lighted the taper and the alcohol and then placed a long [ms. torn] the dish to preserve the flames from the interference of chance. (Ms. cut here) in the air the flame of the alcohol was well formed and very steady The unignited part was very considerable & perfectly distinct It extended above the top of the taper The flame of the taper did not go out on lighting the alcohol but appeared to separate from it and hang over it and shone very bright in the upper part of the alcohol flame commencing immediately from the unignited vapour. You will instantly conceive the explanation I give of this phenomenon, namely that the space in the center of the flame & immediately over the alcohol is pure vapour that as the air mixes with the vapour at the sides entering itself farther & farther as it rises higher so in proportion flame is formed. That where the flame was permanent throughout then oxygen was present even in the center that the volatile parts of the taper will not burn in the pure vapours of Alcohol but did in the flame, & then formed its flame within that of the alcohol and I am not aware of any objections that may arise in your mind respecting them – If a chance breath distorted the flame then as the lower & superficial part approached in its waverings the wick of the taper it lighted up & its flame appeared though still within that of the alcohol and in such cases I supposed that the wick of the taper had come within the oxygenated part of the alcoholic vapour.

Returning for a moment to my first instance of a candle the only part of it where I can suppose any thing like combustion at surfaces to take place is at the lowest part of the flame there you will perceive a very faint blue light more marked at the edges than at the entering parts because there we see more of it at once but the light is at best very little. Even this however evidently results from an intermixture of the vapour with the air (but the two have not penetrated each other far) and upon close examination you will find that even this faint combustible does not commence at the wick but at a small distance from it and that when the vapour of the tallow and the common air are merely in contact & have not had time to mix there is no flame I shall leave this subject with Sir H. D.'s theory of blowing out a candle which operation has never yet been satisfactorily explained – He says that as inflammable gases will only burn in certain proportion with air to extinguish a combustion we must make the mixture pass from these proportions This may be done either by adding more of the inflammable or more of the air by adding more of the inflammable the oxygene is diluted by adding more of the air the inflammable is diluted This last is the case in blowing out a candle. The vapour of the tallow is diluted with so much common air as to be uninflammable and the fl[ame] [ms. torn] exists no longer.

Having unconsciously run on so fast & so far I shall cut off the rest of your letter with brief notices. – I have no hand in the Catalogue – I am writing a second Lecture so that the book is engaged at this moment but is at your service – Is not time a succession of events – by an ignorant person you do not mean a blockhead. If I were to ask you what *Thoan* was and should afterwards tell you by that term I understand a succession of events, would you not say that my *Thoan* and the common word time had the same meaning. – Can you take tea with me on Monday. – our two Lectures on Saturday allow me no spare time at the end of the week and I have forgot your free days.

I heard from Robert the other day that Miss Abbott had a nasty cold. I hope it is much better and more I hope it has no connection with "waddling" "night & morning", Your own words Ben.

Remember me to our friends & believe me,

Ever Yours,
M. FARADAY

[1] Thomas Wheeler (1754–1847), demonstrator of Botany at the Chelsea botanic garden, 1778–1820.
[2] Faraday had served as Davy's assistant in the researches on flame which led to the invention of the miner's safety lamp.

33   M. FARADAY to B. ABBOTT, 23 September 1816
[*R.I., Warner mss., B.J. 1, 223ff*]

R.I.,
Sept. 23[d], 1816

DEAR ABBOTT,

I am obliged to excuse myself for tomorrow evening I confess myself guilty of the highest breach of manners in doing so since it arises entirely from my negligence But I will state to you the circumstances I had promised my assistance to Mr. Cockary[1] in every thing that I could to help him in the two Lectures he had to give us this quarter and I kept my word with respect to his first delivered on last Wednesday week. he has lately called on me for similar aid in the next to be given on Wednesday and I am in consequence necessitated to be with him at Dorset St tomorrow evening to arrange This circumstance I had entirely forgotten when I arranged with you and have thus rendered myself culpable but I hope you will forgive me by consenting to come some other evening as soon as convenient It happens that this week I have no other evening but on Friday at liberty on which if you will come I shall be happy If not choose your own next week (excepting Wednesday & Sat) and let me know as soon as you can.

Whilst in the City I heard a curious charge from Mr. Gray[2] made by you against me I suppose in joke but given by him with so serious a face that I was tempted to explain a thing I rarely do to those who have no connection (necessarily) with my affairs – The charge was that I deserted my old friends for new ones – Supposing that you intended this seriously which I do not think you did I shall take the opportunity to explain to *you* how my time is generally occupied The duties of my situation (which is no sinecure) necessarily confine the time which I can dispose to the evenings of these Wednesday belongs to the

Society Saturday to Weymouth St generally; Monday & Thursday come into a system of instruction & may be considered as school evenings which however I at times do though unwillingly break into and Tuesday & Friday I find little more than sufficient to do my own business in so that you will perceive I have not much to spare Business is the first thing to which I am not only tied by necessity but by honor Pleasure is the last and then again there is an intermediate part verging on both to which I consider it a duty to attend I mean the Society After my work I attend to that then to my own affairs & then to my friends This long explanation however looks so serious that I would cut it shorter if I had time for I am confident it must be unnecessary but being here as it helps to fill up I will leave it – I shall hope to see you on Friday if not You will let me know and when you will come

I am as always,
Yours Sincerely
M. FARADAY

Excuse the haste

[1] Cockary was a member of the City Philosophical Society.
[2] See Letter 23, fn. 2.

34 M. FARADAY to B. ABBOTT, 28 October 1816
   [*R.I., Warner mss., previously unpublished*]

Royal Institution
Octr 28 1816

DEAR ABBOTT

I scarcely know how it is and yet there is no one kind of employment whether of pleasure or business that falls to my share which more frequently and strongly impresses on my mind the truth of the old saying "delays are dangerous" than that of letter writing On the eve of scribbling I am frequently diverted from my purpose and it is very seldom that I perform the duty at the exact time I intended Now though this is the fact yet I know no direct way of accounting for it for I do not perceive clearly the cause I am very much amused by writing when once engaged and am never in a hurry from inclination to leave off The defect appears to have some connection with habit perhaps that which induces some and it may be amongst them myself to imagine that to write a letter previous study & thought is requisite My reason for supposing this to be the case is that on a receiving a letter yours for instance I form answers in my mind to the various parts as I read them & incontinently determine to send those answers to you in the evening. – The evening comes but the time appears to be barely sufficient to recollect the matter & not enough to write it also & the affair is therefore deferred to a more convenient time and thus a number of little delays occur each one in itself insignificant but together making us [*sic*] a tremendous sum It is for one such a sum that I have now to apologise for

99

by refering to the dates I find it is as much as 17 days since I received your last and the delay is aggravated by the circumstance that the nature of that letter in some manner required an immediate answer – I have but little to urge in palliation of my offence but one circumstance that may lessen it in your eyes is or rather was my repeated determination to substitute verbal for written communication I intended to have seen you Sunday week I intended it also last sunday and I positively determined to come this evening but preparations for the morning's lecture have turned my occupation from walking & talking into writing i.e.* unless you will come and see me and my uncertainty respecting the health of Mrs. Abbott makes me uncertain whether I should ask you (I am too lazy to scratch out and correct you must therefore put in at the * "and I do not know when I shall see you") – I have made up my mind to be in Long Lane next Sabbath day.

I trust that the bad news contained in your last will be compensated for by an excellent account in your next of the health of Mrs. Abbott & the rest of you and that there will be no alloy of that kind in any future communication for a long time to come – With respect to the blow pipe I asked Mr. Newman at the time that you wrote but he happened not to have one made and at present I am not aware whether he has or whether you continue to want it. He gave me to understand that he did not let out apparatus in general – I suppose you are aware that the flame is very small and quite insufficient to heat a large mass of matter with oxygen & hydrogene you cannot ignite a piece bigger than a pea or small horse bean but with common air & the flame of a spirit lamp the flame is somewhat larger

I do not know that there is any thing new in the Chemical world and having been very dry throughout the whole of this letter I shall end by my remembrance to all friends &

sign myself Yours truly

M. FARADAY

35 M. FARADAY to B. ABBOTT, 31 December 1816
[*R.I., Warner mss., B.J. 1, 234ff*]

R.I.,
Decr 31, 1816.

DEAR ABBOTT,

I have delayed writing for some days that I might when I did do it produce something of importance in size at least and I am in hopes from your last that you will not object to my intentions and reasons the latter are that our mutilated correspondence may be resumed to the advantage of us both The observation contained in yours of the 25th respecting the various causes and influences which have retarded our mutual communication together with my own experience which on this point you are aware has been great make it desirable that our plans should be such as to facilitate the object we have in view in the writing of letters That object is I believe the communication of information between us and the habit of arranging in a proper and orderly manner our ideas on any given or casual subject so that they may be placed with credit and service to ourselves on paper This object it strikes me would in part be attained by giving in addition to the general tone of a liberal & friendly letter something of the essayical to our communications. I do not mean that every letter should be an essay but that when a thought or a series of thoughts on any subject particular for the moment enters the mind that the liberty be allowed of throwing them into form on paper though perhaps unconnected with what has gone before or may succeed it. This indeed I believe is the plan we have actually followed but I am not sure that I had so conceived the thing before at least I had not marked out in my own mind that in pursuance of our object I might set down and scribble to you without preface whatever was uppermost in my mind. However at present you perceive what I aim at and what are my intentions and though as I before observed we have both virtually followed this plan yet I have at this time given it something like form or ground or expression or whatever else you please that I might be more concious [*sic*] of it and make use to a greater extent of the liberty it allows me

I must confess that I have always found myself unable to arrange a subject as I go on as I perceive many others apparently do Thus I could not begin a letter to you on the best methods of renovating our correspondance and proceeding regularly with my subject consider each part in order and finish by a proper conclusion my paper and matter together I always find myself obliged if my argument is of the least importance to draw up a plan of it on paper and fill in the parts by recalling them to mind either by association or otherwise and this done I have a series of major & minor heads in order & from which I work out my matter. – Now this method unfortunately though it will do very well for the mere purpose of arrangement & so forth yet it introduces a dryness and stiffness into the style of the piece composed by it for the parts come together like bricks one flat on the other and though they may fit yet have the appearance of too much regularity and it is my wish if possible to become acquainted with a method by which I may write my exercise in a more natural and easy progression I would if possible imitate a tree in its progression from roots to a trunk to branches twigs [reading doubtful] & leaning where every alteration is made with so much ease & yet effect that though the manner is constantly varied the effect is precise and determined Now in this situation I apply to you for assistance I want to know what method or what particular practice or exercise in composition you would recommend to prevent the orderly arrangement of A1 A2 A3. B1. B2 C1. C2 C3. C4 etc or rather to prevent this orderly arrangement from appearing too artificial – I am in want of all those conjunctions of style those corollaries etc by which parts of a subject are put together with so much ease and which produce so advantageous an effect and as you have frequently in your contributions to our portfolio given me cause to admire your success & my own deficiency on this point I beg that you will communicate to me your method of composing or if it is done spontaneously & without an effort on your part that you will analyse your mental proceedings whilst writing a letter and give me an account of that part which you conceive conducive to so good an end – With this request I shall refer the subject to you & proceed briefly to notice the contents of your letter

With respect to my remarks on Lectures I perceive that I am but a mere Tyro in the art & therefore you must be satisfyed with what you have or expect at some future time a recapitulation or rather revision of them – but your observations will be very acceptable – All the experiments on the blow pipe I have made – In the No. of the Journal R I published this evening you will see among miscellaneous intelligence a report on the subject signed M. F.[1] – your plan of 2 boxes has been proposed by many persons but in the most perfect state by Children.[2] he adds gages to the boxes by which to regulate the emission of air. – You must feel convinced that I regret much the health of Mrs. Abbott mends so slowly but for the fear of being troublesome in a sick house I should have called long since – Remember me to all Friends & Believe me Dear Abbott

Yours as Ever
M. FARADAY

[1] M. Faraday, 'Report on some experiments made with compressed oxygene and hydrogene, in the laboratory of the Royal Institution,' *Q JS*, 2 (1817), 461.
[2] John George Children (1778–1852) was a frequent visitor at the Royal Institution. I do not find that he published anything on the blow pipe at this time. It is probable that his set-up was described to Faraday and Davy in conversation.

36   M. FARADAY to B. ABBOTT, 20 January 1817
[*R.I.*, *Warner mss.*, *B.J.* 1, 246ff]

Royal Institution
Jan.ʸ 20ᵗʰ, 1816 [postmarked 1817][1]

DEAR ABBOTT,

The irresistible propensity in the human breast to draw conclusions before every circumstance has been examined or even before possession is obtained of the necessary data is so general that it passes unnoticed altho constantly active in ourselves until some very flagrant instance in others draws the attention to the results of such irregular and improper proceedings and points out the folly of immature judgements Now though it happens that these flagrant instances occur frequently and are continually reminding us of our own delinquency yet some how or other the fault still retains its ground and even appears at times to increase in strength.

T'would be a source of much useful consideration to endeavour to point out those causes which support & strengthen this ill habit of the mind and the comparative strength of them in persons differing in intellectual powers & tempers – It is not however my intention at this time to take up this subject though I am concious [*sic*] it would * be of much service to me by giving me a more direct and positive knowledge of the peculiar manner in which I am affected to the production of this effect but I have been led thus far into the subject by hearing from Farley[2] that Mr. Murray[3] had informed him Sir H. Davy had stolen some experiments from the french chemists and adopted them as his own

(I received yours of the 27 at the above scratch [*] but being determined to finish my sentence proceeded – to continue).

Murray has told Farley that Sir H. keeps a platinum wire red hot by holding it over ether & he says the effect is produced by the sulphur of the ether combining with the platinum & that the experiment is the same with that of the french chemists where they combine sulphur & copper leaf directly Now least you should be troubled by these queer explanations of an impossible effect I shall (being now permitted) lay this (a) new discovery before you

Sir H. Davy has lately been engaged in an investigation of the nature of flame and combination During the progress of his experiments he observed many appearances which led him to conclude that combustible bodies (the term includes supporters) combined at a temperature *less* than that necessary for their inflammation but a grand difficulty occurred in making this combination if it took place he has however succeeded & produced one of the most beautiful & magical experiments in the science of chemistry Heat a fine wire of platinum coiled at the end in the flame of a spirit lamp to very dull redness or even beneath & then introduce it into a phial of mixed oxygene & hydrogene gases The wire immediately becomes hotter rises to a bright red & fires the mixtures – This effect is produced by the gases combining at that temperature and producing heat which though not sufficient itself to enflame the mixture can elevate the temperature of the wire untill by accumulation the gases are fired – A more beautiful experiment is made with coal gas for not being so combustible as hydrogene it permits the wire to rise to a higher temperature in it before it inflames – Hold a wide mouthed phial over a burner until it is filled with gas & then place the heated platinum wire just in the neck where the common air can mix with the gas & the phenomena will occur with great splendour The wire becoming white hot As it forms a current in the middle air passes by the sides into the phial & renders the whole explosive & then by lowering the wire you will get effects that will astonish you by their brilliancy

The success of the experiment when made with ether depends on the circumstance that it is always rising in a vapour & forming on its surface an explosive atmosphere Into a wine glass put a little ether & then hold the heated platina wire about 3/8 of an inch from [the] surface and rather to one side that a descending current of air may [be] [ms. torn] established The wire will remain red hot as long as any ether is in the glass – This experiment is peculiar from the circumstance of a new substance being formed it rises in vapour from the hot wire has much of the smell of chlorine & I would advise you not to get in the way of the fumes – They produce white vapours when ammonia is near & possess some acid properties

When the experiment with ether is made in a very dark room a pale flame is seen rising from the hot wire & generally most abundant when the wire is not visibly red

These experiments succeed with all the combustible gases & vapours even with that of warm alcohol but the only metals that are efficaceous are platinum & palladium The others possess too much radiating & conducting power – I need not now point out to you the inapplicability of Murrays explanations They will strike you at once and perhaps tomorrow evening should he accost you you will be able to inform him on *this* point as well as on many others

Now in answer to your letter. – I shall be very happy to see your acquaintance but on Thursday Chambers[4] has invited a few of the society to sup with him & as he did it formally and I with others formally accepted his invitation I am fixed Friday & Sat are out of the question – you have a lecture one day & I have *two* the next but suppose we say Monday – or if you like tuesday & let me know if he will take tea or not and at what time you will come (Sunday I had forgotten) – I allow you to scold me as hard as you please for non-appearance at Bermondsy for I deserve it but I must get scolded some-where & I dont know how to choose so I let chance decide it – What with Sir H.——— Mr. Brande, our twofold series of Lectures – original investigations – the Society & its committee – my time is just now so closely cut up that sunday will hardly suffice for my Mother Brother & Sister & as your hospitality constantly presses me to dinner which when accepted as constantly makes me too late I hardly know what to do – I have determined as far as I can to see you next Sunday but write me for fear of a failure

I am very glad to hear Mrs. Abbott is better remember me to her kindly & express warm wishes from me for her recovery – I hope Mr. Abbott Miss Abt & Robert are well remember me to them & I'll thank you for your trouble [reading doubtful] on Sunday

> I am
> Dear Ben
> Yours Ever
> M. FARADAY

I never can get through a letter with any regularity[. Y]ou [ms. torn] must excuse every thing.

¹ A common error at the beginning of a new year. The letter clearly was written in 1817, but Faraday continued to write 1816.
² Perhaps John Farley who had just finished a paper 'On the Fixed Oil of Wine; and on the light emitted by metallic wires of low temperature in certain volatile media,' *PM*, 49 (1817), 209.
³ This is probably John Murray (1778–1843), the publisher who published the *QJS*. Murray's relations with Davy were often stormy. For another example see Samuel Smiles, *A Publisher and His Friends, Memoir and Correspondence of the Late John Murray*, 2 vols., London & New York, 1891, Vol. 2, p. 208.
⁴ Chambers was a member of the City Philosophical Society.

37 M. FARADAY to B. ABBOTT, 15 April 1817

[*R.I., Warner mss., previously unpublished*]

Royal Institution,
March [crossed out and April written in in Abbott's hand] 15ᵗʰ, 1817.

DEAR ABBOTT,

I cannot exactly say how long it is since I wrote to you or since your last arrived here but I fear your mind will not be long in giving an idea of a space by far too considerable at least with myself I must confess that a fearful lapse of time has intervened between then and the present moment and what tends to exaggerate the idea is that the very circumstances which have caused the omission tend to make it appear more considerable For as time is measured merely by the events that succeed each other the more of these that are put together the greater will appear the space over which they are expanded and the more distant will be two objects that bound them – Excepting regret however at these long intervals the only determination which has been raised in my mind by this last one is never to promise positively again and therefore for the future you must get your letters from this part of the world as you can catch them i.e either in bundles or single either in a continued series or insulated like land marks just to shew that certain relations are still existing and remain to be revived

Notwithstanding this cavalier statement on my part I have still some out of sight hopes that you will not be guided by a similar determination or rather that from the effect of a little milk of human kindness – from communicativeness – from listlessness and above all from friendship & an excellent capacity your letters will come tumbling in *upon* me with more speed & in greater abundance than they have done and that though your pocket may not suffer for the shoes of the postman yet that mine may – not that I would encourage the least hopes in you that I shall relax from my determination or that you entice any more promises from me made only to be broken – but that setting me a good example I may par hazard be cheated at some unguarded moment into the writing you a letter even though to the neglect of other things

I am quite ignorant of what your last contained for having left it lying on my desk day after day & week after week waiting for an answer it has at last been lost and this mishap has awakened me to a sense of my neglect – Now however that I am going to write (going do [*sic*] I say) I want a subject and hardly know what to do for one – to make up the loss in the best way I could i.e as far as concerned the filling up of the paper I resolved never once to retrograde in thought untill this sheet was full and in consequence you are likely to get a kind of olio, sallad, coat of many colours – tailors flag, or other compound thing having no one thing with either beginning or end to it in it – you must however find the best excuse for it you can – for I can offer you none and may therefore consider it as the scum that rises after long boiling from a pot of good contents or as the first dirty water that descends from newly running spouts or as – as – as any other bad precursor of a good thing – ah I think I have said too much I am almost promising again but that would not be wonderful in a letter professing like this to have no two parts alike so that what has been said shall all go without alteration Indeed I can neither afford time paper or pen for another letter at this instant

I promised your brother that I would come down (or up) to you on or by next sunday at farthest and I mean to *keep my word* and even to dine with you if you choose c'est-a-dire if you have no objection – in explanation of which last word I w[ish] to say (troublesome politeness being banished that cordiality mak[eth] [ms. missing] her place) if all is convenient

It is hardly proper that I should pretend to write sense in this letter but I cannot help expressing hopes that I shall see Mrs. Abbott & all well when I come &

that I am as ever
Yours
M. Faraday

38 M. Faraday to B. Abbott, 25 July 1817
[*R.I., Warner mss., B.J. 1, 25 off*]

R.I.
Friday Morning, ½ ps 7
25 July 1817[1]

Dear Abbott
I did not get your kind note until last night and have since then been endeavouring to extricate myself from a meeting of some of our people respecting a singing school attached to our meeting house[2] in hopes that I could have said to you "I will come" – It happens however unfortunately that I have been one of the most earnest in bringing the consultants together and that I shall be obliged to be with them plodding over the means of improving

our own singing in place of attending to & enjoying that of other on this evening

It avails me nothing to express my regrets therefore I shall restrain my pen except in saying

I am as always
Yours sincerely
M. FARADAY

¹ Date pencilled in, probably by Abbott.
² Faraday had been raised as a Sandemanian and remained a loyal member of the London congregation all his life. See *LPW*, 2ff. He also had a good baritone and thoroughly enjoyed singing.

39 M. FARADAY to B. ABBOTT, 25 September 1817

[*R.I., Warner mss., previously unpublished*]

Royal Institution
Septr 25th, 1817

DEAR ABBOTT,

I hasten at present to send that answer to your last which it appeared to require immediately but which for two or three reasons I have delayed 'till now These were first the intimation in yours that no arrangement could be made for this week with your friends Secondly that my next week was so filled I wanted a few days grace to make room in it for you Thirdly that I wished to send Robert an account of his water but was puzzled by some curious appearances in it

Now that I am always glad to see you & your friends you cannot doubt though the tone of your letter implies so much hesitation therefore I pass over all your scruples to to [*sic*] the appointment of a day – Now as Tuesday & Friday are rejected on your side it follows that we must look to Monday Wednesday Thursday or Saturday – With me Monday is school night – Wednesday Lecture night Thursday Smarts Lecture to which I am engaged & Saturday Business night – I have been endeavouring to get back Thursday but have not succeeded therefore I am obliged to point out Monday night as the one on which I can be at home & be glad to see you the school being the only engagement I can break I am sorry for this as it gives but so short a notice to you but I cannot now help it & would have written before but I hoped yesterday for a later day – on monday evening therefore I shall see you

Now with respect to the water¹ Robert left me it is a very pure one containing only 8.9 grs per pint of solid products the salts I at first considered as Sulphate & Muriate of soda with the least possible quantity of Muriate of Lime but at the end of the processes I found a quantity of carb of Soda which I cannot satisfactorily account for. It appears to belong to the water but it may have got in by accident if it is a part of the mineral contents of the water it is very curious &

I should like to ascertain the fact on a fresh portion of the water mine being all gone

The Specific Gravity of Mr. W's sea water is 1027.6 The SG of common sea water is said to vary from 1026.9 to 1028.5

> I am Dear Ben
> Yours as ever
> M. FARADAY

If you could come early on Monday & take also an early tea with me twould be well for I this moment remember that it is Quarterly night with our School[2] & that we have some quarrels to settle If possible I should like to be in the city by 9 o'clk but supposing that will trespass [on] [ms. missing] you I will give up the idea – however let me know tomorrow if you can & do just what you like with me & the night too.

> MF

[1] Faraday began his scientific career as an analytical chemist and performed literally hundreds of analyses of water samples sent to him from all over England. There is a manuscript volume at the Royal Institution in which is carefully recorded each of these analyses. This provided a considerable income to him in the 1820's.
[2] I have been unable to identify the school.

40 M. FARADAY to B. ABBOTT, 27 February 1818
[*R.I.*, *Warner mss.*, *B.J. 1, 283ff*]

> Royal Institution
> Friday Feb.ʸ 27ᵗʰ, 1817 [but postmarked 1818][1]

DEAR BEN

I was extremely shocked at the Note I received from you the other day for the circumstance came on me entirely unexpected[2] I thought you had all been perfectly well & was regretting that though I had been negligent in our intercourse I neither saw nor heard from *you* – It is not necessary Ben that I should offer you consolation at this time you have all the resources necessary within yourself but I scruple not though at the risk of reagitating your fatigued feelings to express my sorrow at the event and condolence with you – It has been my lot of late to see death not near me it is true but around me on all sides and I have thought and reasoned on it until it has become in appearance harmless and a very commonplace event I fear at times that I am becoming too torpid and insensible to the awe that generally and perhaps properly accompanies it but I cannot help it and when I consider my own weak constitution the time I have passed & the probable near approach of that end to all earthly things I still do not feel that inquietude [reading doubtful] & alarm which might be expected It seems but being in another country

But I must shorten these reflections I have not time nor you I imagine serenity to bear them – but philosophise or if you please moralise – the world may laugh as long as it pleases at the *cant* of those terms – so long as they alter not the *things* they are welcome to their enjoyment you will find your best resources in reason & I am sure that conscious of *that truth* you have gone to it in distress.

You say you left many messages at Mr. Grays I have not heard them but I have been little there or any where except on business so that they missed me – I have been more than enough employed We have been obliged even to put aside lectures at the Institution – and now I am so tired with a long attendance at Guildhall Yesterday & today being subpoenaed with Sir H Davy Mr. Brande Phillips[3] Aikin[4] & others to give chemical information on a trial which however did not come on that I scarcely know what I say

I fear Dear Benjamin that the desultory character of my letter will hurt rather than console your feelings but I could not refrain longer from acknowledging yours & the pain it gave me

Make my kindest remembrances to all & believe me Dear Ben

Yours as Ever

M. FARADAY

[1] Above the date there is a pencilled note, probably written by Abbott: 'The date below appears to be erroneous This letter referring to the death of my mother which occurred in Feb *1818* – See the postmark'.

[2] News of Abbott's mother's death.

[3] Faraday's friend, Richard Phillips, who had become a chemist and was soon to be the editor of the *Annals of Philosophy*.

[4] Arthur Aiken (1773–1854), a mineralogist and chemist.

41   M. FARADAY to S. COCKS, August 1818[1]

[*Wellcome Medical Historical Library, previously unpublished*]

Royal Institution
August 1818

DEAR SIR

I called on Mr. Hume[2] this Morning on returning from the Office but am not sure any thing he said will influence you. He talked much of what was irrelevant to my object and I could not get him to say distinctly that the Malt (i.e like yours) was made by Mr. —— of —— before your patent for the purpose of colouring beer: he could not fill up the vacuities in name and place or would not – But he said this much that he had been in Herefordshire to a kiln where he believes he was not expected – that they were not at work but by desire of the master or others *set to work* – that he ascertained the temperature of the kiln and found it to be in all places above 400° – that this was not in the air alone *but in the grain* – that he used among other means alloys of metal fusible at different points and that pieces of these alloys not fusible below 400° fused among the malt in the kiln – that the malt produced was called high dried brown malt. – He further says that the malt I enclose (being some I took out of a parcel he shewed me) was made at the kiln in Herefordshire before the date of your patent – this however he could not state on his own authority but said that the Men are ready and were in court with samples like that to swear it was made before that date – He further observed that he was with Mr. Ronalds[3]? of Apothecaries Hall when the experiments were made by which malt like yours was prepared under 400° and could swear to it but observed it took a very long time – and he did not explain to me the anomaly of it being prepared under & not above 400° as is implied in their affadavits – He talked a good deal of sugar starch &c which I could not distinctly understand but concluded by observing that out of the many points that would destroy the patent it would fall by that of previous preparation of the Malt as to be sworn by the Malsters men to the samples they would bring

I must confess I do not know what to make out of all this. There will be many oaths against you and these oaths they say are tack'd to facts Mr. Hume's confidence in his experiments on the temperature of the malt makes me doubt his confidence on the other points certainly, and almost the honesty of the defendants I do not see any thing in his experiments, though well looking, that make me alter my opinion of the Malt; but You and Your counsel must be careful to point out or to draw out fully the chemical relations of metals to heat as regards their capacity and conducting power or his experiments, with the alloys, will appear to have great weight, though I believe they have none. But this can be explained better to you verbally by some of us [ms. torn but some words written in]

Mr. Hume tells me he has been making an affadavit this morning & that More business is to be done tomorrow I regret that success is not certain where it ought to attend. Mr. Wheeler[4] said it was possible I should be wanted tomorrow and that I was to leave word where I should be I shall be somewhere at Hampstead and if required you will be able to ascertain the exact spot by inquiring of Mr. Barnard[5] or of his family 34 Paternoster Row

Yours Obediently
M. FARADAY

[1] Faraday was sometimes, in these years, involved in legal cases requiring expert testimony. This is one of them, dealing with the question of whether a patent could be issued for a new process of making malt for beer. For another case, see *LPW*, 107 and Letter 46. For this case, see Richard Vaughan Varnewall and Edward Hall Alderson, *Reports of Cases Argued and Determined in the Court of the King's Bench with Tables of the Names of the Cases and the Principal Matters*, London, 1819, 345.
[2] Probably George Walter Hume of Long-acre, later a member of the Society of Apothecaries.

3 Henry Ronalds, Apothecary.
4 Walter Daniel Wheeler took out a Patent on a new process for drying and preparing malt in 1817.
5 Faraday was to marry Sarah Barnard in 1821.

42 M. FARADAY to G. DE LA RIVE,[1] 6 October 1818

[*Bibliothèque publique et universitaire de Genève, ms. 2311, f. 53–4, B.J. 1, 286ff*]

Royal Institution
Octr 6th 1818

DEAR SIR

Your kindness when here in requesting me to accept the honor of a communication with you on the topics which occur in the general progress of science was such as almost to induce me to overstep the modesty due to my humble situation in the Philosophical world and to accept of the offer you made me: But I do not think I should have been emboldened thus to address you had not Mr. Newman since then informed me that you had again expressed a wish to him that I should do so and fearful that you should misconceive my silence I put pen to paper willing rather to run the risk of being thought too bold than of incurring the charge of neglect towards one who had been so kind to me in his expressions

My slight attempts to add to the general stock of chemical knowledge have been received with favourable expressions by those around me but I have on reflection perceived that this arose from kindness on their parts and the wish to incite me on to better things I have always therefore been fearful of advancing on what had been said lest I should assume more than was intended and I hope that a feeling of this kind will explain to you the length of time which has elapsed between the time when you required me to write and the present moment when I obey you

I am not entitled by any peculiar means of obtaining a knowledge of what is doing at the moment, in Science to your attention and I have no claims in myself to it I judge it probable that the news of the philosophical world will reach you much sooner through other more authentic and more dignified sources and my only excuse even for this letter is obedience to your wishes and not an account of any thing interesting for its novelty

That my letter may not however be entirely devoid of interest I will take the liberty of mentioning and commending to you a new process for the preparation of gas for illumination Its valuable points are that the furnace and fire is much smaller than usual that the purification is simply washing in water that the gasometer is reduced much in size that the gas is a purer and more highly carbonated substance and that the whole operation is performed in a clean and neat manner and with very little trouble. This method is that of distilling oil in a heated cast Iron tube and it was first done I believe and the apparatus formed by J & P [reading doubtful] Taylor of this city[2] Their furnace is a neat square piece of Iron work having a sand bath or other application at the top and not more than 3 feet 6 inches long 3 feet high and 24 inches wide The oil used is the worst possible that called pilchard dregs which appears almost like a black mud is excellent it does not cost here more than 2/6 per gallon The gas obtained contains no sulphuretted hydrogen but only a little Sebacic acid or sebate of ammonia and that is washed out by water Compared with Common coal g[as] its rate of consumption is as 2.25 to 6 i.e., 2 1/4 c[ubic] feet of this gas will supply an argand burner for 1 ho[ur] [ms. torn] which would require 6 of common coal gas; and the diminution of the gasometer which I before referred to may as you will perceive be in this proportion

A great advantage of this apparatus is that being small it is not expensive and this with the little care required in managing it will effectually do away with all monopoly; when eighteen or twenty lights are wanted it is applicable with great advantage and two or three shopkeepers may join together and have one amongst them with very little cost

I am afraid that with all my reasons I have not been able to justify this letter If my fears are true I regret it but it was your kindness that drew it from me and to your kindness I must look for an excuse

> I am Dear Sir
> With Great Respect
> Your Obedient Humble Servant
> M. FARADAY

I regret that I have not a copy of my experiments on flame in tubes of which to buy [reading doubtful] your acceptance They are only in the Journal of Science edited here but I presume ere this they will have caught your attention

MF

[1] Charles Gaspard de la Rive (1770–1834) was a member of the Genevan aristocracy who fled before the revolutionary wave created by the French Revolution. He received his medical degree at Edinburgh and practised for a few years in London. Faraday met him in Geneva during his trip on the continent with Davy.
[2] For an account of the problems encountered in the introduction of gas lighting in London, see Stirling Everard, *The History of the Gas Light and Coke Company, 1812–1949*, London, 1949 and Charles Hunt, *A History of the Introduction of Gas Lighting*, London, 1907.

[*R.I., Warner mss., B.J. 1, 321ff*]

Royal Institution
April 27th, 1819.

DEAR ABBOTT,

I hasten to write to you in return for yours of Yesterday though what I can say to you will be little better than silence or absence as you will see before we arrive at the end of this letter I am sorry to hear of the continued illness and dullness of your house and sympathise deeply with you in the care with which you must consequently be burden'd – You make me a singularly systematic statement of the reasons which prevent my seeing you here and I am sorry they are of such a nature and so cogent I cannot help fancying that you require a similar one from me to account for my absence from Bermondsy and to satisfy you I will detail to you my employments.

You will be aware that Business of the Institution must press hard upon me at this time and during the whole of the Lectures To this is added much private employment which will not admit of neglect With reference to my evenings they are thus arranged on Monday evening there is a scientific meeting of Members here and every other monday a dinner to both of which my company is requested on Tuesday Evening I have a Pupil who comes at 6 oclk and stops till 9 engaged in private lessons.[1] On Wednesday the Society requires my aid Thursday is my only evening for accidental engagements Friday my pupil returns and stops his three hours and on Saturday I have to arrange my little private business Now you will see that, except on Tuesday and Friday after 9 oclk that I have no Evening but Thursday for any thing that may turn up Now for Thursday next I have engaged with a party to see Matthews[2] whom as yet I have not seen but on the Thursday following I shall expect you if you can find it convenient

I must now hasten to my crucibles so for the present adieu.

Yours Very Sincerely
M. FARADAY

[1] Faraday gives no hint as to the identity of his pupil nor what subject he was teaching. Presumably, it was chemistry.

[2] Matthews was a member of the City Philosophical Society.

44   SIR H. DAVY to M. FARADAY, 1 November 1819

[*R.I., previously unpublished*]

Rome,
Nov.ʳ 1,

DEAR MR. FARADAY

I shld be much obliged to you if you will send this letter to my Brother.¹ –

I will thank you likewise to ask Mr Moore whether he has received the Deed I executed from the [illeg.] of Green [reading doubtful] & whether the money is paid into Drummonds.²

I have read Berzelius' paper which is a wretched composition.³ There is as much difference between his estimates & those of Dulong as between his & mine – If he does not make his experiments with more care than he reads the papers he criticizes they must owe their coincidence *to calculation*. –

Pray write to me at Naples.

> I am Dear Mr. Faraday
> > Your sincere friend *and* wellwisher [reading doubtful]
> > H DAVY

¹ Dr John Davy (1790–1868).
² This clearly refers to some bit of Davy's private business about which I can find nothing further.
³ J. J. Berzelius, 'Note. Sur la composition de l'acide phosphorique et de l'acide phosphoreux,' *AC*, 10 (1819), 278. Berzelius attacked both Davy and Faraday in this paper. See *LPW*, 46. The reference in *LPW* is incorrect.

45   M. FARADAY to G. DE LA RIVE, 20 April 1820

[*Bibliothèque publique et universitaire de Genève, ms. 2311, f. 55–6, B.J. 1, 327ff*]

Royal Institution
April 20ᵗʰ, 1820

DEAR SIR

I never in my life felt such difficulty in answering a letter as I do at this moment your very kind one of last year. I was delighted on receiving it to find that you had honored me with any of your thoughts and that you would permit me to correspond with you by letter But I fear that my intention of meriting that honor has already made me unworthy of it for whilst waiting continually for any scientific news that might arise to send you I have delayed my answer so long as almost to forfeit the right of permission to send one at all I hope you will attribute my tardiness to its right motive, diffidence of my worthiness to write to you; and that it will not injure me in your estimation. I will promise if you still grant me the liberty of correspondence never to err so again

I am the more ashamed of my neglect because it is a neglect of gratitude as well as of respect. I am deeply indebted to you for your kind expressions respecting my paper on the sonorous tubes[1] and its value is very much increased with me by your praise I regret however on the same subject that you should imagine I thought but little of your experiment with mercury.[2] I made it immediately and was very much surprised by it and I only refrained from noticing it because I was afraid of myself and thought I should apply it wrongly and thus intrude on your subject without any right or reason. Indeed I had hopes that you would take up the subject again and after reviewing the various sonorous phenomena of different kinds as produced in different ways would undertake what I had not ventured to do namely to draw general conclusions and develope the laws to which they (the phenomena) were obedient.

You have honored me by many questions and no regret can be greater than mine that I have suffered time to answer them rather than myself – In every line of your kind letter I find cause to reproach myself for delay – The next I will answer more readily and the fear will be that I shall trouble you too often rather than too seldom

You honor me by askng for scientific news and for any little information of my own. I am sorry that both sources are very barren at present but I *do hope* that both will improve Mr Stodart & myself have lately been engaged in a long series of experiments and trials on steel with the hope of improving it and I think we shall in some degree succeed[3] we are still very much engaged in the subject but if you will give me leave I will when they are more complete which I expect will be shortly give you a few notes on them. I succeeded by accident a few weeks ago in making artificial plumbago but not in useful masses. I had heated iron with charcoal dust two or three times over and in that way got a dark grey very crystalline carburet of Iron of I believe a definite composition but the outside of the button which had been long in close contact with the charcoal was converted into excellent plumbago. Since then I have observed amongst the casters of iron that when they cast on a facing of charcoal dust as is the case in fine work that the surface of [the] casting is frequently covered with a thin film of plumbago evidently formed in the same way as in the above experiment

We have lately had some important trials for oil in this metropolis in which I with others have been engaged.[4] They have given occasion for many experiments on oil and the discovery of some new and curious results. One of the trials only is finished and there are 4 or 5 more to come As soon as I can get time it is my intention to trace more closely what takes place in oil by heat and I hope to bribe you to continue to me the honor & pleasure of your correspondence by saying that if any thing important turns up I will make it the matter of a letter.

I am My Dear Sir with the Highest respect Your Obliged & Humble

M. FARADAY.

¹ 'On the Sounds produced by flame in tubes &c.,' *QJS*, 5 (1818), 274.

² G. de la Rive, 'Notice sur les sons produits dans les tubes par la flamme du gaz hydrogène,' *BU*, 9 (1818), 111.

³ M. Faraday and J. Stodart, 'Experiments on the alloys of steel, made with a view to its improvement,' *QJS*, 9 (1820), 319, and 'On the Alloys of Steel,' *PT* (1822), 253. See also *LPW*, 109ff., and L. Pearce Williams, 'Faraday and the Alloys of Steel,' in Cyril Stanley Smith, editor, *The Sorby Centennial Symposium on the History of Metallurgy*, New York, 1965, 145. Faraday's work on steel is treated in great detail in Sir Robert A. Hadfield, Bt., *Faraday and his Metallurgical Researches*, London, 1931.

⁴ See *LPW*, 107.

46   M. FARADAY to R. PHILLIPS, 30 May 1820

[*Burndy Library, Norwalk, Conn., Michael Faraday Collection M1, previously un-published*]

May 30ᵗʰ Tuesday. In White cross Street. [postmarked 26 Ju 1820]

Operated with Boiler No. 1.¹ The same as used before Took out a bottle full of the oil and removed the short thermometer which was found safe and unbroken. – The man-hole and all other parts were close except the vent pipe of 2 feet in length.

   Began to raise the heat in the boiler at.

14.50′ —the temperature was 367° by long thermometer

—55′ —375°

— 57′ —381° no inflammable vapour.

      382° apparently inflammable vapour in very small quantity

—59′.5—390° very slightly inflammable

24. 2′ —400° Phillips & Bostock saw the inflammation

— 3′ —407°

— 5′ —417° Burst of vapour & bumping

— 7′.5—435° Plenty of vapour combustible

—10′ —445°

—12′ —455° flame continued a few moments – Saw pale flame

—15′ —463°

—15′.5—485° flame continuous some moments like a gas burner

      tube now heightened to 3 feet 10 inches

—17′ —495° long bright flame

—19′ —500° flame 2 feet long

—20′ —507° used a pan (about 2 quarts) as a hood – fired the vapour within.

      – The vapour fired by a light held 6 inches above the pipe.

—21′ —520°

—23′.5—527° More water in the vapour now than before. A small tub used as

      a steam-bin filled readily with vapour and easily fired at a light

—25′ —543° A large barrel now used as a steam bin easily inflamed the
         vapour inside
—26′ —545° Do.
24.27′ —560° Do.
         565° Tub filled with flame very bright
Oil now boiling Tub filled with vapour in less than 15″ and the flame when
fired immense After some trials in the tube the wood itself took fire and burnt –
At the time when the small barrel was placed over the pipe and the vapour in it
fired it inflamed a piece of paper just in the inside and even the wood itself

The jet of flame from the end of the tube at last reached up to
& played against the beam above.
                                                              M. FARADAY

[1] See the end of Letter 45.

47 M. FARADAY to G. DE LA RIVE, 26 June 1820
[*Bibliothèque publique et universitaire de Genève, ms. 2311, f. 57–8, B.J. 1, 330ff*]

Royal Institution
London
June 26th, 1820.

MY DEAR SIR

Not long since I troubled you with a letter in which I said I would shortly
send you an account of some experiments on steel made by Mr. Stodart &
myself.[1] A paper will appear in the next No. of our Journal which will contain
all we have as yet ascertained on the subject and as the results seem to me to be
interesting I hope you will not be sorry that I keep my promise by mentioning
the principal of them to you. In the small way in which only we have as yet
worked they are good and I hope that no failure will occur when the processes
are transferred to the Manufactory.

It is possible you may have observed an analysis of Wootz or the Indian
steel published in one of our Journals some time since[2] I could at that time find
nothing in the steel besides the Iron & carbon but a small portion of the earths
or as I presume their metallic bases. On the strength of this analysis we endeavoured to demonstrate the particular nature of Wootz synthetically by
combining steel with these metallic bases and we succeeded in getting alloys
which when worked were declared by Mr. Stodart to be equal in all qualities
to the best Bombay Wootz. This corroboration of the nature of Wootz received
still stronger confirmation from a property possessed by the Alloys in common
with Wootz namely their power of yielding damasked surfaces by the action
of acids. When Wootz is fused & forged it still retains so much of the crystalline
structure as to exhibit when acted on by very weak sulphuric acid, for some time

117

a beautiful damasked surface. This we have never yet seen produced by pure steel but it *is* produced in our imitation of wootz or alloys of steel with the metal of Alumine

I must not forget to tell you how we formed our alloys. Many attempts failed the following method succeeds. Fuse Iron in small pieces with charcoal powder. If the button produced is malleable break it up & re-fuse it with more charcoal. In this way a carburet of Iron will be formed which has its place between steel & plumbago. It is fusible when broken has a dark grey colour and is very highly crystalline It is so brittle that small pieces of it may be rubbed to powder in a mortar. Some of this powdered carburet was then mixed with pure alumine & the whole strongly heated. A portion of the alumine was reduced by the carbon of the carburet and a compound of Iron Aluminium & carbon was obtained Then English cast steel being mixed with about 10 per cent of this alloy the whole was fused and our artificial wootz obtained.

I presume that the properties of Wootz are so well known to you that I need not stop to say what are the supposed improvements in steel when it is converted into Wootz

Whilst making the carburet above mentioned we also succeeded in forming plumbago but I am afraid this artificial production of it will not be very useful in its application If Iron be heated highly and long enough in contact with charcoal plumbago is always formed. I have some buttons of metal here weighing 2 or 3 ozs that appear to be solid plumbago The appearance however is deceitful for it is only on the surface & to the depth perhaps of the 1/40 of an inch that the plumbago has been formed The internal part is composed of the crystalline carburet before mentioned What is plumbago is very good and marks excellently well and though we have never yet been able to fuse powdered plumbago into a mass yet I think that if it were required to form it in a compact state to work up into pencils it might be done by embedding plates of Iron about the 1/20 of an inch thick in charcoal & heating intensely for a long time This we have not yet had time to try but intend to do so.

You will readily suppose that during nearly 2 years that we have been at work on this subject a great deal of useless matter except as furnishing experience has accumulated. All this you will rather wish away so that I shall pass over unimportant alloys to write of those which promise good results

Perhaps the very best alloy we have yet made is that with Rhodium Dr. Wollaston[3] furnished us with the metal so that you will have no doubts of its purity and identity. One & a half per cent of it was added to steel & the button worked. It was very malleable but much harder than common steel & made excellent instruments In tempering the instruments they required to be heated full 70°F. higher than is necessary for the best cast steel and from this we hope it will possess greater degrees of hardness & toughness. Razors made from the alloy cut admirably.

Next to the alloy of Rhodium comes that of silver about which there are many curious circumstances. Silver refuses to combine with steel except in very small proportions and this want of affinity is much greater when the metals are cold than when hot. If for instance 100 steel & 1 silver be fused together cooled hammered &c. &c. and then laid in weak sulphuric acid for 10 or 12 hours its structure will be developed & it will be found to be a congeries of fibres of steel & silver the one distinct from the other but intimately mixed in every part Now the perfect dispersion of the silver throughout all parts proves that it has been taken up by the steel whilst in fusion but its separate state of existence shews that it has been rejected from the alloy as it solidified Indeed this refusal of the silver by the steel as it cools is so remarkable that if the hot alloy be observed globules of silver may be seen extruded from the surface as the temperature falls.

But however; we went on diminishing the quantity of silver as long as its separate existence could be observed in the alloys and when we arrived to a $1/500$ part we found that the whole remained in combination with the steel. This Alloy was excellent, all the cutting instruments made of it were of the best quality & the metal worked without crack or flaw and with remarkable toughness & malleability under the hammer.

The Alloy of steel and platinum is not so marked by an acquir[ed] [ms. torn] superiority as the two I have already mentioned and yet platinum in quantities from 1 to 3 per cent does seem to be of advantage to steel but we are now continuing this subject. The powerful affinity with which platinum combines with the metals generally, meets with no exception when tried with Iron or Steel; they unite in all the proportions we have tried from 1 platinum to 100 steel up to 90 platinum to 20 steel We expect a good deal from some of these higher compounds

I think the affinities of platinum & silver for steel are worth comparing together Though they stand almost together in an electrical arrangement of the metals and both of them very far from Iron or Steel still they do not exhibit attractions for steel at all comparable Platinum will combine in any proportion apparently with steel or Iron and at temperatures so low that the two metals may be welded together at heats barely sufficient to weld Iron whereas it is with difficulty that a $1/500$ part of silver is made in any way to combine with steel

I hope my Dear Sir I have not tired you yet for I am now going to begin writing across but I will promise not to detain you very much longer either by excuses or details – We have been induced by the popular idea that meteoric Iron would not rust to try the effect of Nickel on Steel & Iron We made alloys of Iron & Nickel varying the latter metal from 3 to 10 per cent and we thought we found that they were not quite so oxidable as Iron alone when exposed with it in greenhouses & in our laboratory But Nickel alloyd with steel gave us no hopes It appeared more oxidable than simple steel and this fault was not compensated for by any other good quality. So for the present we have dismissed that metal from our experiments though I expect as we go on we shall find many occasions to resume thoughts and intentions which we may have laid down

Mr Children[4] has obliged us with an accurate analysis of the Siberian Meteoric Iron and he finds it to contain a very large proportion of nickel In the mean of three experiments it amounts to 8.96 per cent.

You cannot imagine how much we have been plagued to get crucible that will bear the heat we require and use in our experiments Hessian, Cornish, Pipe clay crucible all fuse in a few minutes if put into the furnace singly and our only resource is to lute two or three one within another together so that the whole may not fuse before our alloy has had time to form in the centre. I have seen Hessian crucibles becomes [*sic*] so soft that the weight of 500 grains of metal has made them swell out like a purse and the upper part has fallen together in folds like a piece of soft linen and where three have been put together the two outer ones have in less than half an hour melted off & flown down onto the grate below

From these circumstances you will judge of the heat we get and now I will mention to you an effect which we obtain & one we can't obtain both of which a little surprised us. The positive effect is the volatilisation of silver – We often have it in our experiments sublimed into the upper part of the crucible and forming a fine dew on the sides & cover So that I have no doubts at present on the volatility of silver though I had before. – The non effect is the non reduction of titanium – We have tortured Menachanite pure oxide of titanium the carbonate &c in many ways in our furnace but have never yet been able to reduce it not even in combination with Iron and I must confess that now I am very sceptical whether it has ever been reduced at all in the pure state.

Now I think I have noticed the most interesting points at which we have arrived Pray pity us that after 2 years experiments we have got no farther but I am sure if you knew the labour of the experiments you would applaud us for our perseverance at least We are still encouraged to go on and think that the experience we have gained will shorten our future labours. And if you find the contents of this well covered sheet of paper interesting I shall at some future time do myself the honor & pleasure of sending a continuation of it [to you] [not clear on photocopy; may be crossed out in original]

If you should think any of our results worth notice in the *Bibliotheque*[5] this letter is free to be used in any way you please Pardon my vanity for supposing any thing I can assist in doing can be worth attention but you know we live in the good opinion of ourselves & of others and therefore naturally think better of our own productions than they deserve

I am My Dear Sir

Very Truly & Sincerely
Your Obliged
M. FARADAY.

[1] See Letter 45.

[2] 'An analysis of Wootz or Indian Steel,' *QJS*, 7 (1819), 288.

[3] William Hyde Wollaston (1766–1828), was the discoverer of Rhodium.

[4] John George Children (1778–1852) was a chemist who served for many years as one of the Secretaries of the Royal Society.

[5] G. de la Rive was the founder of the *Bibliothèque Britannique* which later became the *Bibliothèque Universelle*.

48 M. FARADAY to A. MARCET,[1] 3 January 1821
[*R.I., previously unpublished*]

Royal Institution
Janry 3rd 1821.

SIR

I received the Volume of Memoirs[2] you were so kind as to permit me to look at, in safety; but too late unfortunately for any notice to be taken of it in the Journal as I had the same day sent the last sheet of the miscellanea back to press The volume appears to me to be highly interesting and augurs well I trust to the series of which it is to be the commencement: at the same time I am not a competent judge of by far the greater part of it and I think I mentioned to you that I had not much influence in the journal except in the Miscellanea which partly falls under my management. I am afraid therefore I should not be able to take that notice of the book which it deserves but if you could spare it again in the course of a month or six weeks, I could give it into the hands of Mr. Brande or you could do so with much better effect and I have no doubt he would be glad of the opportunity of making it known I have been and am still so very busy that I have only looked slightly over the volume and I am sorry that in addition to these reasons I have to add the paucity of my knowledge also has prevented me from enjoying many of the good things contained in it.

I am Sir
with great Respect
Your Obd. Humble Servt.
M. FARADAY.

[1] Alexandre Marcet (1770–1822), like G. de la Rive, was an emigré during the French Revolution. He also obtained his medical degree at Edinburgh. His wife, Jane (1769–1858), wrote popular books on science, one of which had considerable influence on Faraday when he first became interested in chemistry. See *LPW*, 19ff.

[2] I have been unable to identify this volume. It is not by Marcet for it does not appear in the printed catalogue of the British Museum. From the context, it would seem to be a collection of papers, most probably on medicine, which formed the first volume of either a new journal or of a multi-volume collaborative work.

49   R. PHILLIPS to M. FARADAY, 4 September 1821
[*R.I., previously unpublished*]

Primrose,
4 Sept [postmarked 1821]

MY DEAR FARADAY —

I have this day read the Electromagnetic paper,[1] & I need hardly say that it has my entire approval, being exactly the thing I wanted. I confess however that I do feel no little regret that I should have been the cause of so much trouble & annoyance to you — I did not suppose that this w^d have been the case, or I w^d not have proposed the undertaking to you, much as I am pleased with the execution of it -- I am not in the least "*frightened*" with what you call the '*mass of matter*', especially after the specimen which you have given — that specimen I wish had been longer, but that is of secondary consequence — I shall take all pains to keep the name private, but should not have the slightest objection to make it known when you wish — *tout au contraire* — the sooner the better. Send to the engraver to wait upon you for the plate — he is a civil but rather a stupid dog — his name is Shury [reading doubtful] Charterhouse House Street [*sic*], Charterhouse Square — Has not Herapath's[2] brother sent an [illeg.] of a balance — ? What like is it — ? If not good let him remain till I return which will be in about 3 weeks — With best respects to Mrs Faraday

I remain [reading doubtful], dear F.
Yours ever truly
R. PHILLIPS

[1] See Faraday's 'Historical Sketch of Electromagnetism,' *AOP*, n.s., 2 (1821), 195, 274.
[2] William Herapath (1796–1867), Professor of chemistry and toxicology at the Bristol School of Medicine. For the 'balance', see W. Herapath, 'Description of a new balance,' *AOP*, n.s., 2 (1821), 291.

50   M. FARADAY to G. DE LA RIVE, 12 September 1821
[*Bibliothèque publique et universitaire de Genève, ms. 2311, f. 61–2, B.J. 1, 354*]

Royal Institution
Sept. 12th, 1821.

MY DEAR SIR

I was extremely gratified the other day on receiving your very kind letter and also you beautifull [*sic*] little apparatus.[1] I owe you many thanks for them and have been using the latter I hope you will say with some effect I have not seen Mr. Prevost[2] so have not heard any news of your delightful place except what your letter contains but I trust all is well

I am much flattered and encouraged to go on by your good opinion of what little things I have been able to do in science and especially as regards the chlorides of carbon I put a copy of my paper on them into the hands of Dr. Ure[3] for you some time since He intended to visit Geneva & I trust long ere this you will have seen him and the paper. You will probably have seen since that was printed that Mr. Phillips[4] and myself have developed a new chloride of carbon so that now there are three of these interesting bodies and I anxiously look for a fourth A short account is in the Annals of Philosophy Aug. 1821[5] which I presume you have seen I expect in a few days to have a copy of the paper to send you. In saying this I may express how much I should be gratified if you could and would point out a way whereby I may send you such or any other papers in the quickest & safest manner. Can I do it by [illeg.] & Wurtz the Booksellers or how? For I am so much flattered by your kindness that I shall always intrude my papers on to it if I may be allowed. I have not seen M Prevost or M Macaire.[6]

Sir H Davys paper[7] is not yet printed and I hardly know what it is for Sir H. left town for the country almost before his ideas were put into order on the subject on which he was working

You partly reproach us here with not sufficiently esteeming Amperes expts on Electro-magnetism Allow me to extenuate our opinion a little on this point. With regard to the experiments I hope and trust that due weight is allowed to them but these you know are few and theory makes up the great part of what M Ampere has published and theory in a great many points unsupported by experiments when they ought to have been adduced At the same time M Amperes experiments are excellent & his theory ingenious and for myself I had thought very little about it before your letter came simply because being naturally sceptical on philosophical theories I thought there was a great want [reading doubtful] of experimental evidence.

Since then however I have engaged on the subject and have a paper in our Institution Journal[8] which will appear in a week or two and that will as it contains experiment be immediately applied by M Ampere in support of his theory much more decidedly than it is by myself. I intend to enclose a copy of it to you with the other & only want the means of sending it.

I find that all the usual attractions and repulsions of the Magnetic needle by the conjunctive wire are deceptions the motions being not attractions etc or repulsions nor the result of any attractive or repulsive forces but the results of a force in the wire which instead of bringing the pole of the needle nearer to or farther from the wire endeavours to make it move round it in a never ending circle and motion whilst the battery remains in action I have succeeded not only in shewing the existence of this motion theoretically but experimentally and have been able to make the wire revolve round a magnetic pole or a magnetic pole round the wire at pleasure The law of revolution and to which all the other motions of the needle and wire are reducible is simple and beautiful Conceive a portion of connecting wire[9] north and south the north end being attached to the positive pole of a battery the south to the negative. A north Magnetic pole would then pass round it continually in the apparent direction of the sun, from east to west above & from west to east below Reverse the connections with the battery & the motion of the pole is reversed Or if the south pole be made to revolve the motions will be in the opposite directions as with the North pole If the wire be made to revolve round the pole the motions a [tear in ms.] according to those mentioned. In the apparatus I used there were but two plates and the direction of the motions were of course the reverse of those with a battery of several pair of plates and which are given above Now I have been able experimentally to trace this motion into its various forms as exhibited by Amperes helix [reading doubtful] etc & in all cases to shew that the attractions & repulsions are only appearances due to this circulation of the pole, to shew that dissimilar poles repel as well as attract and that similar poles attract as well as repel and to make I think the analogy between the helix & common bar magnet far stronger than before But yet I am by no means decided that there are currents of electricity in the common magnet. I have no doubt that electricity puts the circles of the helices into the same states as those circles are in that may be conceived in the bar magnet but I am not certain that this state is directly dependant on the electricity, or that it cannot be produced by other agencies and therefore until the presence of Electrical currents be proved in the magnet by other than magnetical effects I shall remain in doubt about Amperes theory.

I have not room here to describe my results more particularly to you but you shall have them as soon as I can possibly send them and I hope they will meet your approbation Allow me to say how much I am indebted to your little ring apparatus for information as I went on and also to say that I have as well by that as by other means been enabled to repeat and confirm an experiment of Amperes that had been doubted by great men here namely the direction of a curve by the magnetism of the earth

Wishing you all health & happiness & waiting for news from you

I am My dear Sir
Your Very Oblgd & grateful
M. FARADAY

[1] G. de la Rive, 'Notice sur quelques expériences électro-magnétiques,' *BU*, 16 (1821), 201.
[2] Probably Jean Louis Prévost (1790–1850) who worked on electricity and its role in physiology.
[3] Andrew Ure (1778–1857), British chemist.
[4] Faraday's friend, Richard Phillips.
[5] 'On two new compounds of chlorine and carbon, and on a new compound of iodine, carbon and hydrogen,' *AOP*, n.s., 2 (1821), 104.
[6] Isaac François Macaire (1796–1869), Honorary Professor at the Académie de Genève, collaborator of F. Marcet in some of his biochemical works.

[7] Probably H. Davy, 'Further researches on the magnetic phenomena produced by electricity; with some new experiments on the properties of electrified bodies in their relations to conducting powers and temperature,' *PT* (1821), 425.
[8] 'On some new electro-magnetical motions, and on the theory of magnetism,' *QJS*, 12 (1822), 74.
[9] 'parallel to the axis of the earth' crossed out in the manuscript.

51   M. FARADAY to J. STODART, 8 October 1821
[*B.J. 1, 339ff*]

Royal Institution,
Monday, October 8, 1821.

MY DEAR SIR,

I hear every day more and more of those sounds, which, though only whispers to me, are I suspect spoken aloud amongst scientific men,[1] and which, as they in part affect my honour and honesty, I am anxious to do away with, or at least to prove erroneous in those parts which are dishonourable to me. You know perfectly well what distress the very unexpected reception of my paper on magnetism in public has caused me, and you will not therefore be surprised at my anxiety to get out of it, though I give trouble to you and other of my friends in doing so.

If I understand aright, I am charged, (1) with not acknowledging the information I received in assisting Sir H. Davy in his experiments on this subject; (2) with concealing the theory and views of Dr. Wollaston; (3) with taking the subject whilst Dr. Wollaston was at work on it; and (4) with dishonourably taking Dr. Wollaston's thoughts, and pursuing them, without acknowledgement, to the results I have brought out.

There is something degrading about the whole of these charges; and were the *last* of them true, I feel that I could not remain on the terms I now stand at with you or any scientific person. Nor can I, indeed, bear to remain even suspected of such a thing. My love for scientific reputation is not yet so high as to induce me to obtain it at the expense of honour, and my anxiety to clear away this stigma is such that I do not hesitate to trouble you even beyond what you may be willing to do for me.

I want you, my dear Sir, to procure me an interview with Dr. Wollaston on his return to town; and I wish for this not only to apologise to him if I have unintentionally done him wrong, but to justify myself from the suspicions that are wrongly raised against me. I feel that Dr. Wollaston is so very far above me that even if he does feel himself wronged, he may not permit himself to think it is of any importance, and may therefore think it unnecessary to allow anything to pass on the subject. But, in that case, I appeal to Dr. Wollaston on my own account. His character and talents have raised him to be a patron and protector of science. All men look to his opinion and judgment with respect. If therefore an impression has gone abroad that I have done him an injustice, surely he will listen to my vindication, if not for his own or even my sake, yet for the sake of that situation in which he stands in the scientific world. I am but a young man, and without a name, and it probably does not matter much to science what becomes of me; but if by any circumstances I am subjected to unjust suspicions, it becomes no one more than him who may be said to preside over the equity of science, to assist in liberating me from them.

With regard to the first charge, I have spoken to Sir H. Davy, and I hope and believe he is satisfied.[2] I wished to apply to him, but knew not where he was till the paper was printed, and immediately I did know I sent him a rough copy of it. How much I regret the haste which made me print the paper in the last number of the Journal, is known to Sir H. Davy and to you.

With regard to the second charge, I have to say that I should have been proud to have put into my paper in a more distinct manner what I knew of Dr. Wollaston's theory and experiments; but that I was afraid to attach to it anything which Dr. Wollaston had not published or authorised. At the same time I must state, that all I knew was what is published in the "Journal of Science," vol. x. p. 363,[3] and that Dr. Wollaston expected to make a wire revolve on its own axis; but I did not see the apparatus of Dr. Wollaston, or the experiment he made at the Royal Institution, or any made elsewhere.

As to the third charge, I had not the slightest notion that Dr. Wollaston was at work, or intended to work, on the subject. It is now near seven months, I believe, since he was at the Royal Institution making an experiment, and I did not know that he intended to pursue it further. If I had thought so I should never have attempted anything on the subject.

The fourth charge is not true. I had assisted Sir H. Davy in nearly all his experiments, and thus had my mind prepared for the subject; but the immediate cause of my making the experiments detailed in my paper was the writing of the historical sketch of electro-magnetism that has appeared in the last two numbers of the "Annals of Philosophy."[4] It was in verifying the positions that I continually had to make mention of in that sketch, that I was led, as described in the commencement of my paper, to ascertain the revolution of the pole round the wire; and then, and then only, Dr. Wollaston's theory came to my mind. I should have been proud and happy here to have mentioned Dr. Wollaston's experiment of the rotation of the wire on its own axis (the only experiment I had heard of), but it did not succeed with me, or Dr. Wollaston's theory as stated in our Journal. But Dr. Wollaston had not published or avowed either, and I judged (perhaps wrongly) that I had no right in that case to mention it.

All I ask is to be liberated from the dishonour unjustly attached to me in these charges. I am anxious to apologise to Dr. Wollaston, in any way that I can, for not having mentioned his theory and experiments, if I may be permitted. I need not again urge reasons why Dr. Wollaston should hear me, or receive into his consideration those circumstances which witness for me in this affair that I have erred innocently. But I hope everything through your kindness. Anxiously waiting to hear from you.

I am, dear Sir,

your very obliged and faithful

'M. FARADAY.'

---

[1] Faraday was accused of having stolen Wollaston's ideas on the possibility of electromagnetic rotation. See *LPW*, 152ff. Though I have not seen the manuscript of this letter, it is of sufficient importance to warrant publishing it here.

[2] Davy kept the issue alive, however, by speaking at the Royal Society in 1823 in such a way as to give the impression that he doubted Faraday's integrity in this matter.

[3] Anon., 'On the Connexion of Electric and Magnetic Phenomena,' *QJS*, 10 (1820–1), 363. The article was written by W. T. Brande and reported on Wollaston's ideas.

[4] 'Historical Sketch of Electro-magnetism,' *AOP*, n.s., 2 (1821).

---

52 M. FARADAY to W. H. WOLLASTON, 30 October 1821

[*B.J. 1, 343*]

October 30, 1821

SIR,

I am urged by strong motives respectfully to request your attention for a few moments. The latter end of last month I wrote a paper on electromagnetism, which I left in the hands of the printer of the "Quarterly Journal," and went into the country. On returning home the beginning of this month, I heard from two or three quarters that it was considered I had not behaved honourably in that paper; and that the wrong I had done was done to you. I immediately wished and endeavoured to see you, but was prevented by the advice of my friends, and am only now at liberty to pursue the plan I intended to have taken at first.

If I have done anyone wrong, it was quite unintentional, and the charge of behaving dishonourably is not true. I am bold enough, Sir, to beg the favour of a few minutes' conversation with you on this subject, simply for these reasons – that I can clear myself – that I owe obligations to you – that I respect you – that I am anxious to escape from unfounded impressions against me – and if I have done any wrong that I may apologise for it.

I do not think, Sir, that you would regret allowing me this privilege; for, satisfied in my own mind of the simplicity and purity of my motives in writing that paper, I feel that I should satisfy you; and you would have the pleasure of freeing me from an embarrassment I do not deserve to lay under. Nevertheless if for any reasons you do not consider it necessary to permit it, I hope I shall not further have increased any unpleasant feeling towards me in your mind.

I have very much simplified and diminished in size the rotating apparatus, so as to enclose it in a tube. I should be proud if I may be allowed, as a mark of strong and sincere respect, to present one for your acceptance. I am almost afraid to make this request, not because I know of the slightest reason which renders it improper, but because of the uncertain and indefinite form of the rumours which have come about me. But I trust, Sir, that I shall not injure myself with you by adopting the simplest and most direct means of clearing up a misunderstanding that has arisen against me; but that what I do with sincerity you will receive favourably.

I am, Sir, with great respect,

your obedient, humble servant,
M. FARADAY.

53 W. H. WOLLASTON to M. FARADAY, 1 November 1821
[*B.J. 1, 344*]

November 1, 1821

SIR,

You seem to me to labour under some misapprehension of the strength of my feelings upon the subject to which you allude.

As to the opinions which others may have of your conduct, that is your concern, not mine; and if you fully acquit yourself of making any incorrect use of the suggestions of others, it seems to me that you have no occasion to concern yourself much about the matter. But if you are desirous of any conversation with me, and could with convenience call to-morrow morning, between ten o'clock and half-past ten, you will be sure to find me.

Ever your most obedient

W. H. WOLLASTON.

I name that hour because I shall have occasion to leave home before eleven.

54 M. FARADAY to G. DE LA RIVE, 16 November 1821
[*Bibliothèque publique et universitaire de Genève, ms. 2311, f. 63–4, B.J. 1, 357ff*]

R Institution
Novr. 16, 1821.

DEAR SIR

Herewith you will receive copies of my papers which I mentioned in a letter I sent to you per post a month or two ago[1] and which I hope you will do me the favour to accept. I also send in this packet a little apparatus I have made to illustrate the rotatory motion on a small scale The rod below is soft iron and consequently can have its inner end made north or south at pleasure by contact of the external end with one of the poles of a magnet To make the apparatus act it is to be held upright with the iron pin downwards the north or south pole of a magnet to be placed in contact with the external end of the iron pin and then the wires of a voltaic combination connected one with the upper platinum wire the other with the lower pin or magnet. the wire within will then rotate if the apparatus is in order in which state I hope it will reach you. Good contacts are required in these experiments.

Now let me know what is doing with you, for I long for news from your southern parts An Italian gentleman who is on his return home will give this packet to you – at least I hope so for I want it to reach you safe – I am excessively busy too much so at present to try my hand at any thing more or even to continue this letter many lines further but I hope soon to have a little news on steel to send you

I am my Dear Sir As Ever

Your Very Obliged and faithful
M. FARADAY.

A single pair of plates 2 or 3 inches square or 4 inches square is quite large enough for the apparatus –

Yours Ever,
M.F.

¹ See Letter 50.

55   M. FARADAY to A. MARCET, 15 January 1822
[*R.I., previously unpublished*]

Royal Institution,
Tuesday Jany 15th 1822.

SIR

I am very much obliged indeed by your kindness in permitting me a perusal of M Berzelius' letter and hasten to return it to you with many thanks. It does not contain many of M Berzelius' own ideas of electromagnetism but consists rather of observations on M. Ampere's theory. I cannot gather from it whether M Berzelius retains the same opinion that he gave in his letter to M Berthollet and which was published in the Annales de Chimie[1] He still speaks of an alternation of poles and refers to the number he formerly gave of two pair but does not say that they are sufficient to explain the phenomena. It appears to me that no succession of poles round the wire however numerous will account for the phenomena indeed the fact of rotation is decidely [*sic*] against such a supposition: but even the phenomena mentioned by Oersted cannot be explained by it for take any particular point on the surface of the wire however small and it may be made apparently either to attract or repel either one pole or the other of a magnetic needle merely by changing the position of the needle to the wire

With regard to the theory of M Ampere it is but justice to that philosopher to say that M Berzelius does not seem to have an exact conception of it, or at least of the position of the currents which it supposes. In the diagram of the earth M Berzelius has assumed one small current in the plane of the magnetic equator M Ampere assumes a current or currents parallel to the equator but not I believe confined to it If I understand him right he assumes many currents in various directions but the general tendency is to a direction round the earth & parallel to the equator a supposition which admits of having terrestrial currents even up to the pole & yet parallel to the equator – In the Magnet M Ampere has not yet decided whether he shall put the currents concentric to each other and having the axis of the magnet for their axis or whether they shall be placed round each atom of matter the axis of all the currents being then however parallel to each other & to the axis of the magnet

All the objections urged by M Berzelius to M Ampere's theory founded on the difficulty of supposing an electromotive force in steel & nickel or currents in the magnet &c. &c. &c. remain with full force and though M Ampere seems very well satisfied with his theory in its present state yet certainly much more must be done with it and much more proved by experiment for it before a cautious philosopher will receive it into his stock of knowledge or think it at all approaching to invulnerable.

I am Sir
Your Oblgd & faithful Servant
M. FARADAY.

[1] J. J. Berzelius, 'Lettre à M. Berthollet sur l'état magnétique des corps qui transmettent un courant d'électricité,' *AC*, 16 (1821), 113.

56   M. FARADAY to A.-M. AMPÈRE, 2 February 1822[1]

[Staatsbibliothek, Marburg/Lahn (Stiftung Preussischer Kulturbesitz), acc. Darm-staedter, 'Trans. of the Newcomen Society', 3 (1922–3), 119]

Royal Institution,
Feby 2nd. 1821.

SIR

I am very much flattered by the letter you did me the honor to send me and by the present of the Exposé[1] for which I beg leave to return you my best thanks Having occasion to write to M Hachette[2] I have promised to accompany my letter to him by this to you and venture a few observations on you [*sic*] beautiful experiment of the rotation of the magnet[3] &c &c. I repeated the experiment the day after I received your letter and using Hare's calorimoter[4] [*sic*] an instrument equivalent to a very large pair of plates instantly obtained the revolution I found it convenient to cement a small piece of glass tube on the upper pole of the magnet which forming a cup to receive the mercury made contact very easy without the chance of touching the solid parts of the arrangement.

You mention your opinion that this experiment will be competent to decide the question whether the currents of electricity assumed by your theory exist round the axis of the magnet or round each particle from which I gather that the view you take of it differs from the one I at present have, since to me it seems a modification of the revolution of a wire round a pole. I presume much in differing from yourself on this subject and more in stating the differences to *you* but I do not hesitate a moment in concluding that in the true spirit of philosophy you are anxious to hear (or at least willing) even the doubts of one young in the subject if there be the smallest possibility that they will either correct or confirm previous views.

The rotation of the magnet seems to me to take place in consequence of the different particles of which it is composed being put into the same state by the passing current of electricity as the wire of communication between the voltaic poles, and the relative position of the magnetic pole to them.

Thus the little arrows may represent the progress of the electricity; then any line of particles parallel to them except that line which passes as an axis through the pole (represented by a dot) will be in the situation of the revolving wire and will endeavour to revolve round the pole and as all the lines act in the same direction or tend to go one way round the pole the whole magnet revolves. That this is the way in which the magnet revolves is I think evident from the consideration above; from the revolution being in the same direction as with the wire and from the following analysis of the experiment I took a piece of 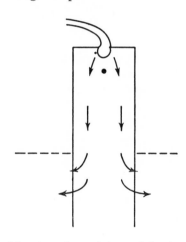 copper wire similar in form to the magnet and having floated it upright in mercury placed a little cap on the top to contain a globule of mercury and then connected the voltaic poles just as they were with the magnet then placing the pole of a strong magnet beneath the cup containing the mercury. it when exactly in a line with the axis of the wire made it rotate slowly on its own axis In this experiment it appears to me that every thing was in the same state as in the former experiment except that the pole was removed out of the revolving mass but preserved in the line of its axis and the rotation of the wire on its own axis seems to me an effect produced exactly in the same manner as the rotation of the magnet on its axis.

I have been thus diffuse in giving my view of the rotation because if it be the true one I do not see how the experiment determines the position of the currents

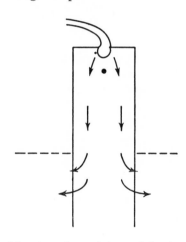

131

more than the one in which a wire rotates round a pole: perhaps however you have the same view of it but see explanations I do not. I regret that my deficiency in mathematical knowledge makes me dull in comprehending these subjects. I am naturally sceptical in the matter of theories and therefore you must not be angry with me for not admitting the one you have advanced immediately Its ingenuity and applications are astonishing and exact, but I cannot comprehend how the currents are produced and particularly if they be supposed to exist round each atom or particle and I wait for further proofs of their existence before I finally admit them. Permit me to express my respect for your high philosophical character and to apologise for thus intruding on your time

I am Sir

Your Obliged & Humble Servant

M. FARADAY

[1] There are considerable difficulties in determining the date of this letter. It cannot be 1821 for Ampère had not discovered the rotation of a current-carrying magnet about its own axis until December of 1821 and it is hardly likely that Faraday would have mistaken the month in which he wrote. As in Letters 36 and 40, there is the strong possibility that Faraday continued to use the previous year in his letters at the beginning of 1821. Thus, I have dated the letter 1822. *But*, Ampère's *Exposé méthodique des phénomènes électro-dynamiques* was not published until 1823 and this is the only *Exposé* Ampère ever wrote. I cannot believe that Faraday waited two years after Ampère's publication (see below) of the fact of the rotation of a magnet on its own axis – an effect which he had sought for in vain – before writing to Ampère about it. Perhaps Ampère sent Faraday a manuscript of his *Exposé*. This is the only suggestion I can make to escape the dilemma.

[2] Jean Nicolas Pierre Hachette (1769–1834) was a friend that Faraday had made on his tour with Davy. He was to be the source of considerable chagrin to Faraday in 1831 when he published Faraday's account of the discovery of electromagnetic induction. See *LPW*, 201ff. and Letter 124.

[3] A.-M. Ampère, 'Expériences relatives aux nouveaux phénomènes électro-dynamiques obtenus au mois de décembre 1821,' *AC*, 20 (1822), 60.

[4] The calorimotor was a voltaic cell using very large plates and, thus, producing large currents. See Robert Hare, 'A new theory of Galvanism, supported by some experiments and observations made by means of the Calorimotor, a new galvanic instrument,' *AJS*, 1 (1818), 413.

57 P. BARLOW to M. FARADAY, 14 March 1822

[*R.I., previously unpublished*]

Roy[l] Art[ry] Acad[y],

March 14th 1822

DEAR SIR

You will be pleased to hear how well I have succeeded in the construction of my new galvanic apparatus, which in the present form does every thing I can wish. I have repeated all your very interesting rotating experiments, and have added one very curious one, which although it throws no new light on the subject is very interesting in the exhibition. I enclose you a drawing of the machine

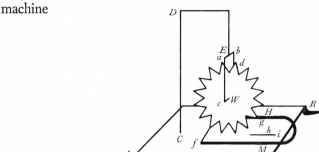

AB is a piece of wood, *CD* a stout brass or copper wire; *abcd* a rectangle of smaller wire soldered at *E*; *W* is a light pointed copper wheel, the lower teeth of which are slightly immersed in the receiver of mercury *fg*: *hi* is a channel of mercury merely for making the contact and *HM* a pretty strong horse shoe magnet, which of course may be supplied by two bar magnets. The mercury being now poured into the receiver and the contact made at *D* and at *i*; the wheel begins to rotate, with an astonishing velocity, and thus exhibits a very pretty appearance –

I have some other experiments in progress which if they succeed to my mind I will inform you of; and when I have got through these I shall proceed to examine the effects with reference to their mathematical laws[1] in which I have some hopes of success. I have repeated the copper cylinder experiment which you showed me when I had the pleasure of seeing you and found it to answer admirably.[2]

I hope you and Mrs Faraday will bear in mind your promised visit to Woolwich during the Easter recess – pray make my compliments to Mrs F, and believe me

Dear Sir yours
very Truly
P. BARLOW

P.S. I enclose you a little of the powder I mentioned when I saw you; if you can find an opportunity of examining it I should be glad to know the result for the satisfaction of my assistant who is a very ingenious fellow (note by Faraday)

Is sulphate of copper with a little charcoal – is soluble in water (nearly all of it.)

---

[1] See Peter Barlow, 'Account of a new series of Electro-magnetic Experiments, with observations on the mathematical Laws of Electro-magnetism,' *EPJ*, 8 (1823), 368.
[2] The only experiment described by Faraday that uses anything resembling a copper cylinder is to be found in Vol. 1, 46. The entries in the Diary are very sparse for this period.

58 M. Faraday to A.-M. Ampère, 3 September 1822[1]

(Arch. de l'Académie des Sciences, Paris, CGA, 3, 928]

R.I.
Septr 3, 1822

Sir

I have been much flattered and gratified by the honor you have done me in your repeated communications and particularly by your last important letter for which I have nothing I can offer as a return but my best acknowledgements I have been *tempted* by favourable opportunities to trespass on your kindness by a correspondence which though it must occupy time to you of great value brings you nothing in return. Anxious as I am to hear from time to time of the progress you make in a branch of science that owes so much to you yet I cannot help but feel that I am the unworthy gainer and you the loser by a correspondence between us, and that though I receive so much I contribute nothing to it. Nevertheless I am still encouraged to write and acknowledge your kindness.

I have but just returned from the country or I should before have returned my earnest thanks for the memoirs I have received through the hands of Mr. Underwood and Mr: Dockray[2] I have as yet only read them hastily and have to reperuse them as well as your last excellent letter more carefully and steadily I am unfortunate in a want of mathematical knowledge and the power of entering with facility into abstract reasoning I am obliged to feel my way by facts closely placed together so that it often happens I am left behind in the progress of a branch of science not merely from the want of attention but from the incapability I lay under of following it notwithstanding all my exertions. It is just now so I am ashamed to say with your refined researches in electro-magnetism or electrodynamics On reading your papers and letters, I have no difficulty in following the reasoning, but still at last I seem to want something more on which to steady the conclusions I fancy the habit I got into of attending too closely to experiment has somewhat fettered my powers of reasoning and chains me down and I cannot help now and then comparing myself to a timid ignorant navigator who though he might boldly and safely steer across a bay or an ocean by the aid of a compass which in its action and principles is infallible is afraid to leave sight of the shore because he understands not the power of the instrument that is to guide him – With regard to electromagnetism also feeling my insufficiency to reason as you do, I am afraid to receive at once the conclusions you come to (though I am strongly tempted by their simplicity & beauty to adopt them) and the more so because I have seen the judgements of such men as Berzelius Prechtel[3] etc. etc. stumble over this subject. Both these philosophers I believe and others also have given theories of electro-magnetism which they stated would account not only for known facts but even serve to predict such as were not then known and yet when the new facts came (rotation

134

for instance), the theories fell to pieces before them These instances are sufficient to warn such feeble spirits as myself and will serve as my apology to you
for not at once adopting your conclusions. I delay not because I think them
hasty or erroneous but because I want some facts to help me on.

I cannot help thinking there is an immense mine of experimental matter
ready to be opened and such matter as would at once carry conviction of the
truth with it. I do not think I shall have to wait long for it though I have no
idea where it should come from except from you – I am not aware of the experiment of M de La Rive to which you refer but shall see it soon I dare say in the
Bibliothèque universelle.

Allow me to beg your acceptance of the inclosed paper as a very small mark
of respect and estime [*sic*] for one who is proud to sign himself your obliged
and humble Correspondant and Servant.

M. F A R A D A Y.

[1] See *CGA*, 2, 586 for Ampère's letter to Faraday.
[2] T. R. Underwood (1772–1835) was a geologist who spent a good deal of time in France.
I am unable to identify Dockray.
[3] Johann Joseph Prechtl (1778–1854). See *LPW*, 140.

59 G. D E L A R I V E to M. F A R A D A Y, 24 September 1822
[*I.E.E., previously unpublished*]

Geneve
24th 7bre 1822

D E A R S I R

I am quite ashamed for having been such a long time without answering to
your kind letters of the last autumn, and without thanking you for the charming
apparatus which you sent to me by an Italian Gentleman. I was always waiting
till I could send to you some piece of scientific news worth your attention, and
at last I take the pen without having obtained what I wished for. – You have
perhaps seen in the *Annales de Chimie* in a letter to Mr. Arago that I had made
some experiments to ascertain whether it was possible or not to prove by
experiment the existence of Galvanic currents at the Surface of the Earth going
from East to West according to Mr Ampère's Theory:[1] For that purpose I
tried to analyse the Rectangle contrived by Mr A. which turning around a
vertical axis, and placed in *the Galvanic* Current, always took a diversion
perpendicular to the Magnetic Needle. – I did Show that the diversion did not
depend from the Inferior horizontal branch. as Mr A. believed, but that it was
highly probable that the Rectangle took its direction from the Influence of the
two vertical branches. – My Eldest Son[2] who is [a] very active labourer [in] that
part of the Science, undertook to make a Complete analysis of that Rectangle,
and contrived for that purpose an apparatus by means of which it was possible
to take away the one after the other any of its branches, and even three at a time,

and that without troubling the diversion of the Current – (That apparatus is described in a paper which shall be published in the *Biblioth. universelle* and of which I shall send you a Copy by the first opportunity.)[3] – By means of that apparatus he proved that the horizontal branches were of no use in the production of the Phenomenon of diversion, and that the vertical ones were only necessary for that production. – He found afterwards that a single vertical wire, which may turn around a vertical axis, when placed in the Galvanic Current, always forces itself to *the East* if the Current is *descendent*, and always to *the West* if the Current is *ascendent*. This experiment as you may see is quite concordant with your views – By means of the same apparatus he has Shown that in the *turning circle* of Mr Ampere the vertical Branches are of no use whatever, the force produced in the one being destroyed by the equal adversary force produced in the other, but that the whole Phenomenon is depending on the horizontal part of the apparatus, and is the consequence of what you had observed with regard to the horizontal motion of a wire when it receives a Galvanic Current – If such a wire is fixed by one of its extremities it is acted on by parallel forces, and it turns round the point to which it is fixed, because, as you have Shown, these parallel forces act in every position while the wire remaines horizontal and carries the Galvanic Current. Now in Mr Ampere's Apparatus you have two (or more) horizontal wires, and as the Galvanic Current [illeg.] in the middle, goes on the right and left side in an opposite direction, of course the parallel forces act on each side of the point of suspension in a direction proper to make the wire turn around the point and thus is produced the rotary motion – These forces are by means of the apparatus put beyond any doubt whatever. – Mr Ampere who came to Geneva this summer has been convinced of their truth and accordingly he has made some alterations to his former supposition, He thinks always that our Globe is surrounded by Galvanic Currents going from East to west, but that their principal energy is at the Magnetic Equator, with that supposition, he may explain pretty well the above mentioned facts. – While Mr Ampere was at Geneve he made in my Laboratory two new Experiments.[4] – Having a Strong disposition to believe that a Repulsion was taking place in all the parts of a Galvanic Current he contrived to demonstrate that repulsion by Experiment. – He took a dish of Earthenware separated in two parts by a piece of glass, the two semicircular portions were filled with Mercury; then he took a piece of wire surrounded with Silk, a part of that wire was parallel to the Glass, and floating on Mercury, the wire passed afterwards on the other side of the glass and had [reading doubtful] another leg parallel to the first, also on the Mercury, the extremities of each leg were in a Metallic contact with the quick Silver drawing as shown on the [illeg.]+and–were put in each Semicircular portions of the dish the wire was sent back to the opposite side – This experiment has some analogy with yours in which there was a loss of weight, with the difference, that in this the Current is both in Mercury and in the wire, in an horizontal direction, while in yours it is horizontal in the Quick silver and vertical in the wire ————————

Be kind enough Dear sir as to write to me if you have some Scientific news, you will see Dr. Marcet who is coming to Geneva if you had some papers of yours

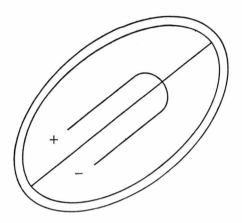

to send to me I should be very much obliged to you – At any time if you have such papers be good enough as to send them to Messrs. *Morris and* [*illeg.*] ———— in the City They will forward them to Geneva – Believe me Dear Sir

Yours for ever
G. DELA RIVE

I have always forgot to thank you for the honorable mention you had made of my little floating apparatus.

The other experiment Mr Ampere made, is this – He placed a piece of Copper very near a strong galvanic current without being in contact with it, and he found that when the current was being intense, the piece of Copper was through influence, made Magnetic, so that it was attracted or repulsed by a Magnet; as soon as the Galvanic Current ceased, the Magnetic property disappeared.[5]

You may do what you please of the facts contained in this letter.

[1] G. de la Rive, 'Lettre du Professeur de la Rive à M. Arago, sur de nouvelles expériences relatives aux actions des courans galvaniques,' *AC*, 20 (1822), 269.

[2] Auguste de la Rive (1801–73) was a good friend of Faraday's. He did important work in electrochemistry and on electrical theory in general.

[3] A. de la Rive, 'Mémoire sur l'action qu'exerce le globe terrestre sur une portion mobile du circuit voltaïque,' *BU*, 21 (1822), 29.

[4] See the article by A. de la Rive, cited above.

[5] Ampère was later to urge this experiment as his claim to the discovery of electromagnetic induction.

[*Bibliothèque publique et universitaire de Genève, ms. 2311, f. 65–6, previously un-published*]

Royal Institution
Octr 9th 1822

MY DEAR SIR

I received your kind letter on Saturday and finding that Dr. Marcet is even now preparing to leave London I am anxious to write to you by him although I have time only for a short letter for Dr. M. requests to have it immediately. I was half afraid you had forgotten me and then again I was half in hopes that you were so busy in the pursuit of science that you had not time to think of me. I am glad indeed on both accounts to find the latter true and am very anxious to see the full account of your experiments I am delighted with them not only because they correct opinions which were before generally received and make them more in accordance with natural phenomena but also because they serve as a vindication to myself for the doubts or rather for the reserve I have entertained respecting M Ampere's theory in its fullest extent Its beauty I admire but I have been unwilling to admit it into my own mind to a rank with those theories in other branches of physical science which are accompanied continually by experimental proofs because though it accords pretty well with most if not all the phenomena yet there are many parts in it that seem to me to be mere assumption – I expressed not many days since to M Ampere my persuasion that there were an immense number of facts still to be made out between the place to which actual experiment has brought us and the extent of his theory and your experiments come very opportunely to strengthen that persuasion

I have really been ashamed sometimes of my difficulty in receiving evidence urged forward in support of opinions on electro magnetism but when I confess my want of mathematical knowledge and see mathematicians themselves differing about the validity of the arguments used it will serve as my apology for waiting for experiment

M Amperes experiments which you mention are I think very important especially that of the production of magnetism in a piece of copper by mere vicinity to a voltaic circuit without actual connection with it I am glad to find M. Ampere has modified the view he took of my little expt of apparent loss of weight and that his present opinion coincides so nearly with mine I remember in my note on E Mag motions I stated the effect to be "equivalent to a diminution of the cohesive attraction of the mercury." I hope he will make out & support the idea of a repulsion in the whole length of the current.

I intend to send one of our papers on Steel by Dr. Marcet[1] and we beg your acceptance of it – I find on looking for it the paper on Electro Magnetical apparatus & the Note on new E. Mag. motions which I thought I had sent you but the name & dust on the outside makes me afraid I have never done so This makes me conclude I have not sent you the paper on the third Chloride of Carbon[2] by Mr. Phillips & myself and I therefore put it into the packet begging that you will receive them as marks of my anxiety to shew you respect.

You kindly mention that I may make what use of the facts you mention in your letter that I please Had I any thing to do with the *Journal of Science* etc I should gladly have availed myself of the liberty But I have nothing to do with it not even with the Miscellania now and I am anxious you should know this. There have been many things in the form or reviews observations etc. that have appeared in it wh[ich] were very adverse to my feelings and I am desirous that ther[e] should not be the least chance of your attributing any [of] the kind to me For the future do not consider me as having a[ny] thing [ms. torn] to do with any articles but such as have either my name or my initials to them.

I have not a particle of news to send you but I hope for some I am at present making a few expts on vapour with reference to the short paper of mine which you have probably seen in the Annales de Chimie and the observations by M Gay Lussac upon it[3] I have been surprised by his remark on the temperature of vapour from saline solutions & so have most of the chemists I have mentioned it to. However I find the point a nice one to determine experimentally but think I now have unexceptionable means. Now that I know how to send to you I dare say I shall often trouble you

> I am dear Sir With great respect
> Your Obedt & faithful
> M. FARADAY

[1] M. Faraday and J. Stodart, 'On the Alloys of Steel,' *PT* (1822), 253.
[2] M. Faraday and R. Phillips, 'On a new compound of Chlorine and Carbon,' *PT* (1821), 392.
[3] 'On the vapour of mercury at common temperatures,' *QJS*, 10 (1821), 354, translated into French and published in *AC*, 16 (1821), 77.

61 M. FARADAY to G. DE LA RIVE, 24 March 1823

[*Bibliothèque publique et universitaire de Genève, ms. 2311, f. 67–8, B.J. 1, 371ff*]

> Royal Institution
> March 24 1823.

MY DEAR SIR

Though it is now some time since I wrote to you yet the event connected with it is so fresh on my mind that it seems but a week or two ago – Dr. Marcet called on me not much more than a week before his death to say how glad he would be to take any parcel or letter in charge for you and I accordingly wrote a letter and put together such copies of my papers as I had by me and which you had not received that you might have them at his hands. Alas[1] *The Event.*

I do not know whether you have received or are likely to receive these things from the persons into whose care Dr. Marcets papers fell – I hope you will for I have not other copies of them and I am anxious they should be honored by being placed in your hands. But I thought I would write you by the post rather than not write at all. I wish & beg to express my best acknowledgements to M de la Rive your son who has honored me with a copy of his excellent memoire[2] – I hope for the sake of this new branch of science that he is pursuing it. That which he has done proves what he may do. I hope you will do me the kindness to speak of me to him in the best way you can for I am always anxious to obtain the good will and commendation of those who are themselves worthy of praise.

I have been at work lately and obtained results which I hope you will approve of – I have been interrupted twice in the course of experiments by explosions both in the course of 8 days One burnt my eyes the other cut them but I fortunately escaped with slight injury only in both cases and am now nearly well – During the winter I took the opportunity of examining the hydrate of chlorine and analysing it – the results which are not very important will appear in the next Number of the Quarterly Journal[3] over which I have no influence) Sir H. Davy on seeing my paper suggested to me to work with it under pressure and see what would happen by heat &c. Accordingly I enclosed it in a glass tube hermetically sealed, heated it obtained a change in the substance and a separation into two different fluids and upon further examination I found that the chlorine and water had separated from each other and the chlorine gas not being able to escape had condensed into the liquid form. To prove that it contained no water I dried some chlorine gas introduced it into a long tube condensed it & then cooled the tube and again obtained fluid chlorine Hence what is called chlorine gas is the vapour of a fluid

I have written a paper which has been read to the Royal Society[4] and to which the President did me the honor to attach a note pointing out the gene[ral][5] applicat[ion] and importance of this mode of pro[ducing] pressure [with] regard to the liquefaction of gases. He immediately [for]med liquid Muriatic acid by a similar means an[d pu]rsuing the experiments at his request I have since [ob]tained sulphurous acid – carbonic acid – sulp[hure]tted hydrogen – euchlorine – and nitrous oxide in the fluid state quite free from water – Some of these require great pressure for this purpose and I have had many explosions

I send you word of these results because I know your anxiety to hear of all that is new but do not mention them publicly (or at least the latter ones) until you hear of them either through the journals or by another letter from me or from other persons because Sir Humphry Davy has promised the results in a paper to the Royal Society for me and I know he wishe[s firs]t to have them *read there* After that they are at [your service.]

I expect [to be able to red]uce many other gases to the liquid form & promise
myself the pleasure of writing you about them. I hope you will honor me with a
letter soon

I am dear Sir
Very faithfully
Your Obliged Servant,
M. FARADAY.

1 Dr Marcet died before he could carry out this commission.
2 See Letter 59, fn. 3.
3 'On fluid Chlorine,' *QJS*, 15 (1823), 71.
4 'On the condensation of several gases into liquids,' *PT* (1823), 189.
5 There are a number of breaks in the photocopy of this letter.

62   M. FARADAY to T. HUXTABLE, 25 March 1823
[*B.J. 1, 373ff*]

Royal Institution,
March 25, 1823

DEAR HUXTABLE,

I met with another explosion on Saturday evening, which has again laid up
my eyes. It was from one of my tubes, and was so powerful as to drive the
pieces of glass like pistol-shot through a window. However, I am getting better,
and expect to see as well as ever in a few days. My eyes were filled with glass at
first.

When you see Magrath, who I hope is improving fast, tell him I intended
calling upon him, but my second accident has prevented me.

Yours ever,
M. FARADAY.

63   D. H. CONYBEARE to M. FARADAY, 4 April 1823[1]
[*I.E.E., previously unpublished*]

Brislington nr. Bristol
April. 4.

MY DEAR SIR

I take up my pen rather with the design of expressing my thanks for your
obliging attention to my enquiries than in the hope of being able to throw any
new light on the difficulties you suggest – & yet even at the risk which I feel
I shall incur of only expressing my own ignorance I shall venture a few words
on these also – but first permit me to say how flattering I feel the attentions to
wh. I have alluded, coming as they do from a person whose merits as
a discoverer I esteem of a very high order & whose reputation I am certain will
encrease [*sic*] almost with every experiment he makes –

When I consider how many lurking & unsuspected causes may interfere to prevent the success of an experiment I confess I am inclined to hesitate before I admit the absence of reaction in one of the cases you mention (namely when the wire was in the middle and the pole outside) as yet fully established – in the other case (when the pole is central) my own views w^d have led me to expect the result you found – yet from one circumstance you mention I doubt whether those views are not erroneous. I will first state what those views are –

I have always referred the phenomena to a circular electro Magnetic current revolving round the wire *only* – & tending to drive a particle of north polarity in one direction (say that of the apex of the apex [*sic*] of the black triangles in the accompanying diagram) & the part.^{le} of S. pol^y in the opposite direction (towards their base)

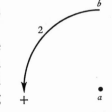

The revolution of the magnetic pole round the wire is a necessary corollary – because it is placed exactly in the same circumstances as the single particle above supposed – The revolution of the wire round the magnet I explain thus if a north polar particle +. fig. **2,** be brought within the sphere of this current it is as we have seen repelled from the apex of the triangle – and of course it equally repels that apex – hence if + be fixed & the wire movable, the wire will move in the direction from *a* to *b* – & as it is always confined at one end must necessarily move in a circle –

On this view there would be no tendency in the nature of the reaction to make the particle + rotate on its own axis – therefore the result is thus far exactly what I should have expected (for I consider the pole of a magnet as obeying the same law as a single polar particle).

You mention however having produced the rotation of a magnet on its own axis. I have overlooked in some way this experiment Where is it recorded?[2] Where [*sic*] the circumstances such as would be inconsistent with the above views?

With regard however to the case in which the wire was central it ought certainly according to this view to have rotated on its axis ——— & a priori it appears to me certain that (unless for some obstacle of an extraneous & accidental nature it would do so) – for I will reason thus

Suppose an apparatus were constructed with a great number of wires arranged so as to form a hollow cylinder moving on two spindles *Z* & *C* – connected with the Zinc & Copper ends of the battery & the north pole *N* of a magnet presented; there can I imagine be no doubt that from the action of the pole on each of these wires the cylinder would be made to rotate on its axis –

Now this being the case – suppose the diameter of the cylinder were reduced till all the wires were brought into contact & formed a close fasciculus I cannot conceive why the rotation should be destroyed by this change

Nor do I see how a single wire differs from such a fasciculus

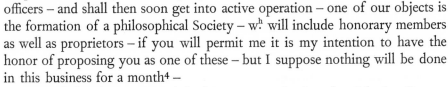

At any rate I think the phenomena might be greatly cleared up by trying first the effect of a cylinder thus composed the wires not being in contact – & afterwards a cylinder formed of a continuous sheet of metal[3] –

With regard to my own apparatus I am provoked not by its failure – (for one must be prepared in all new subjects to grope ones way & to learn as much from the failure as the success of experiments) but because I find it impossible to understand the cause of that failure –

I was much interested in the important information you communicate with regard to the liquifaction of Chlorine &c – you have rendered correct the blunder of a friend of mine who in beginning a course of Chemical experiments sent for a bottle of Carbonic acid –

Our institution at Bristol is now placed on a permane-[ent] [ms. torn] basis – the regulations proposed by the provisional Com[mittee] having been unanimously adopted on Monday last. On [the] 21. we meet to elect officers – and shall then soon get into active operation – one of our objects is the formation of a philosophical Society – w.h will include honorary members as well as proprietors – if you will permit me it is my intention to have the honor of proposing you as one of these – but I suppose nothing will be done in this business for a month[4] –

So much has been accomplished in your Institution that I look w.th very sanguine views to the acquisition of a similar instrument of science in our neighbourhood – had it existed twenty years earlier S.r H. Davy might perhaps remained amongst us – & the experiments w.h have illustrated your laboratory have immortalised ours –

We have expended our whole capital in our building but desire an annual income from subscription & we are also raising funds from donations to furnish our Museum with cabinets & to provide apparatus – on the latter head I shall be very desirous to consult with you as to the best & most economical forms of galvanic batteries &c – the younger institutions must always look up to the older for assistance & information – believe me My dear Sir

very truly y.rs
CONYBEARE

143

P.S. Should any thing bring you this way I shall have much pleasure in shewing you everything interesting in the way of science in this neighbourhood & in affording you introductions to the Iron works of Sth Wales – & shall have a bed at your service –

1 The letter can be dated with considerable confidence from the reference to the liquefaction of chlorine. Faraday's paper 'On fluid chlorine' was read to the Royal Society on 13 March 1823.
2 See Letter 56, fn. 1.
3 It would appear that Faraday had anticipated Conybeare here. See Letter 57.
4 For the activities of the Bristol Institution, see *Proceedings of the Bristol Institution*. The first volume appeared in 1823. Publication ceased in 1836 with Vol. 13. The Institution no longer exists.

64   M. FARADAY to J. J. BERZELIUS, 1 July 1823
[*Kungl. Vetenskapsakademiens Bibliotek, Stockholm, previously unpublished*]

R.I.
July 1, 1823

SIR,

– It is now several weeks since I was surprised and very highly gratified by a Messenger from Mr. Allen[1] who brought a bottle containing a quantity of Selenium mixture and a note stating it had been sent me by your directions. I should have hastened immediately to express my sense of the very high honor you had done me but that I was fearful of troubling you merely with my unworthy thanks and I hoped that by the delay of a few weeks I might have an opportunity of stating some new fact or other which would have given a degree of interest to my letter. But I am now ashamed of having waited so long and beg to return my sincerest thanks for the honor & kindness you have done me and to assure you that the notice you have taken will be no small stimulus and encouragement to me to pursue the paths of Science.

I have been very anxious to work on the mixture you sent me and repeat your important experiments but with the number of lectures and other business which is pursued in our laboratory, nearly all my time is occupied in drudgery. During the summer however I look for a few spare weeks and shall endeavour to employ them on the Selenium.

I have lately been engaged in condensing several of the gases into liquids. You have probably seen notice of the results in the Journals. It is my intention if you will allow me the liberty to send a copy of my papers to you through the hands of Messrs. Tothe & Co. and I hope you will honor me by accepting them. They are at present in the hands of the printer.

If I am not mistaken a young Gentleman of the name of Namier has the advantage of being in your Laboratory. If so will you oblige me by mentioning my name to him with best remembrances to him and his father.

> I have the honor to be Sir
> Your very Obliged & faithful Servant
> M. FARADAY

[1] William Allen (1770–1843) was a chemist and Member of the Royal Institution.

65 T. R. ROBINSON[1] to M. FARADAY, 13 July 1823
[*I.E.E., previously unpublished*]

> Dublin
> July 13th/23

DEAR SIR

On arriving here I heard of the death of Mr Higgins,[2] Professor of Chemistry at the Dublin Royal Society You instantly occurred to me as one who might be certain of success if he offered himself I do not know the emoluments of your present situation, but the others stands thus. The professor has a salary of L. 500 per annum, his lectures are gratuitous, but he may have assistant pupils who pay (or did in Higgins's time) 10 Guineas for the course. All expenses of his lectures defrayd [*sic*] by the society and a very complete establishment of apparatus &c. I am not myself a member of this society, tho I believe my opinion would have some weight with many of them; its most influential persons are Hon. George Knox, John Leslie Foster MP. and Joy the Irish Solicitor General: if you have access to any of these there would be no doubt of your success – You will perhaps wonder at my taking the liberty of counselling one whom I never saw but twice, but there is a free masonry of science, and they who wish to be thought to belong to the *Craft* are always anxious to force themselves on the notice and acquaintance of its true brethren. If you make any application to the D. Society, the attestations of capacity wh [*sic*] are usually produced on such occasions might be from Wollaston and Davy who are most admired here of all yo[ur] [ms. torn and missing] luminaries – If on the other ha[nd] [ms. torn and missing] you think the thing not worth seeking there is no harm done but the writing an idle letter. Believe me

> yours very sincerely
> T. R. ROBINSON

My direction is
    Observatory
    Armagh

[1] Thomas Romney Robinson (1792–1882), astronomer and Fellow of Trinity College, Dublin.
[2] William Higgins (1766–1825).

[Historical Society of Pennsylvania, previously unpublished]

Royal Institution
Feby 14, 1824.

Dear Sir

Whenever I open my writing book I am ashamed to see your last kind letter of Septr last[1] remaining there unanswered but at the same time I have always the excuse at hand of having nothing important to write to you about and having no right to disturb you except about things of importance

I have however at last passed over this argument and am determined to thank you without farther delay for your continual kindness and for the good offices which I am sure I am indebted to you for at the Royal Academy of Sciences The honor conferred on me by that body is so far beyond what I had any right to expect that I cannot return my thanks to it and my friends in it as I ought to do and have little more to do than accept it with gratitude & in silence

I am now to beg for information from you which perhaps you will do me the kindness to send at any convenient opportunity I am sorry to say there is no hurry for it on my part because of my incapacity I wish to ask you whether in the event of my ever writing any more papers of a respectable kind it would not be a matter of propriety and duty in me to send one to the Royal Academy of Sciences as a token of gratitude for the mark of distinction they have bestowed upon me – whether it would be acceptable – and what would become of it – I beg you to understand I do not promise to do this because I am not sure I shall ever do any thing more worth describing and because also the next paper I may produce is claimed by the Royal Society, but if I should be fortunate enough to have two papers more then I should like to do as I have hinted above provided it be proper

I was a little startled the other day by one of the numbers of the Annales de Chimie[2] In the account it gives of the proceedings of the Academy of Sciences for Septr 15th. 1823. it mentions that MM. Braconnot[3] & Hatchett[4] were elected Corresponding Members in the Section of Chemistry and I was afraid I had been assuming those honors which belonged really to another and though M Braconnot deserved them more than I did I should have been sorry to have resigned such a prize. However the Official Letters sent to me by Baron Cuvier[5] and also an announcement in the following Number of the Annales de Chimie of my letter of thanks to the Academy for the honor it had done me satisfied me that it had been a mistake of the press & that I had not done wrong in assuming the title

I beg with this letter to introduce Dr. Symes to you He is a friend's friend and is very anxious to know what you have done in France with the new vegetable alkalies I have encouraged my friend to hope that you will introduce

146

Dr. Symes to M Baruel [reading uncertain] who I suppose has an immense store of practical information on the subject

Whenever you honor me with another letter pray let me know how I may direct send or otherwise convey to you I know not whether I shall ever have the pleasure of seeing you at Paris but I please myself with the expectation

I have the Honor to be

Dear Sir

Your Very Obliged & faithful Servant

M. FARADAY

[1] See *CGA*, 2, 652 for the letter from Ampère to Faraday.

[2] *AC*, 2 s., 24 (1823), 318.

[3] Henri Braconnot (1781–1855), Professor of Natural History at the Lycée de Nancy and Director of the Nancy Botanical Gardens.

[4] Charles Hatchett (1765–1847), English chemist.

[5] Georges Cuvier (1769–1832), famous comparative anatomist and paleontologist. He served for many years as *Secrétaire Perpetuelle* of the *Académie des Sciences*.

67   SIR J. F. POLLOCK[1] to M. FARADAY, 26 March 1824

[*Cornell University, previously unpublished*]

Northern Circuit

Friday Evg

March 26th, 1824

MY DEAR SIR

I beg to return you my grateful acknowledgements for your very satisfactory communication on the subject of the rendering liquid certain gaseous fluids – Mr. Brougham[2] had not heard before of the success with which you had conducted your experiments and the reduction of carbonic acid gas to the liquid state appeared to him so extraordinary & important that he was incredulous till I showed him your letter – had I possessed the means on the circuit of referring to the transactions of the Royal Society I shd. have had no difficulty in convincing him – but a reference to the author of the papers was better still – I hope you will be cautious in your experiments as far as the safety of your own person is concerned & record your triumphs without being obliged to mention your wounds. –

Believe me Ever

Your faithful & obliged

Servt.

[?] FRED POLLOCK

[1] Sir Jonathan Frederick Pollock (1783–1870) was a famous jurist.

[2] Henry Brougham (1778–1868), amateur physicist and Lord Chancellor of England after 1830.

68 M. FARADAY to B. ABBOTT, 16 December 1824[1]

[*Harvard University, previously unpublished*]

R Institution,
Dec.ʳ 16, 1824

DEAR ABBOTT

I have received yours and was very glad to see any thing to remind me of old & pleasant times Though things have altered with us both & we are thrust much more forward into life than perhaps we expected yet I should be sorry if our younger pleasures & feelings were forgotten amid the cares which I at least am now immersed in. (as Cockary [reading doubtful] would say.

I am now lecturing here in the Laboratory and that does not diminish my labours or increase my spare time – However none of my evenings are fixedly engaged except Wednesdays and Saturdays though the others are frequently picked up as they float about a week before hand – I trust however I shall see you on some of them

I am glad to hear the school prospers. I am a good deal amused at observing how much your hand writing is altered I can guess at the causes but shall get you to explain to me philosophically when I see you

I am Dear Ben
Yours Ever
M. FARADAY

[1] This, so far as I can determine, is the last letter Faraday wrote to Abbott.

69 P. BARLOW to M. FARADAY, 4 May 1825

[*R.I., previously unpublished*]

Royl Artry Acady
May 4 1825

DEAR SIR

I am much obliged to you for your hint about Arago's experiments.[1] I had heard indistinctly of them before but after the receipt of your letter Marsh[2] and I set to work and we made them succeed very satisfactorily I have since had Herschel down and I have been *spinning* with him and Babbage in town[3] – but at present the explanation is in the dark. The following will reach most if not all the facts at present known – viz. That a certain attraction takes place between either pole of a magnet and copper, and all other metals, but too small to be distinguished in a general manner, besides being equal on both poles it has no tendency to disturb the needle unless one pole is much nearer than the other; but by revolving the plate and consequently the point to which the pole is attracted the needle has a tendency to move with it. We obtain a similar result with or without plate provided one pole of the needle is brought very near. On a trial

148

of different metals their powers appear to be in the following order Iron Copper Zinc tin lead bismuth and antimony. The former besides its property common with the other metal has the other property which I found by revolving my ball, and which as I am inclined to explain, both results differ from the latter only in this, that the effect I observed depended upon the induction of magnetism in the iron ball from the Earth, whereas the result which Arago has noticed is due to the magnetism induced in the metal by the magnet itself. We must therefore suppose copper and all metals perhaps are substances to be slightly magnetic (Partially) except when intensely excited and then existing only in a very slight degree.

It is said that when Arago's copper plate is cut in radii the effect is diminished and by some experiments I have made it does appear to be so; this perhaps is a little at variance with my explanation – but I should be glad to do without vortices if I can.

Compliments to Mrs Faraday

Dear Sir yours truly
P. BARLOW

My paper is to be read on Thursday[4]

[1] Francois Arago, 'L'action que les corps aimantés et ceux qui ne le sont pas exercent les uns sur les autres,' *AC*, 28 (1825), 325.
[2] James Marsh (ca. 1790–1846), chemist and inventor ot the Marsh test for arsenic. Marsh was at the Royal Academy at Woolwich at this time with Barlow.
[3] See Charles Babbage and J. F. W. Herschel, 'Account of the repetition of M. Arago's experiments on the magnetism manifested by various substances during the act of rotation,' *PT* (1825), 467. Also *LPW*.
[4] Peter Barlow, 'On the temporary magnetic effect induced in iron bodies by rotation,' *PT* (1825), 317. (Read 5 May 1825.)

70   J. F. W. HERSCHEL to M. FARADAY, 13 September 1825
[*R.S., previously unpublished*]

Slough,
Sep. 13, 1825

DEAR SIR,

I am most obliged to you for your copy of your Paper with the notes (?). I will take care that they shall be inserted in the end of the volume.

I received some time ago a packet of specimens of the Glass of Exp. 1. with a paper of determinations of the Specific gravities of different portions & from different situations in the pots.[1] This I presume was from you though with no name. – The difference of S. G. between the top & bottom in one case exceeds anything I could have supposed possible. It is evident that no accidental defect in mixing could have produced it. A separation, by subsidence, of one fluid within the other, has evidently taken place. This is very remarkable, and indicates that we ought to aim at making atomic compounds, or at least compounds *capable* of permanent mixture I therefore

[The following paragraph is crossed out in ms.] On comparing the dispersive powers of the glass in these three pots and those analyzed at the R. Institution before the commencement of the experiments, with a series of dispersive powers of 5 kinds of Flint-glass of which I have given an account in the Edinb. Trans. Vol. X.[2] I am surprised to find that while the *refractive indices* differ very little, the dispersions of the former glasses are [word inked out] much greater The mean of the Refractive indices of nine specimens now examined is 1.60 The mean of their dispersive indices 0.081 The mean of the Refractive indices of 5 specimens formerly examined is 1.59 that of their dispersive indices 0.064.

The quantity of Lead therefore exerts a much greater influence on the dispersive than on the refractive power.

[The following sentence has a line drawn through it.] Yet this is true only within certain limits. I have [end of line] formed an atomic silicate of Lead (S̈ L̇).[3] Its refractive index came out so high as 2.123 for Extreme Red rays & therefore probably as high as 2.2 for mean, which approaches to the refraction of Phosphorus and exceeds glass of Antimony. Its dispersion is Enormous – so much so that I could not measure it with my usual apparatus. A prism of 21° 12′ required to be opposed by three prisms of flint glass of 30° to neutralize the colour This glass however is too soft, and cannot be cooled in large masses quick enough to prevent crystallizing & losing its transparency – but, what is very singular is that I could not obtain it otherwise than *full* of streaks & veins though its fusion is as liquid as water & it was well agitated before

[1] The Royal Society appointed a Committee in 1824 to seek means of improving the quality of optical glass, especially for telescopes. A sub-committee consisting of Faraday, John Herschel, already famous as a physicist, and George Dollond, a practising optician, was named to carry out the actual investigation. See M. Faraday, 'On the Manufacture of Glass for Optical Purposes,' *ERPC*, 231ff. Also *LPW*, 115ff.

[2] See J. F. W. Herschel, 'Practical Rules for the Determination of the Radii of a Double Achromatic Object-Glass,' *EPJ*, 6 (1822), 361. This is the tenth volume of the journal, but the sixth which is edited by both Jameson and Brewster; the numbering started anew when Brewster became co-editor.

[3] It was an accepted practice at this time to indicate the atoms of oxygen in a compound by dots. Thus this compound in modern notation would be $PbSiO_3$. The modern symbols were only beginning to come into use in the 1820's.

M. FARADAY to J. F. W. HERSCHEL, 4 October 1825
[*R.S., previously unpublished*]

Royal Institution,
Octʳ 4. 1825

MY DEAR SIR

I was very much surprized yesterday at perceiving that Mr Taylor had printed my paper in the Philosophical Magazine[1] even *before* the Publication of the part of the Philosophical Transactions containing it. From a note which Mr. Taylor has sent me today I understand it was entirely a mistake and not from any want of respect to the request of the President & Council I enclose Mr. Taylor's note and should be obliged if you would express my regret & explain to the President & Council how it so happened.

I am now engaged in examining & analyzing some of the glasses. The difference in gravity is as Mr Hudson[2] has stated it and depends upon lead having sunk whilst alkali has risen in the pots I suppose before the action was completed. I will send you the results as soon as I have them correctly.

Perhaps you will have the goodness to preserve Mr Taylors note or return it to me after having explained to the council – lest any future explanation should be required.

I am Dear Sir
Yours Very faithfully
M. FARADAY

[1] 'On new compounds of carbon and hydrogen, and on certain other products obtained during the decomposition of oil by heat,' *PM*, 66 (1825), 180.
[2] It is impossible to identify Mr Hudson with any degree of certainty. He may have been an employee of Pellatt and Green, glassmakers; if so, he has left no further traces in history. Or, he may have been James Hudson (1804–59) who became Assistant Secretary of the Royal Society in 1829.

72 M. FARADAY to J. F. W. HERSCHEL, 7 November 1825
[*R.S., previously unpublished*]

Royal Institution
Novʳ 7, 1825

MY DEAR SIR

I send you the results of the analyses of some specimens of glass from the pots No. 1 and 3 of our experiment

I. Glass from top of Pot No. 1 – slightly green in colour – Specific Gravity

3·33

Silica	49.2
Protoxide of lead	33.04
Potash	17.3
Trace of oxide of iron	
	99.54

II. Glass from bottom of Pot No. 1. Strong green colour and very much mottled – Specific Gravity 3.73

Silica ————————	49.8
Protoxide of lead ———	38.4
Potash ————————	11.6
Trace of oxide of Iron ——	small
	99.8

III. Glass from top of Pot No. 3.
         Colourless mainly – but streaky

Silica ————————	52.0
Protoxide of lead ———	34.25
Potassa ————————	13.75 deduced

IV. Glass from bottom of Pot No. 3 – Yellowish green – mottled

Silica ————————	33.9
Protoxide of lead ———	51.7
Potash ————————	14.4 deduced

The difference in the potash of the specimens from the top & bottom of the Pot No. 1. is very remarkable and is the reverse of that in the specimens from No. 3 Indeed later altogether the results indicate very great irregularities in the pots

I am dear Sir
Yours Very faithfully
M. FARADAY

73   M. FARADAY to J. F. W. HERSCHEL, 14 November 1825
[R.S., *previously unpublished*]

Royal Institution,
Nov. 14th. Monday[1]

DEAR SIR

I am quite of your opinion with regard to the fritting[2] & think that an operation similar to that which commences the *crown glass* maker's proceedings is what is wanted though I dare say I [crossed out] we shall have to feel our way a good deal by experiment before we attain the best or even a good mode of doing it. I am afraid we shall not do much by the present desultory mode of describing the matter (i.e. by notes & at a distance from each other) and think that the sooner we can meet at the works to examine the annealing furnace and turn it or other parts of the place to account as fritting furnaces the better. One thing I think is pretty certain, that we shall want many pots probably both open & covered and I should think the man might as well get a stock ready made It is hardly worth while making three only & then waiting two or three months for three more. And though it may be objected that we do not at present know the best material with which to line them yet I think that is of but minor importance *until* we have learnt how to treat the materials we put in as to get them combined into one homogeneous substance – *that done* we may proceed to the discovery of the best method of preventing it from being spoiled again by the matter of the pot

I must confess I should like very much to have some of the old glass after being heated & thrown into water pulverized sifted well mixed and two pots filled with it, one well stirred up according to an early suggestion of yours – the other taken out thrown into water pulverized mixed – re-fused & & – I should like too to have a small pot in the hot corner containing *good glass* to see whether by fusion & time any separation of parts would take place

I suppose you will soon be enabled to authorize our meeting and working at the glass house

> I am dear Sir
> Very faithfully yours
> M. FARADAY

¹ Postmarked 1825 15 November.
² 'Fritting' was the practice of using glass from other batches, in broken pieces, as the material for a new batch, rather than starting with the raw materials themselves.

74 M. FARADAY to A.-M. AMPÈRE, 17 November 1825
[*Burndy Library, Norwalk, Conn., Michael Faraday Collection B1, previously unpublished*]

> Royal Institution
> Novʳ 17. 1825.

MY DEAR SIR

I have had great pleasure at different times lately by the receipt of your kind letters sent by our mutual friends M. De la Rive, Mr. South¹ and Mr. Underwood though it has so happened that by my absence from town &c. none but that by Mr. South has reached me in due time. I beg at this opportunity to return you my sincere thanks for your kindness in sending me copies of your papers these I value highly not only for their intrinsic merit but also because they are so many marks of your kind estimation of myself. and I hope you will never fail to make them as from yourself by writing on the title page. I only wish that I were competent more frequently to make proper acknowledgements for them by similar returns.

Every letter you write me states how busily you are engaged and I cannot wish it otherwise knowing how well your time is spent. Much of mine is unfortunately occupied in very commonplace employment and this I may offer as an excuse (for want of a better) for the little I do in original research

I am sorry to find by one of your letters that you experience an unworthy opposition to the fair & high claim you have to the approbation and thanks of your fellow Philosophers. This however you can hardly wonder at I do not know what it is or by whom exerted in your case but I never yet even in my short time knew a man to do anything eminent or become worthy of distinction without becoming at the same time obnoxious to the cavils and rude encounters of envious men. Little as I have done, I have experienced it and that too where I least expected it.

I think however and hope that you are somewhat mistaken in your opinion of the feeling here It is true that some of your views were at first received here with great reserve but I think that now all your facts are admitted and are all properly attributed to you With regard to your theory it so soon becomes mathematical that it quickly gets beyond my reach at the same time I know that it has received the consideration of eminent men here – I am not however competent to tell you exactly how it is accepted. for in fact being a very busy man and somewhat retired in habits I am all day long in my Laboratory, do not go much among scientific men and am in some sort an anchorite in the Scientific world Hence I have neither time nor opportunity for scientific conversation and am frequently surprized at information which is new to me when old to every one else.

Be assured however that whenever the opportunity occurs *I* do full justice to your important investigations for as far I can go with them I am convinced of their accuracy & great value.

Many thanks to you for M. De Monferrand's book.[2] I had it only a day or two ago – and though I have not yet read it have looked over the table & agree with you in its accuracy

> I am My dear Sir
> Your Very Obliged & faithful friend
> M. FARADAY

[1] James South (1785–1867), astronomer.
[2] J. B. Demonferrand, *Manuel d'électricité dynamique*, Paris, 1823.

75 J. GUILLEMARD to M. FARADAY, 10 January 1826
[*R.S., previously unpublished*]

> Royal Institution,
> 10th Jany. 1826

SIR,

I enclose a Copy of a Minute of the proceedings of the Committee of Managers on the 9th Instant.

> I have the honour to be
> Sir,
> Your most obedient Servant
> J. GUILLEMARD, *Sec. R.I.*

Mr. Professor Brande having suggested that in consequence of the rank which Mr. Faraday holds in Science, and his many important avocations it would be proper to relieve him from his attendance as Assistant upon the Professor of Chemistry at his lectures.

Resolved, That the suggestion of Mr. Brande be adopted. – And that Mr. Faraday's attendance upon him be no longer required.

Extracted from the Minutes of the Managers of the 9*th* of January 1826.   JOS. FINCHER
Asst Secretary

76   M. FARADAY to J. F. W. HERSCHEL, 25 April 1826

[*R.S., previously unpublished*]

Royal Institution
April 25, 1826

DEAR SIR

In consequence of the extreme pressure of business which I have been subjected to for some time past and am still subject to I doubt very much whether I can be at the Glass Committee on Thursday I send you therefore the results of some analytical experiments made on the glass of the Pot No. 1 with specimens taken from the top and the bottom I did not think it worth while nor have I had time to examine the other pots

Glass from the top
    Specific Gravity – mean of two experiments 3.5467.
    100 parts contained Silica —————— 43.1
           Protoxide of lead   —   39.57
           Potash &c ————— 17.33
Glass from the bottom
    Specific Gravity – mean of two experiments 3.5472
         Silica ——————— 43.5
         Protoxide of lead   —   39.76
         Potash &c ————— 16.74.

You will immediately see how accordant these results are with the apparent homogeneity of the glass The slight difference which does exist is probably in part due to errors of experiment and perhaps in part to the circumstance of the lower specimen having been taken from the vicinity of the pot from which it may perhaps have gained a little siliceous matter

You will observe that this glass is not as yet equal to Guignand's[1] in density or in the proportions of oxide of lead & that it surpasses all the flint glasses that were analysed in the quantity of alkali present. There is no reason to suppose that this great quantity of alkali which is half as much more than that contained in some flint glasses is requisite and it may perhaps be usefully replaced by lead

I am dear Sir
Very Truly Yours
M. FARADAY

[1] Pierre Louis Guinand (ca. 1745–1826), Swiss optician. See Anon., *Some Account of the late M. Guinand, and of the discovery made by him in the manufacture of flint glass for large telescopes*, London, 1825.

77   C. DAUBENY[1] to M. FARADAY 25 April 1826
[*I.E.E.*, *previously unpublished*]

Magdalen College Oxford
April 25th 1826

MY DEAR SIR,

I have somewhere met with a statement as to the effects of compression on water which appeared to me of so anomalous a kind that I should be glad to learn whether there be any truth in it, and I know no one so well able (in such a subject more particularly) to give me information, as yourself. –

The fact stated was, that when water expos'd to an high temperature underwent a certain quantum of pressure, as in one of Perkins' Engines[2] it was resolv'd into its elements, or at least that Hydrogen was evolv'd. Now if such be the case, are we to imagine, that a still *greater* degree of pressure would compensate for a lower degree of temperature, and if that is the case, the bottom of the ocean must be compos'd of a mixture of the two elements of water, supporting a mass of that fluid. – The whimsical notion thrown out by Professor Leslie in the supplement to the Encyclop. Britann.[3] immediately suggests itself, but your researches would lead us to imagine that in all probability neither of the Elements of water under such pressure would be in a gaseous state. – This circumstance however would not probably prevent the Oxygen from acting as a supporter of combustion, so that volcanoes might thus continue to burn under the sea without access to air – It is true that if the metals of the Earths & Alkalies are the *cause* of the volcanic action, water itself would act as a supporter, but even then we should have to account for the sulphurous Acid so commonly given off, the existence of which seems to imply the *presence* of Oxygen in an uncombin'd state. – Allow me, whilst on this subject, to ask your opinion on the mode in which I have attempted to explain the fact that Lavas of submarine origin appear to have evol'd more slowly than those which have flow'd in the open air –

I account for this by the slow conducting power of liquids, and I contend, that the two causes which contribute to cool with such rapidity heated bodies thrown into *shallow* water, ought not to operate (to the same extent at least) at so great a depth. – The first of these, the change of the water into steam, could not probably take place at all; the second the expansion of the aqueous particles nearest the source of heat would be [ms. torn] [in some] measure contracted by the compress- [ms. torn] [-ion of] the water itself at so great a depth. – I think it appears from Perkins' experiments on the compressibility of water,[4] that if the ocean be 10 Miles deep, it would at the bottom be near 18 pr.ct. denser than at the top. Consequently if the expansion of water by heat follows the same ratio above 212° as it is found to do below, the lower stratum of the ocean would require to be rais'd nearly to 1000 of Fahrenheit, before it would acquire the same density as that at the surface estimated at 50° or 60°. – Ought not this circumstance to retard the circulation which would otherwise take place in the strata of water at the bottom of the ocean, when heat were applied. –

I cannot ask you to devote much of your valuable time to the consideration of these, probably crude, speculations, but I shall be oblig'd by a line informing me whether the fact relating to the decomposition of water be correct or not, as I am preparing a work on Volcanoes in which I ought to allude to it. – May I also ask you, whether you have ever examin'd a Quack Medicine sold by a Dr Salamè an Italian Empiric, as I have been ask'd its composition, and should not wish to throw away my time in analyzing it, unnecessarily. It is a brownish powder, soluble in water, & not affected by heat. This is all I know about it at present.

I take the opportunity of a friend's hand to send you this letter which I hope you will not think too troublesome. I feel much oblig'd by your kind present of your interesting paper on Napthaline [*sic*] and remain

dear sir with much esteem
Yrs truly
CHARLES DAUBENY

[1] Charles Daubeny (1795–1867) was Professor of Chemistry and Botany at Oxford University. He was interested in the theory of volcanoes and published a number of papers on volcanic action. See *RSCSP*.
[2] Jacob Perkins, 'A new Steam Engine and its application to engines of the old construction,' *EPJ*, 9 (1823), 172.
[3] *Supplement to the Fourth, Fifth, and Sixth Editions of the Encyclopaedia Britannica*, 6 vols., Edinburgh, 1815–24, 5 (1822), article 'Meteorology,' 326. Compressed air, Leslie suggests, lies at the bottom of the ocean and it is this air which feeds volcanic fires.
[4] Jacob Perkins, 'On the compressibility of water,' *PT* (1820), 324.

[*Burndy Library, Norwalk, Conn., Michael Faraday Collection W33, previously unpublished*]

Royal Institution
May 2 1826

DEAR SIR

I do not recollect any such statement as that you mention respecting the decomposition of water at high temperatures and pressures independent of the chemical action of other substances present Is it any thing about the experiments of Cagniard de la Tour[1] or Perkins[2] with his engine that has originated the idea in your mind? I should be very sceptical indeed of such an operation and should require to see the experiments two or three times before I should believe it. I think all the probabilities are against it and that pressure would rather produce combination than destroy it. Indeed I have two or three facts or rather Mr Brande has confirmatory of the latter opinion. At the same time they are imperfect & do not bear directly on the point

Going as in the second page of your letter to the notion that the oxygen & hydrogen are actually separated I do not see how it would facilitate explanations of combustions supposed to depend upon the presence of the free oxygen I can imagine the oxygen leaving the hydrogen only because it from some cause or other is no longer in the relation of a supporter of combustion and if it be imagined to lose its power of combination with hydrogen I see no reason why it should retain its power of combination with sulphur: or in more general terms I think the relative situation of oxygen to the different combustibles under great pressure must be the same as at the earths surface

With regard to your explanation of the appearances depending upon the different rates at which lava may have cooled in shallow & very deep water I go with you at once as to the effect produced in shallow water by evaporation and not produced in deep water but I do not see that the circulation should be diminished by the increase of density beneath – whatever the increase of density may be there can be little doubt that of two *contiguous* particles of water the one which is warmed more than the other will ascend and if it continues warmer than those it comes into contact with it must ultimately reach the surface for as it ascends it in consequence of being relieved from the pressure of the particles above which it had passed would expand and from its superior temperature would still retain a less specific gravity than the particle next above it It seems to me that in an ocean of water even though the lower stratum should be several times more dense than the upper, that an appreciable increase of temperature at the bottom would immediately cause circulation ultimately extending throughout. I am of course speaking of those ranges of temperature not including the anomalous expansion of water below $40.°F$

I have not seen the Quack medicine.

I am dear Sir

Very Truly Yours
M. FARADAY

158

[1] Baron Charles Cagniard de la Tour (1777–1859), 'Exposé de quelques résultats obtenus par l'action combinée de la chaleur et de la compression sur certains liquides tels que l'eau, l'alcool, &c,' *AC*, 21 (1822), 127, and 'Sur les effets qu'on obtienne par l'application simultanée de la chaleur et de la compression à certains liquides,' *AC*, 22 (1823), 410.
[2] See Letter 77.

79 M. FARADAY to J. F. W. HERSCHEL, 26 May 1826
[*R.S., previously unpublished*]

Royal Institution
May 26 1826

Private

MY DEAR SIR

I believe yours are the hands into which I should put a paper intended for the Royal Society. I have shewn it to Sir Humphry Davy[1] who thinks pretty well of it but does not seem quite satisfied with the argument I cannot however alter my view and for my comfort and more my fullest confidence Dr. Wollaston is quite satisfied with it

I hope you will take the trouble of glancing over it and that you will be of Dr. Wollaston's opinion and that afterwards you will tell the President you have the paper.

I am dear Sir
Yours Very faithfully
M. FARADAY

[1] Davy was P.R.S. at this time.

80 J. F. W. HERSCHEL to M. FARADAY, 26 May 1826
[*R.S., previously unpublished*]

May 26, 1826.[1]

DEAR SIR

I have read with much interest your paper on the limit of Vaporisation[2] – and certainly can see no objection to the Argument which appears to me as nearly demonstrative as the nature of physical Argument admits, & altogether a material step made towards settling our notions on the point of the constitution of the atmosphere.

Gravity acts perpendicularly to the horizon – therefore suffering by a vaporific nisus, atoms to be detached from the *under* surface of silver at common temperatures – they will fall to the ground in *dust* of *infinite* i.e. atomic tenuity – but as in so doing from resistance of the air they will occupy an enormous time – their mutual elasticity will urge them asunder in a *horisontal* plane & end by covering the whole surface of the Earth with disseminated simple atoms of Silver

From the *upper surface* no vapour can rise at all.

But the Silver itself exerts a *gravitating* force which in that almost infinite state of tenuity competent to its vapour below 100 Fahr. may be sufficient to restrain *lateral* vaporisation

Assuredly however the attraction of cohesion which must extend to some small distance may have (at such distances as separate the particles of vapour from the surface of the Silver in initio) force enough to restrain its further dispersion – Or we may regard the vaporizing nisus at all temperatures as in a state of perpetual antagonism with the cohesive force – and only then 1st capable of overcoming it when the temperature reaches a certain limit.

The elasticity of particles in the state of vapour is as T/x ($x = $ dist). The cohesive force is as a/x where T is a coefficient increasing with the temperature – and x some function of a increasing much faster than a. Therefore when T/a equals a/x the equilibrium subsists and the limit marked by this is a surface surrounding the silver at a distance which *is greater* the *less* T is. Within this surface all is attraction – without all repulsion If therefore the vaporative nisus have intensity sufficient to urge a particle beyond this surface it will remain aeriform if not it will recondense into silver.

Now if this nisus be a force decreasing as the temperature decreases (which surely will be admitted) then it is clear that a limit MUST arrive when it cannot carry the particle up to the point of indifference – for 1st that point becomes more remote & the attraction within it is stronger – and 2dy the force urging the particle outwards becomes weaker as the temperature sinks. [The following sentence is interpolated in Faraday's hand.] In this case there will *fall no dust* even from the undersurface.

It seems to me that this amounts to demonstration. I mentioned this view of the subject to Sir H. D. when speaking of your ideas.

I am inclined as you will see by this to make a distinction between cohesion attraction which exists in fluids – and the crystallising forces of your elegant camphor experiment.[3] N.B. the crystals of Iodine so formed are of singular size & beauty.

Yours truly

J. F. W. HERSCHEL

[1] Inset round the date is the following: [Two words illeg.] Not a Copy – material alterations & improvements in that sent.

[2] 'On the existence of a Limit to Vaporization,' *PT* (1826), 484; *ERPC*, 199.

[3] *ERPC*, 203.

[*R.S., previously unpublished*]

Devonshire Street,
May 27, 1826.

DEAR SIR

I have read with much interest your paper on the limit of vaporisation and certainly can see no objection to the general argument which appears to me as nearly demonstrative as the nature of physical sciences admit and altogether a natural step made toward settling our notions on the constitution of the Atmosphere. Allow me however to pursue the matter a step or two into particulars. Gravity acts perpendicularly to the horizon – therefore supposing Atoms to be detached by a vaporific nisus from the *under* surface of Silver at common temperatures – they will be vapour to all intents and purposes till they reach the ground and to this they will fall not merely as *dust* of infinite or rather of atomic tenuity – but, exerting all the while their full repulsion on each other in a horizontal direction in virtue of which they will recede from each other and spread themselves ultimately over the whole surface of the earth – as *discrete* atoms. The same kind of *dusty vapour* will emanate from the sides of the silver. But from the upper surface no vapour can rise, because gravity ex Hypothesis is too strong for it to overcome –

Were the *Earth's Gravity* then *only* considered – all solid bodies would still be in a continual state of diminution by vaporization and your argument would be untenable. Let us see what other forces we can call in

The silver itself exerts a *gravitating* force towards itself in all directions which in that almost infinite state of tenuity competent to its vapour at 100 Fahrenheit *may* be sufficient to restrain the lateral vaporization – But not that from the under surface

The attraction of *Crystallization* does not exist in fluids or is counterbalanced. That of *Cohesion* however does and it appears to me that it is amply sufficient to establish your point

We may regard the vaporizing nisus as a force urging the particles of a body from its surface and decreasing as the temperature decreases.

The elasticity of a particle of Silver (i.e. its gaseous repulsion) is directly as some power or function of the temperature and inversely as its distance from the neighbouring particles (and may therefore be represented by T/x).

The cohesive attraction is inversely as some very high function of the same distance x and is probably independent of the temperature – or if it do depend on it is *inversely* as a power or function of it. It may therefore be represented by $1/T'X$

Therefore the total force retaining the atom on the surface at the distance a in opposition to the *vaporific nisus* is $1/(T'X) - T/a$ consequently when this vanishes there is nothing to oppose it. This condition establishes a surface of indifference about the silver within which all is attraction & without – all repulsion

The distance of this surface from the Silver is that value of a which satisfies the equation and without entering at all into its form, it is clear from its general constitution, $(x/a = 1/TT')$
that a must necessarily be *Greater* as the temperature t is *less*.

Moreover within this surface of indifference the total retentive force is Greater as the temperature is less.

Now from both these considerations – 1st that the sphere of attraction is increased in *extent* by a decrease of temperature and 2*ndly* that by the same cause the retentive force within its limits is *increased*, it clearly follows, that the vaporific nisus, which *decreases* as the temperature Sinks – must ultimately be incapable of urging an atom to the distance of the Surface of indifference – and that vaporization will cease altogether. In this case there will be no dust falling from the under surface, after a certain decrease of temperature

This view of the subject I mentioned to Sir Humphry Davy when first I heard of your idea of a limit to vapour and it seems to me to amount to full demonstration

I remain

Dear Sir

Yours very truly

J. F. W. HERSCHELL.[1] [*sic*]

[1] This is not Herschel's autograph, but a note which was written by someone else. See Faraday to Herschel, May 30, 1826. This accounts for the misspelling of Herschel's name. What it does not account for is the difference between this document and the preceding one. This latter was probably only an abstract, kept by Herschel, of the actual letter to Faraday.

It does not follow Faraday's published paper.

82 M. FARADAY to J. F. W. HERSCHEL,[1] 30 May 1826

[*R.S., previously unpublished*]

Royal Institution,
May 30th, 1826

DEAR SIR

I am exceedingly obliged to you for your attention to my paper and beg to thank you heartily for your excellent and instructive note. I should have written to you sooner but from press of business could not find time to copy your letter. This however I have had done by another and now return it begging you will have the kindness to let it accompany the paper since it will add so much value to it Knowing your liberality in scientific communication I am pretty confident you will not refuse my request, and in that case when the paper goes in to the R S. the copy I have sent can be attached to it.

I am dear Sir

Very Truly Yr Oblgd

M. FARADAY

I forgot when I last saw you to make a remark or rather ask a question relative to an observation of yours respecting the difference between the light of Lieut Drummond[2] ball of lime & the light produced by salts of lime in flame. When experimenting with the salts of lime it is the *flame* that is coloured reddish &c – with the light of the ball of lime although that emanating from the ball itself be of the nature you describe yet the *flame* of alcohol around the ball is of another colour and as far as my rough observation without a prism of the same kind as that produced by salts of lime. Is it so or not? The colour of the flame around the ball is very distinct & decided.

MF

[1] The identity of the recipient is clear from the context.
[2] See Thomas Drummond, 'Description of an apparatus for producing intense Light visible at great distances,' *EJS*, 5 (1826), 319. This is the original limelight. See Letter 95, fn. 1.

83   J. F. W. HERSCHEL to M. FARADAY, 31 May 1826
[*R.I., previously unpublished*]

May 31. 1826.

DEAR SIR,

My note[1] was merely *conversational*, nor had I at the time of writing it the slightest idea of in any way appending my own crude notions to a finished production like your paper. I wrote merely to clarify my ideas, and I ought

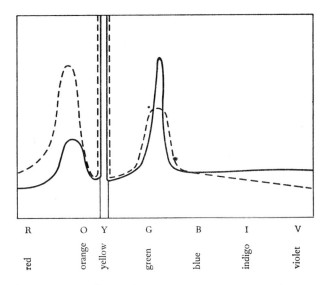

rather to apologise to you for making you accessory to such a process, than to wish to see it in print. There is the less need of this as the comment is one which most of your readers will easily enough make for themselves

163

With regard to the light of Mr Drummond's lamp.[2] It is very true that lime colours flame red (Brick-red) – It is true also that the general tint of Mr. Drummond's lamp seen after an oil lamp or after Candle light – verges to greenish or bluish But if we examine the ruddy flame of alcohol containing Prussiate of lime in solution, we *shall* find in it the green line which distinguishes the light of the ball – only the red line in its Spectrum is far more prominent.

The relation of the two lights may be represented thus the Black line represents the lines whose ordinate is proportional to the intensity of the light in different points of the Spectrum in the light of the ball – the dotted line is the flame-light

I remain dear Sir
Yours very truly
J. F. W. Herschel

[1] See Letter 80.
[2] See Letter 82.

84   J. F. W. Herschel to M. Faraday, 8 June 1826
[*R.I., previously unpublished*]

Thursday June 8, 1826.

Dear Sir,

I deferred answering your note under an impression I might possibly meet you at the RS tonight – that not being the case though late, I will make no further apologies, but merely state that my opinion as to the propriety of appending the remarks in my note to your paper remains unaltered, even by your expression of a wish that they should be so – which I hope you will understand in the sense I mean it as originating in a sense of something like indelicacy towards the Society in its Secretaries publicly commenting on the contents [reading doubtful] of papers, which necessarily come into their hands before those of the Members & (however perfectly understood in particular cases) might tend to establish a precedent that might prove very inconvenient in future. I hope therefore you will not take it amiss if I still require you to look on the remarks as purely conversational, and I remain

dear Sir
Yours very truly
J. F. W. Herschel

Niton
July. 23, 1826.

MY DEAR EDWARD

Many thanks to you for your instructive letter I cannot for shame longer delay answering it though I have no inclination for letter writing generally and contrive that Sarah shall do all that is possible. You know my occupation and will understand why I avoid writing as often as I can. Poor Sturt! – I thought he could not last long. The Medical men said the hot weather must soon bring his life to a close. I am amused and a little offended at Upcots hypocrisy.[1] He knows well enough that to the world an hours existence of our Institution is worth a years of the London and that though it were destroyed still the remembrance of it would live for years to come in places where the one he lives at has never been heard off [*sic*] Unless he comes with perfect good will & feeling in every part of the way I do not think I at least shall meet him for that nonsense of his though it may amuse once twice or thrice becomes ridiculous if it is to be thrown into every affair of life both common & serious and would probably be in our way. I think it would not be a bad joke to touch him up behind and say one cant imagine how it is that he is only assistant librarian at such an Unknown Institute as the London and that one cant help but imagine there must be some cause or other or he would be aiming at a higher character in the house or would endeavour to get into a more public place *etc. etc. &.* I think I could make the man wince if I were inclined and yet all in mere chat chat over a cup of tea. But this is all nonsense which however he brings to mind by the corresponding nonsense of his own affectation.

Now Hennell[2] is a plain common sense man without any particular varnish over his conduct & manners and when he speaks one knows what he means. I feel much therefore for his disappointment and think it altogether an unwise thing in some to be so neglectful of his desires & feelings in this case as they have been. Why should not we Philosophers tempt recruits by every honourable means? and when Hennell had so worthily earned the reward of pleasurable feelings why should they not be gratified when it might have been done with so little trouble? It annoys me as much I think as it will Hennell himself for I felt a great anxiety to see a copy of *his first paper* to the Royal Society

Will you have the goodness to call or send to Mr Nicol the printer[3] applying either to Mr. Nicol or Mr Batsford – I left word that proofs of my paper on vapour should be sent to me here by post,[4] – and also that a hundred copies should be printed off for myself as usual. All I want is to know that this has not been forgotten I do not care so much about the proofs but should be sorry if the copies were forgotten. I saw Mr. Batsford [and] [ms. damaged] told him &

therefore think things are safe as he [ms. illeg.] & cannot always be there – just look after [ms. torn] things for me.

I am glad to hear all is so well arranged for the Oxford trip – I am writing away here[5] & get on pretty well but it will be a more laborious job than I expected – I tire of writing day after day but have stuck too [*sic*] pretty well this far.

Mrs Faraday desires to be remembered to you – I am dear Magrath,

Very Truly Yours
M. FARADAY

[1] Sturt and Upcot were clearly members of the circle of friends Faraday had made in the days when he was an active member of the City Philosophical Society. Upcot was Assistant Librarian of the London Institution.
[2] Henry Hennell (?–1842), a chemist at Apothecary Hall in London. His first paper in the *PT* was 'On the mutual action of sulphuric acid and alcohol, with observations on the composition and properties of the resulting compound,' *PT* (1826), Pt. 3, 240. I have been unable to discover the source of Faraday's annoyance here.
[3] William Nicol of 58 Pall Mall, had been printer to George III.
[4] 'On the existence of a limit to vaporization,' *PT* (1826), 484. See also Letters 79–83.
[5] This probably refers to the one book (as such) that Faraday wrote, *Chemical Manipulation*, London, 1827.

86 M. FARADAY to J. F. W. HERSCHEL, 16 August 1826
[*R.S., previously unpublished*]

Niton,
Isle of Wight,
Aug 16 1826

DEAR SIR

I have but lately received your letter at this place and in answer to your enquiries am sorry to say that I have had no opportunity of examining the smallest portion of the iron you speak of none of it having come into my possession The occurrence of lead in it is a very odd thing especially if as you mention it exists in notable quantity I several years ago made experiments on the alloys of lead with cast iron they were of a very rough nature and I have forgotten every thing of the results except the possibility of alloying lead in small quantities with the iron which was effected in several instances

I have always been struck by the circumstance that notwithstanding the apparently independent sources of meteoric matter both stones and alloys with iron and also the minute chemical examination which has frequently been made of them that no new metal or element of any kind has been found in them nothing but what has previously been recognized in the materials of our globe.

I think that if meteoric masses had been unexamined and I had been looking out for something in which to discover new bodies I should at once have gone to them.[1]

I am Dear Sir
Truly Yours
M. FARADAY

[1] It was not at all clear at this time where meteorites came from. See the relevant papers by F. Arago and E. F. Chladni as listed in *RSCSP*.

87 M. FARADAY to J. F. W. HERSCHEL, 21 August 1827

[*R.S., previously unpublished*]

Royal Institution,
Aug 21 1827.

MY DEAR SIR

I have just returned to town and have your letter of last month Pray excuse me for being (necessarily) unable to attend to your desires. – I called on you twice before I left town and not finding you had some conversation with Dr. Young[1] about the furnace which you probably heard of.[2] We agreed that there were some points which must be well considered & provided against as for instance the emission of much smoke and the chance of our neighbours disturbing us by calling the furnace a nuisance and also that it would be proper to defer the creation of it till I could watch it in every part I shall now remain in town except for a day or two at a time & have written to the builder to come & discuss certain points in his specification and after having seen him I should be glad to see you. If I knew what your days & hours were at Slough I would come down by the coach – I could make nobody hear at your house this morning but heard from Mr Babbages[3] servant that you were at Slough to which place I now write. Favour me with a line & let me know how we can meet for half an hour. I was unlucky yesterday in trying to see Mr Dollond but hope to meet with him in a day or two.

I am sorry to hear you have resigned the Secretaryship[4] I hope it does not imply that you must withdraw your attention from the glass committee It would alter my views of the Committee & its usefulness very much if you were

I am dear Sir
Truly Yours
M. FARADAY

[1] Dr Thomas Young (1773–1829) was a member of the Royal Society's Glass Committee and the English champion of the undulatory theory of light.
[2] Faraday found it increasingly difficult to work at the glass works and wished to move operations to the Royal Institution. To do this, a furnace had to be constructed at the R.I. *LPW*, 116.

³ Charles Babbage (1792–1871) was to earn fame as the inventor of a computing engine for the determination of various mathematical functions. At this time, he was best known for his work on the reform of mathematical notation in England which he accomplished with the collaboration of Herschel.

⁴ Of the Royal Society.

88 M. FARADAY to D. LARDNER,¹ 8 October 1827

[*B.J. 1, 405*]

Royal Institution,
October 6, 1827

MY DEAR SIR,

My absence from town for a few days has prevented your letter from receiving an answer so soon as it ought to have done; and to compensate for the delay I should have called upon you yesterday evening, but that I prefer writing in the present case, that my reasons for the conclusion at which I have arrived may be clearly stated and understood.

You will remember, from the conversation which we have had together, that I think it a matter of duty and gratitude on my part to do what I can for the good of the Royal Institution in the present attempt to establish it firmly. The Institution has been a source of knowledge and pleasure to me for the last fourteen years, and though it does not pay me in salary for what I *now* strive to do for it, yet I possess the kind feelings and good-will of its authorities and members, and all the privileges it can grant or I require; and, moreover, I remember the protection it has afforded me during the past years of my scientific life. These circumstances, with the thorough conviction that it is a useful and valuable establishment, and the strong hopes that exertions will be followed with success, have decided me in giving at least two years more to it, in the belief that after that time it will proceed well, into whatever hands it may pass. It was in reference to this latter opinion, and fully conscious of the great opportunity afforded by the London University of establishing a valuable school of chemistry and a good name, that I have said to you and Mr. Millington² that if things altogether had been two years advanced, or that the University had to be founded two years hence, I should probably have eagerly accepted the opportunity. As it is, however, I cannot look forward two years and settle what shall happen then. Upon general principles only I should decline making an engagement so long in advance, not knowing what might in the meantime occur; and, as it is, the necessity of remaining free is still more strongly urged upon me. Two years may bring the Royal Institution into such a state as to make me still more anxious to give a third to it. It may just want the last and most vigorous exertions of all its friends to confirm its prosperity, and I should be sorry not to lend my assistance with that of others to the work.

I have already (and to a great extent for the sake of the Institution) pledged myself to a very laborious and expensive series of experiments on glass, which will probably require that time, if not more, for their completion; and other views are faintly opening before us. Thus you will see, that I cannot with propriety accede to your kind suggestion.

I cannot close this letter without adverting to the honour which has been done me by my friends, and I may add by the Council of the University, in their offering me the chemical chair in so handsome and unlimited a manner; and, if it can be done with propriety, I wish you to express my strong sentiments on this point to those who have thought of me in this matter. It is not the compliment and public distinction (for the matter is a private one altogether), but the high praise and approbation which such an unlimited mark of their confidence conveys, and which, coming to me from such a body of men, is more valuable than an infinity of ordinary public notice. If you can express for me my thankfulness for such kind approbation, and the regret which I feel for being obliged by circumstances to make so poor a return for their notice, I shall be much obliged to you.

You will remember that I have never considered this affair except upon general views, for I felt that unless these sanctioned my acceptance of the Professorship, it would be useless to inquire after such particulars as salary, privileges, &c. I make this remark now, that you may not suppose these have been considered and approved of, supposing other things had been favourable. I have never inquired into them, but from general conversation have no doubt they would have proved highly satisfactory.

I am, my dear Sir, yours very truly,

M. FARADAY.

¹ Dionysius Lardner (1793–1859) was Professor of Physics and Astronomy at London University from 1828 to 1840. The letter which follows seems important enough to warrant reprinting. I have not seen the manuscript.
² John Millington (1779–1868) was Professor of Mechanics at the Royal Institution from 1817 to 1819. He was also the vice president of Dr Birkbeck's London Mechanics' Institution out of which the University of London grew.

89   J. CLARK¹ to M. FARADAY, 30 April 1828

[*I.E.E., previously unpublished*]

George Street
April 30th 1828

MY DEAR SIR

I have long wished to have some conversation with you on the subjects of examination in Chemistry, but I know how much your time is occupied & now intrude upon you reluctantly.

In the first place I have my doubts whether our descriptive schedules will not rather prove a license to idleness than a stimulus to exertion both to Teachers and Pupils; – whether they may not lead to a system of grinding on particular subjects, than an encouragement to the acquisition of comprehensive information. –

If the extent of the examination on the subjects stated in the schedule applies not only to these but all other subjects of chemistry – these being given merely as examples, to shew the kind & extent of information required, it is all well; otherwise I should fear it would have the effects I have predicted.

In the Classics it is more easy to specify the examination by stating the authors on which the candidates will be examined, and in Mathematics the same thing may be done; but in Natural Philosophy, & more especially in the department of Chemistry, it appears to me that the syllabus of the lectures (& I hope each recognized lecturer will be required to publish a syllabus of his lectures) would seem a good guide for regulating the subjects & extent of examination and better than any partial schedule.

If the Descriptive schedule is preferred I would submit to you whether it should not comprehend some of the practical branches of Chemistry. As our Bachelor's degree is intended for men who ought to be acquainted with the more important applications of the science, ought he not to be required to possess some knowledge of even the leading chemical manufactures – Might not the following practical subjects be added to the schedule;

The Materials & Process for manufacturing Sulphuric acid.

The same for Carbonate of Soda

The same for acetic acid –

The ores of Iron & the Process for making cast Iron the same for Lead – for Zinc & for Copper –

These are the leading Chemical manufactures of Britain which have passed under the domain of Science, & every man who has received a moderate Chemical education can easily comprehend & ought to know them. What relates to Fermentation also, and the arts depending upon it, might be properly included among the practical subjects of examination – as Malting – the Vinous Fermentation – the acetic –

In the schedules on Physics & astronomy they require a knowledge of the principal instruments by which the phenomena of the science is shown & exhibited, and for an equally strong reason it appears to me that the practical processes by which Chemistry is illustrated & its importance shewn, should form a part of the examination.

I venture to make these suggestions to you with great deference, & would not have done so had you not mentioned to me one day at the Senate that you had drawn up your plan without having had time to consider the subject much. – I beg you not to think it necessary to make any reply to these lose [*sic*] hints written in haste, they are merely meant to call your attention to the subject.

On looking over the schedules there appears to me a great omission in no notice being taken of Geology & Meteorology – what think you of this? – We require our candidates to know all that is known of the distant planets, whilst he may be perfectly ignorant of the nature of the planet which he inhabits.

Believe me, dear sir,
Very truly yours
JA CLARK

1 James Clark (1788–1870) was a noted London physician. He served for many years in the Senate of London University. See Letter 363, fn. 1.

90 M. FARADAY to J. F. W. HERSCHEL, 24 July 1828

[*R.S.*, *previously unpublished*]

Royal Institution,
July 24, 1828

DEAR SIR

Our furnace is breaking away at the top so fast that I am afraid we cannot make more than 2 or 3 more experiments in it. I have therefore had Ramsay[1] to look at it & he has sent me the accompanying estimate for what repairs & alterations we thought fit. Now it would be an excellent job done whilst I am out of town (& I leave London next Tuesday) for it would partly employ Anderson[2] in watching the men & seeing they do work rightly and also would be drying for us again on returning to London. Can this be done? Can we do it or can you report to a council of the Royal Society so as to get it done? Although perhaps this Council may not decide before I go out of Town, Yet if you thought it likely I could have Anderson so far instructed that he could when you gave him authority inform Ramsey & let the work proceed.

I have not spoken to Mr Dolland [*sic*] for I have but just got the paper and am anxious to save the post.

I am dear Sir
Truly Yours
M. FARADAY

1 Mr Ramsay was the contractor who undertook the task of reinforcing the furnace. See Royal Institution, Minutes of the Meetings of the Managers, 7 (1825–32), 214.
2 Sgt Anderson was Faraday's faithful laboratory assistant, hired specifically to aid in the investigation of glass. He was to remain at Faraday's side throughout Faraday's scientific career.

[Staatsbibliothek, Marburg/Lahn (Stiftung Preussischer Kulturbesitz), acc. Darm-staedter, previously unpublished]

Royal Institution
Aug. 29th. 1828

DEAR PHILLIPS

I do not know whether my country rambles are concluded for this year or not I am afraid they are and indeed ought not to grumble except that they have not as yet enabled me or us to see you I have refrained from writing in the obscure hope that perhaps I might have a laugh with you this summer, but I have been obliged to laugh without you so far and must still endeavour to be chearful [*sic*] notwithstanding your absence I can't help wishing that you had stopped in London for though acquaintances offer themselves in abundance I do not find that my list of friends increases

Sarah & I have been rambling about for nearly two months – I have not been at home many days. – I am very much better for the country &c and think I begin to feel as usual: all I am annoyed about are the nervous headaches and weakness they unsettle me & make me indisposed to do anything but they are much better than they were.

I hardly know any thing that is doing here I have not seen the journals these two months – nor have I seen any one to inform me of general proceedings. The London University opens its schools early in October I have not heard a guess about the probable success of the establishment – Nor have I heard any thing about the King's College except that it is liberally supported by subscriptions in all parts of the country Pray how does Cooper[1] get on in the Borough? perhaps I ought to ask Dr. Booll [reading doubtful] that question rather than you seeing you are so far from the spot – I am so indifferent to most things except the success of this particular house (the R Institution), that I cannot help laughing myself at the surprise which strangers feel when they begin to talk to me about scientific concerns in London expecting that I shall be fully informed upon all points & mightily concerned about them and find me less instructed & more indifferent than the merest town-talker And then my bad memory does not mend the matter – I am sorry to say it gets worse

Now about Mrs. Phillips and my wife for they ought to share with us in these communications seeing they are so scarce (wives or communications?). You did not say a word about your wife in your last and we want to hear a little on that point as well also as about the numerous hopes of your family from Miss Phillips to Master Richard – (Sarah tells me there is a smaller hope than him – I had forgotten it) So in your next let us have a fuller account – I think if Mrs. Phillips wrote it it would be more circumstantial.

I began this letter directly after breakfast and it is now three o clk. All the rest of the time has been wasted in nearly useless conversation with callers there is no end to them in this house They leave me no time to write my letters Farewell dear Phillips for the present. Sarah begs to be remembered to you & Mrs. Phillips and to Miss Phillips and the rest of her acquaintance and I wish to be remembered [also] [ms. torn] I never can close one of these letters in reasonable compass without leaving out some important point but the whole comes to this that we do not forget any of you.

Very Faithfully Yours
M. FARADAY

[1] It is possible that this refers to Sir Astley Paston Cooper (1768–1841) who was then at the peak of his fame as a physician. The mention of another doctor (Dr Booll whom I am unable further to identify) strengthens this possibility.

92 M. FARADAY to J. F. W. HERSCHEL, 25 November 1828

[*R.S., previously unpublished*]

Royal Institution,
Nov 25 1828

DEAR SIR

On Saturday I made a piece of glass 5 inches square. On Monday took it to Mr Dolland [*sic*] Today he reports its good with the exception of one run which will *grind out*.

I was excessively cramped in making this piece of glass because of the smallness of our furnace. I have asked Mr Dolland whether he sees objection to laying out £10 or £15 in constructing a small furnace in the Glass furnace room here which will work properly – he sees none – do you? I shall make sketches & tell Ramsey to give me an estimate – hoping that what will be required will not be objectionable. I expect the estimates by Friday.

Let me know whether you object to this course I cannot make large specimens without some other means than those we have here & I think the large specimen just made is sufficient to prove the applicability of the principles when properly attended to

The piece just made is full of bubbles That was inevitable in the present furnace.

I am dear Sir
Very Truly Yours
M. FARADAY

93 M. FARADAY to B. SMITH,[1] 26 March 1829

[*American Philosophical Society, previously unpublished*]

Royal Institution
March 26, 1829.

DEAR SIR

At your Brothers request I write to you in haste hearing that you will soon leave England for your trip to America. I have asked Mr. Brande whether he could suggest any thing which your kindness & willingness could do for the

Institution and he agrees with me that it is only in the way of Minerals that we can recommend things to your attention The American Philosophical reports are so uncertain that we do not know how to trust them but it is said that very fine minerals large & beautiful are abundant Now with us these are desirable. Strontian specimens from Lake Erie are amongst the number

Your Brother told me of your plan of flying kites and wished me to write you my opinion as to danger from the Electric fluid I should think you had very little reason to fear from that agent but I certainly should advise that you have a metallic communication as a chain or rod descending from the string at the distance of a few yards from the ship (if convenient) and touching the water even entering it for a few feet if that can be allowed and also that a wire run up the string from this chain perhaps 30 or 40 feet – If the conductor cannot be dropped from the string into the water then it ought to be continued by good metallic communication from the string over the ship & down the side until it touch & enter the water but I should prefer the first method Much must be left to your own observation & judgement but attend to this one point never have a *broken or interrupted* conductor let the different metallic parts touch each other

If your plan succeeds I hope you will send us an account if it Serve [reading doubtful] as a subject for one of our Friday Evenings describing the arrangements both successful & unsuccessful which you had occasion to make in the passage.

I am Sir
Your Very Obedt Servant
M. FARADAY

¹ Benjamin Smith was a brother of one of the Members of the Royal Institution. See Letter 117.

94   M. FARADAY to E. MITSCHERLICH,¹ 5 June 1829
[*Deutsches Museum, previously unpublished*]

Royal Institution
June 5th 1829.

MY DEAR SIR

I have not forgotten the pleasure I received from the few short visits you formerly made me in London and am quite unwilling to allow your remembrance of me to be altogether lost A friend of mine Mr Halswell intends passing through Berlin and I am desirous upon the occasion of writing to you for a double or triple purpose One as I have before said & the leading one to keep your remembrance of me alive. Another the introduction of Mr Halswell to you as a gentleman & a scholar whom you will be pleased to know and the third a favour which I am going to ask of you only on condition that you will refuse it if it incurs too much trouble.

There is manufactured at the Royal Porcellain works at Berlin such basins for chemical operations as infinitely surpass any thing we have in London I would write to the works directly for them but do not know the sizes & prices & could not therefore well describe what I want. Now You as a chemist know perfectly. If I understand rightly it is only evaporating basins which are particularly useful to chemists and such as are from 3 to 5 inches in diameter I imagine to be those that will suit me best A few down to 2 inches and a few up to 6. 7 or 8 inches in diameter but I may not go to an expence of more than eight or ten pounds sterling altogether and therefore I must be economical Now if you would take the trouble of ordering these for me according to your discretion it would be a great favour done me If they manufacture any thing else you think useful & not expensive then put a specimen or two in.

If you could look them out & order them: the people at the works I hope would take the trouble of packing them up & shipping them addressed to me to the Care of Messrs. Bingham Richards & Co. Kings Warehouse Custom House London – At the same time sending a letter per post to Messrs. Bingham Richards & Co. Kings Arm Yard. Coleman Street. London advising them of the shipment

As to the payment at Berlin I intend to ask Mr Halswell the bearer of this letter to pay to you or at the Porcellain works the expence incurred I am in hopes you can arrange to do this though the goods may not be shipped until afterwards

I hear of your progress and continually regret that my ignorance of the German Language entirely prevents me from arriving at the correct knowledge of what is doing in a very active part of the scientific world. But time gets shorter & shorter with me business accumulates more & more.

Believe me to be
My dear Sir
Your Very Obliged & faithful
M. FARADAY

[1] Eilhard Mitscherlich (1794–1863), chemist and crystallographer, Professor of Chemistry at the Friedrich-Wilhelms Institute in Berlin.

95 M. FARADAY to T. DRUMMOND,[1] 29 June 1829
[*B.J. 1, 408*]

Royal Institution
June 29, 1829

SIR,

In reply to your letter of the 26th, and as a result of our conversation on Saturday, I beg to state that I should be happy to undertake the duty of lecturing on chemistry to the gentlemen cadets of Woolwich, provided that the time

I should have to take for that purpose from professional business at home were remunerated by the salary.

But on this point I hardly know what to say in answer to your inquiry, because of my ignorance of the conveniences and assistance I should find at Woolwich. For the lectures which I deliver in this Institution, where I have the advantage of being upon the spot, of possessing a perfect laboratory with an assistant in constant occupation, and of having the command of an instrument maker and his men, I receive, independent of my salary as an officer of the establishment, 8l. 15s. per lecture. The only lectures I have given out of this house were a course at the London Institution, for which, with the same conveniences as to laboratory and assistance, I was paid at the same rate. Since then I have constantly declined lecturing out of the Royal Institution because of my engagements.

I explained to you on Saturday the difficulty of compressing the subject of chemistry into a course of twenty lectures only, and yet to make it clear, complete, and practically useful; and without I thought I could do this, I should not be inclined to undertake the charge you propose to me. Now twenty lectures, at the terms I have in this house, amount to 175l. per annum, and therefore I should not be inclined to accept any offer under that; the more expecially as, if I found that the times and hours of the students allowed it, I should probably extend the course by a lecture or two, or more, that I might do the subject greater justice.

Notwithstanding what I have said, I still feel the difficulty of estimating labour, the extent of which I am ignorant of.

Were the lectures of that class which do not require to be accompanied by experiment, or were the necessary experiments and illustrations of such a nature that (as in mechanics) the preparations, once made, are complete and ready when wanted for future courses, I should not feel the difficulty. But in many parts of chemistry, and especially in the chemistry of the gases, the substances under consideration cannot be preserved from one course to another, but have to be formed at the time; and hence, if the illustrations are to be clear and numerous, a degree of preparatory labour, which has to be repeated on every occasion.

For these reasons I wish you would originate the terms rather than I. If you could make the offer of 200l. a year, I would undertake them; and then, supposing I found more work than I expected, I should not have to blame myself for stating an undervalue for my own exertions. I have no thought that the sum would overpay, because, from my experience for some years in a chemical school founded in the laboratory of the Royal Institution, I have no doubt that the proportion of instruction to the students would expand rather than contract.

Allow me, before I close this letter, to thank you and the other gentlemen who may be concerned in this appointment, for the good opinion which has induced you to propose it to me. I consider the offer as a high honour, and beg you to feel assured of my sense of it. I should have been glad to have accepted or declined it, independent of pecuniary motives; but my time is my only estate, and that which would be occupied in the duty of the situation must be taken from what otherwise would be given to professional business.

I am, Sir, your most obedient servant,

M. FARADAY.

[1] Col. Thomas Drummond (1797–1840) was Lieutenant Governor of the Royal Military Academy at Woolwich. See Letter 96. He had attended Faraday's and Brande's lectures at the Royal Institution and was undoubtedly instrumental in obtaining the invitation to Faraday to lecture at the RMA.

96 T. DRUMMOND to M. FARADAY, 16 December 1829
[R.S., *previously unpublished*]

Royal Military Academy,
Woolwich,
16 Dec. 1829

SIR

I beg leave to inform you that I received a letter last night from Lord Downes Secretary to the Master general of the Ordinance acquainting me that His Lordship approves of your being appointed to deliver a Course of Chemical Lectures at this Institution for which you are to receive a Salary of £200.

His Lordship has further decided that the Course shall consist of not less than 25 Lectures in the year.

The vacation commences on the 19 Inst. and the Cadets will not return until the 1st February. I shall take an early opportunity of calling upon you with a view to making the necessary arrangements.

I am Sir
Your ob. Servt.
TH. DRUMMOND
Col., Lt. Gov., R. M. Academy

97 M. FARADAY to J. A. PARIS, 23 December 1829
[B.J. 1, 54]

Royal Institution,
December 23, 1829.

MY DEAR SIR

You asked me to give you an account of my first introduction to Sir. H. Davy, which I am very happy to do, as I think the circumstances will bear testimony to the goodness of his heart.

When I was a bookseller's apprentice I was very fond of experiment and very adverse to trade. It happened that a gentleman, a member of the Royal Institution, took me to hear some of Sir H. Davy's last lectures in Albemarle Street. I took notes, and afterwards wrote them out more fairly in a quarto volume.

My desire to escape from trade, which I thought vicious and selfish, and to enter into the service of Science, which I imagined made its pursuers amiable and liberal, induced me at last to take the bold and simple step of writing to Sir H. Davy, expressing my wishes, and a hope that if an opportunity came in his way he would favour my views; at the same time, I sent the notes I had taken of his lectures.

The answer, which makes all the point of my communication, I send you in the original, requesting you to take great care of it, and to let me have it back, for you may imagine how much I value it.

You will observe that this took place at the end of the year 1812; and early in 1813 he requested to see me, and told me of the situation of assistant in the laboratory of the Royal Institution, then just vacant.

At the same time that he thus gratified my desires as to scientific employment, he still advised me not to give up the prospects I had before me, telling me that Science was a harsh mistress, and in a pecuniary point of view but poorly rewarding those who devoted themselves to her service. He smiled at my notion of the superior moral feelings of philosophic men, and said he would leave me to the experience of a few years to set me right on that matter.

Finally, through his good efforts, I went to the Royal Institution, early in March of 1813, as assistant in the laboratory; and in October of the same year went with him abroad, as his assistant in experiments and in writing. I returned with him in April 1815, resumed my station in the Royal Institution, and have, as you know, ever since remained there.

I am, dear Sir, ever truly yours,

M. FARADA

98 M. FARADAY to R. PHILLIPS, 10 January 1830

[*Imperial College, London, previously unpublished*]

Royal Institution,
Jany 10. 1830

DEAR PHILLIPS

I received your packet of Alkali and regret that I have been obliged by business to delay answering your letter respecting it. But I have examined & think it a very fine article. It is as nearly caustic as may be only a trace of carbonic acid being present there is only a trace of sulphates and besides caustic soda I find little else than water & common salt There is a small portion of insoluble matter consisting of sulphuret of iron & carbonate of lime but it can be of no consequence in the applications of the substance

The quantity of alkali present i-e of soda is above 56 per cent. probably equal to 56.5 – In dry carbonate of Soda equivalent to 94.5 per cent.

Compared with American Potash the substance may be considered as pure and I know of no reason why it should not surpass that alkali in most applications In many cases I think it must be preferable. Thus for the bleachers it is quite caustic & ready for use for the soap makers it is the alkali they want – & they have no occasion to refer to double decompositions whether they require some carbonic acid present or not I cannot certainly say – In glass making if soda give results equal to the promises given by the experiments already made your articles must be of great importance

What experience I have of the alkalis induce me to conclude that the powers of Soda & potash upon organic bodies as in bleaching &c is according to their equivalent powers You will understand that I mean 32 of Soda produce as much effect as 48 of potassa. At least that is the impression on my mind and I expect to hear it confirmed by all those who use the alkalis

I do not know of any other important point referred to in your letter If I have forgotten any thing remind me of it

I am Dear Phillips
Ever Truly Yours
M. FARADAY

You may make what use you please of this letter provided you do not publish it

MF

99   M. FARADAY to E. MAGRATH, 26 March 1830
[*R.I., previously unpublished*]

R Institution
Mar 26. 1830

DEAR MAGRATH

It is pleasant to have some note of you again but I was sorry to hear from Dr Nicholl[1] this morning that you gained strength only slowly. I was in hopes Greenwich would have done you good. I unluckily missed you at Greenwich & have missed you at the Athenaeum too but in fact I am missing every where and find myself any thing but what I ought to be My strength fails my nerves grow feeble and I am become a patient that does no credit to any one. Dr. Nichol was here this morning & is very kind but I want rest & he cannot give me that

I was to have dined at the Athenaeum today with him but feel unable to do so. I ought to give an evening next friday I have no one ready & feel almost indifferent to it. Even Woolwich lectures have done me no good in health yet for this last month I have in [*sic*] all sorts of indispositions

However I shall write you no more folly of this kind I would be glad to retire to the sea side if I could for a week or two & hope to do so at Easter. I feel no spirits for anything

Hoping we shall both meet to laugh at our present miserable state I recommend to you what I am forced to have myself Patience.

Ever Dear Magrath
Truly Yours
M. FARADAY

[1] Dr Whitlock Nicholl (1786–1838) was Faraday's personal physician. He also helped Faraday to coin new terms when such were demanded by his researches into the nature of electricity. See S. Ross, 'Faraday consults the Scholars: the Origins of the terms of Electrochemistry,' *NRRS*, 16 (1961), 187.

100 M. FARADAY to DAVIES GILBERT,[1] 13 May 1830
[*PRO, Adm. 1, 3471*]

Royal Institution
May 13th. 1830

DEAR SIR

At your request I have been making enquiries that I might be enabled to judge what would be the probable expence of continuing & perfecting the glass experiments at this place

I am induced to suppose that from £75 to £80 would pay the wages and buy the materials necessary to enable me to ascertain the full value of the process already described in the paper you have made the Bakerian Lecture[2] – and that if afterwards it were required to extend the process to plates of glass 18 or 20 inches in diameter £100 more would build the furnace – pay wages etc. for that purpose

I purposely avoid reading the articles that my friends tell me appear in the public prints But the mere mention of them by others induces me to remind you that the expence incurred by the Sub Committee at the Royal Institution by leave of the Authorities is not above a fourth or a fifth I believe of that incurred by Sir H. Davy and the Committee which he appointed at the outset of the investigation

I further wish you most distinctly to understand that I regret I ever allowed myself to be named as one of the Committee. I have had in consequence several years of hard work; all the time that I could spare from necessary duties (and which I wished to devote to original research) been [*sic*] consumed in the experiments and consequently given gratuitously to the public I should be very glad now to follow Mr Herschells [*sic*] example & return to the prosecution of my own views and it is only because I do not like to desert my post at the most critical time if you and others think it worth while to keep it filled that I am willing to pursue the experiments further

I am Dear Sir
Your Obligd & faithful Servt
M. FARADAY

[1] President of the Royal Society.
[2] M. Faraday, 'On the manufacture of glass for optical purposes,' *PT* (1830), 1. See also *LPW*, 116ff.

101 M. FARADAY to E. MITSCHERLICH, 4 August 1830[1]

[*Deutsches Museum, previously unpublished*]

Royal Institution
4th. August 1830.

MY DEAR SIR

Your letter which I received some time since gave me great pleasure and I have many times been on the point of taking up my pen to answer it but have been prevented by some sudden occupation My situation is such that I am liable to be constantly disturbed and for 8 or 9 months in the year am thoroughly tired with continued business Although I date from the R Institution I am at this moment a little way from town resting from recent fatigue & recovering from ill health

Your kind attention to my letter was no more than what I expected from your kindness although I knew very well I had no claim upon it for my opportunities of making your acquaintance in a worthy manner have been very few – far fewer than I desired. Your kindness in the porcellain the filtering paper & other things is fully appreciated by me and I hope soon to have the pleasure of examining the box you promised to send me[2] You refer to other to other [*sic*] things which with you are far cheaper than with us and if you obtain this letter before the box leaves or if any other opportunity occurs I should be very glad to have an ounce or two of potassium also some sodium – some bromine and also cadmium if not very dear – We have selenium which came from Germany but it is mingled with a great deal of sulphur – If it is not hoping too much I should be delighted to find that you would think for me and put up any thing you may suppose we have not or which is dear with us Many things are so expensive with us that they limit our experiments.

I am quite anxious to see the cahier of your treatise which you mention in your letter and your doing so encourages me to speak to you relative to a work which is in contemplation here. You are aware that a Quarterly Journal of Science has been published in London Edited by Mr. Brande & continued for many years past. This Journal is to cease and the Managers of the Royal Institution are desirous of establishing a Quarterly Journal according to their

Charter & which shall be truly scientific and excluding illnatured reviews shall include as much foreign science as possible. The latter has been sadly neglected here & it is their wish that every means should be taken to supply the deficiency in the new Journal. The Bookseller will of course have his profits but the work is to be no source of profit to the R Institution or to the Managers On the other hand everybody who contributes scientific matter is to be paid. The rate of payment will vary from five to ten guineas a sheet according to the character of the person who writes & the originality & quality of the contribution. If the work succeeds every thing it produces is to be expended upon its own improvement. Now I have thought that perhaps you could help us to science of an original kind from your part of the globe either by telling us of person [*sic*] who would contribute or sending us papers & I promised the Managers to ask you whether you could not let us have a popular but scientific account of your own discoveries not too profound & mathematical but yet clear & good & fit to be an authority, something indeed like Fresnels account of the undulatory theory of light which in fact Dr. Young translated for Mr. Brande's Journal.[3]

The first Number of the new Journal will appear on the first day of October & it is hoped that every number will be an improvement.[4] If we can get men like yourself to help it, it will be sure to succeed and will quickly become a pleasure to those who support it. Any thing which you may like to say upon the subject communicate to me & I will lay it before the Committee.

With the strongest recollection of your kindness and the highest respect to your talents, I am My dear Sir

Your Most Obliged & faithful Servant
M. FARADAY

I hope the address of this letter will enable it to reach you

[1] The latter half of the photostat of this letter was too poor to show the punctuation clearly.
[2] I have been unable to locate Mitscherlich's letter to Faraday in which he clearly offered to send chemical apparatus and reagents to Faraday.
[3] A. Fresnel, 'Elementary view of the undulatory theory of light,' *QJS*, 23 (1827), 127, 441; 24 (1827), 113, 431; 25 (1828), 198; 26 (1828), 168, 389; 27 (1829), 159.
[4] The Journal was short-lived, lasting only from 1830 to 1831 and complete in two volumes.

102 J. N. P. HACHETTE to M. FARADAY, 22 August 1830
[*R.I., B.J. 1, 416*]

Paris,
22 aout 1830.

MONSIEUR

vous avez probablement Reçu un petit memoire sur des Experiences hydrauliques, que je vous ai envoyé le 17 juillet passé.[1] en même temps que je Reçus Votre Memoire sur le verre, un autre memoire de M. Davies Gilbert s'y trouvait joint.[2] j'ai traduit ce dernier memoire, et la traduction sera publiée dans le bulletin de la Societé d'encouragement, cahier de juillet.[3] j'ai ajouté quelques notes a cette traduction, qui j'espere, seront accueillies par M. Davies Gilbert. j'esperois pouvoir vous envoyer avec cette lettre, quelques exemplaires de mes notes precedées du memoire; mais l'imprimeur du bulletin ne me les a pas encore renvoyées – je profiterais de la premiere occasion, pour me Rappeller a votre Souvenir, a celui de M. Davies Gilbert qui a bien voulu me gratifier d'un exemplaire de son Memoire sur les Machines à vapeur du Cornwall –

Parmi les evenemens qui ont Signalé les journées des 27, 28 et 29 juillet,[4] vous aurez remarqué l'influence des Sciences sur la population parisienne. des jeunes gens, de l'age moyen 19 ans, formant l'Ecole polytechnique, habitent un ancien college, placé aux extremités de Paris; là ils etudient tranquillement les ouvrages des Lacroix, des *Poissons*, de Monge, &c. l'analyse mathematique, la physique et la chimie enrichie de vos decouvertes sont leur unique occupation. un detachement armé se presente a eux, les invite a Marcher avec lui pour la defense de la charte violée,[5] cette jeunesse humble, modeste, sans armes, revetue de l'uniforme qui rappelle la defense de Paris en 1814, sort du College, et a l'instant chaque groupe armée proclame un eleve Polytechnique son commandant; elle se croit invincible; puis que la Science et l'honneur la precedent; elle Marche avec confiance, parcequ'elle a l'assentiment de tout ce qui porte un coeur genereux. les principes Mathematiques (Principia Mathematica) et les principes de gouvernement se donnent donc la main; les deux premieres nations du Monde se Rapprochent; puisse la raison triompher de tous les prejugés qui s'opposent au perfectionnement des Sociétés!

en france, le Savant, l'artiste, l'ouvrier sentent toute la dignité de sa position sociale; chacun ajoute un peu de bien, au bien qui existe; la plus petite decouverte dans les Sciences est un bienfait pour l'humanité; les grandes decouvertes sont pour notre Siecle les actions heroiques. en vous exprimant mon opinion sur l'influence des Sciences, j'eprouve un sentiment bien vif d'estime et de Reconnaissance pour Vous et vos compatriotes, qui consacrez votre vie entiere aux Recherches Scientifiques.

j'ai l'honneur d'etre bien affectueusement Monsieur

Votre devoué Serviteur
HACHETTE

---

[1] Probably J. N. P. Hachette, 'Expériences sur le mouvement des fluides aériformes et des liquides,' *JGC*, 9 (1830), 377.
[2] Davies Gilbert, 'On the progressive improvements made in the efficiency of steam-engines in Cornwall, with investigations of the methods best adapted for imparting great angular velocities,' *PT* (1830), 121.
[3] [J.N.P.] Hachette, 'Notice sur le travail mécanique des machines à vapeur du comté de Cornouailles, comparé à la dépense en combustible,' *BSd'E*, 29 (1830), 255.
[4] The July Revolution in which Charles X of France was overthrown.
[5] The constitutional Charter granted to the French people upon the accession of Louis XVIII to the throne after the defeat of Napoleon.

103 A. DE LA RIVE to M. FARADAY, 21 October 1830

[I.E.E., previously unpublished]

Genève, le 21 octb^{re} 1830

Mon père me charge de mille amitiés pour vous; nous parlons tres souvent de vous ensemble. Je vous prie de me rappeler au souvenir de Mr *Margrath.*[1] dont je n'ai pas oublié toutes les bontés à mon égard.

Permettez moi, Monsieur, de venir me rappeler à votre souvenir & vous faire en même temps une demande qui j'espere ne vous dérangera pas. Je viens d'apprendre par le dernier numéro du *Quarterly Journal of Sciences* que ce journal alloit être remplacé par un autre publié directement par l'Institution Royale;[2] croyez-vous qu'il seroit possible d'organiser une échange entre ce nouveau Journal & la Bibliothèque Universelle qui se publie à Genève; ainsi que nous l'avons deja fait la plupart des autres Journaux Anglois. Auriez vous la bonté de vous charger de cette negociation & de me faire ensuite savoir si elle a reussi; vous nous rendriez un grand Service, car un des principaux agrémens que nous eprouvons de notre cooperation à la redaction de la Bibl.Universelle, c'est de nous procurer facilement par les échanges, une collection complete des journaux Scientifiques étrangers. – Si l'échange est accepté nous enverrons à l'adresse que vous nous indiquez la collection de 1830 de la Bibl. Univ. & vous aurez la bonté de faire parvenir les numéros du nouveau Journal à mesure qu'ils paroitront à l'adresse de la *Direction de la Bibliothèque Universelle* chez *Bossange, Barthes & Lowell, booksellers 14, Great Marlborough Strt London.* – Si je m'adresse à vous pour cette affaire, c'est d'abord que je connais votre complaisance & que de plus je présume & j'espere que vous devez prendre une grande part à la redaction du nouveau Journal.

J'ai encore un service à vous demander; il s'agirait de nous mettre quelquefois au courant de vos travaux & de nous adresser de temps à autres quelques détails sur les recherches que vous avez faites & sur les mémoires que vous allez publier. Si vous pouviez y ajouter quelches nouvelles Scientifiques principalement en ce qui concerne les arts industriels, ce seroit un mérite de plus à une correspondance qui en auroit déjà beaucoup pour nous sans celà. Nous venons d'organiser un arrangement semblable avec quelques savans de l'Italie & de l'Allemagne & nous serions bien heureux que vous voulussiez consentir à nous favoriser aussi quelquefois de vos lettres. Pour éviter les frais de port vous pourriez les adresser sous forme de papiers ou de notes à mon adresse comme *redacteur de la Bibl. Universelle,* chez les mêmes libraires que j'aie indiqué ci dessus. Je serais aussi & meme plus reconnaissant quand vous voudriez m'écrire directement par la poste.

Nous avons bien besoin de nouvelles Scientifiques; car ici, comme en France, on ne fait pas grand chose, tandique [*sic*] vous venez de publier votre beau travail sur la fabrication de verre dont nous avons recu des exemplaires &

que nous avons traduit [illeg.] dans le Bibl. Univ. Nous vous remercions beaucoup de ces exemplaires & nous attendons avec impatience quelque nouvelle production de vous qui sans doute ne tardera pas. – Je m'occupe toujours de recherches sur l'électricité & d'un travail complet sur le sujet qui j'espère sera achevé au printemps prochain, quoique j'aie encore bien a faire.[3] Les évênemens politiques ont absorbé dernierement bien du temps & de l'attention; il n'en restait pas beaucoup pour la Science. Marcet[4] & Macaire ont recu aussi les exemplaires de votre mémoire & vous en remercient.

Encore une négociation pour laquelle je comptais écrire au Dr Roget,[5] mais que vous voudrez peut-etre bien suivre. Il s'agiroit de l'échange des *Transactions philosophiques* avec les mémoires que publie notre *Société de Physique & d'Histoire Naturelle*. Depuis cette année cette publication sera regulière & il paraitra deux cahiers in 4° par an. Nous avons déjà obtenu la faveur d'une échange avec presque toutes les Sociétés Savantes de l'Europe & entr'autres l'Institut de France; nous serions heureux d'avoir le meme succès auprès de la Société Royale. Seriez vous assez bon pour arranger cette affaire ou croyez-vous que je doive en écrire au Dr Roget. Vous voudrez bien peut-être me répondre un mot à cet égard, comme sur les autres demandes que je vous adresse. Permettez moi de vous adresser ici, mes excuses pour mon indiscretion l'expression de la haute considération & de l'attachement que vous a voué votre tout dévoué

AUGT DE LA RIVE

J'aurais aimer avoir quelques nouvelles Scientifiques à vous donner; mais nous sommes bien pauvres dans ce moment. Un travail sur la decomposition des huiles par l'electricite et sur les [illeg.] specifiques des composés par compression à leurs élémens, voilà ce que je ferais paraitre de plus prochain. – J'aurais soin, si cela peut vous intéresser de vous en communiquer les résultats.

[1] Edward Magrath, Faraday's long-time friend and Secretary of the Athenaeum.
[2] See Letter 101.
[3] Auguste de la Rive's *Traité d'électricité théorique et appliquée* appeared in three volumes at Paris between 1854 and 1858(!).
[4] François Marcet (1803–83) was the son of Alexandre and Jane Marcet whose main scientific work was done in biochemistry. He was one of A. de la Rive's companions in Geneva.
[5] Peter Mark Roget (1779–1869) of Thesaurus fame was one of the Secretaries of the Royal Society at this time.

[Bibliothèque publique et universitaire de Genève, ms. 2316, f. 51, previously unpublished]

Royal Institution
Nov.ʳ 22 1830.

MY DEAR SIR

It is long since I received your letter but absence in the country and other causes have prevented me from answering it before this time. I am glad of any circumstance that keeps your recollection of me alive. Our Managers immediately ordered the exchange you requested to be made & the first No of the New Journal was sent three weeks ago to Your Bookseller here as you requested. If Bossange will take the trouble of sending your Bibliotheque to the Royal Institution it will save us the necessity of making frequent enquiries after its arrival

At present I write by post as a quick way of reaching you but shall I in future send *all* communications through the bookseller to you? Copies of papers notes etc? and may I send copies of papers etc. to Marcet etc. in the same way under cover to you? or will that embarras [*sic*] your pockets?

I take great interest in the New Journal & wish it earnestly to succeed but my time is so exceedingly occupied that I cannot pledge myself to [*sic*] much for it. – The same want of time prevents me from pursuing *glass* as I wish the same want will prevent me from assisting you by communications of news etc for it prevents me from going out into the world & hearing much news – I hope soon however to be able to arrange for more leisure that I may be able to work at philosophy & send you a paper or two i.e. copies as heretofore

With respect to the New Royal Institution Journal the Managers wish to make it good and with that view are anxious to obtain communications from Men of Science from all parts of the world. The work is to be no source of profit to the Institution or the Managers but all it produces which the Bookseller does not claim is to be expended in supporting & improving it. All papers are to be paid for at so much per printed sheet 4.5.6.7.8 or even 10 guineas according to its merits experimental character & character of its Author. Such payment helps to defray the expences of the experiments Now we are in hopes that such men as yourself will be willing to communicate your papers to us – Not that you should not put them in the Bibliotheque but because of the distance between Geneva & London we consider that if you sent us a manuscript so that it might be published at the same time here as at Geneva it would be here an original paper and so so [*sic*] your discoveries & investigations would be more rapidly & widely diffused than at present. If you think well of this when you send a paper send it so that it may be published in the next No of the Journal in due time. You will be aware of the periods of publication of the time required for the transit and that for arrangement & printing. Such payment as may be necessary we will make according to your direction. If you come in contact with other *good* men and think the arrangement expedient perhaps you will mention it to them

I am going to the Royal Society council this afternoon & will try to make the arrangement of transfer as you request – I have just left the Council – I am told the RS does not exchange with any Society – they present Transactions to Royal & National Societies and I find that the Secretary of Your Society must apply formally to the Sec. of the RS if the Transactions be desired

With earnest remembrances to your father & any [reading doubtful] friends I am Dear Sir faithfully yours

M. FARADAY

105 G. MOLL[1] to M. FARADAY, 24 December 1830
[*I.E.E., previously unpublished*]

Utrecht
24 December 1830

I am much obliged to you my dear Sir! for the kind notice which you have been pleased to take of my paper on the invention of telescopes.[2] In future I shall be most happy in submitting to the approbation of the proprietors of the Journal of the Royal Institution any paper of mine which might appear to me not to be unworthy of appearing in such a respectable publication. I cannot indeed refrain from stating that I have a great mind to say a few words to Mr Babbage about his recent publication on the state of Science in England.[3] I believe indeed that he took an erroneous view of the question and that many things which he admires in foreign countries are far inferior to what he might have found at home. You justly observe that you ought not remain ignorant of what is done elsewhere; but there is a great difference between a just estimate of foreign exertions and extolling them beyond measure above what is done in your own country. We certainly must endeavour not to suffer ourselves to be swayed by national prejudice but we must take equal care not carry [*sic*] our admiration of foreigners so far, as to be unjustly severe against our own countrymen. This, I apprehend, is the case with Mr Babbage and with many other Englishmen, who cherish his opinions. You have long been, in a great measure ignorant of what was done on the continent; this want of information naturally occasioned self complacency, and very often it was with great reluctancy that English writers did justice to the conspicuous merits of french, Italian, and German philosophers. From this unjust contempt some amongst you have run in the other extreme of unbounded admiration. I believe you have been mistaken in both ways, and the truth lays between. The national, Imperial or royal Institute of France, is alike undeserving the sneers which have been

187

thrown out against it, and of the high encomiums which have bestown upon its members [*sic*]. There, and every where there is much which is bad, mixed with a greater and smaller proportion of good. But be that ratio what it may, I do not see that Mr Babbage is at all justified in thus undervaluing what is done in his own country. My friend now Sir James South,[4] follows on the same side, he is determined to see everything in black in England and to speak highly on the Scientific institutions of foreign countries. But he himself, the identical Sir James South is a direct proof of the fallaciousness of his own words. Show me such another man, show me a Surgeon in France, who rose to such a Scientific eminence in any thing except surgery. Mr Bailey[5] [*sic*] is another proof of the contrary of what I understand him & his friends to assert. Let it be shewn that there exists amongst the 30 millions of frenchmen, one broker, nay even one merchant, who is an astronomer. Where am I to find on the exchange of Paris a merchant like Mr Roscoe.[6] They accuse the present Royal Astronomer of Selling the copies of the Greenwich observation [*sic*] to a grocer; at the Royal Observatory of Paris there can be little danger of such an irregular proceeding, since I heard it publicly stated by an eminent German Astronomer, at the late meeting of Philosophers at Hamburg that in the space of eight months, not even an Observation was made at Paris for ascertaining the rate of their clock! But all this would led [*sic*] me too far, and I will not enter deeper in to such an abundant source of recrimination.

The last article of your kind letter requires a distinct answer. The object of the proprietors of the Quarterly Journal is not profit, no more is mine! I have been publishing pretty much, perhaps too much; but I can safely swear that I never got the least pecuniary reward for my labours; nay, my country men will very often take it into their heads that it is my bounden duty, to giv[e] [ms. torn and missing] my opinion upon any scheme which they may think proper to lay befor[e me] [ms. torn and missing] and that my time and exertions must be entirely at their disposal. Un[der] [ms. torn and missing] such circumstances I cannot accept the proposals of your Committee, but I would feel obliged to them if they would favour me with a few copies of my paper to be given to my particular friends; half a dozen will satisfy my utmost wishes. If when in London, they will confer upon me the favour of being admitted to the library & collections of the Royal Institution I will certainly feel exceedingly obliged to them.

At the close of this year, I cannot, I presume, make you a better wish, than that you may succeed entirely in the course of the next, in furnishing opticians, with such flint glass, as may give full scope to the skill and dexterity of your own Dollonds[7] and Tullys.[8]

I am Dear Sir!
Yours very truly
G. MOLL

Any parcel directed to H. Braaksma Esq 71 Great Queensstreet Lincoln's Inn fields will come to hand, as will any letter, which latter may be also simply directed to Prof. Moll Utrecht

1 Gerrit Moll (1785–1838), Professor of Mathematics and Physics at the University of Utrecht. None of Faraday's letters to Moll have survived.
2 G. Moll, 'Geschiedkundig onderzoek naar de eerste Uitrinders der Verrekijkers, uit de aanteekeningen van wijle den Hoogleeraar van Swinden, zamengesteldt,' *Nieuwe Verhandelingen der Eerste Klasse van het Koninklijk Nederlandsche Instituut van Wetenschappen, Letterkunde en Schoone Kunsten te Amsterdam*, 3 (1831), 103. An English translation appeared in the *JRI*, 1 (1831), 319, 483.
3 Charles Babbage, *Reflections on the Decline of Science in England*, London, 1830. See also *LPW*, 350ff.
4 Sir James South (1785–1867), trained as a surgeon, was an astronomer of some note and a close friend of Faraday's. He published an attack on the Royal Society in 1830 entitled 'Charges against the President and Councils of the Royal Society' (London, 1830), which added to the heat generated by Babbage's book.
5 Francis Baily (1774–1844) was a stockbroker with a burning interest in astronomy. He was a moving force behind the creation of the Royal Astronomical Society and served for many years as its President.
6 Thomas Roscoe (1791–1871) was a wealthy merchant noted primarily for his literary labours.
7 The Dollonds were a family of opticians having passed down the skills of their craft from one generation to another. George Dollond (1774–1852) collaborated with Faraday and Herschel on the project for improving optical glass.
8 The Tulleys, like the Dollonds, were a family of opticians whose technical skills were handed down from father to son. A Tulley was still carrying on his trade in 1830. See Sir George Biddell Airy's *Autobiography*, Cambridge, 1896, 38, 54, 90 and 110.

106   M. FARADAY to A.-M. AMPÈRE, 24 December 1830

[*Harvard University, previously unpublished*]

Royal Institution
Dec.ʳ 24th 1830

MY DEAR SIR

Having a few moments to spare from the continual business which oppresses me I secure them to write a few words to you not that I have any particular scientific news to tell you but to acknowledge your constant kindness in sending me copies of your papers to answer a letter of yours which I have had on my desk before my eyes many weeks for that purpose and to exchange feelings of kindness & friendship with you at the same time that I express my respect for you.

I can never forget that the commencement of the kindness I have always experienced from French philosophers was by M Hachette sending me a copy of your first papers on Electro-magnetism – I knew neither him nor you directly at that time and the favour was so much the more valuable[1] Whenever

Mr Underwood is in London he tells me all about your health and your un-
wearied pursuit of Science I wish there were more labourers like you and I wish
I were more worthy of your companionship; but I live in hopes I shall have
more leisure and may be able to do something which shall deserve a little more
praise

I trust you received the copy of my paper on glass? I am anxious to complete
that investigation and then proceed to some other branch of enquiry.

I do not know when I shall be able to see France but I do look for that pleasure some time: till when and always I am

My dear Sir
Your Obliged & faithful Ser [ms. torn]
M. FARADAY

¹ This would indicate that Faraday had not met Ampère when he visited Paris with Sir
Humphry Davy.

107   M. FARADAY to W. WHEWELL, 21 February 1831
[*Trinity College Library, Trinity College, Cambridge, previously unpublished*]

R. Institution
Feb. 21, 1831

SIR,

Mr. Daniell¹ has put your letter into my hands because the note you refer
to passed through me into the journal. When a friend from Cambridge (who
had received it from a friend of yours) gave it to me to put into the journal if
thought fit for that purpose you may suppose I did not hesitate a moment in
my opinion.² Nor have I any hesitation with regard to your offer of further
explanation on the subject but shall (as far as I have influence) be very glad to
have it for the next number

Your remarks upon chemical notation with the variety of systems which have
arisen with regard to notation nomenclature scales of proportional or atomic
number &c had almost stirred me up to regret publicly that such hindrances to
the progress of science should exist – I cannot help thinking it a most unfortunate thing that men who as experimentalists & philosophers are the most
fitted to advance the general cause of science & knowledge should by the
promulgation of their own theoretical views under the form of nomenclature
notation or scale actually retard its progress – It would not be of so much
consequence if it was only theory & hypotheses which they thus treated but
they put facts or the current coin of science into the same limited circulation
when they describe them in such a way that the initiated only can read them

You will easily suppose that I am not referring to the value which would
belong to the application of any acknowledged & received mode of expressing

190

facts of one kind; to another kind but I am objecting in general to what you object to in particular when you reprove the introduction of a new mode of notation whilst the one already received & known is amply sufficient

> I am Sir
> Your Obedt Servt
> M. FARADAY

Mr. Daniell wished me to ask you where we could pay to your account the sum (I think Seven Guineas) for the paper on Arches[3] &c

> MF

Let us have the paper as soon as convenient – Not later than the end of April Sooner if possible.

[1] John Frederic Daniell (1790–1845), was Professor of Chemistry at King's College, London, from its creation in 1831. He was the inventor of the Daniell cell producing a constant e.m.f.
[2] W. Whewell, 'On the Employment of Notation in Chemistry,' *JRI*, 1 (1830–1), 437.
[3] See M. de Lassaux, 'Description of a Mode of erecting light Vaults over Churches and similar Spaces,' communicated by Professor Whewell of Cambridge, *JRI*, 1 (1830–1), 224.

108   G. MOLL to M. FARADAY, 11 March 1831
[*I.E.E., previously unpublished*]

> Utrecht
> 11 March 1831

MY DEAR SIR!

With your very kind and obliging letter of the 1 instant, I received a copy of the No 2 of the Journal of the Royal Institution, although I had already received this number from the bookseller, this copy was not less acceptable as it will afford me an opportunity of making a present of it to a friend. The kind letter of the Managers of the Institution lays me under great obligations to them, and if this Mr Singer[1] who subscribed the letter, is that Mr Singer who wrote a book on electricity and galvanism, I ought to be grateful to him also for the very useful information which I derived from his writings.

I find in the same number some electro-magnetic experiments of mine, which I would very much like to have repeated by skilful hands Perhaps they might do well enough for an evening lecture in the Royal Institution, and I should be very happy to hear that they succeeded well. I mention the circumstance because I found many philosophers rather sceptical on the subject, and my old and excellent friend Van Marum[2] was with great difficulty worked into persuasion when he had the evidence of his own senses. Many indeed did not succeed because the surface of their apparatus was either to [*sic*] small, or the iron which they employed not sufficiently soft.

191

Allow me to point out some errors of the preface my paper [*sic*] on the invention of telescopes printed in the Journal of the R.I. They may be easily corrected in an erratum added to the following number. First, then Pierre Borel[3] is not a native of *Chartres* as I, and not the printer, erroneously stated but of Castres in Languedoc. Thus p 230 line 4 from the underpart, stands *Chartres* read *Castres*.

p. 325 line 5 from beneath *vitro-crystal lines* read *vitro-crystallines*
p. 329 line 16 from above stands *Bussi* read *Russi*.[4]

„ ibid	„ 22	„	„	„	Teannin read Jeannin[5]
„ ibid	„ 23	„	„	„	*Bussi* read *Russi*.
„ 330	„ 25	„	„	„	*Tansz* read Jansz[6]
„ ibid	„ 2 from beneath	„			*Tansz* read *Jansz*
„ 331	„ 6 from above	„			what *Borel says,* read *what Boreel*[7] *says*
„ 332	„ 5	„	„	„	*translate Borel's name* read *Boreel's name*
„ 332	„ 7 from beneath	„			*That he left the Hague* read *Thus he left the Hague*
„ „	„ „	„	„		*produced a telescope* read *procured a telescope.*

It is certainly not be wondered [*sic*] that outlandish handwriting and hard names led the printer to some mistakes.

I just finished a paper, which goes with the present, which, if it suits the purpose of the managers of the Institution is very much at their service. It goes on the comparison of the french Kilogramme and the British Troy, and some other weights.[8] It is very strange and vexing that after all what is done [*sic*] and has been written on the subject of weights and measures, we are still in the dark as to the real value of so important a weight as the french unit of the kilogramme. I, for one, do not know what it is.

I really do not recollect what I wrote you about the present state of Science in England, but certainly I do not think it all worth printing. Still I am not ashamed to own my opinions. The English have quite enough of their natural and foreign political and scientific enemies, without waging a civil-scientific war amongst themselves. I have not the slightest doubts but that the Counts, Marquesses and Barons of the french Institute will be highly amused in seeing some of the English Philosophers so overanxious to level to the ground the venerable fabric of the Royal Society in order to have it reconstructed in the more modern form of the french Institute.[9] Still I am one of those who are of opinion that the experiment of such a radical reform as appears to be contemplated for the Royal Society will prove an utter failure. No foreigner and no person not belonging to the Society can judge, and perhaps ought to abstain from judging, of its internal management, but a neutral foreigner (if however such there be) who inquires impartially into the state of science in England and in other countries cannot help seeing with regret, Englishmen scoff and rail at things which ought to have been looked upon as the pride of their country. Babbage, for example, is lost in admiration of the meeting of German Philosophers and Physicians, which he attended in Berlin, now two years ago. No doubt many excellent persons are assembled on these occasions, and the pleasure of enjoying the company of so many eminent men must be exceedingly gratifying to any rational being. But if we come to consider the really scientific business which is transacted in those assemblies, if we are to separate the genuine corn from the chaff, we will find very little of the first and great abundance of the latter. I was present at the last meeting in Hamburg, and I must say that very often I was quite astonished at what I saw and heard. But I must not take up any more of your valuable time.

[No signature]

[1] S. W. Singer, then Librarian of the Royal Institution.
[2] Martyn van Marum (1750–1837), Dutch chemist and physicist, most famous for his work in electrostatics utilizing the great electrostatic generator of the Teyler Museum in Harlem.
[3] Pierre Borel (ca. 1620–89) wrote on the invention of the telescope. See his *De vero telescopii inventore, cum brevi omnium conspiciliorum historia*...Hagae Comitum, 1655.
[4] Possibly Georgius Russi of Padua.
[5] Pierre Jeannin (1540–1622), President of the Parlement of Paris. In the paper, Moll refers to *Lettres et Negotiations du Président de Jeannin*, Paris, 1656.
[6] Zacharias Jansz, a spectacle maker of Middelburg.
[7] Willam Boreel (1592–1668), cited by Borel as playing a role in the discovery of the telescope.
[8] G. Moll, 'On the comparison of British, French, and Dutch weights,' *JRI*, 2 (1831), 64.
[9] See Charles Babbage, *Reflections on the Decline of Science in England*, London, 1830.

109   C. WHEATSTONE to M. FARADAY, 23 March 1831

[*I.E.E., previously unpublished*]

March 23d 31

DEAR SIR,

I have perused your paper and am quite satisfied that the inferences you draw from your experiments are correct.[1] But I must differ from you in one thing; you state it as your opinion that it is of much less importance to establish the real cause of the phenomena than to show that Savart's[2] explanation is erroneous. Now this is paying too much deference even to a highly merited reputation, and were this the sole utility of your experiments the end might have been obtained with much less time and ingenuity than you have bestowed upon the task. The fact that we do not hear these presumed co-existent sounds, is alone a sufficient evidence of their non-existence, nor can it be alleged in justification of the supposition that they are too feeble to be heard, for if they exist they are sufficiently intense to form acoustic figures; neither will the explanation avail by which the late Dr. Young attempted to account for the phenomena exhibited by liquids on vibrating elastic surfaces when I repeated my experiments to him, viz: that they might indicate the coexistence of vibrating motions so rapid as to exceed the limits of audibility; for the sounds assumed in Savart's explanation were in general not more than two octaves above the fundamental sound. Another way by which Savart's hypothesis can be satisfactorily disproved, is by an application of my optical means for decomposing vibratory motions with which you are acquainted; this was the form of the experiment. I took a square plate of glass and at the middle of one of the edges I cemented a bead such as used in the Kaleidophone, and by applying a violin bow at the middle of another edge I caused the plate to vibrate in the mode of division with two diagonal quiescent lines; the light of a candle reflected from the bead formed a luminous line equal in length to the amplitude of the vibration which, on moving the plate rapidly in its own plane, was decomposed into a zig-zag line ⌒⌒⌒ or ∧∧∧⌒ but without any trace of another zigzag line with more numerous bends and of lesser amplitude, which always occurs when in the vibrations of a string a higher sound coexists with the fundamental.

The real value of your experiments is that of assigning the true cause of phenomena, which was so little obvious as to have escaped the observation of such experienced philosophers and successful experimentalists as Chladni,[3] Oersted[4] and Savart; and this discovery has a twofold importance, it will render the investigation of the residual phenomena of elastic surfaces less complicated, and it promises some further valuable information from the application of similar considerations to other phenomena with which they are intimately connected.

I remain

Dear Sir

Yours Truly

C. WHEATSTONE

[1] M. Faraday, 'On a peculiar class of acoustical figures, and on certain forms assumed by groups of particles upon vibrating elastic surfaces,' *PT* (1831), 299.

[2] Felix Savart (1791–1841) is best known for his work (with Biot) on electrodynamics and the magnetic forces associated with electrical currents. His main interest, however, was in the nature of sound. For his many papers on this subject, see *RSCSP*. The specific point Faraday criticized is to be found in 'Recherches sur les vibrations normales,' *AC*, 2 s., 36 (1827), 187. See M. Faraday, *ERCP*, 314.

[3] Ernst Friedrich Chladni (1756–1827) founded the study of vibrating plates. Chladni figures are the regular forms taken up by light powders strewn upon such plates when the plates are caused to vibrate by the application of a violin bow. For his many papers on such figures, see *RSCSP*.

[4] For Oersted's work on Chladni figures, see *RSCSP*.

110 M. FARADAY to P. ROGET,[1] 15 April 1831
[*R.S., previously unpublished*]

R. Institution,
April 15, 1831

DEAR SIR

I have spoken to Mr. Daniell & as far as we can answer questions without Committee that of Mr Swanson's to you is answered in the affirmative i.e. that Mr Swanson[2] should cut the Engravings. But it is irregular to order engravings && before the Committee know any things about the paper & Mr. Daniel [*sic*] tells me that from the arrangements made there might perhaps not be room There is a Journal Committee on Monday. Can Mr Swanson or You send us the paper for that meeting && so as to put things in right order.

I return you E. Davy's[3] paper. I am not sure he is not right in the main point of a compound between Chlorine & Nitrous gas but the reasons are put so vaguely & embarrassed by so much little particular detail that weakens instead of strengthens the argument that the paper would not convince me & I should be obliged to make experiments before I should feel satisfied. This I have not time to do nor should it be expected. The paper ought to tell the story clearly. If the compound exists & if the account of it had been of one half the length of the paper I should say it would be fit for the Transactions

You will be aware that for the Next three Thursdays I shall not be able to be at the R S. Council (should they happen to fall on those days).

Ever Dear Sir
Truly Yours
M. FARADAY

[1] See Letter 103, fn. 5.
[2] Possibly William Swainson, the naturalist, whose works were heavily illustrated. Swainson had published in the *JRI* so was known to Faraday.
[3] Edmund Davy (1785–1857) was Sir Humphry Davy's cousin. See his 'On a new combination of chlorine and nitrous gas,' *PRS*, 3 (1831), 27.

111 G. MOLL to M. FARADAY, 25 April 1831
[*I.E.E., 'Isis', 52 (1961), 88*]

Utrecht
25 April 1831.

MY DEAR SIR!

It is a good while ago since I sent you a paper on the comparison of french english and other weights.[1] I hope it came safely to hand. I am in no hurry whatever to see it published all I want to know is whether you received it, and whether you are inclined to publish it at all.

In a former letter I stated to you my opinion on Mr Babbage's book. This has given occasion to the inclosed tract,[2] in which I endeavoured not to refute Mr Babbage for he offers no proofs nor arguments, but to point out some glaring errors in which he suffered himself to be induced. It is indeed a sorry sight how many of your Journals reecho Mr Babbage's sentiments, and in general how prone Englishmen are nowadays to give exclusive admiration to whatever is French. You may depend upon their not returning the obligation, and John Bull may hold himself assured that his neighbours on the other side of the Channel bear him as violent a hate as ever. But there is nothing like experience and John must be left to find that out for himself, which I have no doubt will be done soon enough. You will see in my paper that I do not belong to the blind admirers of Napoleon and for this simple reason, that I hate a tyrant whatever may be his talents. It is an error that Napoleon did much for Science. What has he done? Given a Galvanic battery to the Polytechnic School; erected a Galvanic Society? What experiments of any importance were made with that battery? What was done by the society. Nothing!

I wonder that no mention whatever was made in Dr Paris's book[3] of the discussion between Sir Humphry Davy and Messrs Thenard[4] and Gay Lussac[5] which happened I believe in 1810 or 1811. Messrs Thenard & Co refused to insert Mr. Davy's paper in the Annales de Chimie upon which it was sent by Sir Humphry to de Lamétherie[6] editor of the Journal de Physique. Sir Humphry wrote to Lamétherie that the paper *was trusted to his love of truth and justice.* I heard Lametherie, in his public lectures in the College de France, state, that Gay Lussac and Thenard threatened him to cause the Journal de Physique to be suppressed by the police if Sir Humphry's paper was inserted. I believe it was the paper about the decomposition of the kalis. I have not the volumes of the Journal de Physique at hand, but, for curiosities [*sic*] sake, I will inquire into the matter, and you must of needs recollect some of the circumstances.

The paper which I send you with this, is at your disposal to print where and how you think best.[7] I do not wish however to have my name prefixed to it, but it does not appear necessary to conceal it from anyone who may happen to know me. At all events some body must read it over before it is printed, and correct at least part of the bad Grammar and bad English. If printed I shall receive with pleasure a few copies.

Believe me dear Sir!
Very sincerely Yours
G. MOLL

---

[1] See Letter 108.

[2] Faraday edited the manuscript and it was published anonymously as '*On the Alleged Decline of Science in England, by a Foreigner.*' See *LPW*, 351.

[3] J. A. Paris, *The Life of Sir Humphry Davy*, London, 1831. There was also a 2-volume edition the same year.

[4] Louis Jacques Thenard (1777–1857) with Gay-Lussac was the guardian of the tradition created by Lavoisier. His most important work was done in analytical chemistry.

5 Joseph Louis Gay-Lussac (1778–1850), Professor of Chemistry at the Ecole polytechnique, best known for his law of combining volumes.
6 Jean Claude Delametherie (1743–1817) was editor of the *Journal de physique* from 1794 until his death. He opposed Lavoisier's new system of chemistry and, thus, was delighted by Davy's discoveries of sodium and potassium. That the oxides of these two metals formed the strongest bases known seemed to strike directly at Lavoisier's theory that oxygen was the principle of acidity.
7 See fn. 2.

112   G. MOLL to M. FARADAY, 7 June 1831
  [*I.E.E., previously unpublished*]

Utrecht
7 June 1831.

MY DEAR SIR!

All I can say in answer to your kind letter of 30th last, is that you have my full authority to print my paper, where and in such a form as you may think proper. I am however with you of opinion, that if it is to have any good effect, this must arise principally from the circumstance of its being written by a foreigner. I have however not the slightest objection, if it is at all thought expedient, to let the editor of the Quarterly publish it as he pleases; only I do not wish to see any alteration made in my statements. I was indeed exceedingly astonished to see the quarterly adopt Babbage's notions, and even going beyond them.[1] I would have been much less surprized if it had been the Edinburgh but something strange must have crossed the minds of the editors of the Quarterly, to allow such things to find their way, in a Journal which has a right to call itself so eminently *english*.

I have been toiling very much these days, in endeavouring to repeat the American electro-magnetic experiments, but without success.[2] I could not convince myself that by increasing the number of coils the power of the temporary magnet was increased in the least degree. First, the horse shoe of weak iron of 26 inches long, and one inch in diameter, was coiled round with 79 feet, of brass bell wire of $\frac{1}{16}$ [reading doubtful] inch diameter, in 5 different and successive coils, making in all 251 [reading doubtful] turns, and weighing about 5 lb in all. The galvanic apparatus consisted of a copper trough in which a zink [*sic*] plate of [blank in ms.] feet square was inserted. It supported about 56 lb.

The same horse shoe, which I had used in former experiments, was coated with silk, over this was coiled an iron spiral of [blank in ms.] inch thick making [blank in ms.] turns. Over this coil a second silk coating was put and over this second silk bag, a second coil, similar to the first. Using the same galvanic apparatus of my former experiments, the horse shoe was unable to carry an anvil of 202 lb. but it very freely took 180 lb. Therefore no increase of power whatever was obtained. Finding myself thus foiled in this attempt, I endeavoured to try what effect a very small galvanic apparatus would have, on a large horse shoe.

A horse shoe of 24 inch in length (when stretched out) and weighing about 29 lb and 2 inches thick, was coated in silk and surrounded with *one* coil of iron wire of [blank in ms.] inches thick. The galvanic apparatus was a small brass trough with a zinc plate of 9 inch square, the weight supported by the temporary magnet was about $8\frac{3}{4}$ lb.

A larger horse shoe of 3 inches thick, and 22 inches arch was now taken, coated, as usual, with silk, and a spiral of iron coiled round it $\frac{3}{16}$ of an inch thick, and making 165 turns. The weight of this horse shoe and coil was about 102 lb. It was first ascertained that the horse shoe, did not

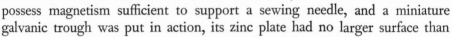

22 inch

possess magnetism sufficient to support a sewing needle, and a miniature galvanic trough was put in action, its zinc plate had no larger surface than $\frac{7}{8}$ square inch. And this sketch represents its real size. The horseshoe, by the means of such a feeble power, became capable of supporting 7 lb. The conducting fluid ($\frac{1}{60}$ nitric acid $\frac{1}{60}$ sulphuric acid I diluted) did no*t* exceed one drachm, it was little more indeed than a thimble could contain.

This experiment appears rather curious, especially, as it would seem that, when large galvanic apparatuses are used, the force which the sam[e] [ms. torn and missing] magnet acquires, does not increase very materially when a stronger galv[anic] [ms torn and missing] power is used. In all these experiments I always use, *one* zink [*sic*] plate in a copp[er] [ms. torn and missing] trough.

I shall be very happy to learn whether you have been more successful in repeating the American experiments. My anvil of 202 lb is still a limit to which I have been gradually approaching, but which I have not yet been able to reach.

9th June My temporary magnet supported today 240 lb; I could not go [illeg.] beyond. The zink [*sic*] plate had 7 square feet surface.

10ʰ June 1831. It supported 254 lb, but I could not obtain more.

[1] See the review of Babbage's book in *QR*, 43 (1830), 305.
[2] This refers to Joseph Henry's work with powerful electromagnets. See Joseph Henry, 'On the application of the principle of the galvanic multiplier to electro-magnetic apparatus, and also to the development of great magnetic power in soft iron, with small galvanic elements,' *AJS*, 19 (1831), 400. See also *LPW*, 181.

113   M. FARADAY to P. ROGET, 4 July 1831

[*R.S., C.R. Weld, 'A History of the Royal Society', 2 vols., London, 1848, 2, 399; also B.J. 1, 401*]

Royal Institution,
July 4th, 1831

SIR

I send you herewith four large and two small volumes of Manuscript, relating to optical glass, and comprising the Journal book and the Sub-Committee-book since the period that experimental investigations commenced at the Royal Institution.[1]

With reference to the request which the Council of the Royal Society have done me the honor of making, namely, that I should continue the investigation, I should under circumstances of perfect freedom assent to it at once. But, obliged as I have been to devote the whole of my spare time to the experiments already described and consequently, to resign the pursuit of such philosophical enquiries as suggested themselves to my own mind, I would wish, under present circumstances, to lay the glass aside for a while, that I may enjoy the pleasure of working out my own thoughts on other subjects.

If at a future time the investigation should be renewed, I must beg it to be clearly understood I cannot promise full success. Should I resume it, all that industry and my abilities can effect shall be done: but to perfect a manufacture not being a manufacturer is what I am not bold enough to promise.

I am
Sir
Your Obedt. Servant
M. FARADAY

[1] For an account of the experiments with glass, and some excerpts from these notebooks, see *LPW*, 116ff.

114   J. J. BERZELIUS to M. FARADAY, 10 August 1831

[*Kungl. Vetenskapsakademiens Bibliotek, Stockholm, previously unpublished*]

Stockholm,
10 Aout, 1831

MONSIEUR,

Je prens la liberté de recommander à votre bienveillante acception le porteur de cette lettre Mr. Ekman,[1] Ingenieur de Mines, de beaucoup de mérite, qui par un tour à l'angleterre cherche a amplifier ses connaissances et profiter des lumières, dont votre patrie abonde dans la fabrication du fer. Je vous prie de vouloir bien lui etre utile par vos conseils et par votre intercession, dont il aura probablement fort souvent besoin.

Jai a vous remercier pour votre admirable travail sur le verre optique, par lequel l'astronomie et la physique deviendront tributaires a la chimie. Mr Ekman vous remettra de la part de M. Sefstrom[2] a Faklun un petit paquet contenant du Vanadiate d'Ammoniaque afin que puissiez prendre connaissance de ce corps interessant par autopsie.

Agrez [*sic*] l'expression de la toute consideration et de la parfaite estime avec lesquelles j'ai l'honneur d'etre,

Monsieur
Votre très humble et obeissant
Serviteur,
JAC. BERZELIUS

[1] I am unable to identify Mr Ekman further.
[2] Nils Gabriel Sefström (1787–1845), who rediscovered and gave the name to the element vanadium.

115 M. FARADAY to J. W. PARKER,[1] 19 August 1831
[*Wellcome Medical Historical Library, previously unpublished*]

R Institution
Aug 19 1831

DEAR SIR

I am sorry I missed you yesterday, indeed I have been very unfortunate in my endeavours to see you all together

I have been so tired of delays about Molls paper that I had arranged with an old friend Mr Boosey[2] to publish it. I therefore send you the title & should be glad to see a review [reading doubtful].

I shall want 500 copies Mr. Boosey will send 500 of his bills to be stitched up with the pamphlet – When stitched send all to me and I will send to Boosey's

Every Truly Yours
M. FARADAY

Do you observe what a muddle the plates of the last No. are in; the only one belonging to that No. is left out

[1] John William Parker (1792–1870), printer and publisher.
[2] Thomas Boosey (1795–1871), bookseller at 28 Holles St., London.

116 W. V. HARCOURT[1] to M. FARADAY, 5 September 1831
[*I.E.E., previously unpublished*]

Wheldrake near York,
Sept. 5. 1831

DEAR SIR

I was extremely sorry to hear that your engagements would prevent your being able to attend the scientific Meeting at York at which your presence both in your philosophical & social character, however you may disdain the latter, would have been especially acceptable.

Though you do not come yourself it may perhaps be in your power to send us some scientific novelties, some account for instance of Vanadium,[2] the history of which its discoverers seem to be very slow in communicating. You may also have an opportunity of inducing the authors of any new inventions or discoveries which may be afloat to exhibit them on this occasion, and as the R. Institution is not sitting you are under no temptation to monopolise them; At this time of the year the *Lions* may be allowed to perambulate the country.

I hope however that at this meeting we shall do something more than shew or see the Lions. There are hopes I think of setting an Association on foot which may give a fresh & active impulse to scientific research in this country. The plan respecting which I am in correspondence with Mr. Herschel, Dr. Brewster, Mr. Whewell & others, is to form an association of all members of all the scientific societies in Great Britain to meet annually to receive & discuss Reports made to it by Committees or Individuals selected from among its number on the state of the several sciences & the points in each most immediately inviting investigation, & therefrom to charge such of its members with the proposed researches as may be most competent for the task, either severally or jointly. In particular cases the expense of experiments may be defrayed, or prizes may be offered; & supposing the Association to possess not only numbers but character & also some courage & freedom of discussion it might obtain more influence with the Government of the country than science has hitherto enjoyed & command for it some degree of national encouragement.

To give efficiency to such a plan as this it must have the active support of all or the greater part of the most eminent cultivators of science & without some promise of that support it would be in vain to propose it Will you assist in carrying it into execution? Would you for instance make one of a Committee to report on the state of Chemistry the points of theory most requiring investigation & the experimental data to be first established or supposing such a report made, would you take a part in conducting the researches so designated & resolved upon?

If it strikes you that this plan or any modification of it may help to raise a spirit of enterprise & exertion in science & give a systematic direction to its present loose & disjointed efforts, pray give your mind to it and write me any suggestions which may occur to you as soon as you can, either as to the constitution of the proposed Society, or as to the points in science coming under your own observation which it should undertake to have investigated.

I am dear Sir
Yrs truly
WM. VERNON HARCOURT

[1] William Vernon Harcourt (1789–1871) was, with David Brewster, the moving figure behind the formation of the British Association for the Advancement of Science.
[2] See Letter 114.

117 M. FARADAY to E. MAGRATH, 5 September 1831
[*R.I., previously unpublished*]

3 Priors Cottages.
Hastings 5 Sept 1831

DEAR MAGRATH

Here we are at our old Quarters and I find we do not know your Sister's address I write therefore by post & just in post time to ask you for it for I think we might as well know where each other resides

We had a very wet day on our journey here but caoutchouc did good duty and we were both warm & dry. I do not think any body ever fares so well on a coach as we do. Others on the outside were wet & cold those within dry but so stewed up that I envied not their lot

Mr Smith (Adams Smith) was on the coach with us He is an M.R.I. and was going to his Brothers house at Robertsbridge (Benjamin Smith)[1]

Mrs. Faraday sends her remembrances.

I am Dear Magrath in haste
Truly Yours
M. FARADAY.

[1] See Letter 93.

118 M. FARADAY to C. BABBAGE, 22 September 1831
[*British Museum, Add. mss. 37186, f. 95, previously unpublished*]

Royal Institution
Septr 22 1831

MY DEAR SIR

I returned to town only yesterday and hasten to answer your letter

The number for Bromine is uncertain. Balard[1] made it 9.326. – Liebig 9.411.[2] Berzelius nearly 9.94.[3] Oxygen being 1. I have no experiment of my own to quote. but knowing the general accuracy of Berzelius in experiment I should trust him most

Chlorine. I believe to be 36. Hydrogen being 1. i.e. $4\frac{1}{2}$ oxygen being 1. Such is the result of my experiments on former occasion [*sic*] as well as of other persons and I know of no reason at present to doubt it

Iodine judging of its number from Expt (analytical) only doubt would hang about it Berzelius makes it nearly 16.06. Gay Lussac 16.2[4] & Prout 16.473.[5] I have no quantitative experiment to quote: I made many formerly with Sir H. Davy but have not the notes. He had them The number 15.8 is perhaps a mean of results deduced from the S.G of its vapour & of hydriodic acid

I am not aware of any thing specific which Serullas[6] has done relating to solid liquid & gasiform bi-carbonated hydrogen. Having done a little myself that way I should be glad to be referred to any views of that clever & active chemist

I am

Dear Sir

Very Truly Yours

M. FARADAY

[1] Antoine Jérome Balard (1802–76) was the discoverer of bromine. See his 'Mémoire sur une substance particulière contenue dans l'eau de la mer (le Brome),' *AC*, 32 (1826), 337.

[2] Justus Liebig (1803–73), 'Sur la brome,' *AC*, 33 (1826), 330.

[3] J. J. Berzelius, 'Poids atomistique de l'Iode et du Brome,' *AC*, n.s., 40 (1829), 430.

[4] Joseph Louis Gay-Lussac, 'Mémoire sur l'iode,' *AC*, 91 (1814), 5.

[5] [William Prout] (1786–1850), later acknowledged authorship of the article, 'On the relation between the Specific Gravities of Bodies in their Gaseous State and the Weights of their Atoms.' It was in this article that the hypothesis, known as Prout's hypothesis, was put forward that all elements have atomic weights which are integral multiples of hydrogen.

[6] Georges Simon Sérullas (1774–1832) wrote a number of papers on the halogens. See *RSCSP*. I have been unable to find any paper on unsaturated hydrocarbons.

119   C. DAUBENY to M. FARADAY, 12 November 1831

[*I.E.E., previously unpublished*]

Oxford,

Nov. 12th, 1831

DEAR SIR,

I have to thank you for a copy of your late Memoir,[1] which arrived the other day with one for Professor Rigaud.[2]

I am send [*sic*] you a Prospectus of the British Association for the promotion of Science which I hope you will approve, though I am sorry to find it is uncertain whether we shall have the advantage of your personal cooperation – Actively engaged as you always are in the advancement of knowledge You have doubtless the best possible right to consult your own feelings in this matter, and I only hope that if you should not feel yourself equal to visiting us on this public occasion, I shall have the pleasure of seeing you here at a time of less bustle, whenever you may find a little change of scene agreeable –

As you are engaged in experiments on Magnetism, I will state to you a fact which seemed to me curious, though I am not well enough read in the recent discoveries on that branch of Physics to feel confident as to its novelty – Having constructed a temporary Magnet of soft Iron in a horse-shoe form after Professor Moll's[3] method which supported from 100 to 140 lb. – I was surprised to find, that after the communication with the battery was interrupted, it still supported the Armature weighing 3 lb, and weights attached amounting to about 17 lb. – Now this was not owing to any induced Magnetism, for the Iron exerted no influence upon the needle or on the lightest Iron filings brought near it and when the Armature had been removed for a single second, the Iron did not attract it in the least – I conceive the effect could only arise from the adhesion between the two smooth surfaces of the Iron, and Armature, and yet the surfaces presented by each extremity of the horse-shoe magnet, were not more than 1¼ Inch in diameter, each. If so, the experiment appears a good illustration of the extreme nearness of contact brought about by magnetic attraction between two metallic surfaces and proves to us that in estimating the force of a magnet, we ought to make a deduction for the weight which the Armature takes up in consequence of its adhesion to the attracting surface. –

Are you aware of the extreme incombustibility of coke completely deprived of its bitumen? I have a specimen from a coal pit of Ld Fitzwilliam's which had caught fire, extremely light owing to its reticulated or honeycombed structure wh. [ich] I have been unable to burn even by exposure to the Oxy-hydrogen blowpipe, by which I have often readily inflamed the Diamond – Its non-inflammability is I suppose in part owing to the thinness [reading doubtful] of its texture, which causes it to have a large surface radiating heat in proportion to the substance in which heat can be accumulated – I have also tried without success to burn it away by heating it red hot with nitrate of ammonia –

I shall send you the copy of a paper of mine, which will appear in the next number of Jameson's Journal in wh.[ich] I hope to prove two points 1st. that warm springs are for the most part of volcanic origin & 2dly. that their products can only be explained by the chemical theory of volcanoes wh.[ich] I have adopted.[4]

Believe me Yrs most truly
CHAS. DAUBENY

[1] Most probably M. Faraday, 'On a peculiar class of acoustical figures, and on certain forms assumed by groups of particles upon vibrating elastic surfaces,' *PT* (1831), 299. 1831, of course, was the date of Faraday's discovery of electro-magnetic induction but the printed paper did not appear until 1832.
[2] (Stephen) Peter Rigaud (1774–1839) was Savilian Professor of Astronomy at Oxford.
[3] See Letter 112. Also, fn. 2 which refers to Henry's work which, in turn, refers to Moll's.
[4] Charles Daubeny, 'On Thermal Springs and their Connexion with Volcanoes,' *ENPJ*, 12 (1832), 49.

120   G. MOLL to M. FARADAY, 13 November 1831
   [R.I., previously unpublished]

Utrecht
13 November 1831

MY DEAR SIR!

Many avocations and frequent absences have prevented me thus long, to give you my most sincere thanks for your trouble in causing my pamphlet to be forwarded to the press.[1] Alas! you have been but poorly rewarded for your pains, and someone, perhaps Dr Brewster himself, whilst he gave me, or endeavoured to give me a good thrashing, has levelled some smart hits at yourself.[2] If you take this matter in the same light as I do, it must not have caused you much anxiety; for my part, I cannot help laughing when I see people becoming restive because they are told that they are not so bad, as they wish to be considered. When people are in the wrong they generally become angry, and nothing of what the writer of the article in the Edinburgh Journal has said, brings me to alter my first opinion. I still maintain that no proof is adduced of the decline of Science in England, and that many may be adduced to the very contrary. In my opinion, the writer of this article has perverted my arguments and very often my own words; of this however others, not I, must be the best judges.

As for your *negotiating a loan of foreign talent, and of subsidizing foreigners*, you know best how this matter stands, but I unhesitatingly declare those expressions scurrilous and ungentlemanlike, nor do I have the least apprehension that anyone who knows me, either in this country, or in England, will think them well applied either to you or me. I am accused of *flattering the English*, but the accuser may be firmly persuaded, that on this side of the water, there is very little disposition, or cause to flatter the English. Any Englishman travelling here, at present, must be conscious of that fact. Indeed recent political events scratched the scars from old wounds, and I am sorry to say that national antipathy, is as strong as ever.[3] I am really in a ludicrous predicament in this respect, both at home and in England, I am blamed for defending English character. However I will assert my right to my own opinion, and speak it out, reckless of consequences.

The Scotch Journalist represents me to have asserted, that Sir Humphry Davy, Sir James South, Mr Babbage and others, were not actuated by noble and patriotic motives. This I utterly deny; no one except a knave or a fool, would have dared to question the honour & the integrity of the highly distinguished individuals just mentioned, though one might happen to differ in sentiment with them on some particular topics.

I cannot follow my scotch foe, through all his arguments. I will not now attempt to show, that when he contrives to bring my arguments in the form of a syllogism, he makes use of the most egregious sophistry.

But of one thing, of which he accuses me, I want to clear myself, it is the attack, which he contends I made on the Duke of Wellington. With the noble Duke's politics I have nothing to do. I merely stated the fact of his Grace's being at present unpopular. Now, Sir! when a Minister, from prudential motives, declines attending on his Sovereign on a public procession, (I mean the intended dinner at Guildhall), when his windows are smashed by the mob, when the firmness of a brave soldier only prevented the rabble to attack his official mansion in Downing street, when verses, like the following are applauded at public dinners,

His* name shall descend on the bright page of Story
While the laurels of Waterloo fade on the brows
Of him who has fought for his country with glory,
But to sink in the ranks of her worst civil foes.

If the Duke had remained Commander in chief, none of this would have happened; and I said no more. My words could never be construed into the sense that none but Earl's sons could be officers in England, but I said that if the Duke had been a common soldier, & like Murat, Soult[4] &tc he could never have risen in the English Army. Dupin,[5] long before me, in a work much admired in England, said pretty much the same of Lord Nelson. If he had entered the army as a Soldier, he certainly would have been made a Sergeant, but it is highly improbable that he would have been an officer. But if both M. Dupin and myself are mistaken in this respect, if in England private soldiers, by force of merit are promoted to the rank of officers, let Dr Brewster's correspondent in the long list of british Generals, point out those who have been promoted from the ranks; let him indicate in what number of the gazette we are to look for the promotion of a Sergeant from the Halbert to a commission. With the archiepiscopal mitre on the Woolsack we have at present nothing to do. I said, and believe to this very moment, that had the Duke of Wellington been the son of a mechanic or a farmer, and entered in the army as a private soldier, he might have carried the halbert to this very moment.

Dr Brewster's friend is probably no inhabitant of London. Should he come there, he is anxious for an invitation at dinner. He says that he sat down with Cavendish, Sir Wm Herschel, James Watt, Maskeline, [sic] Playfair, Hutton, Davy, Wollaston, Young, and Chenevix,[6] and he wants to know with what mighty living, he is to be invited next. Well, if you should happen to know him, invite him with Sir Frederic Herschell [sic], Sir James South, Capt Kater, Mr Babbage, Mr Barlow, Mr Bailie, [sic] Capt Perry, Lieut. Collonel [sic] Colby, Mr Robt Brown, Mr Troughton, Prof Leake, Dr Brewster (if this last can be made to agree) Sir Robert Sappings, Mr Wallace, Mr Airy[7] &c &c, and he must be very fastidious indeed if he does not like the company.

Do not give yourself the trouble, as our northern friend wants you to do, to tell me whether you were more gratified by being a member of the Royal Society or a correspondent of the Institute. That a man of your standing should be a member of the first Scientific body of your own country must be a matter of course. But in order to state the question fairly, we ought to ask a german, a Swede, a Prussian, an Italian whether they should prefer belonging to the Royal Society or the Institute.

What is said about calumniating the french is mere humbug. Was there, or was there not, in the french Senate a Commission for preserving the liberty of the press, and another for the preservation of individual liberty? Was it, or was it not the duty of the Senate to preserve the liberty of the french people? Did that Senate even so much as remonstrate against Napoleon's tyranny? Did they not disgracefully abandon their former master when fortune forsook him? Let the discourses of Lacepede to Napoleon be read,[8] and it will appear that a more disgusting specimen of abject flattery cannot be found in history. Did Monge[9] sign or not the death warrant of the unfortunate Louis XVI? Was or was Carnot[10] not a regicide? Human nature certainly shudders at those things, but they are not imputations, they are historical facts, and if our Reviewer wants proofs, let him recur to the *inflexible Moniteur*.[11] Let him read the history of the french revolution by Montgaillard,[12] and let him then talk of calumny and shuddering. And you Sir! you are called upon to approve by your silence of such acts; you are not to suffer, on pain of the indignation of our Scotch friend, that any one testifies his abhorrence of the part which the french savans took in the horrors of the french Revolution, in the murder of Louis XVI; you are not to allow any one to state how much he despises the vile abettors of Napoleon's tyranny. If it should come to this, if [MS. torn and missing] Regicide, murder, slavish subservience to a foreign despot, could find many defenders amongst the learned of England, then indeed, it could be said, not that Science, but that virtue and morality were declining in that country.

Believe me, my dear Sir
Very sincerely yours
G. MOLL.

Did you succeed in repeating Dr ten Eycks experiments?[13] I do not well understand how he manages his apparatus.

* The words 'The King's' were written in the margin of the letter here.
[1] See Letter 115.
[2] *EJS*, n.s., 5 (1831), 1, 334 is a review of Moll's pamphlet. It was written by David Brewster and is a slashing attack on both Moll and Faraday.
[3] In 1830, Holland and Belgium split apart with the English siding with the Belgians.
[4] Marshals in Napoleon's army who had risen from the ranks of the army of the *ancien régime*.
[5] See François Pierre Charles Dupin, *View of the History and Actual State of the Military Force of Great Britain*, translated with notes by an officer, 2 vols., London, 1822.
[6] Henry Cavendish (1731–1810), experimental physicist. Sir William Herschel (1738–1822), astronomer. James Watt (1736–1819), inventor of the separate condenser for steam engines. Nevil Maskelyne (1732–1811), Astronomer Royal. John Playfair (1748–1819), mathematician and popularizer of James Hutton's geological theories. James Hutton (1726–97), geologist, farmer and metaphysician. Sir Humphry Davy. William Hyde Wollaston (1766–1828), chemist and experimental physicist. Dr Thomas Young (1773–1829), proponent of the wave theory of light. Richard Chenevix (1774–1830), chemist and crystallographer.
[7] John Frederick Herschel (1792–1871), astronomer and physicist. Sir James South (1785–1867), astronomer. Henry Kater (1777–1835), astronomer and metrologist. Charles Babbage (1792–1871), mathematician. Peter Barlow (1776–1862), mathematician and physicist. Francis Baily (1774–1844), astronomer. John Perry (1670–1732), civil engineer and traveller.

Thomas Colby (1784–1852), surveyor. Robert Brown (1773–1858), botanist. Edward Troughton (1753–1835), scientific instrument maker. William Martin Leake (1777–1860), geographer. David Brewster (1781–1868), physicist. Sir Robert Sappings (1768–1840), naval architect. William Wallace (1768–1843), mathematician. George Biddell Airy (1801–92), astronomer.

8 See Bernard-Germain Comte de Lacépède, *Discours, Séance publique du 1ᵉʳ janvier 1806. Reception et inauguration des 54 drapeaux dont S. M. l'Empereur et roi a fait présent au Sénat* (Paris, n.d.).

9 Gaspard Monge (1746–1818), mathematician.

10 Lazare Carnot (1753–1823), mathematician and engineer.

11 The *Moniteur Universel* was for many years the official newspaper of the revolutionary and Imperial governments.

12 See Abbé Guillaume Honoré Rocque de Montgaillard, *Histoire de France, depuis la fin du regne de Louis XVI jusqu'à l'année 1825* ..., 8 vols., Paris, 1827.

13 Philip Ten Eyck of Albany collaborated with Joseph Henry in some of the latter's work on electro-magnetism. See *AJS*, 19 (1831), 402 and 20 (1831), 201.

121 M. FARADAY to J. G. CHILDREN,[1] 21 November 1831
[*R.S., previously unpublished*]

Royal Institution,
Nov. 21, 1831

SIR

I find myself constrained to leave town for 8 or 10 days for health's sake and as I shall therefore be unable to attend the next Council I feel bound to submit to the President and Council through you such reasons as are in favour of the proposition I had the honor to make of a Medal to Berzelius

An Edition of Berzelius' Treatise on Chemistry in French[2] is now in course of publication. It will consist of 8 vols and four of these have appeared in the successive years of 1829, 1830, 1831. It is under the arrangement of M Berzelius himself whose preface from Stockholm is dated November 1828, and he says it will contain all new matter up to the date of its publication It has done so as far as it has proceeded and will no doubt continue to do so to the end

Since 1827, and therefore within the limit fixed for the medal, Berzelius has published many important papers in the Annales de Chimie some of which have already been embodied in the Edition referred to. I therefore think that work a full & sufficient reason for adjudging the medal to the author because its date as a compilation and the date of original matter in it are both within our limits of five years.

There are fifteen papers in the Annales de Chimie since 1827, amongst which are the *Analysis of Platina minerals with new observations on Iridium & Osmium,* an *account of the new earth Thorina* (*the true Thorina*) *Demonstration of the peculiar nature of Lactic acid Analysis & comparison of the Tartaric & racemic acids,*[3] two bodies which with the same composition have different qualities

I have not thought it necessary to insist upon Berzelius' deserts No one who knows anything of chemistry can doubt but that he merits it most highly. I have only endeavoured to shew that according to our own rules he is eligible to receive it

I am Sir

Your Very Obedt. Humble Servant

M. FARADAY

[1] J. G. Children (1778–1852), chemist and, for many years, one of the Secretaries of the Royal Society.

[2] J. J. Berzelius, *Traité de chimie minérale, végétale et animale*, trans. by A. J. L. Jourdan, 8 vols., Paris, 1829–33.

[3] 'Recherches sur les métaux qui accompagnent le platine, et sur la méthode d'analyser les alliages natifs ou les minérais de platine,' *AC*, 2 s., 40 (1827), 51, 138, 257, 337.

'Recherches sur un nouveau minéral, et sur un nouvel oxide qu'il renferme,' *AC*, 2 s., 43 (1830), 5.

'Sur l'acide lactique,' *AC*, 2 s., 46 (1831), 430.

'Composition de l'acide tartrique et de l'acide racémique (traubensäure) (1); poids atomique de l'oxide de plomb, et remarques générales sur les corps qui ont la même composition, et possèdent des propriétés différentes,' *AC*, 2 s., 46 (1831), 113.

122 M. FARADAY to R. PHILLIPS, 29 November 1831

[*B.J. 2, 6*]

Brighton,
November 29, 1831

DEAR PHILLIPS,

For once in my life I am able to sit down and write to you without feeling that my time is so little that my letter must of necessity be a short one; and accordingly I have taken an extra large sheet of paper, intending to fill it with news. And yet, as to news, I have none, for I withdraw more and more from society, and all I have to say is about myself.

But how are you getting on? Are you comfortable? And how does Mrs. Phillips do; and the girls? Bad correspondent as I am, I think you owe me a letter; and as in the course of half an hour you will be doubly in my debt, pray write us, and let us know all about you. Mrs. Faraday wishes me not to forget to put her kind remembrances to you and Mrs. Phillips in my letter.

To-morrow is St. Andrew's day,[1] but we shall be here until Thursday. I have made arrangements to be *out* of the Council, and care little for the rest, although I should, as a matter of curiosity, have liked to see the Duke in the chair on such an occasion.[2]

We are here to refresh. I have been working and writing a paper that always knocks me up in health, but now I feel well again, and able to pursue my subject; and now I will tell you what it is about. The title will be, I think, "Experimental Researches in Electricity:" – I. On the Induction of Electric

Currents; II. On the Evolution of Electricity from Magnetism; III. On a new Electrical Condition of Matter; IV. On Arago's Magnetic Phenomena.[3] There is a bill of fare for you; and, what is more, I hope it will not disappoint you. Now the pith of all this I must give you very briefly; the demonstrations you shall have in the paper when printed.[4]

I. When an electric current is passed through one of two parallel wires, it causes at first a current in the same direction through the other, but this induced current does not last a moment, notwithstanding the inducing current (from the voltaic battery) is continued; all seems unchanged, except that the principal current continues its course. But when the current is stopped, then a return current occurs in the wire under induction, of about the same intensity and momentary duration, but in the opposite direction to that first formed Electricity in currents therefore exerts an inductive action like ordinary electricity, but subject to peculiar laws. The effects are a current in the same direction when the induction is established; a reverse current when the induction ceases, and a *peculiar state* in the interim.[5] Common electricity probably does the same thing; but as it is at present impossible to separate the beginning and the end of a spark or discharge from each other, all the effects are simultaneous and neutralise each other.

II. Then I found that magnets would induce just like voltaic currents, and by bringing helices and wires and jackets up to the poles of magnets, electrical currents were produced in them; these currents being able to deflect the galvanometer, or to make, by means of the helix, magnetic needles, or in one case even to give a spark. Hence the evolution of *electricity from magnetism*. The currents were not permanent. They ceased the moment the wires ceased to approach the magnet, because the new and apparently quiescent state was assumed, just as in the case of the induction of currents. But when the magnet was removed, and its induction therefore ceased, the return currents appeared as before. These two kinds of induction I have distinguished by the terms *volta-electric* and *magneto-electric* induction. Their identity of action and results is, I think, a very powerful proof of M. Ampère's theory of magnetism.

III. The new electrical condition which intervenes by induction between the beginning and end of the inducing current gives rise to some very curious results. It explains why chemical action or other results of electricity have never been as yet obtained in trials with the magnet. In fact, the currents have no sensible duration. I believe it will explain perfectly the *transference of elements* between the poles of the pile in decomposition. But this part of the subject I have reserved until the present experiments are completed; and it is so analogous, in some of its effects, to those of Ritter's[6] secondary piles, De la Rive[7] and Van Beek's[8] peculiar properties of the poles of a voltaic pile, that I should not wonder if they all proved ultimately to depend on this state. The condition of matter I have dignified by the term *Electrotonic*, THE ELECTROTONIC

STATE. What do you think of that? Am I not a bold man, ignorant as I am, to coin words? but I have consulted the scholars.[9] And now for IV.

IV. The new state has enabled me to make out and explain all Arago's phenomena of the rotating magnet or copper plate, I believe, perfectly; but as great names are concerned (Arago, Babbage, Herschel, &c.), and as I have to differ from them, I have spoken with that modesty which you so well know you and I and John Frost[10] have in common, and for which the world so justly commends us. I am even half afraid to tell you what it is. You will think I am hoaxing you, or else in your compassion you may conclude I am deceiving myself. However, you need do neither, but had better laugh, as I did most heartily when I found that it was neither attraction nor repulsion, but just one of my *old rotations* in a new form.[11] I cannot explain to you all the actions, which are very curious; but in consequence of the electrotonic state being assumed and lost as the parts of the plate whirl under the pole, and in consequence of magneto-electric induction, currents of electricity are formed in the direction of the radii; continuing, for simple reasons, as long as the motion continues, but ceasing when that ceases. Hence the wonder is explained that the metal has powers on the magnet when moving, but not when at rest. Hence is also explained the effect which Arago observed, and which made him contradict Babbage and Herschel,[12] and say the power was repulsive; but, as a whole it is really tangential. It is quite comfortable to me to find that experiment need not quail before mathematics, but is quite competent to rival it in discovery; and I am amazed to find that what the high mathematicians have announced as the *essential condition* to the rotation – namely, that *time is required*, – has so little foundation, that if the time could by possibility be anticipated instead of being required – i.e. if the currents could be formed *before* the magnet came over the place instead of *after* – the effect would equally ensue. Adieu, dear Phillips.

Excuse this egotistical letter from yours very faithfully,

M. FARADAY.

[1] The day of elections to the Council of the Royal Society and annual meeting of the Society.
[2] H.R.H. The Duke of Sussex had just been elected P.R.S., beating out J. F. W. Herschel whom Faraday had supported. See *LPW*, 353ff.
[3] This was, of course, Faraday's first paper in the series of Experimental Researches in Electricity which were to flow from his pen for almost thirty more years.
[4] For the experiments upon which the statements that follow are based see *ERE*, *1*, 1ff.
[5] This state Faraday christened the 'electrotonic state' and it was to play a central role in his further experiments. See *LPW*, 198, 205, 285, 383.
[6] Johann Ritter (1776–1810), 'Expériences sur un appareil à charger d'électricité par la colonne électrique de Volta,' *JP*, 57 (1803), 345. Ritter invented the storage battery or 'secondary pile' as Faraday calls it.
[7] A. de la Rive, 'Recherches sur la cause de l'électricité voltaïque,' *AC*, 2 s., 39 (1828), 297.
[8] Albert van Beek (1787–1856), 'Sur un phénomène extraordinaire concernant l'influence continue qu'exerce le contact de métaux hétérogènes sur leurs propriétés chimiques, longtemps après que ce contact a cessé,' *AC*, 2 s., 38 (1828), 49.

14-2

[9] Most probably Whitlock Nicholl, M.D. See *NRRS*, 16 (1961), 191.

[10] (footnote by B.J.) A pushing acquaintance who, without claim of any kind, got himself presented at Court.

[11] *ERCP.*

[12] See Letter 69. Also F. Arago, 'Note concernant les phénomènes magnétiques auxquels le mouvement donne naissance,' *AC*, 2 s., 32 (1826), 213; 'Note sur de nouvelles actions magnétiques dues au mouvement de rotation,' *NBSP* (1826), 85.

123   C. DAUBENY to M. FARADAY, 1832[1]
[*R.I.*, *previously unpublished*]

MY DEAR SIR,

There has been some talk amongst the friends of Science in this University about soliciting the Heads of Colleges to propose Honorary Degrees for a few of the more distinguished persons who are expected here at the approaching Meeting, but before a list is made out, we are desirous of ascertaining whether we are to expect the pleasure of your attendance during any part of the time, and whether such a mark of distinction would be acceptable to you, as well as gratifying to the body who would confer this mark of their consideration I cannot help flattering myself that as when I last saw you, you told me you had not entirely given up the intention of coming, the circumstance I have stated may decide you in favor of being here, and that you would value this tribute to your services to Science the more, as coming from a Body of men, by whom such honors to Men of Science has hitherto been but rarely paid Pray inform me in the course of the week, whether on the count of your Honorary Degree of D.C.L. being determined on, we may reckon on your attendance for a day or two during the week of meetings

> and believe me
> Yrs. very truly
> CHARLES DAUBENY

[1] The meeting of the *BAAS* at Oxford was in 1832. Faraday was awarded an honorary doctorate there.

124   J. N. P. HACHETTE[1] to M. FARADAY, 7 January 1832
[*R.I.*, *previously unpublished*]

Paris
7 janvier 1832 –

MONSIEUR ET CHER CONFRERE

le 26 decembre 1831, j'ai communiqué a l'academie Royale des Sciences la lettre que vous m'avez fait l'honneur de m'ecrire le 17 du même mois.[2] cette communication a été fort bien accueillie. le plaisir que j'ai eprouvé en apprenant vos nouvelles decouvertes, a été partagé par tous mes collègues, notamment par MM. Arago, ampére, [*sic*] et Savart. M. Arago notre secretaire perpetuel a lû l'extrait de votre lettre, que je lui avois Remis avant la Seance – .

Je desire apprendre comment vous avez operé pour produire les Courans electriques par les aimants, et comment un plateau metallique tournant se change en Machine electrique. je vous Remercie mille fois de la lettre Savante et philosophique que vous aviez voulu m'adresser.

Veuillez bien agreer mes Salutations très affectueuses,

HACHETTE

Rue St hyacinthe, St Michel 8.

t.s.v.p.

P.S. Vous trouverez cy joint deux feuilles du lycée,[3] qui Rendent compte de la Communication que j'ai faite d'aprés votre lettre du 17 decembre 1831 –

H.

[1] See Letter 56.
[2] It was this letter from Faraday to Hachette which announced the discovery of electromagnetic induction. The account given in *Le Lycée* was seized upon by two Italian physicists, L. Nobili and V. Antinori who published a paper which appeared to give them priority for the discovery. See *LPW*, 201.
[3] *Le Lycée*, 29 December 1831.

125 M. FARADAY to J. BARROW,[1] 8 January 1832
[*PRO, Adm. 1, 4610, Prom. Lett., previously unpublished*]

R Institution
Jany 8, 1832

DEAR SIR
There are certain bills as follows

Newman	33.	9.	6
Ramsey[2]	1.	6.	2
Wedgewood[3]	3.	14.	6
Miscellaneous	47.	5.	3
	85.	15.	5

which Dr. Roget tells me he has sent to you and you say are ordered for payment months ago but of which we can get no account at Somerset house (Pay officer)

I find so little progress made in clearing up the matter by writing to Dr Roget that I intrude on you to ask whether they are or are not passed and if so where my man should go for the money. The tradesmen ought to have had their money a twelvemonth ago.

If you could tell my Messenger who wants what to do next it would very much oblige

Yours Very faithfully
M. FARADAY

[Two notes at the end in other hands]: What appears Nothing more than the inclosed ltr [reading doubtful] – You will however perceive that the amounts vary as well as the number of the claimants

[1] John Barrow, later Sir John (1764–1840), was secretary of the admiralty. The letter refers to expenses incurred in the work on glass.
[2] See Letter 90.
[3] Probably the firm of Wedgewood, rather than an individual. The sum most probably was to pay for the crucibles used in the glass researches.

126   M. FARADAY to C. BABBAGE, 30 January 1832

[*British Museum, Add. mss. 37186, f. 228, previously unpublished*]

Royal Institution
Jany. 30, 1832

MY DEAR SIR

The person I thought of for chemistry has left his occupation & can be of no use to your friend

Do you think my assistant Mr Pearsall[1] would do. (not my own servant Anderson whom you saw today). He is engaged all day but could have his evenings as a favour but he cannot have pupils in the laboratory I have not spoken to him but if you think he would do; and he knows plenty for the purpose being really a good chemist but very prosy & prolix in his language, he should call on your friend – only let terms be made before business is entered upon for then there can be no mistake

Your shilling is an alloy of Silver and Zinc i.e of standard silver & zinc. The copper in it is no more I believe than the usual alloy of silver There is no nickle – I have not ascertained proportions

Will you allow me to offer you a copy of my last paper[2] If you look at it I wish you would *begin* at the *end*. I am really anxious to obtain an opinion however vague from such a man as yourself or Sir John Herschell on the paragraphs 128. 129. at page 340 – But do not go from more serious matter to it Only take it up as recreation when you wish to forget the Engine[3]

I am
Dear Sir
Yours Very Sincerely
M. FARADAY

[1] Thomas J. Pearsall, minor chemist.
[2] The First Series of Experimental Researches in Electricity.
[3] Babbage was engaged in constructing a calculating engine which qualifies as the first modern computer.

127 M. FARADAY to R. DUNDAS and J. D. THOMSON,[1]
10 February 1832

[*PRO, Adm. 106/1520, previously unpublished*][2]

Royal Institution
Feby 10th. 1832.

GENTLEMEN

Since I received the sheet of bronze I have been engaged in experiments on it, with the endeavour if possible to find some test of its comparative durability, relative to copper, when on ships [*sic*] bottoms.

The bronze is an alloy of copper and tin; and yields me nearly 6.2 per cent of the latter metal. I can discover only very minute traces of other metals, not more than occur in ordinary copper, and I believe they are accidental

But I have been more anxious to find, if possible, indications of the properties of the bronze as a whole, than to search after its minute composition; inasmuch as the former could by no means be deduced from the latter. – On comparing the bronze voltaically with copper, I do not find that its energies are less; they appear to be as nearly as possible the same; from which I should be led to expect, that their chemical action, relative to sea water, (upon which the corrosion depends) would also prove nearly the same.

Then again, I have compared the action of an artificial sea water upon similar pieces of this bronze and of sheet copper. I find them both corroded; and the action is so nearly equal, that I cannot say whether it is greatest upon the copper or the bronze. Out of many specimens, some of bronze may be selected surpassing others of copper; but it is just as easy to select some of copper surpassing others of bronze.

I am of opinion, therefore, that it is only by actual trial and comparison with copper of *equal weight*, upon ships bottoms, that a true and useful result can be obtained; and though from the facts I have stated, I should not expect any superiority in the bronze; yet it is possible that when tried under the circumstances of time, motion, &c. &c. attending upon the sheathing of a ship, it may, from corroding more equally, (for corrode it certainly will) or in some other way not to be anticipated, exhibit some point of superiority.

Its broken and cavernous surface might be expected rather to assist chemical action. The coat of oxide upon it may perhaps be favourable as an envellope, or it may be voltaically injurious; But I think it useless to speculate in this report upon points which can only be correctly and usefully ascertained by a practical experiment. I am

Gentlemen
Your Very Obedt Humble
Servant
M. FARADAY

[1] Robert Dundas, Viscount Melville (1771–1851), was First Lord of the admiralty from 1812 to 1827 and continued his interest in the Navy throughout his life. I am unable to identify John Dean Thomson.

[2] During the years when Faraday was working intensively on electromagnetic induction and the nature of electricity, he was also a consultant on chemistry for the admiralty. See *LPW*, 106.

128 M. FARADAY to E. W. BRAYLEY,[1] 24 February 1832
[*R.I., previously unpublished*]

R Institution
Feb 24th 1832

MY DEAR SIR

I owe you many thanks for your note – I have adopted your second form with a little alteration

The mistake which you have made about the Progress of Foreign Science is an illustration of what I wish to guard against – *No part of it is mine* – Nor are abstracts of foreign Memoirs *etc. etc.* except they are found in the MISCEL-LANEA & even there several papers are from other hands

I send you a very hasty & badly written report of my evening[2] – but I want time sadly. If you would like to be considered as Editor or Sub Editor of the Phil Mag I may send you a ticket to the Evenings for the Season To night we have a subject which is expected to be very interesting. *The Philosophy of Improvisation* by an Italian Improvisatore.

If you like to come come & then let me know whether you would wish to be free for the season.

Ever Truly Yours
M. FARADAY

Alter the report as to wording any way you like

– M.F.

[1] Edward William Brayley (1802–70), had studied at the Royal Institution in Brande's courses on chemistry. He was at this time, joint librarian of the London Institution and one of the editors of the *PM*.

[2] Probably a report on his lecture 'On the first two parts of his recent researches in electricity; namely, volta-electric induction, and magneto-electric induction,' *PM*, n.s., 11 (1832), 300.

129 M. FARADAY to J. G. CHILDREN, 12 March 1832
[*R.S., previously unpublished*][1]

Royal Institution,
March 12, 1832

MY DEAR SIR

Will you do me the favour to ask permission for me that the accompanying sealed paper be deposited in the Strong box of the Royal Society It contains certain views of magnetism & Electricity arising from my late investigations which are I believe peculiarly my own I wish to work them out experimentally but as that will require time I am anxious to place a record of my views in a sure place so that if they prove important, a date may be referred to at which they may be proved to be my own.

I am Dear Sir,
Yours Most faithfully
M. FARADAY

[1] See Letter 130.

130 Sealed note signed M. FARADAY, 13 March 1832

[R.S., *LPW*, *181. Also Royal Society – occasional notices*, 2 (*1937*), *9; and Wireless World*, *42* (*1938*), *400–1*, (*5 May*)]

Royal Institution,
March 12th 1832

Certain of the results of the investigations which are embodied in the two papers entitled *Experimental researches in Electricity*, lately read to the Royal Society, and the views arising therefrom, in connexion with other views and experiments, lead me to believe that magnetic action is progressive, and requires time; i.e. that when a magnet acts upon a distant magnet or piece of iron, the influencing cause, (which I may for the moment call magnetism,) proceeds gradually from the magnetic bodies, and requires time for its transmission which will probably be found to be very sensible.

I think also, that I see reason for supposing that electric induction (of tension) is also performed in a similar progressive way.[1]

I am inclined to compare the diffusion of magnetic forces from a magnetic pole, to the vibrations upon the surface of disturbed water, or those of air in the phenomena of sound, i.e., I am inclined to think the vibratory theory will apply to these phenomena, as it does to sound and most probably to light.

By analogy I think it may possibly apply to the phenomena of induction of electricity of tension also.

These views I wish to work out experimentally; but as much of my time is engaged in the duties of my office, and as the experiments will therefore be prolonged, and may in their course be subject to the observation of others; I wish, by depositing this paper in the care of the Royal Society, to take possession as it were of a certain date, and a lone right, if they are confirmed by experiments, to claim credit for the views at that date: at which time as far as I know no one is conscious of or can claim them but myself.

M. FARADAY

[1] In *LPW*, the last word in the second paragraph was mistranscribed as 'time.'

131 M. FARADAY to the EDITOR of the 'Literary Gazette', 27 March 1832

[*Burndy Library, Norwalk, Conn., Michael Faraday Collection U1, LPW, 201*]

R Institution
March 27th 1832

MY DEAR SIR

Will you let me call your attention for a moment to the Article Electricity & Magnetism at p 185 of your last Gazette. You there give an account of Nobili's experiments[1] and speak of them as if independent of or any thing but a repetition of mine. But if you had seen Nobilis paper you would have found that my name is on every page; that the experiments in it were a consequence of his having seen a copy of my letter to Paris, which letter he translates into Italian & inserts; & that he tried and obtained the spark with the magnet, because in my letter, I said that I had obtained the spark in a particular case. Nobili, so far from wishing to imply that the experiments & discovery are his; honors me by speaking of the "nuove correnti di Faraday"

I should not have noticed the matter but that in the Gazette it is said "researches of Mr Faraday which were rapidly tending to the same discovery"[2] whereas they are my own experiments which having gone first to Paris & then to Italy have been repeated & studied by Signori Nobili and Antinori

Perhaps the mistake may have risen from the circumstance of the Number of the Antologia[3] bearing date November 1831 But that date is no guide for the work was not published, or printed even, till long after that; & Nobili's paper in it is dated January 1832.

Excuse my troubling you with this letter, but I never took more pains to be quite independant of other persons than in the present investigation; and I have never been more annoyed about any paper than the present by the variety of circumstances which have arisen seeming to imply that I had been anticipated

I am
Dear Sir
Very Truly Yours
M. FARADAY

[1] See Letter 124, fn. 2.
[2] *LG*, 185.
[3] *Antologia; giornale di scienze, lettere et arti*, published at Florence.

[*R.I., previously unpublished*]

Naples,
3 Avril, 1832.

Monsieur, et très estimable Professeur,

J'ai l'honneur de vous adresser cette lettre, pour vous entretenir d'un phénomène que je dois à vos très-belles theories relatives aux inductions. J'ai fait construire un cylindre en fer doux dont le diamètre était de 40 millimetres, et le poids de 7 chilogrammes [*sic*] a peu près. Autour du cylindre j'ai enroulé 200 métres de fil de cuivre vêtu de soie; et j'ai lié les extremités aux fils conjonctifs d'un multiplicateur à deux aiguilles. La jonction faite, j'ai tourné le cylindre du nord au sud, et *vice versa*: l'aiguille du multiplicateur a commencé à osciller; et aprés cinq à six tours du cylindre a parcouru 180°. Quand elle était là parvenue j'ai continué à tourner le cylindre, avec la precaution d'alterner le mouvement chaque fois que l'aiguille décrivait la demicirconference; alors la rotation est devenue continuelle, et n'a cessé qu'en cessant de tourner le cylindre en demicircle, ou le tournant en sens contraire. La vitesse de rotation de l'aiguille croissait avec l'acceleration du mouvement du cylindre.

Avec le même cylindre j'ai essayé de mettre en rotation l'aiguille d'un multiplicateur qui en avait une seule; mais l'aiguille aimantée, aprés avoir parcourue 95°; revenait vigoreusement tirée par le magnetisme terrestre. Je me suis aperçu que pour y reussir, il faut augmenter la masse du fer ou le fil de cuivre ou tous les deux ensemble.

Vous voyez bien, Monsieur, que par les successives separations et compositions que le magnetisme naturel du fer subit, dans le mouvement du cylindre, j'obtiens deux courans lesquels appliqués parallelement et en sens contraire aux deux poles de l'aiguille la mettent en rotation. Vous voyez aussi, si je ne me trompe pas, que mon appareil merite quelque attention pour sa simplicité; et qu'il repand plus de jour sur le magnetisme en rotation, decouvert par M. Arago. Mais j'attends là-dessus votre trés-appréciable jugement. M. Auldjo s'est chargé de vous consigner ma lettre, et de vous temoigner les sentimens d'éstime et de consideration avec lesquels je suis

Votre trés-humble et respectueux
Serviteur
Lorenzo Fazzini.

[1] Lorenzo Fazzini (1787–1837), Professor of Mathematics, Physics, Logic and Metaphysics at the University of Naples. He does not appear to have published on the subject of this letter.

[Bibliothèque Nationale, N.A. Fr. 1304, f. 8, previously unpublished]

Royal Institution
April 5, 1832

MY DEAR SIR

On writing to you at present it is merely to announce that I shall be able to send you a copy of my recent papers on Electricity &c &c in the course of a week provided I find means of conveyance. I thought of writing to you immediately after I had written to M Hachette some time ago but the experiments delayed me at first and then I found I could tell you so little in a letter and that little as in the case of my letter to M Hachette was so liable from my bad writing perhaps to be misunderstood that I thought it better to wait 'till the paper was printed

The time between the reading & the printing has been however sadly prolonged in consequence of new regulations at our *Royal Society* and has far exceeded what I thought would be required

I hope that when you receive the papers you will think them worth having: I have felt great pleasure in carrying on the investigation and think it is an important step; but no man is well fitted to judge his own works

I have heard in some way that you have not received a copy of my paper on the *arrangements of particles on vibrating surfaces* &c &c which I sent to you with several others to MM. Gay Lussac, Arago, D'Arcet,[1] Berthier,[2] Hachette, Despretz[3] Serullas, Becquerel[4] and the Academy of Sciences & Philomatic Society I sent them by the means of our Assistnt [*sic*] Secretary to the Academy of Sciences with the *Royal Society Box* being assured they would be given to those friends to whom they were addressed

If you really have not received it I must send you another copy but I hope you will when you write me again tell me how I shall send I am afraid my other friends have not received their copies

I am still hard at work on Magnetism &c &c & hope yet to get new results

I am My dear Sir
Your very Oblgd &
faithful Servant
M. FARADAY.

[1] Jean Pierre Joseph d'Arcet (1777–1844), Warden of the French Mint and chemist.
[2] Pierre Berthier (1782–1861), analytical chemist and Inspector of Mines.
[3] César Mansuète Despretz (1792–1863), physicist, Professor at the Ecole polytechnique.
[4] Antoine-César Becquerel (1788–1878), chemist and student of electricity.

Greenhill
Edinburgh,
13th. April 1832

My dear Sir

I felt so extremely interested in your fine experiments in Electro-Magnetism that on my return to Scotland I could not resist immediately repeating them which I did with entire success.

I have now the satisfaction of informing you that I have obtained repeatedly before witnesses sparks from a natural magnet. I first got a spark so far back as the 30th. of March but as it was only once & from a want of coinciding circumstances which I did not then understand I could not repeat it, & I therefore declined giving any account of it. Believing then that it would be impracticable to obtain it with any degree of certainty at pleasure from a *momentary* current of magnetism I constructed an apparatus for producing a continuous current, which failed from a peculiarity in the construction which I have since met with a parallel of & which puzzles me a good deal; perhaps in another letter I may trouble you with some questions about it.

Driven back to the original simplicity of my apparatus; I availed myself of a set of experiments I had in the meantime made to determine the conditions under which a spark could easiest be obtained from weak galvanic currents of low intensity. Today I am happy to say I have obtained numerous sparks. The mode in which I proceeded was the following. I had prepared a helix of copper wire about 7 inches long & containing about 150 feet of copper wire (I had one with double that length). A soft iron canister which I had properly adapted to the poles of a very large [reading doubtful] natural magnet belonging to Dr. Hope[1] professor of chemistry here was made to traverse its axis & the magnetic current was created by making the contact with the poles of the magnet. The excellence of the contact proved to be of essential importance. One end of the helix wire was terminated in a cup of mercury whilst the other was connected with an Iron wire one end of which was brought to a fine point & was capable of being brought at pleasure in contact with the surface of the mercury in this cup. I devised the means of bringing the canister with speed & accuracy up to the magnet in the dark which an assistant did at my direction at the instant in which I *broke* the connection of the circuit formed at the junction of iron point with the mercury I found the instant of breaking better than that of *making* the circuit, & that it was more efficacious at the *sides* of the mercurial curved surface than in the centre. Perhaps you will favour me by informing me how the information of Nobili's Experiment published in the Literary Gazette came to this country & also if you know how he performed it. I have not heard of it except as a rumour, I think from yourself. I cannot help again expressing the strong sense I feel of the liberality with which you have put your fine experiments into the hands of the Scientific world at so early a period. Will you have the kindness to communicate my result to Christie[2] & any-one else who may be interested in it: & believe me my dear Sir yours very sincerely

JAMES D. FORBES

[1] Thomas Charles Hope (1766–1844), after whom the mineral Hopeite was named.
[2] Samuel Hunter Christie (1784–1865), specialized in the study of magnetism, and later became Secretary of the Royal Society.
See James D. Forbes, 'Account of some experiments in which an Electric Spark was elicited from a natural magnet,' *PM*, 3 s., 1 (1832), 49.

135 J. D. FORBES to M. FARADAY, 18 April 1832

[*I.E.E., previously unpublished*]

Greenhill
Edinburgh
18th Apr. 1832

MY DEAR SIR

Your welcome & prompt reply to my letter has just reached me: & I seize an opportunity of acknowledging it. I am most anxious to see your paper & hope Hudson[1] lost no time in forwarding it.

If I understand you rightly, no one but Nobili had got a spark from a *Natural* Magnet before me I have often repeated my experiment & got it quite under my command. I have shown the spark to Sir John Leslie, Dr. Hope & many others.

The history you gave me of the transfusion of Information is a lesson to discoverers.[2]

You would oblige me much by sending me Nobili's paper as I am going to print immediately in the R.S. Ed. Transactions[3] a notice of my experiment which will be out in a few days. If it is too large for an Admiralty Frank which Mr. Hudson could probably procure for me, you would very much oblige me by addressing it to me, care of Sir William Forbes & Co[4] Edinburgh.

Believe me dear Sir Yours
most sincerely
JAMES D. FORBES

[1] James Hudson (1804–59), Assistant Secretary to the Royal Society from 1829 to 1838.
[2] This undoubtedly refers to Faraday's experience with Hachette, Nobili and Antinori. It shows how strongly he felt that he would recount the tale, obviously in some detail, to Forbes.
[3] Forbes' 'Account of some experiments in which an Electric Spark was elicited from a natural magnet' did not appear in the *TRSE* until 1837, 197. See Letter 134, fn. 2.
[4] A banking firm founded by James Forbes' father.

[*I.E.E., previously unpublished*]

Paris, 29 avril 1832
Rue St hyacinthe
St Michel 8

MONSIEUR ET TRÈS HONORÉ CONFRERE —

vous aurez appris par les journaux que j'avois communiqué a l'Academie des Sciences de l'institut la lettre du 17 decembre 1831, par laquelle vous avez annoncé au Monde Savant l'heureuse et Brillante decouverte de l'influence reciproque des Courans electriques; ou electro-Magnetiques.[1] nous attendons avec impatience le memoire imprimé que vous avez presenté a la Societé Royale, et qui nous fera connoitre Votre maniere d'operer. —

Je vous envois une copie d'un vieux memoire imprimé en 1804,[2] presenté a l'academie le 31 octobre 1803. Vous me ferez bien plaisir de me donner votre avis sur les faits contenus dans ce memoire. ces faits nous ont paru tres singuliers pour l'epoque ou nous les avons observés, mais alors, il nous fut bien impossible d'en trouver une explication plausible. nous avons obtenu par la rotation d'un plateau de cuivre, une electricité Spontanée etincelante; d'après la nouvelle construction du doubleur, cette electricité ne provenoit ny du frottement de l'axe du plateau mobile sur les tourillons; ny du Reservoir commun, ny du Contact de deux Substances heterogenes; ainsi la Cause de l'electricité produite par la Rotation d'un plateau, nous etoit tout a fait inconnue, cette electricité etincellante n'etoit pas une electricité d'abord très foible mise *a priori* dans les plateaux fixes. ces plateaux etant bien isolés et a l'etat naturel electrique, on faisoit tourner le plateau mobile, et après un petit nombre de Revolutions, l'etincelle partoit entre les fils de l'electrometre de Bennet, mis en Communication avec les disques fixes. Je pense, Monsieur, que vous avez souleve le voile qui nous cachoit la verité, et je suis porté a croire que l'aimant terrestre joue un grand Role dans les phenomenes que nous avons observés sur le doubleur de notre Construction. —

Cette lettre Vous sera Remise par Melle Vara anglaise; qui demeure avec nous pour l'instruction de ma petite fille agée de 12 ans; plus tard avec ma fille, j'auray l'honneur de vous presenter mon second enfant, qui est agé de 21 ans, et qui est eleve de l'Ecole polytechnique.

Agreez, Monsieur, l'assurance de la plus haute Estime et du plus Sincere attachement de

HACHETTE

[1] See Letter 124.
[2] J. N. P. Hachette and Charles Bernard Desormes, 'Du doubleur d'électricité,' *AC*, 49 (1804), 45.

[I.E.E., previously unpublished]

Freeland,
Perthshire
2ᵈ May 1832

My dear Sir

I had the pleasure of receiving yours from Brighton two days ago. The same day I saw in the Annales de Chimie for December all that our continental friends have made of the Discovery:[1] with a translation of Nobili & Antinori's paper which bears date 31st Jan.[2] (from your mentioning that it was in the Antologia for November I had fancied it was much earlier). I must say they have made but poor pickings of your Discovery, & it is quite a specimen of French fact to see how they have patched together all their little experiments & additions (sometimes perfect trifles) with all the formality of the 1° 2ᵈᵒ &c. But what is most provoking is to see Ampere bringing together in formal array his old Geneva Experiments which we may be sure he would have had out long ago if he had made anything of them;[3] but it is wonderfully easy to connect crude & unintelligible fragments when another has furnished the key.

It was very interesting to me to see how exactly Nobili had followed the subject as I did & that he met with the very same difficulties & succeeded in the very same way which I did. This you will see in my paper which I shall soon send you. It is to be [reading doubtful] published in the Edinburgh. S. Transactions & I put it into the hands of the printer before I saw anything of Nobili's paper.

I was a good deal vexed at not getting your Paper when you were good enough to say that if you were not convinced I had already got it you would have sent me another copy. I was at Mr. Buchanan's[4] house the day before yesterday & he had heard nothing of it. If Mr. Hudson cannot explain why it has not come to hand you would extremely oblige me by sending a copy by coach addressed to me care of Sir William Forbes & Co Edinburgh My reason for being in a hurry is that I must add a postscript to my paper, about Nobili's experiment & should think it necessary to see yours first.

Do not doubt my dear Sir that you will get all the credit due to you for your fine experiments on this subject All the nibbling of the Français will not do you much harm. I am yet very imperfectly informed as to the extent of your experiments on induction of electric currents, as till I read yesterday in the *Annales* your letter to Hatchette[5] the only tangible information I had on the subject & the only guide which led me to my experiments & discovery of the spark, was contained in the few hints you were kind enough to give me one evening after the Royal Institution Lecture.

I return to Edinburgh in two days in order to observe the Transit of Mercury. I am Dear Sir

Yours very sincerely
James D. Forbes –

¹ 'Diverses notices sur les courans électriques produits soit par d'autres courans, soit par des aimans', *AC*, 2 s., 48 (1831), 402.
² *Ibid.*, 412.
³ (A.-M.) Ampère, 'Expériences sur les Courans électriques produits par l'influence d'un autre courant,' *ibid.*, 405.
⁴ David Buchanan (1745–1822) had founded a printing establishment and was a publisher in Edinburgh. This Mr Buchanan was probably his son.
⁵ *AC*, 2 s., 48 (1831), 402.

138   M. FARADAY to J. J. BERZELIUS, 5 May 1832
[*Kungl. Vetenskapsakademiens Bibliotek, Stockholm, previously unpublished*]

R Institution,
London
May 5th, 1832

DEAR SIR,

We have been alarmed here by reports of your death but rejoiced again by finding it was false. This circumstance must account to you for the delay in sending you a copy of my paper on *Experimental researches in Electricity* but of which I now beg your acceptance

I have to thank you for being the means some time since of sending me some Vanadiate of Ammonia from M Sefstrom.¹ I have written to him since & sent him a paper by another channel & hope my communication has reached him for I thought that it had as through you been closed for ever.

That you may long live to advance Chemical Science and interest and delight your contemporaries is the earnest wish

of Dear Sir
Your very Oblgd & faithful
M. FARADAY

¹ See Letter 114.

139   M. FARADAY to C. BABBAGE, 7 May 1832¹
[*British Museum, Add. mss. 37186, f. 382, previously unpublished*]

Royal Institution,
May 7ᵗʰ 1832

MY DEAR SIR

I send you all the authorities I have looked at there is not even an exception in favour of *Quinine*

{ HENRY. Elements 11th Edition²
{ *Quinia*. Cinchonia. Atropia Voratria Delphia Picrotoxia etc etc
{ PHILLIPS Translation of Pharmacopaeia³
{ *Quinia*. Cinchonia Morphia

{ PARIS. Dr. Medical Chemistry & Pharmacologia[4]
{ *Quina* [*sic*] Cinchon*ia* Strychn*ia* Morph*ia* Delph*ia*
{ Atrop*ia* etc etc
{ TURNER Dr. Elements of Chemistry[5]
{ *Quina* [*sic*] Cinchon*ia* Morph*ia* Delph*ia* Strychn*ia* etc etc
  Turner says *once* on its history "or Quinine" but in title & elsewhere
  Quina
{ Brande – Manual[6]
{ Quin*ia* Cinchon*ia*. Morph*ia* Delph*ia* etc etc
{ *Christison* on Poisons[7]
{ Says Atrop*ia* Strychn*ia* etc etc but as he speaks of Poisons only has not
{ the analogous bodies, Quin*ia* etc.
  Hare Dr. of Philadelphia United States Chem Compendium[8]
  Quin*ia* Cinchon*ia*. Vevatr*ia*, Delph*ia* etc etc
  He says however once for each "or Quinine" Cinchonine Vevatine"
  Delphine" etc etc –
  The French say. *Quinine Cinchonine Vevatrine Delphine Morphine* etc.
  etc. throughout

If you write *Quinine* only, you will be as far as I have looked for authorities
the only English Scientific writer who has done so.

                                                        I am

                                           Dear Sir

                                              Very Truly Yours
                                                M. FARADAY.

---

[1] In an earlier letter, not published here (British Museum, Add. mss. 37186, f. 269), Faraday
had counselled Babbage against using the term 'quinine'. The letter that follows indicates
how seriously Faraday took the problem of proper terminology.
[2] William Henry, *The Elements of Experimental Chemistry*, 11th ed., 2 vols., London, 1829.
[3] Richard Phillips, *A Translation of the Pharmacopoeia*, London, 1824.
[4] John A. Paris, M.D., *The Elements of Medical Chemistry*, London, 1825, and
Pharmacologia, 6th ed., 2 vols., London, 1825.
[5] Edward Turner, M.D., *Elements of Chemistry*, Edinburgh, 1827.
[6] William Thomas Brande, *A Manual of Chemistry*, London, 1819.
[7] Sir Robert Christison, Bart., *A Treatise on Poisons in relation to Medical Jurisprudence,
Physiology and the Practice of Physic*, Edinburgh, 1829.
[8] Robert Hare, M.D., *A Compendium of the course of chemical instruction in the Medical
Department of the University of Pennsylvania*, Philadelphia, 1827.

[*I.E.E., previously unpublished*]

Paris 18 Mai 1832
Rue St. hyacinthe St Michel 8

Monsieur

lorsque vous eutes la bonté de m'informer de vos decouvertes sur les influences momentanées des Courans electro-Magnetiques, de la publication que vous en aviez faite a londres par la lecture de votre Memoire presenté a la Societé Royale, j'ai cru que deja autorisé par vous a montrer votre lettre a mon confrere M. Ampere, je pouvois dans votre propre interet, et avec le desir d'assurer la priorité de votre invention a son auteur, communiquer votre lettre a l'academie en Seance.[1] si je n'ai pas rempli vos intentions, je vous prie de croire que c'est par erreur, et j'espere que mon caractere vous est assez connu, pour ne pas mettre en doute le sentiment qui m'a dirigé en publiant votre lettre. vous rendre justice entiere, vous assurer toute priorité, voila mon unique but – votre lettre a été traduite de l'anglais en français, par un jeune Medecin, qui habite la france depuis long temps, et dont le pere est un Ministre attaché a la Maison de votre Roi. dans une note du Memoire imprimé que vous avez eu la bonté de m'adresser, vous dites qu'il y a quelques erreurs dans cette traduction. il est vrai qu'on a lu *tomes*, mot de votre lettre imaginé par vous, *tome*, au lieu de *tonic*, mais comme vous ne mettez pas les points sur les *i*, on a pu se tromper, et d'ailleurs je ne vois pas d'autres erreurs. Les Resultats de vos Recherches ont été bien compris et a florence et a Paris; mais on attendoit avec impatience votre très beau Memoire, pour Repeter vos experiences. M Savary[2] m'a dit qu'on traduisoit en ce moment votre Memoire, pour le publier dans les annales de chimie et phisique –.[3] Je conserve votre derniere lettre, avec celle que vous eutes la bonté de m'écrire en octobre 1821, en y joignant le joli petit appareil du fil de cuivre tournant autour d'un aimant –.

Cette lettre vous sera Remise par M. Rousselle,[4] de Paris, qui voyage pour son instruction; ayez la bonté de lui faire voir votre etablissement *Royal institution*.

Agreez, Monsieur, l'assurance de mon bien sincere attachement

Votre bien devoué Confrere
HACHETTE
de l'institut

[1] See Letter 131.
[2] Felix Savary (1797–1841), Professor of Astronomy and Geodesy at the Ecole polytechnique, writer on electrodynamics.
[3] A French translation of Series 1 appeared in the *AC*, 2 s., 50 (1832), 5, 113.
[4] Possibly Martial Roussel of Amiens, student of the mechanical arts.

[*British Museum, Add. mss. 37186, f. 445, previously unpublished*][1]

R. Institution
May. 31st 32

MY DEAR SIR

You are quite right in your recollection of sulphate of baryta precipitate I have had that substance in suspension under particular circumstances for 18 or 24 hours together in glasses not containing more than four inches of water & the liquid turbid even at the end of that time

But I cannot express even generally how long a particular substance or a fine precipitate takes to settle for the same substance varies very much according to the circumstances under which its particles have aggregated & become solid in smaller or larger masses

As you are considering the suspension of solid particles for a longer or shorter time according to their magnitude. Are you aware that Girard[2] has something particular about the influence of solid particles in liquids I have referred to it at p 60 of my Manipulation[3] 2nd Edition but you will find his paper in the Mem de l'Académie Royale. IV. 1819. 1820

Oxide of tin made by pouring nitric acid on tin foil is when rubbed so fine a powder. it can hardly be washed in any reasonable time in pure water Add salt to the water. which increases the S.G. & the oxide separates far more readily.

Ever Dear Sir
Very Truly Yours
M. FARADAY.

I send you two pennyworth of Manufacture. The things are made at Nuremburg. sent here and sold retail with a profit for the above small sum I think there are 30 pieces including box & lid

[1] Babbage, at this time, was interested in the problem of sedimentation in geology. See his letters to Charles Lyell in these years in this collection.
[2] P. S. Girard, 'Mémoire sur les atmosphères liquides, et leur influence sur l'action mutuelle des molécules solides qu'elles enveloppent,' *MAS*, 4 (1819–20), 1.
[3] M. Faraday, *Chemical Manipulation*, 2nd ed., London, 1830.

142   M. FARADAY to J. D. THOMPSON, 3 July 1832

[*PRO, Adm. 1, 4610, Prom. Lett., previously unpublished*]

Royal Institution
July. 3, 1832

SIR

Some time since the Navy Board applied to me professionally through you to analyse & experiment on certain specimens of Bronze & Copper The charge for my labour is ten guineas but I am ignorant how to carry on that part of the affair and beg to ask your instructions

I would willingly give help to the Government Gratis were I at all in circumstances to justify me in doing so but my time is my only estate

I am Sir
Your Very Obedt Servt
M. FARADAY

[1] See Letter 127.

143   J. N. P. HACHETTE to M. FARADAY, 9 July 1832

[*I.E.E., previously unpublished*]

Paris,
9 July 1832

MON CHER MONSIEUR ET CONFRERE.

J'ai Reçu la lettre que vous m'avez fait l'honneur de m'écrire le 24 mai. Je suis tout à fait de votre sentiment sur l'Empressement de certaines personnes à cultiver le champ du voisin à leur profit particulier.[1] les publications que vous avez faites à la Société Royale, confirmées par la Communication à l'académie Royale des Sciences de Paris, ne laissent aucun doute sur la priorité de vos decouvertes, dont l'honneur vous appartient sans partage.

vos principales expériences ont été repetées le mois passé au Cours de phisique de la faculté des Sciences de paris, admirablement bien fait par M. Pouillet;[2] elles ont parfaitement reussi en presence de plus de 800 personnes. Je joins ici la figure geometrale des fers a cheval qui ont Servi a montrer l'etincelle electrique. le premier fer *ANS* etoit enveloppé par le fil de cuivre couvert de soie, dont les extremités plongoient a volonté dans les capsules a Mercure communiquant aux poles de la batterie galvanique. le second fer *A'NS* en contact avec le premier par les cercles *N* et *S* portoit un autre fil dont l'observateur tenoit les extremités, a une petite distance l'une de l'autre, et près de son oeil. chaque fois que le Servant de l'observateur plongeoit les extremites du fil enroulé sur le premier fer a cheval dans les Capsules a Mercure, ou les retiroit de ces capsules, on voyoit parfaitement l'etincelle.

Substituant au premier fer a cheval *ANS* et au fil qui l'enveloppe un aimant artificiel d'acier capable de Supporter un poids de (lisez 35) 35 kilogrammes,[3] la Separation ou le Contact de cet aimant avec le fer a cheval *A'NS* donne

229

egalement l'etincelle aux extremités du fil enroulé sur ce fer – ces deux experiences reussissent toujours; l'etincelle est visible pour le plus nombreux auditoire, en placant un chapeau noir derriere les fils entre lesquels l'etincelle part.

J'ai rendu Compte a la Societé philomatique du memoire imprimé que vous avez bien voulu m'envoyer le bulletin qui en fera mention, s'imprime actuellement, et j'auray l'honneur de vous l'adresser.

Je crois qu'on s'occupe de la traduction du Memoire entier pour l'insertion aux Annales de chimie et de phisique redigées par MM. Gay Lussac et Arago – on imprime cette traduction.[4]–

aujourd'huy 9 juillet, l'academie des Sciences a nommé M. Dulong[5] en Remplacement de M. G. Cuvier Secretaire perpetuel[6] – et M. de Blainville;[7] Professeur d'anatomie Comparée et de zoologie, en remplacement du même M. Cuvier – Je vous envois deux opuscules de M. Dumas,[8] qui est sur les Rangs pour Remplacer a l'academie, M. Serrulas, enlevé par le cholera – agreez, Monsieur et cher confrere, les complimens les plus affectueux

HACHETTE

Rue St hyacinthe St Michel 8 –
Paris 9 juillet 1832

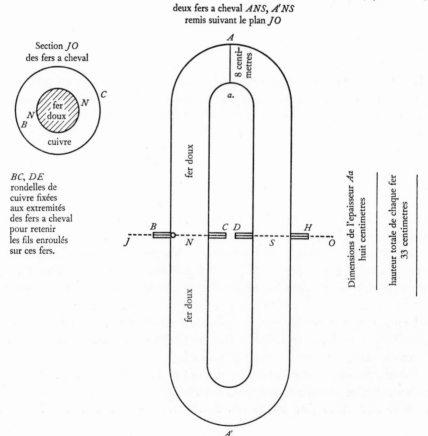

deux fers a cheval *ANS, A'NS*
remis suivant le plan *JO*

Section *JO*
des fers a cheval

fer
doux

cuivre

BC, DE
rondelles de
cuivre fixées
aux extremités
des fers a cheval
pour retenir
les fils enroulés
sur ces fers.

8 centi-
metres

a.

fer doux

fer doux

Dimensions de l'epaisseur *Aa*
huit centimetres

hauteur totale de chaque fer
33 centimetres

Cette lettre vous sera Remise par M. Nobile,[9] de naples, qui s'occupe d'astronomie, et qui voyage pour son instruction.

H

chaque fer a cheval pèse 18 kilogrammes. le fil de cuivre enroulé sur chaque fer
étoit de Mille Metres en longeur, et pesoit 6 Kilog 3/4 sans soie, et avec
quatre couches de soie sur chaque fil 7 Kilogrammes 1/2:

en aimantant l'un des deux fers a cheval par une Batterie galvanique de 24
plaques (cuivre et zinc), de 10 sur 16 centimetres, on pouvoit suspendre au
second fer un poids de 4 à 500 Kilogrammes.

Paris 9 juillet 1832
H

[1] See Letter 137.
[2] Claude Pouillet (1790–1868), Professor of Physics in the Faculty of Sciences at the
University of Paris.
[3] The figure originally written was 75. This has been written over to turn it into a rather
illegible 35. Hence, Hachette's verbal directions.
[4] *AC*, 2 s., 50 (1832), 5, 113.
[5] Pierre Louis Dulong (1785–1838), famous for his work with A. T. Petit on specific heats
of elements and their relation to atomic weights.
[6] Georges Cuvier (1769–1832), the great paleontologist and comparative anatomist.
[7] Henri Maris Ducrotay de Blainville (1778–1850), Professor in the Faculty of Sciences of
the University of Paris and in the *Ecole normale*.
[8] Jean-Baptiste Dumas (1800–84), chemist and, later, Faraday's friend.
[9] Antonio Nobile (1794–1863), Neapolitan astronomer.

144 J. PLATEAU[1] to M. FARADAY, 24 July 1832
[*I.E.E.*, *previously unpublished*]

Bruxelles
le 24 Juillet 1832

MONSIEUR

J'ai reçu, par Mr Forbes,[2] Votre mémoire et la lettre dont vous avez bien voulu
m'honorer, et je prends la liberté de vous adresser mes remerciments [*sic*].
Bien loin qu'il y ait eu quelque chose de désagréable pour moi dans la petite
affaire de priorité qui a motivé l'envoi de ma lettre aux Annales de physique
et de chimie, ma premiere pensée, en apprenant que vous aviez publié des
observations analogues aux miennes,[3] a été de m'applaudir de ce que de semblables phénomenes, que j'osais à peine croire dignes d'intérêt, vous avaient
cependant paru mériter une attention particuliere; et maintenant Je me félicite
doublement d'une circonstance qui m'a procuré, à moi débutant dans la carriere
des sciences, l'honneur de correspondre avec vous. Permettez-moi de profiter
de cet avantage et veuillez ne pas vous offenser si je prends la liberté de vous
demander un exemplaire de votre mémoire sur ces illusions d'optique. J'ai
cherché inutilement ici à me procurer soit le memoire lui-même, soit une analyse
détaillée de ce qu'il contient: je vous serais donc bien reconnaissant, Monsieur,

si vous pouviez disposer d'un exemplaire en ma faveur. Comme je continue à m'occuper des sujets analogues et que j'espere publier bientôt un travail sur la formation et l'évanouissement des impressions de la rétine,[4] j'attache un prix infini à me procurer toutes les observations qui peuvent avoir quelque rapport avec ce genre de recherches et j'espere, Monsieur, que vous apprécierez le motif d'une demande qui, sans cela, pourrait vous paraitre indiscrete.

En profitant de l'observation qui vous est due qu'on produit une image fixe en faisant tourner une roue devant un miroir, j'ai construit des anamorphoses du genre de celle que j'ai l'honneur de vous envoyer ci-joint: j'ai pensé que cette application de l'une de vos idées pourrait vous être agréable. Pour que l'effet soit bien visible, il doit être observé le soir en plaçant une bougie entre le cercle et le miroir; le cercle doit être tenu le plus près possible de la glace et le plus loin possible de l'oeil qui ne doit pas se placer dans le prolongement de l'axe autour duquel la figure tourne, mais à une certaine distance vers la droite et un peu au dessus: enfin il faut ne regarder que d'un oeil. J'ai indiqué à peu pres ci-dessous les positions relatives de la glace, de la bougie, du cercle et de l'oeil, le tout en projection horizontale. ab est le miroir, c la bougie, df le cercle

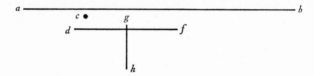

tournant autour de l'axe gh, et K la position de l'oeil. De cette maniere on voit l'image completement immobile d'un petit cheval parfaitement régulier, mais qui devient difforme dès que l'oeil n'a pas exactement la position convenable. Si l'on regarde des deux yeux, on voit deux images l'une réguliere et l'autre difforme qui se nuisent mutuellement, enfin si l'oeil est trop près du cercle, on ne peut plus obtenir d'image bien réguliere: il doit en être le plus loin possible. Il est inutile de dire que la figure difforme doit être tournée vers la glace et que c'est à travers l'espece de gaze [sic] que produit dans son mouvement la fente percée dans le cercle, qu'on aperçoit l'image réguliere. Au reste vous trouverez aisément par vous même les conditions les plus favorables pour produire l'effet désiré.

J'ai pris la liberté, Monsieur, de joindre encore à ma lettre un exemplaire de ma dissertation sur les impressions de l'organe de la vue;[5] c'est bien imparfait, et l'on peut y reconnaître l'ouvrage d'un étudiant sortant à peine de l'université: il y a d'ailleurs assez long-temps que cela a été publié; mais j'espere pouvoir dans quelque temps terminer un travail plus complet sur ce sujet,[6] et alors je me ferai un devoir et un plaisir de vous l'offrir aussitôt.

Veuillez, Monsieur, agréer l'assurance des sentiments les plus profonds d'estime et de respect avec lesquels j'ai l'honneur d'être

Votre très-humble et très
obéissant serviteur
JH PLATEAU

P.S. Si vous daignez m'envoyer un exemplaire de votre mémoire sur les illusions d'optique, veuillez avoir la bonté de l'adresser à Monsieur Quetelet,[7] directeur de notre observatoire.

[1] Joseph Plateau (1801–83), Professor of Physics at the University of Ghent. The letters from Faraday to Plateau, so far as I have been able to determine, have not survived. *RSCSP* gives Plateau's first name incorrectly as Jean.
[2] James D. Forbes.
[3] See J. Plateau, 'Sur une illusion d'optique,' *AC*, 2 s., 48 (1831), 281, and M. Faraday, 'On a Peculiar Class of Optical Deceptions,' *JRI*, 1 (1831), 205 and *ERCP*, 291.
[4] J. Plateau, 'Sur quelques phénomènes de vision,' *QCM*, 7 (1832), 288.
[5] *Dissertation sur quelques propriétés des impressions produite par la lumière sur l'organe de la vue*, Liège, 1829.
[6] *Essai d'une théorie générale comprenant l'ensemble des apparences visuelles qui succèdent à la contemplation des objets colorés et de celles qui accompagnent cette contemplation*, *MASB*, 8 (1834).
[7] Adolphe Quételet (1796–1874), astronomer and social statistician.

145 M. FARADAY to J. BARROW, 10 October 1832
[*PRO, Adm. 1, 4610, Prom. Lett., previously unpublished*]

Royal Institution
10th Oct.r 1832.

SIR

I hasten, on my return to town, to acknowledge your letter and the honor done me by My Lords Commissioners of the Admiralty in requesting my opinion in conjunction with others upon Mr. Brunels[1] application of the condensed gases as mechanical agents. As the discoverer of the condensation of the gases I think it would be inexpedient for me to be joined with the gentlemen you name; for on the one hand I think such a committee should give a report uninfluenced by my views and on the other as I mean with Mr. Brunels kind permission to examine the apparatus very closely I may probably remark some philosophical point which I should feel inclined to pursue alone.

I would beg you however to state to my Lords Commissioners of the

Admiralty that if their Lordships consider my opinion as at all worth having I shall feel honored in giving it after the Committee have reported and after I have carefully examined the apparatus: but in that case I would beg the favour of you to state rather more explicitly than in your last the points to which their Lordships would desire my answers

I am

Sir

Your Humble Servant

M. FARADAY

[Two notes at bottom in other hands: "Has he not been told that the meeting was put off? "Yes, Sir, by letter of 2nd Oct –.]

[1] Marc Isambard Brunel (1769–1849), engineer, who designed and supervised the construction of the Thames tunnel, completed in 1843. Brunel spent some ten years attempting unsuccessfully to use condensed gases to provide the motive power of engines.

146   M. FARADAY to J. G. CHILDREN, 23 October 1832

[R.S., previously unpublished]

Royal Institution,
23rd October 1832

SIR

I have been honored by the receipt of your letter requesting to know on the part of His Royal Highness the President[1] and Council of the Royal Society whether I could accept the office of a Member of Council if recommended & elected for the coming year

In reply I beg respectfully to decline the probability of election: not that I undervalue the character of that high and responsible office or esteem lightly the favourable opinion which would recommend me to it But the time I can spare from imperative duties is already so small that I am anxious to devote the whole of it to original investigation and I entertain a hope that his Royal Highness the President and the Council will think that in so doing I am performing to the best of my abilities my duties to Science & the Royal Society[2]

I am
Sir
Your Obedt. Humble Servant
M. FARADAY

[1] H.R.H. The Duke of Sussex.
[2] Faraday felt the defeat of the 'professionals' in the contest between Herschel and Sussex keenly and withdrew temporarily from active participation in the governing of the Royal Society. See LPW, 354.

147 M. FARADAY to SIR J. F. W. HERSCHEL, 10 November 1832

[*R.S., previously unpublished*]

Royal Institution,
10 Nov 1832

MY DEAR SIR

I received your letter introducing Dr Robinson[1] but fear he was hardly worth such an honor from you. At his request I wrote to Cambridge introducing him as the Dr Robinson you had introduced to me and I find that he has been borrowing Money of the persons there Professor Lanning [reading doubtful] & others as he has also done of me. I cannot say he will not repay but under all circumstances I think I ought to let you know the result, that he may not use your name more than you would like elsewhere.

I am glad you like my last experiments and I have the more pleasure in receiving your commendation than that of another person – not merely because there are few whose approbation I should compare with yours but for another circumstance. When your work on the study of Nat. Phil. came out,[2] I read it as all others did with delight. I took it as a school book for philosophers and I feel that it has made me a better reasoner & even experimenter and has altogether heightened my character and made me if I may be permitted to say so a better philosopher.

In my last investigations I continually endeavored to think of that book and to reason & investigate according to the principles there laid down.

I am therefore
My dear Sir
Your much indebted & oblgd
M. FARADAY

[1] Possibly Thomas Romney Robinson, D.D. (1792–1882), Irish astronomer at the Armagh Observatory. The charge levelled by Faraday is not at all characteristic of Robinson.
[2] John F. W. Herschel, *A Preliminary Discourse on the Study of Natural Philosophy* (London, 1830). See *LPW*, 178ff. for effect of this work on Faraday's ideas.

148 M. FARADAY to M. GAY-LUSSAC, 1 December 1832[1]

[*AC, 2 s., 51 (1832), 404. Also ERE, 2*]

Institution royale,
1er décembre 1832[1]

MON CHER MONSIEUR,

J'ai désiré vous écrire une lettre sur l'électro-magnétisme, et je vous prie de l'insérer dans les *Annales de Chimie et de Physique*, si vous pouvez m'accorder cette faveur. Je crains que cette lettre n'occasionne plus de controverses que je ne voudrais; mais les circonstances sont telles que je suis forcé à prendre la plume; car si je gardais le silence, ce silence serait regardé comme l'aveu d'une erreur, non-seulement sous un point de vue philosophique, mais encore sous un point de vue moral, et dans une occasion où je me crois exempt de ces deux sortes d'erreur.

Vous comprenez sans doute que je veux parler du Mémoire de MM. Nobili et Antenori.[2] [*sic*] Je vous écris, parce que vous avez jugé assez bien de la matière pour insérer mon Mémoire dans votre excellent et véritablement philosophique journal, et parce que, y ayant inséré aussi le Mémoire de MM. Nobili et Antenori, tout ce qui a été écrit sur ce sujet se trouve renfermé dans les *Annales*. Je puis donc espérer que vous ne me refuserez pas ce que je viens vous demander ici.

Le 24 novembre 1831, mon premier Mémoire fut lu à la Société Royale, c'est celui que vous m'avez fait l'honneur d'insérer dans les *Annales* du mois de mai 1832 (p. 5–69). Ce Mémoire fut la première annonce que je fis de mes travaux sur l'électricité. Le 18 décembre 1831, j'écrivis une lettre à mon ami M. Hachette, qui me fit l'honneur d'en donner communication à l'Académie des Sciences, le 26 du même mois.* Cette lettre fut aussi insérée dans le numéro des *Annales* de décembre 1831 (p. 402). La seconde série de mes recherches, qui date du 21 décembre 1831, fut lue à la Société Royale, le 12 janvier 1832, et trouva place dans les *Annales*, mois de juin 1832 (p. 113–162). Ce sont là les seules publications (excepté quelques notes jointes à des Mémoires dus à d'autres auteurs) que j'aie faites jusqu'à présent sur cette matière; et tout cela a été écrit et lu antérieurement à quoi que ce soit d'un autre savant quelconque.

Pendant ce temps, la lettre que j'adressai à M. Hachette, et que vous m'aviez fait l'honneur d'insérer dans les *Annales*, avait attiré l'attention de MM. Nobili et Antenori, et ces savans laborieux publièrent un Mémoire dont la date remonte au 31 janvier 1832, et qui est en conséquence postérieur à tous mes écrits. Ce Mémoire a obtenu une place dans les *Annales* du mois de décembre 1831 (p. 412–430). Un second Mémoire, intitulé: *Nouvelles expériences électro-magnétiques*, par les mêmes savans, et daté du 24 mars 1832, a aussi paru et a été inséré dans les *Annales* de juillet (p. 280–304).

Je crains que la lettre que j'écrivis à M. Hachette, et que, dans sa bienveillance pour moi, il me fit l'honneur de lire à l'Académie des Sciences, ne soit devenue une source de malentendus et d'erreurs, et n'ait eu pour résultat de nuire à la cause de la vérité philosophique, bien loin de la servir. Et cependant je ne sais comment je dois expliquer ce point, et rétablir les choses à leur vraie place, sans avoir l'air de me plaindre en quelque sorte de MM. Nobili et Antenori, ce qui est pour moi une chose on ne peut plus désagréable. J'honore ces messieurs pour tout ce qu'ils ont fait, non-seulement pour l'électricité, mais encore pour la science en général; et, si ce n'était que le contenu de leurs Mémoires m'oblige à parler et me place dans l'alternative ou d'admettre ou de nier l'exactitude de leurs assertions, j'aurais mis de côté les erreurs scientifiques que je crois qu'ils renferment, laissant à d'autres le soin de les relever. Ces savans n'avaient eu malheureusement d'autre connaissance de mes recherches que par la courte lettre que j'adressai à M. Hachette, et, ne se souciant pas de recourir à mes Mémoires (quoique, ce me semble, ils eussent dû le faire dans cette circonstance), ils se sont mépris tout d'abord sur le sens d'une phrase qui se rapporte aux belles observations de M. Arago, et ils ont prétendu que je n'avais pas fait auparavant ce qu'ils supposent avoir fait eux-mêmes, et finalement ils avancent ce qui me paraît être de fausses idées sur les courans magnéto-électriques, et donnent ces idées comme des *corrections* des miennes, lesquelles n'étaient pas encore parvenues sous leurs yeux.

D'abord, qu'il me soit permis de rectifier ce que je regarde comme la méprise la plus grave de toutes, la fausse interprétation donnée à mes paroles; car il eût été facile de relever avec le temps les erreurs commises dans les expériences.

MM. Nobili et Antenori disent (p. 428 des *Annales*, tom. XLVIII): "M. Faraday considère le magnétisme de rotation de M. Arago comme entièrement lié au phénomène qu'il a découvert il y a dix ans. *Il reconnut* ALORS, *comme le dit la notice, que, par la rotation d'un disque métallique sous l'influence d'un aimant,* on *peut donner naissance dans la direction des rayons de ce disque, à des courans électriques en quantité assez considérable pour que ce disque devienne une nouvelle machine électrique.* Nous ignorons entièrement comment M. Faraday a reconnu ce fait, et nous ne savons pas comment un résultat de cette nature a *pu rester* SI LONG-TEMPS *généralement ignoré, et, pour ainsi dire,* OUBLIÉ dans les mains de l'auteur de la découverte; du reste, etc."

Maintenant, *je n'ai jamais dit ce* que MM. Nobili et Antenori m'imputent ici. Dans ma lettre à M. Hachette, citée en tête de la notice, je donnai un court exposé de ce que j'avais récemment découvert et lu à la Société Royale, le 24 du mois précédent. Cette notice se trouve à la page 402 du même numéro des *Annales*, et on y lit: "La quatrième partie du Mémoire traite de l'expérience aussi curieuse qu'extraordinaire de M. Arago, laquelle consiste, comme on sait, à faire tourner un disque métallique sous l'influence d'un aimant. M. Faraday considère le phénomène qui se manifeste dans cette expérience comme *intimement lié* à celui de la rotation magnétique qu'il a eu le bonheur de trouver il y a dix ans. *Il a reconnu que, par la rotation* du disque métallique sous l'influence d'un aimant, *on peut* former, dans la direction des rayons de ce disque, des courans électriques en nombre assez considérable pour que le disque devienne une nouvelle machine électrique."

Je n'ai jamais dit, ou je n'ai jamais eu l'intention de dire que j'avais obtenu ces courans électriques par la rotation d'un disque métallique, à une époque plus reculée que la date du Mémoire que j'étais en train d'écrire; mais j'ai dit que l'effet extraordinaire découvert par M. Arago était lié dans sa nature avec la rotation électro-magnétique, que j'avais découverte plusieurs années auparavant, car tous les deux sont dus à une action tangentielle; et je dis que, par la rotation d'un disque près d'un aimant, je pourrais (maintenant) faire que des courans d'électricité s'échapperaient ou tendraient à s'échapper dans la direction des rayons, constituant ainsi le disque d'une nouvelle machine électrique ; et cela, je pense, est tout-à-fait prouvé dans la partie du Mémoire dont je donnai un aperçu : on peut le voir à la page 65-118 du tome L des *Annales*.

J'ai le plus ardent désir de voir relever cette erreur, parce que j'ai toujours admiré la prudence et la réserve philosophique de M. Arago, en résistant à la tentation de donner une théorie de l'effet qu'il avait découvert ; tant qu'il ne put pas en découvrir une qui s'y appliquât entièrement, et en refusant son assentiment aux imparfaites théories des autres. Tout en l'admirant, j'adoptai sa réserve à cet égard, et peut-être, par là même, j'avais les yeux ouverts pour reconnaître la vérité, dès qu'elle se présenterait.

Arrivons maintenant à ce qui touche la philosophie de mes écrits. Mon Mémoire du 24 novembre 1831 contient, dans sa quatrième partie, mon opinion sur la cause du phénomène de M. Arago ; opinion que, encore aujourd'hui, je ne vois aucune raison de changer. MM. Nobili et Antenori, dans leurs écrits du 31 janvier et du 24 mars 1832, prétendent relever certaines erreurs de mon fait, et donnent des développemens étendus sur les phénomènes magnéto-électriques. Je n'ai nullement remarqué que les écrits de ces savans ajoutent un seul fait à ceux que contiennent mes Mémoires, si ce n'est qu'ils font mention de l'étincelle obtenue par l'aimant ordinaire ; résultat que j'avais obtenu moi-même auparavant, mais seulement au moyen de l'électro-aimant. D'un autre côté, je pense que les Mémoires de ces messieurs contiennent des idées erronées sur la nature des courans magnéto-électriques, et qu'ils se méprennent sur l'action et la direction de ces courans dans le disque tournant d'Arago. Ces savans disent : "*Nous avons récemment vérifié, étendu, peut-être rectifié dans quelques parties les résultats du physicien anglais, etc.*" (*Ann.*, p. 281, t. L.) Et ensuite, à la page 298, d'après ce qu'ils pouvaient *supposer* être mes idées (car quoiqu'elles eussent été lues, et qu'elles soient maintenant publiées, ils n'avaient pas jugé à propos de les consulter) ils disent : "Nous avons déjà dit notre avis sur cette idée ; mais si, dès le commencement de nos recherches, elle ne nous sembla pas pouvoir facilement se concilier avec la nature des courans découverts par M. Faraday même, qu'en dirons-nous après toutes les nouvelles observations qu'il nous est arrivé de faire pendant la continuation de nos recherches ? Nous dirons qu'on avait dans le galvanomètre le juge compétent, et que c'était à lui à résoudre la question."

Avec le plus grand désir de me voir repris quand je suis dans l'erreur, il m'est cependant impossible de découvrir dans les écrits de ces messieurs aucune rectification dont je puisse faire mon profit ; mais j'admets entièrement la compétence du galvanomètre, et je procéderai aussi brièvement que possible à soumettre à son jugement nos idées différentes, en ce qui touche le phéno-mène d'Arago ; et je suis si satisfait présentement des faits et des résultats consignés dans les Mémoires que j'ai publiés (quoique je pusse faire des change-

mens dans quelques-unes de leurs parties, si j'avais à les écrire de nouveau)
que je n'aurai nul besoin de renvoyer à des expériences qu'ils ne renferment pas,

Ce n'est pas mon intention de m'étendre davantage sur le premier Mémoire
des savans italiens. J'ai fait des notes de correction à une traduction anglaise
qui a paru dans le *Philosophical Magazine*; j'ai eu l'honneur d'en envoyer
quelques exemplaires à vous et aux auteurs. J'ai maintenant en vue de comparer
la seconde partie de leurs écrits avec la quatrième partie de mon premier
Mémoire et avec quelques parties des autres Mémoires, comme jetant du
jour sur les principes généraux. Les deux écrits ont pour but de donner une
explication du phénomène d'Arago, et tous deux se trouvent heureusement dans
le cinquantième tome des *Annales*, de façon qu'il est facile de s'y reporter. Je
renverrai à mes Mémoires par les nombres indiqués ainsi (F. 114), et aux écrits
de MM. Nobili et Antenori par la seule indication de la page des *Annales*.

A la page 281, après quelques remarques générales, on lit: "Nous avons
récemment vérifié, étendu, peut-être rectifié dans quelques parties les résultats
du physicien anglais; *nous avons dit alors* que le magnétisme de rotation trouvait
un véritable point d'appui dans les nouveaux faits de M. Faraday, et que par
conséquent la théorie de ce magnétisme *nous paraissait* à présent tellement
avancée, qu'elle méritait bien qu'on entreprit enfin de développer les principes
physiques dont elle dépend. *L'écrit que nous faisons paraître est destiné à remplir
ce vide, etc.*" Je ferai seulement remarquer, à ce sujet, que, tout juste quatre mois
auparavant, le Mémoire que je lus à la Société Royale avait dit la même chose, et
avait donné ce qui deviendra, je l'espère, un exposé exact et vrai de la philosophie
de l'effet dont il s'agit (F. 4–80).

A la page 282, on lit: "Nous avons déjà signalé ces courans dans nos premières
recherches, c'est-à-dire dans le premier écrit qui fut inséré dans le numéro de
décembre (p. 412); mais j'avais "déjà parlé de ces courans" quatre mois
auparavant (F. 90).

A la page 283, se trouvent décrits "les explorateurs ou sondes galvanométriques," lesquels ne sont que ce que j'avais décrit auparavant et désigné
sous le nom de *collecteur* ou *conducteur*. (F. 86, etc.)

Au commencement de l'investigation de l'état du disque tournant d'Arago
dans le voisinage d'un aimant, on choisit deux positions relatives de la
plaque et de l'aimant: l'une appelée (p. 284) "*disposition centrale*", où le pôle
magnétique se place verticalement sur le centre du disque; l'autre (p. 285)
"*disposition excentrique*," dans laquelle l'aimant agit en dehors de ce point.

Eu égard à la *disposition centrale*, on lit (p. 284): "En ce cas, l'aimant agissant
sur le centre du disque, les *sondes* ne transmettent au galvanomètre aucun signe
de courant, *quelque part qu'elles soient placées*; et si on remarque par hasard de
petites déviations, ce n'est que par défaut de centralisation; de sorte qu'on n'a
qu'à *corriger ce défaut* pour voir disparaître aussitôt tous les signes de source
équivoque, etc. Effectivement, qu'arrive-t-il à une spirale électro-dynamique qui

239

tourne tout autour de son propre centre, toujours en face du même pôle magnétique? *Rien absolument*. C'est une *circonstance indifférente* que celle de tourner. La formation des courans *tient à une tout autre condition*, car ils *ne se manifestent* que dans le moment qu'on *approche* ou qu'on *éloigne* les spirales des aimans. Tant que les spirales *demeurent en présence*, qu'elles se *meuvent ou non*, il n'y a *point de courant*; de la même manière qu'il *n'y en a pas* dans le cas de rotation centrale où les points du disque restent constamment à une même distance du pôle magnétique, en renouvelant ainsi la combinaison de présence continuée, à laquelle les *nouvelles lois* des courans de M. Faraday N'ASSIGNENT *aucun effet*."

Cette assertion est tellement erronée dans chacune de ses parties, que j'ai été obligé de la citer dans toute son étendue. En premier lieu, des courans d'électricité *tendent bien* à se former dans le disque tournant, dans le cas de "disposition centrale," ainsi que dans tout autre cas (F. 149–156); mais leur direction est du centre à la circonférence, ou *vice versa*, et c'est à ces parties qu'on devrait appliquer les collecteurs. C'est précisément le cas qui fait du disque tournant une nouvelle machine électrique (F. 154), et c'est sur ce point que MM. Nobili et Antenori se sont tout-à-fait trompés dans leurs deux Mémoires. Cette erreur se retrouve dans tout le courant du Mémoire que je compare en ce moment avec mon premier écrit; et, sauf erreur, voici, à mon avis, dans toutes ses parties la théorie du phénomène d'Arago donnée dans ce Mémoire.

On trouve à la page 284 qu'il n'arrive *absolument rien* lorsqu'une hélice tourne sur son axe concentriquement avec un pôle magnétique, et que la circonstance de la rotation est indifférente. J'ose dire, quoique je n'aie point fait des ex-périences, qu'un courant électrique tendra à passer transversalement à l'hélice, et que la circonstance de sa rotation, au lieu d'être indifférente, renferme dans ces cas la seule condition essentielle exigée pour produire les courans. L'hélice, en effet, peut être considérée comme analogue à un cylindre qui occuperait sa place, si ce n'était qu'elle n'est nullement aussi bonne, parce qu'elle se trouve coupée en un long fil enroulé. L'hélice peut aussi être considérée comme un simple fil qui serait placé en un lieu quelconque occupé par ce cylindre, et j'ai montré que ceux-ci produisent des courans dans leur état de rotation, s'ils touchent par leurs extrémités opposées à un galvanomètre.

Il est dit, à la page 284, que la formation des courans "tient à une *tout autre condition*, car ils ne se manifestent que dans le moment qu'on approche ou qu'on éloigne les spirales des aimans; tant que les spirales demeurent en présence, qu'elles se meuvent ou non, *il n'y a point de courant*, de la même manière qu'il n'y en a pas dans le cas de *rotation centrale*, etc." Maintenant, dans mon premier écrit j'ai montré que la condition essentielle était, non l'approche ou l'éloigne-ment, mais simplement que le métal qui se mouvait coupât les courbes mag-nétiques (F. 101, 116, 118, etc.); et qu'en conséquence, toutes choses égales d'ailleurs, le mouvement sans changement de distance est le plus effectif et le plus puissant moyen d'obtenir le courant, au lieu d'être la condition dans laquelle rien absolument n'arrive. Dans mon second écrit, *je prouvai* que le mouvement à travers les courbes magnétiques était la seule condition nécessaire (F. 217); et que, loin que l'éloignement ou le rapprochement fût nécessaire, l'on produirait les courans par l'aimant lui-même en le tirant seulement dans sa propre direction (F. 220).

Finalement, en parlant de cette "disposition centrale," et de l'absence supposée d'effet, lorsque "les points du disque restent constamment à une même distance du pôle magnétique," MM. Nobili et Antenori disent (p. 285): "En renouvelant ainsi la combinaison de la présence continue à laquelle les *nouvelles lois* des courans de M. Faraday *n'assignent aucun effet*; " et puis ont lit dans une note: "Ces lois se réduisent à trois," qui sont spécifiées, d'abord pleinement et dans une forme plus resserrée, comme il suit: " 1re LOI. Pendant le rapprochement: courant produit contraire au courant producteur; répulsion entre les deux systèmes. 2e LOI. La distance ne variant pas. Point d'effet. 3e LOI. Pendant l'éloignement. Courant reproduit dans la même direction que le courant producteur. Attraction entre les deux systèmes."

Je n'ai jamais donné moi-même ceci comme les simples lois qui gouvernent la production des courans que je fus assez heureux pour découvrir; et je ne comprends pas davantage que MM. Nobili et Antenori disent ici que ce sont *mes* LOIS, quoiqu'à la page 282 une de ces lois soit ainsi appelée. Mais je décrivis ces trois cas à la fois dans mon premier Mémoire (F. 26, 39, 53), ainsi que dans la Notice, c'est-à-dire dans ma Lettre à M. Hachette, comme les effets que j'avais observés. Il a été démontré par ce que j'ai déjà dit, que ce ne sont pas les lois de l'action de l'électricité magnétique, car le simple fait d'obtenir des courans d'électricité au moyen de la révolution d'un cylindre (F. 219) ou d'un disque (F. 218), lié à un aimant, ou de l'aimant lui-même (F. 220), contredit chacune de ces lois. UNE DE CES LOIS, qui renferme la totalité des effets, est donnée dans mon Mémoire (F. 114, 116, etc.), et celle exprime simplement la *direction* dans laquelle le corps mouvant conducteur *couperait* les courbes magnétiques. Cette loi de direction étant donnée, je m'efforçai de récapituler le tout en général (F. 118) dans les termes que je vais répéter ici: "Tous ces résultats font voir que l'induction des courans électriques est excitée circulairement par une *résultante magnétique* ou *axe de puissance*, tout de même que le magnétisme circulaire dépend d'un courant électrique, et est représenté (*exhibited or excited*) par lui."

J'ai voulu citer dans toute son étendue ce passage des savans italiens, parce qu'il contient presque toutes nos différences, quant aux faits et aux idées qui concernent cette partie du sujet. Ayant ainsi fait voir toutes les erreurs que ce passage renferme, on me permettra d'être plus concis, en montrant, *à l'aide du galvanomètre*, les erreurs qui, en étant découlées, se trouvent répandues dans tout le reste du Mémoire. Il est, en vérité, très curieux de remarquer comment, avec des indications galvanométriques généralement correctes, ces savans se sont laissés égarer sous l'influence d'idées arrêtées d'avance. Par exemple, à la page 287–288, et dans la fig. 11, pl. III, on voit le résultat d'un examen, par le galvanomètre, des courans dans un disque tournant; ces courans sont représentés, presque correctement à l'aide de flèches; et néanmoins les *deux conséquences* qu'on en a tirées s'accordent avec la théorie énoncée, et sont diamétralement opposées aux faits.

"L'une de ces conséquences (p. 287) ressort de l'inspection immédiate des flèches qui marquent les courans dans les deux régions du disque (fig. 11) et c'est que *sur les parties qui entrent, il se développe un système de courans contraires à celui qui se produit de l'autre côté.* L'autre conséquence, on l'obtient en comparant les courans produits sur le disque avec les courans de la cause productrice, et c'est que *sur les parties qui entrent, la direction des courans est contraire à celle des courans producteurs, tandis que de l'autre côté il y a identité de direction dans les deux systèmes.*"

Mais j'ai montré, dans mon premier Mémoire (F. 119), "que lorsqu'un morceau de métal passe ou devant un simple pôle ou entre les pôles opposés d'un aimant, ou près de pôles électro-magnétiques, soit ferrugineux ou non, on obtient des courans électriques à travers le métal transversalement à la direction du mouvement. Ce fait est prouvé au moyen de fils (F. 109), de plaques (F. 101) et de disques (F. 92, etc.), et, dans tous les cas, le courant électrique était dans *la même direction*, soit que le métal s'approchât ou s'éloignât de l'aimant, pourvu que la direction de ses mouvemens ne changeât point. Dans le disque tournant d'Arago, l'électricité, que dans une infinité d'expériences je pus tirer d'une de ces parties, s'accorda toujours avec ces résultats (F. 92, 95, 96) et conséquemment (F. 119, etc.) je les ai récapitulés dans une courte description, comme cela se présente dans le disque d'Arago, établissant surtout (F. 123) que les courans produits près ou sous les pôles sont déchargés ou retournent dans les parties du métal situées de chaque côté de la place du pôle et plus éloignées de cette même place, là où l'induction magnétique est nécessairement plus faible."

J'ai représenté cet état de choses sous une forme générale dans la figure ij jointe au mémoire, que j'ai fait correspondre aussi bien que je l'ai pu quant aux flèches, à la désignation des parties, etc., etc., avec la fig. 11, pl. III du Mémoire des savans italiens. Je vais maintenant faire voir comment elle s'accorde avec les résultats galvanométriques obtenus par ces savans, ainsi qu'avec leurs *conclusions.*

Eu égard aux résultats galvanométriques, ma figure pourrait servir en place de la leur, sans occasionner aucune différence; et je n'ai pas la moindre raison de dire qu'ils sont inexacts. Relativement à "l'une de ces conséquences qui ressort de l'inspection immédiate des flèches qui marquent les courans dans les deux régions du disque," ou de tout autre examen attentif et expérimental, on voit que les courans n, n, n, en entrant, au lieu d'être dans *une direction contraire* à ceux qui sont dans les parties s, s, s, qui s'écartent, suivent exactement la même direction; c'est-à-dire que, quant au mouvement général, près du pôle ils vont de haut en bas, ou de la circonférence vers le centre, transversalement aux lignes que les diverses parties décrivent dans leur cours; et à une grande distance (F. 92) de chaque côté du pôle, ils sont dans la direction contraire. A mesure qu'une partie de la ligne décrite par un point est plus voisine du pôle, un courant la traverse, commence et s'accroît en intensité jusqu'à ce qu'il parvienne à la plus courte distance, ou un peu au-delà, à cause que le temps entre dans cet effet comme un élément. Ensuite à cause de la distance, le courant diminue en intensité sans avoir jamais changé sa direction relative à sa propre course. C'est seulement quand elle est arrivée aux parties les plus éloignées où l'électricité excitée se décharge, qu'un courant se manifeste dans la direction *opposée*, ou plus ou moins oblique. Je crois qu'il est tout-à-fait inutile de parler du changement partiel dans la direction des courans à travers les parties les plus rapprochées du centre ou de la circonférence; les deux ou trois courbes que j'ai grossièrement tracées montreront dans quelles directions s'opèrent ces change-mens.

La seconde conséquence qui ressort du Mémoire des savans italiens (p. 288) est que, "sur les parties qui entrent, la direction des courans est contraire à celle des courans producteurs," (c'est-à-dire ceux qui sont considérés comme existant dans l'aimant); "tandis que, de l'autre côté, il y a identité de direction dans les deux systèmes." Cette assertion est exactement le contraire de la réalité (F. 117). Au moyen des flèches (fig. 11 et fig. 1), j'ai indiqué la direction des courans dans le pôle magnétique; et c'est la même que la direction donnée par MM. Nobili et Antenori, dans la fig. 1, pl. 111. Mais ma figure ii, ainsi que les indications du galvanomètre, montrent évidemment que les parties entrantes n, n, n, en approchant de l'aimant, ont des courans qui passent à travers dans la *même* direction que le courant dans ce côté du pôle de l'aimant; et que les parties qui s'éloignent s, s, s ont des courans qui suivent une direction contraire de ceux qu'on suppose exister dans le côté du pôle magnétique dont ils s'écartent.

Je m'imagine, mais je ne suis pas tout-à-fait sûr, que MM. Nobili et Antenori supposent que des courans circulaires sont excités dans la partie métal voisine du pôle, de la même manière et absolument comme ceux qui se forment dans l'hélice, quand on l'approche d'un aimant, et que lorsque cette partie du disque s'éloigne, les courans circulaires sont en quelque façon renversés, comme cela arrive dans l'hélice lorsqu'elle s'écarte de l'aimant. Un passage de leur premier écrit et un autre à la fin de la page 284 paraissent impliquer que telle est leur idée. Cette idée me vint il y a plus d'un an; mais je vis bientôt, après de nombreuses expériences (je viens d'en citer quelques-unes), qu'elle n'était nullement satisfaisante; et lorsque j'eus vérifié que l'action de l'hélice, en se rapprochant et en s'éloignant du pôle, s'expliquait entièrement (F. 42) par la loi (F. 114), je fus forcé d'abandonner mes idées antérieures.

Le Mémoire continue ensuite (p. 288) à expliquer les phénomènes du disque tournant d'Arago; mais après avoir fait remarquer que la théorie est en général basée sur deux conclusions qui sont le contraire de la réalité, il ne sera pas nécessaire d'en faire un examen minutieux. Il n'est pas possible qu'elle puisse représenter les phénomènes avec exactitude. Ceux qui sont curieux de connaître le véritable état de choses, seront à même de décider, à l'aide d'un petit nombre d'expériences, si les idées que j'ai publiées dans l'écrit qui annonça le premier la découverte de ces courans sont vraies, ou si les savans italiens ont eu raison de déclarer que j'étais dans l'erreur, et ont publié des idées plus justes sur ce sujet.

Tout le monde sait que, lorsque M. Arago publia sa remarquable découverte, il dit que l'action du disque sur l'aimant pouvait se résoudre en trois forces: la PREMIÈRE, perpendiculaire au disque, et il trouva que celle-ci était répulsive; la SECONDE, horizontale et perpendiculaire au plan vertical renfermant le rayon au‑dessous du pôle magnétique; celle-ci est une force tangentielle, et occasionne la rotation du pôle avec le métal; la TROISIÈME est horizontale et parallèle au même rayon; à un certain point vers la circonférence, elle devient nulle; mais plus rapprochée du centre, elle tend à pousser le pôle vers le centre, et plus près de la circonférence, elle tend à l'écarter du centre.

A la page 289, MM. Nobili et Antenori donnent l'explication de la première de ces forces. Comme nous l'avons déjà dit, ces savans considèrent les parties voisines de l'aimant comme ayant des courans contraires à ceux qui se trouvent à côté du pôle dont ils approchent, et en conséquence ils sont répulsifs, et ils considèrent les parties qui s'éloignent comme ayant des courans identiques en direction avec ceux qui sont à côté de l'aimant dont ils s'éloignent, et en consé‑quence ces parties sont attractives. La somme de chacune de ces forces diverses est égale l'une à l'autre; mais en ce qui concerne l'aiguille ou l'aimant, cette distribution n'est pas la même, "les forces répulsives étant les plus proches, envahissent le disque jusque sous l'aiguille, et obtiennent ainsi la prépondérance sur l'action des forces contraires qui s'exerce plus obliquement et de plus loin. En somme, ce n'est qu'une partie des forces répulsives qui est balancée par les forces attractives; le reste ne trouve aucune opposition, et c'est ce reste qui produit l'effet."

Mais j'ai démontré dans cette lettre que les courans, dans les parties qui s'approchent ou s'éloignent, sont exactement le contraire de ce que supposent les savans italiens; et qu'en conséquence, là où ils attendent de l'attraction, ils auront de la répulsion, et là où de la répulsion, de l'attraction; de sorte que, suivant leur opinion, corrigée par l'expérience, le résultat devrait être de *l'attraction* au lieu de *la répulsion*. Mais M. Arago a raison de dire que c'est de la répulsion; et, en conséquence, la théorie de l'effet donné ne peut pas être la vraie.

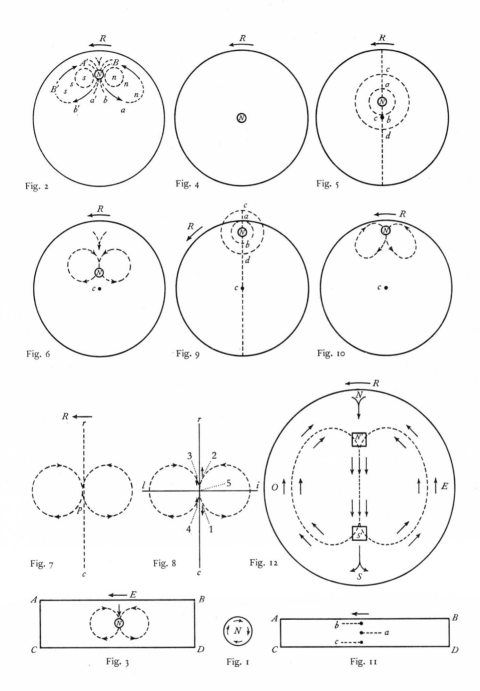

Fig. 2

Fig. 4

Fig. 5

Fig. 6

Fig. 9

Fig. 10

Fig. 7

Fig. 8

Fig. 12

Fig. 3

Fig. 1

Fig. 11

On trouvera dans mon premier Mémoire mes vues sur l'effet dont il s'agit. J'ai examiné s'il serait possible ou probable (F. 125) que le temps fût un élément nécessaire pour le développement du plus grand courant dans le métal. Dans ce cas, la résultante de toutes les forces serait en avant de l'aimant, lorsque c'est la plaque qui tourne; ou en arrière, quand c'est l'aimant que l'on fait tourner; et une ligne qui joindrait cette résultante avec le pôle, serait oblique au plan de mouvement; alors la force dirigée suivant cette ligne peut se résoudre en deux autres, l'une parallèle, l'autre perpendiculaire au plan de mouvement ou de rotation; celle-ci serait une force répulsive, produisant un effet analogue à celui qui a été remarqué par M. Arago.

La seconde force est celle qui fait que l'aimant et le disque se suivent mutuellement. En nous reportant à la page 290, fig. I ou II (on peut se servir aussi de ma figure II), on lit: "Il existe en s, s, s des forces d'attraction vers lesquelles il (l'aimant) est attiré, et il y a en n, n, n des forces répulsives qui le poussent vers ce même côté." En conséquence, l'aimant se meut après ou avec le métal; mais les courans, et conséquemment les forces, sont justement le contraire de ce qu'on a supposé, comme je viens de le montrer. L'aimant et le disque devraient donc se mouvoir dans des directions opposées, si les forces agissaient de la manière que l'on suppose. Cependant, comme ils ne se meuvent pas par le fait dans des directions opposées, il est évident que la théorie qui explique leur mouvement, en renversant les faits, doit être elle-même erronée.

La troisième force est celle qui tend à transporter le pôle magnétique ou vers le centre ou vers la circonférence, de chaque côté d'un point neutre situé sur le rayon au-dessus duquel se trouve l'aimant; cet effet est décrit à la page 281, et dans une figure (4) qui accompagne le Mémoire, et que je crois tout-à-fait correcte. Le Mémoire continue à expliquer cet effet en se reportant à la force répulsive admise (p. 289) pour rendre compte du premier effet qu'a observé M. Arago : à savoir, la répulsion verticale du disque; et supposant que cette force répulsive soit répandue sur une certaine étendue du disque sous l'aimant, on établit (p. 292, fig. v) que si le pôle est situé fort près de la circonférence, la portion du corps d'où émane cette force est diminuée, étant coupée par la circonférence elle-même; et conséquemment les parties les plus voisines du centre sont plus puissantes et poussent le pôle en dehors; tandis que si le pôle est placé fort près du centre, l'étendue d'où émane cette force dépassera le centre, et comme cette partie excédante est considérée, quoiqu'à tort, comme inactive, alors la portion qui se trouve vers la circonférence est plus puissante, et pousse le pôle vers le centre.

Il se présente une ou deux petites objections à cette opinion, mais elles ne sont rien, pour ainsi dire, en comparaison de celle qui s'élève, quand on se rappelle que, conformément aux propres idées de l'auteur sur les actions des courans, l'erreur dans la direction de ceux qui sont excités près du pôle, nous oblige à substituer l'*attraction* à la *répulsion*, comme je l'ai fait voir en parlant de la première de ces forces: en conséquence, tous les mouvemens qui se lient à la troisième force devraient être dans la direction contraire à ceux qui se présentent actuellement; et la théorie qui, quand elle est corrigée par des expériences faites avec le galvanomètre, indique de tels mouvemens, doit être abandonnée.

A la page 292, je trouve que le Mémoire renvoie à la "IIe loi" de M. Faraday. Comme je l'ai déjà dit, je ne donnai jamais ces trois assertions comme des lois. Je regrette beaucoup, en vérité, qu'une lettre qui ne fut jamais destinée à donner des détails minutieux, mais seulement quelques faits recueillis à la hâte parmi des centaines de faits décrits auparavant dans le Mémoire lu à la Société Royale; je regrette, dis-je, que cette lettre, que je ne pensais jamais voir imprimer, ait pu induire en erreur les savans italiens. Mais cependant, après avoir examiné de nouveau tous les faits, je ne vois nullement que je doive être responsable de l'erreur qu'ils ont commise, comme ayant avancé des résultats erronés, ou, quant à ce qui concerne le Mémoire, pour n'avoir pas donné au monde scientifique les détails les plus complets aussitôt que cela m'a été possible.

Je n'ai pas encore publié mes idées sur la cause de la troisième force signalée par M. Arago; mais comme les savans italiens, en donnant les hypothèses que j'ai justement regardées comme inexactes, disent (p. 293): "En effet, quelle autre hypothèse pourrait concilier la *verticalité* que l'aiguille conserve dans les deux positions n, s, n″, s″ (4e fig. avec l'autre fait de la répulsion de bas en haut qui soulève l'aiguille dans la seconde position s″, n″?" Je suis tenté d'en offrir un autre à cette place, en prévenant toutefois que les directions et les formes que je pourrais tracer comme celles des courans magnéto-électriques excités, doivent être considérées seulement comme des approximations générales.

Si un morceau de métal suffisamment large pour contenir, sans les briser aucunement, tous les courans qui peuvent être excités dans toute son étendue par un pôle magnétique placé au-dessus de lui, se meut dans une direction rectiligne sous le pôle, alors un courant électrique traversera la direction de son mouvement dans les parties du voisinage immédiat du pôle, et retournera dans la direction opposée de chaque côté dans les parties qui, se trouvant plus éloignées du pôle, sont sujettes à une force inductive plus faible; ainsi le courant sera complété ou déchargé (voyez la figure III). Soit *ABCD* représentant un morceau de cuivre se mouvant dans la direction de la flèche *E*, et *N* le bout nord de l'aimant placé au-dessus, alors des courans d'électricité seront produits dans le morceau de métal, et quoiqu'ils s'étendent, sans aucun doute, de la partie au-dessous du pôle à une grande distance à l'entour (F. 92), et qu'à la fois ils diminuent d'intensité et changent de direction en s'éloignant de cette partie, cependant les deux cercles peuvent servir à représenter la résultante de ces courans; et il sera évident que le point de l'action la plus intense est là où ils se touchent, et immédiatement sous le pôle magnétique, ou à cause du temps exigé un peu en avant. De là, cette portion des forces qui agit parallèlement au plan du métal, portera le pôle en avant dans la direction de la flèche *E*, parce que les forces sont également puissantes du côté *AB* du pôle, que du côté *CD*; et cette portion qui, à cause du temps nécessaire pour la production des courans excités est perpendiculaire à la direction du métal, sera, comme nous l'avons déjà dit, répulsive, et tendra à pousser le pôle en dessus ou en dehors.

Mais supposons qu'en place de ce métal qui se meut dans une direction *rectiligne*, on substitue un disque circulaire tournant sur son axe, et d'abord considérons le cas du pôle magnétique placé sur son centre (fig. IV), il n'y a alors aucune production des courans électriques, non parce qu'ils ne tendent pas à être produits, car j'ai déjà dit dans cette lettre, et démontré dans mes Mémoires (F. 149, 156, 217), qu'au commencement où le disque se meut, les courans sont aussi prêts à se mouvoir, mais parce qu'ils tendent à se former dans la direction des rayons de la circonférence au centre; et comme toutes les parties sont également influencées, aucune d'elles n'ayant un excès de puissance sur l'autre, et toutes étant distantes également du centre, aucune décharge ne peut avoir lieu, et en conséquence aucun courant ne peut se développer. Comme aucun *courant* ne peut exister, aucun effet dépendant de l'action d'un courant sur le pôle ne peut se produire, et là donc il n'y a ni *révolution*, ni répulsion de l'aimant. De là, la cause de la *verticalité sans répulsion* qui a lieu à cette place.

Considérons maintenant le cas où le pôle de l'aimant, au lieu d'être placé au-dessus du centre du métal, est à l'un de ses côtés comme en *N*, figure V. La tendance à former des courans électriques est due au mouvement des parties du disque à *travers* les courbes magnétiques (F. 116, 217), et lorsque ces courbes sont d'intensité égale, les courans électriques s'accroissent en force, en proportion de l'augmentation de la vitesse avec laquelle se meuvent les parties du disque qui coupent les courbes magnétiques (F. 258). Traçons maintenant un cercle *ab* autour d'un pôle magnétique, comme centre, et il représentera la projection des courbes magnétiques d'*intensité égale* sur le disque; *a* et *b* seront les points du rayon qui passe immédiatement sous le pôle, situés à une égale distance du pôle; mais comme la partie *a* passe sous le pôle avec une vitesse beaucoup plus grande que la partie *b*, l'intensité du courant électrique qui est excité dans cette partie est proportionnellement plus grande. Cela est aussi vrai pour des points dans tout autre rayon coupant le cercle *ab*, et cela sera aussi vrai pour tout autre cercle tracé autour de *N*, comme centre, et représentant, en conséquence, des courbes magnétiques d'intensité égale; excepté que lorsque ce cercle s'étend au-delà du centre *C* du disque tournant, comme à *c d*, au lieu de l'existence d'un courant plus faible au point *d* qu'au point *c*, c'est alors un courant opposé qui tend à être produit.

La conséquence naturelle de ces actions des diverses parties est que, comme la somme des forces tendant à produire le courant électrique dans la direction de *c* à *d* est plus grande sur le côté *c* du pôle magnétique que sur le côté *d*, la courbure ou le retour de ces courans par la droite et par la gauche commence aussi de ce côté; et maintenant les deux cercles qu'on peu regarder, ainsi qu'auparavant, comme pouvant représenter les résultantes de ces courans, ne se touchent pas exactement sous le pôle, mais à une plus ou moins grande distance du pôle vers la circonférence, comme à la fig. VI.

Cette circonstance seule n'occasionnerait aucun mouvement dans le pôle forcé de se mouvoir seulement dans la direction du rayon, mais étant combinée avec celle qui résulte du *temps* nécessaire pour le développement du courant, et à laquelle on s'est reporté auparavant comme expliquant la *première* de ces trois forces, par lesquelles M. Arago représente l'action du pôle et du disque magnétiques, elle expliquera, j'espère, entièrement tous les effets qu'on recherche, et prouvera aussi l'influence du temps, comme élément; car, soit *c* (fig. VII) le centre d'un disque tournant, et *r c* une partie du rayon sous le pôle magnétique *p*, comme nous venons de le faire voir, le contact des deux cercles (représentant les courans) est sur le côté du pôle en dehors du centre *c*; mais à cause de l'élément du temps et de la direction de la rotation *R* de la plaque de métal, il est aussi un peu à la gauche du rayon *r c*; de sorte que le pôle est soumis, non avec symétrie, mais obliquement, à l'action des deux ordres de courans. La conséquence nécessaire est que s'il est libre de se mouvoir dans la direction du rayon, et dans celle-là seulement, il se mouvra vers le centre *c*, car les courans produits par un pôle marqué (nord) sont exactement tels que, d'après leur action mutuelle, ils devraient pousser le pôle dans cette direction.

Ce rapport des courans avec le pôle qui les engendre est aussi facilement prouvé par l'expérience que par le calcul. J'ai fait voir (F. 100) que lorsqu'un pôle marqué (nord) est au-dessus d'un disque tournant dans la direction des flèches *R*, dans les figures du Mémoire des savans italiens, ou dans la mienne, les courans (indiqués par les cercles) sont comme dans les fig. III, VI ou VII. Alors, en tendant un fil de métal qui conduirait le courant dans cette double direction (fig. VIII), et mettant au-dessus un pôle marqué (nord) assujéti à pouvoir seulement se mouvoir parallèlement à *r c*, je trouvai que, placé en un point quelconque dans la ligne *r c*, il n'a aucune tendance à se mouvoir. Il y avait aussi une autre ligne perpendiculaire à la première, et qui la traversait au contact des cercles, dans laquelle le pôle n'avait aucune tendance à se mouvoir. Placé en tout autre lieu que dans ces deux lignes, il se mouvait dans un sens ou dans l'autre, et lorsqu'il était placé dans les positions marquées 1, 2, 3, 4, il se mouvait dans la direction des flèches attachées à ces points. Maintenant la position du pôle, eu égard aux courans dans l'expérience d'Arago, quand l'aimant et le disque sont disposés comme dans la fig. V ou VII, est exactement celle du point 1 dans la fig. VIII, et de là ce pôle a une tendance vers le centre *C*.

Portons maintenant notre attention vers ce qui arriverait si nous transportions graduellement le pôle du centre vers la circonférence. Soit la figure IX qui représente le nouvel état de choses en un temps quelconque, comme la figure V a représenté le premier état, il est évident que la vitesse des parties *a*, *b* du rayon sous le pôle ne diffèrent pas l'une de l'autre autant qu'elles différaient précédemment, étant seulement à peu près comme $1:\frac{1}{2}$, au lieu de $1:6$; et avec toutes les courbes d'égales intensités comprises dans ce cercle, la différence sera donc moindre. Cela seul peut faire que la place du pôle et le lieu de contact des cercles qui représentent les courans (fig. VII) se rapprochent l'une de l'autre dans la direction de la ligne $r\,c$, et portent par conséquent le pôle en 1 (fig. VIII) plus près de la ligne neutre $l\,i$. En jetant les yeux sur le second cercle $c\,d$, fig. IX, des courbes magnétiques d'égale intensité, on verra que comme le disque ne s'étend pas jusqu'à c, ou même au-delà de a, il n'y a rien à ajouter à la force du courant sur ce côté du pôle; tandis qu'en d le rayon en se mouvant à travers les courbes magnétiques ajoute à l'intensité du courant excité en b, et partout ailleurs de ce côté du pôle; et peut facilement, suivant la position du pôle sur la plaque de métal (c'est-à-dire plus près ou plus loin du bord), rendre leur somme ou égale ou plus grande que la somme des forces sur l'autre côté, celui de la circonférence. Si la somme des forces est égale, alors le pôle sera quelque part dans la ligne $l\,i$, comme en 5, fig. VIII, et n'aura aucune tendance ou vers le centre, ou vers la circonférence, quoique sa tendance à se mouvoir avec le disque ou au-dessus du disque reste la même. Ou si la somme des forces est plus grande sur le côté d que sur le côté c, alors le pôle sera dans la position 2, fig. VIII, et sera poussé en dehors dans la direction du rayon, en conformité avec les résultats d'Arago.

Outre cette cause de changement dans le mouvement du pôle parallèlement au rayon et qui dépend de la position du pôle près de la circonférence, il y a une autre cause qui, je crois, se présente en même temps, et aide l'action de la première. Quand le pôle est placé vers le bord du disque, la décharge des courans excités en arrière s'entrechoque sur le côté du bord, par le défaut de matière conductrice, ainsi, dans la figure X, au lieu d'avoir la forme régulière des figures VII et VIII, les courans sont arrêtés dans leur course vers la circonférence, tandis qu'ils ont toute la latitude nécessaire pour leur mouvement, dans les parties qui se dirigent vers le centre; cela seul doit faire que le point de la plus grande force tombe un peu plus près du centre que la projection de l'axe du pôle magnétique, et aide à placer le pôle dans la position 2, fig. VIII. J'ai une telle confiance dans cette opinion, que, quoique je n'aye pas eu occasion de faire moi-même l'expérience, j'ose prédire que si, au lieu de faire usage d'un disque tournant, une lame ou une plaque de métal de cinq à six pouces de large, comme A, B, C, D, figure XI, se mouvait dans une direction rectiligne, conformément à la flèche sous un pôle magnétique situé en a, le pôle tendrait à se mouvoir en avant avec la plaque, ainsi qu'au-dessus, mais non vers la droite ni vers la gauche; tandis que si le pôle était placé au-dessus du point b, il se dirigerait aussi vers le bord AB, ou s'il était placé au-dessus de c, il tendrait à se mouvoir aussi vers le bord CD.

Ayant ainsi répondu à la question de "quelle autre hypothèse, etc., etc.," posée par les auteurs du Mémoire à la page 293, je puis maintenant continuer l'examen de ce Mémoire. A la page 294, se trouve répétée l'erreur relative à la nature des courans, c'est-à-dire leur inversion supposée; cela est assez vrai avec une hélice et quelques formes d'appareil. Mais le courant simple et élémentaire, engendré dans le passage d'un fil devant un aimant, n'est pas renversé lorsque le fil de métal s'éloigne (F. 171, 111, 92).

A la page 295, on suppose que lorsque la rotation est lente, "la révolution des courans est circonscrite dans d'étroites limites, et on a *peu à ajouter* aux résultats qui ont servi de fondement à toute la (nôtre) théorie." Mais quand le mouvement est rapide, les courans enveloppent le disque tout entier, "de manière à devenir une espèce de labyrinthe." Pour ma part, je crois que les courans ont la même direction générale que nous avons déjà donnée dans les figures, soit que la rotation soit lente ou rapide, et la seule différence est une augmentation de vitesse.

On choisit alors une circonstance réellement simple, quoiqu'elle paraisse d'abord compliquée; par exemple, celle où les pôles opposés de part et d'autre du centre. Cette circonstance avec la direction du mouvement, et le courant produit, se trouve dans la figure VII du Mémoire des savans italiens. Il est tout-à-fait inutile de citer les pages 296, 297 qui expliquent cette figure; mais je donnerai la figure XII qui correspond, et qui est selon mes idées et mes expériences; de sorte que les deux figures peuvent être comparés entre elles. Il est tout-à-fait satisfaisant pour moi de voir que dans cette partie du Mémoire, ainsi que dans la première, je ne trouve aucun résultat d'expériences importantes contraire aux idées que j'ai publiées, quoique je sois bien éloigné d'adopter les conclusions qu'on en a tirées.

Si on examine la figure XII, on verra à l'instant qu'elle résulte de la manière la plus simple possible des deux pôles. Ainsi, en ce qui concerne le pôle supérieur, ou pôle nord seulement, les courans sont comme dans la figure VI. Mais comme avec ce pôle le courant qu'il détermine va de la circonférence vers le centre, alors avec le pôle sud, dans la même position ou la position correspondante, les courans iront du centre à la circonférence (F. 100); et en conséquence, dans la fig. XII, ils se continueront le long du diamètre N, S, à travers le centre de la plaque, pour retourner dans la direction des flèches sur les côtés E, O. Les points où je ne me trouve pas d'accord avec les *indications du galvanomètre* qu'ont obtenues MM. Nobili et Antenori sont premièrement la direction des courans en N et en S, laquelle est le contraire de ce que j'obtins, et secondement l'existence de tout axe oblique de puissance comme P, Q, dans leur figure 7.

Le Mémoire finit, du moins en ce qui me concerne, à la page 298, en faisant de nouveau mention de l'erreur (mais non comme erreur) relative au disque tournant, qui devient une *nouvelle machine électrique*. Au commencement, les auteurs, peu familiarisés avec les principes sous l'influence desquels on obtient un tel résultat, le nient; et quoiqu'ils disent ici: "Qu'en dirons-nous après toutes les *nouvelles observations* qu'il nous est arrivé de faire pendant la continuation de nos recherches," je ne suis nullement déterminé à rien changer à ce que j'ai publié; et même j'y ai plus que jamais confiance, puisque, si leurs observations s'étaient trouvées d'accord avec les résultats que j'ai obtenus, j'aurais de grandes raisons, après l'examen auquel je les ai soumis, de craindre que mes idées ne fussent erronées.

Je ne terminerai pas cette lettre sans exprimer de nouveau le regret que j'éprouve d'avoir été contraint de l'écrire; mais si l'on se rappelle que les Mémoires des savans italiens furent écrits et publiés *après mes* Mémoires originaux; que leur dernier écrit a paru même dans les *Annales de Chimie et de Physique* après les miens; et qu'il semble en conséquence avoir porté la science au-delà de ce que j'avais fait moi-même; que tous deux m'accusent d'erreurs dans les expériences et dans la théorie, et en outre de mauvaise foi; que le dernier de ces écrits porte la date du mois de mars, et qu'il n'a été suivi d'aucune correction ou rétractation de la part des auteurs, quoique nous soyons en décembre, et que je leur aie envoyé, il y a plusieurs mois (à l'époque où j'en fis parvenir à vous et à d'autres personnes) des exemplaires de mes Mémoires originaux, et des copies de notes sur une traduction de leur premier Mémoire; et si l'on considère qu'après tout je n'ai à me reprocher aucune des erreurs dont on m'accuse, et que les Mémoires de ces messieurs sont conçus de telle sorte que j'ai été obligé de répondre aux objections qu'on m'a présentées, j'espère que personne ne dira que je me suis trop hâté d'écrire une chose qui aurait pu être évitée, ou que j'aurais fait preuve de respect pour la vérité, et que j'eusse rendu justice à mes propres écrits, ou à cette branche de la science si, connaissant des erreurs si importantes, je ne les avais point fait remarquer.

Je suis, mon cher Monsieur, tout à vous bien sincèrement, FARADAY.

* D'après le compte rendu de cette séance qu'a donné le *Lycée*, au n° 35.
[1] The letter was written originally in English, not French. See Letter 244. I have been unable to find the original.
[2] See Letter 137.

149   M. FARADAY to J. BARROW, 4 December 1832
[*PRO, Adm. 1, 4610, previously unpublished*]

Royal Institution,
4th Decr 1832.
SIR

I beg to enclose to you for the information of my Lords Commissioners of the Admiralty a report embodying the substance of the analyses and experiments I have made on certain samples of meal from the Surrey Convict ship which you did me the honor to send to me for that purpose on the 30th Ultima

I am Sir
Your most Obedient
Humble Servant
M. FARADAY

Report on five samples of oatmeal received from the Admiralty on the 30th November [1832] said to be from the Surry [*sic*] Convict ship

Sample (*No. 1. Oatmeal – Contractor Inglis*[1] *sent by Mr. Wyse*[2] *to the Admiralty*) This meal is evidently different to good samples of meal and more gritty – I could not discover that barley meal had been mixed with it but at the same time I should state that in certain proportions it would be difficult to gain positive evidence of its presence

On proceeding to analysis abundant reason was discovered why this meal should be of bad quality: for it has been mingled and adulterated with more than 10 per cent of some calcareous matter, I believe, ground chalk. That no doubt might arise as to its improper presence I ascertained by analysis the proportions of earthy and saline matters in this and the other samples so that a fit judgment can be drawn of the quantities which being derived from the soil or during grinding &c &c. are inevitably present. The present sample contained per cent 0.5 of silica – 0.7 of phosphate of lime – 1.3 alumina and soluble salts and 10.7 carbonate of lime the remaining 86.8 parts being meal – water &c.

The silica alumina & salts were to be expected and are not in quantities larger than may be allowed as accidental. The phosphate of lime is in too small a quantity to be considered as having been purposely added yet being one of the substances in burnt bones it excites suspicion: I would rather however consider it accidental The calcareous matter is no doubt an adulteration and it will appear that in good meal I could find none of it

Sample (*No. 2. Oatmeal. Contractor Waugh sent by Mr Wyse to the Admiralty*) This was very good in all its evident qualities – Upon being analysed only 1.5 per cent of earthy and saline matter was found in it Of this nearly 0.4 was silica &c. and 1.1 alumina & salts. There was a trace of lime present but so small as to render its proportion inappreciable. The proportion of earthy and saline matter here is very small and must be allowed as that which could easily enter during the growth of the grain – or afterwards during the necessary operations even in the most careful hands.

Sample marked (HUBBERT *sent by Mr Wyse to Deptford and thence to the Admiralty*) This had all the characters of good meal. Being analysed it gave 2.3 per cent of earthy and saline substances of which 0.7 was silica &c. and 1.6 alumina salts &c. There was no lime here or at most the merest trace. There is no reason from the analysis to have any suspicions of this meal

Sample marked (*Oat.* [abbreviation doubtful] 10.4 *Inglis E.x* [reading doubtful] *21 Sept '33 sent by Mr Wyse to Deptford & thence to the Admiralty*) This sample had all the characters of the first sample It contained a large proportion of Carbonate of lime but as I had no doubt it was a sample of the same meal I did not pursue the analysis so as to obtain proportions which would have occupied time and caused delay

Sample marked (*Oat!* [abbreviation doubtful] *1–6 Waugh E.x* [reading doubtful] *12 Oct.'33 sent by Mr Wyse to Deptford & thence to the Admiralty*) This sample had all the characters of good meal. Believing it to be a duplicate of the second sample, I examined it only generally & found it to agree in all points

I then obtained a sample of oatmeal from a dealer in whom I have all confidence and analysed it. It contained 2.3 of earthy and saline matters of which 0.8 was silica and 1.5 alumina & salts: a minute trace of lime was present. This sample therefore agrees with those from *Waugh* and *Hubbert* and like them is in strong contrast to that from *Inglis*

As barley meal was supposed to be present in the sample from *Inglis*, I procured some *Barley meal* to ascertain its proportion of earthy & saline matters and whether calcareous matter is present in it. It yielded 3.1 per cent of inorganic matters of which 1.3 was silica and sandy particles; 1.8 alumina & salts. But here there was only the merest trace of lime present so that it stands strongly contrasted to the sample from *Inglis*

M. FARADAY

¹ The various contractors for supply of oatmeal mentioned below have left no further imprint upon history.
² Possibly Thomas Wyse (1791–1862), later Sir Thomas, then M.P. for Tipperary.

150 M. FARADAY to J. BARROW, 12 December 1832
[*PRO, Adm. 1, 4610, previously unpublished*]

Royal Institution,
12 Dec\[r\] 1832

SIR

In reply to your note of yesterday I beg to say I will report to you immediately I have analysed the meals and therefore after that report the man who brought the samples can have them back again

Your last letter says I am to ascertain "if any of them contain the like proportion of calcareous matter which the former ones did" The extract from the report of the Solicitor recommends that the samples "be submitted to a similar test of analysis and if similar results be produced, etc. etc."

Now I am able to say at present that the samples are (all of them) similar to the former samples from Inglis and all contain calcareous matter. But if you require me to speak to proportions *in each case* it involves the accurate analysis of each one for the quantity of calcareous matter present and requires far more care and time. It will require at least a week more to make such analysis satisfactory to myself

Will you have the goodness to tell me whether you think that a report on the general similarity in which I can give a strong opinion as to similarity of proportion also will be sufficient or whether you wish me to proceed with the quantitative analysis of each for the carbonate of lime

I am
Sir
Your Very Obedt Servant
M. FARADAY

151 M. FARADAY to J. BARROW, 12 December 1832
[*PRO, Adm. 1, 4610, Prom. Lett., previously unpublished*]

Royal Institution
12th Dec.ʳ 1832

SIR

I have the honor to inclose for the information of My Lords Commissioners of the Admiralty a report upon thirty one samples of oatmeal received on the 8th instant for analytical examination

and have the honor to be
Sir
Your Obedt Humble Servt
M. FARADAY

12th Dec.ʳ 1832 Report on thirty one samples of oatmeal received from the hands of Thomas Griffiths on the 8th. Dec.ʳ 1832.

These samples of oatmeal were numbered from 1 to 31 inclusive and were sealed up separately On submitting them to analytical examination I found that they were generally of the same class and character with two which I had the honor to refer to in a former report (of the 4th instant.) labeled Inglis etc etc All of them contained calcareous matter: evidently added for fraudulent purposes the proportion appeared to be nearly that of the former samples i.e. between 10 and 11 per cent but I am not able to speak accurately to the quantities without being allowed more time & pursuing the analyses in a more refined manner

M. FARADAY

[*I.E.E., previously unpublished*]

Bruxelles,
le 8 Mars 1833

M<small>ONSIEUR</small>

Permettez-moi d'abord de vous offrir mes bien Vifs remerciments pour la bonté que vous avez eue de m'envoyer votre mémoire sur les illusions d'optique,[1] je l'ai lu avec un plaisir extrême et je me suis empressé de produire les effets que je ne connaissais pas encore. Nous nous sommes rencontrés en plusieurs points; mais votre notice renferme des experiences extrêmement interessantes qui vous sont entierement propres, telles que les effets des roues tournant devant un miroir et dont certaines parties semblent se mouvoir, tandis que d'autres paraissent immobiles; telles encore que l'illusion produite par une brosse circulaire et par laquelle vous donnez une explication plausible du phénomene que présentent les rotiferes. Vos expériences sur les roues tournant devant une glace m'ont inspiré l'idée d'un nouveau genre d'illusions qui m'ont paru très-curieuses et qui, en modifiant convenablement la maniere de les produire, pourraient peut-être recevoir d'autres applications, par exemple, dans la Fantasmagorie. Je prends la liberté de vous envoyer, ci-joint, un exemple de ces illusions que vous concevrez probablement à la seule inspection du cercle et des figures, et sur lesquelles vous trouverez d'ailleurs des détails dans le N° de la *correspondance de l'observatoire*[2] que M<small>r</small> Quetelet vous envoie; je vous recommende seulement de ne pas vous placer trop près du miroir, car les petites figures deviennent alors confuses, et aussi de faire plutot l'expérience le soir; Enfin vous aurez sans doute bientot trouvé toutes les conditions les plus favorables. Je vous prie d'accepter en même temps un petit instrument destiné à recevoir le cercle de carton: vous concevrez aisément, en voyant ce petit appareil, la maniere de vous en servir; je crois seulement necessaire de vous prévenir qu'il se termine par une vis munie de son écrou, comme vous le voyez ci-dessous où j'ai séparé les deux pieces: de sorte que, pour l'employer, on introduit d'abord la vis dans le trou percé au centre du cercle de carton, puis on y place l'écrou que l'on serre suffisamment. De cette manière le cercle se trouve solidement attaché à la piece de cuivre *ab*, et on peut le faire tourner avec la plus grande facilité autour du fil de fer qui sert d'axe, sans qu'il puisse s'incliner de côté ou d'autre; enfin cet axe est legerement aminci dans la plus grande partie de sa longueur, de sorte que la piece cylindrique *ab* n'éprouve de frottement que dans un tres-petit nombre de points.

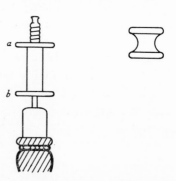

Vous verrez, Monsieur, dans l'article de la *correspondance* relatif à ce genre d'illusions, que je me suis hâté de saisir l'occasion de répondre au désir que vous m'aviez manifesté, et de faire connaître l'empressement et l'obligeance que vous aviez bien voulu mettre à reconnaître la priorité de mes observations.

Je prends la liberté de vous envoyer en même temps un autre N° de la *correspondance* dans lequel j'ai inséré un aperçu du travail dont je m'occupe maintenant sur une grande classe de phénomenes de la vision, qui comprend, entr'autres, la durée de la sensation de la vue.[3] Depuis l'insertion de cet article, cependant, mes idées se sont légerement modifiées, mais seulement de maniere à rendre la chose encore plus simple: j'espere pouvoir dans peu de temps vous offrir le mémoire dans lequel ce sujet, que je n'ai fait qu'indiquer dans la correspondance, sera traité avec développement.[4]

Le vif intéret que doit porter un physicien à tout ce qui regarde le sujet dont il s'occupe spécialement, et le désir qu'il doit avoir de connaître tout ce qui a été fait sur cette matiere seront, j'espere, mon excuse auprès de vous, Monsieur, et j'ai la confiance que vous voudrez bien ne pas regarder comme indiscrete la demande que je prends la liberté de vous faire de quelques renseignements relatifs au genre de recherches sur lesquelles j'ai eu l'honneur de me rencontrer avec vous: Dans votre mémoire, vous dites que Mr Wheatstone s'occupe de recherches plus générales et qui renferment les effets produits par les roues; comme je me suis aussi occupé d'effets plus généraux et dont ceux des roues sont des cas particuliers, ainsi que vous l'avez vu dans ma lettre aux rédacteurs des annales de physique et de chimie, vous concevrez combien je dois désirer de savoir si Mr Wheatstone a publié son travail, ou de connaître au moins, d'une maniere un peu plus précise, de quoi il traite.[5] Je le désire d'autant plus vivement que peut-être ces renseignements necessiteraient des modifications ou des additions au mémoire auquel je travaille. vous parlez aussi, dans votre mémoire, à propos de la durée de la sensation de la vue, des effets du *Kaleïdophone*,[6] instrument dont je n'ai aucune connaissance: J'aurais donc une obligation à ajouter à celles que je vous ai déjà, Monsieur, si je pouvais obtenir de vous quelques éclaircissements à l'égard du travail de Mr Wheatstone et à celui du Kaleïdophone, éclaircissements que je me reproche à moi-même de vous demander, quand je songe combien votre temps est précieux et de quelle maniere vous savez l'employer.

Si vous me faites l'honneur de me répondre, veuillez, Monsieur, avoir la bonté de m'adresser directement votre lettre, par le service des postes, chez Monsieur Quetelet, à l'observatoire, autrement les lettres et paquets restent ordinairement plusieurs mois en route.

Veuillez me croire, Monsieur, avec tous les sentiments d'estime et de con-sidération

Votre très-humble et très-dévoué

serviteur

J^H PLATEAU

[1] See Letter 143, fn. 3.
[2] J. Plateau, 'Sur un nouveau genre d'illusions d'optique,' *QCM*, 7 (1832), 365.
[3] 'Sur quelques phénomènes de vision,' *ibid.*, 228.
[4] See Letter 143, fn. 6.
[5] Charles Wheatstone's first papers on physiological optics appeared in 1838. See *RSCSP*.
[6] See Charles Wheatstone, 'Description of the Kaleidophone, or Phonic Kaleidoscope; a new philosophical toy, for the illustration of several interesting and amusing acoustical and optical phenomena,' *QJS*, 23 (1827), 344.

153 M. FARADAY to E. MITSCHERLICH, 17 August 1833[1]

[*Deutsches Museum, previously unpublished*]

Royal Institution
17 August 1833

MY DEAR SIR

On returning from the country I find your very kind letter, your present of fluids, & the accompanying diploma and I write in haste that I may not be found wanting in respect to the Academy which has done me the honor of electing me a Corresponding member.[2] May I ask you to express my warmest thanks for this mark of approbation saying also that I feel it a strong stimulus to the earnest pursuit of that which has already been the cause of my receiving the approval of the Academy – I would answer by letter to the Secretaries but thought it perhaps more proper to acknowledge the favour through the same channel by which I received it.

Your hydro-carbons are to me exceedingly interesting for I have long resolved to pursue certain views which I entertain of the nature of these bodies, but the experimental researches in Electricity have drawn me off & will still keep me from that subject.[3] You know how laborious experiments are and will not I think believe me lazy.

I hope in a month or two to have two other papers on Electricity to send you. Is the channel by the Royal Society's box a good one by which to convey such things to you or can you tell me of a better. I must close this letter and meet an engagement. I have only time to thank you for all your kindness and say what pleasure I feel in your remembrance of me. I shall be delighted to see your results in the work you speak of & also to pay the bill I have so long owed you or the works.

My dear Sir
Most Truly Yours
M. FARADAY

[1] The photostat of this letter was too poor to check the punctuation closely.
[2] This refers to Faraday's election as Corresponding Member of the Academy of Sciences of Berlin.
[3] This probably refers to Mitscherlich's paper 'Ueber das Benzin und die Säuren der Oel und Talgarten' which appeared in French translation in *AC*, 2 s. (1833), 41.

Faraday never returned to his chemical studies.

154 J. N. P. Hachette to M. Faraday, 30 August 1833

[*I.E.E., B.J.* 2, *51*]

Paris,
30 août 1833

MONSIEUR ET TRÈS CHER CONFRERE,

Ayant fait un petit voyage vers ma ville natale (Mezières, Ardennes), j'ai trouvé a mon retour votre lettre du 17 juin et la 3eme Serie de vos recherches electriques; qui sera bientot suivie d'une 4eme serie.

en lisant la dernière page (64) de votre memoire sur la 3ème Serie, j'ai remarqué ces mots: *my first unfortunate Letter to M. Hachette*; Je vous avoue que je ne puis pas concevoir rien de malheureux dans l'annonce d'une decouverte, qui vous place au rang des plus heureux et grands physiciens.

Supposez pour un moment qu'un membre de la Société Royale ait fait part de votre lecture, dans une lettre particulière, que cette lettre ait tombé par hasard entre les Mains d'un physicien qui auroit repété vos experiences et qui auroit la pretention de les avoir inventées. Vous pourriez alors dire, *O, unfortunate Letter*. tout le Contraire arrive; vous annoncez une grande decouverte a la Societé Royale; elle est transmise de suite a Paris en votre nom; toute la gloire de l'inventeur vous est assurée; que pouviez-vous desirer de plus? que personne ne travaille dans la mine que vous aviez ouverte; cela est impossible. l'excellence de votre decouverte est en raison des efforts que chaque physicien fera, pour l'etendre. ne lisez-vous pas avec plaisir la feuille du journal français, *le temps*, qui chaque Mercredi, donne la Seance de l'academie des Sciences, du lundi precedent. y at-il [*sic*] un academicien français qui se plaigne de cette prompte communication? non; c'est le contraire. les routes en fer ne donnent pas encore aux nouvelles Scientifiques, la vitesse de la pensée, et sous ce rapport, elles sont encore tres imparfaites.

Je ne me pardonnerois pas, si j'avois a me reprocher une communication qui auroit été pour vous la Cause d'un vrai Malheur, mais permettez-moi de vous dire qu'en cette circonstance, le Malheur n'est que dans votre imagination; je crois avoir contribué a etendre votre gloire, votre renommée, a vous rendre la justice qui vous est due, et je m'en felicite. J'espere que vous partagerez mes sentimens. agreez l'assurance de mon bien-Sincere attachement –

HACHETTE

155 M. FARADAY to E. W. BRAYLEY, 10 October 1833

[*The Literary Repository, no. 4, 1957, pub. by G. Stevens, Bookseller, Beaminster, Dorset*]

R.I.,
Oct. 10, 1833.

DEAR SIR,

I prefer Mr. to Dr. but as letters, papers, etc, etc, are continually reaching me addressed Dr. I am obliged to acknowledge the title or they would miss their object. This it is which constrains me in part to assume the designation but whenever I am at liberty I like Mr. best. Somehow it happened that the running title to the first and second series of researches was headed Dr. and I believe more for uniformity than any thing else it was continued in the third. I do not know how it is in the fourth; but in the fifth and future I think it shall return to Mr.

Very truly yours,
M. FARADAY

156 G. MOLL to M. FARADAY, 15 November 1833

[*I.E.E., previously unpublished*]

Utrecht
15 November 1833.

MY DEAR SIR!

Your kind letter of 9th September last gave me infinite pleasure. I am very happy indeed that one standing so high as yourself in scientific reputation, has still the goodness to remember me. I certainly had some idea of visiting England at the time of the Cambridge meeting,[1] but other affairs prevented my executing so pleasing a scheme. Since however I wanted to turn to some advantage the time I had to dispose of, I made an excursion to Germany and visited the celebrated University of Göttingen. If I had not been thoroughly persuaded of the truth of what I stated in my pamphlet against the declinarians, I could have acquired here the fullest conviction of the correctness of my opinions. No one doubts but that Gauss[2] is a man of Genius, perhaps the first mathematician living, still he is not a good lecturer, and so far useless, and his observatory as well as that of Harding[3] looks much as if little use was made of it. Stromeyer[4] has certainly a neat laboratory, but nothing like what may be seen in twenty places in England, besides that in my opinion there is a great want of apparatus. In the department of natural philosophy, mechanics, natural history &c the apparatus belonging to the university is next to nothing, and if I am not mistaken the lectures of old Blumenbach[5] would scarcely draw an audience to the lecture room of a mechanics Institution. Their library however, it must be said, is excellent, and challenges, as far as usefulness is concerned, any other in existence. Gauss has got up a very pretty apparatus, a sort of magnetic tele-graph. Two bar magnets of a pound weight, are suspended in different places in a distance of ab^t 1½ miles (english), each has wires coiled round but not touching them, these wires communicate, through the open air over roofs and steeples and the action of a couple of galvanic plates in one place all [reading doubtful; 'all' is apparently crossed out] gives motion to the magnet placed at the distance of 1½ miles. The thing at any rate is very curious.

I have read with the greatest pleasure your new series of experiments.[6] They are sure to carry your name down to posterity as long as there will be anything existing like science. I do not know how the declinarians are to dispose of you, unless they want to hold you up as an exception confirming the general rule.

There is at present here a person of the name of Dr Keil, who boasts much in general, but in particular of your acquaintance, and that of Dr Barlow.[7] He talks of magnets carrying 400 and 200 lbs and certainly he has some horse shoe magnets of great but not of such enormous force. Many people here imagine him to be a phoenix, for my part I take him to be a arrant knave, and an impudent quack. However, as I know not much of him, I may be mistaken. I am indeed induced to believe that he intends to cheat our government, out of some of their, or rather of the public money, and as we cannot well afford, at present, to incur any useless expenses, I should like to prevent his design. You will confer therefore a great Obligation on me, if you will favour me, as soon as possible, with an account of this persons [*sic*] proceedings in England, and what is your opinion on his scientific merits. He must have had some dispute with Mr Christie,[8] concerning some experiments which he exhibited at the Royal Society. He also professes himself to be a great friend of Mr Barlow;[9] in one word he tells so much, that the capacity of my belief is even too small for one half of it. If your occupations should not allow you to write me on this subject next post, I will direct Mr Braaksma to call upon you to receive such verbal information, as you may think proper.

A good while ago, I sent to Sir David Brewster an account of some electro and thermoelectric experiments, which appeared not altogether uninteresting. I never since heard of the knight, nor did he publish the exp[eriments] [ms. torn and missing]. I think he owes me a grudge, for abusing me in his Journal, on account [of] [ms. torn and missing] the declinarian question. Perhaps this is the first time that a man has been abused for telling people that they are not so bad, as they fancy themselves to be.

I request my best compliments to your Lady, and believe me ever

Yours
MOLL

Pray do favour me with copies of your publications.

261

[1] The *BAAS* met in Cambridge in 1833.
[2] Karl Friedrich Gauss (1777–1855), one of the foremost mathematicians of the nineteenth century.
[3] Karl Ludwig Harding (1765–1834), Professor of Astronomy of Göttingen.
[4] Friedrich Stromeyer (1776–1835), Director of the Chemical Laboratory at Göttingen.
[5] Johann Friedrich Blumenbach (1752–1840), Professor of Medicine at Göttingen.
[6] Series 3, 4 and 5 all appeared in 1833.
[7] Peter Barlow, of the Royal Artillery Academy, Woolwich.
[8] Samuel Hunter Christie, one of the Secretaries of the Royal Society.
[9] Rev. John Barlow, one of Faraday's close friends.

157 D. LARDNER[1] to M. FARADAY, 8 January 1834
  [*I.E.E., previously unpublished*]

Manchester,
8 Jany 1834

MY DEAR SIR

As I think it would be a pity that a subject so suitable to your friday evening meetings as Babbages Machinery[2] should not find a place at them, it has occurred to me that a general view of it might be given as an introduction to the more detailed account which will form the subject of the proposed course of three lectures – I could shew the general arrangement of the parts and give some account of one or two of the most material points in it, referring for details to the subsequent lectures –

If you approve of this you may "*book me*" – for one friday Evening. I cannot however undertake any thing before the end of April or beginning of May.

There is another invention which I think even more important than the machine and which arose incidentally out of it – I mean the "Mechanical notation" – Babbage and myself have lately put our heads together and have made some improvements in this and have applied it to the Steam-engine – If you call at Dorset street I will shew you a *map* of the working of a steam-engine which we have constructed – If you think this a desirable subject for one of your fridays you may command my services –

I shall not impose upon you the trouble of answering this – You will probably see Babbage and as he will be writing to me from time to time I shall hear of you –

Believe me Dear Sir
Yours faithfully
DION: LARDNER

[1] Dionysius Lardner (1793–1859), was Professor of Astronomy at London University at this time.
[2] See Letter 87, fn. 3.

158 M. FARADAY to E. W. BRAYLEY, 11 January 1834

[*R.I., previously unpublished*]

R Institution
11 Jan.ʸ 1834

DEAR SIR

In reply to yours I send you an answer on the other side – The names I think excellent & hope they will at all events find entrance into public use[1]

Mr Conybeare is not aware probably of the admirable Magneto electric machines now constructed by Newman & others An account of their construction has never yet been published. Mr. Caxton[2] first fitted them up in that form & ought to send you a paper & drawing. I have had a continuous shock from one equal to what I have felt from a very powerful voltaic battery

Every Truly Yours
M. FARADAY

[1] I am unable to discover to what names Faraday here refers.
[2] Caxton was a scientific instrument maker who was one of the first to construct a reasonably powerful dynamo.

159 M. FARADAY to MRS M. SOMERVILLE,[1] 1 March 1834

[*Bodleian Library, Oxford, previously unpublished*]

Royal Institution
Mar. 1, 1834

DEAR MADAM

I cannot refuse myself the pleasure any longer of thanking you for your kindness in sending me a copy of your work.[2] I did intend to read it through first; but I cannot proceed so fast as I wish because of constant occupation

I cannot resist saying too what pleasure I feel in your approbation of my late Experimental Researches The approval of one judge is to me more stimulating than the applause of thousands that *cannot* understand the subject

I am
Dear Madam
With Every Respect
Your faithful Servt
M. FARADAY

[1] Mary Somerville (1790–1872), popularizer of science and amateur astronomer and mathematician.
[2] Mary Somerville, *On the Connexion of the Physical Sciences*, London, 1834.

160 M. FARADAY to W. WHEWELL, 24 April 1834

[*Trinity College Library, Trinity College, Cambridge, NRRS, 199*]

Royal Institution,
24th April 1834

MY DEAR SIR,

I am in a trouble which when it occurs at Cambridge is I understand referred by every body in the University to you for removal and I am encouraged by the remembrance of your kindness and on Mr. Willis'[1] suggestion to apply to you also But I should tell you how I stand in the matter.

I wanted some new names to express my facts in Electrical science without involving more theory than I could help, & applied to a friend Dr Nicholl who has given me some that I intend to adopt for instance a body decomposable by the passage of the Electric current, I call an "*electrolyte*" and instead of saying that water is *electro chemically decomposed* I say it is "*electrolyzed*" The intensity above which a body is decomposed beneath which it conducts without decomposition I call the "Electrolytic intensity", *etc etc* What have been called the poles of the battery I call the *electrodes* they are not merely surfaces of metal but even of *water* & *air*, to which the term poles could hardly apply without receiving a new sense. *Electrolytes* must consist of two parts which during the *electrolization* are determined the one in one direction the other in the other towards the electrodes or poles where they are evolved these evolved substances I call *zetodes*, which are therefore the direct constituents of electrolites.

All these terms I am satisfied with but not with two others which I have used thus far. It is essential to me to have the power of referring to the two surfaces of a decomposable body by which the current enters into & passes out of it, without at the same time referring to the electrodes. Thus let *a* be a decompos-

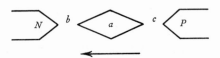

able body & P & N the pos & neg poles which may *or* may not be in contact with *a* at the points *b. c* and shall yet transmit the electricity which passes through *a*. Admitting the usual mode of expression & talking of a current of Electricity proceeding from the positive pole *P* through *a* to the negative pole *N* my friend suggested & I have used the term *eisode* for *c* and *exode* for *b*. the points where the *zetodes* are rendered and a zetode going to *c* I have called a *zeteisode* & another going to *b*. a *zetexode*

But the idea of a current especially of *one* current is a very clumsy & hypothetical view of the state of Electrical forces under the circumstances The idea of *two* currents seems to me still more suspicious and I have little doubt that the present view of electric currents and the notions by which we try to conceive

264

of them will soon pass away and I want therefore names by which I can refer to *c* & *b* without involving any theory of the nature of electricity In searching for a reference on which to found these I can think of nothing but the globe as a magnetic body If we admit the magnetism of the Globe as due to Electric currents running in lines of latitude their course must be according to our present modes of expression from East to West and if a portion of water under decomposition by an electric current be placed so that the current through it shall be parallel to that considered as circulating round the earth then the oxygen will be rendered towards the east or at *c* in the figure & the hydrogen towards the west or at *b* in the figure I think therefore that if I were to call *c* the *east-ode* & *b* the *west-ode* I should express these parts by reference to a natural standard which whatever changes take place in our theories or knowledge of Electricity will still have the same relation But Eastode & Westode or Oriode & Occiode are names which a scholar would not suffer I understand for a moment and *Anatolode* and *dysiode* have been offered me instead

Now can you help me out to two good names not depending upon the idea of a current in *one direction only* or upon Positive or negative and to which I may add the prefixes Zet or Zeto, so as to express the class to which any particular *Zetode* may belong.

I am making very free with you but if you feel inclined to help me I shall be very much obligd & if not may[2] no ceremony in saying that you cannot assist me.

I am Dear Sir
Your faithful Servt
M. FARADAY

¹ Rev. Robert Willis (1800–75), Fellow of Caius College, Cambridge, had lectured at the Royal Institution. *NRRS*, 195.
² Ross, *NRRS*, 16 (1961), 200, reads 'make' here which does make more sense, but the word seems undeniably to be 'may.'

161 W. WHEWELL to M. FARADAY, 25 April 1834

[*I. Todhunter, William Whewell, 2 vols., London, 1876, 2, 178, and NRRS, 16 (1961), 201*]

Trinity College,
Cambridge,
April 25, 1834.

MY DEAR SIR,

I was glad on several accounts to receive your letter. I had the pleasure of being present at the R.S. at the reading of your paper, in which you introduced some of the terms which you mention, and I was rejoiced to hear them, for I saw, or thought I saw, that these novelties had been forced upon you by the novelty of extent and the new relations of your views. In cases where such causes operate, new terms inevitably arise, and it is very fortunate when those, upon whom the introduction of these devolves, look forwards as carefully as you do to the general bearing and future prospects of the subject; and it is an additional advantage when they humour philologists so far as to avoid gross incongruities of language. I was well satisfied with most of the terms that you mention; and shall be glad and gratified to assist in freeing them from false assumptions and implications, as well as from philological monstrosities.

I have considered the two terms you want to substitute for *eisode* and *exode*, and upon the whole I am disposed to recommend instead of them *anode* and *cathode*. These words may signify *eastern* and *western way*, just as well as the longer compounds which you mention, which derive their meaning from words implying rising and setting, notions which anode and cathode imply more simply. But I will add that, as your object appears to me to be to indicate opposition of direction without assuming any hypothesis which may hereafter turn out to be false, *up* and *down*, which must be arbitrary consequences of position on any hypothesis, seem to be free from inconvenience even in their simplest sense. I may mention too that *anodos* and *cathodos* are good genuine Greek words, and not compounds coined for the purpose. If however you are not satisfied with these, I will propose to you one or two other pairs. For instance, *dexiode* and *sceode* (*skaiode* if you prefer it) may be used to indicate *east* and *west*, agreeably to Greek notions and usages, though their original meaning would be *right* and *left*: but I should say in this case also, that right and left, as it cannot be interpreted to imply a false theory, any more than east and west, would be blameless for your object. Another pair, *orthode* and *anthode*, which mean *direct* and *opposite* way, might be employed; but I allow that in these you come nearer to an implied theory. Upon the whole I think *anode* and *cathode* much the best.

I have already said that I liked most of your new words very well, but there is one which I should be disposed to except from this praise; I mean *ʒetode*. My objections are these. This word being grouped with others of the same termination might be expected to indicate a modification of electr*ode*, as eis*ode*, and ex*ode*, or an*ode* and cath*ode* do. Instead of this, it means a notion altogether heterogeneous to these, and the *ode* is here the object of a verb *ʒete*, contrary to the analogy of all the other words. It appears to me that, as what you mean is an element, all that you want is some word which implies an element of a composition, taking a *new* word, however, in order that it may be recollected that the decomposition of which you speak is of a peculiar kind, namely, *electrolytical* decomposition. Perhaps the Greek word *stecheon* (or *stoicheion*) would answer the purpose. It has already a place in our scientific language in the term *stoecheiometry*, and has also this analogy in its favour, that whereas

266

your other words in *ode* mean *ways*, this word stecheon is derived from a word which signifies to *go in a row*. The elements or zetodes are two things which *go*, or *seek to go*, opposite ways. I might add that, if you want a word which has a reference to your other terms, the reference must be to the process of decomposition by which these elements are obtained. You might call your zetode, an *electrostecheon*, especially if you had occasion to distinguish these elements obtained by *electrolytical* processes from others obtained by *chemolytical* processes, that is, the common analysis effected by the play of affinities. Elements obtained in the latter way might be called *chemostecheons* in opposition to *electrostecheon*. But I am afraid I am here venturing beyond my commission and out of my depth; and you must judge whether your stecheons or zetodes, or whatever they are to be, are likely to require the indication of such relations. If you were to take anode and cathode and adopt stecheon, I think *anastecheon* and *catastecheon* might indicate the two *stecheons*. If you stick to zetode, *anazetode* and *catazetode* would be the proper terms; but perhaps *zetanode* and *zetocathode* would be more analogous to zetode, which is a word that, as I have said, I do not much like.

My letter is become so long that I will recapitulate: *anode, cathode, zetanode, zetocathode* fulfil your requisitions; *anode, cathode, anastecheon, catastecheon* are what I prefer. With great interest in your speculations, and best wishes,

Believe me, yours very truly,
W. WHEWELL.

162   M. FARADAY to SIR C. LEMEN, 25 April 1834
[*W. H. Browning*,[1] *previously unpublished*][2]

R. Institution,
April 25, 1834

DEAR SIR,

I am much obliged to you for a sight of Mr. Fox's[3] letter. At present my mind is very unsettled with regard to the nature of the Electric agent. The usual notions attached to Positive and negative and to the term current I suspect are altogether wrong but I have not *a clear view* of what ought to be put in their places.

It is very easy to imagine forces with certain directions as a kind of abstract notion of electricity but that is saying little or nothing although all the phenomena may be accounted for in such a way. It is the cause of the forces that one wants to lay hold of. I have one idea that in what we call the current in the decomposition of bodies anything but a resolution and recombination of forces seems between contiguous particles but I want to see clearly *how* these changes come about and as yet cannot.

That being the case I have no opinion to offer on our friends [*sic*] views but to hope that he will go on either strengthening them or correcting them by experiment.

I am dear Sir
Very Truly Yours
M. FARADAY

¹ Mr W. H. Browning, Chiddingstone, Bexley Road, Eltham, S.E.9.
² All but the last paragraph appears in *LPW*, 268. The letter was transcribed by Mr Browning, and not seen by the present editor.
³ Robert Were Fox (1789–1877), geologist.

163 M. FARADAY to W. WHEWELL, 3 May 1834
[*Trinity College Library, Trinity College, Cambridge, NRRS*, 16 (*1961*), *203*]

R. Institution,
May 3, 1834

MY DEAR SIR,

I have waited very impatiently for a proof of my paper that I might send it to you with my letter of thanks for your kindness¹ But I am afraid I have involved by that a charge of unthankfulness towards you, which however I assure you I do not deserve

All your names I and my friend² approve of or nearly all as to sense & expression, but I am frightened by their length & sound when compounded As you will see I have taken *dexiode* and *skaiode* because they agree best with my natural standard East and West I like Anode & Cathode better as to sound but all to whom I have shewn them have supposed at first that by *Anode* I meant *No way*

Then *Stechion* I have taken although I would rather not have had the hard sound of *ch*. here especially as we have similar sounds in both the former words. But when we come to combine it with the two former as *dexio-stechion* & *skaio-stechion* especially the latter I am afraid it becomes inadmissible simply from its length & sound forbidding its familiar use. For I think you will agree with me that I had better not give a new word than give one which is not likely to enter into common use

It is possible perhaps that by this time some other shorter word may have occurred for *Stechion* if so will you favour me with it. If not I think I must strike out the two compounds above and express my meaning without the use of names for the two classes of stechions though they are very very much want(ed)

It was the shortness & euphony of *Zeteisode* & *Zetexode* which were their strong recommendations to me.

I am My Dear Sir
Your Obliged &
faithful Servant
M. FARADAY

Can you give me at the bottom of the pages the greek derivatives *etc. etc.* that when you return me the leaves I may have them right for the printer They are of course uncorrected at present.

MF

[1] The Seventh Series of Experimental Researches in Electricity was 'On electro-chemical decomposition' and 'On the absolute quantity of electricity associated with the particles or atoms of matter.'

[2] Whitlock Nicholl, M.D. See *NRRS*, 16 (1961), 188.

164   W. WHEWELL to M. FARADAY, 5 May 1834

[*I. Todhunter, William Whewell, 2 vols., London, 1876, 2, 181 and NRRS, 16 (1961), 204)*

Trinity Coll.
Cambridge,
May 5, 1834.

MY DEAR SIR,

I quite agree with you that *stechion* or *stecheon* is an awkward word both from its length and from the letters of which it is composed, and I am very desirous that you should have a better for your purpose. I think I can suggest one, but previous to doing this, I would beg you to reconsider the suggestion of *anode* and *cathode* which I offered before. It is very obvious that these words are much simpler than those in your proof sheet, and the advantage of simplicity will be felt very strongly when the words are once firmly established, as by your paper I do not in the least degree doubt that they will be. As to the objection to *anode*, I do not think it is worth hesitating about. *Anodos* and *cathodos* do really mean in Greek *a way up* and *a way down*; and *anodos* does not mean, and cannot mean, according to the analogy of the Greek language, *no way*. It is true that the prefix *an*, put before *adjectives* beginning with a vowel, gives a negative signification, but not to substantives, except through the medium of adjectives. *Anarchos* means *without government*, and hence *anarchia, anarchy,* means *the absence of government*: but *anodos* does not and cannot mean *the absence of way*. And if it did mean this as well as a *way up*, it would not cease to mean the latter also; and when introduced in company with *cathodos*, no body who has any tinge of Greek could fail to perceive the meaning at once. The notion of *anodos* meaning *no way* could only suggest itself to persons unfamiliar with Greek, and accidentally acquainted with some English words in which the negative particle is so employed; and those persons who have taken up this notion must have overlooked the very different meaning of negatives applied to substantives and adjectives. Prepositions are so very much the simplest and most decisive way of expressing opposition, or other relations, that it would require some very strong arguments to induce one to adopt any other way of conveying such relations as you want to indicate.

If you take *anode* and *cathode*, I would propose for the two elements resulting from *electrolysis* the terms *anion* and *cation*, which are neuter participles signifying *that which goes up*, and *that which goes down*; and for the two together you might use the term *ions*, instead of *zetodes* or *stechions*. The word is not a substantive in Greek but it may easily be so taken, and I am persuaded that the brevity and simplicity of the terms you will thus have will in a fortnight procure their universal acceptation. The *anion* is that which goes to the *anode*, the *cation* is that which goes to the *cathode*. The *th* in the latter word arises from the aspirate in *hodos* (way), and therefore is not to be introduced in cases where the second term has not an aspirate, as *ion* has not.

Your passages would then stand thus:

"We purpose calling that towards the east the *anode*†, and that towards the west the *cathode*‡. . . . . I purpose to distinguish these bodies by calling those *anions*§ which go to the *anode* of the decomposing body, and those passing to the *cathode*, *cations*¶. And when I have occasion to speak of these together I shall call them *ions*

† ἀνά, upwards, ὁδός, a way: the way which the sun rises.
‡ κατά, downwards, ὁδός a way; the way which the sun sets.
§ ἀνιόν, that which goes up (neuter participle). ¶ κατιόν, that which goes down."

I am so fully persuaded that these terms are from their simplicity preferable to those you have printed, that I shall think it a misfortune to science if you retain the latter. If, however, you still adhere to *dexio* and *scaio*, I am puzzled to combine these with *ion* without so much coalition of vowels as will startle your readers. I put at the bottom of the page the explanation, if you should persist in this.* I would only beg you to recollect that even violent philological anomalies are soon got over, if they are used to express important laws, as we see in the terms *endosmose* and *exosmose*; and therefore there is little reason for shrinking from objections founded in ignorance against words which are really agreeable to the best analogies. The existing notation of Chemistry owes its wide adoption and long duration to its simplicity.

I am afraid you will think I am fond of playing the critic if I make any further objections, otherwise I would observe on your Article 666, that if you are not sure that you will want such words as *astechion*, it is throwing away your authority to propose them. If what I have written does not answer your purpose pray let me hear from you again, and believe me,

Yours very truly,
W. WHEWELL.

P.S. If, adopting the term *ion* for *stechion*, you do want the negative *astechion*, I do not think there will be any difficulty in devising a suitable word.

* δεξιός, on the right hand, and hence, the *east*; σκαιός, on the left hand, and hence, the west. [This note is Dr Whewell's.]

165   M. FARADAY to W. WHEWELL, 5 May 1834
[*Trinity College Library, Trinity College, Cambridge, NRRS, 16 (1961), 206*]

R. Institution,
Monday, (May 5, 1834)

MY DEAR SIR,

Hoping that this sheet of paper will reach you before you write to me I hasten to mention two names instead of eisode & exode which are free I think from objection as to involving a point of theory Namely *Voltode* and *Galvanode*

My friend Dr. Nicholl proposes *Alphode* and *Betode*

Then the compound are good in sound *Volta-stechion, Galva-stechion* or *Alphastechion* & *Beta-stechion.*

Ever Truly Yours
M. FARADAY

166   W. WHEWELL to M. FARADAY, 6 May 1834
[*R.I., NRRS, 16 (1961), 206*]

Trin. Coll.
Cambridge.
May 6. 1834

MY DEAR SIR,

You will have received my letter of yesterday and perhaps will have formed your opinion of it. I still think *anode* and *cathode* the best terms beyond comparison for the two electrodes. The terms which you mention in your last show that you are come to the conviction that the essential thing is to express a *difference* and nothing more. This conviction is nearly correct, but I think one may say that it is very desirable in this case to express an *opposition*, a contrariety, as well as a difference. The terms you suggest are objectionable in not doing this. They are also objectionable it appears to me, in putting forwards too ostentatiously the arbitrary nature of the difference. To talk of Alphode and Betode could give some persons the idea that you thought it absurd to pursue the philosophy of the difference of the two results, and at any rate would be thought affected by some. Voltode and Galvanode labour no less under the disadvantage of being not only entirely, but ostentatiously arbitrary, with two additional disadvantages; first that it will be very difficult for any body to recollect which is which; and next that I think you are not quite secure that further investigations may not point out some historical incongruity in this reference to Volta and Galvani. I am more and more convinced that *anode* and *cathode* are the right words; and not least, from finding that both you and Dr Nichols [*sic*] are ready to take any arbitrary opposition or difference. *Ana* and *Kata* which are *prepositions* of the most *familiar* use in composition, which

271

indicate *opposite* relations in *space*, and which yet *cannot* be interpreted as involving a theory appear to me to unite all desirable properties.

I am afraid of urging the claims of *anion* and *cation* though I should certainly take them if it were my business – that which *goes to* the *anode* and that which goes to the cathode appears to me to be exactly what you want to say. To talk of the two as *ions* would sound a little harsh at first: it would soon be got over. But if you are afraid of this I think that *stechion*, as the accepted Greek name for element, is a very good word to adopt, and then, *anastechion* and *catastechion* are the two contrary elements, which I am sure are much better words than you can get at by using dexio and scaio or any other terms not prepositions.

I expect to be in London on Friday and Saturday, and if I am shall try to see you on one of those days and to learn what you finally select. Believe me

Yours most truly
W. WHEWELL

167 M. FARADAY to W. WHEWELL, 15 May 1834
[*Trinity College Library, Trinity College, Cambridge, previously unpublished*]

Royal Institution,
15 May 1834

MY DEAR SIR

I ought before this to have thanked you for your great kindness in the matter of the names respecting which I applied to you; but I hoped to have met you last Saturday at Kensington and therefore delayed expressing my obligations

I have taken your advice and the names used are *anode cathode anions cations* and *ions* the last I shall have but little occasion for. I had some hot objections made to them here and found myself very much in the condition of the man with his son and Ass who tried to please every body; but when I held up the shield of your authority it was wonderful to observe how the tone of objection melted away

I am quite delighted with the facility of expression which the new terms give me and shall ever be your debtor for the kind assistance you have given me

I am My dear Sir
Your Obligd & faithful Servant
M. FARADAY

[*R.I., previously unpublished*]

Utrecht
1 June 1834.

MY DEAR SIR!

Although I have not had since an age the pleasure of any direct communication with you, still I have to thank you for your very valuable papers on electricity which you had the goodness to transmit to me. Mr Braaksma wrote me what you said about the pseudo Dr Keil,[1] and I was happy to find that my humble opinion about this individual coincided with that of more able judges. Nevertheless the impudent Scoundrel, by the assistance of some fools, succeeded in squeezing from the public purze [*sic*], about three hundred pounds, for pretended improvements on marine compasses, none of which, I am persuaded is worth a farthing. He is now in Amsterdam, where he is practising on the credulity of the public. If you would take the trouble to sit down for five minutes, and put in my hands some efficacious means of exposing the ignorance and cunning of this quack, you would render a service to humanity.

The Gentleman who is to deliver this letter to you, is a young man belonging to one of the first families of this country, he is a man of fortune, and if you should give him an opportunity of enjoying your conversation, I dare say, you will find an excellent and Gentlemanlike companion. However he does not belong to our class, he is not scientific, and therefore is not likely to become a bore, but there is one service, which you rendered me on my last visit, and which, I hope, you will bestow on him, which is to get him introduced to the Athenaeum club. I was so much pleased, with an Institution of that sort, that I would always make it a particular point on any visit to England, to endeavour to get admission to this place. I almost forgot to mention my friends name, it is Mr de Jonge van Ellemeet.[2] I apprehend you will find it rather hard to pronounce and full more difficult to remember.

I believe I shall have the pleasure of seeing you this summer. If nothing comes in the way to prevent me, it is my intention to part from hence in the beginning of July, and if once safely landed on British ground, you may depend that I shall not be slow in making my appearance in Albemarle Street.

Believe me very sincerely
Sir!
Yours truly,
MOLL.

[1] See Letter 156.
[2] Willem Cornelis Mary de Jonge van Ellemeet (1811–88), later a lawyer and Dutch magistrate.

169   M. FARADAY to W. V. HELLYER,[1] 12 June 1834

[Brig. M. D. Jephson,[2] previously unpublished]

R. Institution,
June 12, 1834

MY DEAR SIR,

I can only give general answers to your questions. I have no doubt that either asphaltene or wood and asphaltene could be used instead of coal but they would require alterations in the furnaces to consort with their mode of combustion and make the heat available and then the effect would probably come near coal. The relation of heating power obtained from coal and asphaltene must be obtained by experiment on a good large scale. The quantity of steam will be obtained at the same time. The stowage will depend upon the quantity of each fuel required to give an equal quantity of steam and will therefore be told by the same expts. I should expect that good coal would be the best, at least until repeated trial and improvement have given the most perfect mode of applying the combustion of asphaltene to the raising of steam.

I am Dear Sir
Most truly yours,
M. FARADAY

[1] William Varlo Hellyer, civil servant.
[2] Brig. M. D. Jephson, Mallow Castle, Co. Cork, Ireland.

170   M. FARADAY to F. O. WARD,[1] 16 June 1834

[A. W. Hoffman, 'The Lifework of Liebig in Experimental and Philosophic Chemistry...' in 'Chemical Society, Faraday Lectures', 1869–1928, London, 1928, 118]

Royal Institution
16th June, 1834.

SIR,

I have no hesitation in advising you to experiment in support of your views, because, whether you confirm or confute them, good must come from your exertions.

With regard to the views themselves, I can say nothing about them, except that they are useful in exciting the mind to inquiry. A very brief consideration of the progress of experimental philosophy will show you that it is a great disturber of pre-formed theories.

I have thought long and closely about the theories of attraction and of particles and atoms of matter, and the more I think (in association with experiment) the less distinct does my idea of an atom or particle of matter become.

I am, Sir,
Your very obedient servant,
M. FARADAY

[1] F. O. Ward was then a twenty-year-old student at King's College, London and had written to Faraday to ask if he should experiment to confirm his new theory of atomic structure.

171 M. FARADAY to W. WHEWELL, 17 June 1834

[*Trinity College Library, Trinity College, Cambridge, NRRS, 16 (1961), 208*]

Royal Institution,
17 June, 1834

DEAR SIR

I beg to offer you a copy of the 6th & 7th Series *etc.* and am anxious again to thank you for your kindness in the matter of the names. I felt during the printing very well pleased with the way in which they read.

I take the liberty of putting 3 or 4 other copies into the parcel but have some suspicion that I am using too much liberty with you. I hope however you will excuse me & I will endeavour to find out some other means of transfer hereafter.

I am
Dear Sir
Your Very Oblgd Servt
M. FARADAY

172 R. W. FOX[1] to M. FARADAY, 18 June 1834

[*I.E.E., previously unpublished*]

Eastwick Park
near Leatherhead,
18 6 mo, 1834[2]

DEAR FRIEND

I had the gratification of attending thy last lecture at the R. Institution when it was stated that Berzelius had referred the phenomena of flame & combustion to the evolution of electricity. This view of the subject I have entertained for many years, & mention'd it on various occasions, indeed I find on referring to a copy of a letter which I took the liberty of addressing to thee dated 24/ 11mo (Novr) 1827.[3] that I alluded to my opinions on this subject in the following words. – "Heat, Light, & electricity appear to have strong analogies & possibly a greater degree of identity than has been supposed" xxxxxxx "May not heat & light or else electricity, be combined with different kinds of matter in definite proportions, & be set free & neutralized (referring to the opposite polarities) in case of inflammation when matter also combines in definite quantities? When we consider the vast store of heat & light which may exist in chemical union, & also in a more mechanical state between the particles & interstices of matter as in mica, &c, for instance, perhaps the objections of the opinion of their materiality founded on friction, percussion &c are not valid." Thou wert so obliging as to acknowledge this letter on the 30 Nov.[4] I have hesitated to send thee the extract not being willing to intrude on thy valuable time, but I thought thou wouldst allow me to allude to my opinions on the subject which I have long entertained. But possibly Berzelius may have expressed these ideas before I did, was that the case?[5]

Very sincerely thine
R. W. Fox

By the enclosed paper it appears that Prony [reading doubtful] or Botto has produced decomposition by the agency of *thermo* electricity.[6] The paper belongs to Dr Hogdkin[7] & I will thank thee to return it to me at Barclay Brothers & Co 12 Austin Friars

[1] See Letter 162, fn. 3.
[2] Quaker notation for 18 June.
[3] I have not been able to discover this letter.
[4] I have not found this letter either.
[5] See Letter 162.
[6] See Giuseppi Domenico Botto (1791–1865), 'L'action chimique d'un courant thermo-électrique,' *BU*, 51 (1832), 337.
[7] Possibly Dr Thomas Hodgkin (1798–1866), after whom Hodgkins disease is named.

173   M. FARADAY to R. W. FOX, 20 June 1834
[*W. H. Browning, previously unpublished*[1]]

Royal Institution,
June 20, 1834

MY DEAR SIR,

I have but a faint recollection of your letter of Novr. 1827 most probably because I have been in the habit of supposing that the general views you refer to have long been as it were common property. Every one who has thought on the subject must have had some such notions on his mind but they all stand in the same level until by some fortunate occurrence or series of facts the one truth which is mixed up with the ninety and nine suppositions equally plausible to the general observer is taken from its fallacious companions and proved to be the only one deserving of attention.

Playfair[2] I think somewhere speaks of cohesion, affinity, heat, light, magnetism, electricity, galvanism, etc. and considers the probability of their all being referred to one common principle – Berzelius views are not twenty one years old. You will find some of them in the annals de chimie for 1813 tome LXXXVI.[3] page 146 and. especially p. 159 if my memory would serve me I could refer you to other authors: but I daresay you can feel with me how in the multiplicity of things one either forgets or remains ignorant of matters put forth to the world and which when one do come to their knowledge tend to prove there is nothing new under the sun.

Professor Botto's letter[4] I have had some time ago and in relation to that matter it proves just what I have been saying above for Becquerel in his new work Traite de l'electricite[5] tome 1. page 551 says that he obtained chemical and heating effects from thermo electricity *many years ago.*

I am

My dear Sir

Most truly yours,

M. FARADAY

[1] This letter was transcribed by Mr Browning, and not seen by the present editor.

[2] John Playfair, *Outlines of Natural Philosophy*, 2 vols., London, 1812–14.

[3] J. J. Berzelius, 'De l'influence de l'électricité sur les affinités,' *AC*, 86 (1813), 146.

[4] See Letter 172.

[5] Antoine César Becquerel, *Traité de l'Electricité et du Magnétisme*, (ultimately) 7 vols., Paris, 1834–40.

174 M. FARADAY to R. W. FOX, 23 July 1834

[W. H. Browning, previously unpublished[1]]

R.I.,

July 23, 1834

MY DEAR SIR,

I had great pleasure in receiving your letter as you will perceive by its drawing upon you an answer per post but I have such opinion of your good will to us that I do not think I shall annoy you although I have time to say but little.

I had two papers waiting for you when your letter came to me. They are both in Col. McInnes[2] hand and I hope you will like them. Two others are in the hands of the R. Society and I have one upon the stocks and there are four more in prospect – So I continue to work whether to purpose or not the scientific world will soon be able to judge.

I think more myself of the *Seventh Series* than of any other. In it I have determined and proved the *definite* action of *Electricity*. But as I have often seen other men mistake themselves so I have some fears until others shall have examined and admitted or refused my data and principles.

If I ever come your way I shall not for a moment doubt your kindness but make my appearance at once. But I see no prospect at present. In the meantime when your instrument[3] now at Mr. Watkins'[4] is complete will you let it stand upon our table some Friday evening for the transactions of our Members at the Meeting?

I am My dear Sir

Very truly Yours,

M. FARADAY

[1] This letter was transcribed by Mr Browning, and not seen by the present editor.

[2] I have been unable to identify Col. McInnes. There is a Col. MacInnis (1779–1859) who commanded the 73 N.I. from 1831 to 1842 and this might be the person to whom Faraday refers.

[3] Robert Were Fox, 'Notice of an instrument for ascertaining various properties of terrestrial

magnetism, and affording a permanent standard measure of its intensity in every latitude,'
PM, 3 s., 4 (1834), 81.
4 Possibly C. F. Watkins who published a paper on the Aurora of 1848, thus indicating his
interest in terrestrial magnetism. See *PRS*, 5 (1849), 809.

175 M. FARADAY to E. MAGRATH, 30 July 1834
    [*R. I., previously unpublished*]

> Mr. Turtles
> Pier Street
> Ryde
> Isle of Wight
> Sat. Evng 30 July 1834

DEAR MAGRATH

Here we are after some twists and turns and yet I doubt whether we shall
stop here more than a week. In a fortnight from this time I intend being at home
again My health is excellent my knee as I suppose it will be for a few months or
perhaps more. It limits my motions too much and I fear that it will increase my
tendency to follow your example i.e. to grow fat Who would have thought
20 years ago, or a little earlier in Dorset Street of ever seeing you & I in the
form of a couple of little fat paunchy men.

I have had a letter from my nephew James James [*sic*] Faraday[1] about the
Athenaeum Gas lighting Few things would please me more than to help my
brother in his business – or than to know that he had got the Athenaeum work,
but I am exceedingly jealous of myself lest I should endeavour to have that done
for him as my brother which the Committee might not like to do for him as a
tradesman, and it is this which makes me very shy of saying a word about the
matter If he had the business I believe he would do it well

> Ever My dear Magrath
> Yours
> M. FARADAY

[1] The son of Faraday's elder brother, Robert. Robert Faraday was a gas-fitter.

176 M. MELLONI[1] to M. FARADAY, 7 August 1834
    [*I.E.E., previously unpublished*]

> Paris,
> le 7. Aout 1834

MONSIEUR!

Je prends la liberté de vous adresser deux exemplaires de mes Memoires sur
la transmission immediate de la chaleur rayonnante par les corps solides et
liquides:[2] me pardonnerez-vous Monsieur si j'y ajoute la demande encore plus
hardie d'un rapport verbal de votre part à la Société Royale de Londres?

Mon ouvrage est une marchandise d'une qualité tellement inferieure que pour le faire accepter à vos savants Collegues il faut en hausser la valeur en l'associant en quelque sorte à l'eclat d'une illustration scientifique: or dans ce cas, comme dans beaucoup d'autres; il vaut mieux pêcher par excès que par défaut; voilà pourquoi je vous ai choisi, quoique privé de l'honneur de vous connaitre personnellement.

Mais puisque la necessité m'oblige à vous demander l'appui de votre nom, et que d'autre part si vous avez la bonté de me l'accorder il me restera un *excès de credit* près de ces Messieurs, je pense qu'il serait fort convenable de l'employer, dans mon interet, à me procurer une petite place de Correspondant de la Société. Il est vrai que je n'ai encore rien fait pour Elle, mais je tâcherai d'y suppléer par la suite si je suis assez heureux pour obtenir votre puissante intercession.

Ainsi tout depend de vous Monsieur. Acceptez de grace ma comission et mes excuses: ce sera une veritable *bonne oeuvre* dont vous recevrez la recompense dans l'autre monde car ici-bas, vous n'y gagnerez rien, absolument rien....[3] à moins que vous ne contiez [*sic*] pour quelque chose la reconnaissance bien vive et bien sincère de celui qui a l'honneur d'être

de vous Monsieur
le très humble et très obeissant servit[r]
MACEDOINE MELLONI

ancient [*sic*] prof.[r][4] de physique à l'Université de Parme, et resident provisoirement à Paris Rue Boucherat n° 2 (au marais)

[1] Macedonio Melloni (1798–1854), Neapolitan physicist, whose most important contributions were to the knowledge of radiant heat. His letters in French are signed Macedoine Melloni.

The letters from Faraday to Melloni have not survived, Melloni's papers being burned (along with many others) by the Germans in World War II when they prepared to evacuate Naples.

[2] M. Melloni, 'Mémoire sur la transmission libre de la chaleur rayonnante par différents corps solides et liquides,' *AC*, 2 s., 53 (1833), 5; 'Nouvelles recherches sur la transmission immédiate de la chaleur rayonnante par différents corps solides et liquides,' *ibid.*, 55 (1833), 337.

[3] The use of dots here does not mean that a passage has been omitted; it follows Melloni's usage. The complete letter is transcribed.

[4] Melloni participated in the Revolution of 1830 in Italy and later emigrated to Paris.

177 D. LARDNER to M. FARADAY, 5 October 1834

[*I.E.E., previously unpublished*]

Manchester
5 Octr 1834

MY DEAR SIR

If in making your friday evening arrangements for the ensuing season you should find nothing more attractive it would give me great pleasure to give you two subjects – 1. Comets – 2. The progress & prospects of locomotion – The latter I could illustrate by very beautiful models – the former by drawings – but I entreat that you may not postpone any other subject of greater interest than these for them – I have so much of public exertion that I assure you my appetite for it is more than satisfied and my object in offering this is merely to contribute even in a minor degree to the objects of the institution –

I have arranged the heads of a course of popular lectures which I think would prove highly interesting in as much as they would bring within the comprehension of unmathematical people a class of problems which elementary teachers have rarely ventured to grapple with – The subject is *the modern discoveries in astronomy* – among these would be comprised such questions as the true figure of the earth, the tides, the trade winds, the weights and densities of the planets, the periodic and secular inequalities of the system – and in a word most of the remarkable consequences of the principle of gravitation as manifested in our system – Also the stellar & nebular discoveries effected by the modern improvements in space-penetrating power – I can conceive nothing more interesting or attractive nor (in a popular form) more novel –

If your committee should at any time want to *fill a gap*, I should be happy to endeavour to supply it by such a course –

Do not put me down for the fridays till after the 1st March as I shall be absent from London – but meanwhile letters addressed to 8 St James Square will reach me.

Ever yours truly
DION: LARDNER

178 M. MELLONI to M. FARADAY, 16 October 1834

[*I.E.E., previously unpublished*]

Paris, 16 Octobre 1834.
Rue Boucherat n° 2

MONSIEUR

Je commencerai par vous demander mille excuses si je ne vous ai pas repondu immediatement: je vous remercierai ensuite de votre charmante lettre et de toutes les choses obligeantes qu'elle contient à mon egard.

Les demandes que je faisais relativement à la Société Royale de Londres, etant necessairement conditionnelles, j'espere Monsieur que vous voudrez bien *me les passer* attendu mon ignorance complete des reglements de cette Societé. C'est deja beaucoup pour moi d'avoir obtenu votre bienveillance, et si le projet que vous m'annoncez à la fin de votre lettre se realise, je serai au comble de mes voeux –

Les experiences que j'ai faites sur la transmission immediate de la chaleur rayonnante sont extrêmement faciles à repeter: elles ne manquent jamais lorsqu'on possede un bon thermo-multiplicateur: mais cet appareil presente plusieurs difficultés de construction qui ne peuvent être vaincues que par des essais multipliés. Ce serait un veritable sacrilege de pretendre que M Faraday employât son tems à de semblables travaux – Dans un [*sic*] autre epoque Monsieur, je vous aurai supplié d'accepter un de ces instruments et vous n'auriez pas été assez cruel pour me refuser; mais les suites de l'emigration m'ont privé de la possibilité de me donner une telle jouissance....et bien d'autres encore!... Je me trouve donc dans la triste necessité de ne pouvoir vous offrir que mes faibles services: c'est-à-dire que si vous le désirez, je surveillerai soigneusement à l'execution d'un appareil complet avec lequel vous pourrez repeter non seulement les experiences de transmission, mais toutes celles qu'il vous plaira de vérifier, ou d'entreprendre sur l'emission directe de la chaleur rayonnante, et le pouvoir reflecteur des corps. Mr Gourjon,[1] qui a confectionné plusieurs thermo multiplicateurs avec une rare perfection, se chargerait aussi du votre et des additions que je me propose d'y faire: la depense totale ne depasserait pas les 400 francs, et je suis presque certain, qu'en examinant les differents usages auxquels on peut l'employer, vous vous trouveriez content de votre acquisition....Mais peut être les rentes des etablissements, que vous dirigez si heureusement pour la diffusion et le progres des sciences, ont-elles deja reçu une autre destination. Alors Monsieur ne pourriez-vous pas engager dans cet achât quelque *amateur ?elé* et habitant de votre magnifique cité? Pardonnez-moi de grace une insistance qui pourrait même passer fort raisonnablement pour une belle et bonne indiscretion. Mais mettez-vous à ma place Monsieur. Eloigné de ma famille et de mon pays, n'ayant d'autre consolation que l'étude, le moindre pas que j'ai pu faire dans la carriere entreprise est devenu pour moi un evenement d'une certaine importance. Il y a bientôt deux ans que mes experiences ont été repetées ici en presence de plusieurs physiciens. M Arago, qui s'etait chargé volontairement d'en faire un rapport à l'Institut semblait plein d'enthousiasme – les belles promesses de sa part ne manquerent pas – elles continuent encore – mais, l'espoir est anéanti. Or si je desirais faire ressortir ma petite oeuvre en l'exposant à la lueur d'une étoile scientifique dont la lumière pâlit incontestablement depuis quelques années, il est bien naturel que je tâche de rassembler avec ardeur les moyens necessaires pour obtenir la clarté d'un astre qui brille dans tout son eclat! Je demande que la verité, *la seule verité,* paraisse sous un jour favorable; qui pourra me blâmer d'une telle intention?..

Agreez Monsieur les respectueux hommages de votre

très devoué et très obeissant serviteur
MACEDOINE MELLONI

¹ Scientific instrument maker at Paris.

179   R. J. KANE¹ to M. FARADAY, 28 October 1834
[*I.E.E., previously unpublished*]

Royal Dublin Society House
Kildare St
October 28 1834.

SIR.

When I had the honor of seeing you in Dublin,² you kindly gave me permission to refer to you, of which I now avail myself in consequence of the following circumstance.

In the Dublin Journal of Medical and Chemical Science, January 1833,³ I published a little paper showing that Ether might be considered as the oxide of a radicle composed of (4C+5H), Alcohol as its Hydrate, the Oxacid Ethers as Oxi-Salts, as Benzoic Ether etc and the Hydracid Ethers as Binary compounds of the Radicle viz Hydriodic Ether the iodide, etc. In the Annales de Chimie September 1833 there appeared a paper by Berzelius translated from Poggendorf's [*sic*] Annalen No 8 for 1833⁴ (consequently later than January) wherein he proposes exactly the same view except that he made Alcohol an oxide of a distinct radicle in place of an hydrate of Ether as I had proposed. In february 1834 a paper appeared in the Annales de Chimie from Liebig⁵ in which he adopted the idea of Ether being an oxide but differed from Berzelius as to the nature of Alcohol. He showed that Alcohol should be considered as an hydrate of Ether, thus bringing Berzelius hypothesis to a perfect coincidence with mine.

A few nights since, I read at the Royal Irish Academy, a notice of the above mentioned facts, I showed the three memoirs, and proved from a comparison of dates, the indubitable priority of mine. Although Berzelius brings forward the hypothesis as new and Liebig attributes to him originality in the idea of it, yet a member of the Academy has stated that the matter has been long familiar to Chemists "that the idea of Ether being an oxide of a radicle (4C+5H) was proposed long since & by many persons."⁶

Now it is curious, that if such were the case Berzelius and Liebig, should not have made any remark upon it, and that it should not have been remarked by the Editors of the Annales de Chimie, who must be supposed to be moderately well versed in Chemical Literature, and that in a careful examination of the French English and Some German Periodicals for the last few years, I should not have found any trace of the idea prior to the appearance of my own paper. The statement although totally unsupported by reference to any work in which the idea is contained, has had such influence as to demand a refutation.

Now as Berzelius and Liebig evidently consider the hypothesis as proposed by them to be original, and as I cannot find any trace of it in books, I am at a loss to know to what the Gentleman alluded. I shall therefore feel much obliged by your letting me know as soon as you have leisure whether you have heard of any person, prior to 1833, having proposed to consider Sulphuric Ether as an oxide of a radicle (4C+5H), Alcohol as its hydrate, Muriatic Ether as the Chloride of the same radicle, Oxalic ether as the oxalate etc. I am now trying to devise experiments by which the truth of the theory may be tested, but in the mean time, I am anxious to determine finally the priority of announcement.

I have latterly tried in every way I could think of to unite Arsenieuretted Hydrogen with Hydriodic Acid, to generate the body corresponding to the Hydriodate of Phosphoretted Hydrogen. I have not yet given up hopes of succeeding, although the frequent operations on that gas made me sick and I had to leave off for a time. At present I am employed galvanising the Hydriodate of Phosphoretted Hydrogen, a substance on which in consequence of its rapid decomposition by water even in the state of vapour in the air, it is very difficult to obtain accurate results.

You will have the goodness to let me know about the Ethers soon, and in the mean time I beg leave to subscribe myself

Your Obedient and
Humble Servant
ROBERT J. KANE

[1] Robert John Kane (1810–90), later Sir Robert, chemist.
[2] The *BAAS* met in Dublin in 1834.
[3] Robert John Kane, 'Miscellaneous contributions to chemical science,' *DJMCS*, 2 (1833), 345.
[4] J. J. Berzelius, 'Ueber die Constitution der organischen Atome,' *AP*, 104 (1833), 617; *AC*, 2 s., 54 (1833).
[5] J. Liebig, 'Mémoire sur la Composition de l'Ether et de ses Combinaisons,' *AC*, 2 s., 55 (1833).
[6] I am unable to locate the source of this quotation. From the context, it appears probable that the remark was made in conversation and does not occur in print.

180 W. WHEWELL to M. FARADAY, 3 December 1834

[Trinity College Library, Trinity College, Cambridge, NRRS, 16 (1961), 212]

Trin. Coll.
Cambridge,
Dec 3, 1834

MY DEAR SIR,

I contrived to get off for Cambridge by Sunday evening's mail, and so did not come to see your devices on Monday which I wanted very much to do; but engagements must be kept and lectures given at the appointed time; – a scientific work of which you have, I dare say, seen the value before this time. If I had seen you I wanted to say a word in connexion with what you intimated, that you did not like the word *ion* as a general term for the two elements the anion and the cation – or that your readers did not like it. You may recollect that at first I mentioned this as a term which I was not satisfied with. If you think it worth while to make the alteration, I would propose *stechion*, "element" as a general term which shall mean the anion and cation together. The Greek term (στοιχειον) is the proper word for "element", and occurs in our derivative stoicheometry, a word sometimes used in chemical literature; but the word *stechion*, the proper English form of it, is not used, and therefore you may introduce it in what sense you like – moreover the termination of stechion will especially harmonize with anion and cation which it is to put people in mind of, and so will keep them in their places.

Perhaps you will not think this suggestion of any importance. I do not say it is of much; but as it occurred to me I have sent it you – Many thanks for your eighth series –

Believe me
Yours truly,
W. WHEWELL

181 M. MELLONI to M. FARADAY, 27 December 1834

[I.E.E., previously unpublished]

Paris,
27 Decembre 1834

MONSIEUR!

Ma joie a été bien vive lorsque Mr Fioruzzi[1] m'a remis votre aimable lettre et le Memoire qui l'accompagnait: j'ai vu par là que loin de m'oublier vous aviez la bonté de vous interesser à moi bien au delà de tout ce que je pouvais esperer. La belle recompense dont vous me parlez aurait été pour moi d'un tres grand prix dans tous les tems, mais elle deviendrait d'une valeur immense après la conduite tant soit *peu charitable* que l'on a tenue ici à mon egard.

Je ne sais point quelles sont les conditions scientifiques qu'une decouverte doit remplir pour meriter la medaille de Rumford. Si vous croyez qu'il soit convenable de presenter dans un cadre tres reserré les principaux résultats de mes recherches, je dirai qu'il me semble n'avoir montré d'une maniere bien nette. 1° Le passage *immediat et instantané* de la chaleur rayonnante à travers les corps solides et liquides, phenomene qui n'etait pas encore generalement admis par les physiciens. 2° La difference qui existe entre *les deux transparences*, lumineuse et calorifique. 3° La transmission immediate du calorique rayonnant par des substances solides *completement opaques*. 4° L'existence d'une veritable *coloration calorifique* invisible dans les milieux diaphanes incolores. 5° *L'absorption egale* que les matieres colorantes continues dans les verres colorés (le vert excepté) exercent sur les rayons de chaleur qui parviennent à traverser la matiere vitreuse. 6° La refraction de la chaleur emanée des corps *chauffés par l'eau bouillante*. 7° *La transmission constante* à travers un corps solide de toutes sortes de chaleurs rayonnantes, depuis celle de la flamme la plus brillante jusqu'à l'émanation calorifique de la main. 8° *La non polarisation* des rayons calorifiques par leur transmission, à travers les plaques de tourmaline. Je me trompe fort, ou ces derniers resultats changent totalement les idées; que l'on s'etait formées sur la nature de l'agent qui produit les phénomènes du calorique rayonnant, d'aprés les observations de Berard,[3] Brewster[4] et De la roche.[5]

Mes experiences sur le changement de position du maximum de temperature dans le spectre (surtout les dernières dont un extrait est insere dans *l'Institut* du 17 Dec.[bre] cour.[t]) me paraissent etablir deux faits d'une grande importance pour l'analyse des rayons calorifiques solaires, savoir la transmission égale de ces differents rayons par le sel gemme, et leur absorption variable dans toute autre substance diaphane incolore.

Enfin je viens de terminer une serie de recherches sur les pouvoirs *emissif et absorbant* [*sic*] des surfaces. Elles m'ont conduit à des resultats fort curieux que je communiquerai bientôt à l'Academie des Sciences. Je crois qu'il est inutile de les definir car vous les releverez aisément à la simple inspection du tableau qui suit –

(Je ne vous confie pas ces resultats sous le secret, de maniere que vous pouvez en faire tel usage qu'il vous plaira.)

Presque toutes mes experiences *ont été repetées un tres grand nombre de fois* et en presence des physiciens les plus distingués de Paris et de plusieurs savants etrangers. M Forbes vient de les repeter aussi avec un plein succès à Edimbourgh et Mr Nobili à Florence (Voir l'opuscule intitulé *Descrizione di due nuove pile thermoelettriche e loro uso nelle ricerche calorifighe* [reading doubtful]). Si l'on exigeait une *espece de certificat* de la part de M Ampere, Arago, Biot ou Dulong, je me chargerai de vous l'envoyer sans delai.

Quelle que soit l'issue du debat qui se tiendra à mon egard entre vous et vos collegues de la Societé Royale, soyez bien certain Monsieur, que je vous serai

Surfaces couvertes de	*Pouvoir emissif* sous l'action de l'eau bouillante		*Pouvoir absorbant* sous l'action			
			d'une flamme d'huile	du platine incan-descent	du cuivre à 400° C.	du cuivre à 100° C.
Noir de fumée	100	:	100	100	100	100
Carbonate de plomb	100	:	53	56	89	100
Colle de poisson	91	:	52	54	64	91
Encre de chine	85	:	96	95	87	85
Gomme laque	72	:	43	47	70	72

toujours infiniment obligé de tant de bienveillance.... Daignez donc accepter l'expression des sentiments de la plus vive reconnaissance que vous offre avec une veritable effusion de coeur

votre tres humble et tres devoué serviteur
MACEDOINE MELLONI

1 Probably a fellow émigré from Italy.
2 See M. Melloni, 'Account of some recent experiments on radiant heat,' *BAASR* (1833), 381.
3 Jacques Etienne Bérard (1789–1869), 'Mémoire sur les propriétés des différentes espèces de rayons qu'on peut séparer au moyen du prisme de la lumière solaire,' *MSA*, 3 (1817), 1.
4 I am unable to identify the paper by Brewster to which Melloni here refers.
5 François Delaroche (1743–1812), 'Observations sur le calorique rayonnant,' *JP*, 75 (1812), 201.

182 M. FARADAY to J. BARROW, 13 January 1835
[*PRO, Adm. 1, 4613, Prom. Lett., previously unpublished*]

Royal Institution
13 Jany 1834[1]

DEAR SIR

By your direction I analysed twenty samples of oatmeal for the Admiralty in November 1832, for which I have a note against the Admiralty in my books of twenty guineas[2]

Perhaps I ought not to mention this to you; but rather make enquiry in the offices somewhere But I have thought once or twice that you sent them to me as one engaged by the Admiralty; being unaware that that engagement ceased long ago. Should such a mistake have occurred with you and the affair is therefore out of the usual order do not trouble yourself any further about it

I am Sir
Yours Very Truly
M. FARADAY

[Note at bottom] Bill paid

1 Really 1835.
2 See Letter 149.

183   D. LARDNER to M. FARADAY, 16 January 1835
[*I.E.E., previously unpublished*]

Paris,
16 Jany 1835

MY DEAR FARADAY.

In case you continue to desire that I should endeavour to give some sketch of the circumstances attending Halleys comet I should wish to do so if it be convenient to you on either the first or second friday in february I have however some fears that the subject will want novelty since there is a very able article on it in the companion to the British almanack for the present year from the pen I suspect of Lubbock.[1] If however notwithstanding this you think the matter will not have the flatness of a twice told tale I will do the best I can with it.

If you should decide to have it, there are one or two little matters which being previously prepared would greatly facilitate the explanation and as I shall most probably not arrive in London till a day or two before the time fixed for the lecture you will perhaps have the goodness to cause the things to be prepared by some one connected with the institution.

I enclose a paper describing what I think would be desirable – The little contrivance of circular & elliptic rings of wire will save a world of explanation and will indeed do what no explanation could equally well effect – I fear you will think the figures to be written on paper too long, yet I do not very well see how we can either dispense with or abridge them – Indeed in addition to them I shall want the use of rather a large black board –

If you thought that two evenings on comets would not be wearisome we might, with very interesting matter respecting Encke's comet, and the comet of 1770, the comet of 1680 (supposed to have been the proximate cause of the deluge &c) in addition to Halleys, occupy the two first fridays in feby. I could not at present undertake any friday evening except one or both of these because I am not certain when I shall be in town – I shall be obliged to leave town the third week of feby.

ever yours faithfully
DION: LARDNER

Any letter addressed to St James Square will be forwarded to me thro the embassy –

[1] Lubbock published a short article 'On the elements of the orbit of the comet of Halley in 1759,' in *PRS*, 3 (1835), 332, and this is probably why Lardner attributes the authorship of the anonymous article in the British Almanack to him.

184 D. LARDNER to M. FARADAY, 23 January 1835
[*I.E.E., previously unpublished*]

Paris –
23 Jany 1835

MY DEAR FARADAY.

I received yours of the 10th but had previously written to you. If you confine the comets to one evening let it be the 6th and say "*Notice of Halleys Comet*" – If you extend it to two evenings say – "*Notice of the most remarkable comets especially those whose return will take place in 1835*" –

The people here have made many and kind enquiries after you – Biot especially says he would give much to have you for a few hours with him. He thinks he has made an important discovery respecting the application of circular polarisation to chemical investigations[1] – He has also shewn me some very extraordinary experiments on radiant heat which throw Leslie's[2] altogether into the shade – I hope to exhibit them at the next meeting of the association[3] –

Immense improvements have been lately made in the observatory which Arago has shewn me and which, when the second circle is finished, will make it a more efficient thing than Greenwich –

I shall (D.V.) be in London on Monday 2nd Feby.

ever yours faithfully
DION: LARDNER

[1] J. B. Biot, 'Mémoire sur la polarisation circulaire et sur ses applications à la chimie organique,' *MAS*, 13 (1835 – but presented in 1832), 39.
[2] For John Leslie's papers on radiant heat, see *RSCSP*.
[3] Possibly contained in Biot's 'Rapport fait à l'Académie des Sciences sur les expériences de M. Melloni relatives à la chaleur rayonnante,' *MAS*, 14 (1838 – but presented in 1836), 433.

185 M. Melloni to M. Faraday, 4 February 1835

[*I.E.E., previously unpublished*][1]

Paris
le 4 Fevrier 1835.

Monsieur

Il y a dans la vie certains evenements qui causent une sensation trop vive pour pouvoir l'exprimer d'une maniere convenable: tel est l'effet qu'a produit sur moi votre noble conduite dans l'affaire de la Societe Royale.[2] Ici, je frequentais des Academiciens puissants qui ne cessaient de me prodiguer des paroles dorées; parmi eux il s'en trouvait quelques uns auxquels j'avois rendu des services, et plusieurs qui se disaient mes amis. Ces messieurs voyaient les obstacles que la malignité opposait à ma carriere scientifique; ils pouvaient les ecarter – je dirai plus – ils le devaient, car c'etait au jugement du Corps savant dont ils font partie que je soumettais le fruit de mes veillees et cependant, la justice que j'avais le droit d'attendre d'eux etait indefiniment prorogée dans la seule crainte d'user leur influence auprès des mechants. On ne pouvait nier en public des faits evidents et connus par la grande masse des philosophes independants; il fallait donc tâcher de les faire oublier par un Silence officiel: on risquait ainsi d'etouffer des germes qui pouvaient devenir feconds pour la Science, mais qu'importe – *Perisse la science et la justice plutôt que nos intérets!* voilà leur devise. Et vous Monsieur qui appartenez à une Societe à laquelle je n'avais rien offert, vous qui me connaissiez à peine de nom, vous n'avez pas demandé si j'avais des ennemis faibles ou puissants, ni calculé quel en etait le nombre; mais vous avez parlé pour l'opprimé etranger, pour celui qui n'avait pas le moindre droit à tant de bienveillance, et vos paroles ont été accueillies favorablement par des Collegues consciencieux! Je reconnais bien là des hommes dignes de leur noble mission, les veritable representants de la Science d'un pays libre et genereux. Ailleurs tout est egoisme ou deception.

Que mille et mille graces soient rendues en mon nom à Mr Faraday et au Conseil de la Societé Royale – je n'y saurais ajouter autre chose pour le moment, mais j'attends avec impatience l'occasion de montrer par des faits les sentiments ineffacables de reconnaissance qui sont profondément gravés dans le coeur de

votre tout devoue Serv. et ami
Macedoine Melloni

Paris ce 4 Fevrier 1835

P.S. Nous aurions besoin Mr Biot et moi de l'appareil de Mr Nicol[3] consistant en deux doubles prismes de spath d'Islande dont les pieces sont collées ensemble au baume de Canada: c'est le même appareil que vient d'employer Mr Talbot[4] dans ses experiences sur l'application de la lumiere polarisée à divers objets vus au microscope. Je vous serai bien obligé si vous vouliez avoir la complaisance

19   289   wsc

d'en acheter un pour notre compte et de l'envoyer à Mr Cardat Conservateur des archives de l'Institut R. de France à Paris (palais de l'Institut): je remettrai de suite la somme que vous aurez deboursée à Mr Pentland[5] ou à telle autre personne qu'il vous plaira de me désigner.

Je vous prierai en même tems de retirer la medaille que vous venez de me faire decerner, et de l'envoyer à la meme adresse.

[1] See *B.J.*, 2, 73, for a major portion of this letter.
[2] Melloni was awarded the Rumford Medal in 1834.
[3] William Nicol (1768–1851) was the inventor of the Nicol prism.
[4] William Henry Fox Talbot (1800–77), pioneer in photography. See his 'Experiments on Light,' *PM*, 3 s., 5 (1834), 321.
[5] Probably Joseph Barclay Pentland (1800–73) who had studied in Paris and was a frequent visitor there.

186   M. FARADAY to SIR J. RENNIE,[1] 26 February 1835
  [*R.I., previously unpublished*]

Royal Institution
26 Feby. 1835

DEAR SIR,

I am very much obliged to you for your kind invitation but am under the necessity of declining it because of a general rule which I may not depart from without offending many kind friends. – I never dine out except with our Presidents – the Duke of Sussex or the Duke of Somerset whose invitations I consider as commands. Under these circumstances I hope you will accept my obligations to you though I cannot accept your favour

I am
dear Sir,
Very Truly Yours
M. FARADAY.

[1] Sir John Rennie (1794–1874), engineer, constructed London Bridge which opened in 1831.

187   M. MELLONI to M. FARADAY, 6 March 1835
  [*I.E.E., previously unpublished*]

Paris
6 Mars 1835

MONSIEUR

J'apprends par votre derniere que l'on vous a consigné les medailles de Rumford,[1] et que vous voudriez savoir quelle serait la voie la plus convenable de me les faire parvenir. Toutes les voies sont bonnes mon cher Monsieur, pourvu que les personnes auxquelles vous aurez la bonté de les adresser soient bien connues de vous ou de moi. Je vous avais indiqué M Cardat ou M Pentland comme appartenant à cette derniere categorie; mais il est entendu que vous pouvez employer tel autre individu qui vous semblera apte à remplir cette commission. Quant au tems vous devinerez sans doute que je serai bien aise de les avoir le plutôt possible: il en est de même de la piece d'optique: mais il importe peu que les deux objets arrivent ensemble, ou separément.

J'ai fait votre commission à Mr Biot qui vous remercie beaucoup de votre souvenir, et me charge de vous dire qu'il va bientôt étudier à fond vos beaux phenomenes d'induction electrique en compagnie de M Poisson[2] qui parait avoir l'intention d'en faire l'objet d'un travail mathematique. Il ne l'a pas fait plutôt parceque, attendu la haute importance du sujet, il sentait la necessité de s'y livrer avec beaucoup de suite, et que le tems lui a manqué jusqu'ici. Il vous prie en même tems de l'informer lui et M. Biot s'il est a votre connaissance que quelques uns de vos compatriotes se soient encore occupés de ses applications de la polarisation circulaire aux phenomenes chimiques, travail dont il vous envoya le premier Memoire dans le tems par Mad^{me} de Sommerville, et qui a été complété depuis par plusieurs autres Memoires inserés dans differents journaux et notamment dans les Annales du Museum d'Histoire Naturelle.[3] Dans le cas de l'affirmative il croirait de son devoir (je me sers de ses propres expressions) d'entrer en communication avec ces Observateurs, et de les aider à vaincre les obstacles qu'ils pourraient avoir rencontrés dans cette nouvelle branche de la Science.

Quant à moi Monsieur, je ne puis que vous remercier de la peine que vous vous êtes donnée de repeter mes dernieres experiences à l'*Institution Royale*;[4] et puisque vous prenez tant d'intêret dans ce qui me regarde, je me fais un veritable plaisir de vous annoncer que MM Biot, Poisson, et Arago ont examine mes resultats dans le plus grand détail; qu'ils en sont *enthousiasmés* et que le premier va bientôt en faire en leur nom un rapport extremement favorable à l'Institut. Pour cette fois la chose est certaine: deja comme [illeg.] le Ministre de l'Instruction Publique m'a accordé une somme de 1200 francs à leur sollicitation. . . . . Je dois de la reconnaissance à ces Messieurs, et j'en aurais. . . . . Mais l'opposition scientifique francaise et mes compatriotes observent que tout cela arrive après le prix de la Societe Royale; et moi, je ne puis m'empécher de reflechir que la Societé Royale n'aurait pas pense à me decerner cette recompense sans vos soins et votre amitié. . . . . Vous voyez donc que je vous dois tout. . . . Aussi mon coeur est-il profondément emu toutes les fois que je me declare

votre tres devoué et tres reconnaissant
MACEDOINE MELLONI

Rue Boucherat n° 2
(au marais)

[1] See Letter 181.

[2] Simeon Denis Poisson (1781–1840), theoretical physicist with whom Faraday disagreed on the nature of electricity. See *LPW*, 284.

[3] For these papers, see *RSCSP*.

[4] On 23 January 1835, Faraday delivered a lecture at the Royal Institution 'On Melloni's recent discoveries in radiant heat.' The manuscript notes for this lecture are at the Royal Institution.

188   M. FARADAY to I. KINGDOM BRUNEL, 4 May 1835

[*Burndy Library, Norwalk, Conn., previously unpublished*]

R Institution
4 May 1835

MY DEAR SIR

I return you the wire suspenders, the Report,[1] &c &c with many thanks for your kindness.

I do not know of such a master as you require. – Probably Barlow can tell you of such a one

I have not read his report through nor should I probably be able to understand all the argument. I happened to open it at random at page 90 & have just scored a consequence there which I don't understand Whilst the one wheel *is falling* surely the weight it before carried is not supported by the other, if so supported, the first wheel *would not fall*: how then can the *whole weight* be considered as supported by *one rail only* for that time

After all I sometimes feel glad that I am not a mathematician for though Mathematical science is sure, I do not find that the conclusions of its professors can be trusted much more than those of other Professors – &c &c &c

Ever Dear Sir
Very Truly Yours
M. FARADAY

Why dont you date your letters from your office or at least from some place – it would very much relieve such bad memories as mine –

M.F.

[1] Peter Barlow, *Second Report Addressed to the Directors and Proprietors of the London and Birmingham Railway, founded on an inspection of, and experiments made on, the Liverpool and Manchester Railway*, London, 1835.

189   W. WHEWELL to M. FARADAY, 9 September 1835
[*Trinity College Library, Trinity College, Cambridge, previously unpublished*]

Trin. Coll.,
Cambridge,
Sept. 9, 1835

MY DEAR SIR

I have been reading your ninth series of "Researches"[1] with the strongest interest, as I read all of them, and especially those which relate to your "Induction." I have a wish to ask a question or two which I dare say you will be good-natured enough to accept as an excuse for my troubling you. In Art. 1077, you say that the supposition of *momentum* or *inertia* is at once set aside by your expts. (1069) and (1089) Now will you allow that there is any force in the following remarks on this? I do not think that it follows that the effects on breaking contact are not produced by inertia, because they are modified by the effect of the wire on itself. Such an effect may alter the distribution of the fluid, so as to affect even its mechanical properties. The mechanical effect of the impulse of the same quantity of water in a water-course will be different when it flows smoothly and when it runs in waves. Then as to (1089) it appears to me to comprise the notion of momentum. When the contact is broken the momentum of the long wire current overpowers that of the shorter one and turns it back. Does not this represent the fact?

I have been strongly impressed with the notion of the inertia of the electro-dynamic current, ever since I read your first series of researches. I state it thus. "A substance when put in motion by another substance, produces, at the *first instant*, an impulse *opposite* to that of the motion; if the velocity be uniform, *no* further *effect* is perceived till the motion is stopped; and at *that instant*, an impulse is produced *in the direction of the motion*." Now this description is a full and exact account of the laws, alike, of electrical currents and mechanical collision. How then can I help identifying the two cases?

I will also take the liberty of making a remark on phraseology, which you know I am used to do. In your first researches you spoke of *volta-induction*, a term which you have since not used. You then employed the term *magneto-electric induction*, which you still, I think, retain. It appears to me that as Ampere did well to introduce the word *electrodynamic* action, to include electro-magnetic, voltaic, and magnetic, after he had shown that the three are identical, so you ought to use a term of like extent for the like reason and call your induction *electrodynamic* induction.

But I have something more to say of the same kind. The facts which occur at making or breaking contact are *not* induction, if induction means, as by analogy it should mean, the condition produced by the neighbourhood of an electric circuit. These facts mark the *beginning* and *end* of induction. Whether

293

there is a permanent condition produced by a neighbouring circuit or not, this class of facts has no right to the name. But allowing the analogy of mechanical action to obtain in the action of electrodynamic wires (I have shown above how strong the analogy is) we see clearly what these facts of instantaneous action are. They are the *reaction* of the current in which motion is produced by induction. You have yourself so called them (1114) You say "a current sustains a state which when allowed to *react*, at the cessation of the original current, produces a second current." I think therefore that in consistence with your own views, all the facts produced by the beginning and end of electrodynamical proximity should be ascribed to *electrodynamical reaction.*

I have always admired how you contrived to get (114) so soon at the very difficult law which governs the direction of an electrodynamical current produced by motion. But I have also wondered, that accepting Ampere's theory, as I think you do, you have never expressed that law and some other of your results, in terms of his theory: but have, on the contrary, determined everything by reference to magnetical directions and curves which according to him are derivative elements. I mention this because I have found that it gave me some trouble to refer your results to his theory.

According to his theory the *convertibility* of electricity and magnetism, of which you speak (1114) as a problematical point, is a fundamental fact. And it seems to me that taking his theory, and supposing the electric fluid to have inertia, the only point in this part of the subject, which remains obscure, is the law of electrodynamic induction properly so called, that is the force by which a current produces a current in a neighbouring substance, whether a current be a vibration, a strain, or anything else.

I shall be glad if you have time to give me any light as to your views on these points. I consider the train of discovery in which you are engaged as so great a thing for us and for posterity that I cannot help wishing to understand the progress of it as clearly as possible. Believe me, my dear Sir, Yours very truly

W. WHEWELL

¹ 'On the influence by induction of an electric current on itself: and on the inductive action of electric currents generally.'

190 M. FARADAY to W. WHEWELL, 19 September 1835
[Trinity College Library, Trinity College, Cambridge, previously unpublished]

Royal Institution
19 Sept ͬ 1835

MY DEAR SIR

Your letter was quite refreshing for I had begun to imagine that I thought more about Electricity and Magnetism than it was worth: and so a notion was creeping over me that after all I was perhaps only a *bore* to my friends by the succession of papers I was bold to send forth, and not that successful labourer for science which I was striving to be. Perhaps you will think so too when I tell you I have the tenth series in print and waiting to reach you; but whatever you may think I am resolved to take your last letter as encouragement to go on.

Your remarks on my phraseology I am quite willing to admit; but let me remind you that I and Ampere use words, i.e. names, in very different ways. My words *Volta-induction – magneto-electric-induction – magneto-electricity – electro-magnetism etc.* are merely intended to indicate how the effects included under them are obtained whereas Ampere by the word "*Electro-dynamic*" essentially implies a theory which theory may be wrong. The origin of all these effects may be something in such a state that when we come to know what it is the word *electrodynamic* may not apply. Perhaps I may be equally wrong, nay more so by far, in the word induction but at all events the prefixes, *Volta*, *magneto*, *magneto electric*, *electro magnetic*, pledge me to no theory, and yet have a certain distinctness of sense which makes them useful. Besides Amperes term, however good it may be, is so general that we must have words as heads of the several divisions into which the great branch of Electrodynamic science practically divides itself, and it is in that way rather than any other I would wish to use mine though I am probably not always consistent with myself

I ought to say that I accept Amperes theory as the best present representation of facts, but that still I hold it with a little reserve. This reserve is more a general feeling than any thing founded on distinct objections to it. Remember I am no Mathematician. If I were one and could go into a closer examination of the theory than is at present possible for me I might have no doubts left; but all my mathematics consist in that rough natural portion of geometry which every body has more or less. Hence the reason why I have never put my facts into terms of Amperes theory; and why I cling to the relations of Magnetic & Electric forces as the simplest I can perceive; these again are readily distinguished in practise and hence the most convenient if not the best for an experimentalist to refer to. I wish most sincerely some mathematician would think it worth his while to do that for the facts which I can not do for them

With regard to your remarks on momentum I can see great force in them. In thinking of momentum I had considered the analogy of a fluid, elastic or not, moving in a tube and acting in proportion to its mass, velocity *etc.* on obstacles in the tube or at least in the current. Perhaps if I could see the true relation of the currents in the phenomena which I have called phenomena of *Volta-induction*, and which relation I think *you say is obscure* I might admit that the idea of momentum is not opposed to the facts or even that it accurately explained them: of course the conclusion at (1077) would, being unfounded, fall to the ground. At present however I feel the difficulty as I did before. Why for instance in the experiment (1090) should the action be transferred from the wire carrying the original current to the neighbouring wire if it be an effect of momentum? The second wire is carrying no current during the time that the electricity is moving through the first, why then on stopping the current in that first wire does not its effect of momentum appear in it also? I am aware however we might talk this matter on a great distance in conversation though hardly by letter

With respect to *induction* remember that when I first used the term I believed that the neighbouring wire assumed & retained a peculiar state (called the *electrotonic state*) as long as the original current was continued (60. 67); and considered the two currents produced only as the particular conditions belonging to the commencement & conclusion of this state. Considered as parts of that induced state I think they might then fairly be called phenomena of *induction*. I have given up this electrotonic state for the time (242) as an experimental result (remember my researches are EXPERIMENTAL) because I could find no fact to prove it but I cling to it in fancy or hypothesis (242. 1114) from general impressions produced by the whole series of results You on the contrary seem to me not merely to admit it but contend for it. You say "a substance when put in motion by another substance produces at the *first instant* an impulse *opposite* to that of the motion; if the velocity be uniform *no* further *effect* is perceived till the motion is stopped and at *that instant* an impulse is produced *in the direction of the motion*" and you say "this is a full & exact account of the laws alike of electrical currents and mechanical collision"; then afterwards you add "we see clearly what these facts of instantaneous action are. They are the reaction of the current in which motion is produced by *induction etc.*" Now if this second current had had an existence during the time that the first current was continued I could have better conceived the notion of momentum As the second instantaneous current does not exist I take it for granted you assume the electrotonic (60) or peculiar (1114) state; but still that will justify the application of the word induction to it either at its beginning its continuance or its termination. Now is it not possible that this state may be a condition accounting for the phenomena on some other principle than that of momentum merely? It is just my ignorance of these things and my inability to view the effects as a mathematician that makes me speak with doubt & hesitation & it may be in great error, but it is the only reason, or rather excuse, I have to offer. I feel that my safety consists in facts; and even these I am but too anxious to pervert through the influence of preconceived notions. To you therefore & such as you I must look for help & assistance and nothing would delight me more than the idea of having, however accidentally or humbly, been the means of setting you of [*sic*] in pursuit of the important object before us

> Ever My dear Sir Most Truly Yours
> M. Faraday

[*R.I., previously unpublished*]

Trinity College,
Cambridge.
Sept. 25. 1835

MY DEAR SIR

I am much obliged by your answer of my enquiries. I should like much to talk over some of them with you and may perhaps have an opportunity of doing so as I expect to be in London for a day or two in the beginning of October; and I will defer to some such opportunity anything more which I have to say on the subject. I feel however we shall probably differ very little for the remarks you make upon my suggestions agree very nearly with my own. The difficulties which you point out as belonging to the opinions which I stated had occurred to me, and it is a matter of great satisfaction to me to find that we look at the matter so nearly in the same point of view. I still think that some of them may be got over; but I am puzzled how to conceive the condition of a magnetic body so that the hypothetical electrodynamic currents which circulate round its particles according to Ampere's theory, shall be absolutely identical with voltaic currents; till this is done, the attempt to identify the circumstances under which the two kinds of currents begin and stop can hardly be successful.

I can hardly conceive how you can even for a moment doubt about the immense scientific importance of your electromagnetic researches. I have all along considered them as the greatest event which ever happened in the history of chemistry. It has for some time been clear that the capital point of chemical theory is the connexion between electrical relation and chemical composition; and you have now got so far as to obtain a numerical measure of the former relation; and some facts belonging to its connexion with the numerical laws of composition. It cannot be doubted therefore that you have made great steps towards the solution of the grand problem; and my own persuasion is that you have before you still greater discoveries than you have yet made. In this point of view I consider Ampere's theory, beautiful as it is, and I think well established, as only a small part of your magnificent subject. Believe me my dear sir

Yours very sincerely
W. WHEWELL

192   M. FARADAY to ADMIRALTY, 27 November 1835
[*PRO, Adm. 1, 4613, Prom. Lett., previously unpublished*]

27 Nov.ʳ 1835

Note of Experiments which should be tried relative to Kyan's process[1]

Wood of large dimensions dipped & left whole
Do ——————————————— cut into planks
Wood of moderate dimensions dipped & left whole
Planks dipped the usual time
Planks dipped & immediately taken out
Planks (dry) washed over with a brush
Larger wood (dry)   Do————————

Of these some put into test situations with corresponding unprepared wood (off the same pieces) put with them – Others placed in ordinary situations with corresponding unprepared wood

The experiments to be made on Oak Elm & Fir – and also upon fresh or green wood

An account of the sizes; – the strength & quantity of liquor; – the time of immersion; – the time of experiment; – the situation where placed etc to be taken in a careful manner and every thing provided so as to give true and impartial results of the goodness or inutility of the process; – and if good the comparative degree of durability which it may confer

M. FARADAY

[1] John Howard Kyan (1775–1850) had devised a process for preserving wood from rotting.

193   G. B. AIRY[1] to M. FARADAY, 2 December 1835
[*I.E.E., previously unpublished*]

30. Woburn Place,
1835 Dec 2

MY DEAR SIR

It is not improbable that some steps may be taken before long for the establishment of regular magnetic observations at the Royal Observatory. And it seems desirable that large bars (similar to those used on the Continent generally) should be used,[2] and that these bars should be powerfully magnetized. Now I wish to learn from you – whether there are not at the Royal Institution powerful horse-shoe magnets which could be advantageously employed for magnetizing such bars – and whether on my application these magnets could be lent to the instrument-maker who might be employed for the construction of the apparatus for the Royal Observatory.

I wish also to learn from you (as a matter of science as well as of practice) whether, supposing a horse-shoe bar of soft iron rendered *pro tempore* intensely magnetic by helices of a galvanic current (connected with the battery &c by flexible wires), such a temporary magnet might not be used to give strong permanent magnetism to a hard steel bar: and in that case, whether any of the apparatus of the Royal Institution could be placed under our management for this purpose.

> I am dear Sir
> Very truly yours
> G. B. AIRY

¹ George Biddell Airy (1801–92) became Astronomer Royal in June of 1835.
² These bars had been introduced by Gauss and W. Weber in their magnetic observatory at Göttingen.

194   W. WHEWELL to M. FARADAY, 11 December 1835
[*Trinity College Library, Trinity College, Cambridge, previously unpublished*]

> Trin. Coll.,
> Cambridge,
> Dec. 11, 1835

MY DEAR SIR,

I think I told you that I was a little dissatisfied with the word *cation* from its resemblance to the common termination of words which is made into *cayshun* in pronunciation. To avoid this I would recommend putting two dots over the i, *catïon*. You might also write *anïon* and *ïon* in the same way, but there is not the same reason for this, though it would prevent your German translators from making your *ïons* into *jons* as they do in Poggendorf [*sic*]. I am desirous your terms should be as unexceptionable as possible because you say you intend to use them freely, and it is easy to see how important are the purposes to which you and your successors will have to apply these terms.

I will mention a notion which has been suggested to me by your experiments and you shall judge if there is anything in it. You show (891, 904, 910) that *electrolysis* is the result of the superior action in the exciting over that in the decomposing cell. You also show (993 *etc.*) that decomposing power increases with the number of exciting cells – of course I suppose the resistance to decomposition might be increased by increasing the number of decomposing cells – If this could be done might we not take such a number of exciting and such a number of decomposing cells that the decomposing force was exactly balanced by the resistance and thus find the ratio of the forces. Thus if 5 cells of iodide of potassium resisting 2 cells of sulphuric acid were not decomposed while 4 cells of the iodide are decomposed, the ratio of the voltaic forces is between 5:2 and 4:2.

299

I am more solicitous to hear of some connection being traced between voltaic action and crystalline structure or crystallising activity, the more I think of it. Crystalline forces are *polar* in their own way, and must, it would seem, be connected with your polar chemical forces.

I trust to your good nature for excusing my troubling you thus and am always,

Very sincerely yours,
W. WHEWELL

Will you allow me to make a request to you? I have all your "Series" of Researches from the 4th to the 10th inclusive: but I have not 1, 2, 3 If you can spare copies of them I should be much gratified by having them from you, as I shall bind you up, when the time comes, in a suitable manner.

195   J. PLATEAU to M. FARADAY, 8 January 1836
[*I.E.E., previously unpublished*]

Bruxelles
le 8 Janvier 1836

MONSIEUR

Je prends la liberté de vous offrir un exemplaire d'un instrument de mon invention,[1] qui se publie maintenant et qui est une conséquence des phénomenes que nous avons étudiés chacun de notre côté. Il y a long temps que j'ai imaginé ce genre d'anamorphoses, et vous vous rappellerez peut-être en avoir vu la premiere idée dans ma Dissertation sur quelques propriétés des impressions & imprimée en 1829;[2] j'y suis revenu depuis à plusieurs reprises dans la correspondance de Mr Quetelet &c.; enfin je me suis déterminé à mettre au jour l'instrument lui-même. Je désire infiniment, Monsieur, que cette bagatelle puisse vous causer quelque plaisir, et je regrette beaucoup que les circonstances qui m'ont empeché jusqu'à présent de mettre à exécution mon projet de voyage en Angleterre ne me permettent pas d'aller vous la présenter moi-même.

Je saisis cette occasion, Monsieur, pour vous remercier des exemplaires de vos belles recherches sur l'électricité que vous avez eu la bonté de m'envoyer. Ces exemplaires me sont bien précieux, offerts par l'homme qui a fait faire de si grands pas à la science des rapports entre le magnétisme et l'Electricité.

S'il vous arrive quelquefois de penser à moi, vous devez me trouver bien paresseux; mais outre la faiblesse de ma santé qui ne me permet pas de travailler autant que je le voudrais, je puis encore apporter pour excuse, que si j'ai publié peu de chose j'ai rassemblé des materiaux; que je travaille maintenant à la seconde section de mon mémoire sur les apparences visuelles &c.; et que j'ai en tête trois autres mémoires sur des sujets relatifs à la vision.

Agreez, Monsieur, l'assurance de la haute considération avec laquelle j'ai l'honneur d'être

> Votre tout dévoué Serviteur
> J^H PLATEAU

T.S.V.P.

P.S. Mr Quetelet me charge de vous faire ses compliments et de vous remercier de l'envoi de vos mémoires.

S'il arrivait quelque dérangement à l'instrument pendant le trajet, ce qui, j'espere n'aura pas lieu si ce n'est peut-être quant à la tension des cordons, j'espere que vous voudrez bien ne juger l'instrument qu'après l'avoir fait remettre en bon état. vous trouverez au fond de la boîte une explication sur la manière de se servir de l'appareil.

[1] Joseph Plateau, 'Sur l'anorthoscope,' *BASB*, 3 (1836), 7. See Letter 143.
[2] See Letter 144, fn. 5.

196 M. FARADAY to W. WHEWELL, 9 January 1836
[*Trinity College Library, Trinity College, Cambridge, previously unpublished*]

> Royal Institution
> 9. Jany 1836

MY DEAR SIR

You will think me long answering your letter but the fact is I hoped to find, what I have not & what I cannot find, a copy of the 1, 2, & 3 series – I have some left but my own which are in constant use. If I can hereafter pick them up you shall have them

Your information about the terms I shall at once make use of. I have been a little reserved about using them myself but I find others are employing them and as they thus approve I shall be decided for the future Perhaps you remember I gave the name of Volta-electrometer to the instrument I used in determining the definite action This Becquerel has translated *Electrometre de Volta* –[1] Daniell advises calling it *Voltameter* which sounds shorter & well; is there any objection?

With respect to the balancing of exciting & decomposing forces in different cells, I once thought to obtain very simple & important results of that kind – in 1007, &c. but was stopped by finding the variations in intensity or in resistance did not follow any evident simple ratio but apparently some more complicated law. – and also by the many interfering causes from change in the state of the plates &c. I have no doubt the subject is a good one but there is much to be cleared away in approaching it

I quite agree with you about the importance of the relation of crystalline &

chemical polarity – but do not pretend to know any thing about it at present though I suspect that it will all burst forth in its true simplicity and beauty some day shortly to some one of those who now think the subject worth considering.

Ever My dear Sir
Most Truly Yours
M. FARADAY

[1] For Becquerel's discussion of Faraday's electrochemical theory see A. C. Becquerel, *Traité expérimental de l'électricité et du magnétisme et de leurs rapports avec les phénomènes naturels*, 8 vols., Paris, 1834–40, 3 (1835), 379ff.

197 J. HERBERT to M. FARADAY, 5 February 1836
[*R.S., previously unpublished*]

Trinity House,
London,
5*th* February 1836

SIR,

At the Court of this Corporation held yesterday, the Deputy Master stated the substance of the communications which have recently taken place between yourself and him –[1] And I have great satisfaction in acquainting you, that it was unanimously Resolved to appoint you, "Scientific adviser to this Corporation in experiments on Light." at a Salary of £ 200 p. annum. –

I have the honor to be,
Sir,
Your very obedient Servant,
J. HERBERT, *Secy.*

[1] Trinity House was hit by a bomb during World War II and burned. Faraday's reports and letters during the tenure of his position as scientific adviser (he resigned in 1865) were destroyed. See *B.J.*, 2, 90 for some of the negotiations here referred to.

198 [Illeg. signature] to M. FARADAY, 15 February 1836
[*R.S., previously unpublished*]

Downing Street,
February 15, 1836.

SIR

In order to carry into full effect the intentions of His Majesty as communicated in His Gracious answer to an Address of the House of Commons on the subject of the Grant of Academical degrees in the Metropolis, the Government have it in contemplation to incorporate by Charter a central board under the title of the Royal University of London. To this body will be entrusted the duty of examining persons duly qualified by Education at the London University College, King's College, and such other Establishments as may from time to time be named by the Crown, & of granting to such persons as may appear duly qualified, Degrees in Arts, Law, & Medicine.

His Majesty's Government are extremely desirous that the persons named in this Royal Charter should be such as to give to the public the fullest security for the effectual & impartial discharge of these new & most important duties, & it will be peculiarly gratifying to me if I am permitted to submit your name to my Colleagues as one of those who we may be enabled to recommend to the Crown as willing to undertake this important & most honourable trust. The duties will be confined to the period of the examination only, and, therefore, will not require any very considerable portion of your time, on which I am aware there are many other claims.

But when it is considered how great is the object to be attained in giving a useful direction as well as affording new encouragement to the intellectual improvement of a numerous Class of the King's Subjects, who without any distinction or exclusion whatever will be admitted under the proposed system to the honor of Academical Degrees, I think that you might be induced to give to the Government your zealous & valuable co-operation.

> I have the honor to be
> Sir
> Your very obt. humble etc,

199 C. Matteucci[1] to M. Faraday, 30 May 1836
[*I.E.E., previously unpublished*]

Florence,
30 mai 1836

Mon cher Monsieur

Je m'empresse de vous faire bien des remercimens de la bonte que vous avez eue de repondre à ma derniere lettre. Personne, Monsieur, est [reading doubtful] plus qui moi convaincu de la date anterieure de votre grande decouverte sur la force decomposante du courant electrique, et vous pouvez regarder cette lettre comme la declaration la plus solennelle. Ce qui m'importe surtout c'est que vous soyez convaincu que la prémiere notice qu'on a eu de celà en Italie, est due a un Numero d'Octobre de l'Institut 1834, à la quelle époque était dejá redigée mon pètit memoire pour les Annales, et j'en avais ecrit aussi à Mr DelaRive[2] — Du reste il y a dans ma petite notice quelque chose qui ne regarde pas cette loi.

Je tiens, Monsieur, a vous persuader que je me croirai l'homme le plus stupide et le plus [illeg.] en publiant ce qui ne m'appartient pas — Je tiens donc seulement à donner une certaine publicité à mes sentimens, et plus que tout autre chose j'aime que vous en soyez convaincu. Je ne connais Mr Poggendorf [*sic*] et je ne connais de quelle maniere, lui proferer cette déclaration. – Permettez encore, Monsieur, que je vous donne une nouvelle demonstration du respect et de la confiance que j'ai en vous. De profonds malheurs domestiques m'obligent a quitter mon Pays. l'occasion est propice et vous pouvez bien m'aider, et je vous prie de ne pas retarder un instant a le faire. Il s'agit de nommer a Corfou, des professeurs Italiens des Sciences Physiques, Chimie ect. [*sic*] Certainement soit par des relations personelles, soit directement vous pouvez avoir de l'influence pour ces élections. Je vous prie de l'employer a mon avantage et le plus tot que vous pourrez – Soit de chimie ou de Physique, mais c'est indiferent. Une lecon n'est pas une découverte.

Agreez, Monsieur, mes remerciemens d'avance, excusez, et croyez moi

C. MATTEUCCI

P.S. Avec l'appareil de M. Jenkin[3] que vous avez si bien etudie, j'ai obtenu, l'etincelle de la torpille, et l'obtiens toujours. –

[1] Carlo Matteucci (1811–68), student of electro-physiology.
[2] See his 'Sur la force électro-chimique de la pile,' *BU*, 58 (1835), 23, and *AC*, 2 s., 58 (1835), 75. The point at issue is Faraday's first law of electrolysis.
[3] See the Ninth Series of *ERE*.

200 F. ARAGO to M. FARADAY, 4 July 1836
     [*Catalogue Charavay, Paris, previously unpublished*]

[Postmarked 4 juillet 1836]

MON CHER CONFRÈRE,

La personne qui vous remettra ces quelques lignes, Mr Le Play,[1] est un ingénieur des mines de beaucoup de mérite que notre gouvernement envoie en Angleterre pour étudier Vos usines à fer et Vos mines de charbon de terre. Veuillez lui procurer quelques lettres de recommandation. Mr Le Play a droit à tout votre intérêt par son zèle, par ses connaissances et comme une des victimes de la Science; la blessure qu'il a reçue aux mains en faisant une opération chimique est une des plus cruelles dont les annales scientifiques aient conservé le souvenir.

Mr Le Play vous dira comment je me suis servi de votre nom à la chambre des Deputés, pour empêcher qu'on n'enlevât à Mr Gay-Lussac la place qu'il remplit auprès de notre comité d'artillerie.[2] Je me flatte que cette citation ne vous déplaira pas.

Agréez mon cher confrère, la nouvelle expression de mon bien sincère attachement

F. ARAGO

¹ Pierre Guillaume Frederic Le Play (1806–82), engineer and economist.
² See *Le Moniteur Universel*, IIIe supplément au No. 160, du mercredi 8 juin 1836, 1349, 2nd column.

Arago concluded his remarks on the importance of retaining Gay-Lussac as consulting chemist for the French artillery with the words:

'Je dirai seulement en terminant que, guidé par les idées que je viens de soumettre à la chambre, le gouvernement anglais vient d'attacher à son artillerie le plus illustre chimiste de la Grande-Bretagne, M. Faraday. Ce n'est pas le même moment que vous choisiriez, Messieurs, pour enlever à l'artillerie française le concours de M. Gay-Lussac. Le contraste serait trop choquant pour qu'une chambre française voulût le sanctionner.'

201 W. NICHOLL to M. FARADAY, 31 October 1836

[*R.I., previously unpublished*]¹

Cottage East Cowes (I.W.)
October 31 1836

MY DEAR FRIEND,

Before I tell you anything of me & mine, I must express my hope that your knee has ceased to trouble you, and that Mrs. Faraday & yourself are well. Your kind call at Shanklin was sadly tantalizing – so short that I could scarcely enjoy the unexpected pleasure of seeing you. We went on that day to Southampton & thence on the day following to Guernsey where we spent a few days, after which we went to Jersey. We were soon more than tired of St. Helier's which we found to be anything but pleasant as a residence, so, hoping, by taking a shorter course homeward, to avoid a few hours' discomfort on the ocean, we came back to Weymouth at which place we arrived at the expiration of four weeks after quitting Southampton. Finding that the air of Weymouth agreed with the boy, we remained there seven weeks, at the end of which time change of weather hinted to us that we ought to seek quarters for the Winter. So we came to Southampton & thence visited Shanklin once again expecting to find a retreat there, but we could not find one. So we came to look at a cottage at East Cowes which I have taken for a year, and of which I took possession on the 25th inst. having waited at E. & W. Cowes during three weeks until the family in possession could give it up to us. It lies very prettily & cheerfully, at the distance of a quarter of a mile from East Cowes, on rising ground, in a gravelly soil, with excellent roads about it. The air is much more fresh & bracing than that of Shanklin & it will I think suit my young man very well. We are very accessible here, as steam-boats to & from Southampton & Portsmouth touch at West Cowes twice a day; & a person coming by mail-coach from London might be here at 10 o'clock on the following morning. It is very comfortable after a pilgrimage of three months to be once more quietly seated in a home. My boy has been very well during our wanderings & he is well pleased to be at liberty in a garden & to be surrounded with his playthings once again.

Pray let me have a line to tell me how you are – how Mrs. Faraday is, & how all are that you are interested about. I take for granted that you are busily engaged in questioning nature & in worming out her secrets, but I am pleased in thinking that you do not fatigue yourself so much [as] (MS. torn and missing) you were wont to do. I am quite sure, that, with my friend Mrs. Faraday at your elbow, you will be reminded sufficiently often that the bow must sometimes be released, & that you will be plied with Quinia & port wine when you need these restoratives. My kind regards to Mrs. Faraday, not forgetting the little Margery[2] Pray offer my kind regards also to Frederic & Edmund Daniell.

> Believe me to be with real regard & esteem
> yrs very faithfully
> WHITLOCK NICHOLL

[1] See *NRRS*, 16 (1961), for a fragment of this letter.
[2] Perhaps a niece and the daughter of Faraday's younger sister, Margaret?

202 M. FARADAY to W. WHEWELL, 13 December 1836
[*Trinity College Library, Trinity College, Cambridge, LPW, 295*]

Royal Institution,
13. Dec.r 1836.

MY DEAR SIR,

I cannot refrain from writing to you. I have just received a short memoire from Sig Mossotti[1] of Turin on the forces which govern matter Have you seen it. I have been exceedingly struck with it & hope it is correct in its mathematical part of which I am no judge. It relates essentially to electricity and deduces all the phenomena of gravitation from it & it is this which makes the interest to me for his view jumps in with my notion which I think I mentioned to you that Universal Gravitation is a mere residual phenomenon of Electrical attraction & repulsion.

He first proceeds to shew that Poissons[2] investigations do nothing as to the settlement of the question whether there be one or two fluids of Electricity He then goes on to shew that the supposed difficulty of allowing that matter (according to the theory of AEpinus[3] & Cavendish)[4] has repulsive powers which are inversely as the square of the distance and also attractive powers in the same ratio does not in reality exist – But that on the assumption of one electric fluid having repulsive powers inversely as the square of the distance – of matter also having repulsive powers in the same ratio whilst the attraction of matter & electricity for each other is in the same ratio but with this addition that the repulsive power of the particles of matter for each other is a little less than the repulsive power of electricity or than the mutual attraction of electricity & matter – then all the phenomena of gravitation – those of statical electricity, and likewise that condition of the particles of bodies by which they are (though not in contact) prevented from approaching each other or receding from each other – flow as natural consequences – the electrical phenomena being as fully explained as they are in Poissons theory

What I want to ask you is your opinion of this paper & of the correctness of the mathematical reasoning. I dare say you have had copies of it sent to Cambridge but if not let me know how I can convey mine to you or let me know that you wish to see it & I will find means of sending it. But I cannot give it to you.

Ever Dear Sir
Most Truly Yours
M. FARADAY

¹ Ottaviano Fabrizio Mossotti (1791–1863), 'On the forces which regulate the Internal Constitution of Bodies,' *TSM*, 1 (1837), 448.

² See Simeon Denis Poisson, 'Mémoire sur la distribution de l'électricité à la surface des corps conducteurs,' *MAS* (1811), 1, and 'Second mémoire sur la distribution de l'électricité à la surface des corps conducteurs,' *ibid.*, Pt. 2 (1811– but appearing in 1813), 163.

³ Franz Ulrich Theodor Aepinus (1724–1802) supported Franklin's one-fluid theory of electricity by arguing that an absolute deficit of electrical fluid in two bodies caused them to repel one another because ponderable matter was endowed with repulsive, as well as attractive, forces. See his *Tentamen theoriae Electricitatis et Magnetismi*, Rostock, 1757.

⁴ Henry Cavendish (1731–1810) supported a theory similar to Aepinus'. See his 'An attempt to explain some of the principal phenomena of electricity by means of an elastic fluid,' *PT*, 1771.

203   W. WHEWELL to M. FARADAY, 29 December 1836

[*Trinity College Library, Trinity College, Cambridge, previously unpublished*]

Dec. 29. 1836

MY DEAR SIR

Thinking over your intended experiments a word occurred to me which, if I understand your arrangements may do very well to express the non-conducting body interposed between two inductive conductors. Call it a *dielectric*:¹ *dia* means *through* and we are familiar with it in scientific words as dioptrice, diaphanous, and recently diathermal I shall be glad if this suits you

I am very truly
W. WHEWELL

¹ See M. Faraday, 'On Induction,' *ERE*, 1, 1168, where the term dielectric is introduced.

The letter from Faraday to Whewell describing his work on induction has not, to my knowledge, survived.

[*R.I., previously unpublished*]

2 A.M. 20 Jan 1837

Dear Faraday,

I do not recollect whether I pointed out to you one of the consequences namely a species of radiation which seems to result from almost any law in which there is one central atom attracting an atmosphere of minor atoms each of which repels all its kindred

Let *A* be the central and let it be surrounded by an atmosphere and let the circle be its limit. Then whatever be the law if any atom of the atmosphere gets beyond the circle or rather spherical superficies then it will go off in a right line in consequence of the repulsion of all its neighbours being greater than the attraction of its central. Now if in any direction *K* for instance a line of atmospheric atoms are driven against the central and its atmosphere – those moving atoms must displace the quiescent ones in consequence of their momentum. They will therefore push some of the supercial [*sic*] ones a little beyond the limits of the atom, and consequently there will go on a continued radiation from all parts of its surface except the point at which the new ones enter. Thus it would appear that the radiation of perhaps to us imponderable matter would result from a multitude of laws besides that of the inverse square – If we conceive more than one body each will radiate in all directions and if through every point of space such lines of atoms passed then it is Le Sage's theory of gravity[1] – I almost fear I cannot hear you tomorrow as I am so occupied if I do it will be incog in the gallery

I scarcely remember what Plàna's[2] letter said but will trust you not to read any part which might appear to an English audience exagerated

Very Truly Yours,
C Babbage.

P.S. Of course such central atoms must have as large atm[ospher]es as they are capable of retaining before radiation commences –

[1] George Louis Lesage (1724–1803) proposed a theory of gravitation based upon the impact of sub-atomic particles moving in swarms throughout space in all directions. Two gross bodies would cast 'shadows' along the lines joining their centres and the impact of the small particles upon them in the unshaded parts would drive them together.
[2] Giovanni Antonio Amedeo Plana (1781–1864), Professor of Astronomy at the University of Turin.

The letter does not appear to have been published.

205 M. FARADAY to E. MITSCHERLICH, 24 January 1837

[*Deutsches Museum, previously unpublished*]

Royal Institution,
24 Jany 1837

MY DEAR SIR

I write at present for the sake of introducing to you either by letter or personally Mr. Crofts a friend of mine who may have occasion to consult you on a matter relating to chemical study. But I will leave him to explain his own object.

I would have sent also some papers, as the most appropriate offering I could make to you but they are not quite ready so that I must wait for another opportunity. Many thanks for all your kind remembrances of me. I have been so electrically occupied of late that I feel as if hungry for a little chemistry: but then the conviction crosses my mind that all these things hang together under one law & that the more haste we make onwards each in his own path the sooner shall we arrive, and meet each other, at that state of knowledge of natural causes from which all varieties of effects may be understood & enjoyed

Ever My dear Sir
Your faithful friend
M. FARADAY

206 T. GRAHAM[1] to M. FARADAY, 22 February 1837

[*R.I., Portfolio, previously unpublished*]

Glasgow,
Feb. 22, 1837.

MY DEAR SIR,

Nobody can deplore more than I do the melancholy occasion of my addressing you at the present moment, the death of our dear friend Dr. Turner.[2] The chair in the London University which he leaves vacant, I am urged by my partial friends to apply for; & altho' I would be well pleased to continue a few years longer labouring quietly in provincial retirement, yet I am satisfied after reflection that it would be imprudent in me to neglect this opportunity of an introduction to the metropolis.

Altho' successful beyond my anticipations as a teacher in the Andersonian Medical School, yet I humbly rest my claim entirely upon my labors in the way of scientific research, which I may at least be allowed to say have been unremitting & disinterested. I make bold to appeal to *your* sympathy in particular upon this ground.

I am well aware that no ordinary effort must be made by myself in the canvass which is likely to ensue, & I am afraid that I will be obliged to tax the kindness of my friends & of yourself especially to the uttermost. In the mean time I am collecting testimonials – I cannot venture to ask you to depart from the rule on which you act in regard to them on my account. But a favorable word from you, the acknowledged head of chemical science in London, to any of the University Professors or the distinguished individuals in the management, particularly at an early period of the canvass, would be absolutely invaluable.

It will probably be required of me to present myself in person, & I propose to repair to London in the course of a few weeks, when I shall do myself the honor to wait upon you.

I remain

Dear Sir

Yours with much regard

THO. GRAHAM

[1] Thomas Graham (1805–69) was, at this time, Professor of Chemistry at the Andersonian Institution in Glasgow. He later (1838) became Professor of Chemistry at the University of London.

[2] Edward Turner (1796–1837), best known for his popular *Elements of Chemistry*, London, 1827.

207   A. QUÉTELET to M. FARADAY, 24 February 1837

[*I.E.E., previously unpublished*]

Bruxelles

le 24 février (1837)

MON CHER MONSIEUR,

Je profite d'un envoi de livres que je fais à la société royale pour vous renouveler mes remercimens pour l'obligeance que vous avez eue de m'envoyer les différens mémoires dont vous avez enrichi la science. permettez moi de vous présenter à mon tour quelques opuscules dont l'un est de moi, et pour lequel je réclame Votre indulgence. c'est un des premiers fruits de notre nouvel observatoire.[1] J'y joins le Volume du bulletins de notre académie pour 1836, parce que je pense que vous y trouverez peut être quelques articles qui pourront Vous intéresser. Le mémoire sur la phloridzine est d'un de nos jeunes chimistes qui essai la carrière où Vous marchez avec tant de distinction; je crois qu'il mérite Votre bienveillance.

Je m'occupe maintenant très activement à mettre en ordre toutes mes observations sur les Variations diurnes et annuelles de la terre. ce sujet a des rapports assez directs avec l'état électrique et magnétique de la terre. Je m'empresserai de vous adresser un exemplaire de ce travail dès qu'il sera imprimé. D'après l'invitation de Mess. De humboldt[2] et Kupffer,[3] je me me [*sic*] suis decidé à entreprendre des observations horaires sur le magnétisme.

Je n'ai pas encore fait construire mon cabinet magnétique; les instrumens seront construits à Berlin.

Je me recommande à Votre bon souvenir, et Vous prie, Mon cher Monsieur, d'agréer les nouvelles assurances de mes sentiments trés distingués et trés affectueux.

Tout à vous
QUÉTELET

P.S. J'ose appeler votre attention sur un article relatif aux étoiles filantes que j'ai inséré à la page 404 des bulletins de notre académie.[4]

[1] Probably A. Quételet, 'Observations faites en 1834 à l'Observatoire de Bruxelles sur la météorologie, le magnétisme terrestre, la floraison, etc.,' *MASB*, 9 (1835).
[2] Alexander von Humboldt (1769–1859), famous German naturalist and traveller.
[3] Adolph Theodor Kupffer (1799–1865), member of the Russian Academy of Sciences and student of terrestrial magnetism.
[4] A. Quételet, 'Sur le nombre moyen des étoiles filantes que l'on peut observer dans une même nuit à une époque quelconque de l'année,' *BASB*, 3 (1836), 404.

208   M. FARADAY to C. W. PASLEY,[1] 27 February 1837
[*British Museum, Add. mss. 41,964, f. 215 (Pasley Papers, vol. 4), previously unpublished*]

R. Institution
27 Feby 1837

MY DEAR SIR

I hoped to have sent you word of your clays[2] before this but the very dangerous & alarming illness of a brother has stopped Lectures & every thing else – He is the least degree better but most of my time is devoted to him – I trust however soon to look at the clays & do what I can with them As however analyses are long things & I have little time to give & should be unable to do more than the two; – if you think time has changed them, you had better send me up two other samples towards the end of this week i.e. about Thursday. and then I trust to return you a quick answer

Ever Dear Sir,
Very Truly Yours
M. FARADAY.

[1] Sir Charles William Pasley (1780–1861), engineer, probably most famous for having successfully removed the wreck of the Royal George at Spithead by underwater detonation.
[2] At this time, Pasley was working on various mortars and cements and the clays mentioned here might have been connected with this. See C. W. Pasley, *Observations on limes, calcareous cements, mortars, stuccos and concrete, and on puzzolanas natural and artificial*, London, 1838.

[*British Museum, Add. mss. 41,964, f. 217 (Pasley Papers, vol. 4), previously unpublished*]

R. Institution
9 Mar 1837

My dear Sir

I have been engaged the last three or four day [*sic*] in analyzing your clays. (You know analyses are very tedious & time consuming things) and now send you the results

The *pit clay* in its moist state has a specific gravity of 2.07. This you required to know though I do not see what use it can be of to you – It contains a trace of carbonate of lime but it also contains little calcareous concretions like small pebbles which would render a specimen carelessly taken very uncertain in its composition In its moist state as sent to me a hundred parts contain the following proportions very nearly

Water		19.0
Sand		30.5
Finer	Silica —	29.8
Particles	Alumina—	16.5
Per oxide of iron		3.7
Carbonate of lime		0.5
		100.0

The Midway clay in its dark coloured & moist state had a Specific Gravity of 1.46 but this of course would vary as the quantity of water varied. – 100 parts gave

Water		50.9
Sand		14.0
Finer Particles 25.6	Silica —	14.8
	Alumina—	10.8
Per oxide of iron		3.4
Carbonate of lime		1.5
Fragments of wood		1.5
Organic matter		3.1

I have put down all the iron as per oxide because it is the best state in which to estimate it. but in the clay whilst dark coloured a portion of it is in the condition of Sulphuret – (the greater portion being even then *per oxide*) and the presence of this sulphuret causes the dark colour & also the evolution of Sulphuretted hydrogen upon the affusion of acids – a little protoxide may also be present

The gases you speak of as existing in the clay do not exist in it really. but are produced from the wood & organic matter – the carbonate of lime & the Sulphuret of iron etc etc by the action of heat

Ever Dear Sir
Very Truly Yours
M. FARADAY.

210   M. FARADAY to C. BABBAGE, 7 April 1837

[*British Museum, Add. mss. 37190, f. 93, previously unpublished*]

R. Institution
7 April 1837

MY DEAR SIR

The simple substances known are fifty three to which if you add fluorine or the *X* which must stand in its place the number will be 54. I hope the progress of discovery will be rather to diminish than increase the number

I am sorry I have not been able to reach your house yet I was hoping for tomorrow night but it may not be – On Wednesday I have business I must attend to

Ever Your Very Obligd
M. FARADAY

211   M. FARADAY to W. JORDAN,[1] 15 August 1837

[*R.I., previously unpublished*]

R Institution
15 Aug. 1837

MY DEAR SIR

I cannot make up my mind whether you are in jest or earnest in last Saturday's L.G.[2] but it looks so like the latter that I thought I should be unkind in leaving you in error respecting my condition, which is what I trust it will always remain, plain *Mister*. This note to you seems to me so unnecessary (can anybody for a moment be mistaken?) that I trust you will not refer to it or me with regard to the matter either in conversation or otherwise

Ever My dear Sir
Very Truly Yours
M. FARADAY.

[1] William Jordan was editor of the *Literary Gazette*.
[2] See *LG* for 12 August 1837, 518. There the announcement is made of the conferral of a knighthood upon Faraday.

[Trinity College Library, Trinity College, Cambridge, previously unpublished]

R. Institution,
12 Oct^r, 1837

MY DEAR SIR

You remember perhaps what I said to you about the possible reference of electric induction to the action of contiguous particles &c. &c. &c. – I have been working & thinking much on the matter & am about to write a paper giving experimental results. At present the bearing of it seems to me *very important* but I wait for a few days when I expect my results will be abundantly decisive one way or the other. – In the mean time I want a word or two

Suppose two insulated bodies electrified P & N are in an inductive relation to each other; we may communicate one with the earth but the induction will not cease being sustained or retained (or anything else that you please) by the other. I put the case thus for convenience sake but it will represent a thousand cases of induction If we call the insulated one *a* and the uninsulated one *b* then I may use these letters to represent the general case. Now *a* may be either Pos or Neg & of course *b* may be either Neg or Pos – Either *a* or *b* may be conducting matter or non-conducting matter *a* & *b* may be parts of the same piece of metal; even the opposite surfaces of the same leaf of gold and yet it is important to express & distinguish *a* & *b* from each other Every case of induction does not include them both for there are plenty of cases where the two states are both *a* and perhaps in Voltaic electricity & thermo electricity we may develope some where both are *b*. Now can you give me two good terms to express these relative states – ie if I bring a glass rod excited positively towards my hand so as to induce in the latter a negative state can you give me a term to express the *determining & sustaining* influence of the rod charge, and the *dependant & sustained* condition of the hand charge.

Whilst on words I will merely mention some other cases where they are wanting Perhaps at some time they may occur to you – One is sadly wanted to replace *current* – Others for Posit. and Negative – and some terms are required to express direction of the force or forces. If Anode *and* Cathode were to be received into use perhaps they would serve as bases: but something still more general and founded rather upon the word to be used instead of *current* would be better.

I hope I am not annoying you with my fancies. If you feel fretted by me put my letter in the fire. I am Dear Sir

Ever Yours faithfully
M. FARADAY

[*Trinity College Library, Trinity College, Cambridge, previously unpublished*]

R. Institution,
25 Oct[r] 1837

MY DEAR SIR

I owe you many thanks for your kind letter.[1] Tomorrow I go to Brighton to write my paper in peace & quietness & shall not be able therefore to see you on the 1st of next month – I have thought over my matter a hundred times and am pretty sure; nevertheless the writing of it may suggest some views which if they occur I would like to catch before I come to you finally for words

The words inductricity, inducteity cathodic & anodic I think are good – but as I shall have occasion to treat of the first principles of Electrical action I will just write my paper & then if the thing still seems to me clear submit the whole view to you at once.

You remember perhaps that I said I thought induction was not directly an action at a distance but an action of *contiguous particles* – *that* I think I shall establish – Again I mentioned that I thought I had proofs that different insulating substances were *not alike* in their power of allowing or sustaining inductive action through them, of this I am not as yet quite so sure but am almost satisfied Now what am I to call this *capacity for induction* if it stands my final test. Put the point thus, (which is almost the form of my experiment) let *a* be an insulated electrified metallic plate & *b* & *c* uninsulated metallic plates with *air* between *a* & *b*, but shell lac between *a* & *c*: if the whole of the inductive force is called 27, then 10 shall be exerted between *a* & *b* whilst 17 is exerted between *a* & *c* though *the intervals are in both cases the same*. In my notes I say the Electric capacity of air being 1, that of shell lac is 1.7 and so on; but I am not quite satisfied with the term *electric capacity* since I view the effect as one depending on the more or less ready polarity or other condition assumed by the *particles* between the inducing surfaces – Remember I am only giving you a case which I am still testing by experiment but I believe the difference exists. To make an *unexceptionable experiment* I have found very difficult

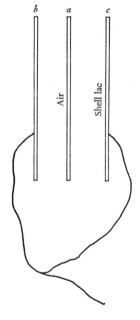

Now do not laugh at me if I ask you not to speak of these things as yet to others. I may be delayed in my final proofs longer than I think, & then should wish to trust as little of my views to the honesty of the world as possible. If they

are correct they must be of the utmost importance to every part of the theory of Electricity and have an influence on every form of its powers & effects: & it is but natural that I should like to review such matters as conduction, discharge, excitation, action of points &c. &c. in the hopes of arriving at some contingent & collateral discovery; – perhaps crystallization; – before others have possession of the key. I do not mean to delay the matter but merely wish to render myself *sure* of the principle before I send it forth.

Ever My dear Sir
Your Oblg^d Servt
M. FARADAY

¹ I have been unable to find this letter.

214 M. FARADAY to J. BARROW, 19 February 1838
[*PRO, Adm. 1, 4615, Prom. Lett., previously unpublished*]

Royal Institution
19 Feby 1838

SIR

In reply to your enquiry respecting my opinion whether hemp in which there is a considerable portion of oil if prepared like Hay and placed below in the store room of steam vessels would not be liable to occasion spontaneous ignition I have to say that such is my opinion and that if ignition occurred I should think it a very natural effect of the circumstances

I have known one case in which hemp being oiled & accumulated in comparatively a small mass has ignited and burnt

I am Sir
Your Obnt Humble Servant
M. FARADAY

215 M. FARADAY to C. BABBAGE, 20 March 1838
[*British Museum, Add. mss. 37,190, f. 399, previously unpublished*]

R Institution
20 Mar 1838

DEAR SIR

I do not know whether you expect any answer to your last note. – yet I would not seem neglectful. I have no thought however to give to Lectures now for I have just lost my *mother*¹ – All I want to say is that there is no change of such lectures this Easter

Yours Very Sincerely
M. FARADAY.

¹ This is literally correct. Mrs Faraday died on 20 March 1838. See Letter 216.

216   M. FARADAY to [E. MAGRATH ?], 22 March 1838
[*R.I., previously unpublished*]

RI.
Thursday 22/3 38

DEAR EDW
My mother died last Tuesday Morning

Ever Yours
M. FARADAY

217   M. FARADAY to A. DE LA RIVE, 10 May 1838
[*Bibliothèque publique et universitaire de Genève, ms. 2316, f. 52–3, previously unpublished*]

Royal Institution
10 May 1838

MY DEAR SIR
Mr Prevosts kindness gives me the opportunity of sending you a copy of a paper on Induction which though printed is not yet published Two other papers of mine developing the consequences of the theory have been read & are now in course of printing and you shall [have] copies as soon as I have them. I am writing a fourth paper on the same subject which I expect will be ready for the Royal Society in a few weeks[1] I have nothing new to say except what is in the papers & sending them will be the best way of informing you

Our library wants certain volumes of the Bibilotheque Universelle & the Librarian says he cannot obtain them at your Agents here. I do not know how the arrangements of the publication is made but if the publisher at Geneva could send them to his bookseller in London with the next Transit of a new number and the bill for them then our Librarian could apply for & obtain them in the regular business like way The volumes are the intire for 1827, namely

34. 35. 36. ———	Literature
34. 35. 36. ———	Sciences
12 ———	agriculture

and for 1831.

46. 47. 48 ———	Literature

making altogether 10 volumes.

With best remembrances to Madame de la Rive, I am My dear Sir

Yours Very faithfully
M. FARADAY

[1] For these papers see *ERE*, 1.

218 R. W. Fox to M. Faraday, 13 September 1838[1]

[*I.E.E., previously unpublished*]

Falmouth
13/9 mo 1838

DEAR FRIEND

At our last meeting of the Cornwall Polytechnic Society held more than eleven months ago, I exhibited specimens of clay which had become *laminated* by long continued voltaic action, & others in which *veins* of oxide of copper &c had been formed by the same agency; the veins & insulated portions of the oxide having been deposited in the *middle* of the clay, which had been previously moistened wh [*sic*] a solution of sulphate of copper. Since then I have obtained veins of oxide of iron, carbonate of Zinc &c, extremely well defined, and I sent a specimen of the latter to Newcastle.

In my first experiments the voltaic action was continued for several months, but from subsequent ones which a friend of mine & I have made, it seems that similar results may be had in a week or two, or less time, by means of Daniells sustaining battery, consisting of four or more pair of plates on rubber cylinders.

The clay may be placed between horizontal or perpendicular plates of metal, (copper & zinc, for instance.) In the former case, horizontal veins are formed & in the latter vertical ones. In part, the veins, as well as the laminae, are always perpendicular to the voltaic currents, & generally very decided cracks or fissures, produced apparently by the same agency, have made their appearance in the clay even when quite hot.

These facts have a decided bearing on very important geological phenomena & it would appear from them that the directions of the laminae of the schistoic & other rocks, ought to indicate those of the electricity.

I have to return thee many thanks for two of thy valued & highly interesting papers rec^d some time ago –

I remain thine very truly
R. W. FOX

[1] Mr W. H. Browning, of Chiddingstone, Bexley Road, London S.E.9, has in his possession a draft copy of this letter which retains the substance of it but differs considerably in its language.

219 M. Faraday to Sir J. F. W. Herschel, 9 October 1838

[*R.S., previously unpublished*]

Royal Institution,
9 Octr 1838

MY DEAR SIR

Your request[1] I esteem a great honor & it will be to me strong encouragement to continue working I sincerely thank you for such encouragement for I sometimes when I set to to revise & criticise my own notions tremble least I have made some great mistake as in the last papers on induction, but then I take courage again remembering that I have not been importantly corrected (in my own opinion at least) in any of the foregone papers and so go on

Your letter has made me search through all my papers for what I believed I had not & it is too true that I have no copies but those for my own use prior to the 8th or 9th series except a waste paper third series which probably contains typographical errors. This I send simply to intimate my anxious desire to attend to your wishes

I have had some thoughts of printing the whole series of papers in a single volume[2] for at present as I know from numerous enquiries they are not to be had for love & hardly for money so expensive is it to purchase them in the Transactions. If I *do* print them you shall have them complete.

Ever Dear Sir
Yours most faithfully
M. FARADAY

[1] The request was for reprints of Faraday's papers on electricity.
[2] These papers make up *ERE*, 1.

220   J. HENRY to M. FARADAY, 9 October 1838
[*I.E.E., previously unpublished*]

Princeton,
College of New Jersey
Oct 9th 1838

MY DEAR SIR

This letter will be delivered, to you, by my Friend and former Pupil, Mr Henry James[1] of Albany, under ordinary circumstances, I would hesitate to give almost any person an introduction to you, knowing how much you are occupied, and how arduous your duties are, but Mr James has some peculiar motives for wishing your acquaintance. Of these however I am but partially informed and must therefore refer you to himself for an exposition of them

You will find him an intelligent, and interesting young gentleman – he is highly esteemed in this country, and belongs to one of our most wealthy and respectable Families – I am deeply interested in his welfare and am principally indebted to his kind attention, to my affairs, for the pleasure and the profit of my late visit to your hospitable shores. Permit me to request as an additional favour to myself that you will give him your candid and free advice and direction relative to the objects for which he seeks your acquaintance. Mr James has devoted himself more to moral and literary subjects than to science and will therefore want one community of feeling with you; you will however find in him qualities of head and heart sufficient to make ample amends for this.

He is aware how much your time is occupied and will not therefore trespass too much on your engagements.

Give my kind regards to your estimable wife and permit me to assure her and you that I shall always retain a lively recollection of the pleasures of my visits to the Royal Institution

I left your country with warm feelings highly gratified with the kindness I had received, and with the unreserve and liberality with which I was instructed in various branches of science.

I had a pleasant and what was then called a quick passage of 26 days across the atlantic Nothing very unusual occured although we had one death in the cabin and was on one night in considerable danger from a violent thunder storm – Every spar and mast for a time was tipped with an electrical brush – the ship was not furnished with a conductor – fortunately however we escaped unscathed.

Since my return my time has been much occupied in making up the leaway of a long absence – I have however devoted some time to some new electrical investigations and hope soon to be able to send you a copy of a paper on the subject

I am very anxious to receive a copy of your late papers and hope soon according to your promises that they will be forth coming – Your investigations are of a very extraordinary character they tend to unsettle what was considered some of the best established laws of statical electricity and were the investigations not from yourself I would be inclined to be some what sceptical in reference to their accuracy – our theories however well they may agree with present knowledge are only expressions for approximate truth and it is only those new facts not immediately referable to them that promise a rich harvest of new development

My Friend Professor Bache[2] arrived safely in the Great Western about a week since I hastened to New York to meet him but we unfortunately missed each other I hope to see him within a few days and to have a long account of all his adventures since we parted in Paris. Give my respects to Prof. Daniel [*sic*] I intend to write to him in a short time I regret that I did not meet with him immediately before my departure from London. Now that steam has become triumphant we may perhaps hope to see him or some of his family on this side of the Atlantic It would give me much pleasure to have an opportunity of reciprocating some of the kindness I received from him.

The account of the meeting of the British association has just been received but I have not yet given it an attentive perusal I have not met with your name on the list and suppose that you were not present.

with Respect and Esteem
I am most sincerely yours
JOSEPH HENRY

[1] Henry James (1811–82), the father of the novelist, Henry James (1843–1916) and the psychologist, William James (1842–1910). The elder James had been very taken with Sandemanianism upon his trip to England in the previous year; hence the 'peculiar motives' mentioned by Joseph Henry.

[2] Alexander D. Bache (1806–67), formerly Professor of Physics and Chemistry at the University of Pennsylvania, and, in 1838, the first President of Girard College. Bache was just returning from a two-year trip through Europe where he had studied the European system(s) of education. See his *Report on Education in Europe, to the trustees of the Girard College for Orphans*, Philadelphia, 1839.

221   H. T. DE LA BECHE[1] to M. FARADAY, 5 November 1838
[*I.E.E., previously unpublished*]

Swansea,
South Wales,
5 Nov. 1838

MY DEAR FARADAY

Barry,[2] the architect, two others and self, lately made a tour by direction of government in order to enquire into the building stone capabilities of our land, the more immediate object being to ascertain what material might be most proper to employ in the construction of the new parliament houses. During the trip we obtained numerous specimens, certain chemical and physical experiments on which would appear very desirable for a right understanding of the subject. I have indirectly heard that you have expressed a willingness to help us in this matter, the management of which, as Director of the Museum of Economic Geology has been handed over to me. Is or is not this news too good to be true? I trust that it is true and that you really will help us; at all events see what is wanted.

1. We have found that the atmosphere acts very differently on buildings and therefore it becomes most desirable to find out, if possible, what difference there may be in the stones employed as regards their chemical composition in the first place. There is no difficulty in distinguishing ordinary mineralogical differences, but more delicate work is required for some materials As for instance, in the case of the magnesian limestones, while some varieties are extremely desirable others decompose very readily. Thus, though both York Minster and Southwell Church are built of this stone, the former is in a wretched state while the last is nearly in as good condition as when erected by the Normans.

In the case again of many sandstones in which the grains are composed of quartz, while some are very durable others decompose readily, arising apparently from differences in the chemical composition of the matter cementing the grains of quartz.

2. Even supposing the chemical composition nearly the same it would often

appear as if the relative porosity of rocks, that is the relative facility with which they imbibe rain, or permit the atmosphere to enter among their particles, causes much difference in the durability of the stone. Some experiments to ascertain this relative porosity become important.

3. As stone which seems to stand well enough in the country does not last when employed in London, as is the case with the best Portland stone, and any newly employed material in London may do the same, it becomes very important to see if there is any thing in the London atmosphere particularly effecting some rocks, such as limestones, which might not effect others in which there is no calcareous matter. Hence if any thing in the London atmosphere may be considered pernicious the specimens might be submitted to an highly dosed with it [*sic*] and the relative effects observed.

I should observe that *Lichens* would appear greatly to protect buildings in the country from atmospheric influences while in London buildings would be without that protection – it being supposed that even on the highest parts of S. Pauls, lichens are not found.

4. As some stones resist the action of frost so much better than others, 1st. in consequence of not imbibing moisture so readily as them, and 2dly. by possessing greater cohesion of parts, experiments to ascertain the relative powers of the specimens to absorb water (both in given short times and when fully saturated) and to see how they respectively resist artificial cold, such as might be considered equal to that of our winters, become valuable and desirable.

5. Experiments to show the relative power of the specimens to resist pressure.

Some fortnight or so since, I wrote to Wheatstone about No. 4 and 5 especially, in consequence of a conversation we had at the Athenaeuam about [illeg.] but have not yet heard from him. As I asked if he could tell me the part [ms. torn] perhaps he is waiting to ascertain it.

Now, my dear Faraday, will you help us [reading doubtful], – pray do, – and assist in dissipating some of the confounded jobbery and humbug which has very generally been hitherto practised as to the stone employed in our public buildings – Pray drop me a line about this and send it to me under cover to T. W. Philipps Esq. &c. &c. Office of Wood, &c, Whitehall Place, putting your name in the corner of your direction to me.

Ever sincerely yours
H. T. De La Beche

¹ Henry Thomas de la Beche (1796–1855), geologist.
² Charles Barry (1795–1860), architect awarded the prize for the design of the Houses of Parliament in 1836. The tour mentioned by de la Beche was connected with the search for materials for their construction. Building began in 1840 and the Houses were opened by Queen Victoria in 1852.

222   G. B. AIRY to M. FARADAY, 14 November 1838

[*I.E.E., previously unpublished*]

Royal Observatory,
Greenwich,
1838 Nov 14

MY DEAR SIR

I am desirous of having your assistance in a practical matter of magnetism. We have here one of Gauss's large bars suspended as a horizontal needle by a bundle of silk: and it seems likely to continue in vibration for ever. The method of checking the vibrations adopted by Gauss is, as I understand, by the *drag* (I use the old word for want of a new one) produced by a curved copper bar completely surrounding the needle in a vertical plane: but none such was furnished to me by the Göttingen artist, and it is not described in the books published by Gauss and Weber.[1] Something of this kind I must have: and I should be glad if you would inform me of what is absolutely necessary in its shape. Must it *surround* the needle, either in a horizontal or vertical plane? or will a horse-shoe at each end, embracing the end of the magnet, be sufficient? Must it be solid, or laminated? What caution must be observed as to the quality of the copper? Is copper ever magnetic? Is any other metal preferable? The suspension of the needle you will understand without any diagram: the horizontal plan is the following

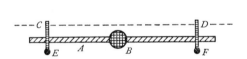

A the needle
B the suspension piece
C a wire-frame
D a lens acting as collimator
E, *F*, counterpoises

The line which must not be interrupted by the copper is *CD*.

I am my dear Sir
Yours very truly
G. B. AIRY

[1] K. F. Gauss and W. Weber, *Resultate aus den Beobachtungen des magnetischen Vereins*, 6 vols., Göttingen, 1837–43. See especially Vol. 2 for a discussion of Gauss's and Weber's method of arranging their instruments.

223 M. FARADAY to S. H. CHRISTIE,[1] 14 November 1838

[*R.S., previously unpublished*]

Royal Institution,
14 November 1838

MY DEAR SIR

Professor Ehrenberg has honored me by requesting that I would in his name present to the Royal Society a copy of his magnificent work on Infusoria &c:[2] you will receive it with this letter I rejoice in having any part in the presentation of such a work from such a man to the Library of the Society.

I also beg you to make application to the President and Council in my name for leave to reprint from the Philosophical Transactions my Experimental researches in Electricity. The cost of obtaining them is so great that those who wish to have them cannot afford the purchase. If leave is granted me, it is my intention to make them into one Octavo volume with an Index. I would also beg the favour of the loan of the plates to the various papers as it is my wish to make the work as cheap as possible

I hope the Council will not think that I am asking too much or overrating the value of the papers to the public Their reward of them at different times by the Copley & Royal Medals must be my excuse in this

I am My dear Sir
Your faithful Servant
M. FARADAY

[1] Secretary of the Royal Society.
[2] Christian Gottfried Ehrenberg (1795–1876), *Die infusionthierchen als vollkommene organismen*, Leipzig, 1838.

224 M. FARADAY to G. B. AIRY, 16 November 1838[1]

[*Royal Observatory, Herstmonceaux, Mag. Insts. to 1848, Sect. 5, previously unpublished*]

Royal Institution,
16 Nov.ʳ 1838

MY DEAR SIR

Remember at the outset that I am writing theoretically & have not seen the magnet which you want to steady or its support & do not know the velocity of the motion which you wish to stop. I do not see any need for a ring in a vertical plane. One in a horizontal plane would be more effective & is near the original form of Arago's Expt. Nor do I see any reason for extending the copper far beyond the extremes of the arc of vibration whatever that may be. The object (on the principle you refer to) is simply to bring a good conductor like copper near to the moving magnetic poles & I should have thought a sort of jacket of this kind might have been applied. If the upper part interferes with the use of the Collimmator & wire frame it would require to be suppressed more or less. The copper should at all events extend beyond the Arc of vibration

I had occasion once to check the Vibration of a galvanometer & yet allow the

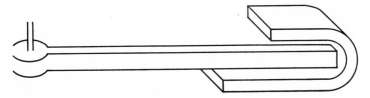

needle to take its true place. I found I could effect this by fixing a small plane under the needle and immersing this plane in water the surface of the water wetting the filament by which it was fixed to the needle. Would any thing of this kind be applicable to your case. For the plane might be used a vane with several fans or perhaps a hollow open cylinder would give rise to fewer disturbances

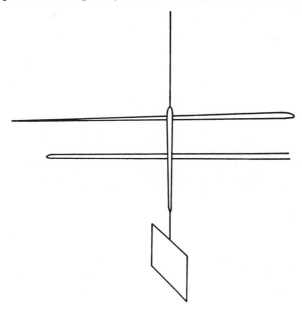

from possible motions in the water than any other form – Instead of water Air in a vessel nearly closed might surround the plane or vane. I have recently found the good retarding effects of a vane in air in stopping the motions of the repelled ball of a Coulomb electrometer

If I could see you we might in talk say something more distinct. I must not say I will come to Greenwich but shall you be in town shortly for instance at the anniversary etc?[2]

Every Truly Yours
M. FARADAY

[1] See Letter 222.
[2] The annual dinner of the Royal Society.

225 M. Faraday to H. T. de la Beche, 16 November 1838[1]
[*Wellcome Medical Historical Library, previously unpublished*]

Royal Institution.
16 November 1838

My dear Sir

I have been out of town until now for my healths sake by Doctors direction & have had no letters sent to me: hence the delay in answering yours. I saw Mr. Barry this morning & had a talk with him on the matter. For myself I can do nothing but talk a little about it; for I am obliged to lay down occupation not take it up – Barry will tell you that he mentioned Daniell to me & if I had spoken first I should have mentioned Daniell to him so you see you have a good man indeed for the purpose a better man than the one you were looking after; I say so with all sincerity of feeling

Your object is a most excellent one and I think must give rise to some good results – From your letter I suspected that you were expecting too much from Chemistry but the conversation with Barry makes me more satisfied

My time is short & as you will hear from Barry: my matter is short too.

Ever My dear Sir,
Most Truly Yours,
M. Faraday

[1] See Letter 221.

226 M. Faraday to J. J. Berzelius, 27 November 1838
[*Kungl. Vetenskapsakadamiens Bibliotek, Stockholm, previously unpublished*]

Royal Institution,
27 Nov. 1838

Sir,

It is with sincere gratitude to the Academy of Sciences of Stockholm that I offer through you my respectful thanks for the very high honor it has conferred upon me[1] I hope that my future exertions will not leave them any occasion to regret the mark of approbation so bestowed.

And to you My dear Sir allow me also to offer my earnest thanks for the value which your name and character has had upon me When I was young and unknown the mere Laboratory assistant of Davy & Brande, I heard you so spoken of by all around especially by the late Dr. Marcet that a lasting impression was made on my mind from which time you have seemed to me as a model of intellect & industry combined worthy the humble imitation of every lover of chemistry & science. I do not say these as words of course indeed I think that on the whole I am too reserved in my manner & communication, and now that the opportunity does occur for a few words I cannot make them altogether a reply to the official part of your letter; but breaking through formality, must let you know that I am not unconscious of or ungrateful for the kindnesses you have at several times shewn me

Your asking for certain papers of mine makes me very proud. I have sent the Series ix x xi xii & xiii to Mr Hudson[2] of the Royal Society for you as they appeared. xi xii & xiii I found a day or two ago were not gone but will go immediately. Series ix & x have I fear been lost on the road or perhaps you will still receive them ix I cannot find but x and xiv I will send by favour of Mr. Tothe

I am preparing a reprint in one volume of the electrical papers & shall then have the honor of sending a copy to the Academy.

I am My dear Baron,
Your Obliged & faithful Servt
M. FARADAY

---

[1] Faraday had just been elected a Member of the Swedish Academy of Sciences.
[2] James Hudson (1804–59), Assistant Secretary of the Royal Society.

227 M. FARADAY to C. BABBAGE, 29 December 1838

[British Museum, Add. mss. 37, 191, f. 68, previously unpublished]

R. Institution
29 Decr 1838

DEAR BABBAGE

The following fixed oils do not thicken by cold or if they do at all but very little[1]

| Almond | Sessimun [*sic*] |
| Linseed | Castor – CD. |

The *linseed* oil of course unboiled The *Sessimun* oil may be obtained at some druggists it is used to adulterate Almond oil. The castor oil should be that having the commercial mark C.D. other castor oil will solidify more or less. Of these the *Almond* is the most fluid the *Castor* the least fluid i.e. thickest.

None of these are very dear in the large way. Even the Castor not more perhaps than 1/6 per pint

As a further assistance to you I may say that spirits of turpentine or the distilled caoutchouc fluid added even in small quantities to some oil thins them much & counteracts the effect of cold more or less But then being volatile. they would evaporate in time though slowly

Ever
Most Truly Yours
M. FARADAY

---

[1] This information was probably desired by Babbage to be applied to the problem of lubricating his calculating engine.

[*I.E.E., previously unpublished*]

Clapham Common
3 Jan 1839

My dear Sir

Mr. Anderson[2] will no doubt have informed you of our failure in obtaining a striking distance with my 320 pairs of the Constant Battery. Mr. Wheatstone suggested that the failure might arise from the Cells not being insulated Since then Mr. Mason[3] prepared 99 Cells which are insulated with great care on Glass well covered with Shellac Varnish – we also had an instrument prepared by Mr. Walker[4] [reading doubtful] with a micrometer screw – but *we could not succeed*

We were however fully compensated for our trouble by obtaining the following result – the entire Battery was afterwards arranged so as to become 9 distinct Batteries of 11 Cells each – the two Voltameters were used with small sharp Electrodes. The action with each used separately was as follows.

With No. 1 Battery of 11 Cells a Cubic In Mix Gases in 70″

2	70″
3	107″
4	111″
5	99″
6	103″
7	104″
8	113″
9	97″

Making a total of 874″ – the mean power being 97″.11 On connecting the 9 pos. into one Cup and 9 Neg into another with the small sized Electrodes we obtained a Cubic in 21″ with the large sized [electrodes] a Cubic in in 10″ and 5 In in 5.3″ with the combined power *by calculation* we ought to obtain the inch in 10″.79 – we obtained it in 10″.4.

The action of the different batteries (whatever may have been the cause) being so varied, I think that with Electrodes of requisite dimensions the Electrolytical effects of *any* number of the Constant Battery may be combined whatever may be the size of the Elements of which they are composed

Were it the custom to canonize philosophers, and a vacancy could be found in the Calendar it ought certainly to be awarded my friend Danielle [*sic*] for the Constant Battery – the Experiments were continued from 4 o clock in the afternoon until 3 next morning and the battery was in as good action as the first hour –

I must not forget to tell you that Brayley is now the Secretary to the Elec.

Socy and I hope under his guidance some good to science may be ultimately obtained by our Exertions. I can only regret that I had not the pleasure of your acquaintance some years ago, however I can only now wish you and yours every happiness this world can afford, and that you may be spared a long life for the cultivation of that science which so many agree is yet only in its infancy

Believe me
My Dear Sir Very Sincerely yours
JOHN S. GASSIOT

P.S. I have sent Mr D an acc^t of the Experiments

---

[1] John Peter Gassiot (1797–1877) was a student of electrical phenomena, particularly of the passage of electricity through evacuated tubes.
[2] Sgt. Anderson, Faraday's assistant.
[3] T. Mason, Jr., constructor of a relatively cheap, constant voltaic battery. See Charles V. Walker, 'An Account of Experiments with a Constant Voltaic Battery,' *TLES*, 1 (1841), 57.
[4] Charles Vincent Walker (1812–65) who later became secretary of the London electrical society.

229 C. W. PASLEY[1] to M. FARADAY, 12 January 1839

[*I.E.E., previously unpublished*]

Chatham
the 12th of Jany 1839

MY DEAR SIR,

I am very much obliged to you for your letter of yesterday. I have got a Battery of 10 cells with porcelain tubes, which cost 4 Shg apiece besides the expense of Carriage and are perfectly rotten & worthless and 3-4ths broken. We have replaced them with Membranes costing 2d apiece. In trying the comparative strength of the detonating powders, we first used only 2 cells, which having failed, we used 3 cells, which fired the detonating powder, but not common gunpowder. 4 fired the common Gunpowder. In our experiments in the Medway, we used *all* our cells, & as our men are Artificers I have ordered 10 more copper cells &c, complete to be made, to double the power of our Battery. The mode we prepare our charges for immersion is this. We inclose our wires in tape sewed round, and covered with water proof composition, composed of pitch, bee's wax and tallow. The ends of these wires are represented by *w,w*. They are led down through a wooden top into a cell *CC* forming a recess in a water proof cylinder, which if we should ever attack the Royal George, will be of very large dimensions, but this cylinder is small in the annexed sketch. The wooden top is shaded. The wires pass through holes in it purposely made large enough not to jam or confine it tight, which we found in some of our previous experiments prevented the ignition of the charge. The two wires are bent at right angles towards each other below the wooden top

329

or lid, to which they are screwed or nailed up by the screws *SS*. The top of the wooden lid has a water proof coating of fine canvas fixed to it, from which rise two canvas collars coated with water proof composition and tied close round the wires near the points *W,W*, in the former figure. This canvas work before it is

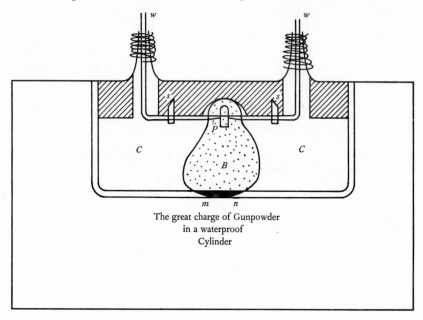

The great charge of Gunpowder
in a waterproof
Cylinder

fixed upon the wood is represented by the figure opposite. *B* is a bag, rendered water proof by a composition of rosin & tallow, containing the powder for firing the great charge, which it does by bursting through the cell into the great charge between the points *m n*, in the first figure. If the explosion of 2 or

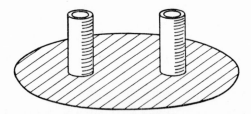

3 ounces contained in *B* should fail no harm is done. The bag *B* is covered with water proof composition. The platinum wire pierces it from one side to the other, being soldered to the extreme ends of the copper wires, pointing towards each other, as I said before. This platinum wire passes through the middle of a small paper cartridge (*P*) containing the detonating powder of nitre sulphur & carbonate of Potash. This little cartridge represented in the first figure is 3/8ths inch in diameter, and surrounded by gunpowder on all sides. The neck of the bag *B* in which it is introduced is only 1 inch in diameter

though it looks larger in the figure, and goes into a cell or groove cut in the wooden top. This day was our most prosperous experiment. We put 100 feet of the copper wires under water with a charge also under water, but there were 470 more of the wires on shore. On trying to explode the whole length 570 feet it failed, but on trying to explode it by the wires shortened to 440 feet it succeeded. We mean next to cover the whole of the wires with the same tapes and water proof composition and to try 450 feet entirely under water, first in a pond & afterwards in the Medway. If 10 cells will not succeed, we will increase the number until it does. 450 feet is the longest wires safety requires even for the largest charges in subaqueous explosions. I have no doubt now of our success. We find that the wire one fifth of an inch in diameter, which I think you recommended, either personally or in your manipulations, will fire gunpowder at twice the distance of the common bell wire about $\frac{1}{16}$th of an inch in diameter which we also used. The way we arrange our wires is thus. We attach them to a rope on contrary sides of it, and bind them round with small cord as in the

annexed figure in which the tape coating covering round the wire is black, the small cord is also black. In this form the wires coil up easily with the tape; but before we fixed them to the rope, the thick wires were very stubborn and intractable.

It was suggested to lay the wires in the seams of the rope in a spiral going round and round, but this mode though it looks much more snug increases the length of the wire too much.

Yours very faithfully
C. W. P A S L E Y

[1] See Letter 208, fn. 1.

230   C. W. P A S L E Y to M. F A R A D A Y, 14 January 1839
[*I.E.E., previously unpublished*]

Chatham
the 14th of Jany 1839

M Y D E A R S I R,

I never paid the smallest attention to the Voltaic Battery, until it appeared to be a better agent for firing Gunpowder under water than any other. To this particular application of its powers, I shall *stick*, I mean *apply without intermission*, until I get its use reduced to something like certainty.

Since I wrote you last, it has occurred to me, that a description of some of our *failures* may not be unacceptable to you. I will describe them.

1st Passing the wires through a wooden top or lid of a waterproof box in which they were jammed tight as in the annexed sketch, the powder being in a bag, *B* covered with water proof composition, and the wooden lid also being coated with a waterproof composition, ignition did not take place.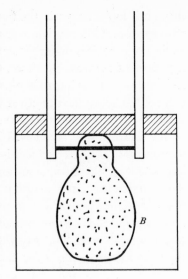

2dly. When the wooden lid was planed smoothe, [*sic*] without any water proof composition over it, the same failure occurred, owing to the tightness of the wires.

Whether we left the copper bare and exposed to the water above the wood, or whether we inclosed it in tape (the tape not being coated with water proof composition, the effect was the same. The powder would not explode.

3dly. On enlarging the holes in the wood, so that the copper wires were not jammed, the explosion always took place, whether they touched the wood on one side or not, and whether the copper was naked or covered.

4th. When we passed the platinum wire through a small tin case containing the powder, and soldered it into the tin as well as to the ends of the copper wires, it failed.

4th [*sic*] When we passed the platinum wire through a tin case as before, but did not solder it to the sides of the case merely putting our water proof composition into the holes, the explosion took place, but we finally abandoned tin and preserved the bag. –

5th. When the platinum wire was fixed round the copper wires by passing it round and round and drawing it close by a pair of pincers, ignition generally failed. When its ends were soldered to the copper, it never failed except from causes not depending on the kind of connection. Even in the open air our battery would not make the platinum wire red hot, when merely passed round the copper, without soldering or pressure.

6th. It being absolutely necessary, that the copper wires should be firmly fixed to the wooden lid, in order to prevent a *pressure from without*, or tension from without, which might by altering their position break the platinum wire, we tried to fix them on the outside of the lid by making a loop or hole in each

of the copper wires thus, and fixing others to the wooden lid, and passing a pair (*PP*) horizontally through them all, as represented by the dotted lines. In this case the experiment failed. We therefore screwed the wires up to the bottom of the lid inside, as represented in the first figure in my former letter, and this has always succeeded.

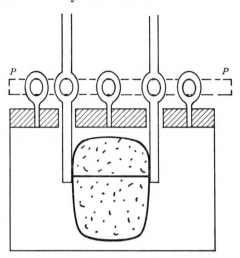

7th. On passing both wires tightly through corks inserted into the lid of hard wood, ignition took place. 8th. On covering the top of each cork and also the top of the hard wood of the whole lid with water proof compositions, the experiment failed. 9th. On covering the corks alone, but not the hard wood with this composition an explosion took place, but this partial coating of the corks only would not answer my purpose, because I know that water will force itself through the pores of wood at the great depths at which I contemplate using the Voltaic Battery, namely from 80 to 100 feet.

Mr. Daniel [*sic*] has repeatedly expressed his surprise to me that the first experiment recorded in this letter should have failed, his opinion being, that it *ought not* to have failed, but we have tried the thing too often to have the smallest doubt of the fact, and I observe in one of your Papers, that you found that ice prevented the action of a powerful battery, which you say was unforeseen by you.

I beg to know, whether there is any objection to our japanning or painting the outsides of the copper cylinders or cells of our Daniell's Battery. Should it do no harm, it will be convenient, and prevent verdigris from collecting?

I remain my dear Sir
yours very faithfully & obliged
C. W. PASLEY

May [reading doubtful] I also beg to know in what way you compare the powers of a Daniells Battery with one of Dr Woolastons. [*sic*]

[I.E.E., previously unpublished]

Chatham
the 9th of Feb. 1839

MY DEAR SIR,

The preparations that I made for securing the Copper wires as a rope &c, have been successful beyond our hopes. Every thing being covered and paid over with pitch &c, each wire in its tape coat, the rope paid over separately then another broad tape covering it, served with hemp yarns &c. all this having rendered our apparatus completely impervious to water, though capable of being coiled up and reeved out from a boat, we fired a charge at the bottom of the Medway from a boat at the distance of 400 feet by 10 cylinders only. I had provided 20 cylinders in readiness, intending if it failed, to add a pair more and make a new trial until it succeeded, and from my former experiments with the wires secured against contact, but not impervious to water, I really thought that 20 would have been required. The dryness of the wires therefore appears to be of very great importance. They were nearly $\frac{1}{8}$th inch in diameter.

With common bellrope wires $\frac{1}{16}$th inch in diameter we could do nothing. 20 cylinders would not fire a charge with them until we reduced the length from 500 to 240 feet. Thus the power of conducting of the small to that of the large wires appears to be as one fourth, rather less than the proportion of their respective diameters; but I think if I recollect rightly, Mr Daniell told me that the power was as the square of the diameter, which would be as 1 to 9 only. I think this must be a mistake, either in *his* rule or in *my* having *misunderstood* him.

My experiment in the Medway was with a very small charge only, as I do not choose to invite spectators to an exhibition with any chance of failure. But I will have another in the course of a fortnight, of which I will give due notice, to sink a cask loaded with gravel to represent a wreck, send a charge of 30 lbs of Powder down to it, and blow it to pieces by the Voltaic Battery from a boat at 500 feet. In short it will be my proposed attack on the Royal George in miniature.[1] The water will be thrown up in a jet and the cask being of [illeg.] [possibly 'firs' – i.e. pine wood] will come up in Fragments to the surface. I will let you and Mr Daniell know in due time & hope you will dine with us. Today I have laid the same Apparatus underground to fire a Mine by the Voltaic Battery for the first time, at 500 feet at which I have invited the officers of the Garrison to be present.

I remain
My dear Sir
Yours very faithfully
C. W. PASLEY

P.S. the Mine failed owing to the negligence of the workman, who soldered the platinum wire to the two copper wires. He had left it too long and it broke, as we ascertained, so that there was no circuit. On Monday I will try the Mine again.

[1] See Letter 208, fn. 1.

232   M. FARADAY to SIR J. F. W. HERSCHEL, 14 February 1839
[*R.S., previously unpublished*]

R. Institution,
14 Feby. 1839

MY DEAR SIR JOHN

In consequence of Saturdays experiments[1] I have had a severe attack of inflammation in the eyes and now am obliged to use these organs very cautiously & for but short periods. This has prevented me from examining the aerolite[2] much and therefore I return it with the letters & no other note than this to you. If you can let me have it again I will go on with its examination & let you have the results as soon as I can.

Ever Dear Sir
Most faithfully Yours
M. FARADAY

[1] Faraday's *Diary* shows no entry between 22 December 1838, and 1 March 1839. In March, however, he was working on volatilized metals at Herschel's suggestion [5081] and this may have been what caused the irritation.
[2] Herschel often called upon Faraday for chemical analyses. The aerolite was of particular importance to Herschel as an astronomer. See Letter 86 for Faraday's views on the theoretical importance of meteorites.

233   M. FARADAY to G. B. AIRY, 2 March 1839
[*Royal Observatory, Herstmonceux, Correction of Compass in Iron Ships, Gen. Corres., 1839–1844, Sect. 9, previously unpublished*]

Royal Institution,
2 March 1839

MY DEAR SIR

I am very desirous of giving a popular account on a Friday Evg to our audience of the relation of a ships [*sic*] compass to the Iron in a vessel and to an iron steam boat and therefore of course to your beautiful correction.[1] I am in hopes you will have no objection and will even assist me by informing me on a few points. That I may however have your wishes I propose calling at the Observatory on Wednesday about 1 o clk if not inconvenient or unpleasant to you

Would you mind dropping me only a single line to say whether I shall lose my labour or no? If I do not hear from you I will take it for granted that I may hope to see you

Ever Dear Sir
Most Truly Yours
M. FARADAY

[1] For an account of this Discourse, entitled 'On Prof. Airy's method of correcting the compass in iron vessels,' see *LG*, 30 March 1839, 201.

234   G. B. AIRY to M. FARADAY, 4 March 1839[1]

[*I.E.E., previously unpublished*]

Royal Observatory,
Greenwich,
1839 March 4

MY DEAR SIR

I am desirous of complying with your wishes, and I am forced to do so with the minimum expenditure of time.

I inclose – 1st [reading doubtful] A copy of a Report to the Admiralty (which please to regard as confidential, though it contains no secrets) 2^d Copy of an address (oral) to the Liverpool Institution. If you will read these, you will be well prepared for further instruction. Please to return them to me very safely on Wednesday if you come, or not later, as I am going out on Thursday morning.

The observations of the dipping needles on deck have been reduced: they agree in results with the other observations: and they shew that there is not much permanent vertical magnetic force.

The dipping needles &c on these shewed that the stern end of the ship attracted the marked end of the compass powerfully. The head end had no particular effect.

The Ironside (the second corrected by me at Liverpool) has arrived safely at Pernambuco[2]: her compasses had gone right all the way. – The arrival of this vessel has been announced in the newspapers with the note that her compasses were true – but the newspapers forgot to say that her compasses had my corrections – you may set this right if you please.

The discovery that the effect of disturbance is due to the separate causes (permanent magnetism and induced magnetism) has necessitated two corrections which were not required before. 1st The possibility of change in the permanent magnetism renders it necessary that observations should be repeated to discover whether it changes with *time*: 2^d The mathematical circumstance that one term of the effect of induced magnetism cannot be distinguished at one place from permanent magnetism and yet will change at other places, renders it necessary that examination should be made in different localities. My conclusion from this is, that the magnetic interests of the Iron Navy ought to be put under the care of one person: if you agree with this I wish you would say so.

I shall expect you on Wednesday not later than 1: if you think any thing else can be extracted [reading doubtful] from me. Probably at all events you would like to see the tables of numbers.

I am dear Sir
Faithfully yours
G. B. AIRY

[1] There is a copy of this letter in the Royal Observatory, Herstmonceux, in Correction of Compass in Iron Ships, Gen. Corres., 1839–1844, Sect. 9.
[2] The port of Recife was commonly known to foreigners, especially seamen, as Pernambuco.

235 W. S. HARRIS[1] to M. FARADAY, 28 April 1839
[*I.E.E., previously unpublished*]

Plymouth
April 28, 1839

MY DEAR FARADAY

I am about to trouble you with a somewhat lengthy communication. I hope your patience will outlive the perusal of it – Having at length completed a closing Paper on the Elementary Laws of Electricity commenced, and in great part worked out, before your last Paper was read – I have sent it forward by this Post to Mr Christie[2] – Your admirable researches on Induction & Attraction, have not of course escaped me. – I have looked them over with exceeding pleasure and Interest – This Paper on the same subject would have been forthcoming before, but that the suffering Illness and death of my Mother, as also of My Aunt her Sister, not long since, together with numerous matters of business always the plague of those engaged in Physical researches in the Country absolutely prevented it. – You well know, we can not invent and make apparatus, & work out results in a loose hurried way – at least if they are to go for any thing hereafter but to proceed. – The Results of my recent Inquiries do not so far as I can see at all oppose themselves to your views of Electrical Induction – I think it highly probable that the action is between contiguous particles in a dielectric as you state modified by the kind of matter through which it is exerted. I hope soon to have a word with you on this interesting subject and if you should think, I can manage to work up a few of the Experiments & results so as to be of Interest for an evening meeting of the R. Institution – I shall be happy to do so I hope to be in London about the 15th of May – The following are some of the principle [*sic*] facts contained in my Paper –

1. Evidence in favor of the conclusion that Electricity is an unknown species of matter differing essentially from common matter

2. That it is in some way associated with the particles of ordinary matter, as to admit of being changed in respect of quantity either in different bodies, or in different parts of the same body –

3. That Induction so far as relating to a given substance is a change of quantity in different parts of it.

4. That the action by which this change is effected, is equal in all directions. Thus whether it take place on a straight line thus —————" or thus ———|" the action upon n is the same – for the same circumstances.

5. The Quantities of Electricity which a neutral Body free ceases to hold in Equilibrio as the distance from the charged body is increased, are inversely proportional to these distances.

6. The Induction upon an *insulated* body indefinitely thin is a vanishing quantity.

7. The Quantities of Electricity which an *insulated* body (in which the opposite Electricity is constant) ceases to hold in Equilibrio as the distance from the charged body is increased, is as the $\sqrt{}$ of these distances –

8. The attractive force between two bodies is not in the inverse ratio of the squares of the distances except one of them be free and the other have an indefinite [*sic*] quantity of charge, in respect of the two opposed surfaces –

9. In all cases of force between a positive & negative surface permanently charged at first, (not by Induction) and which are of small thickness the force is as the distance inversely

10. The Force is as the distance inversely between a charged & *Insulated* neutral body –

11. An Induction similar to that on Conductors can take place in Glass or other dielectrics – when it does it is a sort of forced disturbance of the particles in place – In the conduction there is change as to Quantity in a given point beside. – (I believe when the particles begin to move out of their place in glass or other dielectrics in consequence of violent tension the bodies rupture or break up in some way –)

12. The attractive force upon a thin neutral disc, insulated, may in respect of the force upon the same disc free, become indefinitely great. – In the case I tried it was as 400:1.

13. The attractive as compared with the Inductive power between two bodies one charged the other free are exactly alike –

14. The Quantities of Electricity displaced in an opposed neutral free body by a positively charged body are inversely as the square roots of the distances between the opposed surface and as the Quantity accumulated directly

15. In the attraction between two bodies the quantities existing at different distances on the opposed surfaces, are as the square roots of the distances inversely

16. All the conditions of two attracting bodies are reducible to those of the Leyden Experiment

17. The Attractive force may be calculated between a charged & neutral body of any form whatever, whether planes, Spheres, Cones or Paraboloids &c on the supposition that the forces are parallell [*sic*] – that they are as the number of Points directly and as the squares of the distances between the Particles inversely. –

18. If the neutral body be insulated we may still calculate the forces by the preceding laws. –

19. In every case of attraction between a charged and neutral body – some portion of the charge is continually accumulating on the charged near surface – In the case I have given of a cylinder *A* charged with a given quantity, and acting on *B* neutral and free – about ⅓th of the whole quantity was on *a* alone when *B* was not present – when *B* was placed at, 2 of an inch distance about, 4 more appeared there – at, 4 distance only, 2 more appeared there in addition – and so on as the distances inversely – but the whole quantity at *a* (viz) that originally there + that added by induction was always [word illeg.] as the square root of distance *a x* exactly.

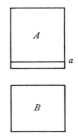

20. The force of attraction is always as the Induced force directly & as the distance inversely – (the Induced force being *constant*) – Untill [*sic*] your researches appeared I could never well understand what these distances had to do with the matter – having been long since convinced, that attraction in Electricity is not to be associated with forces supposed to emanate from a center – I speak of the common attraction between two bodies – you have shewn that it depends upon the domination of the particles of the Dielectric through which the Induction takes place –

With respect to the Elaborate Theorys [*sic*] of Electrical Action, advocated and maintained upon the justly accquired [*sic*] reputation of the French Mathematicians I am disposed to view them with great distrust – At least I *know* that many of the most vital of the physical data upon which they rest, are false, and I believe others begin to think the same now Although – when I first stated that Electricity was not *confined* to bodies by Atmospheric Pressure many of our Mathematicians of excellent Theoretical Learning considered my views as unreal. – In the mean time however not one of them ever tried an Experiment – I remember at one of the Early meetings of the British association, getting something like a civil dressing for what was considered an inconclusive Experiment, at variance with the highest Mathematics of Electricity.

Your researches are the only instances in which the whole subject of Electricity has been fairly grappled with – Every one engaged in this interesting Department of Science – must without any undue praise allow, that you have done more to advance & enrich it than has been effected by the accumulated researches of all your predecessors. I think as to the question of its general nature & properties especially.

The operation of Repulsion has been always a sort of confusion in my mind – It appears to me (anomalous as the expression may be) to be after all, another form of attraction – I mean by Repulsion the separation of two bodies similarly Electrified and free to move – The Inductions go on, or attempt to go on upon each body just as if one was charged & the other neutral – and there is evidently a disposition of the Electricity with which each is charged to change place, just in the same way as the particles would do in a neutral body – only in the accumulated plate, there are more particles, and greater tension –. If we call this repulsion – then I don't see why common Induction is not repulsion – and the first tendency of a charged body is to repel, not attract a neutral body. All the Mechanical Theory of Repulsion by Biot, Hauy & others is evidently a fallacy. It serves however as a Peg to hang out a few equations to dry upon. – Any thing for a differential –

In the attraction also between two bodies, suppose the Planes they say since every particle of Electricity on $A = m$ attracts every particle on $B = n$ therefore force of *one* particle of m to n will be as n and force of all the particles of m to n will be $m \times n$ &c But it must be at least allowed that since the force of one particle say at B is not the same for all the particles on A – that is to say Force on c is less than force on q &c, therefore the attractions are constantly

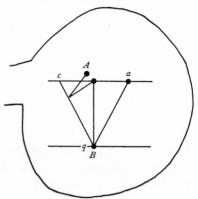

differing & unequal – hence it can not be as $m \times n$ it may be as some function of it – but it surely can not be as $m\, n$ But after all the oblique forces $Ba\ Bc$ &c may (since force is as $1/D^2$) become at last so small, in respect of the exactly opposite and nearest neutralizing Particles that they may be neglected and at last the force be reduced to a system of plle forces thus ⫴ . The fact is we know little about the matter, and I suppose we never shall until you, or somebody of equal Philosophical Power, like you shall tell us –. There is another thing here to be considered. If we suppose two particles + and − to be attracting each other thus

$$+ \qquad\qquad -$$
$$o \qquad\qquad o$$

and we place a minus particle at a thus

$$+ \qquad\qquad \overset{\textstyle -}{}$$
$$o \qquad\qquad o$$
$$-a$$

340

then the force between the first two particles becomes extremely diminished and may be made to vanish altogether by placing a positive particle at *b* thus

+   —

o   *o*

−*a*   +*b*

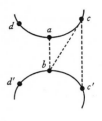

that is to say the actions at −*a* and at +*b* upon the original particles will be exclusive – but something of this kind happens in oppositely attracting bodies say two planes Not only is particle *b* greatly neutralized by near particle *a* and its force on a particle *c* diminished by the increased oblique distance *bc* in addition to this – but the distant particle *c* is also greatly neutralized by an opposite particle *c'* – the same may be said of *d* and *d'* in respect of particles *a* and *b* hence the

forces may at last become parallell [*sic*] forces thus which I really

believe is the case, and the commencement of the proposition will be – Every particle on *A* attracts a corresponding and opposite Particle on *B* – hence in Planes if *f* = force of one Particle and *a* the number of Particles then Whole Force is as $f \times a$ or as $f\,a$ so

Between spheres this expression will vary – as I have shewn in my first papers

Before concluding this long letter – I recall to my mind a kind note which you was [*sic*] so good as to send me in reply to my communication, requesting your opinion upon Lightning Conductors. I was hurried out of London at the Time owing to the illness of my mother. I had not time to say any more about it then – and a good deal of domestic trouble has since prevented me. – The fact is I *ought not* to have *asked* you for any opinion on this subject – but I was at the time a good deal bewildered – and I acted under the suggestion of a friend, who was interested in endeavoring to get the Conductors fairly dealt with by the Government – and who was very intimately acquainted with the Chancellor of the Exchequer. – Pray excuse my having done so Who is there as observed by the celebrated Roman Poet "Wise at all hours" – With respect to my system of defending shipping from Lightning. It is impossible that I should not feel deeply interested in it: not more from personal considerations; than on grounds of general science. One of my principle objects has been to get a History of the cases of Damage by Lightning not only in our Navy, but in the Merchant Service having evidence that ships frequently perish from this source of damage. – The amount in the Navy of damage done, loss of Life &c. is quite frightful – as you may perceive by the accompanying paper. I looked to obtain many important facts connected with Atmospheric Electricity – some I have arrived at, as may be seen by my late Papers in the Nautical Magazine, copies of which I hope soon to send you.[3] We have had no less than 7 ships of the Navy damaged by Lightning within the last 12 months. In one case the Rodney of 92 Guns – the ship was set on Fire – Two men killed, and the M Mast rendered useless – added to which the ship was detained at Malta, under an extensive refit [reading doubtful] in consequence, at a cost of 100 £ a day & upward to the Country – I do not conceive the Naval Department is justified in throwing Science overboard & allowing all this to continue when evidence exists, that it can be prevented – . I have a word or two to say to you respecting your late Papers in the Transactions when we meet

Ever my Dear Sir
Faithfully & truly your sincere friend
W. SNOW HARRIS

P.S. I have sent my Paper to Mr Christie at the RS If you feel any interest about it – I dare say he will let you have it for perusal – previously to its being read

[1] W. Snow Harris (1792–1867) was a military surgeon who published a number of papers on electrostatics.
[2] W. Snow Harris, 'Inquiries concerning the elementary laws of Electricity,' *PT* (1839), 215.
[3] W. Snow Harris, 'On the Protection of Ships from Lightning,' *NM*, n.s., 1 (1837), 394, 449, 531, 584, 738, 824; 'Illustrations of cases of Damage by Lightning in the British Navy,' *ibid.*, 2 (1838), 590, 747.

236   M. I. BRUNEL to M. FARADAY, 24 May 1839

[*I.E.E., previously unpublished*]

Thames Tunnel May 24th May/39
2 am

MY DEAR SIR

I am authorised by our Directors to consult you and Mr. Brande respecting the influence of Gases which frequently burst upon us, proceeding evidently from River deposits which have gradually sunk upon us.

We have attended to your direction of a mixture of Ammonia and Lime in the proportion of 1 to 2 as the men can support the emanating vapour; but it happens at almost every high water, that the deleterious waters or fluid soil which contain those Gases, coming in by sudden bursts, and in great quantities, overpower the antidote prescribed.

Our most efficient men, those who operate in the upper part of the shield, are affected with sickness debility and giddiness to a degree that they have left their parts unfinished and in an incomplete state, without being able to account for it, or in some instances, they have been removed almost senseless, and almost beyond recovery.

I may include in the list of those who are equally exposed, the Gentlemen who are my Assistants in this underdertaking. I say nothing of myself because I am not so often below nor so long;

The only moderator we find, is that of allowing the ground to rest; but this I have not the option of availing myself of.

I send you some portions of the fluid ground, as it has and does come upon us, besides the *black-water* which I have sent you before.

Your early attention to this question is particularly desired.

I am my dear Sir very truly yours.
Mᶜ I. Brunel
[Marc Isambard]

237 M. H. Jacobi[1] to M. Faraday, 21 June 1839
[*PM, 3 s., 15 (1839), 161*]

St. Petersburg,
June 21, 1839

It is some time since, that during my electro-magnetic labours, a fortunate accident conducted me to the discovery that we might by voltaic action make copies in relief of an engraved copper plate, and that a new inverted copy of those in relief might be obtained by the same process, so that the power was obtained of multiplying the copper copies to any extent. By this voltaic process the most delicate and even microscopic lines are reproduced, and the copies are so identical with the original that the most rigorous examination cannot find the least difference. I send you in the accompanying packet two specimens of such plates, which I hope you will accept with kindness.[2] The one which is in relief is the copy of an original engraved with the burin; the second is the copy of that in relief, and consequently identical with the original. The third is the original plate, but covered with reduced copper. I had the intention of making a second copy, but unfortunately the plates adhere so strongly at times that it is impossible to separate them. I cannot tell the cause of this intimate union which occasionally occurs, but it appears to be the case only when the copper at the surface of which the reduction is effected is brittle, and consequently is lamellar and porous. I may dispense with describing more at large the apparatus that I make use of. It is simply a voltaic pair *à cloison* where the engraved plate is used in the place of the ordinary copper plate, being plunged in the solution of sulphate of copper. I have found it necessary that a galvanometer with short wires should always make part of the circuit, so that one may judge of the force of the current and direct the action; the latter being effected by separating the electromotive plates more or less from each other or modifying the length of the conjunctive wire, or finally, diminishing more or less the conducting power

343

of the liquid on the zinc side; but for the success of the operation it is of great importance that the solution of copper should be always perfectly saturated. The action should not be too rapid: from 50 to 60 grains of copper should be reduced on each square inch in 24 hours. The accompanying plates have been formed, one in two days, the other in one day only, and that is the reason why their state of aggregation is not so solid and compact as that of the small piece, No. 4, which has been reduced more slowly.

It is to be understood that we may reduce the sulphate of copper by making the current of a single voltaic pair pass through the solution by copper electrodes; as the anode is oxidized the cathode becomes covered with reduced copper, and the supply of concentrated solution may then be dispensed with. According to theory one might expect that exactly the same quantity of copper oxidized on one side would be reduced on the other, but I have always found a difference more or less great, so that the anode loses more than the cathode gains. The difference appears to be nearly constant, for it does not augment after a certain time, if the experiment be prolonged. A thoroughly concentrated solution of sulphate of copper is not decomposable by electrodes of the same metal, even on employing a battery of three or four pairs of plates. The needle is certainly strongly affected as soon as the circuit is completed, but the deviation visibly diminishes and very soon returns almost to zero. If the solution be diluted with water to which a few drops of sulphuric acid have been added, the current becomes very strong and constant, the decomposition goes on very regularly, and the engraved cathode becomes covered with copper of a fine pink red colour. If we replace the solution of sulphate of copper by pure water acidulated with sulphuric acid, there is a strong decomposition of water even on employing a single voltaic couple. The anode is oxidized, and hydrogen is disengaged at the cathode. At the commencement the reduction of copper does not take place; it begins as soon as the liquid acquires a blue colour, but its state of aggregation is always incoherent. I have continued this experiment for three days, until the anode was nearly dissolved; the colour of the liquid became continually deeper, but the disengagement of hydrogen, though it diminished in quantity, did not cease. I think we may conclude from this experiment that in secondary voltaic actions there is neither that simultaneity of effect, nor that necessity of entering into combination or of being disengaged from it, which has place in primary electrolytic actions.

During my experiments many anomalies respecting these secondary actions have presented themselves which it would be too embarrassing to describe here: in fact there is here a void which it will be difficult to fill, because molecular forces which as yet we know nothing of appear to play a most important part.

With respect to the technical importance of these voltaic copies, I would observe that we may use the engraved cathode, not only of metals more negative than copper, but also of positive metals and their alloys, (excepting brass,) notwithstanding that these metals, &c. decompose the salts of copper with too much energy when alone. Thus one may make, for example, stereotypes in copper which may be multiplied as much as we please. I shall shortly have the honour to send you a bas-relief in copper, of which the original is formed of a plastic substance, which adapts itself to all the wants and caprices of art. By this process all those delicate touches are preserved which make the principal beauty of such a work, and which are usually sacrificed in the process of casting, a process which is not capable of reproducing them in all their purity. Artists should be very grateful to galvanism for having opened this new road to them.

During the last winter I frequently illuminated my saloon, which is of considerable size, by Drummond's light. The mixed gases were obtained in sufficient quantities, that is to say, at the rate of 3 or 4 cubic feet per hour, by decomposing dilute sulphuric acid (specific gravity 1.33,) between electrodes of platina by a constant battery of a particular construction. I only passed the gas through a glass tube filled with chloride of calcium, and there was neither gasometer nor any other provision for it. As soon as the voltaic current was closed the jet might be lighted, and the flame then burnt tranquilly, and of the same intensity for any length of time. The construction and manipulation of the battery, though extremely perfect, was still a little embarrassing. At present, a battery, with a decomposing apparatus which will produce from 3 to 4 cubic feet of electrolyzed gas per hour, occupies little more space than the page of paper on which I write to you (10 inches by 8 inches) and is about 9 inches in height. Behold certainly a beautiful application of the voltaic battery.

In the application of electro-magnetism to the movement of machines, the most important obstacle always has been the embarrassment and difficult manipulation of the battery. This obstacle exists no longer. During the past autumn and at a season already too advanced, I made, as you may perhaps have learned by the gazettes, the first experiments in navigation on the Neva, with a ten-oared shallop furnished with paddle-wheels, which were put into motion by an electromagnetic machine. Although we journeyed during entire days, and usually with 10 or 12 persons on board, I was not well satisfied with this first trial, for there were so many faults of construction and want of insulation in the machines and battery which could not be repaired on the spot, that I was terribly annoyed. All these repairs and important changes being accomplished the experiments will shortly be recommenced. The experience of the past year combined with the recent improvements of the battery give as the result, that to produce the force of one horse (steam-engine estimation) it will require a battery of 20 square feet of platina distributed in a convenient manner, but *I hope* that from 8 to 10 square feet will produce the effect. If heaven preserves my health, which is a little affected by continual labours, I hope that within a year of this time, I shall have equipped an electromagnetic vessel of from 40 to 50 horse power.[3]

In my paper, "On the application, &c.*" I have spoken of the influence which those magneto-electric currents which you had discovered a short time before, would exert on the progress of electro-magnetic machines. They are properly the cause that the expectations which have been entertained regarding these machines have not as yet been fulfilled. But if one examines them more nearly these currents are not so disadvantageous as have been supposed. Experiments which I have made by interposing a galvanometer or a voltameter have taught me that during the action of the machine the electrolytic action of the battery is much less, and sometimes not more than half that which takes place when the machine is stopped, the current still passing by the helices which surround the bars of iron. Thus if on the one part the magneto-electric currents diminish the force of the machine, on the other the electrolytic dissolution of the zinc, which makes the greatest part of the current expense, is at the same time considerably diminished. I have not as yet succeeded in completely developing the mutual relations of the current before and during the working of the machine.

I take the liberty of sending you some memoirs from the *Bulletin scientifique* of the Academy. The result of the joint memoir of myself and M. Lenz[4] is *that the attraction of electromagnets is as the square of the force of the current, or as the square of the electrolytic action of the battery*. It appears that this important law holds good for machines in motion; at least the experiments I have made on that point do not depart from it more than may be admitted as the error of observation or the result of accidental circumstances.

I am, &c.

M. H. JACOBI.

* See Taylor's *Scientific Memoirs*, 1, 503, and 2, (Pt. 5), 1.

[1] Moritz Hermann Jacobi, (1801–74), Professor of civil architecture at the University of Dorpat from 1835 to 1840.
[2] The plates are not reproduced in *PM*. See Letter 238 for Faraday's reaction to them.
[3] *TSM*, 1, 503 and 2, Pt. 5, 1.
[4] Heinrich Friedrich Emil Lenz (1804–65), Professor of physics at the University of St Petersburg and enunciator of Lenz's law.

238 M. FARADAY to M. H. JACOBI, 17 August 1839

[*Archives, The Academy of Sciences, U.S.S.R., photographically reproduced, with partial Russian translation, in* Электричество, *no. 9 (1948), 74*]

Royal Institution
London
17. August. 1839

MY DEAR SIR

Your letter was an honor & a kindness of which I had no expectation; and I thank you most heartily for it. I only wish I had in answering it good news like your own to send but mine will be a very poor letter in comparison with yours, for I have not been strong enough of late to work much and have nothing at present to tell I felt so much interest in your letter & the great results of which you gave me so good an account *that I have translated it* & sent it almost entire to the Editors of the Philosophical Magazine hoping that they will think it fit news for their readers. I trust I have not offended you in this but I wished others to know of your results as well as myself. Somehow or other our means of communication are so bad that we obtain the news from the North of Europe in a very imperfect way, and I who unfortunately do not read German & am too old to learn it am in sad ignorance of the great things in Electrical Science which are described in that language.

I shall hope as soon as convenient to hear in one way or another further results of your exertions especially as regards the application to mechanical purposes & I most fervently wish that your great exertions should meet with the high reward they so richly deserve Of course I am a little desirous of knowing the probable expence of the power obtained but I am also aware that in first applications the cost is no guide to the price at which the power may ultimately be obtained. To think only of putting an electro magnetic machine into the Great Western or the British Queen & sending them across the Atlantic by it or even to the East Indies! what a glorious thing it would be.

The plates too which you sent me are very kind & complimentary but they are also both in theory & practise *exceedingly beautiful* & all who have seen them here admire them, and as to your Drummond Light your account is most exciting. I hope you will soon let us know how your battery is constructed. – and also the arrangement of the other part of the apparatus.

Will you do me the favour to mention me to M M. Lenz & Parrot[1] as also to M Fuss.[2] I do not know them personally or by letter but by their labours I do – and beg to present my sincere respects

I have lately put my Researches (which are getting old fashioned & out of date so fast does electricity progress) into a collected form – they make an 8vo volume I beg to offer a copy to you for your kind acceptance & shall give it into the hands of Mr Hudson at the Royal Society to send by the first opportunity with the Transactions of the R. Society – I hope you will receive it safe

I am My dear Sir
Your Very Obligd & most faithful Servt
M. FARADAY

[1] Georg Friedrich Parrot (1767–1852), Professor Emeritus of physics at the University of Dorpat and Member of the St Petersburg Academy of Science.
[2] Paul Henrich von Fuss (1797–1855), Secretary of the St Petersburg Academy of Science.

[*I.E.E., previously unpublished*]

Royal Mint
Wednesday 11 Oct 39

MY DEAR FARADAY

Many thanks for your very satisfactory note which I assure you has given all of us sincere pleasure. I called yesterday morning on Dr Latham[1] to tell him its contents and ask whether he had any further advice to give you – he says, *none* provided you will continue as you have begun, and remain thoroughly idle – pray act strictly upon this principle. You can have no difficulty in amusing and occupying yourself with what you call trifles – things which do not require thought or consideration – your brain will then regain its tone, and you will be able to make moderate & prudent use of its faculties Dr Latham expressed his sincere conviction that under these conditions all would get quite right again. It grieves me that I cannot offer to be of any effective use to you as regards the friday Evenings, but you know how sad a figure I cut on those occasions – and as to the tact requisite for their general management & arrangement, I can only confess I have it not – However – I will do all and anything I can – and if you will suggest any thing which I can follow up, or point out any enquiries that I can make, or persons to whom I can apply, you have only to send me your hints and orders – Not but that I confidently hope that before their time comes on, you will feel quite up to all business of that kind – I get on tolerably well with with [*sic*] the Electricity Lectures – in Anderson I have an excellent prompter – he tells me that I do better than he could have expected – a plain compliment which I dearly appretiate [*sic*]. At first I began to fear the fate of Phaeton in the Chariot of Phoebus – but by now and then going a little astray from your notes, and following the excellent maxim of not attempting, as the metaphysicians do, to explain what I do not understand I hope I shall not commit myself – I admire your apprehension of having ridden your hobby in improper times and places – no one could say you were not his master. I am afraid they sometimes see that I am mounted upon an animal I am afraid of. You would have been amused the other day had you been present at the Athenaeum House Committee upon the subject of Illumination. The old gas apparatus for that purpose is worn out & it has become necessary to replace it – the question therefore naturally arose as to whether the arrangement and device might not be improved – and it was thought right to consult an artist or two – Accordingly – those two excellent persons as well as artists, Sir A. Callcot[2] and Sir F Chantrey[3] were applied to – The former suggested placing Minerva in a niche of lights – and the latter adopted the notion as a good one, and gave a place for the purpose – it was thought original and highly appropriate – But, when *we* (the common plain members of the committee) came to examine the matter, we found that Minerva would probably have been red hot before the evening was over, or more likely blistered splintered or fused – for to add to the joke, we found on enquiring that to render her *waterproof* she had been imbued with wax – now although Minervas [*sic*] power was very great and her attributes superhuman – I do not remember among them that of being *fireproof*. I shall have some fun with Sir Francis upon this matter.

I made the other day a good modification of your beautiful ice-pail experiment as regards induction – namely – fully charged a large Leyden jar – then removed the knob and wire and searched the inside of the jar with a carrier ball for Electricity and found none – nor of course on the outside – then replace the knob & you have plenty – it well shews the transfer of the Electricity & the place where induction can ensue to the surrounding bodies – After the whole experiment the jar on discharging is found in full force – though no symptom whatever of Electricity can be detected in it, if all sources of induction are cut off – I mean of extraneous induction. I have not said half that I had intended but [word illeg.] my paper. Make my kind regards to Mrs. Faraday – take care of your self and when you feel inclined oblige me with a line or two and set me about anything that I *can* do for you to relieve you of trouble.

> Yours dear Faraday –
> Very sincerely
> W. T. B.

1 Peter Mere Latham, M.D. (1789–1875), Faraday's personal physician since the death of Whitlock Nicholl. Faraday suffered a breakdown in health in 1839 from which he never fully recovered.
2 Sir Augustus Wall Callcott (1779–1844), landscape painter.
3 Sir Francis Legatt Chantrey (1781–1841), sculptor.

240 M. FARADAY to E. MAGRATH, 19 December 1839
[*R.I., previously unpublished*]

> 80 Kings Road
> Brighton
> Thursday 19/12.39

DEAR MAGRATH

Thanks for your kind note & your kinder thoughts. We get on very well here & I think I am now really beginning to feel better in the whole man as well as in the head. Nevertheless we mean to bide our time here according to Dr Lathams instructions

The Newspapers come most regularly & are a great amusement. Remember us to Mrs Hollroyd I hope she is recovering from her serious accident

> Ever Dear Magrath
> Truly Yours
> M. FARADAY.

241   M. FARADAY to E. MAGRATH, 23 December 1839
[*R.I., previously unpublished*]

R Institution
Monday 23 Dec[r] 1839.

DEAR MAGRATH

I came to town on Saturday Evg & I leave again this morning at 10 for Brighton. Dr Latham thinks very well of me & I think very well of myself – With care I think I shall be able to manage the Season very well. – I still have headache & other feelings flying about but I believe rest will be the best cure for this. My general health is very good & I hope yours is too. Whenever I write now I feel as if it was so much about self that I am quite ashamed of it

Ever dear Magrath
Truly Yours
M. FARADAY

242   R. HARE to M. FARADAY, [no date].
[*AJS, 38 (1840), 1*][1]

DEAR SIR,

1. I have been indebted to your kindness for several pamphlets comprising your researches in electricity, which I have perused with the greatest degree of interest.

2. You must be too well aware of the height at which you stand, in the estimation of men of science, to doubt that I entertain with diffidence any opinion in opposition to yours. I may say of you as in a former instance of Berzelius, that you occupy an elevation inaccessible to unjustifiable criticism. Under these circumstances, I hope that I may, from you, experience the candour and kindness which were displayed by the great Swedish chemist in his reply to my strictures on his nomenclature.

3. I am unable to reconcile the language which you hold in paragraph 1615, with the fundamental position taken in 1165. Agreeably to the latter, you believe ordinary induction to be the action of *contiguous* particles, consisting of a species of polarity, instead of being an action of either particles or masses at "*sensible distances.*" Agreeably to the former, you conceive that "assuming that a perfect vacuum was to intervene in the course of the line of inductive action, it does not follow from this theory that the line of particles on opposite sides of such a vacuum would not act upon each other." Again, supposing "it possible for a positively electrified particle to be in the centre of a vacuum an inch in diameter, nothing in my present view forbids that the particle should act at a distance of half an inch on all the particles forming the inner superficies of the bounding sphere."

4. Laying these quotations before you for reconsideration, I beg leave to inquire how a positively excited particle, situated as above described, can react "inductrically" with any particles in the superficies of the surrounding sphere, if this species of reaction require that the particles between which it takes place be contiguous. Moreover if induction be not "an action either of particles or masses at *sensible* distances," how can a particle situated as above described, "*act at the distance of half an inch on all the particles forming the disk of inner superficies of the bounding sphere?*" What is a sensible distance, if half an inch is not?

5. How can the force thus exercised obey the "well-known law of the squares of the distances," if as you state (1375) the rarefaction of the air does not alter the intensity of the inductive action? In proportion as the air is rarefied, do not its particles become more remote?

6. Can the ponderable particles of a gas be deemed contiguous in the true sense of this word, under any circumstances? And it may be well here to observe, that admitting induction to arise from an affection of intervening ponderable atoms, it is difficult to conceive that the intensity of this affection will be inversely as their number as alleged by you. No such law holds good in the communication of heat. The air in contact with a surface at a constant elevation of temperature, such for instance as might be supported by boiling water, would not become hotter by being rarefied, and consequently could not become more efficacious in the conduction of heat from the heated surface to a colder one in its vicinity.

7. As soon as I commenced the perusal of your researches on this subject, it occurred to me that the passage of electricity through a vacuum, or a highly rarefied medium, as demonstrated by various experiments, and especially those of Davy, was inconsistent with the idea that ponderable matter could be a necessary agent in the process of electrical induction. I therefore inferred that your efforts would be primarily directed to a re-examination of that question.

8. If induction, in acting through a vacuum, be propagated in right lines, may not the curvilinear direction which it pursues, when passing through "dielectrics," be ascribed to the modifying influence which they exert?

9. If, as you concede, electrified particles on opposite sides of a vacuum can act upon each other, wherefore is the received theory of the mode in which the excited surface of a Leyden jar induces in the opposite surface a contrary state, objectionable?

10. As the theory which you have proposed, gives great importance to the idea of polarity, I regret that you have not defined the meaning which you attach to this word. As you designate that to which you refer, as a "species of polarity," it is presumable that you have conceived of several kinds with which ponderable atoms may be endowed. I find it difficult to conceive of any kind which may be capable of as many degrees of intensity as the known phænomena

of electricity require; especially according to your opinion that the only difference between the fluid evolved by galvanic apparatus and that evolved by friction, is due to opposite extremes in quantity and intensity; the intensity of electrical excitement producible by the one being almost infinitely greater than that which can be produced by the other. What state of the poles can constitute quantity – what other state intensity, the same matter being capable of either electricity, as is well known to be the fact? Would it not be well to consider how, consistently with any conceivable polarization, and without the assistance of some imponderable matter, any great difference of intensity in inductive power can be created?

11. When by friction the surface is polarized so that particles are brought into a state of constraint from which they endeavour to return to their natural state, if nothing be superadded to them, it must be supposed that they have poles capable of existing in two different positions. In one of these positions, dissimilar poles coinciding, are neutralized; while in the other position, they are more remote, and consequently capable of acting upon other matter.

12. But I am unable to imagine any change which can admit of gradations of intensity, *increasing* with remoteness. I cannot figure to myself any reaction which increase of distance would not lessen. Much less can I conceive that such extremes of intensity can be thus created, as those of which you consider the existence as demonstrated. It may be suggested that the change of polarity produced in particles by electrical inductions, may arise from the forced approximation of reciprocally repellent poles, so that the intensity of the inductive force, and of their effort to return to their previous situation, may be susceptible of the gradation which your electrical doctrines require. But could the existence of such a repellent force be consistent with the mutual cohesion which appears almost universally to be a property of ponderable particles? I am aware that, agreeably to the ingenious hypothesis of Mossotti,[2] repulsion is an inherent property of the particles which we call ponderable; but then he assumes the existence of an imponderable fluid to account for cohesion; and for the necessity of such a fluid to account for induction it is my ultimate object to contend. I would suggest that it can hardly be expedient to ascribe the phænomena of electricity to the polarization of ponderable particles, unless it can be shown, that if admitted, it would be competent to produce all the known varieties of electric excitement, whether as to its nature or energy.

13. If I comprehend your theory, the opposite electrical state induced on one side of a coated pane, when the other is directly electrified, arises from an affection of the intervening vitreous particles, by which a certain polar state caused on one side of the pane, induces an opposite state on the other side. Each vitreous particle having its poles severally in opposite states, they are arranged as magnetized iron filings in lines; so that alternately opposite poles are presented in such a manner that all of one kind are exposed at one surface,

and all of the other kind at the other surface. Agreeably to this or any other imaginable view of the subject, I cannot avoid considering it inevitable that each particle must have at least two poles. It seems to me that the idea of polarity requires that there shall be in any body possessing it, two opposite poles. Hence you correctly allege that agreeably to your views it is impossible to charge a portion of matter with one electric force without the other. (See par. 1177.) But if all this be true, how can there be a "positively excited particle?" (See par. 1616.) Must not every particle be excited negatively, if it be excited positively? Must it not have a negative, as well as a positive pole?

14. I cannot agree with you in the idea, that consistently with the theory which ascribes the phænomena of electricity to one fluid, there can ever be an isolated existence either of the positive or negative state. Agreeably to this theory, any excited space, whether minus or plus, must have an adjoining space relatively in a different state. Between the phænomena of positive and negative excitement there will be no other distinction than that arising from the direction in which the fluid will endeavour to move. If the excited space be positive, it must strive to flow outward; if negative, it will strive to flow inward. When sufficiently intense, the direction will be shown by the greater length of the spark, when passing from a small ball to a large one. It is always longer when the small ball is positive, and the large one negative, than when their positions are reversed*.

15. But for any current it is no less necessary that the pressure should be on one side, comparatively minus, than that on the other side it should be comparatively plus; and this state of the forces must exist whether the current originates from a hiatus before, or from pressure behind. One current cannot differ essentially from another, however they may be produced.

16. In paragraph 1330, I have been struck with the following query, "What then is to separate the principle of these extremes, perfect conduction and perfect insulation, from each other; since the moment we leave the smallest degree of perfection at either extremity, we involve the element of perfection at the opposite ends?" Might not this query be made with as much reason in the case of motion and rest, between the extremes of which there is an infinity of gradations? If we are not to confound motion with rest, because in proportion as the former is retarded, it differs less from the latter; wherefore should we confound insulation with conduction, because in proportion as the one is less efficient, it becomes less remote from the other?

17. In any case of the intermixture of opposite qualities, may it not be said in the language which you employ, "the moment we leave the element of perfection at one extremity, we involve the element of perfection at the opposite"? Might it not be said of light and darkness, or of opakeness and translucency? in which case, to resort to your language again, it might be added,

"especially as we have not in nature, a case of perfection at one extremity or the other." But if there be not in nature any two bodies, of which one possesses the property of perfectly resisting the passage of electricity, while the other is endowed with the faculty of permitting its passage without any resistance; does this affect the propriety of considering the qualities of *insulation* and conduction in the abstract, as perfectly distinct, and inferring that so far as matter may be endowed with the one property, it must be wanting in the other?

18. Have you ever known electricity to pass through a pane of sound glass? My knowledge and experience create an impression that a coated pane is never discharged through the glass unless it be cracked or perforated. That the property by which glass resists the passage of electricity, can be confounded with that which enables a metallic wire to permit of its transfer, agreeably to Wheatstone's experiments, with a velocity greater than that of the solar rays, is to my mind inconceivable.

19. You infer that the residual charge of a battery arises from the partial penetration of the glass by the opposite excitements. But if glass be penetrable by electricity, why does it not pass through it without a fracture or perforation?

20. According to your doctrine, induction consists "in a forced state of polarization in contiguous rows of the particles of the glass" (1300); and since this is propagated from one side to the other, it must of course exist equally at all depths. Yet the partial penetration suggested by you, supposes a collateral affection of the same kind, extending only to a limited depth. Is this consistent? Is it not more reasonable to suppose that the air in the vicinity of the coating gradually relinquishes to it a portion of free electricity, conveyed into it by what you call "*convection.*" The coating being equally in contact with the air and glass, it appears to me more easy to conceive that the air might be penetrated by the excitement, than the glass.

21. In paragraph 1300, I observe the following statement: "*When a Leyden jar is charged, the particles of the glass are forced into this polarized and constrained condition by the electricity of the charging apparatus. Discharge is the return of the particles to their natural state, from their state of tension, whenever the two electric forces are allowed to be disposed of in some other direction.*" As you have not previously mentioned any particular direction in which the forces are exercised during the prevalence of this constrained condition, I am at a loss as to what meaning I am to attach to the words "some other direction." The word *some*, would lead to the idea that there was an uncertainty respecting the direction in which the forces might be disposed of; whereas it appears to me that the only direction in which they can operate, must be the opposite of that by which they have been induced.

22. The electrified particles can only "return to their natural state" by retracing the path by which they departed from it. I would suggest that for the

words "*to be disposed of in some other direction*," it would be better to substitute the following, "*to compensate each other by an adequate communication.*"

23. Agreeably to the explanation of the phænomenon of coated electrics afforded in the paragraph above quoted (1300), by what process can it be conceived that the opposite polarization of the surfaces can be neutralized by conduction through a metallic wire? If I understand your hypothesis correctly, the process by which the polarization of one of the vitreous surfaces in a pane produces an opposite polarization in the other, is precisely the same as that by which the electricity applied to one end of the wire extends itself to the other end.

24. I cannot conceive how two processes severally producing results so diametrically opposite as insulation and conduction, can be the same. By the former, a derangement of the electric equilibrium may be permanently sustained, while by the other, all derangement is counteracted with a rapidity almost infinite. But if the opposite charges are dependent upon a polarity induced in contiguous atoms of the glass, which endures so long as no communication ensues between the surfaces; by what conceivable process can a perfect conductor cause a discharge to take place, with a velocity at least as great as that of the solar light? Is it conceivable that all the lines of "contra-induction" or depolarization can concentrate themselves upon the wire from each surface so as to produce therein an intensity of polarization proportioned to the concentration; and that the opposite forces resulting from the polarization are thus reciprocally compensated? I must confess, such a concentration of such forces or states, is to me difficult to reconcile with the conception that it is at all to be ascribed to the action of rows of *contiguous ponderable particles*.

25. Does not your hypothesis require that the metallic particles, at opposite ends of the wire, shall in the first instance be subjected to the same polarization as the excited particles of the glass; and that the opposite polarizations, transmitted to some intervening point, should thus be mutually destroyed, the one by the other? But if discharge involves a return to the same state in vitreous particles, the same must be true in those of the metallic wire. Wherefore then are these dissipated, when the discharge is sufficiently powerful? Their dissipation must take place either while they are in the state of being polarized, or in that of returning to their natural state. But if it happen when in the first-mentioned state, the conductor must be destroyed before the opposite polarization upon the surfaces can be neutralized by its intervention. But if not dissipated in the act of being polarized, is it reasonable to suppose that the metallic particles can be sundered by returning to their *natural state* of depolarization?

26. Supposing that ordinary electrical induction could be satisfactorily ascribed to the reaction of ponderable particles, it cannot, it seems to me, be pretended that magnetic and electro-magnetic induction is referable to this species of reaction. It will be admitted that the Faradian currents do not for their production require intervening ponderable atoms.

27. From a note subjoined to page 37 of your pamphlet, it appears that "on the question of the existence of one or more imponderable fluids as the cause of electrical phænomena, it has not been your intention to decide." I should be much gratified if any of the strictures in which I have been so bold as to indulge, should contribute to influence your ultimate decision.

28. It appears to me that there has been an undue disposition to burden the matter, usually regarded as such, with more duties than it can perform. Although it is only with the properties of matter that we have a direct acquaintance, and the existence of matter rests upon a theoretical inference that since we perceive properties, there must be material particles to which those properties belong; yet there is no conviction which the mass of mankind entertain with more firmness than that of the existence of matter in that ponderable form, in which it is instinctively recognised by people of common sense. Not perceiving that this conviction can only be supported as a theoretic deduction from our perception of the properties; there is a reluctance to admit the existence of other matter, which has not in its favour the same instinctive conception, although theoretically similar reasoning would apply. But if one kind of matter be admitted to exist because we perceive properties, the existence of which cannot be otherwise explained, are we not warranted, if we notice more properties than can reasonably be assigned to one kind of matter, to assume the existence of another kind of matter?

29. Independently of the considerations which have heretofore led some philosophers to suppose that we are surrounded by an ocean of electric matter, which by its redundancy or deficiency is capable of producing the phænomena of mechanical electricity, it has appeared to me inconceivable that the phænomena of galvanism and electro-magnetism, latterly brought into view, can be satisfactorily explained without supposing the agency of an intervening imponderable medium by whose subserviency the inductive influence of currents or magnets is propagated. If in that wonderful reciprocal reaction between masses and particles, to which I have alluded, the polarization of condensed or accumulated portions of intervening imponderable matter, can be brought in as a link to connect the otherwise imperfect chain of causes; it would appear to me a most important instrument in lifting the curtain which at present hides from our intellectual vision, this highly important mechanism of nature.

30. Having devised so many ingenious experiments tending to show that the received ideas of electrical induction are inadequate to explain the phænomena without supposing a modifying influence in intervening ponderable matter, should there prove to be cases in which the results cannot be satisfactorily explained by ascribing them to ponderable particles, I hope that you may be induced to review the whole ground, in order to determine whether the part to be assigned to contiguous ponderable particles, be not secondary to that performed by the imponderable principles by which they are surrounded.

31. But if galvanic phænomena be due to ponderable matter, evidently that matter must be in a state of combination. To what other cause than an intense affinity between it and the metallic particles with which it is associated, can its confinement be ascribed consistently with your estimate of the enormous quantity which exists in metals? If "a grain of water, or a grain of zinc, contain as much of the electric fluid as would supply eight hundred thousand charges of a battery containing a coated surface of fifteen hundred square inches," how intense must be the attraction by which this matter is confined? In such cases may not the material cause of electricity be considered as latent, agreeably to the suggestion of Œrsted, the founder of electro-magnetism? It is in combination with matter, and only capable of producing the appropriate effects of voltaic currents when in act of transfer from combination with one atom to another; this transfer being at once an effect and a cause of chemical decomposition, as you have demonstrated.

32. If polarization in any form can be conceived to admit of the requisite gradations of intensity, which the phænomena seem to demand; would it not be more reasonable to suppose that it operates by means of an imponderable fluid existing throughout all space, however devoid of other matter? May not an electric current, so called, be a progressive polarization of rows of the electric particles, the polarity being produced at one end and destroyed at the other incessantly, as I understood you to suggest in the case of contiguous ponderable atoms.

33. When the electric particles within different wires are polarized in the same tangential direction, the opposite poles being in proximity, there will be attraction. When the currents of polarization move oppositely, similar poles coinciding, there will be repulsion. The phænomena require that the magnetized or polarized particles should be arranged as tangents to the circumference, not as radii to the axis. Moreover, the progressive movement must be propagated in spiral lines in order to account for rotary influence.

34. Between a wire which is the mean of a galvanic discharge and another not making a part of a circuit, the electric matter which intervenes may, by undergoing a polarization, become the medium of producing a progressive polarization in the second wire moving in a direction opposite to that in the inducing wire; or in other words an electrical current of the species called Faradian may be generated.

35. By progressive polarization in a wire, may not stationary polarization or magnetism be created; and reciprocally by magnetic polarity may not progressive polarization be excited?

36. Might not the difficulty, above suggested, of the incompetency of any imaginable polarization to produce all the varieties of electrical excitement which facts require for explanation, be surmounted by supposing intensity to result from an accumulation of free electric polarized particles, and quantity

357

from a still greater accumulation of such particles, polarized in a latent state or in chemical combination?

37. There are it would seem many indications in favour of the idea that electric excitement may be due to a forced polarity, but in endeavouring to define the state thus designated, or to explain by means of it the diversities of electrical charges, currents and effects, I have always felt the incompetency of any hypothesis which I could imagine. How are we to explain the insensibility of a gold-leaf electroscope, to a galvanized wire, or the indifference of a magnetic needle to the most intensely electrified surfaces?

38. Possibly the Franklinian hypothesis may be combined with that above suggested, so that an electrical current may be constituted of an imponderable fluid in a state of polarization, the two electricities being the consequence of the position of the poles, or their presentation. Positive electricity may be the result of an accumulation of electric particles, presenting poles of one kind; negative, from a like accumulation of the same matter with a presentation of the opposite poles, inducing of course an opposite polarity. The condensation of the electric matter, within ponderable matter, may vary in obedience to a property analogous to that which determines the capacity for heat, and the different influence of dielectrics upon the process of electrical induction may arise from this source of variation.

With the highest esteem,
I am yours truly,
ROBERT HARE.

* See my Essay on the causes of the diversity in the length of the sparks, erroneously distinguished as positive and negative, in vol. v. American Philosophical Transactions.[3]

[1] Also published, with minor alterations in *PM*, n.s., 17 (1840), 44. The editors of the *PM* numbered each of Hare's paragraphs and then edited Faraday's answer (Letter 245) by inserting these numbers where appropriate. The numbers have here been retained.
[2] See Letter 202.
[3] Hare's note.

243 M. FARADAY to SIR J. F. W. HERSCHEL, 18 January 1840
[*R.S., previously unpublished*]

Royal Institution,
Jany 18 1840

MY DEAR SIR JOHN

It is fifty to one that you have tried so many varnishes that any one I might speak of upon first thoughts, you by experience would condemn. The way in which I have seen some specimens of brass keep their polish & character when covered with good shell lac varnish makes me ask you whether you have tried that substance I mean a solution of shell lac in alcohol

I should be afraid to say that the orange yellow deposit is an infallible test of cadmium. I was once troubled with an appearance of that kind which turned out to be iron. I should think you could easily add on the combinative tests of the character of the deposit in acid & of its relation to Sul Hydrogen.

Many thanks for your kind invitation which I should most gladly accept but that I *never* dine out on any occasion. I believe the last time I did do [reading doubtful] so was to *dine with you at the Freemasons Hall*[1] & that was a solitary occasion.

Ever My dear Sir John
Your oblgd Servt
M. FARADAY

[1] The occasion was a dinner in 1833 given in Herschel's honour. See *PM*, n.s., 2 (1833), 391.

244 M. FARADAY to [one of the editors of the *PM*, probably R. TAYLOR], 17 March 1840
[*R.I., previously unpublished*]

R. Institution
17 Mar 1840

MY DEAR SIR

Though your letter is crammed with matter I must answer briefly before I leave for Woolwich

Thanks for the glass. The printings return as you say

I send a dozen of the precipitations & a metal mould – Thanks for the card but I never go out if I can help it

Thanks also for telling me of Hare's letter.[1] I have run it over but I would rather leave you to do what you like (unbiassed by me) about it. I think that probably on reading it more at leisure (whenever that may be) I may perhaps write an answer to him asking him to put it into Sillimans Journal: but I do not know whether this course will seem necessary to me tomorrow or another day

I have looked over the translation[2] & made little alterations here & there but dont let them pass unless as your own or the Editors. It is very flattering to me that you think the letter worth mentioning but still I do not wish to be any party to its appearance in an English dress least I should be charged with *originating* its appearance in the Phil Mag. – and as you know I wish my papers to be treated only as you the Editors may think them worthy & not from personal motives to myself. The French translation in many little points varied my meaning & for that reason I wish I could have found you the original but I cannot & now the French must be considered as the original.

I send the Friday Evgs

I am greatly your debtor for the offer of your help but think the Evgs are all arranged *safely*.

The subject on the 27th is Dr. Gregory Statistics of disease & mortality in London.

[no signature]

[1] See Letter 236.
[2] See Letter 148. The translated text appeared in *PM*, n.s., 17 (1840), 281, and was reprinted in Vol. 2 of *ERE*.

245 M. FARADAY to R. HARE, 18 April 1840
[*PM, n.s., 17 (1840), 54, ERE, 2*]

Royal Institution,
April 18, 1840

MY DEAR SIR,

i. Your kind remarks have caused me very carefully to revise the general principles of the view of *static induction* which I have ventured to put forth, with the very natural fear that as it did not obtain your acceptance, it might be founded in error; for it is not a mere complimentary expression when I say I have very great respect for your judgement. As the reconsideration of them has not made me aware that they differ amongst themselves or with facts, the resulting impression on my mind is, that I must have expressed my meaning imperfectly, and I have a hope that when more clearly stated my words may gain your approbation. I feel that many of the words in the language of electrical science possess much meaning; and yet their interpretation by different philosophers often varies more or less, so that they do not carry exactly the same idea to the minds of different men: this often renders it difficult, when such words force themselves into use, to express with brevity as much as, and no more than, one really wishes to say.

ii. My theory of induction (as set forth in Series xi. xii. and xiii.) makes no assertion as to the nature of electricity, or at all questions any of the theories respecting that subject (1667). It does not even include the origination of the developed or excited state of the power of powers; but taking that as it is given by experiment and observation, it concerns itself only with the arrangement of the force in its communication to a distance in that particular yet very general phænomenon called *static induction* (1668.). It is neither the nature nor the amount of the force which it decides upon, but solely its mode of distribution.

iii. Bodies whether conductors or non-conductors can be *charged*. The word *charge* is equivocal: sometimes it means that state which a glass tube acquires when rubbed by silk, or which the prime conductor of a machine acquires when the latter is in action; at other times it means the state of a Leyden jar or similar inductive arrangement when it is said to be charged. In the first case the word means only the peculiar condition of an electrified mass of matter considered by itself, and does not apparently involve the idea of induction; in the second it means the whole of the relations of two such masses charged in opposite states, and most intimately connected by inductive action.

iv. Let three insulated metallic spheres *A*, *B* and *C* be placed in a line, and not in contact; let *A* be electrified positively, and then *C* uninsulated; besides the general action of the whole system upon all surrounding matter, there will occur a case of inductive action amongst the three balls, which may be considered apart, as the type and illustration of the whole of my theory: *A* will be charged positively; *B* will acquire the negative state at the surface towards *A*, and the positive state at the surface furthest from it; and *C* will be charged negatively.

v. The ball *B* will be in what is often called a polarized condition, i.e. opposite parts will exhibit the opposite electrical states, and the two sums of these opposite states will be exactly equal to each other. *A* and *C* will not be in this polarized state, for they will each be, as it is said, charged (iii.), the one positively, the other negatively, and they will present no polarity as far as this particular act of induction (iv.) is concerned.

vi. That one part of *A* is more positive than another part does not render it polar in the sense in which that word has just been used. We are considering a particular case of induction, and have to throw out of view the states of those parts not under the inductive action. Or if any embarrassment still arise from the fact that *A* is not uniformly charged all over, then we have merely to surround it with balls, such as *B* and *C*, on every side, so that its state shall be alike on every part of its surface (because of the uniformity of its inductive influence in all directions) and then that difficulty will be removed. *A* therefore is charged, but not polarly; *B* assumes a polar condition; and *C* is charged inducteously (1483.), being by the prime influence of *A* brought into the opposite or negative electrical state through the intervention of the intermediate and polarized ball *B*.

vii. Simple charge therefore does not imply polarity in the body charged. Inductive charge (applying that term to the sphere *B* and all bodies in a similar condition (v.)) does (1672.). The word charge as applied to a Leyden jar, or to the *whole* of any inductive arrangement, by including *all* the effects, comprehends of course both these states.

viii. As another expression of my theory, I will put the following case. Suppose a metallic sphere *C*, formed of a thin shell a foot in diameter; suppose also in the centre of it another metallic sphere *A* only an inch in diameter; suppose the central sphere *A* charged positively with electricity to the amount we will say of 100; it would act by induction through the air, lac, or other insulator between it and the large sphere *C*; the interior of the latter would be negative, and its exterior positive, and the sum of the positive force upon the whole of the external surface would be 100. The sphere C would in fact be polarized (v.) as regards its inner and outer surfaces.

ix. Let us now conceive that instead of mere air, or other insulating dielectric, within C between it and A, there is a thin metallic concentric sphere B six inches in diameter. This will make no difference in the ultimate result, for the charged ball A will render the inner and outer surfaces of this sphere B negative and positive, and it again will render the inner and outer surfaces of the large sphere C negative and positive, the sum of the positive forces on the outside of C being still 100.

x. Instead of one intervening sphere let us imagine 100 or 1000 concentric with each other, and separated by insulating matter, still the same final result will occur; the central ball will act inductrically, the influence originating with it will be carried on from sphere to sphere, and positive force equal to 100 will appear on the outside of the external sphere.

xi. Again, imagine that all these spheres are subdivided into myriads of particles, each being effectively insulated from its neighbours (1679.), still the same final result will occur; the inductric body A will polarize all these, and having its influence carried on by them in their newly acquired state, will exert precisely the same amount of action on the external sphere C as before, and positive force equal to 100 will appear on its outer surface.

xii. Such a state of the space between the inductric and inducteous surfaces represents what I believe to be the state of an insulating dielectric under inductive influence; the particles of which by the theory are assumed to be conductors individually, but not to one another (1669.).

xiii. In asserting that 100 of positive force will appear on the outside of the external sphere under all these variations, I presume I am saying no more than what every electrician will admit. Were it not so, then positive and negative electricities could exist by themselves, and without relation to each other (1169. 1177.), or they could exist in proportions not equivalent to each other. There are plenty of experiments, both old and new, which prove the truth of the principle, and I need not go further into it here.

xiv. Suppose a plane to pass through the centre of this spherical system, and conceive that instead of the space between the central ball A and the external sphere C being occupied by a uniform distribution of the equal metallic particles, three times as many were grouped in the one half to what occurred in the other half, the insulation of the particles being always preserved: then more of the inductric influence of A would be conveyed outwards to the inner surface of the sphere C, though that half of the space where the greater number of metallic particles existed, than through the other half: still the exterior of the outer sphere C would be uniformly charged with positive electricity, the amount of which would be 100 as before.

xv. The actions of the two portions of space, as they have just been supposed to be constituted (xiv.), is as if they possessed two different *specific inductive capacities* (1296.); but I by no means intend to say, that *specific inductive capacity* depends in all cases upon the number of conducting particles of which the dielectric is formed, or upon their vicinity. The full cause of the evident difference of inductive capacity of different bodies is a problem as yet to be solved.

xvi. In my papers I speak of all induction as being dependent on the action of contiguous particles, i.e. I assume that insulating bodies consist of particles which are conductors individually (1669.), but do not conduct to each other provided the intensity of action to which they are subject is beneath a given amount (1326. 1674. 1675.); and that when the inductric body acts upon conductors at a distance, it does so by polarizing (1298. 1670.) all those particles which occur in the portion of dielectric between it and them. I have used the term *contiguous* (1164. 1673.), but have I hope sufficiently expressed the meaning I attach to it: first by saying at par. 1615, "the next existing particle being considered as the contiguous one;" then in a note to par. 1665, by the words, "I mean by contiguous particles those which are next to each other, not that there is no space between them;" and further by the note to par. 1164. of the octavo edition of my Researches, which is as follows: "The word contiguous is perhaps not the best that might have been used here and elsewhere, for as particles do not touch each other it is not strictly correct. I was induced to employ it because in its common acceptation it enabled me to state the theory plainly and with facility. By contiguous particles, I mean those which are next."

xvii. Finally, my reasons for adopting the molecular theory of induction were the phænomena of electrolytic discharge (1164. 1343.), of induction in curved lines (1166. 1215.), of specific inductive capacity (1167. 1252.), of penetration and return action (1245.), of difference of conduction and insulation (1320.), of polar forces (1665.), &c. &c., but for these reasons and any strength or value they may possess I refer to the papers themselves.

xviii. I will now turn to such parts of your critical remarks as may require attention. A man who advances what he thinks to be new truths, and to develope principles which profess to be more consistent with the laws of nature than those already in the field, is liable to be charged, first with self-contradiction; then with the contradiction of facts; or he may be obscure in his expression, and so justly subject to certain queries; or he may be found in non-agreement with the opinions of others. The first and second points are very important, and every one subject to such charges must be anxious to be made aware of, and also to set himself free from or acknowledge them; the third is also a fault to be removed if possible; the fourth is a matter of but small consequence in comparison with the other three; for as every man who has the courage, not to say rashness, of forming an opinion of his own, thinks it better than any from which he differs, so it is only deeper investigation, and most generally future investigators who can decide which is in the right.

xix. I am afraid I shall find it rather difficult to refer to your letter. I will, however, reckon the paragraphs in order from the top of each page, considering that the first which has its *beginning* first in the page. In referring to my own matter I will employ the usual figures for the paragraphs of the Experimental Researches, and small Roman numerals for those of this communication.

xx. At paragraph 3, you say, you cannot reconcile my language at 1615, with that at 1165. In the latter place I have said I believe *ordinary induction* in all cases to be an action of *contiguous* particles, and in the former assuming a very hypothetical case, that of a vacuum, I have said nothing in my theory forbids that a charged particle in the centre of a vacuum should act on the particle next to it, though that should be half an inch off. With the meaning which I have carefully attached to the word contiguous (xvi.) I see no contradiction here in the terms used, nor any natural impossibility or improbability in such an action. Nevertheless all *ordinary* induction is to me an action of contiguous particles, being particles at insensible distances: induction across a vacuum is not an ordinary instance, and yet I do not perceive that it cannot come under the same principles of action.

xxi. As an illustration of my meaning, I may refer to the case, parallel with mine, as to the extreme difference of interval between the acting particles or bodies, of the modern views of the radiation and conduction of heat. In radiation the rays leave the hot particles and pass occasionally through great distances to the next particle, fitted to receive them: in conduction, where the heat passes from the hotter particles to those which are contiguous and form part of the same mass, still the passage is considered to be by a process precisely like that of radiation; and though the effects are, as is well known, extremely different in their appearance, it cannot as yet be shown that the principle of communication is not the same in both.

xxii. So on this point respecting contiguous particles and induction across half an inch of vacuum, I do not see that I am in contradiction with myself or with any natural law or fact.

xxiii. Paragraph 4 is answered by the above remarks and by viii. ix. x.

xxiv. Paragraph 5 is answered according to my theory by viii. ix. x. xi. xii. and xiii.

xxv. Paragraph 6 is answered, except in the matter of opinion (xviii.), according to my theory by xvi. The conduction of heat referred to in the paragraph itself will, as it appears to me, bear no comparison with the phænomenon of electrical induction: – the first refers to the distant influence of an agent which travels by a very slow process, the second to one where distant influence is simultaneous, so to speak, with the origin of the force at the place of action: – the first refers to an agent which is represented by the idea of one imponderable fluid, the second to an agency better represented probably by the idea of two fluids, or at least by two forces: – the first involves no polar action, nor any of its consequences, the second depends essentially on such actions; – with the first, if a certain portion be originally employed in the centre of a spherical arrangement, but a small part appears ultimately at the surface; with the second, an amount of force appears instantly at the surface (viii. ix. x. xi. xii. xiii. xiv.) exactly equal to the exciting or moving force, which is still at the centre.

xxvi. Paragraph 13 involves another charge of self-contradiction, from which, therefore, I will next endeavour to set myself free. You say I "correctly allege that it is impossible to charge a portion of matter with one electric force without the other (see par. 1177). But if all this be true, how can there be a *positively excited particle?* (see par. 1616). Must not every particle be excited negatively if it be excited positively? Must it not have a negative as well as a positive pole?" Now I have not said exactly what you attribute to me; my words are, "it is impossible, experimentally, to charge a portion of matter with one electric force *independently* of the other: charge always implies *induction*, for it can in no instance be effected without (1177.)." I can, however, easily perceive how my words have conveyed a very different idea to your mind, and probably to others, than that I meant to express.

xxvii. Using the word *charge* in its simplest meaning (iii. iv.), I think that a body *can* be charged with one electric force without the other, that body being considered in relation to itself only. But I think that such charge cannot exist without induction (1178.), or independently of what is called the development of an equal amount of the other electric force, not in itself, but in the neighbouring consecutive particles of the surrounding dielectric, and through them of the facing particles of the uninsulated surrounding conducting bodies, which, under the circumstances, terminate as it were the particular case of induction. I have no idea, therefore, that a particle when charged must itself of necessity be polar; the spheres $A\ B\ C$ of iv., v., vi., vii., fully illustrate my views (1672.).

xxviii. Paragraph 20 includes the question, "is this consistent?" implying self-contradiction, which, therefore, I proceed to notice. The question arises out of the possibility of glass being a (slow) conductor or not of electricity, a point questioned also in the two preceding paragraphs. I believe that it is. I have charged small Leyden jars made of thin flint glass tube with electricity, taken out the charging wires, sealed them up hermetically, and after two and three years have opened and found no charge in them. I will refer you also to Belli's curious experiments upon the successive charges of a jar and the successive return of portions of these charges*. I will also refer to the experiments with the shell lac hemisphere, especially that described in 1237. of my Researches; also the experiment in 1246. I cannot conceive how, in these cases, the air in the vicinity of the coating could gradually relinquish to it a portion of free electricity, conveyed into it by what I call convection, since in the first experiment quoted (1237.), when the return was gradual, there was *no coating*;

and in the second (1246.), when there was *a coating*, the return action was most sudden and instantaneous.

xxix. Paragraphs 21 and 22 perhaps only require a few words of explanation. In a charged Leyden jar I have considered the two opposite forces on the inductric and inducteous surfaces as being directed towards each other through the glass of the jar, provided the jar have no projection of its inner coating, and is uninsulated on the outside (1682.). When discharge by a wire or discharger, or any other of the many arrangements used for that purpose is effected, these supply the "some other directions" spoken of (1682. 1683.).

xxx. The inquiry in paragraph 23, I should answer by saying, that the process is the same as that by which the polarity of the sphere B (iv., v.,) would be neutralized if the spheres A and C were made to communicate by a metallic wire; or that by which the 100 or 1000 intermediate spheres (x.) or the myriads of polarized conducting particles (xi.) would be discharged, if the inner sphere A, and the outer one C, were brought into communication by an insulated wire; a circumstance which would not in the least affect the condition of the power on the exterior of the globe C.

xxxi. The obscurity in my papers, which has led to your remarks in paragraph 25, arises, as it appears to me (after my own imperfect expression), from the uncertain or double meaning of the word discharge. You say, "if discharge involves a return to the same state in vitreous particles, the same must be true in those of the metallic wire. Wherefore then are these dissipated when the discharge is sufficiently powerful?" A jar is said to be discharged when its charged state is reduced by any means, and it is found in its first indifferent condition. The word is then used simply to express the state of the apparatus; and so I have used it in the expressions criticised in paragraph 21, already referred to. The process of discharge, or the mode by which the jar is brought into the discharged state, may be subdivided, as of various kinds; and I have spoken of conductive (1320.), electrolytic (1343.), disruptive (1359.), and convective (1562.) discharge, any one of which may cause the discharge of the jar, or the discharge of the inductive arrangements described in this letter (xxx.), the action of the particles in any one of these cases being entirely different from the mere return action of the polarized particles of the glass of the jar, or the polarized globe B (v.), to their first state. My view of the relation of insulators and conductors, as bodies of one class, is given at 1320. 1675. &c. of the Researches; but I do not think the particles of the good conductors acquire an intensity of polarization anything like that of the particles of bad conductors; on the contrary, I conceive that the contiguous polarized particles (1670.) of good conductors discharge to each other when their polarity is at a very low degree of intensity (1326. 1338. 1675.). The question of why are the metallic particles dissipated when the charge is sufficiently powerful, is one that my theory is not called upon at present to answer, since it will be acknowledged by all, that the dissipation is not necessary to discharge. That different effects ensue upon the subjection of bodies to different degrees of the same power, is common enough in experimental philosophy: thus, one degree of heat will merely make water hot, whilst a higher degree will *dissipate* it as steam, and a lower will convert it into ice.

xxxii. The next most important point, as it appears to me, is that contained in paragraphs 16 and 17. I have said (1330.), "what then is to separate the principle of these two extremes, perfect conduction and perfect insulation, from each other, since the moment we leave in the smallest degree perfection at either extremity we involve the element of perfection at the opposite end?" and upon this you say, might not this query be made with as much reason in the case of motion and rest? – and in any case of the intermixture of opposite qualities, may it not be said, the moment we leave the element of perfection at one end, we involve the element of perfection at the opposite? – may it not be said of light and darkness, or of opakeness and translucency? and so forth.

xxxiii. I admit that these questions are very properly put; not that I go to the full extent of them all, as for instance that of motion and rest; but I do not perceive their bearing upon the question, of whether conduction and insulation are different properties, dependent upon two different modes of action of the particles of the substances respectively possessing these actions, or whether they are only differences in *degree* of one and the same mode of action? In this question, however, lies the whole gist of the matter. To explain my views, I will put a case or two. In former times a principle or force of levity was admitted, as well as of gravity, and certain variations in the weights of bodies were supposed to be caused by different combinations of substances possessing these two principles. In later times, the levity principle has been discarded; and though we still have imponderable substances, yet the phænomena causing weight have been accounted for by one force or principle only, that of gravity; the difference in the gravitation of different bodies being considered due to differences in *degree* of this *one force* resident in them all. Now no one can for a moment suppose that it is the same thing philosophically to assume either the two forces or the one force for the explanation of the phænomena in question.

xxxiv. Again, at one time there was a distinction taken between the principle of heat and that of cold: at present that theory is done away with, and the phænomena of heat and cold are referred to the same class, (as I refer those of insulation and conduction to one class,) and to the influence of different degrees of the same power. But no one can say that the two theories, namely, that including but one positive principle, and that including two, are alike.

xxxv. Again, there is the theory of one electric fluid and also that of two. One explains by the difference in degree or quantity of one fluid, what the other attributes to a variation in the quantity and relation of two fluids. Both cannot be true. That they have nearly equal hold of our assent, is only a proof of our ignorance: and it is certain whichever is the false theory, is at present holding the minds of its supporters in bondage, and is greatly retarding the progress of science.

xxxvi. I think it therefore important, if we can, to ascertain whether insulation and conduction are cases of the same class, just as it is important to know that hot and cold are phænomena of the same kind. As it is of consequence to show that smoke ascends and a stone descends in obedience to one property of matter, so I think it is of consequence to show that one body insulates and another conducts only in consequence of a difference in degree of one common property which they both possess; and that in both cases the effects are consistent with my theory of induction.

xxxvii. I now come to what may be considered as queries in your letter which I ought to answer. Paragraph 8 contains one. As I concede that particles on opposite sides of a vacuum may perhaps act on each other, you ask, "wherefore is the received theory of the mode in which the excited surface of a Leyden jar induces in the opposite surface a contrary state, objectionable?" My reasons for thinking the excited surface does not directly induce upon the opposite surface, &c., is, first, my belief that the glass consists of particles conductive in themselves, but insulated as respects each other (xvii.); and next, that in the arrangement given iv., ix., or x., *A* does not induce directly on *C*, but through the intermediate masses or particles of conducting matter.

xxxviii. In the next paragraph, the question is rather implied than asked – what do I mean by polarity? I had hoped that the paragraphs 1669. 1670. 1671. 1672. 1679, 1686. 1687. 1688. 1699. 1700. 1701. 1702. 1703. 1704. in the Researches, would have been sufficient to convey my meaning, and I am inclined to think you had not perhaps seen them when your letter was written. They, and the observations already made (v., xxvi.), with the case given (iv., v.), will, I think, be sufficient as my answer. The sense of the word *polarity* is so diverse when applied to light, to a crystal, to a magnet, to the voltaic battery, and so different in all these cases to that of the word when applied to the state of a conductor under induction (v.), that I thought it safer to use the phrase "species of polarity," than any other, which being more expressive would pledge me further than I wished.

xxxix. Paragraph 11 involves a mistake of my views. I do not consider bodies which are charged by friction or otherwise, as polarized, or as having their particles polarized (iii., iv., xxvii.). This paragraph and the next do not require, therefore, any further remark, especially after what I have said of polarity above (xxxviii.).

xl. And now, my dear sir, I think I ought to draw my reply to an end. The paragraphs which remain unanswered refer, I think, only to differences of opinion, or else, not even to differences, but opinions regarding which I have not ventured to judge. These opinions I esteem as of the utmost importance;

but that is a reason which makes me the rather desirous to decline entering upon the reconsideration, inasmuch as on many of their connected points I have formed no decided notion, but am constrained by ignorance and the contrast of facts to hold my judgement as yet in suspense. It is, indeed, to me an annoying matter to find how many subjects there are in electrical science, on which, if I were asked for an opinion, I should have to say, I cannot tell, – I do not know; but, on the other hand, it is encouraging to think that these are they which if pursued industriously, experimentally, and thoughtfully, will lead to new discoveries. Such a subject, for instance, occurs in the currents produced by dynamic induction, which you say it will be admitted do not require for their production intervening ponderable atoms. For my own part, I more than half incline to think they do require these intervening particles, that is, where any particles intervene (1729. 1733. 1738.). But on this question, as on many others, I have not yet made up my mind. Allow me, therefore, here to conclude my letter; and believe me to be, with the highest esteem.

My dear Sir,
Your obliged and faithful Servant,
M. FARADAY.

* *Bibliotheca Italiana*, 1837, lxxxv., p. 417.[1]

[1] Faraday's note. The reference is to Giuseppi Belli (1791–1860), 'Sui residui delle scariche delle bocce di Leida.'

246   M. FARADAY to A. DE LA RIVE, 24 April 1840

[*Bibliothèque publique et universitaire de Genève, ms. 2316, f. 54–5, B.J. 2, 107*]

Royal Institution
24th April 1840

MY DEAR SIR

Though a miserable correspondant I take up my pen to write to you, the moving feeling being a desire to congratulate you on your discernment, perseverance faithfulness & success in the course of *chemical excitement of the current in the* voltaic battery.[1] You will think it is rather late to do so; but not under the circumstances. For a long time I had not made up my mind: then the facts of definite electrochemical action made me take part with the supporters of the chemical theory; and since then Marianini's[2] paper, with reference to myself, has made me read & experiment more generally on the point in question. In the reading I was struck to see how soon, clearly, & constantly you had & have supported that theory and think your proofs & reasons most excellent & convincing. The constancy of Marianini & of many others on the opposite side made me however think it not unnecessary to accumulate and record evidence of the truth & I have therefore written two papers, which

I shall send you when printed in which I enter under your banner as regards the origin of electricity or of the current in the pile My object in experimenting was, as I am sure yours has always been, not so much to support a given theory as to learn the natural truth and having gone to the question unbiassed by any prejudices I cannot imagine how anyone whose mind is not preoccupied by a theory or a strong leaning to a theory can take part with that of contact against that of chemical action. However I am perhaps wrong in saying so much for as no one is infallible & as the experience of past times may teach us to doubt a theory which seems to be most unchangeably established so we cannot say what the future may bring forth in regard to these views.

I shall be anxious some day, if health continues, to make a few experiments on contact with the Electrometer I know of your's, Becquerels, &c but if there are any dimensions which are particular or any precautions which as a practical man you are aware of & know render it more sensible, I am in hopes if you take the trouble to write to me hereafter you would not mind sending me word or referring me to the papers or works which may mention them

And now before I conclude let me ask you to remember me kindly to Madame de la Rive of whose good will & courtesy both I and my wife have a very strong remembrance. I was not well during my journey at that time but still I have a great many pleasant recollections and amongst the most pleasant those of Geneva for which I am indebted to you

I have several papers of your to acknowledge but I cannot recollect them so accurately as to thank you in order for them I am always grateful & very glad to see them. Your historical account of your own researches as regards the battery[3] has been very useful to me. and makes me wish more & more that we had a sort of Index to Electrical science to which one might look for facts, their authors, and public dates. The man who could devise a good scheme for such an index so that it might take in new facts as they were discovered & also receive old and anticipating observations as they should gradually be remembered & drawn forth from obscurity; would deserve well of all scientific men

But I must conclude & am as ever My dear Sir Your Obliged, Grateful & admiring friend.

M. FARADAY

[1] August de la Rive had, since 1833, been an ardent defender of the chemical theory (as opposed to the contact theory) of the origin of electricity in the voltaic battery. See his papers on the subject listed in *RSCSP* from 1833 to 1836.

[2] Stefano Marianini (1790–1866), 'Sulla teoria degli Elettromotori, Memoria IV. Esame di alcune sperienze adotte dal Sig. Faraday per provare che l'elletricita Voltaica nasce dall'azione chimica dei liquidi sui metalli. Con un'appendice sopra un'anomalia che presentario alcune metalli nella decomposizione dell'Ioduro di Potassio operata dall'Elettricita,' *MSIM*, 21 (1837), 205. See *LPW*, 365ff, for a brief account of this controversy.

[3] A. de la Rive, 'Esquisse historique des principales découvertes faites dans l'électricité depuis quelques années,' *BU*, 52 (1833), 225, 404.

[*The Library, King's College (Durham University), loaned by Mrs J. Reid*]

Brighton,
24 April 1840

DEAR ANDREW

Your aunt[2] shewed me your last letter which besides the pleasure it gave as a kindly communication I read with great interest on account of its philosophical character and so to divide things properly we are about to return you a joint answer in which all the useful will be touched upon by your Aunt[2] & the fantastical as you may called [*sic*] it by me. I envy you your stormy evening walk and think if we had been together we might have made some very interesting observations. I do not doubt any part of your description & think that the hissing & luminous appearance which you saw were the natural preparations and precursors of the discharge of lightning which immediately afterwards occurred. Did you happen to observe any luminous appearance on yourself? I have little doubt that if you had held out your hand each finger would have had the light on the tip perhaps however it is as well that you did not happen to do so. It seems to me very likely that the lamp post was struck by the lightning or at all events something near it i.e. in the neighbourhood. Did the light go out? Have you seen the post since & examined the bars to see whether they seemed affected? Is the whole post iron or part iron part wood? Is it a gas lamp or an oil lamp light post? The effect of the snow in making it the post [written above by Faraday with insertion mark] brighter is very curious How was the night altogether? very dark? or was there a sort of luminous haze about? Could you see the ground well or the clouds? and what time of night was it? I have sent you a large lot of questions but you will perceive they are so many proofs that I believe your story. And now I may say I do not think your situation was without danger and am very happy you escaped to be a comfort to your parents & family to whom give the affectionate love of your affectionate Unkle. [*sic*]

M. FARADAY[3]

[1] Andrew Reid was Faraday's nephew by marriage.
[2] Mrs Faraday.
[3] I have omitted the letter added to this one by Mrs Faraday.

24-2

[Arch. de l'Académie des Sciences, Paris, Dossier Faraday, previously unpublished]

Royal Institution
29 April 1840

MY KIND FRIEND

When I came home the other day from the country, where I had been for healths sake, the most pleasant thing to greet me was your affectionate face[1] and your paper still more touching because of the brief but pleasant words upon it: and today on my return from Woolwich I find your most welcome letter and the glasses of M. [illeg.]. Believe me very grateful for your kindness and the more so as I feel quite undeserving of it You know that I am a recluse & unsocial and have no right to share in the mutual good feeling of Society at large, for the man that does not take his share of goodwill into the common stock has no claim on others. Such is not the case I hope from any cold or morose feeling in the heart but from particular circumstances amongst which are especially mental fatigue and loss of memory Do not think therefore that I am unaffected by your kindness of which I feel quite unworthy. It has disturbed my feelings the more as it was quite unexpected, for knowing your high station in science & seeing [reading doubtful] your value as a man I did not think you would spare much thought for me after your return to Paris.

I must not let you mistake me. You speak in your letter of an election and your wish that my name had been chosen. I had not before heard of it but I know that whomever the Academy has chosen must be more fit than myself. I feel ever gratified but still unworthy of the honor the Academy has already done me and I have a consciousness within that the time *is past* in which I could make myself more deserving. It is not for these things that I feel most grateful to you (though for them I earnestly thank you) but for your kindness & affection which is to me of more value than distinction & renown. How I shall ever return your goodness I do not know except by words of acknowledgement for I feel as if all the power of doing pleasant things was on your part & none on mine.

You remind me of two of your countrymen, alas no more, to whom I was most deeply indebted and yet if I remember aright whose faces I never saw, Ampere and Hachette. When a young man and fearful of venturing into science because of the hard feelings I saw around me both these wrote to me when I durst not have ventured to speak to them & cheered me & gave me that confidence to which the little I have done if it is any thing at all is entirely due.

I could run on sometime this way for the subject tempts me but must not. Will you thank M. [illeg.] for me when you see him. I will write to him soon. I have not yet seen Monsieur Thomas[2] but shall call on him this afternoon. I hear he leaves London tomorrow morning but I hope still to see him May every happiness be with you & Madame Dumas to whom offer my humble respects. I would mention a name or two and amongst [reading doubtful] them Arago, Biot & Becquerell, but I must not give you trouble & will write. I am in all sincerity Dear Sir Your obliged and most grateful Servant.

M. FARADAY

[1] Dumas had left his portrait at the Royal Institution for Faraday.
[2] Possibly Frédéric Thomas (1814–83), lawyer and litterateur whose political activities under the July Monarchy may have brought him into contact with Dumas.

249 C. DESPRETZ to M. FARADAY, 12 May 1840
[*I.E.E., previously unpublished*]

12 mai, 1840

MONSIEUR

J'ai ici beaucoup de difficulté à prendre une position où je sois en état de me livrer à mes travaux convenablement.

J'ai été mis le premier, il n'y a pas trois mois, par la section de physique pour une place vacante dans son sein. Quoique le premier, j'ai échoué. il y a une nouvelle place vacante par la mort de Mr. Poisson, qui se trouvait par exception, membre de la section de physique des personnes poussent un Géomêtre, d'autres un experimentateur.

Permettez, Monsieur, que je reclame votre appui dans cette circonstance. J'ai resolu dans ces dernièrs temps, deux questions importantes.[1] celle des maximum de densité des dissolutions salines, acides, &c et celle de la propagation de la chaleur dans les liquides.
Vous Savez mieux que personne, Monsieur, qu'il n'y avait que des doutes sur ces deux sujets.

On donne souvent à Londres des medailles aux physiciens qui ont fait faire un pas à la physique. il me semble, si je ne m'abuse, que ces deux questions resolues meriteraient bien quelque chose. si cela se pouvait, mes travaux en seraient relevés. voyez, Monsieur, si mes prétentions ont quelque fondement. personne plus que vous n'est en mesure d'avoir [une] [ms. torn] opinion éclairée a cet égard.

Quoique nous n'ayons jamais été en rélation suivie, j'ose m'adresser à vous, dans un moment un peu critique pour moi. je comte sur votre obligeance et votre discrétion. je vous prie de m'honorer d'un mot de reponse.
je joins, ici, 2 exemplaires du memoire sur les maximum [*sic*] de densité.
2 exemplaires d'un memoire pour justifier le premier. (dans ce memoire, il y a une legere faute de langage, on a dit racine négative, au lieu, de racine correspondant au radical négatif.

2 exemplaires d'un mémoire sur la propagation de la chaleur dans les liquides.
je vous réitere la priere de me donner un mot de reponse.*

Agréez l'assurance des sentimens distingués avec lesquels je suis

Monsieur

votre très humble
& obt. Serviteur
C. DESPRETZ

*prof. de physique à la
faculté des sciences de
Paris.*

* 2 ex. d'un memoire sur les oscillations de zero.[2]

[1] See his 'Recherches sur le maximum de densité de l'eau pure et des dissolutions aqueuses,' *AC*, 2 s., 70 (1839), 5; 73 (1840), 296; and his 'Sur la propagation de la chaleur dans les liquides,' *CR*, 7 (1838), 933.

[2] C. Despretz, 'Observations sur le déplacement et sur les oscillations du zéro du thermomètre à mercure,' *CR*, 4 (1837), 926.

250   A. DE LA RIVE to M. FARADAY, 15 May 1840
[*I.E.E., previously unpublished*]

Presinge (près Genève)
le 15 Mai 1840

MON CHER MONSIEUR,

Je viens vous remercier de votre bonne & amiable lettre du 22 Avril[1] je suis bien heureux que vos belles & savantes recherches vous aient conduit aux mêmes resultats que moi. Je suis bien impatient de lire votre mémoire & de l'imprimer dans la Bibl. Univ. J'étais aussi sur le point de faire paraitre un travail sur le même sujet dans lequel, analysant les recherches de Marianini, de Fechner[2] & autres, je montrais que leurs objections contre la théorie chimique n'etaient nullement fondées; votre dernier mémoire rendra ma besogne bien facile. Plus je vais en avant & plus je fais d'expériences sur ce sujet, plus je suis convaincu que les notions chimiques existent là souvent où on ne les soupçonnait pas; ainsi qui aurait cru le platine oxidable même à l'air, & cependant c'est un fait indubitable; Berzelius lui-même à qui j'ai fait part de mes dernières expériences sur ce sujet en convient. – Par exemple, faites secher après les avoir bien lavées dans les acides & dans l'eau distillée, deux lames de platine, l'une dans le *vide*, l'autre dans *l'air* ou dans *l'oxigène*, la première sera constamment positive par rapport à la seconde dans de l'eau acidulée. Ainsi encore faites passer le courant par induction à travers de l'eau acidulée ($\frac{1}{10}$ [illeg.] d'acide sulfurique) au moyen de deux fils de platine; vous verrez une poudre noire sur la surface de ces fils, poudre noire qui est du platine parfaitement métallique & qui a été réduit en poussière par l'oxidation & la réduction successives qu'a éprouvées chaque fil sur lequel le courant par induction amenait successivement de l'oxi-gène & de l'hydrogène. Cette dernière expérience peut se faire aussi avec des fils d'*or*, de palladium &c, [2 words illeg.], comme on devait s'y attendre, avec des fils de *cuivre*, *d'argent* &c; elle est très jolie; je désirerais bien que vous la répétassiez. L'appareil que Newman vous fit en 1834 pour produire les courants par induction au moyen d'un aimant est excellent pour produire ces effets. Il faut que les fils aient été bien lavés dans les acides avant l'opération & qu'ils soient très rapprochés l'un de l'autre (à 3 ou 4 lignes de distance seulement); il faut se servir d'acide sulfurique ou nitrique bien purs étendus de 9 fois leur volume d'eau. –

J'ai fait dernièrement plusieurs expériences assez intéressantes avec ces courants d'induction en me servant de métaux différens, pour les transmettre dans les solutions acides. En voici une qui est bien favorable à la théorie chimique de l'électricité voltaïque. – Je plonge dans de l'eau acidulée un couple formé d'un fil de *platine* & d'un fil de *plomb* ou de tout autre métal oxidable, placés chacun à l'une des extrémités d'un galvanomètre, j'ai un courant très faible; je fais passer les courans par induction, allant alternativement en sens contraire, du fil de plomb qui fait partie du couple a un fil de platine plongé dans le liquide qui n'est pas le même que celui qui est lié métalliquement sur le fil de plomb les courans par induction amènent alternativement sur le fil de plomb de l'oxigène & de l'hydrogène; or ce fil ne garde que l'oxigène qui l'oxide; cette oxidation donne lieu à un fort courant qui transporte l'hydrogène sur le fil de platine qui forme un couple avec le plomb. – Or où est ici la source de courant si ce n'est dans l'oxidation du plomb operée de la manière la plus directe par l'arrivée de l'oxigène sur ce métal. Si c'est le contact qui donne lieu à ce courant, pourquoi n'existait-il qu'à un infiniment faible degré avant que l'oxigène arrivât sur la surface du plomb. Il y a dans ce phénomène & d'autres analogues plusieurs détails assez curieux que je ne vous donne pas de peur de vous en ennuyer, mais que vous trouverez dans mon mémoire[3] que je compte vous envoyer en vous demandant, si vous le jugez convenable, d'avoir la bonté de le présenter à la Société Royale. –

Les recherches de Mr Schöenbein sur l'odeur[4] qui accompagne certains effets électriques me paraissent curieuses, mais je n'admets pas, encore du moins, son explication. J'ai souvent observé le phénomène, & je le crois du à quelques particules très subtiles, détachées soit du métal qui sert d'électrode, soit de la solution décomposée; je suis plutôt disposé à croire que c'est un effet de l'oxida-tion légère qu'éprouvait au pole positif, même les métaux les moins oxidables, particules qui oxidées se détachent du reste du métal & surtout à cause de leur extrême ténuité [sont] en suspension dans le gaz. Peut-être aussi reste-t-il un peu d'arsenic dans le métal qui donne lieu à cette odeur.

Je vous ai envoyé par Mr Prevost ma petite notice sur un procédé électro-chimique de dorage;[5] j'espère que vous l'avez reçue. Dès lors j'ai encore perfectionné mon procédé & il est à présent employé en grand à Genève. Indépendamment de l'avantage qu'il présente pour la santé par l'absence du mercure, il a l'avantage d'être beaucoup plus économique que le procédé par amalgamation (plus du 2/3). Indépendamment de l'*argent* & du *laiton*, nous avons réussi à dorer *l'acier* & même *l'argental*. [*sic*] – Le point le plus important c'est que la surface à dorer soit parfaitement propre; la moindre tache de graisse ou d'oxidation empêche complètement l'opération de réussir. L'emploi de l'hydrogène dégagé sur la surface à nettoyer par son immersion dans l'eau acidulée avec un petit morceau de zinc qui lui est uni métalliquement, réussit très bien. – Il faut aussi que le métal ait une composition & une structure bien uniforme; Ainsi l'argent allié avec du cuivre, si l'alliage n'est pas conforme, c. à d. s'il y a des portions qui présentent plus de cuivre que d'autres se dore mal & inégalement. Il s'opère un effet électrochimique entre les différentes parties du même métal qui dérange complètement l'opération. – Je désirerais vivement que vous fassiez quelques essais; avec votre dextérité & habileté ordinaire vous verrez bientôt en quoi le procédé peut être perfectionné. – Je suis à chercher une bonne occasion pour vous envoyer quelques objets dorés par mon procédé, que j'ai là & qui vous sont destinés; j'espère que vous les receverez incessamment & que vous en serez content.

Ne croyez-vous pas qu'on pourrait mettre une petite notice sur ce sujet dans un journal Anglais, par exemple dans l'*Athenaeum* et ne pourriez-vous pas avoir la bonté d'en dire ou d'en faire dire quelques mots par un autre, si votre temps ne vous permet pas de faire vous même (ce qui me serait bien plus agréable) un article de quelques lignes sur ce sujet. Vous pourriez peut-être y joindre quelques mots sur mes expériences relatives à l'oxidation des fils de platine & aux effets divers dont je vous parle des courans par induction.

Vous me faites espérer que vous allez prendre les expériences sur l'électricité *statique* developpée par le contact des métaux; je vous en supplie examiner avec attention ce point comme vous avez examiné les autres & vous arriverez, j'en suis sûr, à la même conséquence savoir que le contact *seul* & *par lui-même* n'est nullement une source d'électricité. Je me suis servi dans toutes mes recherches d'un électroscope à feuilles d'or *sans piles sèches* (Gardez-vous en, c'est une source d'erreur), aussi d'un condensateur de laiton doré de 9 pouces de diamètre environ. – J'ai [reading doubtful] avoir soin de tenir l'intérieur de l'électroscope bien désseché avec du *chlorure de calcium*. – J'ai sur ce sujet un grand nombre d'expériences non encore publiées que j'ai faites avec cet appareil & qui toutes conduisent au même résultat.

Enfin pour terminer cette longue lettre, je vous dirai que la lecture du mémoire de Mr Regnault[6] sur les *chaleurs spécifiques* nous a décidés Marcet & moi à publier, sans tarder, les recherches que nous avons déjà faites sur ce sujet sur les *solides*, les *liquides*, & *les gaz*. Notre procédé fondé sur les lois [illeg.] nous a donné des résultats qui concordent assez bien avec la loi de Dulong & Petit. –

Quant aux gaz nous avons continué à trouver pour les gaz [illeg.] & notamment pour l'*hydrogène*, *exactement* la même chaleur spécifique que pour l'*air*; mais il est des gaz composés qui n'ont pas sous le même volume & la même pression la même chaleur spécifique que les gaz simple [*sic*]; ainsi nous avons trouvé pour le *gaz oléfiant* (hydrogène bicarbure).[7] 1,451° & pour le gaz *acide carbonique* 1,210 l'*air* était 1. – Nous avons obtenu les résultats suivants pour des substances dont la chaleur spécifique n'avait pas encore été obtenue. *Sélénium* 0,08240, *Cadmium* 0,05766, *Tungstène* 0,1306, *Molybdène* 0,06594 [last figure doubtful], *Cobalt* 0,1172 au lieu de 0,1498 qu'avaient trouvé Dulong & Petit, probablement parce qu'ils faisaient usage de cobalt réduit par le charbon & qui en contenait encore un peu, tandis que nous nous [sommes] servis de cobalt réduit par l'hydrogène. – Mais voilà une lettre assez longue. – Ne voudrez vous point nous voir cet été en Suisse. Un voyage sur le Continent vous reposerait & vous ferait du bien. – Nous avons à Presinge des chambres toutes prêtes pour vous recevoir vous & Madame Faraday. – Venez profitez en & croyez moi toujours votre tout dévoué & bien affectionné.

A. DE LA RIVE.

[1] Letter 246.

[2] Gustav Theodor Fechner (1801–87), probably best known as the formulator of Fechner's Law in psychology, had defended the contact theory of electricity in 1837. See his 'Rechtfertigung der Contact-theorie des Galvanismus,' *AP*, n.s., 42 (1837), 481.

[3] A. de la Rive, 'Nouvelles recherches sur les propriétés des courants électriques discontinus et dirigés alternativement en sens contraire,' *AE*, 1 (1841), 175.

[4] Christian Friedrich Schoenbein (1799–1868) of Basle discovered ozone and gun cotton. His correspondence with Faraday was published in 1899. See George W. A. Kahlbaum and Francis V. Darbishire, *The Letters of Faraday and Schoenbein*, 1836–62, Basle and London, 1899.

The paper to which de la Rive here refers is 'On the odour accompanying electricity, and on the probability of its dependence on the presence of a new substance,' *PRS*, 4 (1840), 226. The 'new substance' was ozone.

[5] A. de la Rive, 'Notice sur un procédé électro-chimique ayant pour objet de dorer l'argent et le laiton,' *AC*, 2 s., 73 (1840), 398.

[6] Henri Victor Regnault (1810–78), 'Recherches sur la chaleur spécifique des corps simples et composés. Ier mémoire: Corps simples,' *AC*, 2 s., 73 (1840), 5.

[7] Ethylene.

251   M. FARADAY to W. WHEWELL, 20 May 1840
[*Trinity College Library, Trinity College, Cambridge, previously unpublished*]

R. Institution,
20 May 1840

MY DEAR SIR

I think the word[1] looks & works very well & I shall use it. I perceive also another new & good word the *scientist*. Now can you give us one for the french *physicien*? physicist is both to my mouth and ears so awkward that I think I shall never be able to use it the equivalent of three separate sounds of *s* in one word is too much

You may think that your good opinion is very grateful to me.

Ever Dear Sir,
Your Oblgd Servt
M. FARADAY

[1] I am unable to identify this word.
[2] William Whewell, *The Philosophy of the Inductive Sciences, founded upon their history*, 2 vols., London, 1840. The word 'scientist' was introduced on p. 113 of the first volume.

252 M. FARADAY to C. MANBY,[1] 27 June 1840
[*Wellcome Medical Historical Library, previously unpublished*]

R Institution
27. June 1840

MY DEAR SIR

I do not know of any particular bookseller whose name I could in preference recommend to you The nearest medical or general bookseller would be the one I should take As to the works of Dalton & myself you will not be able to get them complete. Certain volumes of Daltons you can obtain but his papers have not been collected As to myself you will be able to procure nothing but the volume of experimental researches in electricity recently published by Taylor of Red Lion court Fleet Street. My work on manipulation is out of print.

By the bye I have no doubt that Taylor would also get any of Daltons works that can be had –

Ever Truly Yours
M. FARADAY

[1] Charles Manby (1804–84), was Secretary of the Institution of Civil Engineers from 1839–56.

253 J. DALTON to M. FARADAY, 29 July 1840
[*R.I., previously unpublished*]

Manchester,
29th of July, 1840. –

DEAR FRIEND,

I sent up two papers on [*sic*] 1839 (I think it was in May) on the Phosphates & the Arseniates.[1]

You delivered them the 20 of June, 1839, as I find by the Philosophical Magazine, Vol. 15, page 337,[2] for which you have my thanks; there were in all *10* papers on various subjects read at the Society.

As I think it will not be published, there being several papers read since, in the Philosophical Transactions, I would thank to take the trouble to send me down the articles of the *Phosphates* & the *Arseniates*: it follows as matter of course that they should be reclaimed by the Author.

I have an imperfect copy of them; but I should wish to send the *originals*, as I have taken great pains with them.

I have the following Essays by me:

"On the mixture of sulpate [*sic*] of Magnesia & Biophosphate of Soda: no Magnesia in it."

"On the *Acid*, *Base* & *Water* in Salts: they are united in atomic proportions; no ½ or ¼ or ⅛ parts of atoms of water that I have found as yet."

"On the Microcosmic [reading doubtful] *Salt*.

It is my present intention to publish them together with the *Phosphates* & *Arseniates*, as a sequel to my Chemistry.[1]

> I am with great respect
> Yours faithfully
> JOHN DALTON

[1] These papers were privately published. See Frank Greenaway, *The Biographical Approach to John Dalton*, Manchester, 1958, 8.

[2] This reference is wrong for page 337 is in the middle of a paper on electricity. Similarly, the Royal Society met on 21 June, not 20 June and there is no record of any papers by Dalton having been read then.

254   J. C. A. PELTIER[1] to M. FARADAY, 31 July 1840
[*I.E.E., previously unpublished*]

Paris
ce 31 juillet 1840

MONSIEUR

J'ai l'honneur de vous faire hommage du premier volume de météorologie[2] que je viens de publier et de quelques mémoires qui ont paru dans plusieurs recueils. Je désirais trouver une occasion pour vous faire parvenir le témoignage de ma déférence pour vos éminens travaux et pour vous assurer de la profonde estime que je voue à votre ingénieux talent d'observation, j'ai été assez heureux pour rencontrer un jeune Savant, Mr. Peyron,[3] professeur de Physique à Marseille qui a accepté cette mission avec empressement désireux lui-même de connaître un des premiers physiciens de l'époque actuelle.

Dans l'un des mémoires que je vous envoie, vous trouverez une expérience contraire au fait annoncé par Mr. Prevost de Genève, sur le magnétisme obtenu par innervation.[4] j'ai regreté que cette expérience ne vous soit pas connue lorsque vous avez preté l'appui de votre nom à ce fait erroné dans un de vos Derniers mémoires;[5] si le temps vous permet de repeter mon expérience, vous vous convaincrez par vous-même de l'erreur du Physicien de Genève

J'espère, Monsieur, vous faire parvenir dans un temps peu éloigné un second volume de météorologie, dans lequel je traiterai des nuages, de la cause de leurs électricités différentes et de la puissante tension qu'ils peuvent acquérir. Je reviendrai avec détail et avec des preuves d'observations et d'expériences sur les trois nouvelles routes que j'ouvre à la météorologie et j'en indiquerai une quatrième plus générale dont les trois premières ne sont que des accessoires. Recevez, Monsieur, l'assurance de ma considération distinguée

PELTIER

26 rue Poissonnière

[1] Jean Charles Athanase Peltier (1785–1845), clockmaker, was the discoverer of the Peltier effect, i.e. the production of cold when electricity is passed through a bismuth–antimony junction.
[2] J. C. A. Peltier, *Météorologie. Observations et recherches expérimentales sur les causes qui concourent à la formation des trombes*, Paris, 1840.
[3] For Peyron's publications, see *CR*, 13 (1841), 820 and 898.
[4] See 'Sur la constitution des nerfs qui se rendent aux organes de la sensation et sur ceux qui se rendent aux organes de la locomotion,' *PVSP*, 20. For Prevost, see Jean Louis Prevost, 'Aimantation d'une aiguille de fer doux par un courant nerveux,' *CR*, 6 (1838), 19.
[5] *ERE*, 2 (1762).

255 J. DALTON to M. FARADAY, 3 September 1840
[*R.I.*, *previously unpublished*]

September 3, 1840.

DEAR FRIEND
D[r] Faraday,

I have been from home more than a week in Cumberland, having Peter Clare[1] with me & my servant man, partly on business & partly on pleasure & on account of my health.

I am sorry to find You are in the same predicament as to health. You have not been injured as to *Lead*, as I was in London? Lead in *Porter* & lead in *water* was my beverage. I was more than a year in getting rid of this complaint in 1804.

My recent attack of paralysis was from *extreme* cold. Being at York & Chester on trials; I was subject in *winter* to the extremity of *cold*, & being temperate & *regular* in my meals, I was subject to irregularities in present situation [*sic*] which were too much for me.

I shall be obliged to you for copies of my papers on *Phosphate* & *Arseniates* at my expense; they are not long: I suppose 20 or 30 Shillings will be the extremity. I want to publish them forthwith. I have copies, but *verbatim* I shall not say.

I observe the Council have voted the Rev. Mr Farquharson paper[2] as fit for publication in the 2[d] part of 1839. The height of the *aurora* was 1897 *yards* or rather above 1 Mile. I calculated it 100 to 160 Miles (1828).[3] Mr. Cavendish 52 to 71 Miles, (1790),[4] Robert Were Fox, 1000 Miles (1831)[5] This would be an interesting Phenomenon to the *British association* whether its height was 1 – or 1000 Miles.

I am your friend
JOHN DALTON

[1] Peter Clare (1781–1851), member of the Manchester Literary and Philosophical Society and Fellow of the Royal Astronomical Society.
[2] James Farquharson (1781–1843), 'Report of a geometrical measurement of the height of the Aurora Borealis above the Earth,' *PT* (1839), 266.
[3] John Dalton, 'On the height of the Aurora Borealis above the surface of the earth; particularly one seen on the 29th March 1826,' *PT* (1828), 291.
[4] Henry Cavendish (1731–1810), 'On the Height of the luminous Arch which was seen on 23 February, 1784,' *PT* (1790), 101.
[5] Robert Were Fox, 'On the variable intensity of terrestrial magnetism and the influence of the Aurora Borealis upon it,' *PT* (1831), 199.

256 M. FARADAY to C. BABBAGE, 2 November 1840
[*British Museum, Add. mss. 37191, f. 484, previously unpublished*]

R Institution
2 Nov.ʳ 1840

Thanks dear Babbage for your kind invitation to one so unworthy from his habits of that sort of kindness since he never values it enough. I leave town tomorrow morning for Brighton & hope to get rid of a headache there which as some people say I have *enjoyed* for the last four months

Ever Truly Yours
M. FARADAY.

257 M. FARADAY to E. MAGRATH, 23 December 1840
[*R.I., previously unpublished*]

R Institution
23 Decr. 1840

MY DEAR MAGRATH

Dont be troubled about me. I was very glad to have a little chat with you but I cannot stand much with any body or in any subject. I ought to apologise to you for my abrupt conclusion but we have known each other too long & too well to have any difficulties on that score

Ever Yours
M. FARADAY.

[*PM, 3 s., 18 (1841), 465*]

Philadelphia,
Jan 1, 1841.

MY DEAR SIR,

39*. In the month of July last I had the pleasure to read, in the American Journal of Science,[1] your letter in reply to one which I had addressed to you through the same channel. I should sooner have noticed this letter, but that meanwhile I have had to republish two of my text books, and, besides, could not command, until lately, a complete copy of all those numbers of your researches to which you have referred.

40. The tenor of the language, with which your letter commences, realizes the hope which I cherished, that my strictures would call forth an amicable reply. Under these circumstances, it would grieve me that you should consider any part of my language as charging you with inconsistency or self-contradiction, as if it could be my object to put you in the wrong, further than might be necessary to establish my conception of the truth. Certainly it has been my wish never to go beyond the sentiment "amicus Plato, sed magis amica veritas.' I attach high importance to the facts established by your "Researches," which can only be appreciated sufficiently by those who have experienced the labour, corporeal and mental, which experimental investigations require. I am, moreover, grateful for the disposition to do me justice, manifested in those researches yet it may not always be possible for me to display the deference, which I nevertheless entertain. I am aware that when, in a discussion, which due attention to brevity must render unceremonious, diversities of opinion are exhibited, much magnanimity is requisite in the party whose opinions are assailed; but I trust that both of us have truth in view above all other objects, and that so much of your new doctrine as tends to promote that end, will not be invalidated by a criticism, which, though free, is intended to be perfectly fair.

41. In paragraph 11 your language is as follows: – "*My theory of induction makes no assertion as to the nature of electricity, nor at all questions any of the theories respecting that subject.*"

42. Owing to this avowed omission to state your opinions as to the nature of electricity, as preliminary to the statement of your "*theory*," and because I was unable to reconcile that theory with those previously accredited, I received the impression that you claimed no aid from any imponderable principle. It appeared to me that there was no room for the agency of any such principle, if induction were an *action of contiguous ponderable particles consisting of a species of polarity*. It seemed to follow that what we call electricity, could be nothing more than a polarity in the ponderable particles, directly caused by those mechanical, or chemical frictions, movements or reactions, by which ponderable bodies are electrified. You have correctly inferred that I had not seen

382

the fourteenth series of your researches, containing certain paragraphs (38). From them it appears that the polarity, on which so much stress has been laid, is analogous to that which has long been known to arise in a ponderable body, about which the electric equilibrium has been subverted by the inductive influence of the electricity accumulated upon another such body. This is clearly explained in paragraph 4 of your letter, by the illustration, agreeably to which three bodies, *A*, *B*, *C*, are situated in a line, in the order in which they are named, in proximity, but not in contact. "*A* is electrified positively, and then *C* is uninsulated." It is evident that you are correct in representing that, under these circumstances, the extremities of *B* will be oppositely excited, so as to have a reaction with any similarly excited body, analogous to that which takes place between magnets; since the similarly excited extremities of two such bodies would repel each other, while those dissimilarly excited would be reciprocally attractive. Hence, no doubt, the word polarity is conceived by you to convey an idea of the state of the body *B*. If I may be allowed to propose an epithet to convey the idea which I have of the state of a body thus electrified, I would designate it as an electropolar state, or as a state of electro-polarity.

43. It does not appear to me, that in the suggestion of the electro-polarity, which we both conceive to be induced upon the body *B* (4), so long as it concerns a mass of ponderable matter, there is any novelty. The only part of your doctrine which is new, is that which suggests an analogous state to be caused in the particles of the bodies through which the inductive power is propagated. Admitting each of the particles of a dielectric, through which the process of ordinary induction takes place, to be put into the state of the body *B*, it does not appear to me to justify your definition of electrical induction. I think that, consistently with your own exemplification of that process, you should have alleged ordinary induction to be *productive* of an *affection* of particles, *causing* in them a species of polarity. In the case of the bodies *A*, *B*, *C* (4), *B* is evidently passive. How then can we consider as active, particles represented to be in an analogous state? If in *B* there is no action, how can there be any action in particles performing a perfectly similar part? Moreover, how can the inductive power of an electrical accumulation upon *A consist* of the polarity which it induces in *B*?

44. Having supposed (8) an electrified ball, *A*, an inch in diameter, to be situated within a thin metallic sphere, *C*, of a foot in diameter, you suggest, that where one thousand concentric metallic spheres interpose between *A* and the inner surface of *C*, the electro-polar state of each particle in those spheres would be analogous to that of *B*, already mentioned. Of course, if there be any action of those particles, there must be an action of *B*; but this appears to me not only irreconcilable with any previously existing theory, but also with your own exposition of the process by which *B* is polarized.

45. Supposing concentric metallic hemispheres to be interposed only upon

one side of *A*, you aver that, agreeably to your experience, more of the inductive influence would be extended towards that side of the containing shell than before (14). Admitting this, I cannot concede that the greater influence of the induction, resulting from the presence of the metallic particles, is the consequence of any *action* of theirs, whether in *contiguity* or in *proximity*. Agreeably to my view, the action is confined to the electrical accumulation in the sphere *A*. Between the electricity accumulated in this sphere, and that existing in or about the intervening ponderable particles, there may be a *reaction*; but evidently these particles are as inactive as are the steps of a ladder in the scaling of a wall.

46. Suppose a powerful magnet to be so curved as to have the terminating polar surfaces parallel, and to leave between them an interval of some inches. Place between these surfaces a number of short pieces of soft iron wire. These would, of course, be magnetized, and would arrange themselves in rows, the north and south poles becoming contiguous. Would this be a sufficient reason for saying that the inductive influence of the magnetic poles was an *action* of the contiguous wires? Would not the phænomena be the consequence of an *affection* of the contiguous pieces of wire, not of their *action*?

47. As respects the word charge, I am not aware that I have been in the habit of attaching any erroneous meaning to it, as your efforts to define it in paragraph 3 would imply. I have been accustomed to restrict the use of it to the case which you distinguish as an inductive charge, illustrated by that of the Leyden jar. To designate the states of the conductors of a machine, I have almost always employed the words *excited* or *excitement*. In my text book these words are used to designate the state of glass or resin electrified by friction, while that of coated surfaces, whether panes or jars, inductively electrified, has been designated by the words *charge* or *charged*.

48. I understood the word contiguous to imply contact, or contiguity, whereas it seems that it was intended by you to convey the idea of proximity. In the last-mentioned sense it is not inconsistent with the idea of an action, at the distance of half an inch: but by admitting the word contiguous to be ill chosen, you have with great candour furnished me with an apology for having mistaken your meaning.

49. Any inductive action which does not exist at sensible distances (20) you attribute to *ordinary* induction, considering the case of induction through a vacuum as an *extraordinary* case of induction. To me it appears that the induction must be the same in both cases, and that the *circumstances* under which it acts are those which may be considered in the one case as *ordinary*, in the other *extraordinary*. Thus take the case cited in your reply (8, 9, 10). Does the interposition of the spheres alter the character of the inductive power in the sphere *A*?

50. Either the force exercised by the charge in *A* is like that of gravitation, altogether independent of the influence of intervening bodies, or, like that of

light, is dependent on the agency of an intervening matter. Agreeably to one doctrine, the matter, by means of which luminous bodies act, operates by its transmission from the luminous surface to that illumined; agreeably to another doctrine, the illuminating matter operates by its undulations. If the inductive *power* of electrified bodies be not analogous to gravitation, it must be analogous to the power by which light is produced, so far as to be dependent on intervening matter. But were it to resemble gravitation, like that force it would be uninfluenced by intervening matter. If your experiments prove that electrical induction is liable to be modified by intervening matter, it is demonstrated that in its mode of operating it is analogous to light, not to gravitation. It is then proved that, agreeably to your doctrine, electrical induction requires the intervention of matter; but you admit that it acts across a vacuum, and, of course, acts without the presence of *ponderable* matter. Yet it requires intervening matter of some kind, and since the matter is not ponderable, it must of necessity be imponderable. When light is communicated from a luminous body in the centre of an exhausted sphere, agreeably to the undulatory hypothesis, its efficacy is dependent on the waves excited in an intervening imponderable medium. Agreeably to your electro-polar hypothesis, the inductive efficacy of an electrified body in an exhausted sphere would be due to a derangement of electric equilibrium, by which an opposite electric state would be produced at the surface of the containing sphere from that at the centre (26, 27). This case you consider as one of extraordinary induction; but when air is admitted into the hollow sphere, or when concentric spheres are interposed, you hold it to be a case of ordinary induction. Let us then, in the case of the luminous body, imagine that concentric spheres of glass are interposed, of which the surfaces are roughened by grinding. In consequence of the roughness thus produced, the rays, instead of proceeding in radii from the central ball, would be so refracted as to cross each other. Of the two instances of illumination, thus imagined, would the one be described as *ordinary*, the other as *extraordinary radiation?* But if these epithets are not to be applied to radiation, wherefore, under analogous circumstances, are they applicable to induction? Wherefore is induction, when acting through a plenum, to be called ordinary, and yet, when acting through a vacuum, to be called extraordinary? In the well-known case of the refracting power of Iceland spar, light undergoes an *ordinary* and *extraordinary refraction*; not an *ordinary* and *extraordinary radiation*. The candle, of which, when viewed through the spar, two images are seen, does not *radiate ordinarily* and *extraordinarily*.

51. If there be occasionally, as you allege (21), large intervals between the particles of radiant heat, how can the distances between them resemble those existing between particles acting at distances, which are not sensible? The repulsive reaction between the particles of radiant caloric, as described by you (21), resembles that which I have supposed to exist between those of electricity;

but I cannot conceive of any description less suitable for either, than that of particles which do not act at sensible distances.

52. Aware that the materiality of heat, and the Newtonian theory, which ascribes radiation to the projection of heat or light-producing particles, have been questioned, I should not have appealed to a doctrine which assumes both the materiality of heat and the truth of the Newtonian theory, had not you led the way; but, agreeably to the doctrine and theory alluded to, I cannot accord with you in perceiving any similitude between the processes of conduction and radiation (21).

53. Consistently with the hypothesis that electricity is material, you have shown that an enormous quantity of it must exist in metals. To me it seems equally evident that, agreeably to the idea that heat is material, there must exist in metals a proportionably great quantity of caloric. The intense heat produced when wires are deflagrated by an electrical discharge, cannot otherwise be consistently accounted for. Agreeably to the same idea, every metallic particle in any metallic mass must be surrounded by an atmosphere of caloric; since the *changes* of dimensions, consequent to variations of temperature, can only be explained by corresponding variations in the quantity of caloric imbibed, and in the consequent density of the calorific atmospheres existing in the mass which undergoes these changes†.

54. Such being the constitution of expansible bodies agreeably to the hypothesis in question, it seems to me that the process, by which caloric is propagated through them by *conduction*, must be extremely different from that by which it is transmitted from one part of space to another by *radiation*. In the one case, the calorific particle flies like a bullet projected from a gun, but with an inconceivably greater velocity, which is not sensibly retarded by the reflecting or refracting influence of intervening transparent media: in the other case, it must be slowly imparted from one calorific atmosphere to another, until the repulsion sustained on all sides, is in equilibrio. It is in this way that I have always explained the fact that metals are bad radiators, while good reflectors‡.

55. In paragraph 25 you allege that conduction of heat differs from electrical induction, because it passes by a very slow process; while induction is, in its distant influence, simultaneous with its force at the place of action. How then can the passage of heat by conduction be "*a process precisely like that of radiation*" (21), which resembles induction in the velocity with which its influence reaches objects, however remote?

56. Although (21) you appeal to the "modern views respecting radiation and conduction of heat," in order to illustrate your conception of the contiguity of the particles of bodies subjected to induction, yet (in 25) you object to the reference which I had made to the same views, in order to show that the intensity of electro-polarization could not be inversely as the number of the polarized particles, interposed between the "inductric" surfaces. Let us then

resort to the case above suggested, of the influence of the surfaces of the poles of a magnet upon intervening pieces of iron wire. In 1679, 14th series, you suggest this as an analogous case to that of the process of *ordinary* electrical induction, which we have under consideration. Should there be in the one case, a thousand pieces of wire interposed, in the second, a hundred, will it be pretended that the intensity of their reciprocal inductive reaction would be inversely as the number; so that the effect of the last-mentioned number of wires would be *equivalent* to that of the first? Were intervals to be created between the wires, by removing from among the number first mentioned alternate wires, it would seem to me that the energy of their reciprocal influence would be diminished, not only as the number of them might be lessened, but also as they should consequently be rendered more remote.

57. If, as you suggest, the interposition of ponderable particles have any tendency to promote inductive influence (14), there must be some number of such particles by which this effect will be best attained. That number being interposed, I cannot imagine how the intensity of any electro-polarity, thus created in the intervening particles, can, by a diminution of their number, acquire a proportionable increase; and evidently in no case can the excitement in the particles exceed that of the "inductric" surfaces, whence the derangement of electrical equilibrium arises.

58. The repulsive power of electricity being admitted to be inversely as the squares of the distances, you correctly infer, that the aggregate influence of an electrified ball *B*, situated at the centre of a hollow sphere *C*, will be a constant quantity, whatever may be the diameter of *C*. This is perfectly analogous to the illuminating influence of a luminous body situated at the centre of a hollow sphere, which would of course receive the whole of the light emitted, whatever might be its diameter; provided that nothing should be interposed to intercept any portion of the rays. But in order to answer the objection which I have advanced, that the diminution of the density of a "*dielectric*" cannot be compensated by any consequent increase of inductive intensity, it must be shown, in the case of several similar hollow spheres, in which various numbers of electrified equidistant balls should exist, that the influence of such balls upon each other, and upon the surfaces of the spheres, would not be directly as the number of the balls, and inversely as the size of the containing spaces. Were gas-lights substituted for the balls, it must be evident that the intensity of the light in any one of the spheres would be as the number of lights which it might contain: now one of your illustrations (8), above noticed, makes light and electrical induction obey the same law as respects the influence of distance upon the respective intensities.

59. From these considerations, and others above stated, I infer, that if electrical induction were an action of particles in proximity, operating reciprocally with forces varying in intensity with the squares of the distances, their

aggregate influence upon any surfaces, between which they might be situated, would be proportionable to their number; and since experience demonstrates that the inductive power is not diminished by the reduction of the number of the intervening particles, I conclude that it is independent of any energy of theirs, and proceeds altogether from that electrical accumulation with which the inductive charge is admitted to originate.

60. In paragraph 31, you say, "that at one time there was a distinction between heat and cold. At present that theory is done away with, and the phænomena of heat and cold are referred to the same class, and to different degrees of the same power."

61. In reply to this I beg leave to point out, that although, in ordinary acceptation, cold refers to relatively low temperature, yet we all understand that there might be that perfect negation of heat, or abstraction of caloric, which may be defined absolute cold. I presume that, having thus defined absolute cold, you would not represent it as identical with caloric. For my own part, this would seem as unreasonable as to confound matter with nihility.

62. Assuming that there is only one electric fluid, there appears to me to be so far an analogy between caloric and electricity, that negative electricity conveys, in the one case, an idea analogous to that which cold conveys in the other. But if the doctrine of Du Fay be admitted, there are two kinds of electric matter, which are no more to be confounded than an acid and an alkali. Let us, upon these premises, subject to further examination your argument (1330), that insulation and conduction should be identified, "*since the moment we leave in the smallest degree perfection at either extremity, we involve the element of perfection at the opposite end.*" Let us suppose two remote portions of space, one replete with pure vitreous electricity, the other with pure resinous. Let there be a series of like spaces, containing the resinous and vitreous electricities in as many different varieties of admixture, so that in passing from one of the first-mentioned spaces, through the series to the other, as soon as we should cease to be exposed to the vitreous fluid, in perfect purity, we should begin to be exposed minutely to the resinous; or that, in passing from the purely resinous atmosphere, we should begin to be exposed to a minute portion of the vitreous fluid; would this be a sufficient reason for confounding the two fluids, and treating the phænomena to which they give rise as the effect of one only?

63. But the discussion into which your illustrations have led me refers to things, whereas conduction and insulation, as I understand them, are opposite and incompatible properties; so that, inasmuch as either prevails, the other must be counteracted. Conduction conveys to my mind the idea of *permeability* to the electric fluid, insulation that of *impermeability*; and I am unable to understand how these irreconcilable properties can be produced by a difference of degree in any one property of electrics and conductors.

388

64. If, as you infer, glass have, comparatively with metals, an almost infinitely minute degree of the conducting power, is it this power which enables it to prevent conduction, or, in other words, to insulate? Let it be granted that you have correctly supposed conduction to comprise both induction and discharge, the one following the other in perfect conductors within an inexpressibly brief interval: insulation does not prevent induction, but, so far as it goes, prevents discharge. In practice, this part of the process of conduction does not take place through glass during any time ordinarily allotted to our experiments, however correct you may have been in supposing it to have ensued before the expiration of a year or more, in the case of the tubes which you had sealed after charging them. But conceding it to have been thus proved, that glass has, comparatively with metals, an infinitely small degree of the conducting power, is it this minute degree of conducting power which enables it to prevent conduction, or, in other words, to insulate?

65. Induction arises from one or more properties of electricity, insulation from a property of ponderable matter; and although there be no matter capable of preventing induction, as well as discharge, were there such a matter, would that annihilate insulation? On the contrary, would it not exhibit the property in the highest perfection?

66. As respects the residual charge of a battery, is it not evident that any electrical change which affects the surface of the glass, must produce a corresponding effect upon the stratum of air in contact with the coating of the glass? If we place one coating between two panes, will it not enable us, to a certain extent, to charge or discharge both? Substituting the air for one of them, will it not in some measure be liable to an affection similar to that of the vitreous surface, for which it is substituted? In the well-known process of the condensing electrometer, the plate of air interposed between the discs is, I believe, universally admitted to perform the part of an electric, and to be equivalent in its properties to the glass in a coated pane.

67. When I adverted to a gradual relinquishment of electricity by the air to the glass, I did not mean to suggest that it was attended by any more delay than the case actually demonstrates. It might be slow or gradual, compared with the velocity of an electric discharge, and yet be extremely quick comparatively with any velocity ever produced in ponderable matter. That the return should be slow when no coating was employed, and yet quick when it was employed, as stated by you (38), is precisely what I should have expected, because the coating only operates to remove all obstruction to the electric equilibrium. The quantity or intensity of the excitement is dependent altogether upon the electrified surfaces of the air and the glass. You have cited (1632) the property of a charged Leyden jar, as usually accoutred, of electrifying a carrier ball. This I think sanctions the existence of a power to electrify, by convection, the surrounding air to a greater or less depth; since it must be

evident that every aërial particle must be competent to perform the part of the carrier ball.

68. Agreeably to the Franklinian doctrine, the electricity directly accumulated upon one side of a pane repels that upon the other side. You admit that this would take place were a vacuum to intervene; but when ponderable matter is interposed you conceive each particle to act as does the body *B*, when situated as described between *A* and *C* (4). But agreeably to the view which I have taken, and what I understand to be your own exposition of the case, *B* is altogether passive, so that it cannot help, if it does not impede, the repulsive influence. Morever, it must be quite evident, that were *B* removed, and *A* approximated to *C*, without attaining the striking distance, the effect upon *C*, and the consequent energy of any discharge upon it from *A*, would be greater instead of less. If, in the charge of a coated pane, the intermediate ponderable vitreous particles have any tendency to enhance the charge, how happens it that, the power of the machine employed being the same, the intensity of the charge which can be given to an electric is greater in proportion to its tenuity?

69. In reference to the direction of any discharge, it appears to me that as, in *charging*, the fluid must always pass from the cathode to the anode, so in reversing the process it must pursue the opposite course of going from the anode back to the cathode. Evidently the circumvolutions of the circuit are as unimportant as respects a correct idea of the direction, as their length has been shown by Wheatstone to be incompetent to produce any perceptible delay.

70. The dissipation of conductors being one of the most prominent among electrical phænomena, it appears to me to be an objection to your theory, if, while it fails to suggest any process by which this phænomenon is produced, it assumes premises which seem to be incompatible with the generation of any explosive power. If discharge only involves the restoration of polarized ponderable particles to their natural state, the potency of the discharge must be proportionable to the intensity of the antecedent polarity; yet it is through conductors liable, as you allege, to polarization of comparatively low intensity (31) that discharge takes place with the highest degree of explosive violence.

71. Having inquired how your allegation could be true, that discharge brings bodies to their natural state, and yet causes conductors to be dissipated, you reply (34), that different effects may result from the same cause, acting with different degrees of intensity, as when by one degree of heat ice is converted into water, by another into steam. But it may be urged, that although, in the case thus cited, different effects are produced, yet that the one is not inconsistent with the other, as were those ascribed to electrical discharges. It is quite consistent that the protoxide of hydrogen, which, *per se*, constitutes the solid called ice, should, by one degree of calorific repulsion, have the cohesion of its particles so far counteracted as to be productive of fusion; and yet that a higher

degree of the same power should cause them to recede from each other, so as to exist in the aëriform state.

72. In order to found, upon the influence of various temperatures, a good objection to my argument, it should be shown that while a certain reduction of temperature enables aqueous particles to indulge their innate propensity to consolidation, a still further reduction will cause them, in direct opposition to that propensity, to repel each other so as to form steam.

73. In your concluding paragraph you allege, "*that when ponderable particles intervene, during the process of dynamic induction, the currents resulting from this source do require these particles.*" I presume this allegation is to be explained by the conjecture made by you (1729), that since certain bodies, when interposed, did not interfere with dynamic induction, therefore they might be inferred to cooperate in the transmission of that species of inductive influence. But if the induction takes place without the ponderable matter, is it right to assume that this matter *aids*, because it does not prevent the effect? Might it not be as reasonably inferred, in the case of light, that, although its transmission does not require the interposition of a pane of glass, yet, that when such a pane is interposed, since the light is not intercepted, there is reason to suppose an active cooperation of the vitreous particles in aid of the radiation? It may be expedient here to advert to the fact, that Prof. Henry has found a metallic plate to interfere with the dynamic induction of one flat helix upon another. I have myself been witness of this result.

74. Does not magnetic or electro-dynamic induction take place as well *in vacuo* as *in pleno*? Has the presence of any gas been found to promote or retard that species of reaction? It appears that, agreeably to your experiments, ponderable bodies, when made to intervene, did not enhance the influence in question, while in some of those performed by Henry it was intercepted by them. Does it not follow that ponderable particles may impede, but cannot assist in this process?

75. I am happy to find that, among the opinions which I expressed in my letter to you, although there are several in which you do not concur, there are some which you esteem of importance, though you do not consider yourself justified in extending to them your sanction, being constrained, in the present state of human knowledge, to hold your judgment in suspense. For the present I shall here take leave of this subject, having already so extended my letter as to occupy too much of your valuable time. I am aware that as yet I have not sufficiently studied many of the intricate results of your sagacity, ingenuity and consummate skill in experimental investigations. When I shall have time to make them the subject of the careful consideration which they merit, I may venture to subject your patience to some further trials.

* As originally printed for the American Journal of Science, the paragraphs of my first letter to Prof. Faraday were not numbered; but as numbers were attached to the paragraphs in the republication of it in the London and Edinburgh Philosophical Magazine and Journal [vol.

xvii. p. 44], I have directed them to be attached to this, my second letter, in due succession.
† I subjoin the language which I have held respecting the constitution of expansible solids, during the last twenty years.

"The expansion of matter, whether solid, liquid, or aëriform, by an increase of temperature, may be thus explained: –

"In proportion as the temperature within any space is raised, there will be more caloric in the vicinity of the particles of any mass contained in the space. The more caloric in the vicinity of the particles, the more of it will combine with them; and in proportion to the quantity of caloric thus combined, will they be actuated by that reciprocally repellent power, which, in proportion to its intensity, regulates their distance from each other.

"There may be some analogy between the mode in which each ponderable atom is surrounded by the caloric which it attracts, and that in which the earth is surrounded by the atmosphere; and as in the latter case, so probably in the former, the density is inversely as the square of the distance.

"At a height at which the atmospheric pressure does not exceed a grain to the square inch, suppose it to be doubled, and supported at that increased pressure by a supply of air from some remote region; is it not evident that a condensation would ensue in all the inferior strata of the atmosphere, until the pressure would be doubled throughout, so as to become at the terrestrial surface 30 pounds instead of the present pressure of 15 pounds? Yet the pressure at the point from which the change would be propagated would not exceed two grains per square inch.

"In like manner, it may be presumed that the atmospheres of caloric are increased in quantity and density about their respective atoms, by a slight increase in the calorific tension of the external medium."
‡ I will here quote the rationale which has been given in my lectures for the last twenty years: –

"Metals appear to consist of particles so united with each other, or with caloric, as to leave no pores through which radiant caloric can be projected. Hence the only portion of any metallic mass which can yield up its rays by radiation, is the external stratum.

"On the other hand, from its porosity, and probably from its not retaining caloric within its pores tenaciously as an ingredient in its composition, charcoal opposes but little obstruction to the passage of that subtile principle, when in the radiant form; and hence its particles may all be simultaneously engaged in radiating any excess of this principle with which a feeble affinity may have caused them to be transiently united, or in receiving the rays emitted by any heated body, to the emanations from which they may have been exposed.

"We may account in like manner for the great radiating power of earthenware and wood.

"For the same reason that calorific rays cannot be projected from the interior of a metal, they cannot enter it when projected against it from without. On the contrary, they are repelled with such force as to be reflected without any perceptible diminution of velocity. Hence the pre-eminence of metallic reflectors.

"It would seem as if the calorific particles which are condensed between those of the metal, repel any other particles of their own nature which may radiate towards the metallic superficies, before actual contact ensues; otherwise, on account of mechanical imperfection, easily discernible with the aid of a microscope, mirrors would not be as efficacious as they are found to be in concentrating radiant heat. Their influence, in this respect, seems to result from the excellence of their general contour, and is not proportionably impaired by blemishes."

1 Robert Hare, M.D.
2 *AJS*, 39 (1840), 108.

[*R.I., previously unpublished*]

Lake of Brientz.
Augt 14th. 1841.

DEAR MR MAGRATH

Mr Faraday seems very unwilling to write letters he says it is quite a labour to him, and that every one advises that he should take thorough rest and that he is quite inclined to do so. I can certainly say nothing against all this but I am anxious that such an old friend as you are should not be neglected altogether I will therefore take the opportunity of his absence (he is exploring the Pass of The Brunig) to begin a letter for him and to tell you how we are going on –

We have been absent from home six weeks now, which we consider about half our time, and we have had upon the whole favourable weather, and seen a great deal of beautiful scenery – We spent a fortnight at Thun at least my sister and myself staid there that time, Mr. Faraday & my brother[1] made sundry excursions from thence over the Gemm[e part illeg.] & from Thun we came to Interlaken, from thence to Lauterbrunnen, over the Wengern Alps to Grindewald back to Interlaken, & by the lake to this place, which rather disappoints us and we think of leaving it again on Monday and expect to reach Lucerne in about a week any letters sent from England till the 25 of this month may be directed there – I think Mr. Young[2] would be quite satisfied with the way my Husband employs his time, he certainly enjoys the country exceedingly and though at first he lamented on absence from home and friends very much, he seems now to be reconciled to it as a means of improving his general health, his strength is however very good he thinks nothing of walking 30 miles in a day (and very rough walking it is you know) and one day he walked 45 which I protested against his doing again tho' he was very little the worse for it, I think is too much, what would Mr Young say to that, but the grand thing is rest & relaxation of mind which he is really taking. there are not so many calls upon his memory here even to remember peoples names – he dislikes dining at Table d'hotes very much and we avoid it as often as we can but that cannot always be done, at the small places we have been staying at this last fortnight it does not signify so much but at Thun there was always such large companies from 20 to 30 at *One, Three* and *five* o'clock and almost all English – My Brothers occupation[3] is a great resource for us it is always an object and of course guides our movements very much he and Mr Faraday are excellent companions and very generally go together in sketching excursions Michael taking a book & a telescope and wandering about till George is ready to return in the mean time my Sister & myself are glad to rest ourselves or take little walks in the neighbourhood of our home for the time being, and sometimes we are obliged to be very industrious, for travelling makes sad work with the clothes –

I think I need say no more, for Mr. Faraday will speak for himself on the

next page but pray give my kind remembrances & best thanks to Mr Young –
I should like to hear how both your sisters are and to be remembered to them
and believe me to be Dear Mr Magrath

Yours very truly,
S FARADAY –

¹ George Barnard.
² James Young (1811–83), chemist and friend of Faraday.
³ George Barnard was a painter.

260 M. FARADAY to E. MAGRATH, 15 August 1841
[R.I., B.J. 2, 154]

Brientz
15 Aug 1841

MY DEAR MAGRATH

Though my wifes letter will tell you pretty well all about us yet a few lines
from an old friend (though somewhat worn out) will not be unpleasant to one
who like that friend is a little the worse for time and hard wear However if you
jog on as well as we do you will have no cause for grumbling by which I mean
to say that I certainly have not for the comforts that are given me and above all
the continual kindness affection & forbearance of friends towards me are I
think such as few experience – And how are things with you? I must ask the
question whether I can hear the answer or not perhaps as we shall not leave
Lucerne before the 2nd or 3rd of next month I may. I hope they are pretty well
& of all friends with you Remember us most kindly to Mr Young we often have
to think of him for many reasons I will give no opinion at present as to the
effect of his advice on my health and memory but I can have only one feeling
as to his kindness and whatever I may forget I think I shall not forget that –
Amongst other things say that the net for the cloaks & coats is most excellent
& has been several times admired for its utility It is droll to think what odd
gatherings go into it sometimes in a hurry. If you happen to see Mr Brande or
Sir James South remember me very kindly to them I think more of my friends
here than I did when at home and feel as if I had something particular to say to
every one of them. Now as to the main point of this trip i.e. the mental idleness
you can scarcely imagine how well I take to it and what a luxury it is, the only
fear I have is that when I return friends will begin to think that I shall overshoot
the mark; for feeling that any such exertion is a strain upon that faculty, which
I cannot hide from myself is getting weaker, namely memory, and feeling that
the less exertion I make to use that the better I am in health & head, so my desire
is to remain indolent mentally speaking and to retreat from a position which
should only be held by one who has the *power* as well as the will to be active.
All this however may be left to clear itself up as the time proceeds and now
farewell dear Magrath for the present

from Your Affectionate friend
M. FARADAY

[*I.E.E., previously unpublished*]

Paris
20 August 1841

SIR

My friends Broguet and professor Masson[2] in investigating the best way of rendering useful the induced currents in the construction of the electrico-magnetical machine of which I exposed to you last week the general plan – have obtained some results which appear to me a complement in some instances – of your own researches and of those of professor Henry. – This reason induces me to give you a short account of the chief points of their experiments. As soon as a machine will be constructed – I shall take the liberty of making you know if the result answers to my hope – and to ask your advice if it does not.

The voltaic apparatus used in the modification of professor Daniell's constant battery in which the earthen cups are replaced by a membrane separating a copper cylinder from a zinc one – which surrounds it – Each copper cylinder is 8 inches in height and $2\frac{1}{2}$ in Diameter – Each Zinc 8 or 7 and 9 lines. A solution of sulfate of copper fills the first – the second is only plunged in pure water.

The helix is formed of two copper wires twice covered with cotton threads – of $\frac{1}{10}$ of inch in diameter and 605 yards in length. They are levelled [reading doubtful] in juxtaposition and form a hollow cubic cylinder of 8 inches and $\frac{9}{10}$ (Fig 1–2)

$1°$ if the electric current is passed through one of the wires – in breaking it constantly – one receives strong shocks from the handles of the extra-current AB – But as soon as the ends of the second wire are joined together – the extra-current ceases completely.

$2°$ If the ends of the inductive wire $B'A$ are connected with a Voltameter or with an helix formed of a wire of $\frac{1}{300}$ of an inch and 500 yards in length – the effects of the extra-current reappear.

$3°$ On receiving the induced or the extra-current shocks are given – The same effect is produced in grasping the handle ending the Wire A of the extra-current – and the handle ending the Wire B' of the induced current – or the two handles $A'B$ – On the contrary on grasping in the same time AA' or BB' nothing at all is felt.

The handles AB' being kept by one person – as soon as the two handles $A'B$ shall be connected – or shall be touched by another person – the shocks become stronger. The same result takes place with two halves of various lengths superposed and distant of $\frac{7}{10}$ of an inch (Fig 4)

$4°$ Three helices being superposed as it is shewn in the Fig 3 – the first formed of 38 yards of copper wire $\frac{1}{10}$ of an inch in diameter – the second of 176 yards of copper wire $\frac{1}{300}$ of an inch and the third of 230 yards of the same fine wire constituting rings of 6 inches in diameter – if broken currents from

8 in ten [reading doubtful] elements pass through the first – the two ends of the second being united – the third is not induced. But as soon as the ending wires of the second ring are connected with a voltameter – or with the helix above described the induction appears and shocks are received.

5° The two wires in the helix fig 2. being united so as to form a single one of 1210 yards – if the wires of the extra-current are connected with the inductors of the *electrical egg* – between the terminal – gold – silver – platina – cupper [*sic*] – zinc – iron – charcoal balls – shall appear all the series of phenomena obtained with a powerful electrical machine – The positive ball is always surrounded by a constant violet glow rising some inches along the rod which supports it. From the obscure negative balls – flows a red brush reaching the positive – In using cupper [*sic*] balls – red squibs rush out from the negative – ending in brilliant and white darts surrounded by a green glow – connecting the basis of the brush with every point of the surface of the positive ball and rod (Fig. 5). In using platina – if instead of the positive ball – an helix with

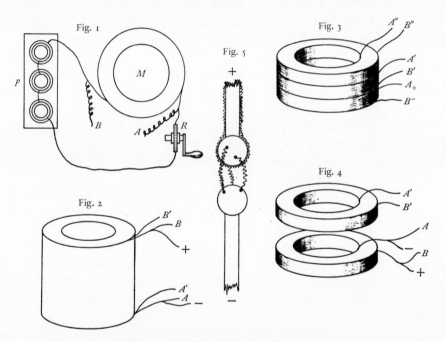

Fig. 1. *P* pile – *M* helix – *R* breaker – *AB* extra-current
Fig. 2. the helix *M* – *AB* inducting wire *A'B'* induced wire + –
    communications with the pile
Fig. 3. Three superposed rings – *AB* receiving the current – *A'B'*
    screening ring – *A"B"* induced ring
Fig. 4. Superposed and distant helices – + – Current – *AB* extra-
    current – *A'B'* induced current
Fig. 5. Light in the vacuum of the electrical egg – copper balls.

loose curls – is applied to the rod – the violet glow is more extended and intense. In every case the brush takes place at a distance and without any previous contact

6° During the preceding experiments an iron cylinder 50 pounds weight being introduced into the hollow of the helix – the shocks grow suddenly weaker – the light diminishes and sometimes vanishes –

I desire that communication to be agreeable to you – There are some new facts not yet cleared up which I shall present [reading doubtful] to you after renewed [reading doubtful] experiments

                 I am Sir

                        Your most grateful and obedient

                             servant

                                   PEYRON

I have undertaken the translation of your Experimental Researches the very *Code* of electricians of which I ambition to endow my own country[3] – I hope that long and difficult task will be completed next year – But before publishing it I shall have the pleasure of submitting my attempt to your approbation.

[In Faraday's hand:]

Dr. Peyron professor of natural philosophy, Marseilles 12 Rue d'Aguesseau, Paris.

1 See Letter 254.
2 Louis François Clément Bréguet (1804–83) and Antoine Philibert Masson (1806–60), 'Mémoire sur l'induction,' *AC*, 3 s., 4 (1842), 129.
3 The catalogue of the *Bibliothèque nationale* does not list a translation by Peyron.

262   M. FARADAY to A. QUÉTELET, 21 October 1841
[*Acad. Roy. des Sciences, Belgique, previously unpublished*]

                                  Royal Institution
                                  21 Octr. 1841

MY DEAR FRIEND

Though ashamed to put you to any expence in the way of postage for a letter so valueless as mine will be yet I cannot let your kindness and your letter to me pass without grateful acknowledgments You would hear that I left England at the Very commencement of June and as I returned only on the 29th of September I lost every chance of seeing you here I had many thoughts of seeing you at Bruxelles for we passed on the rail road from Liege to Ostend on the 27th of September but the extreme activity of the population on the Railroad & still more as they told me at Bruxelles in consequence of the rejoicings, with the necessity of getting home quickly after a long absence, and the doubt whether you were there all drove me home Besides which my companions of whom two were ladies had need to return home quickly also & so I lost the sight of Bruxelles & probably of you also. for I thought afterwards you were almost sure to be there at such a time.

I know you will be glad to hear that I am pretty well & though ashamed to speak of myself yet in answer to your kindness I may tell you that my quiet sojourne in the vallies [sic] of Switzerland where I have scarcely seen a person has been of great service to me. I am still idling, giving myself what I believe is necessary rest. not merely refraining from working but even from reading as yet. This reminds me to thank you heartily for the volumes and papers you left for me you are indeed a worthy example in activity & power to all workers in science and if I cannot imitate your example I can at least appreciate & value it.

But I must conclude
Being as ever [reading doubtful] Most Sincerely Your
Oblgd. M. FARADAY

263 M. FARADAY to J. J. BERZELIUS, 2 November 1841
[*Kungl. Vetenskapsakadamiens Bibliotek, Stockholm, previously unpublished*]

Royal Institution,
2 Nov. 1841

DEAR SIR

Though very unwilling to occupy the time or intrude on the attention of one whose exertions in the cause of science are so invaluable as your own yet I hope you will excuse my present letter both in kindness to myself & for its object to which I will come at once. One of our Noblemen the Earl of Ross[1] [sic] has been deeply & successfully engaged in casting & grinding specula for large reflecting telescopes and is now about to attempt one upon an enormous scale He has been led to think that purity of copper may be of importance to him I believe he intends by experiments to try the value of copper more or less pure but in the mean time is anxious to know the source of the purest in quantities amounting to perhaps a ton or two i.e. from 1000 to 3000 or 4000 lbs. I have promised to ask you whether the commercial copper of Sweden is better or no (in your opinion) than English & whether it can be had. I thought I had heard that Russian copper was the best for alloying with silver but cannot recollect my authority. I should be ashamed to think of putting you to trouble but I thought (& hope) that a word from you would be sufficient for I have reason to know the range & accuracy of your knowledge. For myself I am not prepared to say that the small difference in the proportion of other metals in commercial copper would be important but it might & that point it will be better to test by experiment The great object will be to obtain a speculum metal not readily tarnishing in the air.

With the sincerest respect & the most earnest wishes for your health & happiness.

I am

My dear Sir,

Your Oblgd & Grateful Servt

M. FARADAY

¹ William Parsons, third Earl of Rosse (1800–67).

264   M. FARADAY to [   ], 9 February, 1842
[Wellcome Medical Historical Library, previously unpublished]

9 Feby 1842

In reply to the inquiry why does the ore require or why does the iron take any of the carbon of the fuel   stated that the ore being essentially a carbonate of iron the first action of heat either in the ore kilns or in the furnace is to drive off the carbonic acid & leave oxide of iron and then the further action of the carbon of the fuel (besides sustaining a high temperature) is to abstract the oxygen of the oxide and so to reduce the iron to the metallic state after which a still further portion of the carbon of the fuel combines with the iron bringing it into the state of easily fusible or pig metal

As carbon may be communicated to the ore or iron in two ways distinct in their nature i.e. either by contact with solid carbon as in the proofs of cementation (that by which steel is commonly formed) or from the carbonated gasses either carburetted hydrogens or carbonic acid which occupy nearly every part of the air way of the furnace it would be desirable to distinguish as far as may be in any furnace having a particular form or action what proportion of the whole effect is due to the one mode of carbonization or the other

(Ever Truly Yours
M. FARADAY)

My dear Sir
    Above you have a rush note

265   A. VON HUMBOLDT to M. FARADAY, 18 August 1842
[R.S., previously unpublished]

Sans Souci,
le 19 Aout, 1842

MONSIEUR ET TRÈS ILLUSTRE CONFRÈRE,
    Quoique les lois beaucoup trop sévères de Votre Patrie Vous empechent de porter des ordres étranger s'ils ne sont pas gagnés dans le *carnage* des batailles, mon Roi n'a pas voulu se priver de la satisfaction de voir inscrit sur la liste de

l'ordre pour le merite dans les sciences et les arts, un nom que vous avez rendu si beau par si grandes et admirables decouvertes. Le Roi désire surtout que vous ne renvoyiez pas cette décoration, mais que vous la conserviez comme une marque de la haute estime due à vos travaux. Il espère que visitant un jour la territoire neutre du continent vous porterez l'order du Grand Frederic, lorsqu'il vous invitera à diner avec Lui au chateau de Sans Souci. Je suis toujours atteintes de toutes les privations auxquelles j'ai été imposés pendant les 13 jours de mon dernier séjour d'Angleterre! Une des plus grandes a été celle de ne pas pouvoir jouir de Votre conversation et vous exprimer l'hommage de la haute et affectueux considération que je vous ai voué pour la vie.

Le B<u>n</u> de Humboldt

266 J. C. A. Peltier to M. Faraday, 16 September 1842

[*I.E.E., previously unpublished*]

Paris

16 Septembre 1842

Monsieur

J'attendais une occasion pour vous faire remettre un exemplaire d'un mémoire que je viens de publier sur un point fort important de météorologie; je profite avec empressement de celle que m'offre Mr. Gourjon, Conservateur à l'Ecole Polytechnique. Ce mémoire est le premier d'une série que je me propose de publier afin d'appeler l'attention des Physiciens sur la route nouvelle que j'ouvre à la météorologie.[1] Je ne puis comprendre comment, après les expériences de Saussure[2] et d'Ermann,[3] [*sic*] on a pu méconnaître la puissante tension *résineuse* du globe. Comment on a pu négliger cette action incessante de la terre sur toutes les transformations qui s'opèrent à sa surface ou dans l'atmosphère? mon étonnement vient encore de s'accroître dans le voyage que je viens de faire en Suisse, lorsque j'ai vu les montagnes jouer le rôle de pointes attachées à un corps chargé d'électricité résineuse, et lorsque j'ai vu leur tension croître avec leur hauteur, leur isolement et leur prépondérance sur les autres cimes. La tension des cônes isolés est telle, que mes électromètres se tenaient le plus souvent à leur maximum de déviation, et qu'en présence des plus petites nues, ils étaient influencés à un haut degré en ouvrant la croisée de la chambre dans laquelle ils étaient renfermés.

Dans ce mémoire je n'ai voulu prouver que deux faits quoique je touche en passant à une foule de phénomènes qui s'y rattachent. L'un de ces faits est l'état électrique du globe, état puissant qui réagit sur tous les autres phénomènes. L'autre est la cause de l'électricité des vapeurs; cause qui donne des nuages *vitrés* et des nuages *résineux*; enfin je détruis une erreur introduite dans la science par Volta,[4] Lavoisier et Laplace,[5] celle d'attribuer l'électricité des vapeurs à la simple évaporation. En dehors de ces deux objets, le reste n'est que l'indication des sujets qui s'y rattachent et que je reprendrai dans d'autres mémoires en y faisant intervenir la puissante réaction de haut en bas du courant tropical supérieur, dont j'ai fait abstraction dans ce mémoire pour ne pas rendre trop complexe la démonstration de la tension *résineuse* du globe.

On imprime actuellement à Bruxelles un second mémoire sur les diverses sortes de Brouillards que j'ai classés en cinq espèces. je regrette qu'il ne soit pas encore arrivé pour vous en offrir un exemplaire.

Recevez, Monsieur, l'assurance de la haute considération que je porte à votre beau talent

PELTIER

26 Rue Poissonnière

[1] For Peltier's meteorological papers in 1841–2, see *RSCSP*.

[2] Horace Benedict de Saussure (1740–99), 'Sur l'électricité de l'atmosphère au dessus d'une montagne du Valais,' *JP*, 2 (1773), 271.

[3] Paul Erman (1764–1851), 'Beiträge über electrisch-geographische Polarität, permanente electrische Ladung, und magnetisch-chemisch Wirkungen,' *AP*, 26 (1807), 1, 121.

[4] Alessandro Volta (1745–1827), 'Osservazione sull'elettricità dei vapori dell'Acqua,' *BF*, 1 (1788).

[5] Antoine Laurent Lavoisier (1743–94) and Pierre Simon Laplace (1749–1827), 'Mémoire sur l'électricité qu'absorbent les corps qui se reduisent en vapeurs,' *MAS* (1781), 292.

267 M. FARADAY to T. ANDREWS,[1] 3 October 1842

[*Science Museum, S. Kensington, previously unpublished*]

Octr. 3. 1842
Royal Institution

Private

MY DEAR SIR

Will you excuse a hasty & perhaps an impertinent letter but circumstances & some talk with Graham move me to it. I am asked to name a person *for recommendation* as Professor of Chemistry in the University of Kings College in Upper Canada The emolument would be about £450 per annum with a house & Garden. The person would have to reside at Toronto & would be on the council of the University of which the Bishop of Toronto is President & there would be a sum of money appropriated by the Council for stocking the Laboratory Is this likely to be agreeable to you i.e would you agree to go out to Toronto on such terms being offered to you from the proper authorities If so let me know. If not still tell me but let this letter be quite private that the feelings of others may not be annoyed.

Ever Truly Yours
M. FARADAY

[1] Thomas Andrews (1813–85), best known for his work on the liquefaction of gases. He introduced the term 'critical point.'

[*R.I., previously unpublished*]

London Institution
Saturday Oct 22 1842

MY DEAR SIR

I have just completed a curious voltaic pile which I think you would like to see, it is composed of alternate tubes of oxygen & hydrogen through each of which passes platina foil so as to dip into separate vessels of water acidulated with sulphuric acid the liquid just touching the extremities of the foil as in the rough figure below.

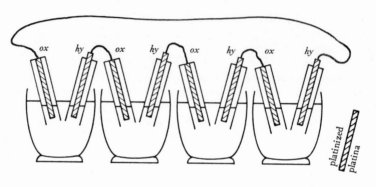

The platina is platinized so as to expose by capillary attraction a greater surface of [liquid] to the gas, with 60 of these alternations I get an unpleasant shock & decompose not only iodide of potassium but water so plainly that a continuous stream of thin bubbles ascends from each electrode Thus water is decomposed by its composition – no oxidable metal is employed. I have reversed the tubes & tried all the counter expts but the phenomena are too marked I think to render any mistakes possible Mr Gassiot was with me today & saw the Expts Can you spare me an hour next week on Tuesday if it suits you or any day except Wednesday at any hour from 11 to 3 – at the Laboratory of the London Institution I cannot but regard the experiment as an important one both as to the chemical & other theories of the pile & as to the catalytic effects of the combination of the gases by platina.

I remain my dear Sir
yours very sincerely
W. R. GROVE

[I.E.E., previously unpublished]

Aberdeen
24th Oct.ʳ 1824[1]

DEAR SIR

I have just received your obliging note. In reference to the second part of the organic chemistry, my duty has been for the most part that of a translator. I regret that I was not concerned in the translation or editing of the first part, which I think might have been rendered more easily intelligible to the student, as well as more interesting. This part, in which the general principles of organic chemistry are developed, was edited by a gentleman who had no practical acquaintance with organic chemistry, and who in consequence committed some mistakes, occasionally even reversing the author's meaning.[2] In the part now published, which contains chiefly details of facts, I could not repair the errors of the introductory part, but I have endeavoured as far as possible to render these details clear and consistent.

In the seventh edition, which will be published in a few days, I have ventured to make considerable additions to the first part of the organic chemistry, with the view of making the subject more easy to the student; but as Prof. Liebig still takes an active share in the execution of the work, I could not rewrite the whole as I could have wished to do; knowing better than he can do, the necessity of being very elementary indeed, for our students, whose previous education is so often imperfect.

In the 7th. edition I have much curtailed the sections on heat and electricity, not that I undervalue these branches, but because without doing so, I could not find space for the briefest sketch of the actual state of chemistry. I have done this with the less regret, because I am convinced that the time has come when the student must resort to works, on these subjects especially, for the information he requires; and that it is absurd even to attempt to give in an elementary work on Chemistry, the matter of such voluminous but absolutely essential works as for example, your own researches on electricity. or those of Melloni and De la Rive.

I have further to mention, that the concluding part of the Organic Chemistry, to be published before Christmas, will be, except the first few pages, written by myself; so that I shall consider myself in reality the responsible editor of that part of the work. Imperfect as I fear it will be, still I have some satisfaction in the consideration that the subjects it contains will be for the first time offered to the British public in their actual state of progress. I omit no endeavours to keep myself fully informed of every thing that is done on the continent, where alone, I regret to say, with hardly an exception, organic chemistry is as yet pursued. I fervently trust that the rising British chemists will take their fair share in the future advancement of this department of our science.

If I might venture to hope to hear from you at your leisure, I should feel deeply indebted to you for mentioning to me the discoveries which in the course of your researches, you cannot fail to make. I am here so much out of the way of scientific news, that any thing of that kind is doubly precious to me.

Within these few days, an arrangement has been made, by which our mutual friend, Dr. Forbes, from an addition to his duties as Professor of Humanity, resigns the Chemistry in King's College to me. As I am henceforth therefore, to lecture on Chemistry, any communication from you will confer on me and my class a very great obligation.

The only new fact (new, at least, to me) that has lately occurred to me, is that in almost all the commercial oxides of manganese, cobalt and nickel are contained, in small but appreciable quantity. When such oxides of manganese are converted into chloride, and digested with carbonate of manganese till the iron is completely separated, the first drop or two of hydrosulphuret of ammonia cause a black precipitate. This I have found to be a mixed sulphuret of cobalt and nickel. Several authors have attributed this black precipitate to an imperfect separation of the iron; but the iron by the above method is separated absolutely, if peroxidised. Perhaps you will think it worth while to cause this experiment to be repeated. If it be new to you, may I ask you to insert a note of it in the Annals of Philosophy or rather Philosophical Magazine.

Mr Davidson[3] of this place, of whom you have heard through Dr. Forbes, has for some weeks been exhibiting his very ingenious and economical method of applying electro-magnetism as a moving power. His apparatus is very neat and efficient, and he has ascertained many points of great practical importance. Believe me

Dear Sir

Yours most respectfully

WILLIAM GREGORY

[1] Although the letter is clearly dated 1824 this is impossible for the work to which Gregory here refers is the seventh edition of Edward Turner's *Elements of Chemistry*, edited by Gregory and Justus Liebig, published in 1842. Gregory must have transposed the 4 and the 2 in this date.

[2] This would appear to be a reference to W. G. Turner who, together with Gregory and Justus Liebig, edited the sixth edition, also of 1842.

[3] Probably Thomas Davidson, an instrument maker.

[*I.E.E., previously unpublished*]

Plymouth
October 26, 1842

My dear Faraday

I was much delighted at seeing your hand writing again – you do not know what great pleasure I experience in hearing from you – . With respect to the expression of Globular Lightning quoted from Arago – & my description of a fire Ball it may be as you say; there is really no such thing – and perhaps I was too indefinite in my language. – I intended to convey however some notion of the impressions made upon those who had witnessed discharges of Lightning productive of mischief in order to fix the attention on the immediate operation of such discharges – in contradistinction to those more playful corruscations and branching sparks which sometimes strike out from clouds and are *lost as it were* in *the air* – at *least apparently so*. That the discharges which do mischief in Lightning Storms – assume to *the senses* the appearance I mention is quite certain. *Almost all the descriptions* given in the Logs of the Navy – contain the expression – "A Ball of fire was seen to Dart" etc. All the sailors invariably speak of Fire Balls If you will look in Priestlys [*sic*] History of Electricity at page 352 and 353 you will find a curious description of this kind – I confess I read this with some suspicion at first – but having met with many such accounts subsequently I now regard it as being rather important.

Some years since a dreadful accident by Lightning happened on the Malvern Hills. I have the Newspaper acct. by me cut out of the Newspaper but unluckily without date – Some Ladies then on a party of pleasure were killed. The account runs thus. It appears that the Party had sought shelter in a Building or Tower of Stone covered with Iron "Miss Margaret Hill was looking out of the door way to see if the storm had passed when she saw the Electric fluid appearing as a mass of fire rolling along the Hill and approaching their retreat &c &c"

In a storm at sea of many years since – the Papers describe the Lightning most triumphantly – On one occasion at midnight the ship was threatened with destruction both by the violence of the Squall and the Electrical discharges which every now & then burst round the ship.. The top sails were lowered on the Caps – The Lightning enveloped the ship for an hour *Once* only in this time a fearful shock burst on the main mast Conductor – The Officer of the Watch says the vivid Light which fell on the Conductor *took away his sight for many minutes*, that a *horrid crash* came at the same time, *simultaneously* – The Carpenter Mr May says it was the same as if all the ship's Guns had been fired at once.. That the ship fairly shook under it, and that he was standing very near the Mast – and observed the Cutlasses & swords stowed in a frame round the Mast; *fairly rattle* in the stand.. They examined the Conductors the next day – but found no ill effects on them – No damage ensued – not a rope yarn [reading doubtful] suffered. Fancy all this in a Southern sea – Pitch dark with a heavy sea – with the Sails round the Mast &c.... This would have been a nice time to have sent the men aloft to shorten in the slack of a chain or wire Rope Conductor – would it not? and if the Chain or wire had been snapped by the violence of the Gale and come partly in board hanging down with a terminating end thus as at *a* what must have happened then?

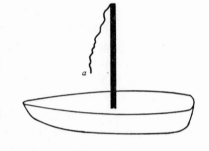

– I consider this a beautiful case – reducible to an experiment on a great scale – All the Seamen on the Ship even have acknowledged the great value of this method of applying capacious Conductors to Ships.

Daniell & Wheatstone have blamed me for meddling with Mr Walkers paper[2].. but I do not know when so great a public question is concerned that I have any pretention to hold my head so high as to think others beneath notice – My Talents do not place me in the position which yours do or Daniells –

– I am now about to ask a favor of you – if you think you can manage to grant it without inconvenience –

I have been requested to draw up a small treatise for the press on this subject – which is now in hand – and in the last pages I have stated your views of Induction, Polarization &c – Would you be so good as to read these 3 or 4 Pages over for me, and say if you think I have put the matter in a clear condensed form, and such as you yourself would not object to?

I wish my Dear Faraday – I could persuade you for your Health's sake to come here next Summer & spend a short time, that I might get you on the Breakwater and with one or two of my medical friends; perhaps we only hope the gratification of giving you our most affectionate & disinterested attention – I am impressed [reading doubtful] with the Idea that were you to venture – you would go back full of Devonshire Cream & Milk. – You should stay here about 2 months – making Philosophy an amusement or Play thing only

Believe me with the most sincere regard & esteem
your very faithful friend
W. SNOW HARRIS

[1] F. Arago, 'Sur le tonnerre,' *ABLP* (1838), 221. Harris is probably referring to the English translation which appeared in *ENPJ*, 26 (1839), 81, 275.
[2] Charles Vincent Walker (1811–82), 'Lightning Conductors,' *TLES* (1843). I have been unable to discover in what Harris' meddling consisted.

[*R.I.* (*copy only*), *previously unpublished*]

Royal Institution
10 Decr. 1842.

MY DEAR BROTHER

The invention may be called a means of ventilating oil and gas lamps for the purpose of carrying away the water, carbonic acid, and other products of their combustion in a *more advantageous manner* than has hitherto been done. It applies to Argand burners, i.e. those with glass or such like chimnies, and consists simply in dipping the end of the pipe which is to serve as a ventilating flue, more or less *into* the glass chimney. Thus if an oil or gas Argand lamp have a burner of 7/8 of an inch in diameter, and a lamp glass on it of the usual proportions, I find that a tube also 7/8 of an inch in diameter, more or less, according to its length and other circumstances, will carry off *all* the results of the combustion of such a lamp, the lower end of the tube being inserted *into* the top of the lamp glass and the upper end carried into a chimney, the open air, or any place where it may be considered convenient to dispose of the burnt air and fuel. The lower end is best placed centrically in the lamp glass; but the degree of its insertion may be more or less at pleasure. In a quiet place, even when almost at the top of the glass it is sufficient; in other cases an inch or more of insertion may be needed. In some of my experiments I have made the burner end of the ventilating tube a little funnel shaped; still however keeping it within the lamp glass, as in the figure: —[1] and in experiments with oil lamps I have introduced a throttle valve into the ventilating tube to govern its draught that the latter might be regulated so as to be strong enough to draw up and carry off all the results of the combustion and yet not so strong as to increase the draught of air by the flame; for when that occurs it causes a quicker charring of the cotton than usual, an effect it may be desirable more or less to avoid.

And now Dear Brother, believing this particular arrangement of the ventilating flue to be my own invention, and having no intention of turning it to any pecuniary use for myself, I am most happy to give freely all my rights in it over to you, or any body you may name for your good; and as Mr. Carpmael[2] says we may legally and equitably make this transfer of rights in this way, I write you this letter describing the principle and arrangement of the invention as far as I have carried it. Hoping it may be productive of some good to you, and of no harm or trouble.

I am My dear Robert
Your Affectionate Brother
M. FARADAY

¹ For a description and illustration of Faraday's invention, see *Rep. Pat. invent.*, 2 (1843), 174, 238.
² William Carpmael (1804–67), author of *The Law of Patents for Inventions explained for the use of inventors and patentees*, London, 1832.

272 W. R. GROVE to M. FARADAY, 19 December 1842

[R.I., previously unpublished]

Hampstead
Monday Dec 19 1842

MY DEAR FARADAY

In forwarding you a copy of my paper¹ I am anxious to say a few words on the subject of our conversation of Saturday last. I was much impressed by your remarks & am convinced that I have been to blame in expressing myself in too few words, in aiming at brevity I have not steered clear of obscurity This did not proceed from thoughtlessness My reasons were twofold 1st I have observed many writers on physics who having in the early part of their career expressed at length theoretical notions have been subsequently obliged to abandon them thus weakening their own authority & giving a character of uncertainty to science or else which is worse, they have been induced by "amour propre" pertinaciously to adhere to erroneous conclusions I was anxious to avoid this to be able thoroughly to mature my judgement before I attempted generalizations which might prove fallacious.

2dly I observe in the present day a tendency to diffuse verbiage & to an accumulation of obvious results, quality diluted & weakened by quantity. I feel now however certain that I have carried the opposite principle too far & I will endeavour to amend in future But although convinced that you are right as to this point of brevity I am not so convinced with respect to the Royal Society. Having contributed one paper which was not published & the reason of their rejection of which I cannot see I do not wish this to happen a second time Unless I strangely misjudge myself it is no sudden [reading doubtful] vanity which renders this view My experience, such as it is, leads me to believe that had I contributed to the Royal Society this paper even in an improved form it would also have been rejected unless I had *made interest* for its insertion & this I will not do – My contributions to science have spoken & shall speak for themselves, if this be pride it is at worst an honest pride. I have made no rash vow on the subject but my present feeling certainly is to have nothing to do with Scientific societies but to publish in periodicals whatever researches appear to me of sufficient importance I conceive that every man has a duty to perform in standing his own ground, if I err it is an error of judgement not of temper I trouble you with this note as I most truly value your esteem & would not have you think meanly of me either as a philosopher or as a man

I remain My dear Faraday
yours very sincerely
W. R. GROVE

¹ I cannot identify this paper with any degree of certainty. See *RSCSP*.

273 M. FARADAY to R. FARADAY, 10 January 1843

[*M. Faraday, previously unpublished*]

Royal Institution,
Jan. 10, 1843

MY DEAR BROTHER,

If I understand the questions in your letter aright they arise upon the supposition of lighting the hall of Devonshire house in three different ways, i.e. either by eighteen of your ventilated gas burners – or by eighteen equal ordinary gas burners – or by oil lamps in the same situation equal in light to the same 18 gas burners – and the questions are which mode will communicate the least heat to the air and which will least affect the air in giving to it impurity.

I believe that your lamps will give the least heat to the air for the following reasons – as compared to the ordinary gas lamp they must give less – because being so near the wall and the pipes soon enclosed the burnt air passing off must go away hot – and so much heat at all events is removed – whereas the ordinary gas lamp gives *all* it heat to the air of the place – As compared to oil lamps giving equal light it is no doubt true that the combustion of the oil for that purpose does not *evolve* so much heat as gas – on the other hand an oil lamp gives all its heat to the air and your lamp does not – and it is my opinion from what I saw of the hall and the proposed place of the lamps that the quantity of heat carried off by the flues would reduce the heating effect of your lamps below that of oil lamps – and perhaps considerably.

As to the sweetness of the air of course neither of the other modes can compare with yours.

Yours affectionately,
M. FARADAY

274 M. FARADAY to T. ANDREWS, 2 February 1843

[*Science Museum, S. Kensington, previously unpublished*]

Royal Institution
2 Feby 1843

MY DEAR SIR

Your hearty letter reached me yesterday & there are two points in it which I cannot allow myself to leave unanswered however unworthy I am to write or lazy I may be or indisposed as I may think myself I am very giddy today more indeed than normal but perhaps writing to you may take it away One curious effect of that kind of feeling with me is to make me cut short the marks representing letters & words and I have no doubt you will find that out before I have *finishd* – behold an example it should have been *finished* – Your kind invitation is most acceptable to me though I have no idea when I can take advantage of it – perhaps never but the thought of your wishing it is itself refreshing & I do sincerely thank you for your kindness. For your papers too[1] I thank you and though I agree with Rochefocault [*sic*] in most things yet my gratitude is something besides a keen sense of favours to come

As to the particular point of your letter about which you honor me by asking my advice I have no advice to give but I have a strong feeling on the matter and will tell you what I should do I have always felt that there is something degrading in offering rewards for intellectual exertion and that Societies or Academys or even Kings & Emperors should mingle in the matter does not remove the degradation for the feeling which is hurt is a point above their condition and belongs to the respect which a man owes to himself: With this feeling I have never since I was a boy aimed at any such prize or even if as in your case they came near me have allowed them to move me from my course and I have always contended that such rewards will never move the men who are most worthy of reward. – Still I think rewards & Honors *good* if properly distributed but they should be given for what a man has done & not offered for what he is to do or else talent must be considered as a thing marketable & to be bought & sold and then down falls that high tone of mind which is the best excitement to a man of power & will make him do more than any common place reward When a man is rewarded for his deserts he honors those who grant the reward, & they give it not as a moving impulse to him but to all those who by the reward are led to look to that man for an example. If I were you therefore I should go on my way & discover & publish (if I can) [reading doubtful] but having done that I see no objection as the time draws nigh to send copies of the papers to the Academy or even such an account of them as may be considered fit and in doing so I should think I was paying a fit mark of respect to the Academy, and giving them the opportunity of marking their sense of what had been done if they saw fit. But I would not depart from my own high position (I mean as respects feeling), for any reward they could give. Excuse my freedom. I have no time to dot ii or cross tt or punctuate. I hope you will find out the meaning.

Ever Most Truly Yours
M. FARADAY

[1] For these papers, see *RSCSP*.

[*I.E.E., previously unpublished*]

King's College
7th Feby 1843

MY DEAR SIR

I have to thank you, which I do most sincerely, for a copy of your Chemical Manipulation, which I have often of late sought for in vain, having given my old copy to a friend some years since. I need not say how much I value it, as every working Chemist must have the same high opinion of it.

I have lately proposed a new method of purifying silver, or rather of obtaining it as *metal* or *oxide* from the chloride. I find that the moist chloride bruised in the dish as much as possible during its washing by decantation, is rapidly converted into oxide by boiling with a solution of caustic potash, of Sp. G. 1.25 to 1.3. The oxide thus obtained is *pure black* and *very dense*. It is sometimes necessary to grind the moist powder (drained first) in a mortar, after 5 or 10 minutes boiling, and then to return it into the liquid and boil for 5 minutes more. Should it, after this, not be entirely soluble in dilute Nitric Acid, it is to be dried and finely ground, which is easily done, and after this, another boiling completes the operation. With small quantities, however, of chloride, if carefully bruised, the first boiling generally succeeds.

It is obvious that the oxide, when pure, yields pure silver by simple heating. But even if it still contain, say $\frac{1}{10}$ of its weight of unchanged chloride, the whole silver is readily obtained by heating the mass with a little borax and salt of tartar without the risk of failure which attends the reduction of the pure chloride, either from insufficient heat, or from a too intense heat, as often happens, causing the alkali to corrode the crucible. I find it much easier to obtain *pure* silver by this process than by any other, for when precipitated by copper, it seems to me generally to contain a trace of that metal, and is almost sure to contain some of the impurities of the copper. At all events it is seldom quite pure. The process is so easy that I dissolved half a crown, and obtained, not only the *pure oxide* but the fused metal quite pure, within two hours. Both the chloride and the oxide, especially the latter, are very quickly washed by decantation. The only precaution is, to make the latter washings of the oxide with *cold* water, as when nearly pure, it has a curious tendency to rise in *hot* water.

This process is admirably adapted for obtaining quickly an absolutely pure Nitrate from common silver. And here also the presence of undecomposed chloride is not injurious, as it is left undissolved by the acid.

The whole process, including the reduction of the silver by the heat of the spirit lamp, from the oxide, is well adapted for the lecture table. The change from the white chloride to the black oxide is very striking.

Finally, we obtain a pure and beautiful oxide, in a new form, quite distinct from that of the oxide precipitated from the Nitrate. I have no doubt that it will meet with many applications. The new oxide dissolves instantaneously in very weak Nitric Acid. It is to be noted that if the chloride have been once *dried* it is decomposed with great difficulty, even by long boiling with potash Still, if first very finely powdered, and, if necessary, again dried and pulverized or levigated, it may be decomposed. I should add that the new form of oxide seems to have the same composition as the common one. It dissolves without effervescence in dilute Nitric Acid.

Yours very truly

WILLIAM GREGORY.

276 Report by M. FARADAY marked 'Private for Committee only', 4 April 1843[1]

[*R.S., previously unpublished*]

4 April 1843

The paper generally does not carry conviction to my mind as to the point with which it sets out & terminates that *metals ~~are always~~ when reduced by electrolysis from aqueous metallic solutions are always reduced by the hydrogen previously evolved.* I held that opinion formerly of some metallic solutions & hold it still of them under certain circumstances: and my present impression is that facts do not bear us out in asserting that the metals are always set free in *one particular way* but that on the contrary the variation of the substances present; their quantity, & other considerations must always be taken jointly into consideration, the final effect being *a resultant of the whole.*

I say thus much for the purpose of adding that I do not perceive any thing in the present paper which at all alters that opinion. – The gas experiments from (9) onwards (as we know by Grove's beautiful Gas battery)[2] may be quoted both ways one (22) is against the direct reduction by hydrogen & for that by a Voltaic circle.

The tone of the paper is too absolute: for after all what can any man say but that he has a certain opinion; – admitting at the same time that he may be wrong – for who is not liable to be wrong in a debateable [*sic*] matter

I can only say in conclusion that if I were the writer of the paper the experiments would not be satisfactory to me.

M.F.

[1] This is a report by Faraday on a paper submitted for publication in the *PT*. So far as I have been able to determine, the paper was not printed. The letter, nevertheless, is interesting because of Faraday's views stated in it.
[2] See Letter 268.

[*I.E.E., B.J.* 2, *168*[2]]

Fort of Ham[3]
the 23[d] of May 1843

DEAR SIR

You are not aware I am sure that since I have been here, no person has afforded me more consolation than yourself. It is indeed in studying the great discoveries which science is indebted to you for, that I render my captivity less sad and make time flow with rapidity.

I submit to your judgment and indulgence a theory of my own on voltaic electricity which was the subject of a letter from me to M. Arago, the 23 of April last, and which I here subjoin. M. Arago was kind enough to read it to the academy[4] but I do not yet know the general opinion on it. Will you have the kindness to tell me sincerely if my theory is good or not, as nobody is a better judge than yourself.

Permit me also to ask you another question that interests me much on account of a work, I intend soon to publish: *what is the most simple* construction to give to a voltaic battery in order to produce a spark capable of setting fire to powder under water or underground. Up to the present I have only seen & employed to that purpose piles of 30 or 40 pairs constructed on Dr Wollaston's principles. They are very large and inconvenient for field service. Could not the same effect be produced by two spiral pairs only, and if so what can be their smalest [*sic*] dimension.

It is with infinite pleasure that I profit of this opportunity to recall myself to your remembrance, and to assure you that no one entertains a higher opinion of your scientific genius than

yours truly
NAPOLEON LOUIS BONAPARTE

I beg to be kindly remembered to Sir James South and to Mr. Babbage.

If you answer me be kind enough to put the direction, A Monsieur Tannert banquier à Ham, departement de la Somme.

[1] The future Napoleon III of France.
[2] There are sufficient errors of transcription in the version published in *B.J.* to warrant republication of the letter here.
[3] Louis Napoleon had been imprisoned after an abortive coup d'état.
[4] *CR*, 16 (1843), 1180.

278 M. Faraday to T. Phillips,[1] 27 January 1844

[*Wellcome Medical Historical Library, previously unpublished*]

R Institution
27 Jany 1844

My dear Sir

I have just been seized with a sharp attack of what feels like lumbago, the first I have had. It may not last long but it makes me catch in breathing – unable to keep a position & will for the present confine me to my room I hope therefore you will excuse me this morning

Ever Truly Yours
M Faraday

[1] Thomas Phillips (1770–1845), portrait painter. His portrait of Faraday hangs in the National Gallery.

279 T. Mayo[1] to M. Faraday, 6 March 1844

[*I.E.E., previously unpublished*]

56 Wimpole Street
March 6th 1844

My dear Sir,

You will, I trust, excuse my troubling you with some remarks on the admirable lecture of which you have very kindly favored me with an abstract.[2].

Believing that no analytical inquiry has ever been set on foot without some preconceived hypothesis, I imagine, also, that theory & hypothesis never need interfere with the *prosecution* of an inquiry.. *Your* discoveries indeed sufficiently shew the value of hypothesis. For no man uses its language more successfully, than you do, as the associating agent in your analytical inquiries.. In this respect your intellectual operations supply a striking proof of the value of a vivid imagination in a Philosopher. –

But I would suggest to you the following doubts, as to the hypothetical expression, w^h you are disposed to substitute, for that, at present in use, of the Atomic Doctrine. –

1$^{\underline{ly}}$ Is it not the substitution of an expression comparatively barren & unproductive, for one 'greatly *used*', as you say, (& I presume greatly *useful,*) 'for the interpretation of Phenomena, especially those of chrystallography [*sic*] & chemistry'? Your atmosphere of force, grouped round a mathematical point, is not, as other hypothetical expressions have been in the course of your remarks, an expression linking together admitted phenomena, but rather superseding the material phenomena, which it pretends to explain. – It resolves in fact, as it would appear to me, all matter into a metaphysical abstraction. For it must all consist of the mathematical point, & the atmosphere of force grouped around it. –

414

2$^{\underline{dly}}$ Might not the difficulty so well pointed out by you, as involved in the prior atomic theory, that it makes space at once an Isolator & a conductor, be removed without *your* hypothesis?

You observe, that in a stick of black sealing wax the particles of *conducting* charcoal diffused through every part of it, are deprived of their conducting power, by a non-conducting body, a resin, intervening & separating one from another; & this appears to you analogous to the condition of atoms generally in respect to conduction or isolation, on the supposition of intervening spaces. – But the atoms of a conducting or isolating body *may* be presumed (I imagine) to have around them an atmosphere of *space* absolutely *indifferent*, & no way interfering with the isolating or conducting power of the homogeneous substance..

But, I will not detain you longer. If my imperfect acquaintance with this class of subjects has occasioned me to write nonsense, pray tear my letter, but Believe me

Your sincere friend & admirer
THOS. MAYO

[Note appended by Mayo to previous letter]

Dr. Faraday ought perhaps to carry his disposition to limit our real knowledge of things to effects & laws, a little farther, & to apply it also to his own hypothesis. – A mathematical point with an atmosphere of force around it, is, in respect to the atmosphere of force, an expression of certain effects. – But what is the mathematical point?

The question which the Philosopher has to answer, in deciding, whether he should accept this, or any other hypothesis, on the subject, is, whether it best interprets phenomena, or is least at variance with them. – The views stated by Dr. Faraday in relation to conduction or Isolation, as regards the atomic theory, are an objection to it, supposing the answer, which I ventured to propose in my letter, be insufficient. – The objection which he takes to atoms on the ground of their uncertain magnitude, is one, which presumes, that we pretend to more knowledge of them, than those who entertain that theory *need* affect to possess. – Indeed the mathematical point of Dr. Faraday is either a simple negation, as having neither magnitude nor parts, or is itself, after all, a material atom. –

The objection that '*The Silver*' (in Dr. Faradays Illustration) '*must vanish if its forces are abstracted*', may prove the necessity of forces to our conception of silver, but does not disprove the necessity of silver to our conception of its forces. – All that we can positively assert as known is effects or forces; but we are organized & irresistibly impelled to assume *substantia*, of which these are properties. – Berkeley permitted himself to philosophise in regard to the external world, just as if he had not proved, that our sensations are all, that we can confidently assert as known to us –

On grounds of this kind I object to Dr. Faradays applying the reasoning contained in his manuscript, in favor of his view, & as destructive of the atomic theory. – It is equally subversive of both as far as it goes. –

If, upon consideration, Dr. Faraday still is of opinion, that his argument *against* the atomic doctrine, founded on its involving the contradictory position, that the intervening space must be both a conductor & an Isolator is satisfactory, I can only say, with becoming humility, that he is more likely to be right, than I am: –

T. MAYO

[1] Thomas Mayo (1790–1871), physician and F.R.S.
[2] M. Faraday, 'A speculation touching electric conduction and the nature of matter,' a lecture delivered on 19 January 1844, at the Royal Institution. For a published version, see *PM*, 24 (1844), 136. It was in this lecture that Faraday declared his belief in the superiority of the point atoms first suggested by Boscovich over those associated with the name of Dalton for explaining physical phenomena. See *LPW*, 376.

280 G. B. AIRY to M. FARADAY, 22 April 1844
[*I.E.E., previously unpublished*]

Royal Observatory
Greenwich
1844 April 22

MY DEAR SIR

I duly received your letter of 9 March[1] (containing the experimental measures of the attractive force of an electrified and a non-electrified plate), but I have not been able to act upon it, because I am and have been very busy and really have scarcely had my thoughts free for a moment.

There is a difficulty (incidental to all cases where attractive force increases as the distance of the attracting bodies decreases), namely that a counterbalancing force must be provided whose variations are extremely rapid. And this is, practically, very difficult to provide and to control.

In order to explain my meaning, I will take the numbers which you gave me as "attraction in grains" for a certain charge, and I will suppose that for two different charges (one $\frac{1}{3}$d and the other $\frac{2}{3}$ds of the same charge) the law of attraction as regards distance is the same, the abolute attractions at equal distances being in the proportion of 1, 2, 3. Then we have –

ATTRACTIONS

Distance	Charge 1	Charge 2	Charge 3
$3\frac{4}{8}$	17	33	50
$2\frac{7}{8}$	25	50	75
$2\frac{4}{8}$	33	67	100

$2\frac{2}{8}$	42	85	125
$1\frac{7}{8}$	50	100	150
$1\frac{6}{8}$	67	133	200
$1\frac{9}{16}$	83	167	250
$1\frac{3}{8}$	100	200	300
$1\frac{3}{16}$	133	267	400
1	167	333	500
$\frac{7}{8}$	200	400	600
$\frac{6}{8}$	233	467	700 grains

Now suppose that I provide a counteracting force whose magnitude at $3\frac{4}{8}$ is 17, at $1\frac{7}{8}$ is 100, and at $\frac{6}{8}$ is 700. Then with a charge 1 the plates would settle at the distance $3\frac{4}{8}$, with charge 2 at the distance $1\frac{7}{8}$, and with charge 3 at the distance $\frac{6}{8}$. And the magnitudes of the forces actually in play at these times would be 17, 100, and 700. Thus to indicate charges whose proportion is 3 to 1, I must actually use forces whose ratio is more than 40 to 1. And this inequality of forces must be included in a comparatively small range: at the same time the apparatus must be so arranged that a similar relation shall be predicable for every diminution of distance as well as for every increase of distance.

I am afraid that this will stop the application of this method.

Repulsive forces are not liable to this objection (supposing them to increase as the distance decreases, which they do). A constant counteracting force would there do perfectly well.

But I fear that (according to the theory of electric attraction) repulsive forces cannot be obtained sufficiently great.

Practical information on this point would be valuable.

I am my dear Sir
Faithfully yours
G. B. AIRY

[1] I have been unable to locate this letter.

281 J. PLATEAU to M. FARADAY, 15 May 1844
[*I.E.E., previously unpublished*]

Gand,
15 Mai 1844

MONSIEUR,

J'ai envoyé, aux savants Anglais, il y a plusieurs mois des exemplaires de mon Mémoire sur les phénomènes que présente une masse liquide libre et soustraite à l'action de la pesanteur,[1] et l'exemplaire adressé à M⁻ Wheatstone était accompagné d'une lettre. Comme, d'une part, cette lettre est demeurée sans réponse, et que d'une autre part malgré la nouveauté et la singularité des faits décrits dans mon mémoire, les Journaux Scientifiques anglais n'en ont fait, à ma connaissance, aucune mention, j'ai conçu quelques craintes sur le sort de mes exemplaires; Dans cette circonstance je viens recourir encore une fois, à l'extrême obligeance dont vous m'avez déjà donné tant de preuves, et vous prier de vouloir bien m'écrire si vous avez reçu l'exemplaire qui vous était destiné.

Je m'occupais activement – de la rédaction de la Seconde partie du mémoire dont il s'agit, lorsque j'ai été arrêté par une affection très grave des yeux qui est loin encore à être guérie et c'est pour cette raison que la présente lettre n'est pas écrite de ma main.

Je saisis cette occasion pour vous exprimer tout le plaisir que J'ai éprouvé en apprenant le complet rétablissement de votre santé, et mes felicitations ne sont que l'écho de celles de tout le monde scientifique. D'un autre côté cependant j'ai quelque peu à me plaindre de vous; autrefois vous me faisiez l'honneur de m'adresser un exemplaire de chacune de vos publications; mais depuis long-temps vous me laissez dans l'oubli. Du reste, j'ai les mêmes plaintes à former, en général, contre vos compatriotes. Sir David Brewster, par exemple, m'avait promis un exemplaire de son mémoire sur les Muscae Volitantes,[2] et je n'ai rien reçu de sa part. Je croyais être lié d'amitié avec Mr Wheatstone et depuis longtemps il ne daigne plus répondre à aucune de mes lettres. Pourquoi cet oubli général? Pendant une couple d'années, il est vrai, J'ai cessé de m'occuper de science, mais depuis deux ans je m'y suis remis activement et il me semble que les travaux que j'ai publiés ne devraient pas ainsi passer inaperçus. Il est bien triste lorsqu'on s'occupe de physique dans un pays qui compte aussi peu de physiciens que la Belgique de ne pas au moins trouver d'écho à l'étranger.

Agréez, Monsieur, l'assurance de ma haute considération   J^h PLATEAU

professeur à l'université, à Gand.

[1] J. Plateau, 'Sur les phénomènes que présente une masse liquide libre et soustraite à l'action de la pesanteur, *MASB*, 16 (1843).
[2] David Brewster, 'On the Phenomena and Cause of Muscae Volitantes,' *BAASR*, 1840 (Pt. 2), 8.

282 J. PLATEAU to M. FARADAY, 12 June 1844
[*I.E.E., previously unpublished*]

Gand,
12 Juin 1844.

MON CHER MONSIEUR FARADAY,

Permettez-moi d'abord de vous remercier bien cordialement pour votre excellente lettre qui m'a causé un extrême plaisir. Ce plaisir cependant a été quelque peu tempéré par les détails que vous me donnez sur le rétablissement non complet de votre santé; mais sans nul doute, le repos vous rendra bientôt toute votre vigueur de tête. Quant à mes yeux, ils sont toujours en mauvais état, et je ne pourrai d'ici à longtemps, reprendre mes expériences. Cependant, grâce à ma petite femme qui veut bien me servir de secrétaire, je continue la rédaction de la seconde partie de mon mémoire,[1] pour laquelle toutes les expériences Sont terminées. Les faits dont se compose cette seconde partie sont d'un genre tout différent de ceux de la première, et ne vous paraîtront, j'espère, pas moins curieux.

J'ai été bien flatté d'apprendre que vous aviez répété quelques unes de mes expériences, et j'ai regretté que vous n'ayez pu mettre à exécution le projet de les reproduire devant votre auditoire. C'eût été un grand honneur pour moi, et je suis presque fâché que vous m'ayez parlé de ce projet avorté; car vous m'avez mis ainsi l'eau à la bouche. En employant des quantités de liquide plus considérables, et en faisant les expériences dans un grand ballon de verre, (voyez mon mémoire §5, et deuxième note du paragraphe 14,) on pourrait donner aux phénomènes des dimensions qui les rendraient visibles à une grande distance. Alors, il est vrai, il semble que l'on devrait employer beaucoup d'alcool; mais en se Servant de votre procédé et en dissolvant dans l'huile une quantité un peu considérable d'oxide de cuivre, on rendrait l'huile beaucoup plus pesante et l'on diminuerait beaucoup la quantité d'alcool nécessaire.

J'ai éprouvé également une vive satisfaction d'amour-propre en apprenant que M.ʳ Richard Taylor[2] insérait mon travail dans les Scientifix [sic] Memoirs. Si vous avez occasion de voir M.ʳ Taylor, seriez-vous assez obligeant pour lui demander s'il ne serait pas possible de tirer à part un exemplaire de cette traduction, et en cas d'affirmative, pour me le faire parvenir. J'espère aussi que vous voudrez bien remercier M.ʳ Taylor de ma part.

Agréez donc mes excuses pour vous avoir injustement soupconné d'oubli à mon égard: l'amitié que vous voulez bien me témoigner est celle qui m'honore le plus, et je m'alarme par conséquent de tout ce qui semble lui porter atteinte.

Je viens de faire la revue des *Series* que j'ai recues de vous et je trouve que les Series 2, 3, 7, 8, 15 et 18 manquent. S'il vous en reste des exemplaires disponibles, vous m'obligeriez beaucoup de me les faire parvenir à la première occasion.

J'ai joint à cette lettre trois exemplaires d'un travail que j'ai exécuté il y a longtemps et que l'Académie de Bruxelles vient d'imprimer.[3] Serez vous assez bon pour faire remettre à leur adresse les exemplaires destinés à M.ʳˢ Daniell et Wheatstone.

Je vous ai demandé bien des choses dans cette lettre, et je serais désolé qu'il en résultât pour vous quelqu'embarras. Si vous me trouvez indiscret ne donnez pas de suite à ces demandes: Je n'en demeurerai pas moins,

Votre tout dévoué
Jʰ PLATEAU
Professeur à l'Université, à Gand.

[1] See Letter 281.
[2] Richard Taylor (1781–1858), printer and founder of the publishing house of Taylor and

Francis. In 1822, he became one of the editors of the *PM*. In 1840, he began publishing English translations of foreign scientific memoirs. This publication ultimately ran to five thick volumes. For Plateau's memoir see *SM*, 4, 16.

3 Probably his 'Sur des expériences d'optique, et sur un appareil pour vérifier certaines propriétés du centre de gravité,' *BASB*, 10 (1843), 310.

283 A. DE LA RIVE to M. FARADAY, 25 August 1844
     [*I.E.E., previously unpublished*]

Genève,
le 25 Aout 1844.

MON CHER MONSIEUR,

J'ai reçu votre petite lettre par le Dr Holland[1] que j'ai eu bien du plaisir à voir; malheureusement la santé de ma femme qui est très mauvaise cet été m'a empêché de recevoir Mr Holland comme j'aurais désiré le faire & comme j'espère le recevoir au printemps à sa [*sic*] retour d'Italie. J'ai appris avec plaisir que sauf votre accident avec le phosphore, votre santé est bonne & je m'en rejouis pour vos amis dans le nombre desquels vous savez que je tiens à être compris & pour votre amie la Science.

Je jouis dans ce moment de trois mois de vacances pendant lesquels j'espère mener à bonne fin bien des travaux ébauchés notamment quelques recherches sur l'aimantation du fer & d'autres sur la combinaison des courants d'induction & des courants électro-chimiques.[2] – Je suis en discussion avec Schoenbein au sujet de son mémoire sur *l'ozone* & sur la composition de l'azote.[3] – Je ne nie point que son hypothèse soit possible, mais je conteste qu'elle soit prouvée. Son grand mémoire a été, je pense, publié trop tôt & il me parait être incomplet quoique très étendu. – Il me traite d'incrédule, de sceptique; mais je vous l'avoue, les preuves que Schoenbein donne de la composition de l'azote & de l'existence de l'ozone comme substance élémentaire *sui generis* ne me paraissent point encore assez concluantes pour que la Science puisse adopter définitivement, pour le moment du moins, cette manière de voir. – Je compte reprendre cet automne avec mon collègue le profr de chimie, Mr Marignac,[4] les expériences de M' Schoenbein et tâcher d'éclaircir la question, très disposé que je suis à trouver qu'il a raison, mais avant tout désirant chercher la vérité.

Il m'est venue une idée que je vous soumets. Ne serait-il point possible que l'odeur que Schoenbein attribue à l'ozone provint d'une petite proportion d'acide arsénieux? Ce qui m'y a fait songer, c'est le fait avancé par un M^r Du Pasquier[5] dans la séance de l'Académie des Sciences de Paris du 12 Aout[6] que cette couche singulière dont le phosphore est recouvert à sa surface est une combinaison d'arsenic (ce qui expliquerait la production de l'ozone par le phosphore); ce même chimiste dit avoir trouvé que l'acide sulfurique le plus pur si c'est celui qu'on retire des pyrites renferme de l'arsenic (ce qui expliquerait la production de l'ozone dans l'électrolysation de l'eau acidulée). –

Quant à la production de l'ozone par l'émission dans l'air de l'électricité ordinaire, je ne pourrais l'expliquer que par un peu d'arsenic que renferme le zinc dont est fait le laiton des conducteurs, arsenic que l'électricité, en sortant du conducteur, emporterait avec elle en [ce] que c'est une substance plus volatile que les autres substances dont est formé le conducteur. – Je ne pretends nullement que l'idée que je mets en avant soit fondée, mais c'est tout au moins une objection contre les conséquences tirées par Mr Schoenbein de son travail, qui vaut peut-être la peine d'examiner. Personne mieux que vous ne pourrait le faire; si vous avez un instant ayez la bonté d'examiner l'idée & de me dire ce que vous en pensez.

La réunion de la Société Helvétique des Sciences Naturelles aura lieu à Genève le 15 Aout 1845. Combien vous seriez aimable si vous veniez nous faire une visite à cette époque; cette Société, la plus ancienne de toutes celles du même genre, ne dure que trois jours. Vous devriez venir & nous amener ou tout au moins, si vous ne venez pas, nous envoyer le profr Daniell & Wheatstone, au souvenir desquels je vous prie de vouloir bien me rappeler. Veuillez aussi présenter mes compliments respectueux à Madame Faraday dont je n'ai point oublié toutes les bontés pour moi l'an dernier & veuillez me croire, mon cher Monsieur, votre dévoué & affectionné pour la vie.

A. DE LA RIVE

1 Sir Henry Holland (1788–1873), physician and amateur scientist.
2 For these papers, see RSCSP.
3 See C. F. Schoenbein, 'De la production de l'ozone par voie chimique,' AE, 4 (1844), 333, and 'Ueber die Zerlegung des Stickstoffs,' MNGB (1844), 109.
4 Jean Charles Marignac (1817–94), Professor of Chemistry in the Geneva Academy.
5 Alphonse du Pasquier (1793–1848), Professor of Chemistry in the Lyons School of Medicine.
6 CR, 19 (1844), 362.

284   M. FARADAY to R. S. MACKENZIE,[1] 5 October 1844
[*Historical Society of Pennsylvania, previously unpublished*]

Royal Institution
5 Octr 1844

SIR

I ought before this to have answered your letter but from a feeling of extreme reluctance to do any thing that might seem to be more or less honoring of myself, have been deterred from replying However I have put down in the accompanying paper the essential answers to your questions & hope you will excuse both their rough condition & the tardiness of their appearance

I am Sir
Your Very Obt Servt
M. FARADAY

Born at Newington in Surrey on the 22nd September 1791. – Appointed Chemical Assistant in the Royal Institution 1st of March 1813. – Director of the Laboratory 7 Feby. 1825. – Fullerian Professor of Chemistry 12 Feby. 1833

Royal Society
Geological Society
Cambridge Phil Society
Royal Soc of Edinburgh
Senate of the University of London
Accademia dei Georgofili di *Firenz*[*i*] [last letter illeg. in photo-copy]
Academy of Sciences of *Paris*
Philomatic Society of *Paris*
Society of Natural Sciences *Heidelbreg*
Imp! Acad Sciences, *Petersburg*
Philadelphia College of Pharmacy
Society [of] Physical Sciences – *Paris*
American Academy of Arts & Sciences
Royal Society of Science *Copenhagen*
Royal Acad of Sciences – *Berlin*
Academy of Sciences &c *Palermo*
Physical Society of *Frankfort*
Royal Society of *Gottingen*
Soc Pharmacy of *Lisbon*
Soc Science in *Modena*
Natural Histy Society of *Basle*
Royal Academy of Sciences of *Stockholm*
American Phil Society – *Philadelphia*
Soc of Useful Knowledge – *Aix la Chapelle*
and others amounting in all to 50 or more.

June 16. 1842 created Knight of the *Order of Merit* – *Prussia* The only separate publication that I remember is the *Chemical Manipulations*. 8.vo three Editions – But now the Electrical papers from the Philosophical Transactions & elsewhere are published together in two volumes 8.vo by Mr. Richard Taylor
  The Journals in which I have published have been

The *Philosophical Transactions*
    Quarterly Journal of Science of the Royal Institution
    & *Philosophical Magazine*

I do not remember that I have published any where else except once in the Annales de Chimie[2]

[1] Robert Shelton Mackenzie (1809–80), M.D., writer and editor of numerous journals and newspapers throughout his life.
[2] See Letter 148.

285   M. FARADAY to J. BARLOW, 18 October 1844

[R.I., previously unpublished]

R. Institution
18 Octr. 1844

MY DEAR BARLOW

I received your letter in due course but could do very little for the cause one thing was that we went to few of the sections[1] and yet my mind & memory became quite bewildered amongst the men & things & I sadly mistook one for another. The subject I thought of more than all others was Dr Falconers gigantic tortoise yet having to go to Newcastle I did not hear his evening.

Though I shall send this to Cavendish Street yet I suppose you are at Horsted Place & I trust thoroughly enjoying & resting yourself Daniel [*sic*] (E.R)[2] called here today but I did not see him.

Mrs. Faraday unites in best remembrances to you & Mrs. Barlow

Ever My dear friend
Yours faithfully,
M. FARADAY

[1] The reference here is to the meeting of the *B.A.A.S.* in 1844 at York.
[2] Edmund Robert Daniell (?–1854), barrister and brother of J. F. Daniell.

286   M. FARADAY to C. L. EASTLAKE,[1] 22 October 1844

[S. M. Edelstein, President, Dexter Chemical Corp., N.Y.C., previously unpublished]

Royal Institution
22 Octr 1844.

MY DEAR SIR

Let me at last report to you my results in reference to the subject to which you called my attention, as well as that of Mr Brande & Dr Reid,[2] namely, the probable effect of hydrogen in its application to lime as proposed by Mr Dinsdale,[3] for the purpose of ameliorating its qualities in regard to the colours used in Fresco painting. Since you directed my thoughts to the matter I have made many experiments, the general results of which are as follows. I have taken well burnt lime, both Dorking and white lime, and have carefully slaked it and mixed it with water. I have then passed hydrogen gas through some portions in a continuous stream for several hours, and other portions I have placed in contact with hydrogen gas in measured & close vessels for days together, using agitation and other means to favour any effect that might occur; but I have never been able to trace the slightest action of the lime and hydrogen on each other, either by *any disappearance* of the hydrogen or by any sensible change of the chemical qualities of the lime.

I have also prepared portions of surface for fresco painting, according to my best ability, after the instructions I received from you; some of them being with the lime in its original state and others with the same lime treated with hydrogen; and I have applied to their surfaces, in the manner of fresco painting, three test colours, namely Vermillion, Cadmium orange, and an Arseniate green. These were applied on the 2nd September and have been observed from time to time. They are all changed more or less, but I cannot perceive any advantage possessed by the hydrogenated lime in its action on them.

I also placed hair pencils in like mixtures of these limes and water, for seventeen days together, moving them frequently & equally in the course of that time, but I cannot perceive much difference amongst them and the little difference that does occur does not point to the hydrogenated lime.

Led by the statement that the keeping of the lime in a slaked condition for a couple of years is a great advantage to it, I took some specimens from the stores which have been so laid up at the Houses of Parliament, for the purpose of examining them in this respect. It appears to me that this lime (which is in a state of paste) is in a very soft and smooth condition in comparison with what would probably be the condition of lime recently slaked; a condition, which seems to be due to its thorough disintegration as a mass and its separation particle from particle. On analysing it I found that it contained a little carbonic acid but not much; for in 100 parts of the dry substance there were but 5¼ parts of carbonic acid; these 100 parts therefore would contain 88 parts of quick or uncarbonated lime and 12 parts of carbonated lime; which considering the processes of burning, carrying, slaking &c that it had to go through, and the necessary time of exposure to air before it was laid up in store, is a very small proportion. I do not believe that the lime which is more than four inches in, from the exterior, has received any portion of carbonic acid during the two years of its inhumation.

The result of these investigations therefore is negative i.e. I have not been able to find evidence confirmatory of M⁼ Dinsdales views.

In respect of the effect of keeping lime for a time, I am led to think, without however having formed any strong opinion on the subject, that the benefit is due to the fine texture which it gradually acquires; and, as there is no doubt that if two surfaces were prepared, the one with fine sand and lime in particles comparitively [sic] coarse, and the other with the same kind of sand & lime in particles comparitively far more perfectly divided, that these two would act very differently both as to the access of carbonic acid from the atmosphere & the transition of lime dissolved in the moisture of the mass from the interior towards the surface; so, there is every reason to expect that there would be a difference in the degree of action upon the colours at that surface and also in the time at which that action would come to a close.

I regret that the general state of my health combined with my necessary avocations prevent me from going further into this subject.

I am My dear Sir
Your Very faithful Obent Servnt
M. FARADAY

[1] Sir Charles Lock Eastlake (1793–1865), painter and historian of art.
[2] David Boswell Reid (1805–63), chemist.
[3] I am able to discover only a W. M. Dinsdale who wrote a short article on dry rot in wood which appeared in *AOP*, n.s., 1 (1821), 45. This article reveals Mr Dinsdale's interest in materials of construction and some familiarity with practical chemistry. It is possible that these interests led him to his supposed discovery of the effect of hydrogen upon lime.

287 J. PERCY[1] to M. FARADAY, 23 October 1844
[*I.E.E.*, *previously unpublished*]

Birmingham,
Oct 23[d]. 1844.

MY DEAR SIR

Be pleased to accept my best thanks for your valuable present which I received last evening You will much oblige me by accepting the specimen of nickel and cobalt. I value a specimen only in so far as it can be rendered subservient to science; and, therefore, have great pleasure in transferring the specimens in question to you. If you require specimens of manganese and tungsten, I think I shall be able to furnish you with them in a short time. I had heard from Mrs. Faraday of your expedition to the North,[2] and I am now glad to hear that that expedition will be attended with benefit, it may be, to thousands of our poor miners; of whom we have so many in the vicinity of Birmingham. It occurred to me when talking over the subject with Mr. Solly[3] one morning recently, that the question resolved itself into two particulars; first, the prevention, by proper ventilation, of the accumulation of the explosive gas; and, secondly, the *detection* and *destruction* of it in the event of its accidental accumulation. And it struck me, – I may have stumbled upon a mare's nest, – that the second object might possibly be accomplished by carrying into the various recesses of the mine a wire, intercepted at proper intervals, wherever accumulation of the gas in question would be likely to occur; so that by connecting this wire with a powerful hydro-electric machine the mine might, in the absence of the miners, be, from time to time, tested in respect to the presence of such explosive mixture. I suppose that by a proper arrangement of this kind, the electric spark might be made to traverse the mine, and to explode any mixture of carburetted hydrogen and air where the former had accumulated to a sufficient extent. One machine might be made available for many contiguous or adjacent mines. Probably, the notion may have long ago occurred to many persons. – You will pardon me, I hope, for thus venturing to obtrude a notion, which may appear to you crude and impracticable upon your attention. –

I do assure you that Mrs. Percy and myself will be delighted again to entertain Mrs. Faraday and yourself. – Your visit was a source of great delight to us both. – And I do indulge the hope that in a short time you will again favour us with your company. You shall do just as you like in every respect. There yet remain many interesting manufactories to entice you. –

I now believe that the notion concerning the transparency of the ultramarine particles originated in an optical illusion. However, I hope to be able to work out the subject satisfactorily. My friend, Mr. Shaw[4] and I have entered upon a long investigation of the *analysis* of photographic phaenomena; and I trust we shall arrive at some correct results in respect to the chemistry of these phaenomena.[5]

Mr. Morrison,[6] whom you saw here, much regretted that he did not mention to you a curious phaenomenon which he observed a long time ago concerning the production of sound by the electric current. – His experiment is this. – Through the axis of a coil of covered wire place a long bar of iron, say six or eight feet long, and let it rest at each end on clay – Then, by passing a current through the coil at the instant of contact and breaking of contact a sound is produced similar to that produced by striking the bar on its end. – He has varied the experiment in a great variety of ways and has apparently avoided every source of fallacy. – No sound is produced when a bar of copper is similarly treated. He has, at the suggestion of Sorby,[7] and others, just sent a paper on the subject to the Philosophical Magazine. –

I must, indeed, apologise for troubling you with so long a letter, and so taking up so much of your valuable time –

With best compliments to Mrs. Faraday and yourself, – in which Mrs. Percy desires cordially to join –

Believe me, my dear sir,
With great respect
Yours very truly
JOHN PERCY

[1] John Percy (1817–89), metallurgist, who later became Professor of metallurgy at the Royal School of Mines.

[2] In 1844, Faraday and Charles Lyell, the geologist, were asked by the government to investigate the causes of a mine explosion at the Haswell Collieries. See 'Report from Messrs. Faraday and Lyell to the Rt. Hon. Sir James Graham, Bart., Secretary of State for the Home Department on the subject of the explosion at the Haswell Collieries, and on the means of preventing similar accidents,' *PM*, n.s., 26 (1845), 16.

[3] Edward Solly (1819–86), chemist. Solly had lectured on chemistry at the Royal Institution in 1841.

[4] Possibly Charles Shaw (1791–1865), merchant of Birmingham.

[5] I can find no publication by Percy on photography.

[6] Possibly Robert Morrison (1822–69), civil engineer and, later, a manufacturer of steam engines.

[7] Henry Clifton Sorby (1826–1908), the great metallurgist.

[Trinity College Library, Trinity College, Cambridge, previously unpublished]

Royal Institution
9 Nov.ʳ 1844.

MY DEAR SIR,

Cagniard de la Tour made an experiment some years ago which gave me occasion to want a new word.[1] will you help me?

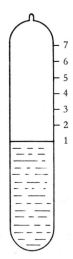

If a glass tube sufficiently strong be nearly half filled with ether & hermetically sealed & then the whole be gradually heated the tension & density of the vapour in the upper part increases & at the same time the liquid ether below expands in volume. Gradually the surface of the liquid ether rises to different heights (1.2.3.4.5.&c. &c.); the difference between it & the vapour above becomes less & less & there is *a* POINT of temperature & pressure at which the liquid ether & the vapourous ether are identical in *all their properties.*

Now I am working on the same point and other fluids and want to express that point. Now what am I to call it? it differs of course both for pressure & temperature for other bodies than ether; but how am I to name this point at which the fluid & its vapour become one according to a law of continuity? Cagniard de la Tour has not named it; what shall I call it –

By having a tube long enough it is easy to have cold fluid below & pure elastic vapour above, yet no line of difference or demarcation any where in the tube.

Ever My dear Sir,
Your Very Oblgd Servt
M. FARADAY

[1] Charles Cagniard de la Tour 'Sur les effets qu'on obtient par l'application simultanée de la chaleur et de la compression à certains liquides,' *AC*, 2 s., 22 (1823), 410.

[Trinity College Library, Trinity College, Cambridge, previously unpublished]

Trin. Lodge.
Cambridge.
Nov. 12 1844

MY DEAR SIR

I am glad to hear that you are working, and come to a point where you wish new words; for new words with you imply new things. I fear I am not sufficiently in possession of the bearings [reading doubtful] of the subject on which you are now engaged to make my help of any use to you. As you are aware, I think the first condition of scientific terms is that they should bear such a relation to one another that the truths of science may be simply expressed. It is therefore difficult to recommend an insulated word. I will however mention to you what occurs to me, and you can make what use of it you will: If I understand right, the point of temperature and pressure special for each fluid, for which you want a name is a more general aspect of the *boiling point* or *dew point*: or perhaps rather like what we may conceive of water at a very high temperature, when it is prevented from flashing in to steam by very great pressure. In this case we may conceive the water to be virtually vapour and prevented from being actual [*sic*] so: and I suppose the same is the case with your fluids – Would it do to call them *vaporiscent*, and this point, the point of *vaporiscence*. As we say a solid liquesces, we may say that a liquid *vaporisces*. Or if you wish rather to say that the liquid state is destroyed, you might say that the fluid is *disliquified*.

We are, as seems to me much in want of a phraseology for describing the solid, liquid, and aery conditions of bodies. To call them the solid, liquid and gaseous *forms*, leads to needless confusion; form has so many other senses. I proposed, in my Philosophy I think, to call them the solid, liquid and aery *consistencies* of bodies: for though consistency does not hang together well with our notion of an air, that is because the air itself does not hang well together for which there is no help.

If I have mistaken your object I should be glad to hear from you again. Believe me

My dear Sir
Yours most truly
W. WHEWELL

290 M. FARADAY to W. WHEWELL, 14 November 1844
[*Trinity College Library, Trinity College, Cambridge, previously unpublished*]

Royal Institution,
14 Nov.ʳ 1844

MY DEAR SIR

I am very much obliged for your kind letter – The word I want is mainly for the purpose of avoiding awkward & clumsy phraseology, for instance instead of saying "In this substance the *Cagniard de la Tour* point occurs at a pressure of etc" I want a word with which to replace Cagniard de la Tour – It seems to me that a word expressing both conditions (vapor liquid) if there be such a one is that which is wanted for at that point the liquid is vapour & the vapour liquid, so that I am afraid to say the liquid *vaporises* or that the fluid is *disliquefied* – It is too bad of me to give you this trouble and then not be content but the beauty of the experiment & its general results has always in my eyes been so great that I have constantly regretted we had not a word wherewith we might talk & write freely about it

Again excuse me & if nothing occurs to you bringing with it at the moment its own conviction of fitness do not take any further trouble – not even to answer.

I am My dear Sir
Your Very Oblgd Servt
M. FARADAY

291   J. LIEBIG to M. FARADAY, 19 December 1844

[*A. W. Hofmann, 'The Life-work of Liebig, The Faraday Lecture for 1875', London, 1876, photocopy of letter at end*]

Giessen
19 Dec. 1844

DEAR FARADAY

I intended to have written you long ago of my safe arrival and that I had found my wife and children well. The opening of my winter course and a mass of work which had accumulated during my absence have hitherto prevented my fulfilling my intentions. Now however that I have a few days of rest during the Christmas holidays, I will not let the opportunity slip, of wishing you, with my whole heart, a merry Christmas and happy new year. Often do my thoughts wander back to the period which I spent in England among the many pleasant hours of which, the remembrance of those passed with you and your amiable wife is to me always the dearest & most agreeable. With the purest pleasure I bring to mind my walk with her, in the botanical garden at York,[1] when I was afforded a glance of the richness of her mind; what a rare treasure you possess in her! The breakfast in the little house with Snow Harris and Graham, and our being together at Bishopthorpe are still fresh in my memory. I wish it were only my good fortune to see and talk with you oftener and to exchange ideas with you.

Nature has bestowed on you a wonderfully active mind, which takes a lively share in every thing that relates to Science. Many years ago your works imparted to me the highest regard for you which has continually increased as I grew up in years and ripened in judgment and now that I have had the pleasure of making your personal acquaintance and seeing that in your character as a man, you stand as high as you do in Science, a feeling of the greatest affection and esteem has been added to my admiration. You may hence conceive how grateful I am for the proof of friendship which you have given me.

I have every reason to be satisfied with my journey in Great Britain, rare proofs of recognition have indeed been given me. What struck me most in

England was the perception that only those works which have a practical tendency awake attention and command respect, while the purely scientific works which possess far greater merit are almost unknown. And yet the latter are the proper and true source from which the others flow. Practice alone can never lead to the discovery of a truth or a principle. In Germany it is quite the contrary. Here in the eyes of scientific men, no value, or at least but a trifling one is placed on the practical results. The enrichment of Science is alone considered worthy of attention. I do not mean to say that this is better, for both nations the golden medium would certainly be a real good fortune.

The meeting at York which was very interesting to me from the acquaintance of so many celebrated men, did not satisfy me in a scientific point of view It was properly a feast given to the geologists, the other Sciences serving only to decorate the table. The direction, too, taken by the geologists appeared to me singular, for in most of them, even the greatest I found only an empirical Knowledge of Stones and rocks, of some petrefacts and few plants, but no Science. Without a thorough Knowledge of Physics & Chemistry, even without mineralogy a man can be a great geologist in England. I saw a great value laid on the presence of petrifactions and plants in fossils, whilst they either do not know or consider at all the chemical elements of the fossils, those very elements which made them what they are

This letter has already grown too long and truly I fear to weary your patience. I cannot however deny myself the pleasure of expressing a sincere wish to see you and your wife here in Giessen next summer Did you know how quietly we live at our German Universities, you would certainly expect from your visit only benefit of your health. Except scientific pursuits we have no other excitements of the mind We take walks in our beautiful green woods and in the evening drink tea at the neighbouring old castles. This is our recreation. I beg of you, dear Faraday to listen to my request, I pray your dear wife to assist me in trying to make you decide on this journey. My wife unites with me in begging this, it would give her the greatest pleasure to make the personal acquaintance of you and your Lady.

Farewell, dear faraday, preserve to me your friendly favor and believe me with all sincerity to be

Yours very truly

Dr. Just. Liebig

[1] Liebig attended the meeting of the *B.A.A.S.* in 1844.

292 M. FARADAY to J. B. DUMAS, 27 December 1844
[*Arch. de l'Académie des Sciences, Paris, Dossier Faraday, previously unpublished*]

Royal Institution
27. Dec.ʳ 1844

What can I say my kindest friend but thanks the most heartfelt thanks to you all for your goodness to me[1] – I cannot understand how I with my reserved habits can have created such a feeling towards myself in such a body of men as constitute your Academy especially too when I remember my moderate standing in science & the little hope that even I entertain of producing much more. I can only account for it by referring it to the innate kindness & heartiness of those who have so thought of & honored me and to the abundant zeal & friendship of yourself. I hope I shall not discredit the honor conferred on me. I will strive to deserve it & should it be my good fortune to produce any contribution to science worthy to be called a discovery the greatest source of pleasure arising to me from it will be the thought that I am helping in some degree to redeem the pledge which you in your earnestness to me & my honor have as it were given to science on my part.

To Mssrs. Arago, Becquerel Chevreul & all say how deeply impressed I am with their undeserved kindness I refrain from multiplying words, for they would not be able to say all I feel.

I conclude that you read my Abstract & I wish the results had been greater

Mrs. Faraday wishes me to remember her to you & though she thinks very well of me still wonders to find that I can create such an interest in you and the Academy. She rejoices in my joy.

Ever My dear friend Your faithful & indebted,
M. FARADAY

[1] Faraday had just been elected *Associé étranger* of the *Académie des sciences*.

293 J. SOUTH to M. FARADAY, 30 December 1844
[*I.E.E., previously unpublished*]

Observatory Kensington
One o'Clock in the Morning of Monday Decr. 30th 1844

MY DEAR FARADAY/

Accept my Congratulations on your being Elected "Associé Etranger del' Academie des Sciences de Paris" – they come to you indeed late; but by no one are they offered with more sincerity than they now quit my pen –

May Providence grant you health and strength, so that you may *very very long* continue, an Honor to old England, and a splendid living Example, that by calling to his aid, industry the most indomitable – perseverance the most unflinching – and honesty the most unsullied, – a poor uneducated Lad, may by God's blessing, make himself, not only one of the first philosophers of Europe, but also one of the most Enviable Characters of the Age –

With kindest regards to Mrs. Faraday, in which Lady South heartily joins me, as well as in every good wish for yourself I remain

My Dear Faraday
Yours Most affectionately
J. SOUTH

P.S. I will call and shake you by the hand the first moment that I can –

294 M. FARADAY to J. B. DUMAS, ca. January 1845
[*AC, 3 s., 13 (1845), 120*]

Je vous remercie de l'intérêt que vous portez à mes expériences. Quoiqu'elles m'occupent depuis six mois, elles seront bientôt rapportées. Vous vous souvenez des expériences de M. Aimé ([1]*Annales de Chimie et de Physique*, 3e série, tome VIII, page 257), qui fit parvenir au fond de la mer divers gaz, ainsi soumis à une grande pression. Les résultats obtenus ne pouvaient pas être observés dans l'état de compression, et ils furent obtenus d'ailleurs à une température ordinaire. Vous vous rappelez aussi les expériences de M. Cagniard-Latour sur l'éther, par lesquelles il prouve qu'à une certaine température, les liquides se transforment en vapeur sans changer de volume.

Or, si ce point de liquéfaction est, comme il le paraît être, le plus bas possible avec les corps les plus volatils et les plus légers existant comme gaz, il n'y a que peu ou pas d'espoir de liquéfier des substances comme l'hydrogène, l'oxygène ou l'azote à aucune pression tant qu'ils seront maintenus à des températures ordinaires, car leur point de liquéfaction est très-probablement au-dessous de la température ordinaire, ou même d'une température considérablement abaissée.

Vous avez par là la clef de ma manière d'expérimenter.

J'ai cherché d'abord à obtenir une température très basse, et, à cet effet, j'ai employé le bain d'acide carbonique solide et d'éther de M. Thilorier;[2] mais, je m'en suis servi en le plaçant sous le récipient de la machine pneumatique. En y maintenant un vide continuel, j'abaissai tellement la température, que l'acide carbonique du bain n'était pas plus volatil que de l'eau à la température de 30 degrés centigrades, car le baromètre de la machine pneumatique était à 28$^{\text{pouces,}}$ 2, le baromètre extérieur étant à 29,4.

Cette disposition terminée, j'ajustai ensemble, au moyen de bouchons et de robinets, de petits tubes de verre et de cuivre, de manière qu'avec le secours de deux pompes je pus forcer et comprimer différents gaz à une pression de 40 atmosphères, et en même temps les soumettre au froid intense obtenu sous la machine pneumatique et en examiner les effets. Comme je m'y attendais, le froid produisit plusieurs résultats que la pression n'aurait jamais pu donner, et principalement dans la solidification des corps ordinairement gazeux. Je vous donne à la hâte ces divers résultats.

Vous vous rappelez les gaz qui ont déjà été condensés, et vous y avez, je crois, ajouté l'hydrogène arséniqué; il est probable, d'ailleurs, que M. Aimé a condensé le gaz oléfiant et l'acide fluosilicique. Voici mes derniers résultats.

Le *gaz oléfiant* est condensé en un beau liquide clair, incolore, transparent, mais il ne s'est pas solidifié; il dissout les corps résineux, les corps bitumineux et les corps huileux.

L'*acide hydriodique* pur peut être obtenu, soit à l'état solide, soit à l'état liquide. L'*acide hydriodique solide* est très-clair, incolore et transparent, en général avec quelques fissures qui traversent la masse; il ressemble beaucoup à de la glace.

L'*acide hydrobromique* peut aussi être obtenu, soit en liqueur limpide et incolore, soit en un corps solide, clair et transparent.

Ces deux acides exigent une distillation très-soignée, dans des vases clos, et sous une forte pression, pour être obtenus purs et incolores.

L'*acide fluosilicique* a été condensé à l'état liquide, mais il faut opérer à la plus basse température. Il est extrêmement liquide, et mobile comme de l'éther chaud. Il produit alors une pression de 9 atmosphères environ, et ne donne aucun signe de solidification. Il est transparent et incolore.

L'*acide fluoborique* et l'*hydrogène phosphoré* m'ont présenté quelques résultats de condensation.

L'*acide chlorhydrique* se liquéfie aisément, à moins de 1 atmosphère de pression, mais il ne se solidifie pas.

L'*acide sulfureux* gèle de suite, comme il fallait s'y attendre.

L'*hydrogène sulfuré* devient solide, et constitue alors une masse blanche transparente cristalline, ressemblant plutôt à du nitrate d'ammoniaque congelé, ou à du camphre, qu'à de l'eau congelée.

L'*acide carbonique*, lorsqu'il passe ainsi de l'état liquide à l'état solide, sans être dispersé en neige, constitue une très belle substance, transparente comme du cristal, de sorte que j'ai douté pendant quelques instants si le tube qui le renfermait était vide ou plein, et j'ai même été obligé, pour reconnaître la présence du corps solide, d'en fondre une partie. L'acide carbonique solide exerce une pression de 6 atmosphères, ce qui m'a prouvé combien facilement l'acide carbonique liquide doit devenir solide, lorsqu'il est lâché à l'air libre.

L'*oxyde de chlore* est une belle substance cristalline rouge-orangé, très-friable; elle ne présente aucun indice de puissance explosive.

Le *protoxyde d'azote* est un des gaz que j'avais déjà condensés autrefois. J'ai vu dans les journaux que M. Natterez[3] [*sic*] a répété mes expériences en employant une pompe pour la compression, et qu'il a obtenu le liquide à l'air libre. Je l'ai également condensé en un liquide, au moyen de ma pompe; mais, de plus, je l'ai solidifié par le bain froid. Il constitue alors un beau corps cristallin transparent ou incolore; mais, dans cet état, sa vapeur ne fait pas équilibre à la pression de 1 atmosphère, et ce résultat s'accorde avec une autre expérience dans laquelle, ayant ouvert un vase contenant ce liquide, une partie s'en est évaporée, a refroidi le reste, mais ne l'a pas solidifié. Le froid produit par cette évaporation est très-grand, ce qui a été prouvé en mettant le tube et son contenu dans un bain d'acide carbonique solide et d'éther dans l'air. Ce bain, qui gèle d'une manière si instantanée le mercure, s'est comporté comme l'aurait fait un vase rempli de liquide chaud, et à l'instant il a fait violemment bouillir le protoxyde d'azote. D'après cela, je me dispose à employer le protoxyde d'azote liquide pour de nouvelles expériences sur l'hydrogène, l'oxygène et l'azote; car, en plaçant un bain de ce protoxyde liquide dans une machine pneumatique, et en expulsant l'air et le gaz, nous pouvons placer le bain de protoxyde relativement à celui d'acide carbonique dans le vide dans le même rapport que ces deux bains observent dans l'air.

Le *cyanogène* gèle, comme l'a déjà prouvé Bussy.[4]

L'*ammoniaque*, parfaitement pure et sèche, peut être obtenue comme une substance solide, blanche, cristalline et transparente, plus pesante que l'ammoniaque liquide, et ayant très-peu d'odeur, à cause de la faible tension de sa vapeur à cette température.

L'*hydrogène arséniqué* et le *chlore* ne passent pas de l'état liquide à l'état solide.

L'*alcool* devient épais comme de l'huile froide, mais ne cristallise pas, non plus que le *caoutchène*, le camphène et l'huile de térébenthine; mais ces corps deviennent visqueux.

Le *bioxyde d'azote* et l'*oxyde de carbone* n'ont donné aucun signe de liquéfaction à la plus basse température et à une pression de 30 à 35 atmosphères.

Tout en faisant ces observations générales, j'ai déterminé beaucoup de nombres relatifs au point de fusion de ces divers gaz, à leur tension à diverses températures, etc. Ces nombres trouveront place dans le Mémoire que je prépare à ce sujet, et où j'espère avoir quelque chose de nouveau à dire sur l'état que l'oxygène, l'azote ou l'hydrogène peuvent affecter en passant à l'état liquide. Ce dernier corps se montrera-t-il sous la forme métallique, comme vous le pensez? L'azote sera-t-il un métal ou bien conservera-t-il sa place parmi les corps non métalliques? C'est ce que l'expérience nous apprendra.

[1] Georges Aimé (1813–46), 'Mémoire sur la compression des liquides.'
[2] See Charles-Saint-Ange Thilorier (1750–1818), 'Solidification de l'acide carbonique,' *CR*, 1 (1835), 194.
[3] Johann August Natterer (1821–1901), 'Leichte Methode, Kohlensäure und Stickgasoxydul in den flüssigen Zustand zu versetzen,' *AP*, 138 (1844).
[4] Antoine Alexandre Bussy (1794–1882), Professor of chemistry at the School of Pharmacy in Paris. I am unable to locate the source for Faraday's statement.

[*R.S., previously unpublished*]

Bâle,
Jan. 18, 1845

My dear Faraday,

As you have taken some interest in my researches on Ozone, I flatter myself that the results of my recent investigations which bear upon a similar subject will engage your attention. After having ascertained that by the slow combustion of phosphorous in atmospheric air a peculiar principle happens to be engendered being in many respects similar to Chlorine I was led to examine those bodies which are capable of exhibiting the same sort of combustion and it is common ether in particular upon which I have lately been making a series of experiments. The results I have already obtained from them are such as will, to my opinion, merit the attention of Chymists. On account of the small space allowed to a letter I cannot state them but in very summary manner. You will however soon have an opportunity to acquaint yourself with the details of the subject.

If a platinum wire being moderately heated at one of its ends be introduced into a mixture of the vapor of common ether and atmospheric air a slow combustion as it is well known takes place and besides aldehydes, aldehydic, formic, and nitric acids, etc. a principle is produced which has hitherto escaped the notice of Chymists and enjoys to a high degree oxidizing and bleaching properties as you will see from the following statements:

1ly. The principle in question destroys Indigo like Chlorine and Ozone.

2ly. It decomposes iodide of potassium and hydroiodic acid eliminating at the same time Iodine; it turns therefore blue the paste of starch being mixt up with the iodide like Chlorine and Ozone.

3. It (slowly) decomposes also bromide of potassium like Chlorine and Ozone.

4. Being in contact with water it changes Iodine into Iodic acid like Chl. and Ozone.

5. Being in contact with water it transforms sulphurous acid into sulphuric acid like Chl. and Ozone.

6. It changes the yellow ferro-cyanide of potassium into the red one like Chl. and Ozone.

7. It turns blue the white cyanide of iron, like Chlorine and Ozone.

8. It transforms the salts of protoxide of iron into the salts of the peroxide, like Chl. and Oz.

9. It makes very rapidly disappear the coloration produced by sulphuret of lead, like Chlorine and Ozone. A number of other sulphurets are also destroyed by it.

10. It is readily taken up by water.

11. Water charged with our principle enjoys all the properties before mentioned.

In comparing the chemical properties of my ozone with those of the bleaching principle produced during the slow combustion of ether in atmospheric air as well as during the rapid one of many other substances we easily perceive a striking similarity between them. The most essential reactions effected by these principals are without any exception the same. From that similarity of properties we might be led to believe that there is either identity or at least some close connexion between the substances enjoying the similarity of properties. Admitting the identity of these principles and starting from the hypothesis I have ventured to suggest regarding the nature of nitrogen, we can rather easily account for the production of our bleaching principle. Heat, in many cases acting like common electricity we might suppose that the former agency determines the oxigen of the air to unite with the hydrogen which I believe to be contained in Nitrogen. Under these circumstances Ozone, the other constituent part of Azote, would be eliminated in the same way as I suppose that principle to be set at liberty by the action excited by common electricity upon atmospheric air. It is at any rate a most remarkable fact that the chemical effects produced for instance by the point of the hydrogen flame are exactly the same as the chemical effects brought about by the electrical brush and such being the case, I at least cannot help thinking that in one respect the same chemical process takes place in both instances. But be that as it may, the facts I have tried to give you the substances of are, to my opinion far from being unfavorable to the view I have taken of the nature of ozone. Just now I am about to ascertain whether the bleaching principle can also be obtained by burning a variety of substances – perhaps a point which is very important to know. Before I conclude I take the liberty to draw your attention upon some facts which appear to be worthy of notice. Whilst Ozone (like Chlorine) enjoys to a high degree the property of polarizing negatively platinum, I have not yet succeeded in obtaining that effect by the bleaching principle produced during the slow combustion of ether in atmospheric air. This neutral state seems to indicate that the said principle is either loosely united to or mixt up with a matter enjoying opposite voltaic, i.e. electropositive properties and it is perhaps from such a compound that results the pungent smell perceived during the combustion of ether. What that matter is I cannot yet say but it may be that the fact I am going to state has something to do with the subject alluded to.

When an aqueous solution of iodide of potassium is repeatedly treated with the atmosphere obtained by slowly burning ether in common air, it becomes reddish brown and if the solution being in that state be heated in a retort only traces of free iodine are given off, but at the same time a crystalline matter distills over, that enjoys all the properties of your ioduret of etherine $(I + C_4H_4)$. As perhaps the pungent matter being produced by the slow combustion of

436

ether our bleaching principle united to the olefiant gas; and is it the latter that does counteract or mask the negative voltaic properties of the former? Ulterior experiments will answer these questions. If you think the contents of my letter such as to be worthy of being communicated to the Royal Society you have full liberty to do so. I have a mind to read myself at Cambridge the report I am charged to draw up on the Ozone affair and to make there the more important experiments regarding that delicate subject. Pray present my humble regards to Mrs. Faraday and believe me,

Yours

most truly

C. F. SCHOENBEIN

[1] This letter does not appear in the published correspondence of Schoenbein and Faraday (G. W. A. Kahlbaum and F. V. Darbishire, editors, *The Letters of Faraday and Schoenbein, 1836–1862*, Bâle and London, 1899).

296 M. FARADAY to J. LIEBIG, 5 February 1845

[*Bayerische Staatsbibliothek, Munich, previously unpublished*]

Royal Institution

5 Feby 1845

MY DEAR LIEBIG

Your very kind letter was to me a source of the highest gratification & pride and I should long since have answered it (aye even the next day) but that I was continually hoping for some great result such as the condensation of hydrogen or nitrogen or at least oxygen and wanted to send you the first word. But to this time notwithstanding all my labour & continued repition [*sic*] of experiments with increased care I have been disappointed – Still I am not cast down & though I have become at last very tired & moreover have an attack of rheumatic influenza – and must for the present rest – yet I trust hereafter to succeed – So my letter will be much poorer in scientific value than I wished – but not my dear friend in the heartiest feelings of affection for your kind expressions which I have by personal knowledge of you learnt to know come from the heart.

My wife often speaks of you and I think has more pleasure in her remembrances thoughts & knowledge of you than of any other amongst scientific men with whom she has become acquainted. Your german feelings of home and wife and other subjects are very congenial to her mind & before she went out knowing that I intended writing to you she desired to be most sincerely remembered to you with many thanks for your good opinion. She thinks you flatter her but I tell her you do not. Talking of my wife reminds me of yours whom you join with yourself in persuading us to come & see you at Giessen Tell Mrs. Liebig that I shape out to myself in fancy such a thing though I hardly hope to see it fulfilled and that I please myself with imagining all about you two, and how much she is like you in feeling and the pleasure that I could have in being at home with you & her & chatting altogether just as we do here in our happiest moments and as you & me have done together – but let it pass. I must put such thoughts aside for the present. – and the reality perhaps for ever – Nevertheless be assured that if things were to shape themselves I would thank you both for your kind invitation by shewing ourselves at your door.

As to my gas experiments – I am still working at them and hope the next time I try I shall have oxygen perhaps the end of this week. Olefiant gas. Phosphuretted hydrogen Hydriodic acid. Hydrobromic acid Fluosilicous & Fluoboric have given way & become liquids and Hydriodic and Hydrobromic acids with Ammonia – Sulphuretted hydrogen – Nitrous oxide – Euchlorine – and dry sulphurous acid have become solids – In working at the tensions of the vapours of these bodies I have been much troubled by irregularities which I can only account for by supposing that they are not always as pure as is supposed. Thus both Olefiant gas & Nitrous oxide gas when condensed give me liquids which must be mixtures of at least two substances of different volatility – and in Olefiant gas the mixture appears to be in very different proportions at different times of preparation as if an alteration in the tempera-ture or in the quantities of materials made alterations in the proportions of the different bodies produced. But I have not yet had time to work this out any further than to its effect in causing great differences in the tension of the vapour produced by the condensed liquid obtained at different times. You know that though I may seem lively enough at times that I soon tire and this with a bad memory soon puts an end to my working for a time Adieu my dear Liebig – That blessings may be on you & yours is the earnest wish of your faithful friend

M. FARADAY

297   M. FARADAY to A. DE LA RIVE, 20 February 1845
[*Bibliothèque publique et universitaire de Genève, ms. 2316, f. 58–9, B.J. 2, 190*]

Royal Institution
20 Feb\ 1845

MY DEAR DE LA RIVE

The thought of writing to you has been so constantly on my mind, and therefore by comparison so fresh, that I had no idea until this minute that I have looked at your letter that I had received it so long ago. – I have waited & waited for a result intending to write off to you on the instant & hoping by that to give a little value to my letter, until now when the time being gone & the result not having arrived I am in a worse condition than ever and the only value my letter can have will be in the kindness with which you will receive it.

The result I hoped for was the condensation of *oxygen* but though I have squeezed him with a pressure of 60 atmospheres at the temperature of 140° F. below o° he would not settle down into the liquid or solid state – and now being tired, and ill, and obliged to prepare for lectures I must put the subject aside for a little while – Other results of this kind i.e of the liquefaction & solidification of bodies usually gaseous which I have obtained you will have seen noticed in the Annales de Chimie[1] – The full account I hope to send you soon from the Philosophical Transactions[2]

As to the Ozone subject – it is exceedingly curious and I am really surprised to think how many results and reasons there appears to be all tending in one direction and yet without any one of them furnishing an overruling and undeniable proof. – I get confused with the numerous reason – my bad memory will not hold them, and with my judgment longs to rest on some one proof such as a little ozone in the separate visible or tangible state Nitrogen is certainly a strange body – it encourages every sort of guess about its nature and will satisfy none. – I have been trying to look at it in the condensed state but as yet it escapes me.

Your kind invitation for the scientific meeting in August is very pleasant to the thought. but I dare not hope much for such happiness. – I long to see Geneva and Switzerland again but there are many things which come between me & my desires in that respect I know the kindness of your heart and how far I may draw upon you if I come and I thank you most truly for not only the invitation you have sent me but for all the favours you would willingly shew me. Do you remember one hot day I cannot tell how many years ago. when I was hot and thirsty in Geneva and you took me to your house in the town & gave me a glass of water & Raspberry vinegar – That glass of drink is refreshing to me still

Adieu my dear friend – Remember me kindly to Madame de la Rive – and if I am not too far wrong in the collocation of thoughts & remembrance of past things – bring me to mind with one or two young friends who shewed me a dolls house once & with whom I played on the green

Yours Most truly & Affectionately

M. FARADAY

[1] Letter 284.
[2] M. Faraday, 'On the Liquefaction and Solidification of Bodies generally existing as Gases,' *PT* (1845), 155.

[*I.E.E., previously unpublished*]

Castle Parsons [reading doubtful] Tower
Tuesday Mar. 4. 45

MY DEAR FARADAY/

As yet I have had nothing to communicate to you concerning our observations with the Leviathan Telescope[1] – for the truth is that not one fine night have we had since I came here. The only Celestial Object we have observed with the large Telescope was the Moon one Evening during the last Junction, and Certainly a Most splendid view of her we had –

The Metal however was then only roughly polished – and its figure was not good – on Tuesday last however it was removed from its tube – on Wednesday – Thursday – and Friday it was re-scoured – on Saturday and yesterday was re-polished – and this day is replaced in its tube –

The weather is extremely unfavorable, and in a few days weather will again interfere with our Nebular Observations – so that when we soon have a change of weather, another 17 or 18 days must elapse before we can do any thing –

There is a necessity for using a watery solution of Ammonia during the process of polishing the large Speculum, and the solution gotten in Dublin, sometimes stains the surface of the metal – nay, occasionally brings out innumerable crystals on the metal face, and that too (as tis said) "because the Ammoniacal Solution Contains Cyanogen" – Whether this be really the Case, or whether it is only hypothesis I know not – it would however be very desirable to obtain some solution of Ammonia which can Certainly Contain none of this "Cyanogen" – I believe the solution of Ammonia obtained from Dublin by Lord Rosse is procured from the Gas works, and as I believe not from Muriate of Ammonia –

Now it seems to me certain that were the Ammoniacal Solution obtained by the decomposition of Muriate of Ammonia, in the good dear old fashioned way, all admixture of Cyanogen with it would be impossible – If you are of that Opinion, can you tell me of any Manufacturer in London on whom Lord Rosse might rely for a supply – Formerly Howard and Gibson of Stratford made all the preparations of Ammonia better than any other persons – whether however they now do so I know not –

Last night we tried the newly polished Speculum of the Leviathan and I am delighted to tell you it performed very satisfactorily – All we want is some clear weather, and I doubt not I should very soon have some very interesting facts to Communicate to you –

How I should be delighted if you could run over to us – is the thing impossible? I am sure it would do you good, and would indeed be regarded as a high honor both by Lord and Lady Rosse – who as well as Dr Robinson desire me to remember them most kindly to you –

Present my best regards to Mrs. Faraday and believe me

Yours Affy
J. SOUTH

PS/ Are you working *in moderation* as you ought – ? A Metal out of Hydrogen, may be obtained too dearly – if at the expence [*sic*] of your health –

[1] The Earl of Rosse had just completed the construction of a six-foot reflecting telescope, then the largest in the world. See his 'On the Construction of large Reflecting Telescopes,' *BAASR* (1844), 79.

299 C. F. SCHOENBEIN[1] to M. FARADAY, 22 March 1845
[*R.S., previously unpublished*][2]

Bâle,
March 22, 1845

MY DEAR FARADAY

I am inclined to believe that I have at last succeeded in solving the problem regarding the nature of ozon [*sic*] and as you were kind enough to pay some attention to my researches on that subject I flatter myself you will peruse with interest the following lines. Having failed in all my apparent attempts at isolating the odoriferous principal and not being able of attaining from those experiments any other results than what consisted in simple effects of oxidation, I was induced to reexamine the circumstances under which Ozon is generated. Resuming the very first idea I started about the nature of the substance five years ago and according to which ozon was to be considered as a peculiar compound consisting of oxygen and hydrogen I recommenced my researches with ascertaining the part which water acts in the formation of our principle. I found out that it is most abundantly produced more abundantly indeed than by any other means known to me by putting phosphorous in immediate contact both with water and atmospheric air at a temperature of about 30°C. Under these circumstances the air of a very *large* bottle may be very richly charged with ozon even within a very few minutes. In exposing phosphorous to the action of common air being deprived of its humidity as completely as possible and suffering the other circumstances to remain the same hardly a trace of ozon makes its appearance, however long the contact of phosphorous with air may last. In making the experiments just mentioned with a gazeous mixture of Oxigen and Carbonic Acid Gas exactly the same results were obtained, ozon was abundantly produced in it when water appeared to be present and the temperature to be sufficiently high, whilst the formation was stopt in the dry mixture. Already five years ago I ascertained the following points 1.) that by heating the points from which electricity is passing into the air the peculiar electrical smell is prevented from making its appearance 2.) that under these circumstances the electrical spark loses its polarizing power 3.) that heated

441

plates of platinum are not polarized by the brush issuing from cold points of [word illegible] 4.) that the voltaic current is not capable of disengaging ozon out of water being heated to a certain degree 5.) that plates of platinum being heated to the same degree do not assume the negatively polar state when placed within an atmosphere of voltaic ozon. Presuming the effects described might be due to a decomposition of ozon carried about by the action of heat I made (with the view of proving the correctness of this conjecture) the following experiments. In the usual way the air of a large bottle was abundantly charged with ozon and an apparatus arranged in such a manner as to allow a current of air in passing through a narrow tube into the atmosphere. After having ascertained that the air issuing from the said tube enjoyed all the properties belonging to ozon I applied heat to part of the tube and no sooner had the latter assumed a certain temperature than the peculiar smell disappeared on a sudden and with it also all the other properties of ozon. In letting cool down again [*sic*] the tube to a certain degree of temperature the air issuing from it reassumed its peculiar smell and along with it all the chemical and voltaic properties. It is hardly necessary to state that voltaic ozon undergoes the same change under the circumstances last mentioned and therefore it appears to be an undoubted fact that ozon, in whatever way it may have been produced is destroyed by heat i.e. decomposed (most [reading doubtful] likely into water and oxigen).

A few days ago M. Marignac a very clever Chymist of Geneva and a friend of mine communicated to me the results of his experiments lately made on ozon. Now they are indeed such as to completely square with mine. In treating powder of silver with large quantities of ozonized air he could obtain nothing but pure oxide of silver and in decomposing iodide of potassium by ozon the Chymist of Geneva got (like myself) iodate of potash some muriate and free Iodine; making use of acidulated water containing a trace of nitrogen and having this fluid electrolyzed, M. Marignac and M. de la Rive[2] obtained ozon as long as the current passed through it provided the liquid was kept cool during its electrolysis. M. Marignac found out that oxigen of itself is not capable of producing ozon with phosphorous and that the latter gas must contain either nitrous acid gas or nitrogen or hydrogen in order to generate that odoriferous substance. From the results obtained both by myself and M. Marignac it appears that nitrogen has directly nothing to do with the formation of ozon, that the latter is an elementary body and that it is produced, if water and oxigen happen to come into contact with one another under peculiar circumstances. This formation of ozon which takes place during the electrolysis of water is easily accounted for but as to the way in which phosphorous or an electrical discharge determines the atmospheric oxigen to unite with water then into ozon [giving rise to?] we do not yet know any thing about it.

My ozon seems to differ very widely from Thenard's peroxide of hydrogen,[3]

442

the latter being inodorous, readily soluble in water, communicating positive polarity to platinum and suffering decomposition by [illeg.] silver, without oxidizing that metal (according to the statement of Thenard) whilst ozon has a peculiar and very strong smell, is scarcely soluble in water, makes platinum assume negative polarity and oxidizes silver. –

Ozon being generated in the atmosphere when the latter happens to be acted upon by common electricity it is to be presumed that the former always contains more or less ozon according to circumstances and that on this account a series of chemical actions taking place within the common air may be traced to the presence of ozon; for instance the slow oxidation of metallic and other substances, the bleaching of vegetable colours &c. I think I can even prove the correctness of these conjectures by direct experiment. Paste of starch mixt up with some iodide of potassium being over long exposed to the action of atmospheric air that happens to be contained within a bottle remains colourless, whilst the same paste turns blue rather rapidly when placed into the open & freely circulating air. I have also ascertained the fact that a solution of iodide of potassium undergoes a slow change by being put in contact with the open air for under these circumstances small quantities of iodate of potash are formed and traces of iodine eliminated. Now ozon acting exactly in the same way upon the said paste of starch as well as upon the saline solution just mentioned we can hardly account for the facts before us in another manner than by admitting the presence of some traces of that highly oxidizing agency in the atmosphere. I entertain therefore little doubt that ozon will turn out after all to be a substance destined to act rather an important and general part in the economy of nature.

As to the evolution of ozon, I think the only way of effecting it is to let pass large quantities of air being richly charged with that component through tubes which are kept as cold as possible, for the facility with which ozon is decomposed leaves very little hope for isolating it by chemical means. Before concluding allow me to say yet a word or two about the phenomenon so long known and so ill understood regarding the [ms. torn and missing] of phosphorous taking place within humid atmospheric air and the oxidation of that [ms. torn and missing] into phosphoric acid. From the facts above mentioned it appears [ms. torn and missing] by some action or other exerted by phosphorous on the atmospheric oxigen and water, these two matters unite into ozon and that the latter reacts upon phosphorous in such a way as to oxidize it into phosphoric acid. From that oxidation proceeds no doubt the principal part of light emitted during the slow combustion of phosphorous within humid atmospheric air for as soon as water is excluded the shining of phosphorous is nearly ended and the formation of ozon entirely stopt and at the same time the oxidation of phosphorous becomes exceedingly slow. Phosphorous acid always mixt up with phosphoric acid is most likely due to the oxidation of phosphorous brought about by free atmospheric oxigen. If you think the contents

443

of this letter interesting enough as to be worthy of the notice of the Royal Society you will oblige me by your communicating them to that learned body.[4] My best compliments to Mrs. Faraday and my most friendly solicitations to Yourself.

Yours most truly
C. F. SCHOENBEIN

[1] See Letter 283.
[2] Not in Kahlbaum and Darbishire, *The Letters of Faraday and Schoenbein, 1836–1862.*
[3] Louis Jacques Thenard (1777–1857), 'Mémoire sur la préparation du bi-oxide d'hydrogène,' *AC*, 2 s., 50 (1832), 80.
[4] A summary of this letter is given in *PRS*, 5 (1843–50), 565.

300   J. PERCY to M. FARADAY, 18 April 1845

[*I.E.E., previously unpublished*]

Birmingham,
April 18 1845

MY DEAR SIR

I write to ask your opinion on one point, and I must apologise for doing so, knowing the value of your time. We have noticed a thousand times the grass in the winter exposed frequently to a cold many degrees below the freezing point. We know that grass contains a large quantity of water. But, although the grass may be exposed to cold sufficiently intense rapidly to freeze water under ordinary circumstances, yet the water in that grass, so far as I have casually remarked, does not when exposed to a considerable degree of cold *appear* to freeze. And when we consider the structure of a leaf, we should be inclined to conclude, that, if the water became solid, the structure of the leaf would be impaired. Now [reading doubtful] the point concerning which I take the liberty of interrogating you is this, – whether water may not, when inclosed in *extremely minute* tubes, say as fine as a hair, remain liquid at the ordinary temperature of congelation. – I have made a few experiments on this point with glass tubes drawn out as fine as a hair; and it appeared to me that *extreme tenuity* of the tube exercised a retarding effect upon the freezing of water contained in them. But I make the statement with *great caution*, as I have not satisfied myself of its correctness by [reading doubtful] frequent repetition. With best compliments to Mrs. Faraday, in which Mrs. Percy desires to unite, I remain, my dear Sir,

With great respect,
Yours sincerely
JOHN PERCY

P.S. There is yet much for you to see in & about Birmingham, & any time you feel disposed to travel this way we shall be delighted to entertain you in our *informal* manner.

[*Smithsonian Institution, previously unpublished*]

Princeton College.
New Jersey.
April. 22. 1845

MY DEAR SIR. –

Permit me to introduce to your acquaintance my friend Professor Cresson of Philadelphia.[1] He leaves his family tomorrow for a few months, to make a short tour in Europe, and with no one abroad is he more anxious to form an acquaintance than with yourself. Permit me to recommend him to your attention as a most worthy, respectable and intelligent gentleman, who is highly esteemed in this country, and with whose acquaintance I am sure you will be pleased.

I have heard that you have had some thoughts of making a visit to this country, to give a course of lectures at the Lowell Institute in Boston. I hope you will conclude to come. You will not find the voyage across the Atlantic an affair of much moment, and the permanent improvement in your health, on account of the tour and relaxation, will more than compensate for the temporary interruption of your pursuits. When you come we shall expect a visit from you and Mrs. Faraday, (for I think it is a settled matter that she will accompany you) at Princeton we are midway between New York and Philadelphia – about forty five[2] miles from each city, on the route of the railroad.

I am rejoiced to learn that you have recovered your health, and that you are again engaged in a series of most interesting experiments, on the condensation of the gases. Permit me to hope that you will remember me in the distribution of the extra numbers of your paper.

I have not published any thing of any importance for some time, although I have on hand a large collection of facts, relative to the dynamic induction of ordinary electricity, which I have deferred publishing until I should have time to make some further investigations. The result, however, has been, that I have been anticipated by others, in some of my discoveries. This, although it may be a matter of some little moment to myself, is of no consequence to the cause of science. I am not very anxious about scientific fame, and I can truly say that I have enjoyed much more pleasure in the pursuit of science, than from any credit I have received for the result of my labors.

With much Respect and Esteem I remain Yours &c.
JOSEPH HENRY

[1] John Chapman Cresson (1806–76), Professor of Mechanics and Natural Philosophy in the Franklin Institute of Philadelphia from 1837 to 1855.
[2] A blank space in the manuscript.

302 M. FARADAY to J. NASMYTH,[1] May 5 1845

[*Wellcome Medical Historical Library, previously unpublished*]

R Institution
5 May 1845

MY DEAR SIR

Next Saturday is my day for a lecture on Iron. May I remind you of your promised kindness, and express a hope that any specimen of cut or punched Iron or other illustration of strength & fracture that you can let me have may arrive here at latest by Friday.[2]

Ever Your Obliged
M FARADAY

[1] James Nasmyth (1808–90), inventor of the steam hammer and pile driver. 'Naysmith' in the manuscript.
[2] See Letter 303.

303 J. NASMYTH to M. FARADAY, 7 May 1845

[*I.E.E., previously unpublished*]

Bridgewater Foundry,
Patricroft,
near Manchester,
May 7 1845

MY DEAR SIR

I am duly favoured with your valued note of the 5th. I had not forgotten the promise I made and which I have had so much pleasure in endeavouring to perform I hope some of the specimens have arrived already as I have had advice of the set of *Equivalents* leaving the Elscan Iron work, Yorkshire a few days since and hope they have come to hand and are in satisfactory Form I only hope they wont [*sic*] too much cumber your lecture table but I trust the clear and definite Idea as to relative quantities of the materials employed on and in the production of a certain mass of wrought Iron will be acceptable to your audience – its [*sic*] a novel mode of Illustrating the subject but I think it is one that has common sense (that of sight) to recommend it I wish I could see a museum of manufactures so arranged it would very materially help to convey sound and lasting impressions a museum of Equivalents? – I should even like to see how large a piece of Bread a glass of Gin represents perhaps something like this I hope you have by this time received more monster shavings from my excellent friend Joseph Miller[1] Esquire Blackwall who I engaged to let you have some specimens which I thought would illustrate the triumph of mechanic art over obdurate material – I hope they have come to hand and are satisfactory

I had also written to my friend Edward Bury[2] superintendent of locomotion Engines on the London & Birmingham for a specimen or two of Broken axle

446

– and hope he also has complied with my request in a satisfactory manner – failing which I might name that there is a collection of most malignant cases under the charge of Sir H De La Beche at Gray's court which might in the absence of suitable specimens from E. Bury supply you with what is desired on that subject, a most interesting and important one it is – I have just received the inclosed from Mr Bury and I fear from its contents he has nothing satisfactory to send on the subject of Railway arches, so I should advise application to Sir H De La Beche – I shall take care to have a small case sent off in time with some specimens of the influence of Cold Swaging or cold hammering in destroying the fibrous fracture of wrought Iron and also of the Effect of annealing at a dull red heat in restoring the strength and that to [sic] in a highly improved degree cold swaging does no harm but quite the contrary *provided* it be followed up by annealing at a dull red heat

Also the little case will contain a specimen of the influence of a few degrees of heat in changing the appearance of the Fracture of wrought Iron from the christaline [sic] to the Fibrous – this is a subject well worthy of attention in as much as that a piece of Iron that was broken *on a cold day* would exhibit a degree of Brittleness and sparkling fracture which 10° or 20° degrees higher temperature would exhibit a totaly [sic] diferent [sic] character of Fracture. I should think this might be worthy of a remark as the quality of Iron might be called in question when it was "John Frost" that was to Blame, it is remarkable how few degrees will make all the difference –

Also it is very important to remark on the strength restoring effects of the process of annealing i e heating the article to a dull red heat and laying it down to cool at its leisure. Chains that have been strained to near their utmost are rendered brittle soon after but if passed through this restorative process the original strength is restored The heat appears to permitt [sic] the particles to again resume a natural relation to Each other – it might be well to Exhibit the Ease with which a piece of Bright new drawn Iron wire can be broken after a bend or two say an $\frac{1}{16}$th of an inch clean Iron wire count the times it will stand bending and unbending say 10 times heat a bit of the same wire dull red hot and let it cool it will then require at least 30 bends and unbends to break it. This would in your! hands convey much valuable information on a very important subject in a few words it directly bears on a class of subjects of the highest practical importance – The Bright wire represents the metal with its particles in a constrained unnatural state. The annealing sets them all comfortable again and they will pay back the kindness ten fold in increased strength and toughness – but perhaps this is just what you were going to do so pray excuse the liberty I am taking in making such suggestions – I am just about to run over to Bolton to try and get a specimen of a bit of clipt [reading doubtful] Iron Bar that will perhaps show the power we have in the serious line of tools – I do like millions by shavings [reading doubtful] [2 wds illeg.] and are satisfactory –

447

Should you toutch [*sic*] on the process of Hardening and tempering of steel it might be as well to say a word on the real distinction between the two processes. The one the primary the other the secondary Hardening by plunging into cold water or mercury which as Every one almost knows hardens the steel. Then comes the modification. Ajust [*sic*] hardness to suit various purposes when we can spare a bit of hardness to get toughness in exchange – *but* in the case of those tools which Engineers use and which are performing such wonders for the cause of civilization in turning and Planing tools &c. for our big machines &c all such are *simply hardened* by heating to *the lowest Red heat at which on plunging into cold water* they will *just harden* This is the grand point

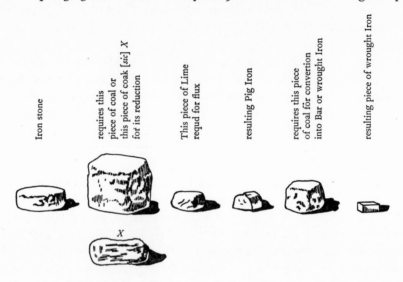

Iron stone

requires this piece of coal or this piece of coak [*sic*] X for its reduction

This piece of Lime requd for flux

resuling Pig Iron

requires this piece of coal for convertion into Bar or wrought Iron

resulting piece of wrought Iron

X

to attain and it is by this simple process alone and no after tempering that the tools in question stand such vast work and peel off such shavings, it is *the* most important point to hit the right heat at which they will just harden Every degree above this is to the damage of the steel as to strength as well as real practical hardness – we never *temper* such tools The simple dip in of the cutting point at the before named lowest-hardening heat is the grand secret if it is so to be termed – pray Excuse the liberty I am taking in perhaps giving in rude form what you knew perfectly well before but the motive is the only excuse I have to offer namely to communicate workshop knowledge on important subjects – I shall put in a specimen of right heated and hardened steel as also a bit of over heated to show the difference of strength and fracture

I doubt not you will be glad to hear that I have had a most gratifying first trial with my pile driving Engine a la Steam Hammer I set it on the top of a blunt log of wood 14^{in} square 16 feet long and let in the steam when off it set a thumping in good Earnest and sent the Pile 15 feet down into hard ground with 20 masterly Blows at the rate of 65 per minute! such pile driving the world never saw before the action of the whole apparatus was perfect and realized in every point what I had anticipated. The following down of the incubus sitting on the head of the devoted pile was laughable in the Extreme for as the pile sunk under the Blows there was the machine following him quicker than sight could detect as I could not detect any difference in time between the sink of the pile and that of the machine following down after him it's realy [*sic*] a laughable scheme this but a truly important one. it is now shipping for Liverpool Dock yard along with a second. They will have lots of work to do there. Pray Excuse this length [*sic*] infliction on your patience from yours Most faithfully

James Nasmyth

1 Joseph Miller (1797–1860), manufacturer of steam engines.
2 Edward Bury (1794–1858), F.R.S. 1844 for improvements in steam engine design.

304 Lord Northampton[1] to M. Faraday, 25 May 1845
[*I.E.E., previously unpublished*]

5 Lowndes St
May 25, 1845

My dear Sir

The question of a new Charter is before the Council of the R. S. but at this moment is waiting for discussion, & for information as to the pecuniary cost of it. If we simply have one, the main object will be to have a more convenient time than the midst of November for our anniversary. There will of course be an opportunity of other improvements which it is advisable not to neglect – I therefore wish the advice of some of the more distinguished members of the society, in addition to that of the council & write to ask you to favour me with any suggestions that may occur to you – It seems to me advisable to make our rule of electing more strict, & I should think it would be better that one Fourth should be sufficient to exclude a candidate, than one Third as at present – Still I think it right to be more liberal than in many other societies, which this would still be –

There is a question on which I should like your advice, but it would not be connected with the new charter – I mean, is it advisable to adopt in some degree, and if so, under what restrictions, discussion *on Papers read* as in many other scientific societies? I am inclined to think it would be advisable, giving however to the president absolute discretion at once to cut it short or to state simply that he did not consider a paper adapted to discussion at all –

Would it be advisable to make any change in the Payments of the Fellows, either admission [illeg.] or Composition Payments? I think the Composition over high, being at Fifteen years purchase, which most often simply makes it

Ten – Besides that the R. S. generally takes in it's [*sic*] members at a more advanced age than other societies.

Would it be better to make the adm.ⁿ Payments Five Pounds? – & the Composition Fifty? – instead of Four & Sixty – Of course this question could only apply to new members –

Yours very truly
NORTHAMPTON

I forgot one very important point. The question whether the Presidency should be unlimited in it's [*sic*] duration – I think *not*. It should not be necessarily *short*, yet in truth a President has much to *learn* which Time alone can teach him before he can be able at all to perform his duties well, I mean, as to *persons*, for I am not alluding to science – But it is not well that he should go on when superannuated, not knowing his own incapacity, & his friends from delicacy not telling him – Moreover a certain degree of change is itself good "New Brooms &c" My idea would be limit it to Ten years – with annual reelection of course.

¹ Spencer Joshua Alwyne Compton, Second Marquis of Northampton (1790–1851), served as P.R.S. from 1838 until 1848.

305   M. FARADAY to SIR E. CODRINGTON,¹ 2 June 1845

[*Burndy Library, Norwalk, Conn., Michael Faraday Collection 20, previously unpublished*]

Royal Institution
2 June 1845

DEAR SIR EDWD

With many thanks for the present and former acts of kindness I return the boat safe I trust from the hands of the Messenger as it now is under my eyes.² I find I make 30 or 40 feet into 5, but I do not wonder at it: for every day brings to me growing proofs of my loss of memory. I was formerly troubled at this but to be troubled by it now would be to spend my life in one strain of regret & disappointment so I bear with it as well as I can & hope my friends will too

Ever Your Obt & Grateful
M. FARADAY

¹ Sir Edward Codrington (1770–1851), Admiral and F.R.S.
² Faraday would appear to have borrowed a model of a ship from Sir Edward. It was probably exhibited in the Library of the Royal Institution.

[*I.E.E., previously unpublished*]

Paris
le 10 juin 1845

Je serais un grand coupable, Mon cher et très honoré Maître, si de trop graves
et de trop puissantes raisons n'excusaient pas le long silence que j'ai gardé
envers vous; mais une longue et très facheuse maladie, dont je ne puis me
délivrer, m'accable depuis trois ans et a mis ma vie en danger pendant plus de
18 mois. C'est une maladie d'intestins, une névrose de l'intestin grêle, qui me
tient ainsi dans un état de souffrance: des rechutes nombreuses s'opposent à ce
que je puisse me livrer à des travaux continus. Du reste Mr. Boutigny,[1] mon
ami, qui vous présentera cette lettre et vous remettra quelques unes de mes
dernières publications, pourra vous dire combien je suis souffrant la plupart du
temps. Mr. Boutigny est un de nos savants les plus ingénieux, dont le nom vous
est assurément connu; c'est l'auteur des belles expériences sur l'état sphéroidal
des liquides[2] et dont les recueils Scientifiques ont parlé plusieures fois. Si vous
desiriez voir ces expériences, je ne doute pas qu'il ne s'empressât de les répéter
devant vous.

Votre lettre du 19 janvier 1843 contenait plusieures observations fort
judicieuses, auxquelles j'aurais repondu immédiatement, si la maladie ne m'avait
tenu éloigné de tout travail sérieux pendant long temps. Lorsque un peu de
mieux se fit sentir, j'employais tous mes moments loisibles à coordonner mes
idées en un Résumé qu'on imprimera sous peu à Bruxelles dans les Mémoires
couronnés de l'Académie.[3] j'avais vu la mort de si près que dans la crainte d'un
retour de sa part, je voulais laisser ce document après moi, puisqu'il lierait les
différentes idées que j'avais émises isolément dans mes publications éparses.
Aussitôt qu'il sera imprimé, j'aurai l'honneur de vous l'offrir. On termine dans
ce moment l'impression d'un Mémoire que j'ai envoyé à la même académie; ce
Mémoire traite de la cause principale de toutes les oscillations barométriques.[4]
C'est un travail tout neuf, qui ne ressemble en rien aux essais antérieurs qu'un
si grand nombre de physiciens ont produits; essais qui n'ont jamais pu lier les
diverses perturbations du baromètre. j'espère vous l'envoyer sous un mois.
Vous trouverez dans ces diverses publications les réponses aux remarques que
vous m'adressiez: il serait donc inutile d'entrer dans des détails que vous
trouverez plus développés dans ces publications.

La hardiesse de mes vues, leur éloignement aux idées reçues produiront
quelques répulsions d'abord; mais j'en appelle à l'avenir, j'en appelle aux
observations et aux expériences faites sans idées préconçues. Déjà, de celles que
j'ai publiées depuis 4 et 5 ans, plusieures avaient aussi été repoussées, telles que
la division des vapeurs élastiques de l'atmosphère, en nuages transparents, en
portions distinctes, dont les unes sont chargées d'électricité négative et les

autres d'électricité positive. Depuis la publication de mon Traité des Trombes[5] plusieurs physiciens observateurs sont parvenus aux mêmes résultats par des routes diverses, et l'existence de ces masses transparentes est maintenant reçue par un grand nombre de savants.

Il en a été de meme de l'état électrique des nuages, lorsque j'ai dit que tout nuage *gris* est *négatif* et tout nuage *blanc* est *positif.* Cela ne fait plus doute actuellement, pour qui a voulu répéter l'observation. Il en est encore ainsi du globe, comme corps chargé d'électricité negative, tandis que l'espace céleste ne possède aucune électricité, et joue par conséquent le rôle d'un corps chargé d'électricité *positive* envers le globe. Dans le mémoire que je vous enverrai, et dont vous trouverez un court abrégé dans un des articles que je vous envoie par M. Boutigny,[6] vous verrez que pour moi il n'existe pas de fluide spécial, auquel on puisse donner le nom d'*électricité*: qu'il y a des phénomènes particuliers qu'on nomme *électriques*, mais que leur cause ne tient pas à un fluide particulier, mais à un état particulier de coercition ou de propagation du fluide universel que l'on nomme *Ether*. C'est là l'idée la plus hardie que j'aurai émise, et qu'on admettra, j'en ai la conviction, non à présent, mais d'ici à dix ans. Les faits, contraires aux fluides spéciaux, s'accumulent trop chaque jour, pour croire qu'il faudra un plus long temps pour démontrer la vérité de cette cause générale de tous les phénomenes électriques. Rappelez-vous tout ce qu'on a dit contre le résultat que j'avais obtenu, celui du froid par un courant électrique. Quoiqu'il ne s'agissait que d'un fait que tout le monde pouvait vérifier, il a fallu trois ans pour le faire admettre; et cette admission n'a été complète que lorsque Mr. Lenz[7] à [*sic*] fait congeler de l'eau par ce moyen.

Je vois par vos beaux et incessants travaux, que vous avez repris toute votre santé, et que rien ne vous arrête plus dans les progrès que vous faites faire chaque jour à la science, recevez en mon sincère compliment, personne n'a pris plus de part que moi à vos souffrances, comme personne ne ressent plus de joie de vous savoir en parfaite santé: la science était en deuil pendant votre maladie, et elle a repris ses habits de fête depuis que vous êtes débarassé de toute souffrance.

Adieu, mon cher et digne Maître, Recevez l'assurance que personne n'a plus de vénération que moi pour votre beau talent et veuillez croire à la haute considération que vous porte

Votre tout dévoué Serviteur
PELTIER
Rue Poissonnière 26

[1] Pierre Hippolyte Boutigny (?–1884), chemist.
[2] P. H. Boutigny, 'Propositions physico-chimiques sur la caléfaction et l'état spheroidal des corps,' *RSAE*, 1 (1841), 167.
[3] 'Essai de coordination des causes qui précèdent, produisent et accompagnent les phéno-mènes électriques,' *MCASB*, 19 (1845–6).
[4] 'Recherches sur la cause des variations barométriques,' *ibid.*, 18 (1844–5).

5 J. C. A. Peltier, *Observations et recherches expérimentales sur les causes qui concourent à la formation des trombes*, Paris, 1840.

6 The memoir mentioned in fn. 3 was abstracted in *BASB*, 11, Pt. 2 (1844), 31.

7 Heinrich Friedrich Emil Lenz (1804–65), 'Ueber einige Versuche im Gebiete des Galvanismus. 1. Ueber Kälte-Erzeugung durch den galvanischen Strom...,' *AP*, 120 (1838), 342.

307 A. DE LA RIVE to M. FARADAY, 12 June 1845

[*I.E.E., previously unpublished*]

Genève,
le 12 juin 1845

MON CHER MONSIEUR,

Je viens vous remercier de votre aimable lettre du 20 février;[1] tout ce qui me vient de vous m'est toujours si précieux par le souvenir qui se rattache à mon père & par la bienveillante amitié que vous voulez bien m'accorder, que je ne puis vous dire le plaisir que m'a fait votre lettre. Je vous remercie de tous les détails intéressants que vous me donnez & je regrette, tout en le comprenant, que vous n'ayez pas poursuivi vos belles expériences.

Nous avons cet été, ainsi que je vous l'ai déjà dit, au mois d'Aout, les 11, 12 & 13 la réunion des naturalistes & physiciens Suisses. Vous savez que cette Société fondée en 1815 est le plus ancien des Congrès Scientifiques qui existent maintenant dans différentes contrées de l'Europe. J'en suis le Président cette année; jugez quelle serait ma joie & celle de tous vos amis & collègues si vous vouliez vous rendre à Genève pour cette époque. Je n'ose l'espérer d'après votre lettre; cependant un petit voyage fait avec Mad^e Faraday vous ferait bien du bien; je vous offre l'hospitalité que je serais, ainsi que ma femme, bien heureux de vous voir accepter. Ce serait une grande joie pour ma femme & pour moi de vous avoir quelques jours à demeurer chez nous avec Mad^e Faraday. Tâchez donc de nous faire cette amitié. – Envoyez-nous également quelques uns de vos compatriotes. Daubeny, Wheatstone, Lyell, &c. devraient bien venir; un mot de vous pourrait les y déterminer. – Nous aurons, j'espère, quelques savants français, allemands & italiens; c'est une raison de plus pour nous de désirer que l'Angleterre ne nous fasse pas défaut. La réunion aura lieu les 11, 12 & 13 Aout à Genève.

Vous avez peut-être vu que Mr Marignac a montré que l'*ozone* de Schoenbein n'était pas le radical de l'azote.[2] Nous avons fait dernièrement une expérience qui confirme l'idée que j'ai toujours eue que c'était simplement de l'oxigène dans son état particulier. – Il suffit de faire passer de simples étincelles électriques à travers un courant d'*oxigène* parfaitement *pur* & *sec* pour lui donner toutes les propriétés de l'*ozone*. Je suis convaincu que tous les autres moyens de préparer l'ozone qui sont indiqués par Schoenbein & auxquels Mr Marignac en a ajouté d'autres, se bornent à électriser par des moyens *mécaniques, physiques* ou *chimiques* l'oxigène, soit celui qui provient de la décomposition de l'eau, soit celui qui est déjà préparé. Ce n'en est pas moins une chose remarquable que cette forme particulière que peut prendre l'oxigène. Cela indiquerait-il que ce n'est pas un corps simple?

Je viens d'achever un assez grand travail sur l'aimantation du fer doux & sur les vibrations que détermine dans les corps conducteurs, mais surtout dans le *fer* le passage des courants électriques *discontinus*, soit alternatifs, soit dirigés dans le même sens. – J'en ai écrit quelques mots a [*sic*] Mr Arago qui a inséré un extrait de ma lettre dans les *Comptes rendus de l'Académie*[3] où peut-être vous l'auriez lu.

Il y a dans tous ces phénomènes des choses bien mystérieuses; ce qui me parait le plus curieux c'est tout ce qui concerne l'arrangement de la limaille de fer & l'action en général exercée sur le fer doux dans l'intérieur d'une hélice dont le fil est traversé par le courant discontinu. J'ai fait construire une hélice dont le fil de cuivre est de plus de 3 à 4 millimètres de diamètre & qui elle même a un diamètre intérieur de 15 à 16 centimètres. Le courant d'une très forte pile en traversant le fil de cette hélice produit, soit lorsqu'il est continu, soit quand il est discontinu, des effets très remarquables. Ainsi, si la limaille de fer est sur un plan horizontal placé au fond de l'hélice qui est elle même verticale, on la voit former comme une forêt de petits arbres hauts de 3 ou 4 centimètres & qui tournaient sur eux mêmes avec une grande rapidité en fuyant en général le centre de l'hélice. Ainsi encore si le plan horizontal sur lequel est la limaille est au haut de l'hélice au lieu d'être en bas, on voit la limaille se porter vers le centre & non vers les bords. – Je vous épargne les effets curieux d'aimantation; je me borne à celui qui se manifeste par les vibrations.

Ces vibrations produisent un très beau son; mais le ton de ce son change pour la même corde de fer tendue de la même manière, selon que l'hélice agit sur certains points ou sur d'autres de la corde. L'intensité varie également de même. Le courant qui traverse le fil de fer y produit le même ton que celui qui y détermine l'aimantation opérée par l'hélice, quoique dans le premier cas le fil ne soit point aimanté; ce fait semble prouver que la modification moléculaire qui résulte de la transmission du courant électrique est la même que celle qui résulte de l'aimantation. Mais quelle est-elle? C'est ce que je cherche à trouver; j'ignore si j'y réussirais.

Je suis convaincu que la propriété du *fer*, du *nickel* & du *cobalt*, d'etre aimantés, tient uniquement à leur constitution moléculaire particulière. L'idée que vous avez émise que cette propriété tient au grand rapprochement de leurs particules me parait recevoir une confirmation de ce que c'est ce même rapprochement qui fait que ces mêmes corps rendent un son par le frottement de leurs particules les unes contre les autres, quand le courant électrique les traverse. En effet le son qu'ils rendent & qui est beaucoup plus fort pour le fer que pour les autres, est tout à fait semblable à celui d'une roue dentée qui en tournant frappe contre un ressort métallique; c'est tout à fait le son d'un métal qui frotte un métal. –

J'ajoute dans l'enveloppe ces quelques mots pour vous demander une faveur. – Vous m'avez donné un volume qui renferme vos memoires jusque & y compris la 14ème Série. – Seriez-vous assez bon pour me donner les mémoires qui suivent? Je n'en ai que quelques uns; je ne les ai pas tous & je désirerais vivement avoir la collection complète. Si vous aviez cette bonté, vous m'obligeriez excessivement en m'envoyant ces mémoires chez *MM. Morris Prevost & C° care of Mr J. L. Prevost* qui doit venir incessamment à Genève & qui me les apporterait.

J'espère que vous avez reçu dans le temps ma notice sur la vie & les travaux de De Candolle[4] que je vous ai envoyée par l'intermédiaire de Mr Baillière.[5]

J'ai appris avec un bien vif chagrin la mort de l'excellent professeur Daniell; c'est une grande perte pour la Science; cette perte a dû vous être bien sensible; car il était d'un caractère si aimable & si bienveillant & il vous était bien attaché.

Votre nomination à l'Académie des Sciences m'a bien rejoui; c'est un acte de justice qui vous était dû depuis longtemps. Il m'a rappelé que vous n'étiez pas Membre honoraire de notre *Société de Physique & d'Histoire Naturelle* & je me suis empressé de demander qu'on vous conférât ce titre bien modeste qui est pour nous une manière non de reconnaitre les services rendus à la Science, nous sommes trop peu de chose pour cela, mais la bienveillance temoignée à votre pays & à ses habitants par des hommes de Sciences. C'est à ce dernier titre seulement, c'est en qualité d'ami de Genève et des Genevois que nous nous sommes permis de joindre votre nom à celui de Arago, de Humboldt, de de Zach,[6] de Becquerel & de quelques autres noms moins célèbres. Colladon[7] qui va aller en Angleterre vous portera le diplôme de ce titre scientifique à ajouter dans quelque petite place à ceux que vous avez déjà.

Je n'ai plus que cette petite place pour vous rappeler, Monsieur, combien je vous suis attaché, vous prier de me rappeler au souvenir de Made Faraday & vous prier de croire aux sentiments respectueux & affectueux de votre dévoué

A. DE LA RIVE

[1] See Letter 297.
[2] Jean Charles Marignac, 'Sur la production et la nature de l'ozone,' *CR*, 20 (1845), 808.
[3] A. de la Rive, 'Des mouvements vibratoires qui déterminent dans les corps, et essentiellement dans le fer, la transmission des courants électriques et leur action extérieure...,' *CR*, 20 (1845), 1287.
[4] A. de la Rive, 'Notice sur la vie et les ouvrages de A. P. DeCandolle,' *BU*, 54 (1844), 75, 303.
[5] Probably Pierre François Philippe Baillière, member of the French family of publishers, who founded a branch of the publishing house in London in 1831.
[6] Franz Xaver Freiherr von Zach (1754–1832), astronomer.
[7] Jean Daniel Colladon (1802–93), Professor of Physics at the Geneva Academy.

[*I.E.E.*, *previously unpublished*]

29 Upp: Southwick Street

Hyde Park Square

July 2, '45

MY DEAR DR FARADAY,

I have rung changes upon two words signifying *form*, & upon three denoting *change* in the hope of finding a word that you may honor by adopting.

$$A \begin{cases} \text{1. } \tau\acute{\upsilon}\pi\text{o}\varsigma = \text{type, character, frame} \\ \text{2. } \mu\text{o}\rho\phi\eta = \text{form, figure.} \end{cases}$$

$$B \begin{cases} \text{1. } \acute{\epsilon}\tau\epsilon\rho\text{o}\varsigma = \text{other, varied, different.} \\ \text{2. } \acute{\alpha}\lambda\lambda\text{o}\varsigma = \text{other} \\ \text{3. } \mu\acute{\epsilon}\tau\alpha = \text{change} \end{cases}$$

These give
1. héterotýpic –
2. héteromórphic –
3. állotýpic –
4. állomórphic –
5. métatýpic –
6. métamórphic –

Nº 6 is in use allready, & so he's out of the question.

No 5 is my favorite – μέτα more than either *heteros* or *allos* denoting *simple* change: The other 2 mean *departure from a type* as in *héterodóxy* & *állophýlic* (a word of Dr Prichard's).[2]

All lie under one disadvantage. The *substantive* form is an awkward one, *e.g. állomórphy métatypy* &c. However, in Geology, they do with the simple adjective *métamórphic* & perhaps the simple form *métatýpic* would serve your purpose.

I don't expect (from the nature of things) to give you words of less than four syllables; but if I can think of one that will work up into good substantives & verbs (so as to ensure you talk of *metatypizing* or *working phenomena of metátypy* by *métatýpic* manifestations) I will trouble you with another lucubration.

Believe me My dear Dr Faraday

Ever most truly yours

R. G. LATHAM

[1] Robert Gordon Latham (1812–88), physician and Professor of English Language and Literature in University College, London.
[2] James Courles Prichard (1786–1848), physician and ethnologist.

[*I.E.E., B.J.* 2, *181*]

Hadley n[ear] Barnet
July 3d. 1845

DEAR SIR,

I have read your lecture on the nature of matter[2] with all the delight, which any one must feel in finding the opinions, which he has long held, so ably vindicated and so clearly illustrated.

There is however one difficulty, which will be felt in adopting the theory of Boscovich, namely that matter, or the physical agens, fills indeed Space, that is by virtue of its forces, as it does not *occupy* it. The ideal points, which are the foci of forces attractive and repulsive, do not present any intelligible conditions for the origination and renewal of the forces. There is a want of the idea of *Substance*. This it is true is unfortunately an equivocal word: but I flatter myself that in the appendix to the "Vital Dynamics", of which I ordered a copy to be sent to you, – namely in the "Evolution of the idea of *Power*", I have given it a correct philosophical import in assigning to it an equivalent meaning with the term "Subject", id quod jacet *sub*, – that it is therefore essentially supersensuous, beyond the possible apprehension of the senses, but necessarily inferred as quovis modo ejusdem generis with that which constitutes our own subjectivity and consciously known as Will, Spirit, Power.

This seems to me to be the true ground and key of all dynamic philosophy: but it has led me further, and I cannot but think that you have been also induced to extend your views in the same direction. Taught by your researches that chemical combination depends upon the equilibrium and neutralization of opposite forces, the liberation of which by decomposition resolves them into voltaic currents, I have been unavoidably forced back upon the question: If the electric forces are the true agents of chemical change what share have the the [*sic*] material substances or chemical stuffs in the phaenomena? And though my knowledge is too imperfect to permit me to come to any satisfactory conclusion I must say that all the arguments I can number bring me to the result: That these supposed stuffs are but the sensuous signs and symbols of the forces engaged in their production. Would that it were my good fortune to communicate with you more at large on this matter. Your obliged

JOS. HENRY GREEN

[1] Joseph Henry Green (1791–1863), surgeon, and Samuel Taylor Coleridge's literary executor.
[2] M. Faraday, 'A speculation touching electric conduction and the nature of matter,' *PM*, 24 (1844), 136.

457

[*Silvanus P. Thompson, 'The Life of William Thomson Baron Kelvin of Largs',* *2 vols., London, 1910, 1, 146*]

St. Peter's College,
August 6th 1845.

Dear Sir – I beg to thank you for your kindness in sending me the Italian memoir which you mentioned to me when I saw you here.[1] I have to apologise for not acknowledging it before, but I did not wish to write till I could say something on the contents, as you were so good as to ask for my opinion. I shall return it to you almost without delay.

The memoir is entirely occupied with the determination of the distribution of electricity on two equal spheres, in contact, which had been examined experimentally by Coulomb, and calculated mathematically by Poisson according to the general theory of Coulomb. The hypothesis which M. Avogadro makes is that the intensity of electricity at any point of the surface of an electrified conductor is proportional to the portion of sky which can be seen from the point projected orthographically upon the tangent plane at the point, or, as he stated it, to the sum of all the portions of a large spherical surface, described round the two spheres, each multiplied by the cosine of the obliquity of the direction in which it is seen. Thus if the two spheres were black, and were exposed to a sky uniformly bright in every direction, above and below (as might be produced by laying them on a perfect mirror, placed horizontally), the intensity of electricity at any point of either would be proportional to the quantity of light which would be received by a small, white piece of paper laid upon the surface at the point. You will readily from this conceive whether the hypothesis is even analogous in any respect to the actual physical conditions of the problem. The numerical determinations differ very widely indeed from the measurement of Coulomb, but the differences are attributed by M. Avogadro to his having neglected the curvature of the lines of inductive action. For an experimental investigation of the curved line of induction, he refers to your eleventh series. The only numbers which he gives are the ratios of the intensities at 30° and 60° from the point of contact, to the intensity at 90° (which latter he, of course, on account of his hypothesis, finds to be the same for all of the unopposed hemispheres). For these ratios he finds .6 and .95. Coulomb's measurements give .21 and .80; Poisson's calculations .17 and .74. The measurements are, as Coulomb himself considers, very uncertain, and may differ considerably from the truth on account of the excessively delicate and precarious nature of his most difficult experiments.

I am at present engaged in preparing a paper, of which I read an abstract at the late meeting of the British Association, for the first number of the *Cambridge and Dublin Mathematical Journal* (a continuation of the *Cambridge Mathe-*

matical Journal), of which a principal object is to show that in all ultimate results relative to distribution, and to attraction or repulsion, it agrees identically with a complete theory based on your views.[2] If my ideas are correct, the mathematical definition and condition for determining the curved lines of induction in every possible combination of electrified bodies are very readily expressible. The distribution of force (or in Coulomb's language, of electrical intensity) on a conductor of any form may be determined by purely geometrical considerations, *after* the form of the curved lines has been found. Thus, let A be an electrified conductor, placed in the interior of a chamber, and let S be the interior surface of the walls, which we may consider as conducting. The lines of induction will of course be curves, leaving the surface of A at right angles, and terminating at S, cutting it also at right angles. By means of these lines let any portion a of A be projected on S, giving a corresponding portion s. The quantity of electricity produced by induction on s will be exactly equal in amount, but of the opposite kind, to that on a, according to your theory (or according to Coulomb's, as follows from a general theorem on attraction). If now we suppose S to be a very large sphere, having A at its centre (and it may be shown that the distribution on A will be very nearly the same as if this were the case, provided every portion of S be very far from A, whatever the form of S), the distribution of the induced electricity on A will be very nearly uniform. Hence the problem of the determination of the distribution on A is reduced to the purely geometrical problem of the determination of the ratio of the s to a. The great mathematical difficulty is the determination of the form of the lines, when curved, as they will always be, except when A is a sphere. In some cases, as, for instance, when A is an ellipsoid, then the curved lines are found with great ease. In other cases, such as that of the mutually influencing spheres, the problem admits of an exceedingly simple solution if attacked from another direction.

It was from the connection with the mathematical theory of Heat (*Mathematical Journal*, vol. iii. p. 75)[3] that I was first able to perceive the relation which the lines of inductive action have to the mathematical theory.

I have long wished to know whether any experiments have been made relative to the action of electrified bodies on the dielectrics themselves, in attracting them or repelling them, but I have never seen any described. Any attraction which may have been perceived to be exercised upon a non-conductor, such as sulphur, has always been ascribed to a slight degree of conducting power. A mathematical theory based on the analogy of dielectrics to soft iron would indicate attraction, quite independently of any induced charge (such, for instance, as would be found by breaking a dielectric and examining the parts separately). Another important question is whether the air in the neighbourhood of an electrified body, if acted upon by a force of attraction or repulsion, shows any signs of such forces by a change of density, which, however, appears to me highly improbable. A third question which, I think, has never been investigated is relative to the action of a transparent dielectric on polarized light. Thus it is known that a very well defined action, analogous to that of a transparent crystal, is produced upon polarized light when transmitted through glass in any ordinary state of violent constraint. If the constraint, which may be elevated to be on the point of breaking the glass, be produced by electricity, it seems probable that a similar action might be observed. – I remain, with great respect, yours faithfully,

WILLIAM THOMSON.

[1] Amadeo Avogadro (1776–1856), 'Saggio di teoria matematica della distribuzione della elettricità sulla superficie dei corpi conduttori nell'ipotesi della azione induttiva escercitata dalla medesima sui corpi circostanti, per mezzo delle particelle dell'aria frapposta,' *MSIM*, 23 (1844), 156.
[2] William Thomson, 'On the mathematical theory of electricity in equilibrium,' *CDMJ*, 1 (1846), 75.
[3] 'On the uniform motion of heat in homogeneous solid bodies, and its connection with the mathematical theory of electricity,' *CMJ*, 3 (1843), 71.

311   M. FARADAY to W. THOMSON, 8 August 1845
[*Silvanus P. Thompson, 'The Life of William Thomson Baron Kelvin of Largs',
2 vols., London, 1910, 1, 149*]

R. Institution,
8 August 1845.

DEAR SIR –

I hasten to acknowledge and thank you for your letter. I reply thus speedily only in reference to your inquiries in the latter part of it.

I have made many experiments on the probable attraction of dielectrics. I did not expect any, nor did I find any, and yet I think that some particular effect (perhaps not attraction or repulsion) ought to come out when the dielectric is not all of the same inductive capacity, but consists of parts having different inductive capacity.

I have also worked much on the state of the dielectric as regards polarized light, and you will find my negative results at paragraphs 951–955 of my *Experimental Researches*. I purpose resuming this subject hereafter. I also worked hard upon crystalline dielectrics to discover some molecular conditions in them (see par. 1688 etc. etc.), but could get no results except negative. Still I firmly believe that the dielectric is in a peculiar state whilst induction is taking place across it. – I am, my dear sir, yours very truly,

M. FARADAY

[*R.I., B.J. 2, 200–4*]

Collingwood
Hawkhurst
Kent
Nov 9, 1845

MY DEAR SIR

I have this morning read with great delight a notice in the Athenaeum of your experiments proving the connexion of Light with Magnetism[2] In the first place let me congratulate you cordially on a discovery of such moment which throws wide a portal into the most recondite arcana of nature If I understand rightly the very meagre account given of your discovery it amounts to this – that the Electromagnetic current is capable of causing *the plane of polarisation* of a ray of light to revolve – for I can put no other probable interpretation on the expression "A beam of polarised light is deflected by the electric current so that it may be made to revolve between the poles of a magnet."

If this be really the state of the case, it is what I have long anticipated as extremely likely indeed almost certain to be sooner or later experimentally demonstrated *Voici mes raisons*

There are 3 distinct classes of phaenomena in which a helicoidal dissymetry occurs – 1*st* the Plagi[hedral] [reading doubtful] faces on Crystals such as quartz which belong to an [otherwise] symmetrical system. These faces in some Crystals indicate a right handed in others a left handed dissymetry of the helicoidal kind. – 2dly the rotation of the plane of polarisation of a ray of light when transmitted through certain solids and liquids indicating a helicoidal dissymetry both in the ray and in the molecules or at least a capacity in the ray to be affected by that peculiarity in the latter. – 3dly in a rectilinear electric current which; [*sic*] deflecting a needle in a given direction as to right & left all around it indicates again a dissymetry of the same kind.

Now I reasoned thus Here are 3 phaenomena agreeing in *a very strange peculiarity*. Probably this peculiarity is a connecting link physically speaking among them. Now in the case of the crystals & the light this probability has been turned into certainty by my own experiments. Therefore induction led me to conclude that a similar connexion exists and must turn up somehow or other between the electric current and polarised light & that the plane of polarisation would be deflected by magneto electricity.

It is now a great many years ago that I tried to bring this to the test of experiment (I think it was between 1822 and 1825) when on the occasion of a great magnetic display by Mr Pepys at the London Institution I came prepared with a copper helix in an earthen tube (as a non conductor) & a pair of black glass plates so arranged as that the 2d reflexion should extinguish a ray polarised

461

by the first after traversing the axis of the copper helix I expected to see light take the place of darkness – perhaps coloured bands – when contact was made. The effect was *nil*. But the battery was exhausted and the wire long and not

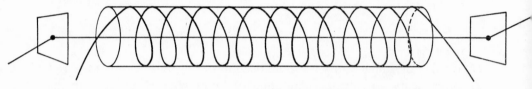

thick and it was doubtful whether the full charge remaining in the battery *did* pass, being only a single couple of large plates. –

There remained to be made another experiment before a negative could be considered as proved – vis to make the light move *along* a strait wire (or a combination of such thus

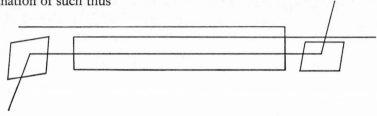

but this requiring preparation on the spot I could not then make and have never since had an opportunity, but the subject has often recurred to my mind and I have made frequent mention of it as a line of experiment worthy to be pursued.

You will be disposed to ask to what all this tends. Assuredly not to interfere for a moment with your claim to a beautiful discovery (for, though I may regret that I did not prosecute a train of enquiry which seemed so promising up to a decisive fact I consider it honour enough to have entertained a conception which your researches have converted into a reality) – but if it be not presumptuous in me to suggest a line of enquiry to you – I would willingly draw your attention to the other member of the triple coincidence above alluded to There *can be now no doubt* of the connexion of the *Crystalline forces* with magnetism & electricity.[3] It seems to me now all but certain that the space or ether? surrounding an electrified wire or a magnet is in the same state with the space or ether intervening between the molecules of a plagi[h]edral Crystal. Polarised light is *the test of that State* – a helicoeidal, [reading doubtful] dissymmetrical State This is the mode in which the phaenomena present themselves to my mind – not that light *is* electricity or magnetism – but that it is affected by them *as* by certain forms of matter; *which* therefore I conclude to be under the influence of magnetic currents in some concealed way circulating about them* – And the line of enquiry I allude to is to ascertain whether crystals formed under the direct influence of magnetic currents or between the poles of magnets may not be thereby made to assume plagi[h]edral faces or shew other indications of assymmetrical action[4] If so the existence of the plagi[h]edral faces on Quartz is accounted for by the presence of such currents during their formation

Believe me
my dear Sir
Yours most truly
J F W HERSCHEL

[1] The copy of this letter kept by Herschel and now in the Herschel papers at the Royal Society differs in some minor respects from this one which was the one sent to Faraday.
[2] *The Athenaeum*, 8 November 1845, 1080.
[3] From here to the asterisk Herschel has written at the bottom of the page to be inserted here.
[4] See [9646–7] for Faraday's experimental test of this suggestion. Also *LPW*, 433, for its context.

313   M. FARADAY to SIR J. F. W. HERSCHEL, 13 November 1845
[*R.S., previously unpublished*]

Brighton,
13 Nov., 1845

MY DEAR SIR JOHN

Your letter was a great pleasure and encouragement to me and I hasten to acknowledge it though so immersed in work I think I may say discovery that (being only a slow worker) I have hardly a moment to spare. The paper which I have sent to the Royal Society contains an account of that which you have rightly understood.[1] I was not aware that there was any thing in the Athenaeum until I received your letter. I have not seen it & do not know who could put it in except as a notion might be gathered up at the Institution from my brief notice to our own members on Monday week. That you did not obtain any result in your experiment is not to be wondered at for in fact you could not with the apparatus you describe even though you had had the strongest battery to act on & in it for *I have not yet been able to discover the effect in air or any gas.* Several years ago I made similar experiments and even used Electrolytes when electric currents were passing through them but obtained nil results. These I published in the Phil Transactions for 1834 Exp Researches 951–955 and Wartman [*sic*] repeating them came to & published similar conclusions.[2] It was only the very strongest conviction that Light Mag & Electricity must be connected that could have led me to resume the subject & persevere through much labour before I found the key. *Now all is simplicity itself.*

The results briefly are these If certain transparent substances be placed between the poles of a magnet so that that line of power commonly called the *Magnetic curve* pass through them & a ray of polarized light be also passed

463

through parallel to the line of magnetic force then the ray is rotated: if the line of Magnetic force pass one way the rotation is in one direction: if it pass the other way the rotation is in the contrary direction. If these same substances be placed in a helix & the electric current be sent round them whilst a polarized ray pass along the axis of the helix it is *in these* substances rotated one way for one direction of the current the other way for the other direction.

Glass, water and thousands of bodies I suppose shew this property but as yet *not gases*. But this rotation does not as yet coincide with that of quartz, oil of turpentine &c. though no doubt it will when we understand the whole subject as for instance let *a* represent a square cell filled with oil of turpentine and *b c* a ray of light passed through it. Let the circles *d* & *e* represent rotation round the oil of turpentine in the one or other direction and finally suppose that the fluid has naturally *right handed rotation*. Then if the ray be passed from *b* to *c* & observed at *c* the natural rotation will be right handed or according to the circle *d*. If the ray pass from *c* to *b* & be observed at *b* the rotation will still be righthanded to the observer at

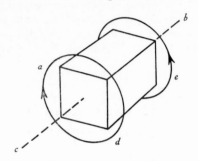

b & therefore according to the circle *e*. Now send an electric current round the fluid in the constant direction of the circle *d*. It will enhance rotation of the ray to the right hand or as the circle *d*, the observer being at *c* but *leave the current unchanged* and change the place of the observer from *c* to *b* now the rotation of the ray will be to the observer's *left hand* not as the circle *e* but still as the circle *d* and the same holds good for the rotation by magnetic force. I would rather not pretend to say more about this at present because I am still at work on the point

As to quartz I cannot say as much for it for a reason you will see presently

As to crystals; being persuaded that their crystalline structure was connected with electrical forces I worked in one direction on the subject, I think now five years ago & gave an account of my negative results in Exp Researches Paragraphs 1692–1695. Quartz will not exhibit any effect on the polarized ray i.e. by the mere influence of magnetic & electric forces though rotating fluids do easily shew the phenomena – so that I cannot say as much for it as for oil of turpentine sugar or tartaric acid As far as I have gone there is this striking relation between crystals & the Electric & Magnetic forces namely that *no doubly refracting* crystal will exhibit the effects of these forces on the ray but only singly refracting crystals as *common salt*, *alum* and *fluor spar*, all of which do so.

I have however (guided by my views of the action of magnets across dimagnetics: [*sic*] Exp Researches 1709–1736) discovered other means of examining the extraordinary state into which bodies generally are thrown by the magnetic forces, than their effect on a ray of light, and not only do doubly refracting crystals but opaque bodies – metals & I conclude all bodies come into subjection. I am so hard at work on this & other matters that I must not take a moment more: for I am here now both to *rest* the head & *work* it at the same time but my next paper to the R.S will contain an account of *new magnetic actions & conditions* of matter. In the mean time let me ask of you to say nothing about this part for I want to make it out as quietly as I can

> Ever My dear Sir
> Yours faithfully
> M. FARADAY

¹ M. Faraday, 'On the magnetization of light and the illumination of magnetic lines of force,' *PT* (1846), 1.
² Elie Wartmann (1817–86), Professor of Physics at the Geneva Academy. For his publications on induction and the state of matter suffering it, see *RSCSP*.

314 W. WHEWELL to M. FARADAY, 20 November 1845
[*B.J.* 2, *208*]

> Trinity Lodge,
> Cambridge,
> November 20, 1845

MY DEAR SIR

I am somewhat scrupulous about trying to take up your time with letter writing, but I cannot help wishing to know a little more than the "Athenaeum" tells us as to your recent discoveries of the relations of light and magnetism. I cannot help believing that it is another great stride up the ladder of generalisation, on which you have been climbing so high and standing so firm. I do not ask you to take the trouble of telling me what your discovery is, but perhaps you may be able to tell me where now, or in a short time, I may see some distinct account of it.

I hope you will have health and strength granted you to follow out this and many more great discoveries.

> Believe me, my dear Sir,
> Yours very truly
> W. WHEWELL.

[Trinity College Library, Trinity College, Cambridge, previously unpublished]

Brighton,
Nov.ʳ 22 1845.

MY DEAR SIR,

I write at the moment of receiving yours. I am here to rest and work, for I have hold of such things that I must not be still; and have no time to describe much. I have not seen the Athenaeum; & if it were here should, perhaps, not look at it; for the light paper seems, for the moment, old & passed *to me* because of that which I am engaged in.[1] But do not say, even, that, you are aware I am so engaged. I do not want men's minds to be turned to my present working until I am a little more advanced.

As to the light, which I shall resume as soon as I can, the chief fact is very simple. Suppose a polarized ray and a magnetic curve (as the lines of magnetic force are often called), passing through a transparent solid or liquid body, having no double refraction, and parallel to each other: – *then the ray is rotated.* If the magnetic line pass in one direction the rotation is one way; if it pass in the other, the rotation is the other way. Or suppose the polarized ray is passing through such bodies as those described above, & an electric current be sent, by a helix, round the substance & the ray; then *again it is rotated*: One way with the current in one direction & the other way with the current in the other direction. It so happens, that, with our conventional understanding of the direction in which an electric current is passing, i. e. from the zinc across the acid to the platinum or copper, – that the rotation is in the same direction as the current; (using Biots mode of expressing the rotation.)

The air, gases, & vapours do not, as yet, shew this property. Neither do those crystalline bodies which have double refraction; – all other transparent solid bodies & all fluid bodies do. Those fluids which rotate per se. have the magneto or electric rotation added to, or taken from, their own.

BUT the change in bodies which is induced by the Magnetic or Electric forces, I can trace by *other properties* than those on light, into bodies crystalline, opaque, metallic [illeg.] & gaseous. *But of this say no word at present.* The paper on light etc. was read at the R. S. last Thursday, I believe: Another or two on the new matter will go in as soon as I can find the mere time to make the multitude of limiting experiments which are needful & write the paper.

I am sure that when *you* have *this discovery you will understand and appreciate it.*

Ever My dear Sir
Yours faithfully
M. FARADAY

[1] Faraday was hot on the trail of diamagnetism. See his 20th and 21st Series of Experimental Researches, *PT* (1846), 21.

[*I.E.E.*, *previously unpublished*]

Genève
le 28 novembre 1845

MONSIEUR & TRÈS ILLUSTRE AMI,

Je viens de lire dans l'*Athenaeum* le titre d'un mémoire que vous avez communiqué à la Société Royale le 18 de ce mois. J'avais déjà aperçu dans un précédent numéro quelques traces de ce travail. Je suis, on ne peut plus impatient, d'en connaitre les détails. – C'est une magnifique découverte que vous avez fait [*sic*] là & vous méritez d'ajouter ce titre à tous les titres scientifiques que vous possédez déjà. Dévoué exclusivement à la Science, d'une activité & d'une persévérance à toute épreuve, & par dessus tout cela doté par la Providence de ce génie admirable qu'on ne peut acquérir si on ne l'a pas, vous méritez de réussir, & grâce à Dieu vous réussissez. Personne plus que moi, soyez en convaincu, ne jouit de vos succès & pour vous & pour la Science.

En attendant que vous vouliez bien m'envoyer votre mémoire imprimé, pourriez-vous m'en transmettre un extrait pour mes *Archives de l'Electricité*, ou tout au moins pour moi, si vous préférez que je ne l'imprime pas encore. Vous me feriez un plaisir des plus vifs & j'en suis digne, je vous assure, par l'intéret que je porte au sujet & par la profonde & respectueuse amitié que j'ai pour vous.

J'avais fait quelques essais sur le sujet que vous venez de travailler avec tant de bonheur, mais je n'avais pas réussi. La seule chose que j'avais cru apercevoir était qu'un rayon transmis à travers l'axe d'une bobine entouré d'un fil traversé par un courant en sortait polarisé. Mais je comptais vérifier ce résultat & m'assurer, ce qui est encore possible, qu'il n'était pas du à quelque réflexion intérieure du rayon de lumière contre les parois du trou de la bobine.

Je ne me permets aucune réflexion, aucune conclusion sur vos découvertes, car je ne les connais que par le titre du mémoire & ce serait prématuré aussi bien qu'imprudent de me lancer dans des discussions de ce genre avant de savoir de quoi il s'agit. Mettez moi donc, je vous en prie, le plus tôt que vous le pourrez, dans le cas de le savoir.

Mon frère qui a été dernièrement à Londres a cherché à vous voir; il a bien regretté de vous manquer soit chez vous, soit chez Madame Romilly[1] où vous avez pris la peine d'aller le chercher; il me charge de vous exprimer ses regrets & l'assurance de ses sentiments respectueux.

Veuillez me rappeler au souvenir bienveillant de Madame Faraday & recevoir vous même, Monsieur & très cher & bon ami, l'assurance des sentiments respectueux & affectueux de votre devoué

AUGE. DE LA RIVE

Si vous voulez bien m'envoyer un extrait de votre travail ne craignez pas de me le transmettre par la poste. Quant au mémoire même dès que vous pourrez

30-2

m'en expédier un exemplaire, ayez la bonté de l'envoyer à mon adresse chez *MM. Morris Prevost & comp.* qui me le feront parvenir le plus vite possible.

1 Probably the wife of Charles Romilly (1808–87), barrister.

317   W. D. CONYBEARE to M. FARADAY, 1 December 1845
[*I.E.E., previously unpublished*]

Axminster
Dec 1

MY DEAR MR. FARRADAY

You must allow me to offer my most sincere congratulations on the late discovery by which you have brought light into connection with the true polar forces of Electro magnetism; I am persuaded that this is as yet only the first opening of a new series of discoveries by which you will throw fresh light on these mysterious & etherial parts of nature, & their relations – when I read of such discoveries I am always reminded of a passage which used to delight me as a boy in Robertsons America[1] where he quotes a letter from one scholar to another writing on the subject of Columbus & his new found World, in which he says, "These are the news which indeed interest minds like ours" – & although I can pretend to little else, yet in the gratification I derive from the progress of science, I believe I yield to few – I only as yet know your late discovery from a slight notice in the newspapers but even this is sufficient to show me its importance, & how much it is likely to add of fresh distinction to a name already so much the first in these branches of science In reflecting on what I read, the idea occurred to me, whether there may not be a connection between that new fact & the polarizing powers exercised by crystalline minerals on light – because your introduction of the electro magnetic current appears simply to produce a partial rotation in these powers – may not therefore the original polarizing powers of crystals likewise in some manner themselves be the result of electromagnetic currents – Crystalline aggregation itself appears clearly a form of attraction following polar laws – & I have always believed it to be closely allied to the only polar force of which we know any thing definitely, namely Electro magnetism – in the tourmaline when warmed we all know that the opposite mineral poles assume an opposite polar electricity. I do wish in your interrogation of nature, you would ask a few questions of all sorts of crystals –

Querie also, might we not hope in Light to detect some manifestation of electical [*sic*] powers if we were to bring into contact two rays of oppositely polarized light, & to find those powers manifested at the point & at the moment when they were brought into union – Of course the idea suggests itself to me from the analogy of the development of Electricity at the moment of the

468

completion of the magnetic circle – has any question to this effect ever been asked of nature I know you are very impertinent in pressing her with home [reading doubtful] interrogations – believe me my dear sir

With much esteem & respect yrs
W. D. CONYBEARE

¹ William Robertson, *The History of America*, 2 vols., London, 1778 and many later editions.

318 M. FARADAY to A. DE LA RIVE, 4 December 1845

[*Bibliothèque publique et universitaire de Genève, ms. 2316, f. 60–1, B.J. 2, 211*]

Brighton
4 Dec.ʳ 1845

MY DEAR FRIEND

Your letter which I received this morning was a very great gratification to me not more for the approbation which it conveyed than for the kindness with which I know it is accompanied. I count upon you as one of those whose free hearts have pleasure in my success and I am very grateful to you for it. I have had your last letter by me on my desk for several weeks intending to answer it but absolutely I have not been able for of late I have shut myself up in my laboratory and wrought to the exclusion of everything else. I learned afterwards that even your brother had called on one of these days & been excluded.

Well, a part of this result is that which you have heard and my paper was read to the Royal Society I believe last Thursday for I was not there and I also understand there have been notices in the Athenaeum but I have not had time to see them & do not know how they are done. However I can refer you to the Times of last Saturday (the 29 Nov.) for a very good abstract of the paper. I do not know who put it in but it is well done though brief. To that account therefore I will refer you.

For I am still so involved in discovery that I have hardly time for my meals & am here at Brighton both to refresh & work my head at once and I feel that unless I had been here & been careful I could not have continued my labours. The consequence has been that last Monday I announced to our members at the Royal Institution another discovery of which I will give you the pith in a few words – the paper will go to the Royal Society next week and probably be read as shortly after as they can then find it convenient

Many years ago I worked upon optical glass & made a vitreous compound of silica boracic acid & lead which I will now call heavy glass & which Amici¹ uses in some of his microscopes and it was this substance which enabled me first to act on light by magnetic and electric forces. Now if a square bar of this substance about half an inch thick and 2 inches long be very freely suspended between the poles of a powerful horse shoe electromagnet immediately that the

469

magnetic force is developed the bar points but it does not point from pole to pole but equatorially or *across* the magnetic lines of force i.e. east and west in respect of the North & south poles. If it be moved from this position it returns to it & this continues as long as the magnetic force is in action. This effect is the result of a still simpler action of the magnet on the bar than what appears by the experiment & which may be obtained at a single magnetic pole. For if a cubical or rounded piece of the glass be suspended by a fine thread 6 or 8 feet long and allowed to hang very near a strong magneto-electric pole (not as yet made active) then on rendering the pole magnetic the glass will be *repelled* & continue repelled until the magnetism ceases. This effect or power I have worked out through a great number of its forms & strange consequences. & they will occupy two series of the Experimental Researches. It belongs to *all matter* (not magnetic as iron) without exception so that every substance belong to the one or the other class – Magnetic or diamagnetic bodies. The law of action in its simpler form is that such matter tends to go from strong to weak points of magnetic force & in doing this the substance will go in either direction along the magnetic curves or in either direction across them. It is curious that amongst the metals is found bodies possessing this property in as high a degree as perhaps any other substance. In fact I do not know at present whether heavy glass or bismuth or phosphorus is the most striking in this respect. I have very little doubt that you have an electromagnet strong enough to enable you to verify the chief facts of pointing equatorially & repulsion if you will use bismuth carefully examined as to its freedom from Magnetism & making of it a bar about $1\frac{1}{2}$ inches long & $\frac{1}{3}$ or $\frac{1}{4}$ of an inch wide. Let me however ask the favour of your keeping this fact to yourself for two or three weeks and preserving the date of this letter as a record. I ought (in order to preserve the respect due to the Royal Society) [not to] write a description to any one until the paper has been received and even read there – After three weeks or a month I think you may use it guarding as I am sure you will do my right and now my dear friend I must conclude. & hasten to work again. But first give my kindest respects to Madame de la Rive & my thanks to your brother for his call.

Ever Your Obedient & affectionate friend

M. FARADAY.

[1] Giovanni Battista Amici (1786–1863), the inventor of the achromatic objective for microscopes.

319   M. FARADAY to C. WHEATSTONE, 5 December 1845
[*B.J. 2, 214*]

Royal Institution,
Friday night, December 5, 1845

Many thanks, my dear Wheatstone, for your note. I have in consequence seen Becquerel's paper,[1] and added a note at the first opening of my paper. It is astonishing to think how he could have been so near the discovery of the great principle and fact, and yet so entirely miss them both, and fall back into old and preconceived notions.

Ever truly yours,
M. FARADAY.

[1] In 1827, Antoine Cesar Becquerel had 'discovered' diamagnetism but had not realized that what he observed was a new magnetic phenomenon. See his 'Sur les actions magnetiques excitées dans tous les corps par l'influence d'aimans très-energiques,' *AC*, 2 s., 36 (1827), 337.

320   M. FARADAY to W. WHEWELL, 8 December 1845
[*Trinity College Library, Trinity College, Cambridge, previously unpublished*]

Royal Institution
8 Decr 1845

MY DEAR SIR,

Think, first of all, of two small bars about 2 inches long & 1/4 or 1/2 an inch in width; and imagine them freely suspended in a horizontal position so that they can revolve on a vertical axis. Let these bars be *Iron* and heavy Glass; or, as a better known thing *Phosphorous*. Place these bars in succession between two powerful magnetic poles N & S. The *iron bar*, as all know, will point axially or from pole to pole, & if nearer one pole than the other, or near a single pole will be *attracted bodily*. – Place the bar of Phosphorous in the same position & it will point equatorially or *across* the magnetic axis & if nearer one pole than the other, or near a single pole will be BODILY REPELLED. With the iron ranks Nickel, Cobalt, Titanium, Manganese, Cerium, (and perhaps another metal Chromium) and *all* their compounds, salts & solutions even, (except perhaps those in which the compound acts the part of an acid): – with the phosphorous ranks *all other* bodies when in the *solid* or *liquid* state.

This is my present discovery which I hinted before to you – and I have not time to go further into it for I am *very hard* at work.

But: – we have used the word Magnetic to indicate an action after the manner of iron Now here is another action which is to that, as Pos is to Neg Electricity, or as any other relation, dual in its character. I have, before the discovery of this power, been in the habit of calling iron etc. *Magnetics*, & the other bodies

471

as water earth etc. *dimagnetics* but now what I am to call this new mode of action? what terms am I to use which shall express for magnetism the *two states* on the opposite sides of the normal or neutral point?[1] We have the Normal condition perfect in Air & all gaseous bodies & I believe I have found one solid substance very near to it.

In Haste

Most Truly Yours

M. FARADAY

[1] See Letter 321.

321 W. WHEWELL to M. FARADAY, ca. 10 December 1845[1]

[*I. Todhunter, 'William Whewell', 2 vols., London, 1876, 2, 365*]

Trin. Lodge,

Cambridge

MY DEAR SIR,

Your discovery is a door into a very wide chamber, though, to my eye, not fully open; but I shall rejoice to see you turn it well round on its hinges, as I know you will.

As to a name for the antithetical classes of bodies, I consider thus. I suppose you called one class *dimagnetic* from analogy with *dielectric*. I think you ought to have said *diamagnetic*; for the bodies *through* (*dia*) which electricity goes would have been called *dia*electric, but that vowels in such cases coalesce. I think you may keep *diamagnetic* for this class, and give to the opposite class a name implying that they *rank along with* magnetic bodies. I propose *paramagnetic*. Will it not do to talk of iron, nickel, &c., as *paramagnetic*, and glass, phosphorus, &c., as *diamagnetic*? Then this new branch of science, for so, of course, it will soon become, will be *Paramagnetism*. I do not see any inconvenience in any of the obvious relations of the word. But it is difficult to judge of this without knowing the relations of the facts better than I do, and, if you find that the words I have suggested will not work well, (for that is the main thing), I will try if I can suggest better.

I give you joy at having such good reason to work hard – I hope you will not work *too* hard.

Yours very truly,

W. WHEWELL.

[1] Todhunter gives 1850 as the date but this is clearly impossible since Faraday only used the term 'dimagnetic' immediately following the announcement of his discovery. The present letter obviously is the answer to Letter 320. I have, therefore, dated it 10 December 1845.

[*Ms. Collection of Dr E. T. Conybeare, OBE, No. 132, Catalogue of Historical Manuscripts Commission, previously unpublished*]

3 Cheyne Walk,
Chelsea,
13th Dec[r] 1845.

My dear Sir,

I fully expected to have been able to call on you this morning, but having to see a Lawyer in situ – Chancery Lane – I was unable. You will naturally ask – What the deuce I wanted to disturb you for? – & I must briefly reply as follows –

Know then, as I was passing into the Royal Society's Rooms last Thursday evening, a special messenger served me with a missive from Sir John Ross,[2] of Polar celebrity, who directed me to place the same before the President & Council of the Royal Society. Thus "pressed" I read the Missive, & forthwith shewed it to Lord Northampton, thinking I had then shot the bolt, – but no, his Lordship directed me to fill up the prayer by placing it before the next R. S. Council: so I passed it on to Mr. Christie.

You ask – What has all this to do with you? Why I'll tell you. The Captain makes a reclamation of Magnetized Light!! and quotes chapter & verse for it.[3] Laud we the Gods!

Such is the mighty matter which I panted to communicate, & now – as I may chant Liberavi animum mecum – believe me always

Your's [*sic*] very truly,
W. H. Smyth: –

No season can be too early or too late for the expression of one's good wishes, I therefore beg to tender my sincere hopes that you will have a happy Christmas & New Year.

[1] William Henry Smyth (1788–1865), Rear Admiral, member of the Council of the Royal Society.
[2] John Ross (1777–1856), arctic explorer.
[3] I have been unable to discover the passages here mentioned in Sir John Ross's published works.

323 Sir J. F. W. Herschel to M. Faraday, 20 December 1845
[*R.S., previously unpublished*]

Collingwood,
Dec. 20/45

My dear sir

Will you bear with me once more if I intrude on your patience with the suggestion of an experiment. I would try it myself – but I cannot lay my hands on any glass fit for the purpose & cannot come up to Town to get it properly executed.

It is very simple – & as follows

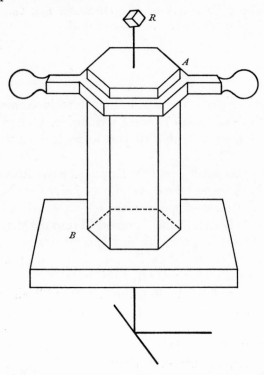

AB is a hexagonal prism of glass (or a circular one with Bipolar ends) of which the two terminal faces are plane and polished – the lower End is fixed in a block to hold it firm i. e. in a hole pierced in it the upper is jammed in a wrench with handles by which it can be subjected to torsion

Pass a ray of polarised light from below up through it in its natural State and set a Rhomb *R* above it to analyse the transmitted ray & adjust to the disappearance or minimum of one image –.

Then apply torsion up to the point (if needed) of rupture of the glass.

Now I should expect the phaenomena of circular polarisation to arise – as in quartz and to have its right or left handed character according to the direction of the torsion

Believe Me Ever
My dear sir
yours very try
J. F. W. HERSCHEL

474

324 M. FARADAY to SIR J. F. W. HERSCHEL, 22 December 1845

[*R.S., previously unpublished*]

R. Institution,
22 Dec[r] 1845

MY DEAR SIR

I received yours this morning & have already given Newman orders for the glass & that I may make your experiment for you. I perhaps shall not be able to make it for a week or ten days for I am now writing my third paper on the magnetic phenomena[1] and I shall hardly be able to finish it. This week I must lay all these things down for a fortnight whilst I deliver six lectures that commence next Saturday.

I will make your experiment but in return I must request you to take care of the accompanying paper[2] not opening it but doing with it as I may hereafter direct. I have certain views and amongst them two which if verified people might say were in some way derived from your suggestions. I do not think it likely your experiment will lead you to them nevertheless least it should do so I wish to guard my own position by putting on sure record before hand what are my expectations in these respects. I have long since ordered the apparatus for both but as I said want time and it may be a month or more before I can work them out.

I am afraid from the wording of your note that you did not receive my reply from Brighton to your former letter[3] I wrote at once.

Ever My dear Sir
Your Most truly
M. FARADAY

[1] Series 21 was read to the Royal Society on 8 January 1846.
[2] See Letter 325.
[3] Letter 313.

325 M. FARADAY, 22 December 1845

[*I.E.E., previously unpublished*[1]]

Royal Institution
Dec[r] 22, 1845

I have reason from experiment to think that a ray is not indifferent as to its line of path but has different properties in its two directions and that by opposing rays end ways new results will be obtained I have ordered apparatus already for the experimental investigation of this point and only want *time*.

I have already made a certain progress in the endeavour to obtain Electric currents or magnetic force from light by the use of circular polarization natural and constrained and also on other principles which I need not advert to here.

M. FARADAY

[1] See *LPW*, 390 and fn. 63, 406.

[*I.E.E., previously unpublished*]

Genève
le 25 X^bre 1845

MONSIEUR & TRÈS EXCELLENT AMI,

Je viens vous remercier de tout mon coeur de votre bonne lettre du 4 X^bre.[1]
– Vous êtes bien aimable d'avoir trouvé le moyen de m'écrire au milieu de
toutes vos occupations & j'en suis bien reconnaissant.

Je n'ai encore eu connaissance de votre première découverte que par l'extrait
de votre Mémoire que renferme l'Athenaeum, extrait qui n'est pas très clair &
qui me parait incomplet. – Cependant d'après ce que j'en ai compris, je n'ai pas,
je l'avoue, tiré de vos admirables recherches les mêmes conclusions que vous.
– Si j'ai bien compris, l'action des electroaimants, des courants électriques & des
aimants ordinaires consiste en ceci qu'elle change le plan de polarisation de
certains corps sur lesquels elle s'exerce. Vous n'avez pas encore trouvé, à ce
que je crois, que cette action eut lieu sur de la lumière transmise dans le vide ou
par un corps transparent quelconque. – J'en conclus que l'action dont il s'agit
s'exerce non sur la lumière, mais sur les corps qui la transmettent, de façon
qu'en modifiant pendant qu'elle a lieu leur structure moléculaire, elle change
leurs propriétés optiques & parconséquent leurs plans de polarisation. Ce
serait ici un effet physique analogue à l'effet chimique qui résulte dans les
expériences de Mr. Biot[2] de la dissolution de certains sucres ou de certaines
substances végétales en plus ou moins grande proportion. On sait qu'il en
résulte des changements dans les plans de polarisation. Qu'un changement dans
la structure moléculaire des corps résulte de l'action qu'exercent sur eux un
électroaimant ou les courants électriques, c'est ce qu'est mis en évidence, à ce
que je crois, les experiences dans lesquelles j'ai réussi à mettre en vibration un
grand nombre de corps, même du bois, en les soumettant à l'action discontinue
de forts électroaimants & de forts courants électriques. C'est ce que vous
trouverez dans la lettre que j'ai adressée à Mr. Arago & qui a été imprimée dans
les Comptes rendus de l'Académie des Sciences d'Avril 1845.[3] Or si cette
action discontinue met tous les corps en vibration, il est évident que ce ne peut
être qu'en modifiant leur structure moléculaire d'une manière passagère, &
parconséquent elle doit la modifier d'une manière permanente si elle est elle-
même continue.

A l'appui de ma manière de voir, j'invoquerai encore vos propres expériences
dont vous me parlez dans votre lettre. – Le fait qu'un électroaimant exerce une
action directe sur les mêmes substances dans lesquelles vous avez observé cette
action sur la lumière qui les traverse, prouve que ces vibrations ne sont pas par
elles-mêmes & indépendamment de la lumière qu'elles transmettent, indifféren-
tes à cette action. N'est-il donc pas plus naturel de croire que le phénomène que
vous avez observé est du à une modification dans la structure moléculaire du

corps plutôt qu'à une action directe exercé [*sic*] sur la lumière qui la traverse? – Je vous soumets ces reflexions qui peut-être tomberont devant une connaissance plus approfondie de vos recherches que je ne connais encore que d'une manière très imparfaite. Si, après en avoir pris une plus ample connaissance, je persiste dans cette manière de voir, je chercherai à vérifier ma conjecture par quelques expériences faciles à imaginer & je vous en soumettrai les résultats, comme je vous soumets dès à présent l'idée que je viens de vous énoncer. – Je vous prie en grâce d'avoir l'extrême bonté de prendre la plume pour me dire en quatre mots seulement ce que vous en pensez, afin que je ne m'en occupe pas davantage si vous me démontrez, comme c'est possible, qu'elle ne mérite pas qu'on s'y arrête.

Permettez-moi, Monsieur & très cher ami, de vous dire à l'occasion des faits intéressants dont vous me parlez dans votre lettre, que j'ai publié en 1829 dans le T. 40ème de la première série de la *Bibl. Univ.* p. 82, des expériences assez analogues aux votres faites par Mr *Le Baillif*[4] à Paris & dont je fus témoin ainsi que Mr Colladon, Mr Savary & je crois Mr Becquerel. Vous verrez que Mr Le Baillif avait très bien démontré la répulsion qu'exercent le bismuth & l'antimoine sur l'aiguille aimantée. Il est vrai que votre expérience est plus générale & qu'elle est faite sur une plus grande échelle. Cependant le fait observé par Mr Le Baillif était très net & très prononcé. Il ne vous en reste pas moins l'immense mérite d'avoir mis ce fait hors de doute, de l'avoir généralisé & d'en avoir trouvé les lois; mais je crois qu'il revient une part de l'observation primitive à Mr Le Baillif & j'ai présumé vous être agréable en vous en prévenant.

A cette occasion saurez-vous me dire pourquoi le *Phil. Mag.* se montre si exclusif à l'égard de nos travaux? Je n'ai pas eu l'honneur depuis bien des années d'y voir insérer une seule de mes recherches. – En particulier il n'a pas dit un mot de mon travail sur les vibrations des corps par l'action des courants électriques, travail qui a pourtant paru dans les Comptes rendus & dans les Archives de l'Electricité & que les Annales de Chimie ont trouvé convenable de reproduire. Il n'a pas non plus dit un mot des expériences que nous avons faites Mr Marignac[5] & moi sur l'*ozone* & notamment de celle dans laquelle nous produisons de l'ozone en faisant passer une série d'étincelles électriques à travers de l'oxigène parfaitement sec & pur. – En général il nous laisse complètement de côté & je crois que je ferai mieux de ne plus adresser nos journaux scientifiques à ces Messieurs. – J'ignore les motifs qu'ils ont d'agir ainsi à notre égard, mais, en tout cas, ce n'est pas aimable. Pardonnez moi ma petite boutade; mais vous êtes vous si bon si juste & si bienveillant pour nous & pour moi en particulier que j'ai pris la liberté de vous faire part de notre mécontentement afin que dans l'occasion vous ayez la bonté d'y avoir égard. – Je termine en vous demandant deux services: le premier, de vouloir bien, quand vous arriverez à quelques résultats intéressants, m'en faire part comme vous avez eu l'extrême bonté de le faire cette fois; le second, de m'expédier le plus vite que vous pouvez votre mémoire afin que nous puissions le traduire immédiatement & avoir le mérite de le faire connaitre les premiers sur le Continent.

Je vous en prie n'oubliez pas de me rendre ce service. – Il me reste à vous prier de présenter mes compliments respectueux à Mad^e Faraday & de me croire votre tout dévoué & tendrement affectionné

A. DE LA RIVE

[1] See Letter 318.
[2] See J. B. Biot, 'Comparaison du sucre et de la gomme arabique dans leur action sur la lumière polarisée ,' *NBSP* (1816), 125.
[3] *CR*, 20 (1845), 1287.
[4] Alexandre Claude Martin Le Baillif (1764–1831), physician.
[5] See Letter 307.

327   J. P. GASSIOT[1] to M. FARADAY, 26 December 1845

[*I.E.E., previously unpublished*]

Clapham Common
26 Decr 1845

MY DEAR FARADAY

I cannot allow yr. note of the 24' In.[2] to remain ever without an early reply. if I have not as yet been among those of yr. friends who have hastened to congratulate you on your recent discoveries – I can nevertheless assure you that I have not been the less an admirer of the same, besides there are some circumstances that may probably have escaped yr. recollection but which have tended to impress them rather more strongly on mine.

Do you recollect my shewing you some apparatus which I had had made for examining Electrolytes under polarized light? – you said to me *go on* – *try it in every shape* – PLACE THE ELECTROLYTE WITHIN A COIL – I did so but not succeeding, I continued my Experiments in another Manner – and subsequently handed all my apparatus over to Grove – who afterwards conducted his Exps at the London Institution – he tells me that I did not name yr suggestion of the Coils but that during the progress of his Exps the same also occurred to him and that like myself he did not use sufficiently powerful apparatus.

When I first heard of yr discovery all the foregoing came to my recollection and I know few things that have given me greater delight than when I found it had fallen in yr hands – had I followed out *your* suggestion as *I ought to have done*, I must have succeeded and there the discovery might have ended – in your hands it is only a commencement – Remember me most kindly to Mrs Faraday, tell her to take care of you, and not to allow you to work *too hard*, as I have told you before you are public property and I as one of that *select* body claim a right to make such a suggestion. – Whenever you feel inclined to pay me a visit do so and I hope you will bring Mrs Faraday with you. I need not say how glad Mrs Gassiot will be to see her – as for any apparatus I have you know it is *all* at your service I shall therefore say no more on that subject – and now for a favor for myself – a literary friend of mine is most anxious to obtain the addition of yr. autograph to a collection he has been making for the last 3 or 4 years and which now contains some of the most eminent for Science & Literature in Europe – they are all written within the red lines of similar papers as I now enclose for insertion in a Book properly prepared – Some have sent him various lines or extracts from their own or other publications and others their family motto. it is I assure you a most beautiful collection

Believe Me My Dear Sir
Most sincerely yrs
JOHN GASSIOT

¹ John Peter Gassiot (1797–1877), best known for his work on cathode rays.
² I have been unable to find this note.

328 M. FARADAY to A. DE LA RIVE, 31 December 1845

[*Bibliothèque publique et universitaire de Genève, ms. 2316, f. 62, previously unpublished*]

R Institution
31 Decr 1845

MY DEAR DE LA RIVE

I recvd your very kind letter yesterday & hasten as you desire to acknowledge it by a few words. It was most acceptable for it gave me the reference I wanted.¹ I remembered some theory of the bismuth repulsion & have referred to the fact in my paper but could not tell whose it was or where published now thanks to you I can do both. I never cease to regret my continually failing memory – Your experiments I have read with the greatest interest & the many others that are daily coming to view respecting magnetic action I am in hopes that by all these joint labours something good will be done for this part of science

I am indebted to you for your remarks on my paper on light & magnetism. but all these views were necessarily early on my mind & I did not lose sight of them in making my final judgment on my experiments – Many here say the same things and it may be with reason Who can as yet say? I cannot but I am persuaded as yet that my view *is right* or else for my own credit's sake I would change it. Whether when the paper appears it may make any alteration I cannot say. – I must not go into detail. I do not recollect the Athenaeums report. the best I have seen is in the *Times* of the 29th November. I think it refers to the difference between the rotation of a polarized ray by quartz sugar – oil turpentine [*sic*] & the 50 other substances that may be used – and *that rotation* which I have induced by Magnetism & Electricity – The two are in direction *essentially* distinct.

As to the Phil Mag. the only reason I can give for what you speak of is that though the names of Philosophers are on the title page. they can take but very little interest in the work. I should almost be led to suppose that Brewster & Phillips do not see the numbers till they are published – but do not say so for I really know nothing except in England we have very few channels. I may say no effective channel to the riches of Philosophy which arise with you or else-where. I regret it deeply but am as a hermit here & do nothing but work. Loss of memory prevents me from interfering in these things. Wishing you & Madame De la Rive every happiness for the new year & for all successive years on this earth I am my dear friend

Very gratefully Yours
M. FARADAY

1 See Letter 326.

329   M. FARADAY to J. B. DUMAS, 9 January 1846
[Arch. de l'Académie des Sciences, Paris, Dossier Faraday, previously unpublished]

Royal Institution,
9 January 1846

MY VERY DEAR FRIEND,

The kindness of your letter has deeply affected me and I should have written the same day but that I was in the midst of a short series of lectures at this place which I could not neglect For all your kind wishes I earnestly thank you and I really do believe that I have strived the more to deserve your good thoughts since I knew that I had them so that you may perhaps even be helping science a little in thinking favourably of me. I am not always sure that what I think good, (being the result of my exertions) is good, but this I am sure of; that your praise makes me strive the more: – and this is not so much that I care for praise on its own account as that I care for the praise which comes from you.

I am a little taken by surprise & startled by your expression of a wish so honorable to me as that I would send some account of my late experiments to the Academy. Our Royal Society which is rather antique in some of its customs, and whose policy I do not on the whole approve of, have a great jealousy of its Fellows sending communications any where but to their meetings, or if sent to the meeting, sending them any where else before they are published in the Transactions. I received a few hints about the notes I sent you respecting condensed gases.[1] Otherwise I should have sent you before this some brief notice of my recent experiments. When I received your last letter therefore I resolved to ascertain from one of the Secretaries the feeling of the Council (having long since ceased to take part personally in the management of the affairs) and the evening before last I saw Dr. Roget. He told me it was against all rules and quoted to me a case in which Fox Talbot[2] having sent a paper to the Royal Society afterwards sent a communication to the Academy which appearing in the *Comptes Rendus* caused that his paper was not printed in the Transactions. This may be all right as it is the old custom but it hardly consists with slow publication. and it prevents me from doing that which would be a great delight to me and what is more if accepted by the Academy would be a great honor Besides which it seems that a number of accounts hastily gathered up by the ear go abroad and any error they may contain remains uncorrected until the Memoire itself appears.

Still I must tell you a little. If the lines of magnetic force generated either by a powerful electro-magnet or a helix be sent through a transparent body parallel to a polarized ray of light passing through it at the same time the polarized ray *is rotated*. The effect takes place with all tranquil liquid bodies and with all transparent solid bodies not possessed of double refracting powers – occurring in different degrees with different substances. In this effect I see a magnetic action on the ray of light but many of my friends here (who however have had no opportunity of considering *all* the facts in the paper) think the effect by no means proves so much: so that you see though I hold my opinion as yet I may be wrong. The ray is rotated to the *right hand* if the magnetic force be in one direction or if the current in the helix go round it in one direction and to the *left hand* if the direction of the magnetic or electric force be reversed. The direction of the rotation is essentially dependant upon the direction of the magnetic or electric force and hence a difference between *this rotation* & any possessed by quartz, sugar, oil of turpentine, etc. of the following extraordinary kind. Place side by side a portion of water in a helix and a tube containing oil of turpentine: – if the oil have right handed rotation send an electric current through the helix clock or right hand fashion and the water in the tube will also have right handed rotation and both will in this respect agree. Now leaving the tubes helices & current entirely alone let the polarized ray be sent in the contrary direction through the tubes & let the observer go to the other end of them to observe etc. He will still find the oil of turpentine rotates the ray to *his right* hand – but NOT SO THE WATER. it will rotate the ray to *his left hand* the rotation being absolutely tied to the direction of the electric current going round it & which seen from this end passes left hand fashion or if instead of water, oil of turpentine be in the helix, & the current of electricity of such force as [just to double – crossed out] to produce a rotation of the ray equal to that which the oil possesses: then, examined by a ray passing in one direction, its rotating power seems doubled; whereas if examined by a ray passing in the other direction, its rotating power is annihilated. This is the chief result on which I rest my opinion against that of my friends (or rather some of them.)

Passing from this subject to the Magnetic condition of matter, I find that all matter in the solid or liquid (& perhaps in the gaseous) state is affected by the magnet but not all as Iron; Matter magnetic as Iron is attracted by the magnet

& an elongated portion points in the direction of the lines of magnetic force; but matter not magnetic, as Iron is *repelled* by the magnet and an elongated portion of it points *across* the lines of magnetic force. Water, Alcohol, Ether, oil, wood, flesh, blood & a thousand other things, have this magnetic rotation but perhaps the best are heavy glass, phosphorous, Antimony & bismuth. Perhaps you may remember that, (I think nearly 30 years ago) M. Le Baillif of Paris shewed the repulsion of a magnet by Antimony and bismuth. I recollected the fact generally & inserted it in my paper Dr. [*sic*] la Rive has more lately referred me to the account of it in the Bibliotheque Universelle. – Having called matter not magnetic as iron, *diamagnetic* I have kept this name to express this new magnetic condition, and so to sum up, I may say that, every solid or liquid substance possesses, & is subject to magnetic power, being either magnetic or diamagnetic in its nature

Out of this property & its investigation, grows a multitude of curious conditions for which I must refer you to the papers which I will send you as soon as I can. Amongst others I have ascertained this point. All the ordinary compounds of magnetic metals are also magnetic – thus, not only are the peroxides of Iron magnetic, as Becquerel & others have shewn but all the salts of Iron are magnetic & all the solutions of the salts if sufficiently strong to counteract the diamagnetic force of the water or alcohol used as a solvent. In this way I have been able to ascertain that Cerium is a magnetic metal for its salts are So also are the salts of Chromium & Manganese. – But I must stop & refer you to the two papers you will presently receive as soon as our R. S. prints them. In the mean time I am at *work*.

My dear Wife thanks you most heartily & begs to be remembered to Madame Dumas in which pray join me. In reference to your observation that she ought to be happy, she thinks, Madame Dumas will be conscious of a happiness which *they* enjoy far beyond any thing that fame can give and it is my firm persuasion that both you & I are sharers in that happiness & the knowledge of it. Still the other is also pleasant perhaps more so than it ought to be.

My brother in law[3] who was here half an hour ago begged me to thank you for your remembrance of him, with his sincere respects and hopes that before the year was out he should see you in England. Speak of me to M Arago & say how gratefully I am his on every recurrence of his *idea* to my mind.

Ever dear Dumas, Yours Affectionately
M. FARADAY

[1] See Letter 294.
[2] William Henry Fox Talbot (1800–77), one of the early workers in photography.
[3] George Barnard.

[*R.S., previously unpublished*]

Royal Institution,
15 Jany. 1846

MY DEAR SIR JOHN

I have at last procured a rod of glass about 2 inches long fit in some degree for the experiment[1] the first two or three pieces when cut were far too irregularly [*sic*] I have also had a rock crystal cut & shaped but it turns out to consist of two or three Macles & to be of no use.

Using the glass a polarized ray was sent along it & examined by a Nicols eye piece the position of the latter being such as to give darkness Then a very little torsion force made this rod act on the ray the luminous image becoming equally visible in any part of it as far as I could judge & increasing much in brightness with the torsion. But there were no signs of rotation of the ray for when the Nicols eye piece was turned the brightness of the image increased & that whether the eye piece was turned in one direction or the other.

I found Mr Hunt[2] at work the other day with crystallizations & magnets & told him generally that you wished an experiment to be made on crystallization but did not describe what. I led him to think that if he offered his services they might be acceptable to you but did not think myself justified in telling him the experiment Probably he has written to you.

I quite grieve to hear of your illness by your letter I heard some others also speaking of it today. Let us hope that it is temporary & that you know how to deal with it and that you really are dealing with it properly & not working hard if rest is required I trust that Lady Herschell [*sic*] is a Tyrant on all those fitting occasions when a wifes best affection is shewn by severity – I owe much to my partner in these respects

As to my paper in your hands I have worked upon both the thoughts contained in it as far as I can at present & must now lay them fallow to resume them when I have sun.[3] So now if it will amuse you open read & burn the paper if you prefer it rather send it back to me.

Ever My dear Sir John
Yours Most Truly
M. FARADAY

[1] See Letter 323.
[2] Robert Hunt (1807–87), chemist and early worker in photography.   [3] See Letter 325.

[*I.E.E., previously unpublished*]

20 Conduit St
Jany 17th 1846

DEAR FARADAY

The repulsion of Bismuth by the magnet was first observed by Brugmans,[1] a Dutch philosopher whose work was published in Latin in 1778. Le Baillif's experiments were announced in the 7^{Th} vol of Férussac's Bulletin des Sciences

Mathematiques et Physiques[2] at page 371, and given in detail in the 8Th vol. page 87; he proved that a magnetic needle was repelled both by Bismuth and Antimony. Saigey's[3] experiments on the mutual repulsion of bodies, of which he considered the former cases to be individual instances, were announced in the 8Th vol of the same work p. 258, and given in full detail in the 9Th vol pp 89, 167 and 239. There is also a paper by Seebeck "on the magnetic polarization of different metals, alloys and oxides between the poles of magnetic bars" to which it may be worth while to refer.[4] It is worthy of remark that Becquerel's, Le Baillif's, Seebeck's and Saigey's experiments were all made about the same time. All together they have done very little towards anticipating the great general principle which [you] have just discovered and demonstrated.

In reference to the experiment I suggested yesterday of submitting to your repelling forces spheres of liquids suspended in another liquid of the same specific gravity, I may mention that when I first read Plateau's interesting memoir[5] it occurred to me that by employing his method a number of instructive electrical experiments might be made.

By floating spheres of a conducting in a non conducting liquid, and charging the former with either electricity, they would be attracted and repelled by excited electrics, and the alterations in their equilibrium shown by their changes of form. The spheres might also be similarly or dissimilarly charged and their mutual actions observed. But what, perhaps, would be a more interesting experiment would be to examine the effects which one of these conducting spheres would exhibit when forming part of a voltaic circuit; to avoid the production of hydrogen gas the negative wire should be coated with per-oxide of lead; the sphere would probably change its form immediately the current is completed, and it would be certainly be [sic] attracted or repelled by a magnet or another similar sphere forming part of the same or a different circuit; rotations would also by certain arrangements be produced. I noted down at the time these and other experiments I proposed, and have several times since thought of setting about them, but other occupations have always interfered, and I have also been somewhat deterred by the consideration that for such experiments to succeed a delicacy and dexterity of manipulation equal to your own would be required.

Yours very Truly

C. WHEATSTONE

[1] Anton Brugmans (1732–1789), *Magnetismus seu de affinitatibus magneticis observationes*, Franequerae, 1778.

[2] *Bulletin des sciences mathématiques, astronomiques physiques et chimiques*, founded by André Etienne Baron d'Audebard de Férussac (1786–1836).

[3] Jacques Frédéric Saigey (1797–1871), scientific instrument maker at Paris.

[4] T. J. Seebeck, 'Ueber die magnetische Polarisation verschiedener Mettale, Alliagen und Oxyde zwischen den Polen starker Magnetstabe,' *AKAWB* (1827), 147.

[5] J. Plateau, 'Sur les phénomènes que présente une masse liquide libre et soustraite à l'action de la pesanteur,' *MASB* (1843).

332   W. WHEWELL to M. FARADAY, 19 January 1846

[*Trinity College Library, Trinity College, Cambridge, previously unpublished*]

Trin. Coll.,
Jan. 19, 1846

MY DEAR SIR,

Prof. Willis[1] gave me an account of your experiment on light shown to the Council of the R. S. which I was sorry I was not there to see. His account leads me to offer a suggestion which most likely you have anticipated, but it did not appear from what he said. I understood him that when you have deviated the plane of polarization by making contact, you prove and measure the change by turning the analyzer till you get the black spot. Now if before the light comes to the analyzer you interpose a double refracting crystal (uniaxal or biaxal) cut so as to give you the rings and cross, or the lemniscate, you will see the cross or the lemniscate *move* out of one position into another on making contact which I should think must be a more striking way of exhibiting the result. It is not likely that this has escaped you.

Willis told me also of your other experiments on magnetism of which I long to see a fuller account.

Believe me My dear sir,

Yours very truly,
W. WHEWELL.

[1] Robert Willis (1800–75), Jacksonian Professor of Applied Mechanics at Cambridge. See Letter 160, fn. 1.

333   M. FARADAY to W. WHEWELL, 20 January 1846

[*Trinity College Library, Trinity College, Cambridge, previously unpublished*]

R. Institution,
20 Jan.ʸ 1846

MY DEAR SIR,

I am greatly obliged by your letter I had not made the experiment however I expected not a *mere move on* but an alteration in the tints I have now set Mr. Durkin[1] about the preparation for it. I understand the papers will not be published until JUNE (end)! As Willis is on the council put a word in for quicker publication.

Ever Your Very Oblgd Svt,
M. FARADAY

[1] I have been unable to identify Mr. Durkin. He would appear to be one of the laboratory aides at the Royal Institution.

[*I.E.E., previously unpublished*]

Collingwood
Jan 22/46.

MY DEAR SIR

A great many thanks to you for all the trouble you have taken. You are used to be better employed than in *proving negatives*. Mr Hunt wrote to me and I told him what I had been thinking of [1] –

You did not surely think me so incurious or rather so deficient in interest respecting the astonishing series of discoveries into which you are now entered fairly – that having your express permission to open and read the paper you sent me sealed, I should not avail myself of it.[2] Accordingly I have done so but I thought it best to reinclose it to you rather than consign it to the flames which I would not do to a bit of your hand writing – Should the first of your views expressed in it be really verified a new field of speculation on the nature of light will be opened as I do not understand what the undulatory or indeed any theory can have to say to a fact of that nature

Go on and prosper – "from strength to strength" like a victor marching with assured step to further conquests – and be assured that no voice will join more heartily in the Paeans that already begin to rise and will speedily swell into a shout of triumph astounding even to yourself than that of

Yours most truly
J. F. W. HERSCHEL

PS. Of course I shall keep silence as to the contents of the paper till you shall yourself break it.

Thanks for your kind expressions about my health. – I have taken the best Medical advice & I hope soon to be set to write again. Already there is an improvement

[1] See Letter 330.
[2] See Letter 324.

335 M. FARADAY to A. DE LA RIVE, 31 January 1846

[*Bibliothèque publique et universitaire de Genève, ms. 2316, f. 63–4, previously unpublished*]

Royal Institution
31 Jany 1846

MY DEAR & KIND FRIEND

I received your letter yesterday and wonder how in the midst of all your avocations and the multitude of your own beautiful and successful labours in the fields of science, bringing forth fresh harvests as you do from day to day you can have so much thought for me I know that your kindness towards me is very great: but I wonder at your physical ability for so much thought directed as it is to such exalted objects and that you can continue it simultaneously with thoughts for every body else. It reminds me of my own imperfection arising I hope not willingly but from want of memory – but for that your kindness is a great compensation

I was not aware that Dumas[1] had caused any part of my letter to him to appear in the Comptes Rendus In fact in that very letter I had to tell him that the Royal Society were very jealous of the appearance of a paper or the matter of a paper elsewhere than in the Transactions and that has been my difficulty in sending *you* any account. for the papers themselves were all sent in last year. I have applied to the Secretary and found the rule to be very strict so strict that a paper by Fox Talbot was kept out of the Transactions because he had sent the matter of it to the Academie des Sciences where it appeared in the Comptes Rendus. – I hope they will now publish quicker – at all events though I must not send you the proof sheets, as soon as ever I can have leave to send you the papers I will not lose a moment in doing so. In the mean time as a part of my letter to Dumas has appeared. (I have not seen it). I will write you a sort of account of my papers here with which you may do as you please

The papers recently sent to the Royal Society form the xix. xx and xxi Series of the Experimental Researches. The xixth has for its title *on the Magnetization of light and the illumination of magnetic lines of force.* and is divided into three parts. The first part is on the *action of magnets on light* and in it I shew by experiments that when any transparent liquid or solid body (not having the power of double refraction) is placed between the poles of a powerful electromagnet and a polarized ray of light is transmitted through it in a direction *parallel* to the lines of magnetic force then withdrawing the magnetic force the transparent substance has no particular extra action on the light but on establishing the magnetic force the ray passing through the substance is rotated in a direction entirely dependant upon that of the magnetic force. and to a degree proportionate to the power of the magnet and the nature and extent of the substance The law of rotation is that if a magnetic line of force be *going from* a north pole or *coming from* a south pole along the path of a polarized ray coming to the observer it will rotate that ray to the right hand or that if such a line of force be coming from a north pole or going from a south pole it will rotate such a ray to the left hand. The rotation continues as long as the magnetic force continues and ceases with it. Fluids possessing the power of rotating the ray can have this magnetic rotation impressed on light in them but then the rotation is in extraordinary contrast with their own rotation being added to it in one direction but at the same moment taken from it in the other. Silicated borate of lead or borate of lead are the substances which most readily shew this exertion of power. – Part 2 of the paper shews by experiment the action of electric currents in helices producing the same phenomenon. The law of action is really the same but its expression becomes more simple for it so happens from our conventional expression of the direction of an electric current; that when a transparent substance is put either into a powerful or a long helix and the electric current sent round it the rotation of the ray is in the same direction as the course of the current: for the current which goes round the helix clock fashion makes the ray rotate clock fashion &c – Part 3 of the paper consists of *general considerations* and contains amongst other points my reasons for believing that the action is a true magnetic action on light.

The xxth and xxist series of Researches are entitled *On new magnetic actions and on the magnetic condition of all matter*. These are divided into Seven parts – Part 1 contains a brief description of the powerful Electro-magnets used and defines the meaning of a few terms amongst others *axial* and *equatorial* direction. *Axial* means that when an elongated body is placed between the contrary poles of a magnet its longest dimension points in the line joining the two poles: *equatorial position* means that the longest dimension of a body placed between the two poles is perpendicular to the line joining the two poles. Part 2 is devoted to *the action of magnets on the heavy glass* in which the effect on light was first observed. It is shewn that a prism of this heavy glass points equatorially and further that this position is due to a simple relation of the magnet & the glass dependant on their power of repelling each other. Either pole of an active magnet will permanently repel a piece of heavy glass: the repulsion is proportionate to the vicinity of the acting bodies and to the intensity of magnetic power. The intervention of metals glass or other substances usually considered not magnetic has no influence in altering the effect. – Part 3. is on *the action of Magnets on other substances not being metals* and here it is shewn that all bodies not being magnetic as Iron are magnetic as heavy glass. or as I have for reason given called it, are *diamagnetic* i.e a portion of any shape will be repelled by the magnet and an elongated portion will point equatorially between the poles. It is very curious to see a tube of water or a piece of meat or a slice of apple or a plane of wood in this way repelled & pointing equatorially between the poles. Phosphorous stands high in this respect. Sulphur & India rubber very well. Division of the mass does not make any difference provided the general form & mass of the substance be retained – Part 4 is on *the action of Magnets on metals generally* and in the first place I find reason to believe that Platinum Palladium & Titanium are truly magnetic metals & must stand in the list with Iron Nickel and Cobalt the two first platinum & palladium taking a very low place. After that I find that all the metals not magnetic in the manner of Iron, are magnetic as heavy glass or are *diamagnetic* for they all point equatorially & are repelled by either pole of the magnet. Bismuth possesses this property in a very high degree equalling and perhaps surpassing phosphorous & heavy glass. The repulsion of bismuth I now find was known to Brugmans as far back as the year 1778. Certain striking phenomena due to Magneto-dynamic induction and produced more especially by copper, silver, and the good conductors amongst the metals are then developed & explained which if left unaccounted for would interfere greatly with the diamagnetic results. – Part 5. takes up *the action of magnets on the magnetic metals and other compounds.* First I find that heat does not entirely destroy the magnetic power of Iron Nickel & Cobalt but that though they fall in force (which takes place not suddenly but by a gradation) they still remain magnetic. being always attracted by the magnet & pointing axially. Next I find that all the salts of Iron Nickel and Cobalt are magnetic and even *all their solutions* so here we obtain the power of preparing media which within a certain degree of strength are magnetic & adjustible in strength. are transparent. and above all are liquid so that the relations magnetic and diamagnetic of other bodies wholly immersed in them can be ascertained. In these solutions the power of the magnetic matter as the iron salt and the power of the water which is a diamagnetic are opposed to each other. so it is easy to prepare a solution which in air presents no appearance of being either magnetic or diamagnetic but is perfectly indifferent. Yet such a solution put (in a tube) into water points axially & is attracted shewing then its magnetic powers whereas if put into a solution a little more ferrugenous than itself it points equatorially & is repelled precisely like a diamagnetic substance. –The magnetism of all the compounds of Iron Nickel & Cobalt. led me to conclude that I could detect the magnetism of metals by the character of their salts. & by examination I find that compounds of Titanium, Manganese, Cerium & Chromium are abundantly magnetic and for these reasons in addition to others I believe them to be magnetic metals. – Part 6 is devoted to *the Action of Magnets in air and gases.* To appearance this action is nul i.e. there is no difference between one gas and another; nor between a gas in its most rare & its densest state. When a tube of air is immersed in mercury or in water oil. alcohol. &c. then it appears to be well magnetic i.e. it points axially & is attracted. When it is immersed in solutions of Iron Nickel Cobalt Manganese. Cerium. Chromium. &c &c of a certain strength then it appears as a diamagnetic pointing equatorially and being repelled. Its place in fact is between the magnetic & diamagnetic class. but whether it constitute a real zero point or have only a differential relation is not I think as yet absolutely decided. – Part 7 contains *general considerations* arising from all the former results and amongst other points their relation to terrestrial phenomena & conditions. & their probable bearing upon the great question of the magnetism of the earth.

Thus my dear friend I have sent you a summary of my experiments or rather of the papers up to the present time. I have not a moment to do more now. and hope you will accept it with all its imperfections as a thank offering for your friendship & kindness to me. Our united remembrances to Madame De la Rive and Yourself. I wish I could once more look at the summit of Mont Blanc in your company

Ever
Most faithfully Yours
M. FARADAY

¹ See Letter 329. Parts of it were published by Dumas in *CR*, 22 (1846), 113.

336   M. FARADAY to R. BROWN,¹ 3 March 1846
[British Museum, Add. mss. 32,441, f. 416, previously unpublished]

Royal Institution
3 March 1846

MY DEAR SIR

In answer to your enquiry respecting Mr. Grove I send you the following as the evidences of his philosophical character First the battery called by his name which though it has not perhaps been formally described is known to every worker in Electricity: it puts into the space of 3 or 4 cubic feet that which at the Royal Institution employed the whole of a large room and because of its power. compactness economy and facility of use is the battery I use to the exclusion of almost every other

Next the Gas Voltaic battery. a very remarkable discovery & application in reference to the principles of voltaic action and which even promises useful practical results

After these come researches on the inactivity of amalgamated Zinc – on Electro Nitrurets – and on the Voltaic action of nonconductors such as Phosphorus Sulphur. & Hydrocarbons with other smaller things

He has published papers in the Philosophical Transactions of 1840. 1843 and 1845. & is at present on the Council of the Royal Society. He has also published many notices in the Comptes Rendus & the Philosophical magazine

In reply to that part of your enquiry which referred to what I should myself do if responsible & as a mode of conveying my opinion in the present case. I may say that if I were on the Committee I should, because of the evidence I have just quoted, support his nomination. but I am anxious in saying this that you should not think I am intruding upon the judgment of the Committee

I am
My dear Sir
Yours Very Truly
M. FARADAY

¹ Robert Brown (1773–1858), botanist and discoverer of Brownian motion.

337 M. FARADAY to C. E. NEEFF,[1] 24 March 1846

[*Darmstaedter Collection, Westdeutsche Bibliothek, Marburg, previously unpublished*]

Royal Institution
London
24 March 1846

SIR

I have had the pleasure of receiving your letter and hope soon to have the further pleasure of reading the papers.[2] I am sorry to say that the German language is a sealed language to me & I have not as yet seen the Archives des Sciences Physiques. but look for it in a few days. – Still I saw (I conclude) a very good account of your experiments in a French paper I think it was the Constitutionelle and from that was glad to find that our researches were in different directions though tending to the same point. – I trust that experimental evidence will now rapidly accumulate in that direction

I have sent through our Royal Society a paper addressed to you which I hope you will do me the honor to accept I mean a copy of my three last series of researches and I hope it will reach you safely in a short time – The Royal Society has at last hastened its publication so that I am set at liberty much sooner than I had reason to expect.

I keep dreaming away with views of matter & its powers that I do not think it wise or philosophic to put forth because I hold them so that they may change with the evidence of experiment: but I use these views as stimulants & guides in some degree into the course of new enquiries and I have as yet had no reason to repent the course I have pursued

I am very much obliged for the Corrigenda I shall put them into your paper before I read it

Believe me to be with great respect

Sir
Your Very Obliged Servt
M. FARADAY

[1] Christian Ernst Neeff (1782–1849), physician and student of electricity.
[2] For Neeff's papers on electricity and magnetism, see *RSCSP*.

338 G. B. AIRY to M. FARADAY, 28 April 1846

[*I.E.E., previously unpublished*]

Royal Observatory
Greenwich
1846 April 28

MY DEAR SIR

There is one modification of the magneto-luminous experiment, which, so far as I find in your paper, has not been made, but which is theoretically important.

It is simply that the plane of original polarization has not been varied.

When I had the good fortune to see the experiments in your cellar[1] – first the light was polarized by a reflector whose plane was necessarily fixed – and then it was polarized by Nichol's prism which was not turned during the experiment.

Now would you do me the favour, when your two Nichol's prisms are mounted, to try with four positions of the plane of primary polarization, namely

and examine the amount and direction of the rotation produced by putting in action the magnetic current (no circumstance whatever being varied except the said plane of polarization) and in a single line acquaint me with the result. I am my dear Sir

Yours very truly
G. B. AIRY

My sister desires me to say that she has lost the pleasure of attending your last Saturday's lecture by absence in Suffolk, but she hopes to avail herself of your kindness now.

[1] Faraday held a 'private showing' of his experiments on the magnetization of light for a few friends at the end of March. The 'cellar' where they were held is the Davy–Faraday Laboratory of the Royal Institution.

339 M. FARADAY to G. B. AIRY, 29 April 1846
[*Royal Observatory, Herstmonceux, Corr. and calcs. on optics to 1848, Sect. 31, previously unpublished*]

Royal Institution,
29 April 1846

MY DEAR SIR

I will make the experiment you desire as soon as I can but it will be 7 or 8 days first. In the mean time I may tell you that early in my experiments I made the plane of polarization (using a reflecting surface glass) revolve about the line passing from the polarizer to the analyser & [?eye]. Thus consider first that the polarized ray passed in an invariably horizontal line in which was the heavy glass or other diamagnetic then the lamp was placed on the right & on the left & above & below & at intervals of 45° with these positions the polarizing reflector being turned in a corresponding degree round the horizontal line as axis. To here were 8 planes of polarization but in all the phenomena were precisely the same i.e if the action of the magnetic force was in any one case to cause a rotation [of] a certain number of degrees to the right hand, it had precisely the same effect in any of the other position. It so happened that partly for convenience with different apparatus & partly on purpose – I did when using magnets make them as it were revolve about this line of the polarized ray – placing the body of the horse shoe or other magnet used sometimes beneath sometimes above sometimes to the right & sometimes to the left but the effect always was the same.

All these cases may be considered as included in the case of a helix & Electric current without a magnet see paragraph 2195. because here no one plane of polarization can be considered as in any way different from another; all are exactly alike.

I do not know whether these facts answer your inquiries if they do not then I have probably not understood your question and may not make exactly the experiment you want – at all events I will make it as soon as I can unless you think it now unnecessary.

> Ever Dear Sir
> Your Most Truly
> M. FARADAY

340 A. DE LA RIVE to M. FARADAY, 1 May 1846
[*I.E.E., previously unpublished*]

Genève
le 1er Mai 1846

MON CHER MONSIEUR,

J'avais promis à mon jeune ami Mr. Alexandre Prevost[1] de lui donner une lettre d'introduction auprès de vous, mais je présume que son oncle Mr. J. L. Prevost vous l'aura déjà présenté. Toutefois je ne veux pas renoncer à cette occasion de vous écrire quelques mots & je tiens à vous dire, ce que vous savez probablement déjà, que Mr. Alexandre Prevost qui marche dignement sur les traces de son grand père Mr. le prof. Pierre Prevost,[2] est un des jeunes savants qui honorent le plus notre pays. Il mérite tout-à-fait de faire votre connaissance & d'être l'objet de votre bienveillante amitié que vous ne refusez jamais à ceux qui sont sincèrement voués à la Science. J'espère que Mr. Prevost aura l'occasion de voir quelques unes de vos belles expériences & qu'il pourra nous donner à cet égard quelques détails à son retour à Genève. –

Je viens de faire un séjour de trois semaines à Paris. On s'y entretenait beaucoup de vos belles recherches. MM. Dumas & Regnault avec qui je m'en suis particulièrement entretenu y mettent un grand intérêt. J'ai vu toutes les belles expériences de Mr. Regnault; c'est admirable de soin & d'exactitude; mais je ne puis trouver, comme je le lui ai dit, les résultats en rapport avec la grandeur des travaux. En fait de Science il n'y avait du reste rien de bien nouveau à Paris. Becquerel travaille toujours ainsi que son fils; ce sont avec Regnault les deux seuls qui me semblent s'occuper actuellement de Science d'une manière sérieuse.

J'ai appris hier par Mr. Grove l'honneur que la Société Royale vient de me faire.[3] J'en suis profondement reconnaissant & je tâcherai de m'en montrer digne. Mais il m'est impossible de ne pas voir dans cette nomination la grande influence d'un homme qui m'a toujours témoigné une bienveillance si vraie, si complète; je n'avais pas besoin de cette nouvelle marque de son amitié pour sentir augmenter chez moi les sentiments que je porte pour lui dans mon coeur; mais Mr. Faraday me permettra bien de lui dire que de même que son amitié le fils est une succession de celle qu'il portait au père, de même aussi le fils a hérité des sentiments d'estime & d'affection que le père avait pour lui.

Veuillez donc, mon cher Monsieur, me conserver cette précieuse affection & me croire votre bien affectueux & respectueux

AUG^E DE LA RIVE

J'ai reçu, il y a un mois, votre bon mémoire ou plutôt vos trois mémoires;[4] [je] les traduit dans ce moment pour les insérer dans la *Bibl. Univ.*

[1] Alexandre Pierre Prévost (1821–73) became a banker in London. He published only a few scientific papers concerning the psychology of vision.
[2] Pierre Prévost (1751–1839), Professor of Physics at the Geneva Academy and author of a large number of scientific papers on a wide range of subjects.
[3] A. de la Rive was named Foreign Member of the Royal Society in 1846.
[4] The 19th, 20th and 21st series of *ERE*.

341 M. FARADAY to G. B. AIRY, 4 May 1846

[*Royal Observatory, Herstmonceux, Corr. and calcs. on optics to 1848, Sect. 31, previously unpublished*]

R Institution
4 May 1846

MY DEAR SIR

I have just made the experiment with the Polarizing Nicoll eye piece in eight positions | / — \ | / — \ and find the effect the same in every position. – Again taking the polarizing & eye pieces in any given position

I then revolved the square prism of heavy glass on the ray passing thrgh it as axis but without the slightest trace of effect on the ray i.e the ray being affected by the magnet & glass suffered no *further* change of any kind by the rotation of the prism

Ever Truly Yours
M. FARADAY

342 M. FARADAY to MRS ROMILLY,[1] 13 June 1846
[*Wellcome Medical Historical Library, previously unpublished*]

R Institution
13 June 1846

MY DEAR MRS. ROMILLY

All the day long I have striving [*sic*] to reach your house & could not because of the lecture & friends who kept me after it, & my wife also has been prevented from calling for me by having to do part of my friend work here. – I wished to learn if Mrs. Marcet was still with you & (remembering a wish expressed by her on a former occasion) to say that on Tuesday next at 11 o clk I should be shewing the diamagnetic & other phenomena to a few friends *in the Lecture room*. There will not be more than 12 or 15 persons and if inclined & well enough to come My old friend would find herself quite at home

Ever Very Truly Yours
M. FARADAY

[1] See Letter 316.

343 W. WHEWELL to M. FARADAY, 7 August 1846
[*Trinity College Library, Trinity College, Cambridge, previously unpublished*]

Cliff Cottage,
Lowestoft,
Aug. 7, 1846

MY DEAR SIR,

I am looking forward with great interest, as I suppose all persons who care for science are, to the continuation of your magnetical researches and speculations; and especially to those which refer to light. The establishment of a connection between magnetical and optical polarity appears to me a capital point, and the laws of this connection must have a wide bearing on our philosophy. I do not know if you have made any further examination of the *amount* of the deviation of the plane of polarization in your experiments (2152) and especially of its amount for different colours. I believe one difficulty in the way of measuring this amount is the feebleness of the action which rotates the plane of polarization. It occurs to me that perhaps you may find some good suggestions as to the mode of making such experimental measures in Biot's researches on a similar subject, the circular polarization of fluids. When he analyzed the emergent ray by a double refracting prism he obtained the two images, neither of which vanished at any angle in consequence of the different amount of rotation of the plane for different colours. But he observed the extraordinary image when it became *darkest*, and noted the series of colours before and after this point, which are blue, *very dark* purple, red; and thus was able to measure the amount of rotation in different cases. His account of these experiments is in the Memoires of the Institut, Math et Phys. Tom xiii. p. 49 (1835). The relative rotation of different colours & other modes of experimenting must be used. You will see that Airy considers the determination of this point as very important.[1] I found after I had sent you some previous suggestions that they were of no value in consequence of the nature of your apparatus and the feebleness of the rotating power.

I am preparing for the press a new edition of my History and Philosophy. If you have observed any mistakes in the former edition, I should be much obliged to your telling me of them.

I am always, my dear Sir,

Yours most truly
W. WHEWELL

[1] See Letter 338.

344   M. FARADAY to W. WHEWELL, 10 August 1846
[*Trinity College Library, Trinity College, Cambridge, previously unpublished*]

Tunbridge Wells,
10 Aug 1846

MY DEAR SIR,

I received your letter here this morning where I am resting a very stupid and giddy head. The head so continually gets out of order that I ~~continually~~ often make up my mind that I shall never do any thing more. I have not much to say to you further about light & magnetism & yet it so happens that what I have to say will meet in some degree part of your letter. My course of study, apparatus, and means do not enable me to supply the careful measures which as you say are so much to be desired but I have fallen upon a method of facilitating their estimation and of very greatly increasing the rotation. The peculiar character of the rotation & its dependance upon the lines of magnetic force led me to conclude that by silvering the polished ends of the diamagnetic employed I should be able to reflect the polarized ray to & fro several times within its substance & so accumulate rotation upon it, for as the rotation is the *same way* as respects the line of magnetic force whichever way the ray was moving in the media so the amount of rotation due to one transit across the glass would be doubled by

496

a second transit and tenfold for ten transits. This proved to be the fact & you will understand the how by allowing the diagram to represent a parallellopiped [*sic*] of glass and the two surfaces *a* & *b* the silvered ends. A ray polarized by a

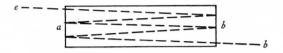

Nicholl eye piece passing from *b* may go diagonally across the glass and out at *e* – or by moving the glass a little it may be made to make two or four (as in the figure) or more reflexions within & then go out to *e*, and this gives rise to a series of images of the luminous object, the first of which is seen directly & the rest after reflexions. I have even traced these images up to the tenth which corresponds to nineteen transits of the ray across the diamagnetic. Placing this piece of glass over the magnet and arranging the apparatus so as to observe the rotation for the images in succession, I obtained for the first or direct image a rotation of 12°, for the second image a rotation of 36° & for the third image a rotation of 60°. Each of these images is of course much weaker than the last but it is easy with a strong light to observe the 4th 5th 6th & 7th which give very high results in numbers – I am just now writing a paper on this matter for the next Phil. Mag. and would rather you should not speak of it except confidentially until that appears.

I am very glad to hear you are preparing a new edition of your great work. I do not remember a single thing that I could point out to you I anticipate great pleasure and instruction from it.

Ever My dear Sir
Most Truly Yours,
M. FARADAY

345 M. FARADAY to J. B. DUMAS, 14 September 1846
[*Arch. de l'Académie des Sciences, Paris, Dossier Faraday, previously unpublished*]

Royal Institution
14 Septr 1846

MY DEAR DUMAS

Whether you will be at Southampton or not during the meeting of the British Association I do not know. if you should I shall be very sorry to have missed you but I was constrained by circumstances at home to return to London and lose many pleasures that I looked forward to. I write now especially to introduce to you my friend the Rev. John Barlow M. A. who is also our honorary & hard working secretary at the Royal Institution and to whom in a great measure our present healthy & prosperous state depends for his exertions in our cause. I am sure you will esteem him. Mrs. Faraday joins me in kindest remembrances to Madame Dumas & constant recollections of her kindness.

> Ever my dear friend
> Your faithful Servt
> M FARADAY

346 W. WHEWELL to M. FARADAY, 4 October 1846
[Trinity College Library, Trinity College, Cambridge, previously unpublished]

> Trin. Lodge.
> Cambridge
> Oct. 4 1846

MY DEAR SIR

I have been reading your paper (P.T. 1845 P. 1) on the liquefaction and solidification of gases; and now see better than I did the importance of what you call "the Cagniard de la Tour state" and the convenience of designating it by a name.[1] Why should you not call it the *Tourian* state? You have so prepared the way for this term by your periphrases that it will scarcely be felt as an innovation.

You say in this paper that C. de la Tour has shown that a liquid under certain circumstances becomes clear gas having *the same* bulk as the liquid. In the account of his expt (in 1823)[2] which I have by me, I find that the gas was 2, 3 or 4 times the liquid. I should be glad if you would give me the reference to the expts you speak of.

I should like much to hear what you think of Dumas's *types*[3] as genera of substances, but must not attempt to involve you in so wide a discussion. Believe me, my dear Sir,

> Yours very truly
> W. WHEWELL

[1] See Letter 288.
[2] C. Cagniard de la Tour, 'Expériences faites à une haute pression avec quelques substances,' *AC*, 2 s., 23 (1823), 267.
[3] See J. B. Dumas, 'Premier mémoire sur les types chimiques,' *AC*, 2 s., 73 (1840), 73. This memoir was followed by a number of others, for which see *RSCSP*.

347 M. FARADAY to W. WHEWELL, 5 October 1846
[Trinity College Library, Trinity College, Cambridge, previously unpublished]

> Royal Institution
> 5 Oct.ʳ 1846

MY DEAR SIR

Many thanks for the name – I think it is *good*.

Now as for the condition of the liquid when the state is assumed. Take (as I have done after Cagniard de la Tours instructions) a strong cylindrical glass tube put into it some ether & then seal it up hermetically so that the liquid ether shall at common temperatures occupy rather less than one half the space. Then gradually heat it. Part of the ether will rise in vapour forming compressed ether steam & the other which remains fluid will expand – As the heat increases the fluid part will enlarge – partly because it expands by the heat & partly because the air or vapour space by such expansion of the liquid becomes less & less and consequently the vapour occupying the space gradually filled by liquid is condensed. If the proportion of liquid to space is well adjusted, the effect will be that in a tube 3 inches long the liquid will increase in volume until not more than 1/8 of an inch of space (containing vapour) remains above it & you may in fact consider the tube full of liquid (*at that temperature*). Now provided the state occurs at that temperature which may be called the Tourian point then the least addition of heat converts all this liquid into vapour & the tube is full of vapour. Since I wrote to you I have looked more carefully at this point of change & it is not the fact that the liquid & vapourous state pass insensibly into one another. The vapour does not occupy more bulk than the liquid or the liquid less than the vapour – and cooling the tube a little brings on the liquid state & heating it again the vapour state – *but* at the moment of change there is an alteration both ways of this kind. Consider the tube as almost filled with liquid & just below the point of change. There is then a faint line of demarcation between the liquid & the vapour space above & both spaces are *clear*. Apply a little heat of a sudden the whole space within becomes obscured for a moment as if by a thick mist This quickly clears & the whole space is full of vapour in which rapid currents are seen (formed by the constant heat of the lamp applied) but no line of demarcation. Cool this & then again the thick mist state comes on which clears away & then there is the line of demarcation liquid and vapour lying in the tube together.

It seems to me that at the moment of the change & mistiness the cohesive attraction of the fluid *comes on* & *goes off* suddenly, which cohesion both Donny & Henry have shewn to be so considerable. Donny's recent & remarkable experiments including the explosion of water I have no doubt you know.[1]

As to types, etc. I really can say nothing The theory of chemistry seems to me to be in a very backward state in comparison with that of many other branches of science.

Ever Truly Yours,
M. FARADAY

[1] François Marie Louis Donny (1822–96), Préparateur of the course in chemistry at the University of Ghent. See his 'On the Cohesion of Liquids and their Adhesion to Solid Bodies,' *PM*, 3 s., 28 (1846), 293.

32-2

[*I.E.E., previously unpublished*]

Obsy. Kensington,
Wedy Night Dec 2.46

MY DEAR FARADAY/

I am very much grieved to find from your kind Letter which I received last night, that you are again teased with a misbehaving knee. I was in hopes that Brodie[1] had effectually secured you against any recurrence of such a Calamity – most sincerely do I hope that the means he is now pursuing may soon produce a radical cure of the diseased part so that you may soon resume your accustomd [*sic*] activity & exercise, the latter of which I believe is very essential to your general health –

As I cannot do it orally I must content myself in making my pen in my *left* hand congratulate you on having two fresh public proofs of the great importance of your recent discoveries – God grant, *great as they are*, that you may still add to their number & honor – you, in the annals of the Royal Society, stand, the solitary instance of 2 of its medals being on the same day presented to the same individual[2] May the almighty Giver of those talents which have enabled you to earn these honors, grant you health and happiness, long to wear them!

Now let me thank you very much for your solicitude about myself – thank God my health is & has been for some time very good – about 6 or 7 weeks ago (as I think you know) I had an attack of pneumonia (illeg.) in consequence of exposure to wet in determining the site for my intended observatory, near the Watford Tunnel, in which I propose making my experiments on the propagation of railway tremors as affecting astronomical observations made from the surface of Mercury – that attack however soon gave way to local bleeding &c – and I had again indulged in my favorite amusement of shooting – and being so occupied on this day fortnight a thorn passed through the nail of the forefinger of my right hand leaving [reading doubtful] in the nail a circular hole (as if it had been punched out) of about a tenth of an inch diameter – it then entered the finger & lay [reading doubtful] pa[*sic*]allel with the finger nail but about the 8th of an inch below it – The pain was instantly most intense – With a Lancet I cut down upon the thorn. and grasping it with a pair of Forceps removed it. it was about 1/2 an inch long about the 1/16th of an inch or a little more at its largest extremity and was a well defined point at the other – Five minutes certainly did not elapse between the thorn's entrance and its removal – yet in this time the first joint of the finger became half as large again as before the Accident – this latter happened about 1 o'Clock P. M. and I continued shooting till dark without inconvenience got 18 shots Killed 14 Cock pheasants, one hen pheasant – and 2 partridges – missing only 1 shot –

On my return home to dinner the point of the finger became somewhat painful on which I poulticed it as I have since done to the present time – the inflammation gradually increased but did not prevent me going down to Watford Tunnel on Friday last –

On Saturday I put my finger under the Care of Mr. South[3] who immediately cut down upon the offending part but without giving me the relief he had anticipated. In the afternoon I went down to Ramsgate to see a sick friend & returned to town on Monday to see Mr South – other cuttings were necessary – these made towards having the pain become less – and altho I got but a bad night it gave me more sleep than I had had for six previous days & nights –

The finger is certainly somewhat less painful than it has been but I fear will not make much more progress without further cut of the knife – It is somewhat curious that yesterday week in the morning for some minutes my jaws were not separable – on Thursday the same but not for so long a period – on Saturday the return was but just sensible [reading doubtful] and this afternoon it remained about a minute – & in all instances without my thinking of it in the least – When I can I will call on you – Kindest regards to Mrs. F——

Yours affectionately
J. SOUTH

[1] Sir Benjamin Collins Brodie, 1st Bart. (1783–1862), physician.
[2] Faraday received both the Royal and the Rumford Medals for 1846.
[3] I am unable to identify this Mr. South. A relative, perhaps?

349 M. FARADAY to G. B. AIRY, 20 May 1847[1]

[*Royal Observatory, Hertsmonceux, Standards vol. 5, Gen. Corr. A–H to 1848 June, Sect. 38, previously unpublished*]

Royal Institution
20 May 1847

MY DEAR AIRY

I wish I could give you an opinion worth the postage of your letter but indeed I have not one of such value in this case. I do not see any reason why a pure metal should be particularly free from internal change of its particles and on the whole should rather incline to the hard alloy than to soft copper & yet I hardly know why I suppose the labour would be too great to lay down the standard in different metals & substances and yet the comparison of them might be very important hereafter for 20 years seems to *do* or *tell* a great deal in relation to standard measures.

I am My dear Sir
Very Truly Yours
M. FARADAY

[1] I have been unable to locate the letter from Airy to Faraday to which this is a reply.

[*I.E.E., previously unpublished*]

Bridgewater Foundry,
Patricroft,
near Manchester,
May 21st. 1847.

MY DEAR SIR

It was with the greatest pleasure I received your valued note by the hands of M. Le Chevalier Cavalli[1] and was most happy in endeavoring to pay him all the attention in my power and furnishing him with such information as he was more particularly in quest of in reference to the main object of his visit – I found him to be a very inteligent [*sic*] man and altho I am but an indifferent linguist what with such scraps of French and Italian and the occasional use of the Chalk and pencil and above all with the help of that sort of free masonry which is natural to all lovers of usefull knowledge – we contrived to get on very well and I trust he was so far satisfied he is about to order some of our handy [reading doubtful] tools and a small Steam Hammer the power and capabilities of which I had much pleasure in exhibiting to him I need not say how much gratified I shall always feel in having a like opportunity to show any little attention in my power to any of your friends or correspondents when visiting these quarters

I am happy to report to you most satisfactory progress with my Steam Hammer and Steam pile driver both of which are now established machines and now in extensive employment in all quarters of the Globe. We are now in hand with Nº 205 Steam Hammer and Nº 18 pile driver so you see I have not let these happy thoughts rest as mere thoughts but sent them forth in material form to do mankind some good service

Our patent agents in the united states are making the St Hammers by the doz^n and being honest fellows send us over with great regularity the proceeds or rather our stipulated portion –

The pile driver has been at work some time on a glorious undertaking namely Damming up the Nile! So as to render all lower Egypt quite independent of the amount rise of the river and furnish the means of Irrigating the whole of that most (when watered) fertile land in the world. if this great work suceed they may then have a nice little innundation every afternoon! and with the bright sun of that glorious old land provide as much corn as feed all the poor of the world and some of the rich into the bargain. It affords me the highest gratification to find my schemes coming to play important parts in such noble undertakings The gratification in this respect is beyond all price and experience –

another pile driver is at work on the piles for the great Railway Bridge at Newcastle upon Tyne having driven the bearing piles down to the rock through 38 feet of gravel and quick sand on which the great piers rest and also made the coffer dams to shut-out the water while the stone work is done. this job is now about over – while another machine is just set to work at Berwick on Tweed in the same way but for a much more extensive bridge Two are just

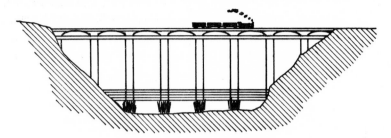

ready to sail for St Petersburgh to drive the foundation of a vast arsenal – and another now loading on the canal barge for Birkenhead Docks to shut out the mersey till its presence is again wanted I am ashamed of bothering your valuable attention with all these matters, but as you were among the first to see the value of the principle of this curious mode of employing momentum for this important purpose, I thought it might interest you to know that your good oppinion [*sic*] of it has been confirmed in actual practice in the most full manner – from 3 to 7 *minutes* according to the nature of the soil is the time required to drive a pile of 50 feet 35 feet into the ground! 24 to 30 *Hours* is about the average for the same performance by the old pile head & battering system. so much for employing momentum in its right *condition* for certain purposes My pile heads are actualy [*sic*] neater after being driven than before. such is the result of a Blow from a massive hammer (35 Cwt.) with 3 foot fall – 80 blows per minute and the whole apparatus sitting the while on the Shoulders of the pile and going down along with it. hammering like, I won't say what, all the way down –

I continue pursuing my intimate acquaintance with the structure of the Lunar surface and find more and more to interest me in it. it is realy [*sic*] a magnificent object and full of the most lasting interest when sedulously studied. I hope to show you some results of these pleasant afternoons ere long – do you know of any scientific Journal that would admit a paper with some Illustrations? living as I do out of the great world but in a very busy little one here I am not in communication with any one who could put me in the way of having some of my investigations recorded in proper form. I should feel deeply obliged if you could name to me any Journal that would think fit to receive a communication now and then which I hope might be worth their paper and space –

But for the profound regard I have for the value of your time I had all but intruded myself on your attention once or twice of late to beg the favor of your permitting me to try what I think might be a rather interesting Experiment in relation to a great mystery – namely the cause of Hardening of Steel than which there is not a process of more value to mankind I know of – civilization rests on it alone what I want to get at is one or two *new* facts by varying the ordinary process – First Exper^t. or *question* – I want [illeg.] to ask Nature is . . what is the Effect in respect to Hardening or otherwise when a bit of steel wire (at usual hardening heat) is plunged into cold water – while the Steel wire in question is at the time part of a pretty powerfull [*sic*] galvanic circuit. – Has such state of circumstances any Effect on the steel as regards *Hardening*?

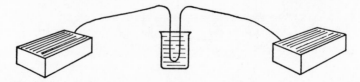

If the Experiment has never been made, it would be well to make it as it might lead to something interesting, perhaps important, and as it is an Experiment that can be made with Ease (perhaps) if Mr Anderson could with your permission permit me to try it some afternoon when he is quite at leisure when I am in town it would indeed be a vast favor to me as I am not possessed of the apparatus – The hardening of steel is so complete a mystery as yet so far as I know that it is by such novel or out of the usual way of treatment that we may hope to stumble on the End of the thread of some interesting facts

I am very much ashamed of thus inflicting such a long winded letter on you and pray your forgiveness.

> Believe me I am
> with the most sincere respect
> yours most truly
> JAMES NASMYTH

¹ I am unable to identify Cavalli. Not to be confused with the student of electricity, Tiberio Cavallo, who died in 1809. This may be a relative whose name would ensure a warm welcome from Faraday.

351 M. FARADAY to J. NASMYTH, 29 May 1847¹
['*James Nasmyth, Engineer, An Autobiography*', London, *1883, 284*]

> Royal Institution,
> 29th May 1847

"MY DEAR SIR   That you should both show kindness to the bearer of my letter, and prove that you did so with pleasure by writing me a letter in return, was indeed more than I ought or could have expected; but it was very gratifying and pleasant to my mind. I only wish that the circumstances of my life were such as to enable me to take advantage of such goodwill on your part, and to be more in your company and conversation than is at present possible.

"I could imagine great pleasure from such a condition of things; but though our desires, and even our hopes at times, spread out beforehand over a large extent, it is wonderful how, as the future becomes the present, the circumstances that surround us limit the sphere to which our real life is circumscribed. If ever I come your way I hope to see your face; and the hope is pleasant, though the reality may never arrive.

"You tell me of the glorious work of your pile-driver, and it must be indeed a great pleasure to witness the result. Is it not Shakespeare who says, 'The pleasure we delight in physics pain'? In all your fatigue and labour you must have this pleasure in abundance, and a most delightful and healthy enjoyment it is. I shall rejoice to see some day a blow of the driver and a tap of the hammer.

"You speak of some experiments on tempering in which we can help you. I hope when you do come to town you will let us have the pleasure of doing so. Our apparatus, such as it is, shall be entirely at your service. I made, a long while ago, a few such experiments on steel wire, but could eliminate no distinct or peculiar results. You will know how to look at things, and at your hand I should expect much.

"Here we are just lecturing away, and I am too tired to attempt anything, much less to do anything just now; but the goodwill of such men as you is a great stimulus, and will, I trust even with me, produce something else praiseworthy. – Ever, my dear Nasmyth, yours most truly,   M. FARADAY."

[1] See Letter 350.

---

352   J. NASMYTH to M. FARADAY, 12 July 1847
[*I.E.E., previously unpublished*]

Bridgewater Foundry,
Patricroft,
near Manchester,
July 12 1847

MY DEAR SIR

Many many thanks for your most kind and most valued letter of the 29 May –

I have taken the liberty to write you on the present occasion in reference to the subject of the interesting experiments which M. Dumas has been making in respect to converting Diamonds into Coke.[1] Under the impression that some facts in intimate connection with this subject may interest you I shall trouble you with them in case they be new to you –

Several years ago it came to me in examining a piece of coke that as Diamond is carbon and Coke is carbon would not Coke *cut* glass so to prove my conjecture I lightly switched a fragment over the face of the pane of glass in the window and as the sun was shining bright through it at the time I was much pleased and interested to find that my conjecture was so far proved as to the identity of Coke with the diamond as that it possessed one of the most remarkable properties of the gem namely that it *cuts* glass. The cuts made in glass by that means are so clean and cut like that they send forth the most beautiful prismatic colours as the rays of the sun happen to strike the plane of the cut at the suitable angle the appearance being exactly similar to that which we see produced by those infinitely delicate fillaments [*sic*] of the gossamers as they flaunt about in the tranquil air of a sunny autumn morning

I enclose you a little morsel of coke so as you may put what I state to proof on the instant provided the sun be shining through your window. you need not fear destroying your Glass as the cuts are so fine and go but small way in but yet are perfect clean *cuts* quite of the Diamond cut family and not mere Scratches –

This "little fact" may peradventure interest you both on its own account and also as a converse proof of Identity of coke with Diamond – and I am inclined to think that in many processes in the arts that Coke Dust would prove to be a most valuable grinding if not polishing material for the Gem Cutters I doubt not it would prove a most usefull and very economical substitute for Diamond Dust

What say you to it as a material for Razor strops. no doubt a very humble application but one which would be no small contribution to the arts of civilization if it made razors do their duty as they sometimes will not do with all the magic powers of a veritable nicchi [reading doubtful]

I earnestly look forward to the happy time when I shall have more leisure to ask Dame nature a question or two toutching [*sic*] carbon in its various forms Especially in reference to its union with Iron which I am more than inclined to think is more in the condition of an alloy in the case of Steel than as a carburet. –

I have to appologize [*sic*] to you for this intrusion on your valuable attention but perhaps you may feel interested in my small fact toutching [*sic*] the glass cutting property [reading doubtful] of Coke.

in making the Window Experiment with the enclosed bit of Coke you have only to Switch it Lightly and at random in such figures as these

so as per Hap Hazard to get some of the minute christals [*sic*] or plates of the coke to be Edge ways with the direction of the motion of the Hand

Believe me I am
most faithfully yours
JAMES NASMYTH

1 I am unable to identify this reference, but see Letter 355.

353   M. FARADAY to J. NASMYTH, 15 July 1847

[E. F. Smith Collection, University of Pennsylvania Library, previously unpublished]

Newcastle upon Tyne
15 July 1847

Thanks my dear Sir to you for your kind letter. I read it here & have successfully made your experiment and I hope that some of your proposed applications of the coke dust will prove as decided in result as they seem likely in theory I have been looking a little at one of your piledrivers here – but cannot give much attention to any thing because of my heavy attack of giddiness – The same circumstance obliges me to be very short in letter writing – for which I know you will excuse me

Ever Yours
M. FARADAY

[*B.J.* 2, *233*]

14 Duke Street,
Edinburgh,
July 29, 1847

MY DEAR LORD,

If I had been in London I should have waited on your Lordship at the Admiralty instantly; as it is, I can only express my readiness to have done so. In reference to your Lordship's request, I will now take the liberty of explaining my position, which I did not very long since in a letter to the Secretary of the Admiralty, to which letter, however, and to a former one, containing the results of serious consideration and much time, I have never received any reply.

For years past my health has been more and more affected, and the place affected is my head. My medical advisers say it is from mental occupation. The result is loss of memory, confusion and giddiness; the sole remedy, cessation from such occupation and head-rest. I have in consequence given up, for the last ten years or more, all professional occupation, and voluntarily resigned a large income that I might pursue in some degree my own objects of research. But in doing this I have always, as a good subject, held myself ready to assist the Government if still in my power – *not for pay*, for, except in one instance (and then only for the sake of the person joined with me), I refused to take it. I have had the honour and pleasure of applications, and that very recently, from the Admiralty, the Ordnance, the Home Office, the Woods and Forests, and other departments, all of which I have replied to, and will reply to as long as strength is left me; and now it is to the condition under which I am obliged to do this that I am anxious to call your Lordship's attention in the present case. I shall be most happy to give my advice and opinion in any case as may be at the time within my knowledge or power, but I may not undertake to enter into investigations or experiments. If I were in London I would wait upon your Lordship, and say all I could upon the subject of the disinfecting fluids, but I would not undertake the experimental investigation; and in saying this I am sure that I shall have your sympathy and approbation when I state that it is now more than three weeks since I left London to obtain the benefit of change of air, and yet my giddiness is so little alleviated that I don't feel in any degree confident that I shall ever be able to return to my recent occupations and duties.

I have the honour to be, my Lord, your Lordship's very faithful servant,

M. FARADAY.

---

[1] George Baron Auckland (1784–1849), was First Lord of the Admiralty at this time.

[*Arch. de l'Académie des Sciences, Paris, Dossier Faraday, previously unpublished*]

Dundee.
Scotland
12 August, 1847

MY DEAR FRIEND

At last I write to acknowledge both the great kindness you favoured me with by M. Le Verrier;[1] and also that received by the hands of M. M. Edwards.[2] It was with great joy I saw them both at the Oxford Meeting; but that did not compensate *to me* for your absence. It is true, I hardly expected you, but Sir Roderic [*sic*] Murchison[3] had greatly raised my hopes; and I am sure I may say the whole meeting longed to see you. Their feelings were not altogether my feelings and none could miss you as I did.

I had undertaken a certain object at the meeting, – the preparation for which and the delay occasioned by the use of unfamiliar and untried apparatus, consumed so much of my time that I saw very little of M. Le Verrier – but I knew him before hand in spirit by his glavanic [*sic*] work; and I shall now not forget his form & appearance. It is a cause of great rejoicing to science that with such mental power and soundness of judgment there is joined a physical *frame*, *health* & *strength* that promises abundant additions to the victories of science. I hope you will give my kindest remembrances to him.

M. Milne Edwards I first knew personally at your house. Here, *i. e.*, at Oxford he was the same kind & hearty friend as there, and gave me your packet with as much delight as I could receive it with. The diamonds & resulting carbon are wonderful; and I hope that a close investigation of the change produced & the attendant phenomena will lead to the reconversion of carbon as coke or charcoal back into diamond – I am not quite sure the result is desirable in relation to the use or value of diamond, but it could not be otherwise than valuable to the cause of science. I shewed the specimens at the section of chemistry & also to the Chairman & others of the Section of Physics; and to many individuals. As Mr Milne Edwards assures me, that you wished me after that, to keep them in remembrance of you, I shall do so; i. e. if I make no mistake in understanding your writing or what he says. But such specimens must be too rare & too valuable to be easily given away or retained.

I left Oxford for London on saturday in the middle of the week of meeting. I was seized in London with a heavy attack of giddiness & confusion in the head which not only prevented my return to Oxford (where I should have seen more of MM. Le Verrier & Edwards) but has not left me to *this day* so that I have been unable to work, think, or write, and this it is which has delayed my answer to your letter. I was sent up into Scotland for change and though better do not feel restored – and am conscious that more than ever I must take care and withdraw from Society – & work – I regret it a little; because I had hoped to do a somewhat [*sic*] more with light and magnetism & still think I see my way further than the bounds of the present state of the subject. – I would much rather be able to send you news and facts than so many useless words; but failing the one I know that I may trust to your kindness in accepting the other. My wife offers her kindest compliments to Madame Dumas and enjoys many remembrances of past favours received by her. I venture also to add mine, though with more fear of their acceptance – for I am afraid that every additional word which I write may be to her an additional trouble. But with other infirmities I feel this, that my hand will not obey my will: and I must cast myself on her gentleness & favour.

Ever My dear friend
Your Most grateful Servt
M. FARADAY

1 Urbain Jean Joseph Le Verrier (1811–77), discoverer of the planet Neptune.
2 Henri Milne-Edwards (1800–85), zoologist.
3 Sir Roderick Impey Murchison (1792–1871), geologist.

356 JANE DAVY¹ to M. FARADAY, 23 August 1847
  [*I.E.E., previously unpublished*]

Park St. [London],
Aug. 23ᵈ, 1847

DEAR MR. FARADAY,

I enclose to you Mr. Herbert Smith's address & his letter to me relative; the latter I beg you will carefully keep. I have written to Lord Selborne for his Artist's name,² whom he recommended, as an excellent Copyiest, & of reasonable demand. You will fully understand, as I wish a very kind feeling toward yourself from me, connected with this gift, I should wish you satisfied. Production, or Size, is of course at your choice, or only Head, just as you prefer; but I think the Thumb in the Hand, gives truth to the beautiful & peculiar Expression of the Head. My finances are not so low even in this Year of demands heavy & sad, as to deprive me, of the real pleasure of gratifying you entirely in this little memorial of earlier Time. Pray do not therefore from mistaken caution, or delicacy, deprive me of my wish; a few Pounds added, if necessary, to ensure what will be valuable to the Artist & creditable, I should willingly add: though about forty £ was what I thought for the larger size. Mr. Piggerskill's [*sic*]³ Talents & his friendliness to you are the best Counsellors; only do not hurry, & repent. I highly approve of your right feeling, about a young Artist; to whom it might be a leading string of healthy Progress. I repeat, your complete & independent enjoyment is my wish; & I shall if this be assured be myself *quite* satisfied. With a kind message to Mrs. Faraday of remembrance I am

Yrs Very truly
JANE DAVY

¹ Jane Davy was Sir Humphry's widow.
² Roundell Palmer, 1st Earl of Selborne (1812–85). The letter refers to Faraday's desire to have a copy made of the portrait of Sir Humphry Davy now hanging in the Royal Society's rooms.
³ Probably the reference is to William Henry Pickersgill (1782–1875), R.A., portrait painter.

357   J. PLÜCKER to M. FARADAY, 3 November 1847
[*I.E.E., previously unpublished*]

Bonn
ce 3 Novembre 1847.

MONSIEUR

J'ai l'honneur de vous addresser deux petits Mémoires contenant des faits nouveaux, qui se rattachent à ceux que vous avez découverts sur le magnétisme et le diamagnétisme.¹ J'ose croire que vous les trouverez dignes pour fixer votre attention. Les pôles d'un aimant sont le centre non seulement de la force magnétique et de la force diamagnétique mais encore d'une force nouvelle qui repousse les axes optiques des crystaux, indépendante de l'état magnétique ou diamagnétique de ces corps. Cette force nouvelle diminue moins vite, avec la distance, que les deux autres forces.

Dans le second mémoire j'ai prouvé que le même corps est magnétique ou diamagnétique suivant la distance des poles.

Je suis très curieux de savoir, ce que vous jugerez des conclusions, que j'ai tiré de mes expériences, que j'ai répeté à plusieurs physiciens, notamment à Monsieur Mitscherlich de Berlin, qui en á [*sic*] été très surpris.

Je continue toujours mes recherches expérimentales dont l'origine remonte à vos belles découvertes. J'ai repeté encore sous des conditions très variées vos expériences sur la rotation du plan de polarisation Pour mieux juger de l'effet que j'ai obtenu, je serai très heureux si vous vouliez bien m'instruire coment je pourrai me procurer un morceau de verre pesant, dont vous vous servez.

Veuillez agréer Monsieur les assurance [*sic*] de mon plus profond respect

Votre
tout devoué Serviteur
PLÜCKER

¹ Probably J. Plücker (1801–68), 'Ueber die Abstossung der optischen Axen der Krystalle durch die Pole der Magnete,' *AP*, 148 (1847), 315 and 'Ueber das Verhältniss zwischen Magnetismus und Diamagnetismus,' *ibid.*, 343.

358 M. FARADAY to J. PLÜCKER, 11 November 1847

[Nat. Res. Counc. Canada, previously unpublished]

Royal Institution
11 Novr. 1847

DEAR SIR

Though I may not write you a long letter because of the present state of my health yet I cannot refrain from thanking you for your letter & also the copy of your papers. I cannot read German which I deeply regret but I gather from your letter the important points of your researches and rejoice that you have been induced to enter this part of physical enquiry. I have not much heavy glass but have this day put a piece of about this size – polished at the ends into the hands of a friend who 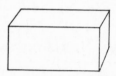 tells me he can send it to you. It will go by a merchants house and may therefore be some weeks on its way, but if after a time you do *not* receive it *and* will tell me how I can send you a piece I will spare another for that purpose

I am Sir
Your Very Obliged & faithful Srvt
M. FARADAY

359 M. FARADAY to W. WHEWELL, 13 December 1847

[Trinity College Library, Trinity College, Cambridge, previously unpublished]

R.I.,
Dec. 13, 1847

MY DEAR SIR

Accept a short paper containing I think very interesting results relating to Diamagnetism

You cannot think how much I rejoice to find that we shall hear you at our table on the 22 Jany. It is to me the full proof of the attainment of that I have so earnestly desired namely that the Royal Institution should be dignified in its scientific character both for what it produces and for those who speak within its walls.

Ever My dear Sir
Yours faithfully
M. FARADAY

[1] M. Faraday, 'On the diamagnetic conditions of flame and gases,' *PM*, n.s., 31 (1847), 401.

360   M. FARADAY to C. R. WELD,[1] 8 January 1848

[*American Philosophical Society, JCE, 26 (1949), 441*]

R Institution
8 Jan.ʸ 1848

MY DEAR SIR

I am happy to say that in England I am not a Sir and do not intend (if, it depends upon me) to become one. The Prussian Knighthood I am in hopes will appear in the list in its due form – for in that I do feel honor, in the other I should not.

Ever Truly Yours
M. FARADAY

[1] Charles Richard Weld (1818–69), assistant secretary and librarian of the Royal Society.

361   M. FARADAY to REV. W. BUCKLAND,[1] 12 January 1848

[*R.S., previously unpublished*]

Royal Institution,
12 Jany. 1848

MY DEAR DEAN

I shall be hard at work at the Trinity House tomorrow evening or I should have made an exertion to reach the Deanery. as it is I shall not be able.

My Soap bubbles were all very good but my Carbonic acid was too recently prepared, indeed only the moment before.[2] I had learnt the lesson before but in the hurry of the moment forgot it again.

I wish I could come tomorrow night that we might blow Soap bubbles against each other. What a beautiful & wonderful thing a soap bubble is?

My sincere respects to Mrs. Buckland.

Ever Truly Yours
M. FARADAY

[1] William Buckland (1784–1856), geologist and Dean of Westminster.
[2] See [10860 ff] for Faraday's use of soap bubbles in determining the magnetic character of gases.

362   J. PLÜCKER to M. FARADAY, 6 February 1848

[*I.E.E., previously unpublished*]

Bonn
le 6 Fevrier 1848

MONSIEUR!

Dans le temps j'ai recu la lettre, dont vous avez bien voulu m'honorer. Le beau morceau de *havy* [*sic*] *glass*[1] m'est parvenu plus tard. Je vous en fais mes remerciments les plus sincères. Si je les fais tardivement, c'est parceque j'aurois voulu en même temps parler de mes experiences. Mais je n'ai put jusqu'ici rien

faire, qui me persuader [*sic*] de l'excellent effet du verre. En ajustant l'expérience de la manière la plus favorable j'ai obtenu une déviation de 23° au moyen
de 3 petits éléments de Grove. J'étois en outre occupé d'un autre travail, que je
désirois terminer, savoir des recherches sur l'état magnétique des gaz et des
liquides.[2] Mon mémoire est parti, il y a quinze jours, pour être inseré dans les
Annales de M. Poggendorff, sans que j'eusse la moindre connaissance de vos
recentes recherches, que dans le même temps "l'Institut" nous parlait à Bonn.
Quant aux expériences avec les différentes flaṁes[3] ma manière d'opérer est
précisement la vôtre, seulement j'ai pris des pointes coniques non arrondies.
J'ai obtenus des superbes paraboles, nettement dessinées, en opérant par
exemple sur les vapeurs d'iode et une flaṁe d'huile de terpentine [*sic*] donnant
beaucoup de fumée. Quelques figures, dessinées d'après nature, sont jointes
á mon Mémoire. Pour les gaz j'admire votre manière vraiment colossale
d'opérer et je sens mon impuissance pour y rivaliser. Seulement j'ai envisagé la
chose encore sous un point de vue différent. L'effet diamagnétique de l'aimant
doit nécessairement produire la *dilatation de l'air environnante*. C'est ce que je
démontre directement en ajustant convenablement un thermomètre á air entre
les deux poles: ce thermomètre montrant, si l'on ferme le circuit, coṁe il aurait
fait en suite d'une augmentation de température, et retournant plus prompte-
ment encore aussitôt que le Magnétisme disparait. Il me parait donc prouvé par
une *expérience directe* que l'air est diamagnétique. En introduisant un peu
d'éther sulphurique dans le vase de l'instrument l'effet a beaucoup augmenté.
L'on pourra mesurer ainsi la force diamagnétique pour les différents gaz.

Veuillez regarder, Monsieur, mes faibles efforts, que je continuerais dans
différentes directions, coṁe provoqués uniquement par votre importante
découverte et me laisser le mérite d'en avoir plus qu'un autre reconnu l'importance

Votre tout dévoué Serviteur
Plücker

[1] See Letter 358.
[2] J. Plücker, 'Experimentäle Untersuchungen über die Wirkung der Magnete auf gasförmige und tropfbare Flüssigkeiten,' *AP*, 149 (1848), 549.
[3] Plücker habitually replaces the second 'm' in a word by a bar over the first one.

363 M. Faraday to Sir J. Clark,[1] 8 April 1848
[*R.S., previously unpublished*]

R. Institution
8 April 1848.

My dear Sir James

My feeling has ever been that the College of Chemistry[2] should be solely
devoted to the *teaching* of chemistry; that the Members should have no other
object, and in consideration of their subscriptions should consider success in

that object as a full return. They should refuse all *personal advantage* & therefore *analyses* or any other occupations for the time & attention of the Director
or the pupils (aside from teaching & research for the good of chemistry as a
whole) should not be undertaken. The idea that the members should have
privileges is derogatory to the purity of their motives & I really believe
inconsistent with the character & success of the college. which if it stands at all
must stand upon the basis of high feeling and utility. If you can help it pray do
not let it enter into the list of bodies which fight for an existence by fits of
expediency shifting from day to day

At the same time I think the College should not be made a greater burden
on the members than is really necessary. There has been too much pretence
about it. & as far as I can judge the house in Harrow Square is both a great
expence & unseemly. One knows that it can be of no real use to the teaching
of chemistry & if not it is worse than a burden for it substitutes an *appearance*
for that which ought to be altogether *reality*.

I especially like pp 15. 16. 17. & 18. of your paper also pp 21. & 22.[3]

I am

My dear Sir James
Ever Truly Yours
M. FARADAY

[1] Sir James Clark (1788–1870), Physician to Queen Victoria and member of the Senate,
London University from 1838 to 1865. Faraday spelt the name 'Clarke'.
[2] The Royal College of Chemistry was founded in October 1845. See Frederick Augustus
Abel, 'History of the Royal College of Chemistry and reminiscences of Hofmann's professorship,' *TLCS*, 69 (1896).
[3] Possibly refers to Sir James Clark, 'Remarks on Medical Reform in a letter addressed to the
Right Hon. Sir James Graham, Bart.,' London, 1842.

364 G. B. AIRY to M. FARADAY, 17 April 1848

[*I.E.E., previously unpublished*]

Royal Observatory
Greenwich
1848 April 17

MY DEAR SIR

I have several times read with infinite pleasure your beautiful experiments
on the diamagnetism {I do not like that word} of flame and gases,[1] and only
trouble you with one remark. You ascribe the gradual beginnings of the effect
to certain supposed mechanical modifications in the effect on, and the means of
receiving the effect by, the ponderable gases. But, inasmuch as there is the same
graduality of beginning of the effect on the circular polarization of light, where
it is impossible that the explanation can find place, does it not appear to arise

from something in some part of the magnetic arrangements which requires time for its development? And if so, is it not an important subject of examination *per se*?

I think it probable that this is not worth reading, and am certain that it is not worth answering; therefore I request that you will not waste any time upon it.

I am, my dear Sir,

Very truly yours
G. B. AIRY

[Note added by Faraday]

Exp. Research 2170. thĕ time in the heavy Glass &c. referred to in letter to Taylor E. Phil Jour Sept 30th 1846.[2]

time in diamagnetism of flame Phil Mag Dec. 1847 p. 402

Time My letter to Gay Lussac – [*ERE*] Vol 2 p 191. 195

E Res Vol 1. Index [illeg.] places.

[1] M. Faraday, 'On the diamagnetic conditions of flame and gases,' *PM*, 3 s., 31 (1847), 401.
[2] There is no letter from Faraday to Taylor in the *Edinburgh Philosophical Journal* in 1846 or in 1847. No such letter is mentioned in Alan E. Jeffreys, *Michael Faraday, A List of His Lectures and Published Writings*, London, 1960, and I have been unable to locate it.

In the September 1846 issue of the *Philosophical Magazine*, there is an article by Faraday which is not, however, in the form of a letter. It does treat the topic referred to above and this is, perhaps, the 'letter' to which he refers. See *PM*, 3 s., 29 (1846), 153.

365 M. FARADAY to G. B. AIRY, 17 April 1848

[*Royal Observatory, Herstmonceux, Astrology & optics, 1849 and 1850, Sect. 14, previously unpublished*]

Royal Institution
17 April 1848

MY DEAR AIRY

Your letters are always real letters & therefore it is a pleasure both to receive & answer them. The *time* has often come into my thoughts & I will tell you briefly on what experiments I rest for my present opinion. Having such a magnet as the one you saw here and placing a copper wire helix either with or without an iron core between the poles having its wires connected with a galvanometer, we observe that when the magnet is made active a current is formed by induction in the *helix* & rendered sensible by the galvanometer – I find this current to have a sensible duration to be strongest at the first moment – & to weaken gradually until insensible – I can make it sensible for a second or even more & though it lasts longest when an iron core *is* in the helix it has duration for a time when the iron is away & the copper helix alone is concerned there being little difference in the two cases as to *time*.

In the next place by breaking & making contact of the helix & galvanometer at one of the wires we can test the rising action of the magnet *or* the helix for any interval, it is easy by a wheel with pins & teeth. to divide the *second* during which the galvanometer shews that the current is continued into 20. 30. or any number of parts & to test for any one of these parts whether the power is then rising in the magnet. In this way *I have ascertained* that the power is rising in the magnet & that it is this continuous rise which makes the current at the galvanometer continuous

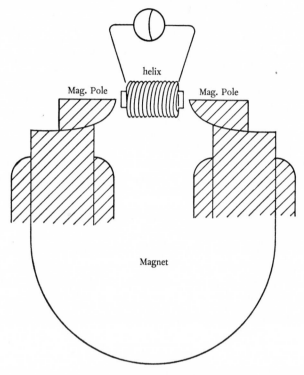

So when on placing a piece of heavy glass between the poles of this magnet I found that its power of rotating a polarized ray rose *gradually* & when on placing the same piece of heavy glass between or within helices *without iron cores* I found that its power rose *suddenly*. I referred the gradual rise to the gradual development of power in the magnet rather than to the time required by the heavy glass to take up a certain state because this time is not necessary when helices alone are used. I do not say that *time* is not involved – but that the time which appeared necessary was necessary from another cause – You will see all this stated briefly in my letter to Taylor. Phil Mag. 1846. vol xxix p. 257.[1]

As therefore heavy glass does not appear to need a sensible portion of *time* to assume its state, so it did not appear to me likely that a gaseous medium would require more time in acquiring the same state.

517

But that the time referred in the case of flame is due to the cause I have assigned to it is to me satisfactorily shewn because it is easy to vary many of the conditions & vary the time with them & trace the currents all the while; & if you saw the experiments (which are long in description, you would see this at once. When a flame is rising between the poles there is of course a strong current of air &c up between the poles. Make the magnet active & the flame gradually shortens & when at a certain depression goes down suddenly still lower & forks out sideways & then there is a current of cold air *downwards* between the poles easily shewn by a little smoke properly applied. It is evident that this conversion of the direction of the currents must take time & I can prolong or shorten the time or stop the change at a particular part of the process at pleasure. Again when the flame is a large one as with ether & so does not shorten or sink down immediately that the magnet is made active one can see the impression made in the two sides of the flame by the currents of air that flow in upon it along the axial line. & the dents there from gradually increase until the flame open out suddenly there & forks as before.

The question of time in the *real* electric or magnetic phenomena is continually on my mind. If you happen to have access to the 8vo edition of my experimental researches, you will find a dozen references to *time* in the first volume & two I think in the second. But as yet I have never been able to lay hold of the matter by a good clear experiment

Your observation on the word *diamagnetic* amused me. I apologized for it on Friday evening stating that the preposition *dia* was applied to bodies when I thought that they possessed no magnetic condition but let the power pass through them unobstructed in its course. After the evening was over *Owen* came to me & said he thought the apology unnecessary & the name or word admirable since the *dia* so well expressed the transverse or cross position which these bodies assumed in the magnetic field. All I can say is that the word *dia* was not applied with that significance but that once having been used and being as a *sound* distinction I thought that to change it was a greater evil than to leave it

Excuse my prosiness & bad writing & believe me to be truly Yours

M. FARADAY

[1] The article to which Faraday refers is, 'On the Magnetic Affection of Light, and on the Distinction between the Ferromagnetic and Diamagnetic Conditions of Matter,' *PM*, 3 s., 29 (1846), 153 and 258.

366 M. FARADAY to MISS DANIELL,[1] 15 May 1848

[*Wellcome Medical Historical Library, previously unpublished*]

R Institution
15 May 1848

MY DEAR MISS DANIELL

I sent some weeks ago & soon after I saw you at Norwood, three letters from your father to me. Two were slight but the third very characteristic – they are all I have for I burn letters generally. I addressed them by Post to Miss Daniell *Norwood* & have heard nothing of them since so conclude Your Sister has them. I should be very sorry to lose them – so both for your sake and mine write to Miss Daniell about them

With best remembrances to your brother believe me

most Truly Yours
M. FARADAY

I purpose going tomorrow to look at a bust.

MF

[1] The daughter of J. F. Daniell who died on 13 March 1845.

367 J. PLÜCKER to M. FARADAY, 5 June 1848

[*I.E.E., previously unpublished*][1]

Bonn
le 5 Juin 1848.

MONSIEUR!

J'ai l'honneur de vous addresser deux petits Mémoires,[2] qui à cause des circonstances politiques me sont parvenus plus tard que d'ordinaire. Je vous ai déja parlé du premier. Le second se rapporte surtout à la polarité diamagnétique, qui maintenant est hors de doute. Vous y trouverez entre autres le fait curieux que l'intensité de la force diamagnétique croît plus rapidement quand on augmente la force de l'Electroaimant que celle de la force magnétique. L'augmentation de la force de l'Electroaimant fait prendre à un morceau de charbon, ayant, d'abord la position d'un corps magnétique, celle d'un corps diamagnétique. Plus tard j'ai constaté cette loi de différentes manières. L'expérience suivante est assez frappante. Si au moyen d'un contrepoids on équilibre un corps quelconque contenant en même temps des substances magnétiques et diamagnétiques (p.ex. du mercure dans un vase de laiton, ce dernier étant magnétique) ce corps est repoussé par l'aimant quand on l'approche de lui et attiré quand on l'éloigne.

J'ai imaginé une méthode qui me permet de comparer exactement l'intensité du diamagnétisme des différents corps diamagnétique coe celle du Magnétisme des differents corps magnétiques. J'exprime par de nombres soit le Magnétisme soit le Diamagnétisme des différents corps solides et liquides, et en même temps je suis parvenu à une foule d'observations curieuses concernant l'induction magnétique et surtout le rapport entre la constitution chimique des corps et leur magnétisme. La difficulté d'obtenir des substances chimiquement pures m'a présenté les plus grands obstacles. Ainsi p. ex. $1/3\%$ d'oxydate de fer melé à une masse d'oxide en doit à moins *doubler* le magnétisme. Le magnétisme des oxydes est *augmenté* par les acides qui s'unissent à eux pour former des sels. En posant le Magnétisme du fer = 100000, je trouve celui d'un même poids d'oxide de Nickel (Ni) égal à 35, celui de ce même oxide à l'état de hydrate $(Ni + \dot{H})$ égal à 142. Le cyanure *jaune* de fer et potasse est diamagnétique, le cyanure *rouge* au contraire (soit en crystal, soit en poudre, soit en dissolution) est décidement magnétique. (Un crystal de ce dernier sel montre très nettement la repulsion des axes optiques par l'aimant, sans y faire attention l'on pourroit facilement le prendre pour un corps diamagnétique). Le sc. ex. J'ai examiné également l'influence de la chaleur. Pour le mercure le soufre, le stéarine je n'ai pas observé la moindre différence soit à haute soit à basse temperature, soit à l'état liquide ou solide. Mais le bismuth á [*sic*] donné des résultats très differents. Dans une de mes expériences il m'a fallu, à la température ordinaire 1,67 gram̃es pour contrebalancer la repulsion diamagnétique d'une masse de 144 gram̃es. À une température élévé [*sic*] il n'en falloit que 0 gr,28, c'est à dire à peu près un sixième. J'y vois une nouvelle analogie entre le magnetisme et le diamagnétisme. Tous les deux diminuent si la température augmente. Il parait en outre que le diamagnétisme du bismuth a sa limite (son minimum) com̃e le magnétisme du fer et du nickel, &c &c

Je me prendrai la liberté de vous addresser mon nouveau Mémoire,[3] qui est maintenant entre les mains de M. Poggendorff aussitot qu'il paraitra . . . Peut être qu'il me sera permis de l'apporter moi même à Londres.

Veuillez agréer, Monsieur, les assurances de mon profond respect   PLÜCKER

[1] See *PM*, 3 s., 33 (1848), 48, for an English translation which is not, however, faithful to the original.

[2] Probably J. Plücker, 'Ueber die Abstossung der optischen Axen der Crystalle durch die Pole der Magnete,' *AP*, 148 (1847), 315, and 'Ueber das Verhältniss zwischen Magnetismus und Diamagnetismus', *ibid.*, 343.

[3] J. Plücker, 'Experimentäle Untersuchungen über die Wirkung der Magnete auf gasförmige und tropfbare Flüssigkeiten,' *AP*, 149 (1848), 549.

368   M. FARADAY to J. PLÜCKER, 12 June 1848

[*Nat. Res. Counc. Canada, previously unpublished*]

Royal Institution
12 June 1848

MY DEAR SIR

I received your letter of the 6 Feby[1] and was glad to find by it that the heavy glass had arrived safe I have no doubt that in your hands it will be more useful than it could be in any others. I also received yesterday another kind letter from you full of beautiful facts and I was so struck with its contents that I instantly sent it to Mr. Taylor to insert (if he was of my mind) in the next number of the Philosophical Magazine. I hope I have not in this done anything you would wish undone but I desired greatly that the facts should be made known to the world Today I have received the printed copy of the two papers you mentioned to me in your letter I had heard of them before in Poggendorf Annalen. It is most tantalizing to me to see your rich results. and yet see them as it were without understanding; – enclosed in a *sealed book* For I cannot read German & I cannot learn it. From day to day my memory grows weaker and if I make an attempt to recover even the little knowledge I had of German words in former times my head grows giddy all things swim around me & I do not recover for some weeks – But it is a shame for me to complain I ought to be content: – and indeed I speak of this matter only that you may not be surprized that I do not rejoice with you in every word that you write as I really should do if I could read them

When your last letter comes back to me from Mr Taylor I shall compare it with the German papers & get some friend to help me and I hope repeat some of the experiments: – but at present I am in my giddy tottering condition and can hardly think of the common place experiments which belong to a couple of lectures I still have to give. After these are over however I trust that a little country air & rest will in part set me up again – At the same time I do not forget that I am nearly 57 years of age – have worked long hours in my life time and as to material strength am somewhat worn. In such cases a man may be patched but he cannot be remade. Wishing you many years of health & such prosperity in science as you have already abundantly tasted

I am my dear Sir
Most truly Yours
M. FARADAY

1 See Letter 362.

369 J. NASMYTH to M. FARADAY, 15 June 1848
[*I.E.E., previously unpublished*]

Barnbro Hall
nr. Doncaster
June 15, 1848

MY DEAR SIR

Your very kind and valued note of the 12th has just reached me here while enjoying a few days holiday with my dear wife at her Fathers nice place here among fine oak trees and green fields, where with pencil in hand I am attempting to Paint "The Alchemist before the Inquisition" from Washington Irvings admirable tale of "The Student of Salamanca".

I greatly wish I could have been present to listen to your Lecture of tomorrow Eving[1] and feel much honoured that you meditate alluding to my views on a similar [reading doubtful] subject – It is rather singular that while the Foreigner should hold that he has discovered that Diamond is Coke, I should long since have held that Coke was diamond in so far as respects its extreme hardness and power of *cutting* Glass. I shall be very happy if by announcing this fact to the world as your mention of it will naturally do, that the discovery of it may in that way be made to thousands who may turn it to some usefull [*sic*] purpose –

I have had no other opportunity or means of making the Experiment as to the grinding power of Coke dust than in the humble application of material for Razor Strop powder in which I find that coke dust infinitely fine and *procured by Levigation,* does certainly set a very keen Edge on a Razor as respects its polishing power I found it *too keen* and in using it in polishing Speculum metals I found it *cut* such very fine *cuts into the* surface as to cause me to lay it aside for that purpose, ie polishing but for *fine grinding* it is I should say quite the thing. These infinitely fine particles of Coke appear to be *thin plates of infinite hardness* which when encountered in the surface you want to cut *Edgeways* appear to send in a very deep cut of great cleavage – just in fact such as the diamond does in the case of Glass.

I am fain to consider Coke as a metalic [*sic*] body or *Carbonium* or very near to it. Steel to be an alloy of this metalic base of Carbon in Iron, but as I have not yet had an opportunity to ask nature the question in the proper manner I am not able to write Q.E.D. to my hypothesis on that hand

The Encouraging opinion which you gave me of the correctness of the principle of my Steam Pile driver has been most fully established in practice. I have made 22 of them which are thumping away in all parts of the world and giving the highest satisfaction. The Emperor of Russia has just sent me a most magnificent Diamond Ring containing 140 Diamonds (which I *dont* [*sic*] intend to reduce to Coke) in testimony of his high satisfaction with the performance of two of my pile Drivers which I have sent him for the Foundation work of a great arsenal at Cronstadt. – I have made 232 steam Hammers already which is not bad progress with a new tool. I am glad to say I have kept clear of all damage from the Late Commercial Earthquake and begin to think I may bring "the cottage in Kent" to a focus and visable [*sic*] to the naked Eye D.V. some time about 1854 when I hope to devote myself to the elaboration of all my pet schemes which the world shall be then welcome to in consideration of their having used me on the whole very well – Telescope making has been the pet hobby of the Evings for the last two years and in respect to the production of most perfect specula in respect to casting, grinding and Polishing by machinery I think I have done some thing good, the polishing process is the work of a machine entirely and leaves nothing to wish for, it is the idea of a friend Mr Lavell of Liverpool. I am still at work on the moon and find it an exhaustless subject of the highest interest.

May I beg to present my most Respectfull [*sic*] regards to Mrs Faraday in which Mrs N wishes to unite.

Trusting you will pardon this very long winded Scribble

Believe me I am
Ever most faithfully yours
JAMES NASMYTH

<hr>

[1] On 16 June, Faraday delivered a lecture 'On the conversion of diamond into coke by the electric flame.' The notes for this lecture are at the Royal Institution.

370   W. THOMSON to M. FARADAY, 27 June 1848

[*Silvanus P. Thompson, 'The Life of William Thomson, Baron Kelvin of Largs', 2 vols., London, 1910, 1, 207*]

Borley Rectory, Sudbury,
Suffolk, June 27, 1848.

MY DEAR SIR—

Since I had the conversation with you last week I have been reconsidering the subject with some care, and I am quite satisfied that the theoretical views which I then mentioned are correct. I should not, however, expect that it would be at all easy, or perhaps possible, to verify experimentally the result that a needle of a diamagnetic substance tends to arrange itself in the direction of the lines of force, when in a situation where there is no sensible variation of magnetic intensity through the space in which it is free to move, since this tendency arises from the mutual influence of the different portions of the diamagnetic substance itself, and is consequently excessively slight. An experiment showing that a diamagnetic needle will be sensibly astatic when the intensity in its neighbourhood is nearly constant would be extremely interesting, as so far confirming the conclusions deduced from theory; but I fear that a complete verification would be unattainable on account of the excessive feebleness of the force of which the existence is to be tested.

The same process of mathematical reasoning enables us to infer that a needle of soft iron and a needle of a diamagnetic substance would both rest stably in the direction of the lines of force, or unstably in a perpendicular direction; but in the former case the directive tendency is extremely sensible, so much so that it may be easily verified by observing the position which a delicately suspended needle of soft iron will assume when acted upon only by the earth.

I have not yet had an opportunity of referring to Poggendorff to find the account of the remarkable researches which you mentioned to me,[1] but as soon as I return to Cambridge I shall read it with great interest . . . . . . – I remain, dear sir, very truly yours,

WILLIAM THOMSON.

¹ See Letters 367 and 368.

371   M. FARADAY to J. B. DUMAS, 3 July 1848
   [Arch. de l'Académie des Sciences, Paris, Dossier Faraday, previously unpublished]

Royal Institution
3. July 1848

MY DEAR DUMAS

   I am very anxious about you & long to know how you and Madame Dumas are My dear wife too joins me in this anxiety You cannot have escaped trouble for it seems to me that in Paris every one must have been in trouble¹ However fourtunate in their personal circumstances they must have been anxious about others. Even at this distance & perhaps as you may think without right we are anxious about you If I could know by a single line how you are it would be consolation in some degree. I am afraid to ask after M. Arago & the many others to whom I am tied by deep feeling for it is scarcely possible all should have escaped trouble but I think of you & them continually.

Ever My dear friend
anxiously & affectionately Yours,
M. FARADAY

¹ In June 1848, General Cavaignac brutally put down an uprising by the working class in Paris. The 'June Days' marked the end of the French Revolution of 1848.

372   J. PLÜCKER to M. FARADAY, 19 July 1848
   [I.E.E., previously unpublished]

Bonn,
19 July 1848

MY DEAR SIR

   I received your very kind letter of the 12 June,¹ and was glad to find by it, that you paid some attention to the new facts I published during the last year. The paper I spoke of in my former letter will accompany the present one and I would give you an extract of it in English, if I had not the intention to pay a visit to England in the first days of August. Then I should be happy to see you and to give every explanation. Allow me only, Sir, to mention, that since I sent my paper to M. Poggendorff, I got very fine curves showing how the intensity of Magnetism and Diamagnetism is depending on temperature. The most expressive curves are those of Nickel and Bismuth, indicating both the same general law, concerning, I think, all bodies. The passage from solidity to fluidity seems to be of no influence.

I did not dream that my last letter would have the honour to be published, but if you thought it convenient, I have nothing to say but only to thank you, for being introduced by you to the English philosophers.

With the best wishes for your health, I am, Sir

Most respectfully yours
PLÜCKER

¹ See Letter 368.

373   J. B. DUMAS to M. FARADAY, 24 July 1848
[*B.J.* 2, *245*]

A la Sorbonne,
le 24 juillet, 1848

MON CHER AMI,

Les événements si tristes, mais, hélas! si bien prévus, que Paris a dû subir n'ont affecté ni moi ni les miens d'une manière directe. Mdme. Dumas et moi, nous avons été bien touchés de votre marque de bonté et de souvenir; c'est une consolation que cette affection des âmes élevées, comme la vôtre, au milieu d'un désordre moral dont rien n'en peut vous donner une idée, et qu'aucune imagination n'aurait certainement pu soupçonner.

Paris etait devenu, depuis six mois, le rendez-vous de tous les scélérats de la France et de l'Europe. Les uns comme chefs, les autres comme instruments, tous ensemble ils s'étaient proposé le pillage, le meurtre, l'incendie, et tous les désordres comme les moyens de *régénérer* notre nation, en détruisant sa bourgeoisie et en livrant tous les pouvoirs, toutes les fortunes, et toutes les familles au despotisme et à la brutalité des classes ouvrières.

Tout est voilé ici; les arts, les lettres, les sciences, tout se ressent du deuil universel. Les fortunes, les prolétaires, les existences, tout a été mis en question par les événements qui se sont succédés.

M. Arago me charge de vous dire combien votre bon souvenir lui a été doux au coeur. Sa conduite dans ces dernières journées de péril a été si ferme et si courageuse, qu'il s'est jeté sur les barricades au milieu des balles avec tant de résolution, que les personnes qui ont pu le voir dans ces circonstances ont pu croire qu'il cherchait une mort glorieuse, désespérant du salut du pays. Il faut bien convenir que nous en étions tous là, et que cette triste pensée ne pouvait guère s'éloigner de nos coeurs quand nous songions à l'immensité des ressources des insurgés et à la faiblesse des moyens de résistance que nous possédions.

Que Dieu vous préserve, mon cher ami, votre pays et vous, de ces lamentables folies! Jamais nous ne cicatriserons les plaies ouvertes et envenimées depuis quelques mois par la presse, les clubs, les sociétés secrètes, et surtout les ateliers nationaux. Partout la haine de toutes les supériorités, la soif de toutes les richesses, la méprise de tout ce que l'homme doit respecter; voilà ce qui a fait la base des écrits, du discours et des associations.

J'interromps ma lettre pour lire le billet qui m'annonce la mort d'un ami, blessé il y a un mois. Tous les jours il en est ainsi; les convois se succèdent, et nous sommes loin d'avoir fini ce compte funèbre.

Adieu, mon cher ami. Pardonnez-moi si je vous réponds si tard, mais votre lettre ne m'est pas parvenue comme elle aurait dû. J'ai changé de logement. Me voici à la Sorbonne; et puis je suis bien découragé, bien triste.

Mes respects à Madame Faraday, je vous prie.

Mille amitiés
DUMAS.

374   J. PLÜCKER to M. FARADAY, 28 September 1848
[*I.E.E., previously unpublished*]

Bonn
28 of Sept. 1848

DEAR SIR!

Being returned home, I feel it my first duty to thank you for the great kindness, with which you received my, [*sic*] when I came to London.[1] I never will forget it, my thank [*sic*] is, believe me Sir, very sincere; so are my sentiments of veneration, but I cant [*sic*] express them in a proper way, and I would not speak in the terms of an English toast at a public dinner. Instigated by the novelty of your discoveries I began, sixteen months ago, my experimental researches. Encouraged by you I'll go on with more pleasure and confidence.

Since a few days I began again to work and I got already some new facts. But, struck by one of your observations, the first thing I did, was to direct my attention to the experiments respecting the different laws of intensity for Magnetism and Diamagnetism. The result has been that these laws are exactly such as I have stated them. The paradox I pointed out to you plainly disappears. Allow me to give you a short account of it.

To repeat my former experiments, I choosed [*sic*] a piece of charcoal, a little longer than I did before. It pointed 1) axially with one of Grove's elements, 2) equatorially with seven and 3) was kept an [*sic*] *intermediate fixed position* with three elements. The third case is a new conformation of the given law, that by increasing power (and particularly by diminuishing [*sic*] the distance from the poles) Diamagnetism increases more rapidly than Magnetism.

I thence concluded that a mixture of magnetic and diamagnetic substances might at a greater distance from the poles be attracted and at a smaler [*sic*] distance repulsed by the Electromagnet; and I proved it by a watchglass filled with Mercury and kept by a Magnet at a short distance (one millimetre) from the poles. The conclusion as well as the experiment and its explication are *correct*. The same experiment may be repeated with a substance showing a very strong Magnetism by suspending it at the balance and increasing the distance from the poles. The experiment, wich [*sic*] in this case at first struck me very much, *proves nothing at all*. The tendency of the balance to return to its position of equilibrium acts here like de [*sic*] diamagnetic force in the original experiment. This tendency increasing more rapidly than the magnetic power, we will have quite the same appearances, even when Diamagnetism had fully disappeared. & Here I have been wrong. The above mentioned experiment with Mercury *where the questioned tendency of the balance may be neglected*, remaining fully conclusive, nevertheless I thought it proper, to afford new proves. I succeded in different way, using allways my large balance. The following experiment is striking.

I brought a watchglass (being magnetic) over the two poles by suspending it at the balance, and put into it a sphere of Bismuth (12mm diameter). The balance was in a state of horisontal equilibrium and the glass at a distance of 5 mm from the poles. The current being produced *by one element* of Grove, the Glass moved towards a fixed equilibrium at a distance of only 2,^{mm} 5 from the poles; but *by using seven elements* the movement of the glass towards the poles was nearly insensible. Therefore the magnetic action of the Electromagnet, instead of increasing, by strengthening the power of the current, considerably diminishes. The balance being then brought into horisontal equilibrium, the glass with the sphere of Bismuth being at a distance of only 2 mm from the poles: with *one* element there was *attraction by Magnetism*, with *seven* elements strong *repulsion by Diamagnetism*.

In trying this experiment I observed that, even in the case of strong diamagnetic repulsion, *at the first moment* there was magnetic attraction. This is in full accordance to my views, the fact being produced either by the increasing power of the Electromagnet, after the current has been established, or there being more resistance (wanting more time) in inducing Diamagnetism than in inducing Magnetism.

In a few days I'll send to Mr Taylor the changement [*sic*] to be made to some numbers of my last paper, happily not yet printed.

I hope my letter will find you in perfect good health

Very truly yours
PLÜCKER

[1] Plücker attended the meeting of the B.A.A.S. at Swansea. Faraday was also there. See *LPW*, 356.

[*Trinity College Library, Trinity College, Cambridge, previously unpublished*]

Royal Institution
7 Nov.ʳ 1848

MY DEAR SIR

It is with great pleasure that I nurse the hope of having you again in one of our Friday Evenings of our coming season. You must have done good to all who heard you but I can testify of myself that the truth you laid down that truth can more easily emerge from error than from confusion has been to me practically useful and a source of continual pleasure in observing that in other things besides those I meddle with it is so

You remember our talk about the connexion which ought to exist between crystalline & electric forces. Well it is beginning to appear. I dare say you know of Pluckers papers in Poggendorfs Annalen on the Magnetic *repulsion* of the *Optic axes of crystals.* I will therefore pass from them to my own matter. I find that certain CRYSTALS are subject to Magnetic force & these may be crystals either of Magnetic or diamagnetic bodies. Bismuth, Antimony, Arsenic, Sulphate of Iron, Sulphate of Nickel are such bodies. If a crystal of bismuth be suspended by a filament of cocoon silk between the horizontal poles of a horseshoe magnet (& a common magnet that will not raise more than 2 or 3 lbs by the keeper can shew the effect if sheltered) the crystal vibrates & points. If the line through the crystal which is then horizontal & equatorial be made vertical the crystal again points & now with its maximum degree of force. If the line which is now horizontal and AXIAL be made vertical, the crystal is indifferent or it is simply repelled as a diamagnetic body ought to be. The form of the piece of bismuth goes for nothing in this experiment the effect depends altogether upon the crystalline structure. This line which places itself parallel to the magnetic axis I have called the Magnecrystallic axis to express the *original condition* of the crystal but as it appears to me that the power by which it points when in the Magnetic field is an *induced* power I have called it the *Magneto crystallic* force.

The Magnecrystallic axis in bismuth is perpendicular or nearly so to the chief plane of cleavage. It is constant for bismuth and for all other bodies in which I find this condition. Thus in Sulphate of Iron it is perpendicular or nearly so to two sides of the rhombic prism

The effect upon the crystal in the magnetic field is not one of attraction or repulsion but of *position* only – and as yet I can find no traces of polarity though the setting force be strong. A crystal of bismuth fixed at the end of a torsion balance is repelled by a single magnetic pole whether the crystal present the end of the Magnecrystallic axis or the side towards the pole i. e. whether it be in the position it would take of itself or whether it be constrained to occupy that the farthest from it or any other position As a diamagnetic body it appears unchanged, & as to polarity there are no signs of it by any difference in the repulsive force. With Sulphate of Iron in which the Magnecrystallic phenomena are very strong there is no alteration in the amount of attractive force. So strong is the tendency to go into *position* that I can make a diamagnetic body approach when it would naturally be repelled or a magnetic body receed when it would naturally be attracted by opposing the magnecrystallic condition to the magnetic or diamagnetic condition. As thus N is an electromagnetic pole – opposite to which is a prismatic crystal of sulphate of iron in which the 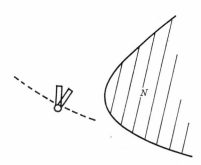 Magnecrystallic axis is represented by the dotted line and which therefore at present is oblique to the lines of force issuing from the pole N. A vertical silken axis is so adjusted that it passes downwards at *a* a little piece of card board is fascened [*sic*] across it & on this the crystal is fixed – so that it can spin as radius round this axis. Now if the torsion be adjusted so that it shall hold naturally the more oblique position the moment the Magnetism is put on it receeds into the other position by the tendency of the Magnecrystallic axis to place itself parallel to the lines of magnetic force. The papers are at the Royal Society & I shall send you a copy as soon as I can. Come in due time and talk to us & encourage me.

Ever Yours –

M. FARADAY

376 M. FARADAY to C. BABBAGE, 9 November 1848

[*British Museum, Add. mss. 37194, f. 212, previously unpublished*]

R Institution
Novr 9. 1848

MY DEAR BABBAGE

Mrs. Faraday cannot call to mind any such paper in Chambers as that I imagined – she has only an impression that the shilling & other exhibitions of London amounts in the Season to £30 which is an estimate of the quantity rather than the productiveness. If I can learn any thing I will let you know.

You have my papers & therefore I will refer you to the numbered Paragraphs 83. etc. – 101 etc. 120 to 130. 138. 250 to 254 & especially the last 254. They are all contained in Series 1 & 2 of the Experimental research 1831–2

As to the effect of *time* that is further considered in a controversial letter printed first in the Annales de Chimie 1832 LI. p 404 or reprinted in the 2nd

Vol of the 8vo Edition of my researches in which latter at p 193. the effect of time is considered as regards Arago's rotation.[1]

When I have the Magnet in action I will shew you the copper effect

Ever Truly Yours
M. FARADAY

[1] See Letter 364.

377 M. FARADAY to W. WHEWELL, 13 November 1848
[*Trinity College Library, Trinity College, Cambridge, previously unpublished*]

Royal Institution
13 Novr 1848

MY DEAR SIR

First let me thank you for your kind reception of the expression of my hope that we should again hear you here. To me your evening discourse was one of the things which gave dignity to the Royal Institution and at the same time I hope not at the expence of the dignity of him who gave it. I am most happy to hear you speak of polarity – though a little timid in hearing you refer to what I have done. But the subject is your own & by your writings is known to be one on which you have thought, and I anticipate much instruction & help from your discourse upon it.

May I tell you that in my two last papers (now at the R S.) I have been drawn to use the word *axiality* in contra distinction to the word *polarity*, meaning thereby an axis of power in which the two extremities are not in different relations, but may be employed indifferently for each other. Such an idea is *not* the same as that which I think you were pleased to approve of in some degree in my definition of the Electric current as an *axis of power* for that has very different properties in the two directions.

I have only used the word suggestively & I would rather you should see how it is used in conjunction with the thoughts that gave rise to its use and these you shall have in the papers when they are printed.

Ever My dear Sir
Most truly Yours,
M. FARADAY

Mr Barlow is in the country but I shall send your letter to him.

M.F.

378 M. FARADAY to W. WHEWELL, 17 November 1848

[Trinity College Library, Trinity College, Cambridge, previously unpublished]

R. Institution
17 Nov.ʳ 1848

MY DEAR SIR

Mr. Barlow rejoices with me in the thought of your discourse and fearing to trouble you too much asks me to ask you what date you will choose We commence on the 19th of January and go on weekly. Will you take the first? or second or third, after that Mr. Brande & I shall arrange our evenings. I should like to hear your thoughts before my evening that I may profit: but all is subject to your convenience & pleasure. "The idea of polarity" is to my mind perfect as a title

Ever Yours Most Truly
M. FARADAY

379 W. WHEWELL to M. FARADAY, 22 November 1848

[Trinity College Library, Trinity College, Cambridge, previously unpublished]

Trin. Lodge.
Cambridge
Nov. 22 1848

MY DEAR SIR

I am encouraged by your approval of my proposed subject to take courage to give you a lecture at the R. I. I am not certain that the 19th of January will be so convenient to me as the 26th; but perhaps you will allow me to leave this point open a little longer. In your letter of the 7th you mention Plucker's papers in Poggendorf [*sic*]. Can you give me the n° of the volume, for I have not been able to find the papers which you refer to.[1]

In the expts on crystals which you describe, you find the axis of maximum pointing force by making vertical the axis which was originally horizontal and equatorial. This I do not understand, because it appears to me that what axis is originally horizontal must depend on an *arbitrary* condition, the original point of suspension. But of course my difficulty arises from not understanding the thing.

I shall want much to see what you say about *axiality*. But we shall have to consider whether *axiality* does not apply to some cases which we have been accustomed to call *polarization*. For instance is not the polarization of light a sort of axiality? A vertical ray polarized in plane NS is not distinguishable from a vertical ray polarized in plane SN. But I see fully the importance of the distinction in electro-chemistry, and have no doubt that the true general

531

distinction will disclose itself as you go on, if it have not done so already. I am quite impatient to see your new paper.

I have been reading over your Researches. I have always had a difficulty about your Induction in curved lines as an original law. I have put down on another paper my difficulty stated as it occurs to me.[2] I should be glad if when you have time you could tell me where I am wrong. I do not ask this in reference to anything I may have to say at the R. I. for I do not foresee daring to touch upon the subject; but I should like to possess your views clearly.

I am always
Very truly yours
W. WHEWELL

[1] See Letter 375. Faraday loaned the papers to Whewell.
[2] I have been unable to find this paper.

380 M. FARADAY to W. WHEWELL, 24 November 1848
[*Trinity College Library, Trinity College, Cambridge, previously unpublished*]

(Royal Institution),
24 Nov.[r] 1848

MY DEAR SIR

In trying to reply to your objections to induction through curved lines I must premise by stating that I have no idea the action is in curved lines, otherwise, than as it is dependant on the action of the intervening & contiguous matter; and that each curve line may for the moment be looked upon as part of a polygon of an infinite number of sides, these sides or straight lines being the distances between the successive particles.

Then, to examine the question; – when an insulated body is charged, P, it will, by induction, induce the contrary state in an *uninsulated conducting* body, N, in its vicinity. I have called the first body P, the *inductric* body, for it sustains the state; to distinguish it from the other, which I have called the *inducteous* body, whose state is sustained entirely by P. Now N has *no relation*, by induction, to any other body than P, and cannot induce on other bodies than P: – for, even supposing an uninsulated conductor at p and assuming that N could act by induction on it, still, N & p are *uninsulated* & therefore in communication with each other; and no induction can take place between bodies which are in conducting communication with each other. They may both be influenced *at once* by P; but they cannot influence each other. Hence, if A in the figure

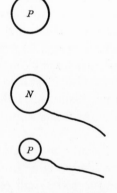

you sent me from (1221), (see next page),[1] be *Pos.*, it will make *C. D.* which is *uninsulated Neg.* (not especially towards the edge *C* except by the accumulation of the ends of curved lines there so to speak; for if the plate *c* be indefinitely extended the maximum of induced effect is at *m*). But *c* being neg. cannot induce towards *f.* or *h.*; first, because all its inductive force is directed towards *A*, by which its state is sustained; & next, because *C, f,* & *h* are always uninsulated & therefore in communication with each other.

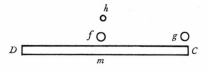

Or; if we suppose that the charge found on *h* is the difference of the effect of *A* on *h*, & the assumed effect of *c* on *h*: – then at all events *A* must act on *h* through curved lines, if *c* does not; for there is no other way for the power to get from *A* to *h*: – unless indeed the difference between *A* & *C* be supposed to be established at *C* and so *C* act with that difference; – but then, *C* ought to be Pos to induce a Neg state in *h*, but it is *always* neg. and cannot be otherwise being brought into that state by Pos *A*.

In place of making *CD* a plate let it be a hemisphere: the effects are equally the same: and in this case, assuming that *C* could induce towards *h*. still *both* its action & the action of *A* must be through curved lines in the air or surrounding insulating body; through which only induction can take place.

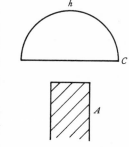

We must remember that it is not the mass of metal which is charged, but solely the surface; and only that part of the surface which is in relation to the Inductric body by inductive action. If the part of the plate *C. D* near the middle be made of gold leaf there is not the slightest trace of action through the gold. Nay more, if the interposed plate *CD* be a series of wires laid side by side all

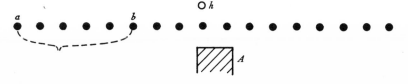

being connected and uninsulated; *A.*, then has *no* power of inducing any state on *h.*, even though *A* may be the knob of a Leyden jar or the conductor of an electric machine in a powerfully excited state & able to give strong sparks to the wires. But if we remove the wires between *a* & *b.* then *h* is affected as in the former case. This is a common experiment with me, using wire gauze in place of wires; & wire gauze of this dimension as to space & metal is a perfect barrier to induction through it.

I do not know whether you are acquainted with Mr. William Thomson of St. Peters College Cambridge, but he has entered, I believe, somewhat deeply into the Mathematics of this part of the subject, and tells me that whether upon Coloumbs [*sic*] hypothesis of an action in straight lines, or mine of an action in curved lines by 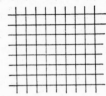 means of contiguous particles, the results ought to be *exactly the same*. His papers are published in some mathematical journal but I do not know the work.[2]

I am My dear Sir
Most Truly Yours,
M. FARADAY

[1] This refers to the diagram appearing below this phrase which is on the second page of the original letter.
[2] See Letter 310.

381 W. WHEWELL to M. FARADAY, 6 December 1848
[*Trinity College Library, Trinity College, Cambridge, previously unpublished*]

Trin. Lodge.
Cambridge
Dec. 6. 1848

MY DEAR SIR

I return the memoirs which you were kind enough to lend me. I hope I have not put you to inconvenience by keeping them so long. I did not hear you speak of the two memoirs. I should be glad to know how far you agree with him in his criticisms that the diamagnetic force is never polar[1] – that the magnetic and diamagnetic force may coexist in the same body, and the like. I conceive that he refers the phenomena too exclusively to the *poles* of the magnet in speaking, as he does, of the one force diminishing faster than the other. The phenomena described in this second memoir are in many respects like yours with crystals.

I think I must settle at once to give you my lecture on the 19th rather than on the 26th.[2]

Believe me always
Truly yours
W. WHEWELL

[1] See Letter 382.
[2] See Letter 379.

[*Trinity College Library, Trinity College, Cambridge, previously unpublished*]

R. Institution,
8 Decr 1848

My dear Sir

It is a fact that if a small bar of charcoal be suspended between the poles of a very strong Electromagnet, the charcoal will *point equatorially* but that if the magnet be weakened – as the poles opened out or the charcoal raised it will at a given distance or for a given weakness stand *axially* being in the first place affected as a diamagnetic body & in the second as a magnetic body. Hence Plucker concludes that the diamagnetic force *increases & diminishes more rapidly* than the magnetic force.

I have formed no *final* opinion on the conclusion he comes to. But this I think I know as a fact that no degree of power can make the magnetic & diamagnetic bodies change places or the individuals of the one class pass into the other.

In all the cases which Plucker mentioned to me there was both a magnetic & a diamagnetic body present and I think he is now of opinion that that is necessary.

Since the paper of Pluckers to which you refer he has adopted rather strongly my supposition (2429.) that diamagnetic bodies may be polarized in the contrary way to iron or magnetic bodies having N & S poles opposite the corresponding N & S poles of the magnet. The proof he gives is brought from the action of a magnet or a piece of iron brought into the magnetic field.

I have similar phenomena produced in the case of crystals but I cannot in the one or the other case admit them as shewing polarity. I shew in my papers how they are a necessary consequence of the new direction given to the resultants of magnetic force –

Weber has I understand a proof of the supposition (2429) of another kind which he considers conclusive as to the correctness of the supposition but the paper is in German & I have not seen it yet in English.[1]

But if a prismatic crystal of sulphate of iron whose length is 5 or 6 times its breadth be suspended in the magnetic field the poles being a certain distance apart it will point equatorially by magnecrystallic power. If the poles be much nearer it will point axially by Magnet power and for a certain distance included within very small limits it will point obliquely. This distance I have called *n*. Now *n* *increases* with increase in the length of the prism; *diminishes* with increase in the magnecrystallic dimension of the crystal – *is not affected* by the vertical dimension of the crystal – & is *not affected* by the *strength of the Magnet*. In a note[2] which I gave into the R. S. last night I think I explain all this by the

Polarity of the crystal as a *magnetic* body – and its mere *axiality* as a Magnecrystallic body.

The oblique set also I have dealt with and find reason to refer it to a small degree of obliquity in the Magnecrystallic axis as respects the length of the prism.

I have told Mr. Barlow that you will take the 19th.

> Ever My dear Sir,
> Most Truly Yours,
> M. FARADAY

¹ Wilhelm Weber (1804–91), 'Ueber die Erregung und Wirkung des Diamagnetismus nach den Gesetzen inducierter Ströme,' *AP*, 149 (1848), 241. This paper was translated into English in *TSM*, 5 (1852), 477. See *LPW*, 423 and fn. 21, 461.
² On 7 December 1848 Faraday delivered the Bakerian Lecture, 'On the crystalline Polarity of Bismuth and other bodies, and on its relation to the magnetic form of force.' The 'note' would appear to be the summary of this lecture which appears in *PRS*, 5 (1843–50), 780.

383   M. FARADAY to J. PLÜCKER, 14 December 1848
[*Nat. Res. Counc. Canada, previously unpublished*]

> Royal Institution
> London
> 14 Dec.ʳ 1848

MY DEAR SIR

Though I date from London yet I ought to say in strict truth that we are at Brighton for the sake of rest & health: – but I received your kind letter in London & shall return thither again in a week or so. It makes me very happy to think that you enjoyed your trip to England and did not consider your excursion to the Association at Swansea lost time.¹ All these minglings do great good, but I am getting too old now to take much part in them. In fancy I enjoy the thought of seeing Germany, but I doubt now whether I shall ever realize the imagination – and indeed the disturbed state of the country is not such as to tempt one.

I have been at work lately and though my first results seemed in striking contrast with yours on the repulsion of the optic axes of crystals yet I come more and more to the conclusion that the power active in both sets of effects are the same. I find that if a crystal of bismuth or antimony or arsenic or a crystalline fragment be subject to the power in the Magnetic field, it is strongly affected & points i.e that there is a line in the crystal which tends to place itself in the Magnetic axis or in the line joining the two Magnetic poles. When this line is placed vertical in a magnetic field having horizontal lines of force then the crystal is in this respect indifferent. This line I have called the *Magnecrystallic axis* – it is strikingly distinguished from the optic axis line because it is *axial*. If a crystallized plate of bismuth i.e one having uniform crystallization through be experimented with. this line or the Magnecrystallic axis will be found to be perpendicular to the chief cleavage planes. If this plate be suspended by the edge the cleavage planes will point or face toward the magnetic poles – but if it be suspended so that this plane is horizontal then the plate does not point at all – Any part of the edge of the plate may then be made to point towards the magnetic poles simply by depressing or raising it above the level. for the vertical plane perpendicular to the inclined plane will always be coincident with the magnetic axis simply because the Magnecrystallic axis of the crystal lies in that plane.

I have sent two papers to the Royal Society which have been read & will I hope shortly be printed[2] & I will send you copies of them as soon as I can.

Mr Taylor has not yet given us your papers in the English dress but I know they are in print & must be out shortly for I have seen copies of the first two which will appear in the next No of the Scientific memoirs.[3] It is a great grief to me that I cannot read German & profit by the beautiful record of Science which Poggendorf gives to the world – But my memory loses power continually & I am obliged to husband the little powers of recollection that I have left least my head should give way altogether – It aches sadly now but will improve I hope. – Writing or thinking makes it feel weary

I am My dear friend
Most truly Yours
M. FARADAY

[1] See Letter 374.
[2] *ERE*, 22nd Series. This was the only paper read to the Royal Society by Faraday in 1848.
[3] J. Plücker, 'On the Repulsion of the Optic Axes of Crystals by the Poles of a Magnet,' and 'On the Relation of Magnetism to Diamagnetism,' *TSM*, 5 (1852), 353 and 376 respectively.

384 A. QUÉTELET to M. FARADAY, 29 December 1848
[*I.E.E., previously unpublished*]

Bruxelles,
le 29 decembre 1848

MON CHER MONSIEUR,

Aussitot après avoir recu la lettre que vous m'avez fait l'honneur de m'adresser, je me suis empressé de communiquer à M. Donny la note que vous avez bien voulu me faire parvenir pour lui. M. Donny a été flatté, comme il devait l'être, de ce temoignage de bienveillance de la part d'un des savants qui font le plus d'honneur à notre époque, et je ne doute pas qu'en ce moment vous n'ayez recu déjà directement tous les témoignages de sa reconnaissance.

M. Donny méritait vos encouragements à plus d'un titre. il est attaché à l'université de Gand et longtemps avant qu'il eut publié ses mémoires, M. Plateau me l'avait signalé comme un jeune savant qui irait fort loin.

à propos de M. Plateau, vous savez qu'il a perdu sans retour l'usage de la vue. malgré cette cruelle infirmité, M. Plateau n'a pas perdu courage; il travaille toujours, mais d'autres doivent faire ses expériences d'après ses indications. il publie en ce moment un travail qui lui fera le plus grand honneur; c'est la continuation de ses recherches sur une masse liquide soustraite à l'action de la pesanteur.[1] le mémoire est un véritable petit chef d'oeuvre pour la clarté et pour la beauté des résultats. vous avez donné déjà des preuves d'un intérêt bien marqué à mon savant et malheureux ami; mais je crois que son nouveau travail méritera tous vos suffrages. Dans la haute position que vous vous êtes faite par votre mérite éminent, vous usez bien noblement, Monsieur, de votre influence pour encourager les jeunes Savants; et ce ne sera certes pas un de vos moindres titres de gloire.

J'ai reçu deux ouvrages nouveaux que j'ose signaler à votre attention: tous deux sont de l'abbé Moigno; l'un sur les télégraphes électriques rend une éclatante justice à notre ami commun M. Wheatstone; l'autre sur l'optique fait également ressortir les beaux travaux de M. Plateau sur les couleurs acciden-telles et sur la Vision.[2]

J'ai aussi reçu, ce matin, une lettre de M. Aug. de la Rive qui reprend un peu courage et se remet à ses travaux sur la physique. il a même commencé un cours de physique à Genève en faveur des artistes.

à la veille du jour de l'an, permettez moi de saisir cette occasion pour vous exprimer mes voeux pour tout ce qui peut vous être le plus agréable. il n'est pas d'homme dont je respecte autant le caractère et les talents, c'est vous dire assez combien je désire que le ciel vous conservé [*sic*] à la science dont vous êtes un des plus dignes ornements. agréez, Mon cher Monsieur, les nouvelles assurances de mes sentiments de respect et d'amitié

Tout à vous
QUÉTELET

Je dois vous remercier aussi pour les [illeg.] et nombreux envois que vous avez bien voulu me faire de vos savants mémoires.

Veuillez me rappeler au souvenir de M. Wheatstone et de nos amis communs.

[1] J. Plateau, 'Recherches expérimentales et théoriques sur les figures d'équilibre d'une masse liquide sans pesanteur (2ème Série)', *MASB*, 23 (1849).
[2] François Napoléon Marie Moigno (1804–84), *Traité de télégraphie électrique*, Paris, 1849, and *Répertoire d'optique moderne*, 4 vols., Paris, 1847–50.